Religio-Philosophical Discourses in the Mediterranean World

# Ancient Philosophy & Religion

*Edited by*

George Boys-Stones (*University of Durham*)
George van Kooten (*University of Groningen*)

*Advisory Board*

Gábor Betegh (*Cambridge*)
Troels Engberg-Pedersen (*Copenhagen*)
Reinhard Feldmeier (*Göttingen*)
Jens Halfwassen (*Heidelberg*)
Matyáš Havrda (*Prague*)
Philippe Hoffmann (*École Pratique des Hautes Études, Paris*)
George Karamanolis (*Vienna*)
Anders Klostergaard Petersen (*Aarhus*)
David Konstan (*New York University*)
Winrich Löhr (*Heidelberg*)
John Magee (*Toronto*)
Maren Niehoff (*Hebrew University of Jerusalem*)
Ilaria Ramelli (*Milan*)
Gretchen Reydams-Schils (*Notre Dame, USA*)
Lautaro Roig Lanzillotta (*Groningen*)
Gregory E. Sterling (*Yale*)
Ilinca Tanaseanu-Döbler (*Göttingen*)
Shaul Tor (*King's College London*)
Robbert van den Berg (*Leiden*)
Peter Van Nuffelen (*Ghent*)

VOLUME 1

The titles published in this series are listed at *brill.com/aphr*

# Religio-Philosophical Discourses in the Mediterranean World

*From Plato, through Jesus, to Late Antiquity*

*Edited by*

Anders Klostergaard Petersen
George van Kooten

BRILL

LEIDEN | BOSTON

Cover illustration: The posthumous encounter of the deceased with the philosophers (1950 NAM 90), relief from the funeral sacrificial table (mensa) in the "House of Proclus" on the Southern slope of the Acropolis at Athens, excavated in 1955, used by courtesy and permission of the New Acropolis Museum in Athens.
© New Acropolis Museum, Athens.

The Library of Congress Cataloging-in-Publication Data is available online at http://catalog.loc.gov
LC record available at http://lccn.loc.gov/2016055789

Typeface for the Latin, Greek, and Cyrillic scripts: "Brill". See and download: brill.com/brill-typeface.

ISSN 2542-3576
ISBN 978-90-04-34146-3 (hardback)
ISBN 978-90-04-32313-1 (e-book)

Copyright 2017 by Koninklijke Brill NV, Leiden, The Netherlands.
Koninklijke Brill NV incorporates the imprints Brill, Brill Hes & De Graaf, Brill Nijhoff, Brill Rodopi and Hotei Publishing.
All rights reserved. No part of this publication may be reproduced, translated, stored in a retrieval system, or transmitted in any form or by any means, electronic, mechanical, photocopying, recording or otherwise, without prior written permission from the publisher.
Authorization to photocopy items for internal or personal use is granted by Koninklijke Brill NV provided that the appropriate fees are paid directly to The Copyright Clearance Center, 222 Rosewood Drive, Suite 910, Danvers, MA 01923, USA. Fees are subject to change.

This book is printed on acid-free paper and produced in a sustainable manner.

# Contents

Notes on Contributors   VII

Introduction: The Religion and Philosophy Debate in a New Key   1

### PART 1
## *Plato*

Plato's Philosophy – Why Not Just Platonic Religion?   9
*Anders Klostergaard Petersen*

Platonic Piety: 'Putting Humpty Dumpty Together Again'   37
*Frisbee Sheffield*

The Real *Euthyphro* Problem, Solved   63
*Nicholas Denyer*

Religion, Philosophy, and the Demons in Between   73
*Lars Albinus*

### PART 2
## *Explorations in an Emerging Common Discourse*

Philosophical Traces in the *Sibylline Oracles*   103
*Helen Van Noorden*

Philosophy and Religion and Their Interactions in 4 Maccabees   126
*Anders Klostergaard Petersen*

The Rapprochement of Religion and Philosophy in Ancient Consolation: Seneca, Paul, and Beyond   159
*Christoph Jedan*

## PART 3
## *Placing Jesus among the Philosophers*

Jesus among the Philosophers: The Cynic Connection Explored and
Affirmed, with a Note on Philo's Jewish-Cynic Philosophy   187
  *Bernhard Lang*

The Last Days of Socrates and Christ: *Euthyphro, Apology, Crito,* and
*Phaedo* Read in Counterpoint with John's Gospel   219
  *George van Kooten*

Criticism of Verbosity in Ancient Philosophical and Early Christian
Writings: Jesus' Critique of the 'Polylogia' of Pagan Prayers (Matthew 6:7)
in its Graeco-Roman Context   244
  *Daniele Pevarello*

## PART 4
## *Reconsidering Early Pagan-Christian Relations*

Christians According to Second-Century Philosophers   279
  *Simon Gathercole*

Epictetus' Views on Christians: A Closed Case Revisited   306
  *Niko Huttunen*

Plotinus, Origenes, and Ammonius on the 'King'   323
  *Harold Tarrant*

Neo-Platonic Readings of Embodied Divine Presence: Iamblichus and
Julian   338
  *Ilinca Tanaseanu-Döbler*

Index of Ancient Sources   375
Index of Modern Authors   396
Index of Subjects   398

# Notes on Contributors

*Lars Albinus*
Associate Professor of Philosophy of Religion, School of Culture and Society, Department of the Study of Religion, University of Aarhus

*Nicholas Denyer*
Senior Lecturer in the Faculty of Classics and Fellow and Senior Lecturer in Philosophy at Trinity College, University of Cambridge

*Simon Gathercole*
Reader in New Testament Studies in the Faculty of Divinity and Fellow at Fitzwilliam College, University of Cambridge

*Niko Huttunen*
Research Fellow in Early Christianity, Faculty of Theology, University of Helsinki

*Christoph Jedan*
Professor of Philosophy of Religion & Ethics, Faculty of Theology and Religious Studies, University of Groningen

*Anders Klostergaard Petersen*
Professor in Early Christianity and Judaism, School of Culture and Society, Department for the Study of Religion, University of Aarhus

*Bernhard Lang*
Professor Emeritus of Old Testament Studies, Paderborn University

*Daniele Pevarello*
Assistant Professor in Early Christianity, Department of Religions and Theology, Trinity College, Dublin

*Frisbee Sheffield*
College Lecturer in Philosophy and Bye-Fellow, Girton College, University of Cambridge

*Ilinca Tanaseanu-Döbler*
Professor for the Study of Religion, Faculty of Philosophy, Georg-August University, Göttingen

*Harold Tarrant*
Professor Emeritus in Classics, University of Newcastle, Australia

*George van Kooten*
Professor of New Testament & Early Christianity, Faculty of Theology and Religious Studies, University of Groningen

*Helen Van Noorden*
Lecturer in Classics and Wrigley Fellow, Girton College, University of Cambridge

# Introduction: The Religion and Philosophy Debate in a New Key

*Anders Klostergaard Petersen and George van Kooten*

In recent years we have witnessed an increased interest in the relationship between philosophy and religion in early Christianity, not least with regard to the presence of philosophical notions and ideas in the texts of the New Testament.[1] From around the turn of the third millennium, classicists and historians of ancient philosophy have likewise begun to focus on the topic of religion in the context of ancient philosophy.[2] In some ways the interest of New Testament scholars in ancient Graeco-Roman philosophy and its potential influence on early Christian texts was a resumption of an older German tradition, dating back to the beginning of the twentieth century, exploring the interactions between philosophy and religion relating to the formation of early Christianity. This movement partly grew out of dissatisfaction with von Harnack's exemption of early Christianity from its Graeco-Roman setting, as he believed that early Christianity was only eventually – and with negative implications – forced to embrace this cultural context. At the same time, this interest was also forged as a reaction against the History of Religions School and its declared interest in the 'mumbo-jumbo' religion of the illiterate masses. This movement, however, was eclipsed by the strong, persistent penchant for thinking of philosophy and religion in dichotomous terms. Bultmann, a student of Wilhelm Heitmüller, a leading representative of the History of Religions

---

[1] See, for instance, the influential works by Abraham J. Malherbe: *The Cynic Epistles: A Study Edition* (Missoula, MT: Scholars Press, 1977); *Moral Exhortation: A Graeco-Roman Sourcebook* (Library of Early Christianity 4; Philadelphia, PA: Westminster Press, 1987); "Hellenistic Moralists and the New Testament," in *Aufstieg und Niedergang der römischen Welt* II.26.1 (ed. Humberto Temporini; New York/Berlin: De Gruyter, 1992), 267–333; Stanley K. Stowers, *A Rereading of Romans: Justice, Jews and Gentiles* (Cambridge, MA: Yale University Press, 1995); and the various books by Troels Engberg-Pedersen, notably his *Cosmology and Self in the Apostle Paul: The Material Spirit* (Oxford: Oxford University Press, 2010) and *John and Philosophy: A New Reading of the Fourth Gospel* (OUP, 2017).

[2] Mark L. McPherran, *The Religion of Socrates* (University Park, PA: Pennsylvania State University Press, 1996); David Sedley, "The Ideal of Godlikeness," in *Plato 2. Ethics, Politics, Religion, and the Soul* (ed. Gail Fine; Oxford Readings in Philosophy; Oxford: Oxford University Press, 1999), 309–28.

School, similarly repudiated philosophical influence on early Christianity by turning to gnostic material in order to reconstruct the religious basis of formative Christianity – in Bultmann's understanding, Gnosticism was a movement entirely independent of the Graeco-Roman world in general and philosophy in particular.

In the 1970s things began to change in two directions. In 1967 Martin Hengel published the first German edition of *Judaism and Hellenism*, but it was not until the appearance of the English translation in 1974 that his main thesis of early Judaism's comprehensive and profound engagement with the Hellenistic world came to exert considerable influence (London: SCM Press). Subsequent to this book, nobody could ignore Graeco-Roman philosophy as a source of influence on Jewish and, thereby, also early Christian thought. At the same time, in the field of classics, John Dillon for the first time drew up the presuppositions of a potentially contextual study of the New Testament with his sketch of the history and development of Middle Platonism.[3] Slightly later, Mark McPherran turned to the religious nature of Socratic and Platonic philosophy over and against a sceptical, profoundly aporetic and irreligious portrayal of Socrates, represented among others by the influential Gregory Vlastos. David Sedley in his turn rediscovered the essence of Plato's ethics as being of a partly religious nature in its orientation towards godlikeness.

These two independent scholarly trajectories, however, have never fully converged. For that reason we decided to organise two colloquia in order to bring scholars from the fields concerned (New Testament scholars, classicists, and historians of ancient philosophy) together in order to examine the potential for engaging in dialogue about the intertwinement of ancient Graeco-Roman philosophy and religion (here confined to Graeco-Roman, Jewish, and Christian religion). The success of such a convergence can easily be hindered by a retrojection of anachronistic, purportedly Enlightenment bifurcations, such as rationality vs. irrationality, reason vs. faith, knowledge vs. revelation, or even within religion between religion proper (that is, reasoned religion) and magic, etc. These antitheses are upheld by both theologians and scholars of the humanities as well as in popular thought. The former often wish to maintain the distinctiveness of their religion and tread the footsteps of the anti-intellectualist Tertullian, who accentuated the incompatibility between Athens and Jerusalem, philosophy and religion by famously exclaiming, "What has Athens to do Jerusalem?" The latter frequently mirror philosophers' repug-

---

3 *The Middle Platonists: 80 B.C. to A.D. 220* (Ithaca, NY: Cornell University Press, 1977; 2nd, revised edition 1996).

nance towards religion. These dualisms have been aptly criticised by Glenn Most – a participant in the colloquia – but nevertheless linger on.[4]

Despite the polemics between philosophy and religion, we are convinced that the scholarly development of the debate moves toward a convergence in which the mutually constructive engagement of ancient philosophy and religion is recognised. Of course these relationships may be construed in a variety of ways. They can be understood in the narrow genealogical sense, in which one text is perceived to exert direct influence on another; they may be conceived in a less narrow sense, in which a thinker is acknowledged to exert influence on another; or they may be understood in a more general manner, in which different people sharing similar discourses are reflecting in a comparable way. Additionally, people living in the same socio-political and cultural environments often display similar patterns of thinking and acting. Finally, one may – at the most general level of analysis – conceive of the ancient Mediterranean Hellenistic world as a *koinē* in which people exchanged their ideas in a common currency. We have left it open to the contributors to decide on the terms in which they want to discuss this relationship and which examples they would like to use in their studies.

In reading the different contributions, we have detected four conglomerates of papers. They are: (1) the religious nature of Plato's philosophy; (2) an emerging common discourse among pagans, Jews, and Christians; (3) contributions that even place the figure of Jesus within the context of Graeco-Roman philosophy; and (4) reconsiderations of the dating and nature of the earliest pagan-Christian relations that acknowledge the potential philosophical character of early Christianity. We shall now introduce the separate conglomerates in more detail, paying due attention not only to their relevance for the issue at stake, but also to their individual stance with regard to it.

In the first conglomerate concerned with Plato, the opening chapter, entitled "Plato's Philosophy – Why Not Just Platonic Religion?" by Anders Klostergaard Petersen, provocatively raises the question of whether Plato's philosophy could be rewritten in terms of religion. Frisbee Sheffield, in her essay entitled "Platonic Piety: 'Putting Humpty Dumpty Together Again,'" offers us a great service in taking up the main focus of McPherran's above-mentioned monograph. Sheffield places great emphasis on the importance of contemplation in Plato's ideas about godlikeness and highlights the assemblage of philosophy, justice, and piety. The *Symposium* and the *Euthyphro* are given

---

4   For the impact of these dualisms, see Glenn W. Most, "From Logos to Mythos," in *From Myth to Reason? Studies in the Development of Greek Thought* (ed. Richard Buxton; Oxford: Oxford University Press, 1999), 25–47, 26–32.

particular attention in Sheffield's treatment. Plato's *Euthyphro*, or rather the so-called Euthyphro Question (Is something good because God voluntaristically commands it? Or does God command it because it is intrinsically good? – reflecting a particular, fundamentalist religious and a philosophical perspective respectively) becomes the sole object of Nicholas Denyer's chapter "The Real *Euthyphro* Problem, Solved." Denyer emphasises the circularity of the argument, but tantalisingly argues for the innocence of this circle, suggesting that a similar congruity is possible in the conceptualisation of the relationship between philosophy and religion. In the final essay of this section, Lars Albinus takes up the issue of demonology in Plato and the Platonist tradition in a chapter entitled "Religion, Philosophy, and the Demons in Between." In his understanding, this topic is particularly pertinent for the discussion of the relationship between philosophy and religion because it counters the assumption that there is unilinear, irreversible development from *mythos* to *logos*. Even *logos* is ambiguously dependent upon the *daimōn* of mythological discourse, but the same applies to *mythos*, which, subsequent to its enlightenment, can never return to a state of naiveté again.

In the next section the focus is directed towards the emergence of a common discourse, which could be designated a religio-philosophical one. As Helen Van Noorden demonstrates in her essay "Philosophical Traces in the *Sibylline Oracles*," it is crucial to pay heed to the common philosophical currency of the age in order to understand what is at stake in a composite Jewish text such as the *Sibylline Oracles*. In Van Noorden's view, this common currency was minted from both Stoic and Platonic sources. Whereas the *Sibylline Oracles* exemplify the lower end of the spectrum at which philosophy and religion engaged, 4 Maccabees exhibits the opposite end. As Anders Klostergaard Petersen in his contribution on "Philosophy and Religion and Their Interactions in 4 Maccabees" shows, this Jewish text of the first century CE is simultaneously a philosophical and a religious discourse. There is no difference between the two. Rather than considering the philosophical dimension of the text as ornamental veneer on solid Jewish material, as the history of scholarship has tended to do, Klostergaard Petersen argues that the two are integral to each other. In the last article of this section, Christoph Jedan, in a chapter entitled "The Rapprochement of Religion and Philosophy in Ancient Consolation: Seneca, Paul, and Beyond," similarly demonstrates how on the subject of consolation it is hardly meaningful to make categorical differentiations between philosophical and religious discourses. The close proximity of consolatory practices in Seneca's and Paul's writings hinges on the emergence of a common religio-philosophical discourse devoted to the consolation of the soul.

The introduction of early Christianity in Jedan's chapter takes us to the third conglomerate of papers, devoted to situating even the figure of Jesus among the philosophers. In Bernhard Lang's contribution – explicitly entitled "Jesus among the Philosophers" – he explores the resemblances between the Jesus of the Synoptic Gospels (Mark, Matthew, and Luke) and the Cynic philosophers. Previously other scholars have also pointed to such similarities, often with the intention of contrasting a non-eschatological Jewish cynic with an eschatological Jewish prophet. This is not the purpose of Lang's enterprise, as he limits himself to a formal comparison that does justice to aspects that are otherwise unexplained from a Jewish perspective, such as the itinerant Jesus. Lang's chapter does not play the cynic Jesus in opposition to the eschatological one. In the next chapter, "The Last Days of Socrates and Christ," George van Kooten argues that the Johannine Jesus is modelled on Plato's portrayal of Socrates in his dialogues on the last days of Socrates. Since in these dialogues (the *Euthyphro*, the *Apology*, the *Crito*, and the *Phaedo*) there is a continuous interaction of religious and philosophical features, John could emulate this kind of portrayal as suitable for his depiction of Jesus. In the concluding essay of this cluster, Daniele Pevarello, in his essay entitled "Criticism of Verbosity in Ancient Philosophical and Early Christian Writings," takes his point of departure from the Sermon on the Mount (Matthew 5–8), in which Jesus warns against the verbosity of pagan prayers (Matthew 6:7–9a). This Matthean motif seems to resonate with the broader philosophical warning against verbosity and also with brevity as a hallmark of proper philosophy. Once again, we are facing a stock motif in the common cultural currency of the day.

Given the previous level of dialogue we have already observed between Judaism, early Christianity, and Graeco-Roman philosophy, it comes as no surprise that contributions in the fourth conglomerate reassess the dominant picture of relations between pagans and Christians. Whereas previous research has emphasised the fully negative attitudes of Greeks and Romans towards Christians, the chapters by Simon Gathercole and Niko Huttunen show a more nuanced picture. In his contribution "Christians According to Second-Century Philosophers," Gathercole gives an excellent overview of the variety of pagan attitudes towards Christianity. He warns against an overly neat, all-encompassing narrative and stresses the pluriformity of the pagan philosophers' positions towards Christians. Yet this does not preclude the existence of certain patterns: they either ignore them, regard them as a threat, or come to see Christianity not only as a real option, but as an attractive and compelling one. Some even make the move of converting to Christianity. In Huttunen's essay entitled "Epictetus' Views on Christians: A Closed Case Revisited," the author zooms in on Epictetus, who already figures in Gathercole's overview, and builds a strong case for Epictetus' semi-positive engagement with Christians. According to Huttunen, Epictetus counted Christians above the category of average men, close to the category of philosophers.

In the final two chapters of this conglomerate we enter into the field of a fully established, direct dialogue on the basis of a mutual exchange between philosophy and theology, between Christian and Neo-Platonist 'philosophers'. Whereas previously, as we have seen, a common discourse arose, and in some cases philosophers even became Christians, the last essays in this book presuppose the existence of an institutionalised Christianity capable of fostering its own teachers, who became dialogue partners with their contemporaneous pagan counterparts. Harold Tarrant's chapter, entitled "Plotinus, Origenes, and Ammonius on the 'King'," demonstrates the common origin of a working vocabulary applied by both pagan and Christian 'philosophers' with respect to God. Astonishingly, Tarrant shows how both philosophies and religions have a surprising ability to forget what had once seemed important and quibble over new hermeneutic issues that were previously not even anticipated. Both were taking part in parallel discussions in which 'proto-Trinitarian' views were articulated. In the final chapter, entitled "Neo-Platonic Readings of Embodied Divine Presence: Iamblichus and Julian," Ilinca Tanaseanu-Döbler even shows how Neo-Platonic philosophers seriously engaged with the Gospel of John. Seen from the perspective of divine presence, highly interesting commonalities and differences both become visible. In this manner, Tanaseanu-Döbler's chapter is a testimony to an insight also highlighted in other essays of the volume – namely, that ancient philosophy and Christianity did not necessarily amount to exactly the same thing: there were both similarities and differences (both between and among philosophies and religions), yet these differences can only be ascertained and acknowledged from within this common religio-philosophical discourse.

Finally, we as editors want to express our sincere gratitude to the Department for the Study of Religion at Aarhus University, the Faculty of Divinity at the University of Cambridge, and Clare Hall in Cambridge for hosting the two colloquia in 2012 and 2014. We also want to express our gratitude to our respective home institutions – the Department for the Study of Religion at Aarhus University and the Faculty of Theology and Religious Studies at the University of Groningen – for their continuous support. We are very grateful to the contributors to this volume as well as to a number of participants at the two colloquia for stimulating debates and reflections, notably Glenn Most, Andrew Smith, David Sedley, Judith Lieu, and Miles Burnyeat. Last but not least, we gratefully acknowledge the fruitful, pleasant cooperation with Loes Schouten, Tessa Schild, and Peter Buschman at Brill, and the great help of Dr Alissa Jones Nelson (Berlin) in copy-editing the manuscript and compiling the indices.

# PART 1

*Plato*

∴

# Plato's Philosophy – Why Not Just Platonic Religion?

*Anders Klostergaard Petersen*

1    Paving the Way for a New Understanding of Plato's Philosophy

Undoubtedly something new is at stake in Plato's comprehensive philosophical authorship and his creation of the literary, philosophical dialogue. This is true whether we compare his thinking with the philosophical predecessors of his time or examine the various forms of religion that permeated his world. The way in which we generally tend to formulate this novelty, however, may lead us down the wrong track when trying to understand what precisely took place in Plato's thinking. I shall take a fresh and provocative look at the topic by suggesting that Plato's innovation does not lie in the turn towards 'philosophy' but in the introduction of a new form of religion.

Needless to say, much of this discussion hinges on what exactly we mean by the terms philosophy and religion, but I do not think the debate can be reduced to a matter of favoured terminology. There is more at play than terminological preferences, since the debate to a great extent also reflects our contemporary stance on the relationship between philosophy and religion, secular discourse and rationality, on the one hand, and irrationality and religious discourse on the other hand. Phrasing the title of this article with Plato's philosophy as an alternative to his religiosity has to do with an asymmetrical relationship between the two. Whereas Plato's philosophy is mirrored in his *oeuvre*, Plato's religion designates the religion observed by Plato, which is not, as we shall see, the same as Platonic religion. Contrary to Plato's religion, Platonic religion designates the type of religion propounded by Plato.

From the perspective of the history of religion, two other issues are involved as well. First, there are some striking similarities between what takes place in Plato's thinking about religion and what we find in a number of contemporaneous cultures. If we restrict the discussion of Plato's philosophy to the Greek context, we prevent ourselves from seeing it as part of a wider cultural pattern. Secondly, the question of whether we think of Plato as an exponent of philosophy or of religion is also inextricably related to a more principal stand: Should we ultimately read Plato in light of the subsequent historical development of a modern philosophical tradition detached from a religious context, or should we rather examine his thinking with an appreciation of what it was a reaction to? Our proclivity to classify him as either a philosopher or an exponent of religion is, I think, often self-revelatory in this regard.

In his contribution to *The Cambridge Companion to Plato*, Michael Morgan observes how religion permeated life in classical Greece and therefore argues that it is hardly surprising that religious vocabulary also pervades Plato's dialogues.[1] Morgan also emphasises how religion as conception, motif, and terminology is an integral part of Plato's thinking. The presupposition of the argument, however, is that Plato, by virtue of being engaged in 'philosophy', was somehow exemplifying something different from religion, and that therefore it may be beneficial to look at Plato from the perspective of Greek religion. I concur with this viewpoint, but at the same time I find the presumed contrast between religion and philosophy problematic.[2] Prior to presenting my own view on this topic, I shall make a detour to Justin Martyr's *Dialogue with Trypho*, which dates to approximately half a millennium after Plato, sometime during the 150s.

In this work the narrator recounts how, by chance, he meets a Jewish man, Trypho, who in the wake of the Bar Kochba Revolt has fled to either Ephesus or Corinth from Palestine.[3] Trypho hails the narrator as a philosopher, revealed by virtue of the cloak he is wearing. When the narrator asks Trypho how he would benefit from philosophy rather than Judaism, Trypho emphasises the intimate relationship between philosophy and God: "Do not the philosophers

---

[1] Michael L. Morgan, "Plato and Greek Religion," in *The Cambridge Companion to Plato* (ed. Richard Kraut; Cambridge: Cambridge University Press, 1992), 227.

[2] Cf. Morgan's conclusion: "I have tried to show how Plato's thinking is immersed in the very complex, variegated phenomenon of Greek religion. He takes its existence for granted, adopts features of it, adapts others, and rejects much of it... Plato also appropriates aspects of Greek ecstatic ritual as a framework for philosophical inquiry. It is this religious dimension that helps to show what makes philosophy so important to him" ("Plato and Greek Religion," 244). There is much to be said for the plausibility of this view, but somehow it does not give religion its due part in the account. See also Gábor Betegh, "Greek Philsophy and Religion," in *Blackwell's Companions to Philosophy. A Companion to Ancient Philosophy* (ed. Mary Louise Gill and Pierre Pellegrin; Malden/Oxford: Blackwell, 2006), 625–39, 625, 633f.; and Mark L. McPherran ("Socrates and Plato," in *The History of Western Philosophy of Religion. Volume 1. Ancient Philosophy of Religion* [ed. Graham Oppy and Nick Trakakis; Oxford: Oxford University Press, 2009], 53–78, 54), who talks about how "Plato has his characters speak of the divine in an unmistakably serious fashion in order to make points that are simultaneously philosophical and religious in nature."

[3] In 1.3, Trypho tells the narrator how he has come to Greece subsequent to the Bar Kochba Revolt and how he chiefly spends his days at Corinth. Eusebius, however, in *Ecclesiastical History* IV.18, locates the conversation with Trypho to Ephesus.

turn every discourse on God? And do not questions continually arise to them about His unity and providence? Is not this truly the duty of philosophy to investigate the Deity?" (1.5).[4] A similar emphasis on philosophy as a form of theology is also evident in the narrator's answer to Trypho: "For philosophy is, in fact, the greatest possession, and most honourable before God, to whom it leads us and alone commends us" (2.1). Subsequently, the narrator proceeds to tell Trypho how he has paid a visit to various individual philosophers (as representatives of respectively Stoics, Peripatetics, Pythagoreans, and Platonists, ibid.) and how at last he has moved on to the Platonists. In this context, he accentuates how the vision of god is the highest goal of Platonism: "And the perception of immaterial things quite overpowered me, and the contemplation of ideas furnished my mind with wings, so that in a little while I supposed that I had become wise; and such was my stupidity, I expected forthwith to look upon God, for this is the end of Plato's philosophy" (κατόψεσθαι τὸν θεόν τοῦτο γὰρ τέλος τῆς Πλάτωνος φιλοσοφίας) (2.6).

The narrator continues to recount how, at long last, he meets an elderly man who introduces him to Christianity as the most perfect among the philosophical schools. Christian truth is portrayed as superior to all other available philosophical strands. The important point to notice, however, is that Christianity is partly put on a par with, partly claimed to be superior to the other philosophical schools (7–8.2). The narrator tells Trypho how, immediately after his meeting with the elderly man, he made a decision to commit himself to the truest form of philosophy. Hence he conceives himself to be a philosopher of Christ: "But straightaway a flame was kindled in my soul; and a love of the prophets, and of those men who are friends of Christ, possessed me; and whilst revolving his words in my mind, I found this philosophy alone to be safe and profitable" (ταύτην μόνην εὕρισκον φιλοσοφίαν ἀσφαλῆ τε καὶ σύμφορον). "Thus, and for this reason, I am a philosopher" (Οὕτως δὴ καὶ διὰ ταῦτα φιλόσοφος ἐγώ, 8.1).

Obviously this portrayal of ancient philosophy is strongly coloured by Justin's Christianity, but that does not detract from the fact that Justin, in the mid-second century, thought this portrayal of philosophy would make sense to his intended audience. Contrary to Michael Morgan's starting point, in which classical Greek religion could be included as a relevant frame of reference for casting light on Platonic philosophy, Justin did not think of philosophy as noticeably different from religion – or perhaps more to the point, Justin did

---

4   This translation is taken from Alexander Roberts and James Donaldson, eds., *Ante-Nicene Fathers. Volume 1. The Apostolic Fathers, Justin Martyr, Irenaeus* (Peabody, MA: Hendrickson, 1995).

not conceive of Christianity as something so different from philosophy that it would preclude a description of Christianity in terms of philosophy.

In this chapter I take my point of departure from Justin's claim, but I want to reverse his argument in two ways. I do not focus on Christianity. Nor am I concerned with philosophy as such. Rather, I want to examine what happens if we turn the tables and try to understand Plato's philosophy in terms of religion. The aim is not to explore how ancient Greek religion may be used to illuminate particular aspects in Plato, but to follow Justin's argument to the point of his juxtaposition of Platonic philosophy with Christianity. If he could think of Christianity – admittedly as an actor's category at the emic level of analysis – as a form of philosophy, then it might be reasonable to conceive of ancient philosophy – slightly differently from Justin – in terms of an observer's category within an etic perspective – as a type of religion *en tout court*. By virtue of the logic involved, such a view not only has implications for the understanding of Plato, but also pertains to other strands of ancient philosophy. Simultaneously, it impels us to pose a question with regard to the time-honoured tendency to understand the relationship between ancient philosophy and religion as a dichotomy.

Plato is generally considered as marking the decisive breakthrough of philosophy over and against religion, although he had a pedigree of philosophical predecessors.[5] In recent years, however, there has been an increasing tendency among classicists to understand Plato and his precursors in terms of religion, as may be seen from the fact that current handbooks and companions to Plato – as well as to ancient Graeco-Roman philosophy in general – often include one or two contributions on Plato and Greek religion.[6] Seen in this light, my essay may be considered simply as carrying coal to Newcastle.

---

[5] See, for example, Hans-Georg Gadamer, *Der Anfang der Philosophie* (Stuttgart: Reclam, 1996), 130.

[6] See, for instance, Morgan, "Plato and Greek Religion;" Glenn W. Most, "Philosophy and Religion," in *The Cambridge Companion to Greek and Roman Philosophy* (ed. David Sedley; Cambridge: Cambridge University Press, 2003), 300–22; and Mark L. McPherran, "Platonic Religion," in *Blackwell Companions to Philosophy. A Companion to Plato* (ed. Hugh H. Benson; Chichester: Wiley-Blackwell, 2009), 244–59. Interestingly enough, Gail Fine's (ed.) *The Oxford Handbook of Plato* (Oxford: Oxford University Press, 2008) neither includes an article on Plato and religion nor has 'religion' as an independent entry in the general index. However, the book does include an essay by Verity Harte on Plato's metaphysics. In the two volumes on Plato edited by Gail Fine for *Oxford Readings in Philosophy*, the second volume bears the title *Plato 2. Ethics, Politics, Religion, and the Soul* (Oxford: Oxford University Press, 1999). This volume includes an article by David Sedley, "The Ideal of Godlikeness," 309–28, in which he, with reference to the famous passage in the *Theaetetus* 176a–b, places emphasis on divin-

Yet it is also characteristic of the present situation that only a few scholars in the field of the study of religion have written on Plato or on ancient Graeco-Roman philosophy in general. Ancient philosophy is commonly understood by students of religion, presumably without any further reflection on the fact, as the prerogative of classicists and scholars of ancient philosophy – a result of the long-standing philosophy-religion distinction. This is detrimental not only to classicists and students of ancient philosophy, but also to the study of religion. Given their particular expertise, scholars of religion ought to have a strong interest in ancient thinkers who invested considerable energy in the discussion of topics such as the notion of piety, the immortality of the soul, divinisation, imitation of the highest good, ascension of the soul, etc. Even more so, they should be attracted to philosophers, who not only occasionally make recourse to myth and religious language in order to make their points, but also instantiate their main protagonist as an intermediary of Apollo. I suppose that the current situation is a result of the time-honoured philosophy-religion dichotomy. In this manner, the reverberations of the old μῦθος-λόγος-debate linger on to the extent that the prevalent scholarly view – outside perhaps the more narrow circles of a few classicists and students of ancient philosophy – as well as general cultural opinion, is to see Plato as a philosopher and, simultaneously, to consider this status as contrasting with religion.[7]

So far I have written about philosophy and religion as if they were self-evident categories, but we need to be cautious about what we impute to these terms. We may easily be enticed to think of them as conflicting categories on the basis of prevalent strands of early Christianity, in which they came to be understood as constituting categorically different modes of thinking. Although the Justinian view had its promulgators during the subsequent Christian his-

---

isation as the overall aim of Platonic philosophy. The volume also includes two essays by David Bostock and Richard Bett on immortality and the soul in, respectively, the *Phaedo* and the *Phaedrus*; see David Bostock, "The Soul and Immortality in Plato's *Phaedo*," 404–24; and Richard Bett, "Immortality and the Nature of the Soul in Plato's *Phaedrus*," 425–49.

7   For the *mythos-logos* debate and its repercussions in contemporary discussions, see Walter Burkert, *Greek Religion* (Cambridge, MA: Harvard Univeristy Press, 1985) 305, 312; Richard Buxton, "Introduction," in *From Myth to Reason? Studies in the Development of Greek Thought* (Oxford: Oxford University Press, 1999), 1–21, esp. 1–13; Glenn W. Most, "From Logos to Mythos," in *From Myth to Reason? Studies in the Development of Greek Thought* (ed. Richard Buxton; Oxford: Oxford University Press, 1999), 25–47; Claude Calame, "The Rhetoric of *Mythos* and *Logos*: Forms of Figurative Discourse," in *From Myth to Reason?*, 119–43; and Geoffrey E.R. Lloyd, *Being, Humanity, & Understanding* (Oxford: Oxford University Press, 2012), 77–80.

tory of reception, it was ultimately the view of the incongruity between philosophy and Christianity (and, thereby, religion) that won the day in terms of how the relationship between the two should be conceived. The austere North African apologist Tertullian, dating to the latter part of the second and first two decades of the third centuries, formulated this position in a vigorous manner. In his *On Prescription against Heretics*, he famously cleaved the bond between Christianity and philosophy into diametrical opposites:

> What indeed has Athens to do with Jerusalem? What concord is there between the Academy and the Church? what between heretics and Christians. Our instruction comes from the "porch of Solomon," who had himself taught that "the Lord should be sought in the simplicity of heart." Away with all attempts to produce a mottled Christianity of Stoic, Platonic, and dialectic composition (*Viderint qui stoicum et platonicum et dialectum christianismum protulerunt*)! We want no curious disputation after possessing Christ Jesus, no inquisition after enjoying the gospel! With our faith, we desire no further belief. For this is our palmary faith, that there is nothing which we ought to believe besides.[8]

The legacy of this adamant and uncompromising emphasis on the incongruity between Christianity and philosophy was exacerbated during the age of the Reformation and even more so during the period of the Enlightenment, in which it was elevated to a general contrast between philosophy and religion.[9] Through this history of reception philosophy came to designate reason and rationality and religion to reflect superstition, irrationality, and revelation. This dichotomy has endured to the present day, in which, as I said, there continues to be a tradition of conceiving the relationship between religion and philosophy in terms of categorically different modes of interpreting the world. Yet to retroject this view onto the period prior to early Christ-religion is problematic to say the least. In such an account any criticism of religion is likely to be understood as *en bloc*. Thereby ancient philosophical critique of contempora-

---

8 Tertullian, *De praescriptione haereticorum* 7.9–13. The translation is from Alexander Roberts and James Donaldson, eds., *Ante-Nicene Fathers. Volume 3. Latin Christianity: Its Founder, Tertullian. I. Apologetic; II. Anti-Marcion; III. Ethical* (Peabody, MA: Hendrickson, 1995).

9 Obviously there have been other important figures during the history of Christianity who have thought differently about the relationship between Platonism and Christianity. One need only think of prominent figures such as Clement of Alexandria, Origen, Augustine, and Thomas Aquinas. That, however, does not detract from the central point that philosophy *per se* was considered to be in opposition to Christianity.

neous religious practices comes to be interpreted as reflecting an entire, principally antagonistic discourse on religion. In this regard, I fully concur with George Boys-Stones in his introductory chapter to the five-volume Durham *History of Western Philosophy of Religion*, where he contends with respect to the Presocratic philosophers:

> Nor is there anything to suggest that their use of this language [traditional cosmological language] is ironic or polemical, for its use is untempered by anything that could seriously be taken as criticism of the religious context from which it is drawn. Occasionally, it is true, reservations are expressed about *particular religious practices*; but even these presuppose the perspective of the religious insider. Far from attacking religion, they question activities and attitudes that risk bringing it into disrepute.[10]

There goes the traditional understanding of the relationship between philosophy and religion. Far from being radical critics of religion, Plato and his predecessors are conceived as religious apologists involved in an effort to reform their contemporaneous religion. As much as I agree with this view, I find Boys-Stones' formulation of this understanding infelicitous or, at least, ambiguous when it comes to Plato. He argues that "[p]hilosophy might be distinguishable now from religion, but in Plato's terms it is its heir, not its other."[11] Apart from the fact that Plato did not have the concept of religion at his disposal, one should remember that he – in company with the other philosophers – did not aspire to replace his understanding of philosophical piety with the traditional worship cultivated by the majority of his fellow-citizens.[12] In fact,

---

10  George Boys-Stones, "Ancient Philosophy of Religion: An Introduction," in *The History of Western Philosophy of Religion. Volume 1. Ancient Philosophy of Religion*, 1–22, esp. 3, cf. 13f. See also the astute comment on Graeco-Roman philosophy by Most, "Philosophy and Religion," 307f.: "In fact, the fundamental tendency of the vast majority of ancient Greek and Roman philosophers is not at all to debunk religion, but to reinforce religiosity. This they try to achieve in two basic ways: either by completing religion, by attempting to satisfy needs and answer questions which, because of the peculiar nature of the ancient religions, these did not seem to be able to supply themselves in a satisfactory manner; or by correcting religion, by modifying those features of traditional myths, cults and beliefs which most clearly violated what were seen to be the demands of reason or of morality, and thereby producing a more philosophically acceptable version of traditional religion."
11  Boys-Stones, "Ancient Philosophy of Religion," 9.
12  Similarly, see Most, "Philosophy and Religion," 308.

it is conspicuous that Plato's critique of existing religion is not directed towards its ritual elements, although he may criticise ritual engagement without the corresponding proper pious attitude (cf. *Laws* X 885b, 888c, 905d–907b), nor is it directed towards the *polis* religion *per se*.[13] In fact, Plato can retain the traditional divine pantheon.[14] The primary problem of Boys-Stones' way of phrasing this view is that it is too reminiscent of the traditional understanding of religion and philosophy as contrasts. Is philosophy really distinguishable from religion, or is it rather, as I am inclined to think, that Plato's philosophy is merely representative of another type of religion, which in the Greek context in particular comes into being in the philosophical trajectory of thinking?

Much of this discussion revolves around what exactly we mean by the term religion. We therefore need to specify its use. From an emic perspective one could argue that there is a marked difference between what Plato designates *philosophia* and what he calls *theologia*, although the term *theologia* only occurs once in his authorship (*Republic* II 379a), and *philosophia* is not used in direct opposition to this category but in contrast to the commercialised learning he associates with the sophists (cf. *Protagoras* 313b–14b; *Sophist* 224c–e.260a). *Philosophia* designates the philosopher's quest for true wisdom, that is the soul's detachment from the body and its desires and subsequent ascent to true cognition with the aim of acting righteously, temperately, and piously, and, thereby, undergoing a process of divinisation by which it becomes godlike (cf. *Phaedo* 12d.32c; *Apology* 28b; *Theaetetus* 176a–b; *Laws* IV 716d).[15] *Theologia*, conversely, refers to that whole set of traditional tales from the poets, predominantly Homer and Hesiod, about the gods. Based on the doubtful moral nature of these gods and the inexpressibility of true wisdom, the stories of the poets cannot convey the one true good (cf. *Republic* II 377b–383c and *Phaedrus*

---

13  Cf. Burkert, *Greek Religion*, 334. It is also noticeable that Plato does not want the lawgiver to interfere with the realm of traditional *polis* religion in *Laws* V 738b–d; cf. *Republic* IV 427b–c. See also Mark L. McPherran ("Does Piety Pay? Socrates and Plato on Prayer and Sacrifice," in *Reason and Religion in Socratic Philosophy* [ed. Nicholas D. Smith and Paul B. Woodruff; Oxford: Oxford University Press, 2000], 89–114, esp. 102–06), who discusses Plato's rejection of prayer and sacrifice as barter in detail (cf. *Laws* X 865b, 905c–09e and *Republic* II 365d–366a) while simultaneously emphasising Plato's adumbration of cult as imitation of god.

14  See also Gerd van Riel, *Plato's Gods* (Ashgate Studies in the History of Philosophical Theology; Farnham: Ashgate, 2013), 54–6.

15  For the importance of the motif of temperance – closely related to the Delphic maxim of "nothing in excess" (μηδὲν ἄγαν) –, see Morgan, "Plato and Greek Religion," 231; and in particular van Riel, *Plato's Gods*, 17–19.

247c); nor can rational discourse. It is not least for this reason that Plato sometimes has recourse to μῦθος in order to express that which he conceives to be fundamentally ineffable.[16] By polemically introducing a distinction between μῦθος and λόγος, however, Plato simultaneously contributes to a redefinition of the term μῦθος.[17] At the same time, the use of μῦθος imbues his account with legitimacy.[18] From the etic perspective, however, Plato's substitution of philosophical religion with an important strand of traditional religion does not diminish the religious character of his worldview. Undoubtedly, Plato's philosophy constitutes another form of religion than the one he criticises, but it still exemplifies religion, defined as "semantic and cognitive networks comprising ideas, behaviours and institutions in relation to counter-intuitive superhuman agents, objects and posits."[19]

---

16   Much has been written on Plato's occasional use of μῦθος. For a fine discussion, see Michael L. Morgan (*Platonic Piety: Philosophy and Ritual in Fourth-Century Athens* [New Haven: Yale University Press, 1990], 71–76), although he identifies Plato's myths as the mythological traditions of the poets, which constituted "the natural vehicle for Plato's philosophical creativity" (75). I do not see how Morgan can come to this understanding. When Plato describes the ascent of the soul and the noetic view of true being, he often does it in language clothed in the terminology of the mysteries; see Burkert *Greek Religion*, 324; McPherran, "Platonic Religion," 255f.; and particularly Andrea Wilson Nightingale, *Spectacles of Truth in Classical Greek Philosophy: Theoria in its Cultural Context* (Cambridge: Cambridge University Press, 2004), 83–89, with respect to *theoria*. Robert N. Bellah (*Religion in Human Evolution: From the Paleolithic to the Axial Age* [Cambridge, MA/London: Harvard University Press and the Belknap Press, 2011], 393), argues that Plato's transitions to express his points in μῦθος should be conceived as an acknowledgement of the fact that rational argument is for the few, whereas myth remains the primary mode of expressing truth. I think this is an underassessment of the role played by μῦθος in Plato.

17   This is a main point in Geoffrey E.R. Lloyd, *Demystifying Mentalities* (Cambridge: Cambridge University Press, 1990), 23.

18   Cf. Radcliffe G. Edmonds III, *Myths of the Underworld Journey. Plato, Aristophanes, and the "Orphic" Gold Tablets* (Cambridge: Cambridge University Press, 2004), 161.

19   This is the shorthand definition of religion given by Jeppe Sinding Jensen, *What Is Religion?* (London: Routledge, 2014), 8. My colleague Lars Albinus, from whom I have benefitted considerably in the writing of this article, would insist, as is evident from his essay to this volume, on the need also to include a pragmatic dimension in the definition of religion. He and I disagree on this point, but I grant him that by introduction of this aspect into the definition, the relationship between philosophy and religion comes out slightly differently than what I argue here. In my view, the emphasis placed by Albinus on the pragmatic dimension of a definition of religion would reduce religious discourses to those containing strong forms of ultimate sacred postulates.

It is on the basis of such an understanding of religion that I shall discuss Plato's philosophy. It exemplifies a form of religion which from an emic perspective we may designate as 'philosophy' or 'philosophical religion',[20] but which from the etic perspective is representative of the wider category of religion.

To move the discussion forward, I suggest that we see the emergence of ancient Greek philosophy from the Pre-Socratics and onwards in the wider context of what has sometimes been dubbed Axial Age religion. Without replacing religion *per se*, the emergence of this type of religion is characteristic of a noticeable transition with respect to previous forms of religion. Archaic forms of religion continued to exist and were for many centuries by far the most prevalent in the cultures involved, but they were contested by the new religious currents that would eventually, in one way or another, win the day. Before proceeding to this topic, however, there is another important point with regard to ancient philosophy and Plato which we need to take into consideration: the close relationship between ancient philosophy and behaviour. This dimension is also important for the discussion of Axial Age religion, since it does not feature as a prominent element in archaic forms of religion. Complementary to the philosophical critique of the poets' portrayal of the morals of the gods, ethics came to play a decisive role in this new form of religion. Pierre Hadot has aptly summarised ancient philosophy under the rubric of choosing a particular course of life. In his seminal *What Is Ancient Philosophy?*, he emphasises this as characteristic of Socrates, Plato, Aristotle, and each of the Hellenistic schools: "La philosophie est amour et recherche de la sagesse, et la sagesse est précisément un certain mode de vie. Le choix initial, propre à chaque école, est donc le choix d'un certain type de sagesse."[21]

---

20   Burkert (*Greek Religion*, 305–37) discusses philosophical types of thinking under the rubric of 'philosophical religion' and asserts that the novelty of philosophical religion consists in the fact that: "Previously religion had been defined by forms of behaviour and by institutions; now it becomes a matter of the theories and thoughts of individual men who express themselves in writing, in the form of books addressed to a nascent reading public." McPherran ("Platonic Religion," 250–58) similarly uses the term philosophical religion with respect to Plato's religion.

21   Pierre Hadot, *Qu'est-ce que la philosophie antique?* (Paris: Galimard, 1995), 161. Cf. Hadot's *Exercices spirituels et philosophie antique* (Paris: Albin Michel, 2002), 290f., 296. The practical aspects of philosophy increasingly come to the fore in the Hellenistic philosophical schools. In different ways, they share the idea that human life is inflicted by desire as the fundamental malady that only philosophy can cure. For an excellent depiction of this transition, see Martha C. Nussbaum (*The Therapy of Desire: Theory and Practice in Hel-*

# PLATO'S PHILOSOPHY – WHY NOT JUST PLATONIC RELIGION?

The cluster of motifs pertaining to self-training, self-transformation, and philosophy as a way of life is embedded in the understanding of philosophy as the means to obtain a form of salvation, which brings us back to the malleability of the traditional philosophy-religion dualism. Its importance in the ancient context also contributes to problems in the contemporary understanding of the relationship between religion and philosophy. Glenn Most has succinctly pointed to this by accentuating a certain ambivalence regarding this element in our thinking about the two. Most underscores our inclination to assert that philosophy today stands in direct continuity with ancient forms of philosophy, whereas there has been a decisive break with ancient (Western) forms of religion, in as much as none of them persisted beyond late antiquity:

> It is the discontinuity between ancient and modern religion that makes it difficult for us to understand ancient religion, but it is the very continuity between ancient and modern philosophy that poses traps for understanding ancient philosophy, for, as we shall see later, the ways in which philosophy was practiced in antiquity shared many of the most prominent features of religion.[22]

In light of these observations, which all point to a far more intricate and indissoluble relationship between philosophy and religion in the ancient world, I shall now turn to the discussion of Plato as an exponent of Axial Age religion.

## 2   Central Elements of Axial Age Religion

In my chapter on 4 Maccabees and the relationship between philosophy and religion (chapter six in this volume), I also touch upon the contested nature and the implications of the term Axial Age religion. A few basic points will suffice to highlight the central ideas of the term. Karl Jaspers was the first to elaborate on the idea of an Axial Age, the idea of which originated in nineteenth-

---

*lenistic Ethics* [Princeton: Princeton University Press, 1994], 33), who also highlights why Platonic philosophy, due to its elite character, is more reticent in pursuing direct practical purposes. For similar emphasis placed on Hellenistic philosophy as therapy of the soul, see André-Jean Voelke, *La philosophie comme thérapie de l'âme. Etudes de philosophie hellénistique* (Vestigia 12; Fribourg: CERF Paris and Academic Press Fribourg, 1993), whose idea about philosophy as "thérapie de l'âme" may advantageously be applied to Plato's philosophy as well.

22  Most, "Philosophy and Religion," 301.

century German thinking, with Hegel and Ernst von Lassaulx.[23] Jaspers used the category to designate a number of Eurasian cultures that, during the period 800–200 BCE, underwent a number of transformations, with striking resemblances between them. These cultures were China, Greece, India, and Israel. Although the first example of Axial Age thinking might have been Akhenaten's campaign to replace the existing cults in Egypt during the fourteenth century with an all-embracing solar cult devoted to Aten, god of light and time,[24] it was not until the sixth century BCE that we find more pervasive forms of Axial Age thinking occurring in these four cultures.

Just as there are uncertainties relating to the precise dating of the beginning of the Axial Age, the same holds true for the end of the period. Some scholars, wanting to include Christianity and Islam in the period, have extended it all the way from 800 BCE to 700 CE. Such a grand periodisation makes it difficult to see the particular gains of operating with a concept meant to bind all these various phenomena together. Therefore, it is clear that we need to make a distinction between axiality as a phenomenon and as a period.[25] Thus we are able to differentiate between different appearances of axial religion, which can take place at different locations and in various periods, provided a number of socio-cultural presuppositions are fulfilled in order to foster such a development. The appearance of Christianity and Islam, for instance, may be thought of as a second wave of Axial Age religion that extended this form of religion to a much wider public. I would therefore opt for a shorter periodisation of the

---

23  For the history of the term and its contested nature, see in particular Hans Joas, *Was ist die Achsenzeit? Eine wissenschaftliche Debatte als Diskurs über Transzendenz* (Basel: Schwabe Verlag, 2014), 8–20.

24  See Assmann, *Death and Salvation in Ancient Egypt* (trans. David Lorton; New York: Cornell University Press, 2005), 144f. Subsequent to the death of Akhenaten, the old cults reemerged, and the solar cult to Aten eventually disappeared. Assmann's view of Akhenaten as an early exponent of Axial Age religion is also related to the emphasis he places on the distinction between true and false religion – the Mosaic differentiation. See Assmann, *Die mosaische Unterscheidung oder der Preis des Monotheismus* (München: Carl Hanser Verlag, 2003). With respect to Egypt as the earliest example of axiality, I take this to be a reasonable possibility, as long as one adds that the socio-cultural presuppositions apparently did not exist for this type of axiality to endure or to leave any lasting impact on subsequent forms of Egyptian religion.

25  Something similar seems to lie behind the distinction in Johann P. Arnason, Shmuel N. Eisenstadt, and Björn Wittrock, *Axial Civilizations and World History* (Jerusalem Studies in Religion and Culture 4; Leiden: Brill, 2005) between a historical and a typological use of the term. See Arnason, "The Axial Age and Its Interpreters," 19–49, 20; and Eisenstadt, "Axial Civilizations and the Axial Age Reconsidered," 531–64, esp. 531.

Axial Age, covering the period from the seventh century until the third century BCE, with the additional clarification that we are obviously not talking about a sharp divide. Like any periodisation, the Axial Age does not refer to a clear-cut divide between a 'before' and an 'after'. It is part of a continuum into which it makes good sense to insert lines of demarcation separating the eighth from the seventh and the third from the second centuries BCE. As I said, the term remains moot in wide scholarly circles; therefore I shall delve into some of the main points of criticism.

In order to discard some of the misunderstandings pertaining to the term, I would like to point to five aspects: (1) Jaspers' notion has been severely criticised for being an echo of a traditional Protestant understanding of religion; this is the most prevalent criticism voiced against the term and the underlying theory. It may well be that critics are right in pointing to a Protestant background for the idea, but of course that does not take away the burden of proof. This is the point at which critics are severely mistaken. Even if Jaspers' understanding can be shown to reflect reminiscences of Protestant conceptions of religion in general and Christianity in particular, Jaspers may well be right. That is to say, if one really wants to repudiate the Jasperian argument, it should be done on the basis of the historical sources and not with 'cheap' accusations resting on Jaspers' alleged Protestantism. (2) There is nothing teleological, unilinear, or irreversible about a development towards an axial form of religion. (3) Subsuming the variously mentioned Eurasian cultures under a common rubric does not require that their paths to an axial form of religion were the same, nor does it imply that an Axial Age type of religion manifested itself in the same manner in these four cultures.[26] That said, however, there are a number of shared elements which, although they may be found in different forms in the relevant Eurasian cultures, resemble each other to such an extent that it is meaningful to subsume them under a common rubric.[27] (4) Emphasising

---

26  Sometimes Persia and Zoroastrianism are also adduced to the example of Axial Age religions, but given the uncertainty about the dating of Zoroastrian sources, I leave it out of the discussion. I am grateful to Prof. Dr. Michael Stausberg for expert advice on Zoroastrianism.

27  For the most important recent literature on this vast topic, see Bellah, *Religion in Human Evolution*, and the various contributions in Robert N. Bellah and Hans Joas (eds.), *The Axial Age and Its Consequences* (Cambridge, MA/London: Harvard University Press and the Belknap Press, 2012). For attempts to test the hypothesis by formalised models, see Nicolas Baumard, Alexandre Hyafil, and Pascal Boyer, "What Changed during the Axial Age: Cognitive Styles or Reward Systems?" *Communicative and Integrative Biology* 8 (2015): 1–5. See also Nicolas Baumard, Alexandre Hyafil, Ian Morris, and Pascal Boyer, "Increased Af-

the higher degree of complexity of one particular form of culture compared to a previous or contemporaneous one does not involve a verdict on its superiority in terms of either truth or ethical stance. Whether one prefers monotheism over polytheism or the reverse is irrelevant, but it is not beside the point that monotheism most commonly presupposes polytheism. (5) As I also emphasise in my chapter on 4 Maccabees, it is a central tenet of a cultural evolutionary approach, as Bellah has epitomised it, that "nothing is ever lost" – that is, nothing decisive.[28] The idea is that new ideas and forms of behaviour are added to already existing ones, which they do not eliminate, but continue to presuppose and build upon.

These clarifications aside, we can resume the debate about the central features of Axial Age types of religion. There is nothing to indicate that the similarities between these cultures are due to mutual interdependencies, which obviously does not exclude the possibility that exchanges did take place. It seems more likely that we shall have to account for the correspondences in terms of convergent evolution, by which I mean that a parallel socio-material development is likely to generate similar patterns of thinking. When it comes to the four cultures under scrutiny, it is likely that a comparable material and social development involving, for instance, growth in population density with a related increase in urbanisation, social stratification followed by enhanced status differentiation, introduction of new and advanced forms of technology, increased wealth, etc., took place during approximately the same period of time. This led to novel forms of thinking. I shall not delve into the various problems relating to specifying the exact nature of the socio-material developments underlying the Axial Age type of religion. There are still many open questions relating to this issue which, one hopes, future research eventually will be able to clarify. Although the discussion on the socio-material presuppositions and, thereby, the causal explanation for the emergence of Axial Age cultures is immensely important, due to my primary topic I shall focus only on the similarities between those manifestations involved in the realm of religion.

---

fluence Explains the Emergence of Ascetic Wisdom and Moralizing Religions," *Current Biology* 25 (2015): 10–15.

28  Robert N. Bellah, "What Is Axial about the Axial Age?" *Archives Européennes de Sociologie* 46 no. 1 (2005): 69–89, 72; and "Nothing Is ever Lost: An Interview with Robert Bellah," interview with Robert N. Bellah by Nathan Schneider, posted on the *Immanent Frame: Secularism, Religion, and the Public Sphere* 14 September 2011; http://blogs.ssrc.org/tif/2011/09/14/nothing-is-ever-lost/; accessed 26 February 2016. Cf. Joas, *Was ist die Achsenzeit?*, 19f., 59f.

In China the transition from archaic forms of religion to Axial Age religion was characterised by individuals such as Laozi – whether he was an actual historical figure or not does not matter, since it is the traditions ascribed to him that are important –, Confucius, and, at a later point, Mencius as well as Xunzi. In the context of India the focus is directed toward Siddhartha Gautama, the Buddha-to-be, and the subsequent development of the two non-brahminical currents of Buddhism and Jainism as well as the broad and many-sided phenomenon which we classify as Hinduism. In Israel the development was typified by the prophets, the emergence of Deuteronomian religion, and the sapiential tradition of the book of Job and Ecclesiastes. The Greek development from archaic to axial religiosity was, as we have seen, not least exemplified by the philosophical current.[29] Despite all the differences between these various cultures and their diverse developments, there are certain features that unite them. As I have already underscored, they were not the same, but they are characterised by sufficient resemblances not only to legitimise their collocation within the same perspective, but also to call for an explanation.

Different scholars place different emphasis on these elements, but I think it is fair to argue that the following are the ones that a majority of scholars are likely to accentuate in their understanding of Axial Age religiosity. More could possibly be adduced, but in my view the following eight are the most crucial – the order in which they are presented is without significance. First, it is noticeable that we see a form of 'thinking about thinking'. In contrast to previous forms of religion, the Axial Age religions were characterised by increasing self-reflexivity, often formulated in second-order concepts and manifested in the ability to understand one's own thinking and practice from an ostensibly external perspective.[30] Second, this form of self-reflexivity is often closely related to a foundational epistemology expressed in spatial categories, whereby differences between opposing views are projected onto a vertical axis,

---

29   For the Chinese, Indian, and Israelite cases I refer to Bellah, *Religion in Human Evolution*, 265–323, 399–566; Arnason, Eisenstadt, and Wittrock, *Axial Civilizations*, 225–83, 361–528; Seth Abrutyn, "Religious Autonomy and Religious Entrepeneurship: An Evolutionary-Institutionalist's Take on the Axial Age," *Comparative Sociology* 13 no. 2 (2014): 105–34; and "The Institutional Evolution of Religion: Innovation and Entrepreneurship in Ancient Israel," *Religion* 45 no. 4 (2015): 505–31 (Israelite religion only). See also the relevant articles in the older edited work of Shmuel N. Eisenstadt (ed.), *The Origins & Diversity of Axial Age Religions* (Albany, NY: State University of New York Press, 1986).

30   This has been particularly highlighted by Yehuda Elkana, "The Emergence of Second-Order Thinking in Classical Greece," in *The Origins & Diversity of Axial Age Religions*, 40–64, esp. 41–43.

manifested as a contrast between the heavenly over and against the mundane perspective. This dualistic spatial staging is frequently projected onto an axis of depth, which implies a parallel contrast between interiority and exteriority, soul and body. Sometimes the ascription of values to these two axes is further developed to include a horizontal, temporal axis. Thereby the difference between the heavenly and earthly positions, the interior and exterior, becomes instantiated as a differentiation between past and present. Third, there is not necessarily a transition from polytheism towards heno- or monotheism, but there is commonly a reduction of the divine pantheon of archaic types of religion. Fourth, Axial Age religions are exemplified by a strong acknowledgement of the existence of rival worldviews that, in terms of thinking, need to be denigrated in order to substantiate one's own truth. Fifth, Axial Age types of religion are distinguished from archaic ones by loosening or even abolishing the ontological differentiation between gods and humans. They enjoin their adherents to imitate the godhead to such an extent that eventually the followers may be said to transcend the ontological differentiation between divine and human.[31] Sixth, Axial Age forms of religion place considerable emphasis on the element of ἄσκησις, understood in the basic Greek sense of training. By engaging in self-improvement exercises, the emulators of different axial worldviews undergo various forms of privation relating to what they consider false values. As they abandon previous values, they strive to inculcate the principles of their new worldview in order to embody them. Seventh, axial types of religion are exemplary of a shift in emphasis from ritual observance of traditional religion to various forms of inner disposition as a prerequisite for proper cultic observance. This is sometimes described as a displacement of importance from ritual to a moral stance. Yet such an understanding is incomplete, since it is not the traditional cult *per se* that is criticised. What is called for is a moral attitude reflecting the new worldview as a prerequisite for observing the rituals. Eighth, the emergence of Axial Age religion typically takes place in a situation of considerable social competition involving religious entrepreneurs' dissociation from the ruling elite – whether political, religious, or both – and defiance of traditional kinship structures and political power.[32]

---

[31] Anders Klostergaard Petersen, "Attaining Divine Perfection through Different Forms of Imitation," *Numen* LX no. 1 (2013): 7–38, esp. 23–34; and David M. Litwa, *We are Being Transformed: Deification in Paul's Soteriology* (BZNW 187; Berlin/New York: De Gruyter, 2012), 58–116.

[32] This is a point that has been especially underscored by Abrutyn. See "Religious Autonomy," 113: "But, what is of central importance was that Axiality came in the form of a new

## 3     The Importance of the Ascent of the Soul in Plato

Based on the previous considerations and underlining of key elements in Axial Age religions, it is time to discuss its relevance with respect to Plato. To what extent is it meaningful to advocate a shift in emphasis from Plato the philosopher to Plato as a prominent representative of Axial Age religion? Before discussing the eight key points mentioned above in the context of Plato, I shall first take a brief look at two pivotal texts in the Platonic corpus, the cave parable of the *Republic* and the myth of the soul in the *Phaedrus*, as my point of departure. They will serve to set the scene for the subsequent discussion of pivotal points.

In the seventh book of the *Republic*, Plato famously compares human nature with regard to education and the lack thereof (παιδεία vs. ἀπαιδευσία, 514a) with prisoners who have since childhood been sitting chained in the most remote part of a subterranean cave. Higher up the cave along an ascending, rough, steep slope and at a distance from the prisoners there is a fire burning. Between the prisoners and the fire there is a road along which a small wall has been built. On the other side of the wall some men are carrying implements of all kinds – human images and shapes of animals wrought in stone, wood, and other materials – which rise above the wall. Some of the men make sounds as well. The shades from these contrivances are projected onto the wall at which the captives are bound to stare. With no other options available, they take the shades and the sounds as reality (τὰ ὄντα αὐτοὺς νομίζειν, 515b). When one of the prisoners is released, compelled to stand up and turn his head, he begins to move towards the light. At first he is overwhelmed by the rays of light radiating into the cave from the outside as well as the light stemming from the fire. Due to the glitter and dazzle of the light, he is unable to discern the objects. Being told that he has spent his life on nonsense and foolishness (φλυαρία) and that he – in his move towards the light – has now come closer to reality (νῦν δὲ μᾶλλόν τι ἐγγυτέρω τοῦ ὄντος), has turned towards more real things (καὶ πρὸς μᾶλλον ὄντα), and sees things more correctly (ὀρθότερον), he is likely to react with confusion, thinking that what he previously saw was more real than what he now sees (515d). Although this captive – due to his inclination to return to his safe, habitual position in the cavern –, with great difficulty, pain, and re-

> institutional sphere becoming autonomous for the first time in human history; and, as opposed to kinship which is always provincial and polity which is always delimited by physical boundaries, this sphere was capable of stretching its boundaries much further because it extended the criteria for membership beyond old local, tribal, or purely ethnic definitions."

luctance, has to be prevented from returning by force, the process is arduous. First, after having seen the burning fire he should be stopped from returning to the other prisoners. Second, subsequent to being confronted with real sunlight, the former prisoner will once again react with anger, annoyed that he has been dragged into the sun, the light of which blinds him and makes him incapable of discerning any of the things conveyed to him as real (τὰ νῦν λεγομένα ἀληθά, 516a). In the end, however, he will obtain clear sight and a lucid perception of things, and he will be happy about the change (αὐτὸν μὲν εὐδαιμονίζειν τῆς μεταβολῆς) and feel pity for his former co-prisoners (516c). Among the captives there have been continuous competitions and prizes given to the man who is the quickest to discern the passing shadows and the best at remembering their customary antecedents (516c). If the released prisoner were once again to return to the cave and participate in these contests, he would, due to his newly won sight, suffer from a lack of habituation to darkness and dimness of vision and perform poorly in the competition. The other captives would deride him, thinking that his eyes have been ruined and his trip out of the cavern has been in vain. Ultimately, were someone to attempt to free the other prisoners from their chains, they would strive to lay hands on the person and try to kill him (516e–517a).[33]

It should come as no surprise that Plato uses simile to illustrate what the lack of insight and the possession of insight into true being means, and how the philosopher – embodied in the fate of Socrates – fares in a world confronted with ignorant people captivated by an overestimation of their own cognitive abilities. Yet the parable is also indicative of a two-tier worldview integral to an Axial Age religious perspective on the world. True cognition can only come into being to the extent that humans detach themselves from the fetters that bind them to this world and by means of the soul's ascent to the intelligible place (εἰς τὸν νοητὸν τόπον) obtain insight into the idea of the good (ἡ τοῦ ἀγαθοῦ ἰδέα, 517bc). Every person has the ability to obtain this knowledge (518c) by means of the divine part of the soul (518e), but only persons who *de facto* turn this part of their soul towards liberating cognition will come to the point of true insight. The ascent to true being (τὰ ὄντα) is indicative of true philosophy (φιλοσοφία ἀληθής, 521c), and it is the task of the philosopher to lead the ignorant to insight (520b–c). It is by virtue of participation in the divine, enabled by the divine part of the soul, that philosophers are capable of liberat-

---

33   For ritual elements in Plato's myths, see Lars Albinus "The Katabasis of Er: Plato's Use of Myths Exemplified by the Myth of Er," in *Essays on Plato's Republic* (ed. Erik N. Ostenfeld; ASMA 2; Aarhus: Aarhus University Press, 1998), 91–105, in which he demonstrates how ritual layers underlie the *Republic*.

ing themselves from the mundane view and obtaining the divine perspective that ultimately grants them insight into the idea of the good. Such a perspective is markedly different from the basic worldview of archaic forms of religion, in which humans uphold their existence by preserving the necessary distance from the divine world (*la bonne distance*). As long as the two realms are kept apart – demonstrably expressed in ancient temple architecture – and humans acknowledge the gods as gods by means of regular sacrifices, the blessings of the gods, in the form of those elements humans need in order to prolong their existence (typically nutrition, offspring, and a long and peaceful life), will continue to flow from the divine world to the human. The implication of this type of religion is that the world as such is basically good. Axial Age forms of religion, conversely, are based on the exact opposite premise – that humans, in order to attain true life, have to detach themselves from this world by gaining access to the divine world. This is cognitively staged in Plato's parable of the cave, which inculcates in humans the need to follow the divine part of the soul in order to gain access to the divine world so that they eventually will be able to see the good.

A similar point is expressed in the famous myth of the soul in the *Phaedrus* (246a–256e).[34] In his second speech in the dialogue, which is centered on love as divine madness (243e–257b),[35] Socrates argues that an account of what the soul really is would require a long, thoroughly divine elucidation, but it is within human power to describe what the soul is like (ᾧ δὲ ἔοικεν) in a brief manner (246a). He then proceeds to compare the soul (ἐοικέτο) with the composite nature of a pair of winged horses and a charioteer. The horses and charioteer of the deities are good and of noble breed, while those of other beings are mixed. Socrates asserts that it is difficult to steer the humans' chariot, since one horse is good and of fine descent while the other is the distinct opposite. This doubleness is the reason for humans being both immortal and mortal. The perfect soul, fully winged, mounts upwards and governs the whole world. When it loses its wings, it descends until it gets hold of something solid, at which point it settles down and takes upon itself an earthly body. By means of the soul, the body is autokinetic.[36] It is this totality of soul and body which is designated a mortal, living being (ζῷον, 246c). Conversely, the gods are com-

---

34  In 265c Socrates alludes to his speech as a μυθικός τις ὕμνος.

35  For the relationship between the speech and its argument of the immortality of the soul and the subsequent myth, see Bett, "Immortality and the Nature of the Soul," 442–44.

36  For the importance of this motif in the speech, see Anne Lebeck, "The Central Myth of Plato's *Phaedrus*," *Greek, Roman, and Byzantine Studies* 13 no. 3 (1972): 267–90, esp. 269. See also the use of this motif in the *Laws* 893b–894c.

posed of a soul and a body that are united for all time.³⁷ The reason why humans might lose their wings has to do with the double nature of the soul.

First, Plato describes how the gods, headed by Zeus in his winged chariot, ascend to the banquet and feast at the top of the vault of heaven. The case is different with humans, whose wings sink due to vileness and evil, which is contrary to the divine (246e). The gods, equipped with divine wings – consisting of that which is beautiful, wise, and good –, proceed to the heavenly zenith through which they pass in order to stand on the outer surface of heaven. From here they behold things outside heaven (247b). Plato acknowledges that no poet on earth was ever capable of worthily describing this, nor shall one ever be able to do so. Yet the figure in Plato's narrative, Socrates, is committed to tell the truth. Therefore he reveals how the immortal souls who have advanced to this place are confronted with truly existing being, which is without colour and form (ἡ γὰρ ἀχρώματός τε καὶ ἀσχημάτιστος καὶ ἀναφὴς οὐσία ὄντως οὖσα, 247c). This being can only be seen by the mind (μόνῳ θεατὴ νῷ), which is the helmsman of the soul (κυβερνήτης ψυχῆς), and only this form of being can be the object of true knowledge (τὸ τῆς ἀληθοῦς ἐπιστήμης γένος, ibid.). The soul rejoices in seeing true being, whereby it is nourished. Subsequent to this extra-celestial travel, the charioteer brings the horses back and feeds them with ambrosia and gives them nectar to drink (247e). Such, claims Plato's Socrates, are the lives of the gods. Although some humans may be elevated to the place outside heaven and join the gods in the heavenly cycle, they are easily disturbed by the horses and, therefore, barely see true being. Other humans aspire to partake in the heavenly journey, but they are unequal to the task. Due to the incompetence of the charioteers, some even have their wings broken, and they never succeed in beholding true being (248a–b). Therefore they have to feed only on opinion (καὶ ἀπελθοῦσαι τροφῇ δοξαστῇ χρῶνται, 248b). Souls naturally yearn for the meadow of truth that nourishes the noblest part of the soul and its wings (a reference to orphic mythological rhetoric).³⁸ Yet, as Plato goes on

---

37  This may appear slightly strange, given that one would expect corporeality also to constitute an impediment to the gods. Yet, the gods are special, among other things, by virtue of the fact that their body is no hindrance to the flourishing of their souls. Van Riel (*Plato's Gods*, 48) takes the combination of body and soul in the gods to be the reason why Plato expresses caution and reluctance towards the account: "It (the living being) is not immortal by any reasonable supposition, but we, though we have never seen or rightly conceived a god, imagine an immortal being which has both soul and a body which are united for all times. Let that, however, and our words concerning it, be as is pleasing to god" (246c–d).

38  See Lars Albinus, *The House of Hades: Studies in Ancient Greek Eschatology* (Aarhus: Aarhus University Press, 2000), 132.

to claim, souls that have managed to follow the gods and thus obtain a partial view of truth shall not suffer until the next period begins. To the extent that these souls continue to succeed in following the gods, they will remain unharmed until time eternal. Most souls, however, are not capable of accomplishing this. Consequently, they will not behold true being; they will suffer from mischance and fall victim to oblivion and evil, and, weighed down by growing heaviness, they will eventually lose their wings and fall to the ground.

Depending on the seriousness of their fall, different souls will be incarnated hierarchically according to their chances of rejoining this celestial, divine travel. At the top of the hierarchy is the soul that has seen the most. This soul shall be incarnated at the birth of a future philosopher, a lover of beauty, or one who follows the Muses and Eros (248d). For all other souls it takes a cycle of 10,000 years before they return to their point of departure and regain wings (249a). Some souls are even reborn as beasts if they have never taken part in truth. The philosopher's soul, however, is unique in its wings. In as much as it is able, through memory, to be in continuous communion with those things that make a god divine (πρὸς οἷσπερ θεὸς ὢν θεῖός ἐστιν, 249c), it succeeds in remaining close to the gods. In language presumably referring to the Eleusinian mysteries,[39] Plato, through the voice of Socrates, goes on to argue that by employing memory rightly, the philosopher "is always initiated into perfect mysteries, and he alone becomes perfect" (τελέους ἀεὶ τελετὰς τελεούμενος, τέλεος ὄντως μόνος γίγνεται, ibid.).[40] Similarly, the philosopher sets

---

39  The usual reference to the Eleusinian mysteries is τὰ μυστήρια, but Plato here employs τελεταί, which seems to be part of a polemic against Orphic interpretation of the Eleusinian mysteries. In the *Republic* 362e–365c there is a similar polemic against Orphic understanding. Here Plato also refers to the τελεταί (365a) aimed to free humans from evils in the other world. Cf. his use of τελεταί in *Phaedo* 69c; *Protagoras* 316d. For Plato's criticism of an Orphic 'take over' of the Eleusinian mysteries, see Fritz Graf, *Eleusis und die orphische Dichtung Athens in vorhellenisticher Zeit* (RVV 33; Berlin: De Gruyter, 1974), 95–121. For a far more cautious view on Orphic influence, see Robert Parker, *Athenian Religion: A History* (Oxford: Clarendon Press, 1996), 100f., although he primarily relates his assertion to the sixth century BCE.

40  See Nightingale, *Spectacles of Truth*, 88. Cf. my note 15 above and *Republic* 251a. The contrast to the philosopher's soul as initiated into the mysteries of true being is the soul that fails to return to this true being. These souls will go away uninitiated into the beholding of being (ἀτελεῖς τῆς τοῦ ὄντος θέας ἀπέρχονται, 248b). The motif was already intonated in 245a in the rejection of the poet who is without possession of the madness of the Muses. Such a poet shall come to the doors of the Muses, confident of his own technical skills, but he will never be initiated (ἀτελὸς αὐτός), and his poetry shall vanish, based as it is on intelligence and not divine madness.

himself apart from human interests and turns his attention towards the divine (πρὸς τῷ θείῳ). The masses will judge him to be out of his mind; his inspiration is concealed from them (ἐνθουσιάζων, 249d3).

At this point, Plato has Socrates close the first part of the discourse. In the second part of the speech (249d4–257b), Socrates discusses the yearning of the soul to regain its previous state. Here he focuses on the lover, because love is the means by which this goal can be reached.[41] Yet recovering what has been lost is a difficult process; all the more so because it is arduous to arrive at images of justice and temperance, and even more so to behold the nature of that which they imitate, by means of the dark organs of sense (250a), since there is no light emanating from their earthly copies (ἐν τοῖς τῇδε ὁμοιώμασιν). Beauty, however, was visible in shining brightness in former times, when some souls in happy company followed Zeus in train, and other souls followed other gods. That was the time during which the souls saw the blessed sight and "were initiated into that which is rightly called the most blessed of mysteries" (καὶ ἐτελοῦντο τῶν τελετῶν ἣν θέμις λέγειν μακαριωτάτην, 250b).[42] Continuing in the wake of the Eleusinian mysteries terminology, Plato relates the souls' celebration of the most blessed of mysteries,

> which we celebrated in a state of perfection (ἣν ὠργιάζομεν ὁλόκληροι), when we were without experience of the evils which awaited us in the time to come, being permitted as initiates (μυούμενοι) to the sight of perfect and simple and calm and happy apparitions (ὁλόκληρα δὲ καὶ ἁπλᾶ καὶ ἀτρεμῆ καὶ εὐδαίμονα φάσματα), which we saw in the pure light (ἐποπτεύοντες ἐν αὐγῇ καθαρᾷ), being ourselves pure (καθαροὶ ὄντες) and not entombed (ἀσήμαντοι) in this which we carry about with us and call the body (σῶμα), in which we are imprisoned like an oyster in its shell. (250b–c)[43]

At this point I shall leave Socrates' speech and relate the text to my previous argument. Similar to the cave parable in the *Republic*, the myth of the soul in *Phaedrus* presupposes a two-tier worldview. The earthly world stands in dire

---

41   Cf. the similar argument in the *Symposium* in Socrates' speech (201d–212c), in particular 210e–212b. Parallel with the speech in the *Symposium*, Socrates' second speech in the *Phaedrus* is given in honour of Eros: "There, dear Eros, you have my recantation which I have offered as well and as beautifully as I could" (257a).

42   When quoting or paraphrasing from the *Phaedrus*, I use a modified version of Harold Fowler's LCL-translation.

43   The last sentence is another echo of Orphic discourse.

contrast to the heavenly world, a dualism which parallels the distinction between interiority (represented by the soul) and exteriority (exemplified by the body). The body is a grave for the soul. True insight can only be attained by gaining access to the divine world. This can only take place by means of that element in humans that already at the outset is united with the divine world. In that regard, this type of religion upholds the notion of a sharp ontological divide between gods and humans, which is characteristic of archaic forms of religion. Contrary to archaic types of religion, however, the myth of the soul in *Phaedrus* emphasises the double nature of humans. By means of the soul, they are capable of gaining access to the divine world. There is also a clear priority. Given the deficient form of being provided by the earthly world, souls should strive for a continuous presence in the divine world in communion with the gods. Similarly to what we saw in the *Republic*, *Phaedrus* also emphasises the ethical aspect. The souls that sink are the ones dragged down by the horse that is the opposite of nobility and good breeding. Perfect souls are not contaminated with vileness and evil. The advantage of the philosopher, similarly, lies in the fact that he – nourished by intelligence and good knowledge – remains, through memory, in perpetual communion with those things that make a god divine.

## 4    Plato as a Representative of Axial Age Religion

On the basis of these two pivotal Platonic texts, I shall return to the eight key features emphasised above as central to Axial Age religion. To what extent do they apply to Plato?

With respect to a form of thinking about thinking or second-order language, this is undoubtedly a prevalent feature in Plato's *oeuvre*. It is not least the existence of this element that qualifies his work as philosophy. In our brief examination of the cave parable and the myth of the soul, we have observed how Plato strives to delineate true being by externalising the view he applies to the world. Simultaneously, we have observed his use of second-order terms, which enables him to subsume different phenomena under more basic categories. Plato's use of the dialogic, elenchic form, although hardly employed in these two Socratic myths, as well as his positioning of logical argument, enables him to criticise habitual thinking and advance critical thinking, which leads to new and more complex insights.

We have also seen how this form of self-reflexivity is spatially reflected in the underlying epistemology. Plato's contrasts between heaven and earth, the interior of the cavern and the outside light, the soul and the body are a spatial mirroring of the difference established between truth and falsehood. In order to obtain a true understanding of the world, one has to engage in that form of activity and beholding that Plato locates in the divine, heavenly world.

Plato speaks interchangeably of god(s) in the singular and the plural, just as he acknowledges the existence of half-gods, heroes, and chthonic divinities.[44] In that regard, one cannot claim that he represents a development towards heno- or monotheism. Yet, as is well known, there are other elements in Plato's *oeuvre* that point in this direction. In the *Timaeus* Plato ascribes to the Demiurge the status of both father and maker of the gods, but also of assuming the role of the highest god (see *Timaeus* 34c–36d). However one interprets the *Timaeus* passage, it unquestionably exemplifies the movement towards henotheism. The same may be said of Plato's notion of true being (τὸ ὄν). The gods and the perfect human souls are capable of reaching the celestial apex through which they pass in order to stand on the outer surface of heaven. From here they behold true being, which can only be appreciated by the mind. Clearly there is an element of henotheism or, more appropriately, heno-ontism in this notion as well.

Throughout Platonic religiosity there is a strong attempt to denigrate, repudiate, and reject sophism as a rival worldview which, in as much as it gains power, threatens the flourishing of true religion – that is, Plato's philosophy. Although there is no direct attack on the *polis*-religion *per se*, there are certainly critiques of it, as may be seen in Plato's rejection of prayers and sacrifices as a form of barter through which people can obtain the favours of the gods (cf. *Euthyphro* 14c–15c; *Republic* 363e–367a; *Laws* 885b–e, 888a–d, 905d–907b, 948b–c). There will be prayers, sacrifices, hymns to the gods, temples, festivals etc. in Plato's ideal city of Kallipolis in the *Laws*, but it is crucial that these institutions should not be abused by the idea that, through them, one can negotiate with the gods.

We have seen how Platonic religion is also characterised by the abolition of the ontological differentiation between gods and humans. By virtue of the divine soul, humans are in possession of something that unites them with the gods and the highest form of being. As highlighted by David Sedley, the notion of divinisation plays a pivotal role in Platonic religiosity.[45] Adherents of philosophy are enjoined to imitate the godhead to such an extent that eventually

---

44  For a list of the different divinities mentioned by Plato, see Aikaterini Lefka, "La presence des divinités traditionelles dans l'œuvre de Platon," in *Les dieux de Platon* (ed. Jérome Laurent; Caen: Presses universitaires de Caen, 2003), 97–117, esp. 98f.

45  See Sedley, ("The Ideal of Godlikeness," 315), who places emphasis on the moral aspect of divinisation. See also Anders Klostergaard Petersen, "Finding a Basis for Interpreting New Testament Ethos," in *Early Christian Ethics in Interaction with Jewish and Graeco-Roman*

they may be said to transcend the ontological differentiation between divine and human. As Mark McPherran has similarly underlined, this development implies that "now the central task of human existence becomes less a matter of assisting gods and more a matter of becoming as much like them as one can."[46]

Closely related to the previous point, Plato places considerable emphasis on self-improvement in the form of philosophy. Contrary to the spread of different types of ἄσκησις in the form of privation as a prevalent feature of Axial Age religion, privation does not feature prominently in Plato's thinking. If, however, we take ἄσκησις in its basic Greek meaning as training and exercise, this element is very noticeable in Plato. The philosopher is called to emulate the worldview his philosophical vocation has committed him to follow. As claimed in the *Phaedo*, true philosophers are the ones who train in death (ἀποθνῄσκειν μελετῶσι, 67e, cf. 81a μελέτη θανάτου). They are hostile to the body and desire to have the soul set apart, by itself, alone (67e). The philosopher should strive, as we saw in the myths of the cave and of the soul, to have his soul ascend to the place at which, nourished by reason, he shall be able to contemplate pure being.

Related to the previous three points, Platonic religion may – comparably to other Axial Age types of religion – be understood as exemplary of a shift in emphasis from the ritual observance of traditional religion to the inner disposition as a prerequisite for proper cultic observance. This is especially obvious in Plato' critique of the idea that, through prayer and sacrifice, one can negotiate with the gods. Although Plato's religiosity does not testify to an attack on the dominant *polis*-religion, it does, by virtue of the type of religiosity it promotes, entail a sort of defiance. By emphasising justice, temperance, and goodness as the moral stance of the philosopher, Plato risks making traditional religious piety superfluous. The man dear to the gods is the one who spends his life becoming like them, whereby he will, of necessity, also come to incarnate the virtues of the aforementioned qualities (cf. *Republic* 613b; *Laws* 896b–897d). Plato avoids critisising the traditional cult *per se*. More accurately, he calls for a moral attitude that reflects the new worldview as a prerequisite for the true cultivation of traditional religion. Thereby, however, similarly to other proponents of Axial Age religion, he came to pave the way for a devel-

---

*Contexts* (ed. Jan Willem van Henten and Joseph Verheyden; STAR 17; Leiden: Brill 2013), 53–81, esp. 75–77.

46  McPherran, "Platonic Religion," 247; cf. *Symposium* 207c–209e; *Phaedrus* 248a.252c–253c; *Republic* 613a–b; *Theaetetus* 172b–177c; *Timaeus* 90a–d; *Laws* 716c For the significance of this motif in Axial Age types of religion, see Petersen, "Finding a Basis."

opment that eventually made the sacrificial institution obsolete – at the very least with respect to sacrificing animals.[47]

Finally, it is reasonable to argue that although Plato represented the Athenian elite, on the basis of his close relationship with Socrates and his subsequent continued philosophical pursuits he also embodied the religious entrepreneur. In principle, Platonic religion is open to all human beings who aspire to engage in philosophical activity and thereby become like the god(s), in as much as this is possible. Despite the fact that Plato continues to uphold the archaic *polis*-religion, his philosophical endeavour makes traditional kinship structures less significant. The status of the good soul in Plato's Axial Age religion is independent of the social status of the persons in question. To the extent that they succeed in becoming true philosophers, they are also able to join the soul's journey to the extra-celestial realm, from where it may behold true being.

This brief application of eight central Axial Age elements to Plato's work has vividly demonstrated the relevance of such a perspective for the examination of Plato. But what does it amount to? I return to my initial question and the overall purpose of this article: Why Plato's philosophy? Why not just designate it his (Axial Age) religion?

## 5   Conclusion

One may reasonably object to my argument that Plato can be seen as a representative of Axial Age religion that I have made the case less demanding for myself by having recourse to two of Plato's famous myths: the myth of the cave and the myth of the soul. In Plato, however, there is always an intrinsic relationship between what is conveyed in myth and the preceding philosophical argument, so there is no contradiction between the two. Simultaneously, his use of myth testifies to the fact that the ultimate goal of Platonic philosophy is to gain insight into that which, by virtue of logical argument, is genuinely ineffable and inexpressible. Yet this fact does not release philosophy from its aspiration to strive for true being. To communicate the content of true being and what it involves, one ultimately has to resort to mythic language as a type of revelatory discourse.

What is expressed in myth, however, may be seen as a spatialisation of the basic epistemological structure contained in philosophical discourse. Plato as-

---

47   See also McPherran, "Platonic Religion," 246.

serts that a true account of the world and, thereby, of being can only be given when looked upon from the outside, from an external perspective. This external perspective happens to be identical with the view taken by the perfect souls located at the top of the vault of heaven. Plato's own designation for this activity is philosophy, but from an etic point of view, we can hardly see this as anything but a novel type of religion in competition with the archaic ones. As it happens, Plato's philosophy is neither singular nor unique in this regard. It is an integral element in a process of cultural evolution through which archaic religions slowly transformed into Axial Age forms of religion. This process occurred more or less simultaneously from the seventh century BCE onwards in China, India, Israel, and Greece. The presuppositions of this process as well as its concrete manifestations were not identical in these various cultures. Yet the number of sufficiently parallel elements support the notion of a recurrent pattern of features and, thereby, the concept of a general development.

When seen through this lens of cultural evolution, Platonic philosophy does not emerge as something categorically different from religion, provided religion is looked upon from the etic perspective. On the contrary, Plato's philosophy is, in fact, religion, in as much as it designates "semantic and cognitive networks comprising ideas, behaviours, and institutions in relation to counterintuitive superhuman agents, objects, and posits" (see note 19 above). We may let go of some of these elements, as they do not really apply to Plato, but it is without doubt that the core elements of this definition are found in his thinking, just as they are in other forms of Axial Age religion. Does this make it superfluous or fallacious to continue speaking of Plato's philosophy? Not at all, as long as we keep in mind that this is a designation that predominantly applies to the emic level of analysis. In terms of overall understanding of Plato and his thinking, however, we had better give up the notion and begin talking about Platonic religion.

Plato's religion refers to the religion cultivated by Plato, about which we know something but not everything. In as much as we can see, Plato was a good observer of the *polis*-religion. At the same time, however, he was a religious reformer, and it is as such that he has exerted an inestimable influence on subsequent developments, both with respect to religion and, at a later time, to philosophy detached from religion. I suggest that we designate this aspect of Plato's religion as Platonic religion in order not to confuse it with the former. Plato's religion became extinct with the end of antiquity. Platonic religion, conversely, lingers on in two forms. First, Platonic religion – together with contemporaneous representatives of Axial Age religion – remains as a basic structure in those forms of religion that have undergone the Axial Age development – that is, the so-called world religions, including Judaism, which strictly speaking is not a world religion. Secondly, Platonic religion endures in later forms of (especially Western) philosophy as a type of thinking that subsequent forms of philosophy have to relate to one way or another. So should we ultimately speak of Plato's philosophy or of Platonic religion? I think the latter is the most adequate historical designation of what was at stake for Plato.

# Platonic Piety: 'Putting Humpty Dumpty Together Again'[1]

*Frisbee Sheffield*

> What is hell? I maintain that it is the suffering of being unable to love.
> FYODOR DOSTOYEVSKY, *The Brothers Karamazov*

∴

Thinking about piety in the dialogues of Plato has become a divided affair. On the one hand there are those who use the so-called 'positive turn' at the end of the *Euthyphro* to develop a 'Socratic' account of piety, where this is supposed to bear some relationship to the historical Socrates. As a result, supporting evidence is restricted to the *Apology*, a work whose views are held to bear greater resemblance to the views of the historical Socrates. In that work, the philosophical practice of 'care for the soul', particularly Socrates' characteristic occupation with uncovering ignorance, is described as a service to the god Apollo (23b, c1, 28e–29a, 29d–30b, 30c7, 30e–31b, 37e–38a), and so it has been thought to provide a specification of that service to the gods, which eluded the interlocutors of the *Euthyphro*. The result of this practice is (ideally) the possession of a specifically human wisdom, which reflects one's proper place in relation to the superior wisdom of the gods.[2] On the other hand, the work

---

[1] This paper was delivered at a conference on Ancient Philosophy and Religion in 2014, and the 2014 meeting of the SAAP in Cambridge, and the Ancient Philosophy workshop in Oxford in 2015. I wish to thank the audiences there for comments; in particular, Gabor Betegh, Sarah Broadie, Gail Fine, Christopher Gill (who suggested the title), Terence Irwin, Lindsay Judson, David Lee, Anthony Long, Malcolm Schofield, David Sedley, and James Warren. I would also like to thank Radcliffe Edmonds, James Lesher, Mark McPherran, Suzanne Ozbrdralek, Christopher Rowe, and Shaul Tor for comments.

[2] See M. McPherran, "Socratic Piety in the *Euthyphro*," *Journal of the History of Philosophy* 23 (1985): 283–309; G. Vlastos, *Socrates: Ironist and Moral Philosopher* (New York: Cornell University Press, 1991); and C. Taylor, "The End of the *Euthyphro*," *Phronesis* 27 (1982): 109–18; who use the *Apology* to interpret the *Euthyphro* and provide a 'Socratic' account of piety, where this, it is often suggested, has some connection to the historical Socrates. See also S. Calef, "Piety and the Unity of Virtue in *Euthyphro* 11e–14c," *OSAP* 13 (1995): 1–26.

of Sedley[3] and Annas[4] has promoted the ethical ideal of god-likeness in the *Theaetetus* and the *Timaeus*, which suggests an alternative account of piety. In this view, our relationship with the gods resides in our becoming like them with respect to contemplative wisdom.[5] Though this shows the gods due reverence, it is not clear whether this is also some kind of service to them and, if so, in what way. These two strands of thinking about human relationships with the divine often fail to intersect (something that works well for those who see a divide between the authentically 'Socratic' and the 'Platonic' in the works of Plato).

There are also significant differences between these views on the exercise of piety as a virtue. For example, Vlastos has argued, with respect to the *Apology*, that piety is or involves moral virtue insofar as it involves care and concern for others: "doing on the god's behalf, in assistance to him, work the god wants done and would be doing himself if he could" and that is specifically work for the benefit of one's fellow men.[6] Annas, by contrast, has argued that the ideal of becoming like god is rather a spiritual ideal of disengagement from the world.[7]

In a recent paper Rowe[8] has provided a bridge between these two views of piety, arguing that intellectual activity in a broad sense, rather than acts of moral virtue, was always central to the accounts of piety in the *Euthyphro* and the *Apology*. He argues for an account of Socratic piety that does not take this to refer in the main to any 'Socrates' that is distinct from 'Plato' and does not take Plato to be committed to the idea – even in these texts – that piety consists in living a moral life;[9] he argues that even in the *Apology* it is not

---

3 "The Ideal of God-likeness," in *Plato: Ethics, Politics, Religion and the Soul* (ed. Gail Fine; Oxford: Oxford University Press, 1999), 309–29.
4 *Platonic Ethics, Old and New* (New York: Cornell University Press, 1999).
5 For various formulations of this idea, see: *Alcibiades* 1 133c1–6; *Phaedo* 80e2–1a10, 82b10–c1; *Phaedrus* 248a1–c5, 249c4–d3, 252d1–3c2; *Republic* 500c9–d1, 501b1–7, 613a4–b1; *Symposium* 207c9–8b4; *Theaetetus* 176a8–b3; *Timaeus* 47b5–c4, 90b1–d7; *Laws* 716b8–d4, 792c8–d5, 906a7–b3.
6 G. Vlastos, "Socratic Piety" in *Socrates: Ironist and Moral Philosopher* (ed. G. Vlastos; Cambridge: Cambridge University Press, 1991), 157–79 at 175.
7 See Annas, *Platonic Ethics*. Those texts highlighted by Sedley and Annas discuss our relationship to the divine in terms of contemplation, and not acts of moral virtue; for such actions are not those in which the gods engage, and the ethical ideal is to become like god; cf. Sedley, "The Ideal of God-likeness," 324. J. Armstrong ("Becoming like God: After the Ascent," *OSAP* [2004]) has questioned the emphasis on disengagement in the 'becoming like god' ideal, however.
8 C.J. Rowe, "Socrates and His Gods" in *Politeia in Greek and Roman Philosophy* (ed. V. Harte and M. Lane; Cambridge: Cambridge University Press, 2013), 313–29, esp. 313.
9 Rowe, "Socrates and His Gods," 321.

clear that helping others is the primary focus of Socrates' activity, rather than cultivating wisdom as such; the important point is that "Socrates saw his life as one of the intellect." This view allows for greater continuity between Plato's treatment of piety in the *Euthyphro* and the *Apology* and the contemplative ideal, which comes to the fore in later works.[10]

I propose to draw the threads of this discussion together by highlighting the role of a text I argue should be foundational for this discussion: the *Symposium*. In that work, Socrates argues that *erōs* is a mediator with the divine and that all relations between men and gods operate through *daimonic* spirits, such as, specifically, *erōs* (202e–203a). Taking my lead from those scholars who see the *Euthyphro's* discussion as basic for an exploration of piety, I attempt to develop an account of Platonic piety in the *Symposium*, using issues raised in the *Euthyphro* as a guide. The specific issues in that work seem to be: (i) to specify how one acts for the sake of the gods in a way that makes it clear one is not benefitting them; (ii) how to specify the *ergon* of the gods in such a way that we can clarify our assistance in this work; and (iii), having done so, how to grasp how this pious work is a part of justice.[11] I argue that the *Symposium* can shed light on all three issues, and it does so in a way that mediates between the other-directed account of piety for which Vlastos argued on the basis of the *Apology* and the contemplative ideal of god-likeness highlighted by Sedley and Annas. It helps to put piety 'back together again' by showing how it functions in a single account. Since this account is one in which *erōs* is central, I also consider whether the relationship between *erōs* and piety is of any lasting significance for Plato and, if so, why that is the case.

1    The *Euthyphro* Puzzles

During the 'positive turn' at the end of the *Euthyphro*, the following claim is explored: "Piety is that part of justice which is our service to the gods" (12e5–8). The connection between justice and piety is first suggested by Socrates, who

---

10    And which, for Rowe ("Socrates and His Gods"), finds expression in Aristotle's *Eudemian Ethics* 8.3 1249b6–23, where he writes of '*therapeuein kai theōrein*' – 'serving and studying god'. Taylor's ("The End of the *Euthyphro*") account of piety in the *Euthyphro* also argues that moral virtue is not essential for Socratic piety (though, unlike Rowe, he does take this account to be authentically Socratic).

11    I am not committed to the claim that the views expressed during the so-called 'positive turn' are those of Socrates, as opposed to those of Euthyphro; they appear within an examination of *Euthyphro's* views. For the purposes of this chapter, what matters is that we accept these views as ones Plato wants us to entertain seriously.

claims that if Euthyphro identifies correctly that part of justice to which piety refers, he will have "learnt sufficiently" what piety is (12e).[12] When clarifying the nature of the service (*therapeia*), Euthyphro confronts difficulties. His proposal is rejected because it implies that the subject of the service is improved or benefitted in a way that is incompatible with the idea that the gods are good and self-sufficient; they stand in need of no improvement by inferior mortals (13b–d). The implication (of 13b–c) is that there is more than one way of acting for the sake of an end. This is borne out in the need to distinguish between horse-breeding and cattle-rearing, where "one aims at the good and the benefit of the object cared for" (b8) while the other, as in the case of the gods, does not aim to make them better (c11–12). This distinction is not clarified sufficiently by the introduction of the new term *hypēretikē* and the notion that the kind of care involved in tending to the gods is that of "servants to masters" (d5); a servant can benefit his master by providing things he needs. This new notion of service captures the asymmetry of the relationship between men and gods, but does not, by itself, resolve the problem of how to construe this relationship in such a way that there is no implication that the object cared for benefits. The issue, more precisely, is not that some benefit or that good arises from the service; the introduction of shipbuilders and doctors shows that many human *hypēresiai* who help with some *ergon* produce some good result (13df.). The specific issue is to clarify the *pankalon ergon* of the gods in such a way that "the many fine things that the gods achieve" (14a9–10) by our service are not such as to benefit them. Socrates indicates that if Euthyphro were able to clarify this issue, then that would have been sufficient for understanding the nature of piety (14b–c). As McPherran argues,[13] this suggests that a promising proposal would explore the following thesis: Piety is that part of justice which is a service (*hypēretikē*) of men to the gods, assisting the gods in their work (*ergon*), a work which produces some good result. The following issues require clarification: (i) how one acts for the sake of the gods in a way that makes it clear one is not benefitting them; (ii) the *ergon* of the gods, which might, in turn, clarify our assistance in this work; and (iii) how assistance in this work might be seen as a part of justice.

---

12  See McPherran, "Socratic Piety," 285; Taylor, "The End of the *Euthyphro*," 116; and Vlastos, *Socrates*, 228 n. 16.

13  Mark L. McPherran, "Socratic Piety in the *Euthyphro*" in *Essays on the Philosophy of Socrates* (ed. H. Benson, Oxford: Oxford University Press, 1992), 220–42 at 223.

## 2    Eros and the Divine

I take these issues in turn and show how the *Symposium* can contribute to addressing them. First let me persuade the reader of the deep connection between *erōs* and the divine in this work. In a neglected passage, Socrates provides an account of *erōs*, which is explicitly said to structure all relations between men and gods. The function or power of *erōs* is that of

> interpreting and conveying things from men to gods and from gods to men – men's petitions and sacrifices, the god's commands and returns for sacrifices; being in the middle between both, it fills in the space between them, so that the whole is bound close together. It is through this that the whole expertise of the seer works its effects, and that of priests, and of those concerned with sacrifices, rites, spells, and the whole realm of the seer and of magic. God does not mix with man: through this it is that there takes place all intercourse and conversation of gods with men, whether awake or asleep; and the person who is wise about such things is a *daimonic* man while the one who is wise in anything else, in relation to one or other sort of expertise or manual craft is vulgar. These spirits, then, are many, and one of them is Eros. (*Symposium* 202e–203a; translated by Rowe)

This is designed to answer a *ti esti* question about *erōs*, the answer to which is that *erōs* is an intermediate *daimōn*, whose function is to mediate with the divine. Indeed, "all society and converse of men with gods and of gods with men" is characterised as *daimonic*, one form of which is *erōs*. So *daimones* more generally are in charge, rather than just Eros, but Eros is listed an as illustrative example of this specific kind of *daimonic* work. Listed here are some of the activities, such as prayers and sacrifices, mentioned by Euthyphro as activities involved in pious relations with the gods (*Euthyphro* 14b3). If this passage (henceforth 'the *daimōn* passage') is taken seriously, by which I mean properly integrated into the rest of Socrates' account, this suggests that all of the productive activities of *erōs* detailed in the lower and the higher mysteries should be seen in this light – that is, as ways in which things are 'interpreted and conveyed' from gods to men and from men to gods. They exemplify *erōs*' function as a mediator with the divine. As we might expect, the intellectual 'ascent' to the form of beauty recalls the language of this passage and is characterised as an 'initiation' into divine mysteries (*ta telea kai epoptika* at 210a1, with *teletas*,

202e8).[14] The aim of all mystery rites – including the Eleusinian Mysteries, to which this text especially refers – was, as Edmonds has argued recently, "to improve the worshipper's relation with the god through a closer contact and experience of the deity;" indeed, "each performance of the ritual was a service to the deity, and a sign of a pious disposition."[15] This particular, philosophical operation of *erōs* in the highest mysteries of the 'ascent' results in the desiring agent "becoming dear to the gods" (212a6), a *pathos* of piety, according to the *Euthyphro*, which all and only pious actions share (9e, 11a6–b1). We have good reason, then, to employ this account in an understanding of Platonic piety.[16]

---

14  On the significance of the mystery terminology, see M. Morgan, *Platonic Piety: Philosophy and Ritual in Fourth Century Athens* (New Haven: Yale University Press, 1990), esp. 80–99. He argues that the religious terminology highlights "Plato's attempt to vindicate Socrates from an old charge and to underscore his own indictment of Athenian piety, by portraying Socrates as a devoted initiate into mysteries even deeper than those celebrated at Eleusis." W. Burkert (*Greek Religion* [Harvard, MA: Harvard University Press, 1987], 92) argues that the distinction between "preliminary initiation" and "perfect and epoptic mysteries... clearly refers to Eleusis." Note the parallels with the *Phaedrus'* characterisation of philosophical *erōs*: the philosopher comes to be perfect (*teleos*) "by always being initiated into perfect rites" (*teleous aei teletas teloumenos*, 249c6–d3; cf. 250b8–c5 on the precarnate vision of Beauty). This is described as a turning towards the divine, and as a possession by the divine (249e1–3).

15  See R. Edmonds, "Alcibiades the Profane: Mystery Terminology in Plato's *Symposium*" (forthcoming).

16  Before we do so, a word of caution. This part of Socrates' speech reports what he heard from Diotima, which may be significant. It may be appropriate for Diotima as a priestess to be describing various aspects of a spiritual realm, without thinking that these reflect Plato's views. One might further wonder; How likely it is that Plato endorsed the expertise of seers, priests, and those concerned with rites and spells? In the *Meno* it is said that they say many fine things but not on the basis of knowledge. In the *Republic* (427b) Socrates says that in Kallipolis they will make no use of religious authorities other than the god at Delphi. The *Symposium* passage does not commit Plato to the view that current seers are wise, and though familiar forms of so-called religious expertise are employed here as examples of *daimonic* work, we have yet to see whether they will be the privileged kind, or whether they will be marginalised, or radically reinterpreted by the end of the account. There are other Platonic dialogues in which Socrates seems to be in receipt of divinatory messages (e.g., *Phaedo* 84d–85b; cf. 60e2, 61b1; with K. Morgan, "The Voice of Authority: Divination and Plato's *Phaedo*," *Classical Quarterly* 60 (2010): 63–81. This suggests that though Plato may not be committed to the expertise of current practitioners of divination, he did not have a problem with these practices as such. As to how committed Socrates/Plato is to the views of Diotima, the proof is in the pudding. Let us not decide that the presence of Diotima is designed to distance Socrates/Plato from the content be-

The work of *erōs* as a *daimonic* mediator is manifested in the attempt to secure *eudaimonia*, explicitly said to be the aim of *erōs* (205d1). The etymology of *eudaimonia* cannot fail to be significant: *eudaimonia* is the proper functioning, the being well, of the *daimōn erōs* in us. As Long has argued, "In order to understand ancient philosophical usage of *eudaimonia* we need to attend to the word's etymology and its implicit reference to goodness conjoined with divinity or *daimōn*."¹⁷ Nowhere is this clearer than in the *Symposium* (and the *Timaeus* 90b–c). The mortal aspiration towards *eudaimonia* is, in fact, an aspiration towards the divine; the gods are paradigmatic examples of those who are "happy and beautiful" (202c7).¹⁸ In desiring to possess the good forever, we desire to become like the gods. The connection between *erōs* and the divine is explicit at many points in Socrates' speech, which moves between the claim that we desire *eudaimonia* and the claims that we desire to possess the good forever, that we desire to participate in the divine (208b3), that we desire immortality (207a), and that we love the "immortal" (208e2). All of these are various specifications of the desire for *eudaimonia*, conceived as the everlasting possession of good and beautiful things, that state which characterises the immortal gods (202c7).¹⁹

The characteristic activity of *erōs* (*ergon*, 206c1ff.) in pursuit of this aim is some kind of productive work (205d1) because, unlike the gods, human beings are subject to flux and change, and productive activity is the mortal approximation to a state of divine possession (207c5–208b5). Pregnancy and procreation, the means by which human nature can participate in the divine (208b5), is a divine affair (206c6). All the various actions and productions detailed in the lower and the higher mysteries are ways in which mortals try "to have a share of the divine" (*athanasias metechei*), to the extent that this is possible (208b5). The various beautiful objects erotically disposed desiring agents

---

fore we know what that content is and how her characterisation might be relevant to it, as I will suggest it is. I thank James Lesher for raising these concerns.

17 A. Long, "*Eudaimonism*, Divinity, and Rationality in Greek Ethics," *Proceedings of the Boston Area Colloquium in Ancient Philosophy* 19 (2004): 123–43 at 126.

18 Compare the definition of god given in the *Platonic Definitions* as an immortal animal sufficient unto itself for happiness (411a3).

19 I move swiftly here over the controversy about whether, and how exactly, all these various specifications of the aim of *erōs* (the good, immortality) are, in fact, related, or whether they are separate goals, as some have argued. On this issue, see C.J. Rowe, "Eros, Immortality, and Creativity" in *Proceedings of the Boston Area Colloquium in Ancient Philosophy* XIV (Leiden: Brill, 1998); and F.C.C. Sheffield, *Plato's Symposium: The Ethics of Desire* (Oxford: Oxford University Press, 2006). For the purposes of this paper, I rely on my arguments in the 2006 volume for an integrated reading of the aim of *erōs* as *eudaimonia*.

pursue promise to deliver the *eudaimonia* characteristic of the divine state (*Symposium* 202c10–d5); the productive work they facilitate allows us to have a share in the divine to the extent possible for human beings (208c5). When we become full of divine *poros* in our creative endeavours, we extend ourselves towards the divine.[20] As Sedley has argued, the *Symposium* is connected to a larger theme in the Platonic dialogues: the ethical goal of "becoming like god."[21] The description of the philosopher as "dear to the gods" at the end of the philosophical ascent (212a6) suggests that he achieves this; as Plato makes explicit in the *Laws* (IV. 716c–717a) and elsewhere, "like approves of like," a passage which suggests an identification between those whom the gods love and those who come to be like them.[22] Becoming like god is not an alternative to the idea that we desire *eudaimonia*; rather, the gods are aspirational ideals for our attempts to secure *eudaimonia*.[23] The entire account, then, is saturated with the presence of the divine, and the operations of *erōs* are expressive of our relationship to the divine.

## 3   Eros and Acting for the Sake of a Divine End

It is not obvious why *erōs* has this role, however. Why is *erōs* that by which we mediate with the divine? Or better, why is *erōs* an appropriate engine of action for the divine?[24] Attending to the characteristic features of *erōs* can, in fact, resolve some of the issues about action in relation to the divine that

---

20  The connection between the divine and the fullness and productive capacity of pregnancy may shed light on the disputed reading at 209b1, where editors have substituted ἤθεος for the MSS readings of θεῖος, since it is hard to understand why Diotima would be talking about the youth who is pregnant in the soul as being divine (θεῖος ὤν) instead of as being a youth when he desires to give birth. If Plato is indeed highlighting the similarity between reproductive capacity and the divine, however, the MSS readings of θεῖος would make sense. I thank Radcliffe Edmonds for this observation.

21  Sedley, "The Ideal of God-likeness," 310.

22  See Sedley, "The Ideal of God-likeness," 312.

23  As Annas (*Platonic Ethics*, 53) has argued: "[becoming like god] is just a specification of what happiness is. Moreover, the idea is also not intended as an alternative to the idea that virtue is sufficient for happiness; for it is explicated, in many of the passages in which it occurs, by the thought that becoming like god is what becoming virtuous is."

24  The intimate connection between *erōs* and the divine recurs in Plato's *Phaedrus*: *erōs* is sent by the gods for our benefit and enables us to follow in the chorus of the gods, i.e., to become like them (244b, 246d, 252c–253c). Here, too, the account is saturated with mystery terminology.

were raised in the *Euthyphro* (or so I shall argue in this section). Consider the following: According to Socrates in the *Symposium*, *erōs* refers specifically to desires for objects considered to be central to our happiness; the aim of *erōs* is *eudaimonia* (205a–d), a divine state. The beautiful objects of *erōs*' pursuit are desired because they promise to deliver that end; they are perceived to be supremely beautiful, perfect, in need of nothing, and, as such, to stand in some relationship to the divine (204c4, *teleon kai makariston*). This specific mode of valuing involved in *erōs* does not require us to suppose that the objects are, in fact, supremely beautiful; the point is just that when one acts for the sake of an object of *erōs* one acts for the sake of an end one perceives to be supremely beautiful and, unlike the lover, in need of nothing.

In the confrontation with the object of desire, an asymmetry is made vivid to the desiring agent in question, which is characteristic of *erōs*. Confronted by an experience of beauty of this kind, one is made aware of how far one falls short of some ideal the object embodies and of how resourceful one is in trying to secure whatever it is that is thought to bring one's own life closer to that of the blessed gods. In this way the experience of *erōs* prompts us to attend both to our mortal limitations and to a more-than-human ability to transcend those limitations. This is figured in the aetiological story about Eros personified by the mortal Penia, responsible for the experience of lack and longing, and the divine Poros, responsible for resourcefulness.[25] This is one of the ways in which the mortal and the divine are 'bound close together' in someone subject to *erōs*.

Since the erotically disposed agent is after *eudaimonia*, some good for himself (206a4), and perceives the object of his pursuit to be capable of delivering that, one who acts for the sake of an object of *erōs* acts in a very distinctive manner; the desiring agent in question desires to affect some change in himself and not, primarily at least, in the desired object, which is perceived to be perfect and blessed (204c, *teleon kai makariston*). This is the import of *erōs*' characteristically productive work in the beautiful (206c1f.). Since the object is valued as something that, above all, makes one's own life worth living, one does not just want to gaze at its value or possess it in the sense in which one wants to get a bit of cake. For the activity of *erōs* to meet the demands of its aim – *eudaimonia* for the agent – a particular kind of change needs to be effected, which is significant, lasting, and transformative for the agent's life. Nor does one desire to care for the object in such a way that the beloved thing is benefitted, for the objects of *erōs* are seen as beautiful, perfect, and blessed

---

25   Poros is implicitly described as a god (203b2–3) and joins the feast of the gods (203b5–7).

(*teleon kai makariston*: 204c4–5) and are viewed as having some relationship to the divine. The desiring agent does not desire primarily to effect a change in the beloved object, to love and care for it in such a way that it will be benefitted and changed. Rather, he desires to change himself, particularly to obtain a measure of divine happiness, by coming to possess some good that the valuable object manifests for him and of which he perceives himself to be in need. Whether it is in relation to beautiful women, beautiful souls or cities, or the beauty of wisdom, the work of *erōs* is, fundamentally, that of self-creation, as we strive to reproduce the value we see in the world and capture it in a life of our own – as parents, poets, legislators, or philosophers. This explains the characteristically productive mode of activity, which is the way in which mortals creatures like ourselves try "to have a share in" the divine *eudaimonic* life (208b5).[26]

The specific mode of valuing involved in *erōs*, the asymmetry of this desire, and its characteristically 'reproductive' action are features that make it a uniquely appropriate term of desire in which to characterise the pursuit of divine ends, such as intelligible forms. Consider the appropriateness of this structure of erotic desire when considering action 'for the sake of' (*hou heneka*) the divine form of beauty. This is an end of a specific kind: it is supremely beautiful, divine, and does not suffer change in any way (210e–211a). Forms are perfect, changeless, self-sufficient, and divine (211a1, 211b3–5, 211e3), and as such, any desiring relationship we have towards these forms must be one that honours not only the supreme value of the object (as *erōs* does), the asymmetry between the desiring agent and the object (as *erōs* also does), but it must also be one that clarifies the specific nature of how one acts for the sake of such an end (as *erōs* also does).[27] When we act 'for the sake of' the

---

26  One might wonder how this focus on self-creation fits the *Phaedrus*. At 253a7–b1 the lover tries to make his beloved as much like the god he resembles as possible, so he is trying to change his beloved in some way, as well as himself. I thank Nancy Worman for raising this objection. The thought here need not rule out change in another. If we return to the *Symposium*, law-givers such as Solon and Lycurgus are clearly trying to make a change in the cities for which they legislate (209d–e); this is how such desiring agents try to achieve *eudaimonia*, given their specification of that aim and the importance of honour to its acquisition. The point is just that insofar as this is an expression of *erōs*, the primary purpose of that activity is to effect a change in the desiring agent himself, namely to secure a name for himself and win renown to satisfy his desire for *eudaimonia*. So although *erōs* does not rule out a change in the relevant object, this is not the central purpose of its activity.

27  For forms as divine, see also *Phaedo* 80b1, 84a9; *Republic* 517d4–5, 500c9–d1; *Phaedrus* 246d8–e1.

form (210e6, 211c2), we act for its sake in the sense that it is the ultimate object to be attained, but we act ultimately for our sake in the sense that the goal is to change ourselves in accordance with it. We do not act for the sake of the form in the sense that we desire to benefit it, any more than we desire to benefit the gods when we attend to them in the *Euthyphro*; *erōs* is a different kind of caring relationship than cattle-rearing in this respect (13b–c). Both the asymmetrical nature of this desiring relationship and its characteristic work – some productive change in the agent to capture the value of the object for ourselves – make it a uniquely appropriate term to characterise how one acts for the sake of a perfect and divine object (the form of Beauty) in order to secure for oneself a share of divine happiness.[28]

Plato drew on such features of *erōs* elsewhere in a way that clarifies its use in capturing an orientation towards an entity of 'supreme dignity and power'. In the *Philebus* a distinction is drawn between *genesis* and *ousia* with the example of the lover and the beloved (53cff.). This serves as an illustrative example of the phenomenon because one kind is "sufficient to itself, the other in need of something else... the one kind possesses supreme dignity, the other is inferior to it." Further, the one exists 'for the sake of something', and the other is 'that for the sake of which the former is always coming into being'. This is used to clarify the way in which *genesis* changes in accordance with being, just as a lover changes in accordance with his beloved; for the other (the beloved/being) is in need of nothing, since it is already in possession of supreme 'dignity'. The use of *erōs* in this context highlights the asymmetry of the relationship, the non-reciprocal nature of the relationship, and how one changes in accordance with the other.

The significance of this structure of *erōs* when characterising a relationship to a divine end was arguably also not lost on Aristotle. Here I am indebted to the work of Gabriel Lear, who brings out the significance of Aristotle's use of Platonic *erōs*.[29] In *Metaphysics Lambda*, Aristotle confronts a puzzle about how unmoved movers move. For Aristotle, that which has the power to move things without itself being moved is an object of desire or thought – *to orekton*

---

28   One might be concerned that embodying the value of the desired object, or "having a share of" (208b3), is not a form of productive activity, which is *erōs'* characteristic work (206cf.), though one might note that in the *Sophist*, imitation belongs to the art of making (219b1). The productive work detailed here, such as delivering physical offspring or psychic virtue of some kind, is how desiring agents try to capture the value of their beautiful object for themselves.

29   Lear, *Happy Lives and the Highest Good: An Essay in Aristotle's Nicomachean Ethics* (Princeton: Princeton University Press, 2004).

*kai to noēton* (1072a26–7). When we desire something, the *kalon* object moves our faculty of desire, which then moves us to action without itself changing in any way. So if there is some supremely beautiful object that the first heaven desires, this could be an unchanging cause of the motion of the heavens. Aristotle then goes on to make a distinction between two kinds of 'for the sake of which' relations. The first is when the object is an object of benefit; the second is when the object is to be attained or realised (*Metaphysics Lambda* 1072b1–3). Since it is central to some ends 'for the sake of which' we act that they are changeable (for instance, when they are benefitted), Aristotle needs to rule out such cases; in order to do so, he employs this distinction between two ways of acting for the sake of an end. Objects of desire are among ends to be attained, which we pursue to improve our own condition rather than theirs. After Aristotle has made this specific distinction, he goes on to claim that the Prime Mover moves the heavenly bodies as something loved (*hōs erōmenon*, 1072b3).[30] Though Aristotle previously talked about unmoved movers in general as objects of desire with terms such as *epithumia, boulēsis*, and *orexis* (1072a26–29), he now shifts specifically to the use of *erōs*: the Prime Mover moves as an object of *erōs* does.[31] Merlan, Elders, and Lear connect this with the *Symposium* to articulate a notion of final causality as imitation;[32] in other words, it indicates that the object in question is pursued in a way that seeks to improve our own condition, not that of the object. As Lear argues, "Plato called the urge to approximate a superior mode of being love."[33] Attending to the specific structure of this desire does indeed show why *erōs* is a uniquely appropriate term in which to characterise a way of acting for the sake of a divine

---

30  As Sedley argues ("*Metaphysics* Lambda x" in *Aristotle's Metaphysics Lambda* [ed. M. Frede and D. Charles; Oxford: Oxford University Press, 2000], 327–51, 334), "The language of desiring and imitating is too prominent in these passages to be ignored."

31  One need not suppose that the first heavens actually experience *erōs* for the Prime Mover. The claim is that the Prime Mover moves as an object of *erōs* moves (without itself being literally an object of *erōs*). The point is that *erōs* demarcates a particular way of acting for the sake of an end.

32  P. Merlan, "Aristotle's Unmoved Mover," *Traditio* 4 (1946): 1–30, esp. 3; L. Elders, *Aristotle's Theology: A Commentary on Book Lambda of the Metaphysics* (Assen: Van Gorcum, 1972), 35–6, 174; Lear, *Happy Lives*, 79, 209.

33  Lear, *Happy Lives*, 72; citing *Symposium* 206e2–207a4. Kyung-Choon Chang ("Beauty in the *Symposium* versus the Unmoved Mover in the *Metaphysics* (Λ)," *Classical Quarterly* 52 [2002]: 431–46) also highlights parallels between Plato and Aristotle here, though he places the emphasis on the objects in each case and argues for a similarity between Plato's treatment of the Beautiful and "Aristotle's understanding of the Unmoved Mover in its nature and function."

end. *Erōs* is an asymmetrical relationship, one in which the object is seen as supremely beautiful and in need of nothing, and (as a result) a relationship in which one seeks to affect a change in oneself and not in the object for whose sake one acts, for this is 'sufficient to itself'. *Erōs* allows both Plato and Aristotle to articulate a specific mode of acting for the sake of a good end, one in which one seeks to have a share in (*metechein*) the value of the desired good end; this is the precise mode of activity needed for Plato when characterising the philosopher's pursuit of forms and for Aristotle when characterising the movement of the first heavens towards a divine end that remains unchanged.

This use of *erōs* has a long history. The hallmarks of this desire were also employed by Neo-Platonists, such as Plotinus and Proclus, who made *erōs* central to their own accounts of the movement of all things towards the One. Its characteristically imitative action is used to illustrate how each entity becomes the best image of its progenitor. Plotinus explicitly associates *erōs* with the notion of *homoiōsis*, 'becoming like' (VI 7, 31, 10), and compares the erotic movement towards intellect and the One with the experience of lovers who wish to see their beloved, to become like them, and to become one with them. *Erōs* becomes the movement of 'religious adoration', uniquely suited to capture action for a divine end.[34]

## 4    Eros and Contributing to the Work of the Gods

So far, I have explored why *erōs* is an appropriate engine of action for a divine end by appealing to its structure (asymmetry) and its characteristic effects (its productive work that attempts to embody the value of the object for the desiring agent himself); I have not yet explored how the pursuit of such divine ends (e.g., forms) is expressive of *erōs*' function as a mediator with the gods. In the

---

[34]    I take the phrase 'religious adoration' from S. Broadie, "Aristotelian Piety," *Phronesis* 48 (2003): 54–70, 56 n. 11). On Plotinus and *erōs*, see A.H. Armstrong, "Platonic *erōs* and Christian *agape*," *Downside Review* 3 (1961): 105–21, reprinted in *Plotinian and Christian Studies* (ed. A.H. Armstrong, London: Variorum, 1979) and W. Beierwaltes, "The Love of Beauty and the Love of God," in *Classical Mediterranean Spirituality: Egyptian, Greek, Roman* (ed. A.H. Armstrong, London: Routledge & Kegan Paul, 1986), 189–205 at 204. Cf. Proclus (*In Alcibiadem* 61.3–5): all that exists is moved towards the One by *erōs*. He also discusses 'assimilation to the origin'. Note also *erōs* as 'the binding guide of all things' (64). On Proclus' use of *erōs*, see G. Quispel, "God is *Erōs*," in *Early Christian Literature and the Classical Tradition: In Honorem Robert M. Grant* (ed. W.R. Schoedel and R.L. Wilken; Paris: Éditions Beauchesne, 1979), 189–205.

*daimōn* passage *erōs* is said to interpret and convey things from men to gods and from gods to men – men's petitions and sacrifices, the god's commands and returns for sacrifices; "being in the middle between both, it fills in the space between them, so that the whole is bound close together." So how are we to explain the philosophical activity described as the fulfillment of *erōs* – capturing the value of the divine form of beauty ("he will give birth not to mere images of virtue, but to true virtue, because it is not an image that he is grasping but the truth," 212a5–6) – in the light of this passage, as we are encouraged to do in the return of the language of 'rites' here (*ta telea kai epoptika* at 210a1, with *teletas* at 202e8)?

Let us start with the role of the gods. It is said that the gods transport 'ordinances and requitals' to men via *daimons* such as Eros, and with purpose: "so that the whole is bound together with itself" (202e7). Could this be a candidate for the *ergon* of the gods, something in which our activity somehow assists them? Strictly speaking, it is *erōs* that "being midway between the two, makes each to supplement the other, so that the whole is bound together with itself," but insofar as the gods are active in relation to this specific end, it seems reasonable to take it that this whole, whatever it is, is of concern to them, and that maintaining this whole via *daimons* such as Eros might be their 'one chief product', to return to the language of the *Euthyphro*. Identifying *to pan*, and the work of 'binding' (*sundedesthai*, 202e6–7) this whole, will be instructive for our account.[35]

Since the parts of the whole specified here are the mortal and the immortal (203a2), it seems that this 'whole' at the very least includes the realm of the mortal and the immortal taken together, though it is less clear what falls

---

35  Some scholars have argued that there is a problem in attributing an *ergon* to the gods. L. Versenyi (*Holiness and Justice: An Interpretation of Plato's Euthyphro* [Lanham: University of Press of America, 1982]: 110), for example, has argued that "if the gods are already as good as possible and possessed of all that is good for them, then they can have no needs still outstanding and thus no motivation for action." But as McPherran, "Socratic Piety," 225 has argued, there is good evidence for divine activity (he cites *Apology* 33c, 41d and the *Phaedrus* 247a, which notes that each god has his own *ergon*). There may be a way to specify the *ergon* of the gods in a way that does not imply that their action is motivated by needs they themselves possess. The fact that they have concern for us does not indicate that the divine nature itself is lacking. McPherran ("Socratic Piety," 298) argues that though there is an *ergon* of the gods, we cannot know anything about this *ergon* other than that it is good; Socrates claims to have no wisdom of things 'more than human' (*Euthyphro* 6a–b; *Apology* 20e). He later reformulates this and claims that we cannot have 'infallible and complete knowledge of the gods' purposes'. This reformulation is compatible with the view developed in this paper.

under those categories. What is clear is that normative terms are strongly connected to the work of *erōs* – beauty is a prerequisite of its activity, for "what is beautiful is in harmony with all that is divine" (206d1–2). For both Plato and Aristotle, the *kalon* is associated with proportion and order.[36] If the *kalon* is a precondition of *erōs*' binding work (whatever that is), we might allow this to tell us something about the nature of the whole to which *erōs*' work contributes. Whatever this emergent whole turns out to be, it will, at best, be a harmonious and unified ordering of the realm of the mortal and the immortal (whatever that includes), and the binding of this whole will be an activity reflective of, or constitutive of, the harmony and unity of that end.

As the ascent shows, the proper functioning of *daimonic erōs*, which is active in relation to this end ('binding the whole'), occurs by means of, or is constituted by, philosophical activity, particularly contemplation of the divine form of beauty; for it is here that the philosopher comes closest to the divine and becomes "dear to the gods" (212a). The philosopher makes cognitive contact with the form and is said to "look there and behold it with that by which he ought," a phrase which elsewhere in the dialogues refers to *nous*.[37] Now, if the activity which brings the philosopher closest to the divine, and in that way somehow contributes to the maintenance of a unified realm between men and gods, is intellectual (noetic) activity, then this feature of the account relates the *Symposium* to other works in which intelligence or *nous* is responsible for 'binding' things together in the proper way. Intelligence or *nous* is characterised as 'the truly good and binding' and said to be responsible for order in Socrates' autobiography in the *Phaedo*. This is also a theme of the *Philebus*.[38] *Nous* is repeatedly linked in the dialogues to arranging things in relation to what is best (e.g., *Phaedo* 99b–c; *Philebus* 28d5–29a4). These details indicate that the whole is bound together in a harmonious and unified way by intellectual activity of a certain kind.

We can be more precise. The privileged work of *erōs* is the activity of making one out of many in dialectical work, looking for what is 'one and the same' amongst various classes of beautiful things, which is to say, pursuing the *eidos* of beauty (210b2), until one can place sensible particular things in the appropriate relationship to their divine end, the form (211e). It is possible, then, to

---

36  In the *Philebus* (64e–65a) the relationship between beauty and proportion is explored. See also Aristotle, *Metaphysics* 1078a31–b1: "The most important kinds of *kalon* are order, proportion and definiteness."

37  R.G. Bury, *The Symposium of Plato* (Cambridge: Heffer, 1932), 132. notes the similarity of this turn of phrase with *Phaedrus* 247c; *Phaedo* 65e; and *Republic* 490b, 518c, 532a.

38  See V. Harte, *Plato on Parts and Wholes* (Oxford: Oxford University Press, 2002), 209.

give content to this notion of 'binding' as that dialectical work which brings together the beautiful particulars and their proper end – the divine form – in which their unity is made manifest. The *kaloi logoi* generated in the ascent will be beautiful to the extent that they show that unity and begin the work of ordering the various beautiful particulars in relation to their proper end. These *logoi* will manifest the proper relationships between the mortal particulars and the divine form in the sense that sensible particulars are not considered to be all there is to know about beauty; the philosopher does not take the image for the original, but sees particulars in their proper relationship to their divine end. In this way, the activity of interpreting the mortal world of sensible experience in the light of the divine form can be seen as an example of *erōs' daimonic* work – a case of divine hermeneutics (202e3). This activity of collecting the particular instances at each level and bringing them together into a unity in the mind recalls the processes of collection and division in the *Philebus* (16b) and the *Phaedrus* (273e), where the activity of collecting particulars also leads one closer to the divine. By such means the philosopher can come into closer contact with the divine entity (the form) in which all these particulars share as well as with the gods (212a1–6), whose own divinity is said elsewhere to rely on their proximity to forms (*Phaedrus* 249d).

Philosophical practice can be seen to operate back again from the divine realm (202e3–6) if the philosopher interprets the mortal world of particulars in light of the divine form and sees that all beautiful things "partake of it" (211b). He might also engage in the more other-directed practice of persons such as Diotima who reveal the highest mysteries of the ascent to mortals. She is an example of a *daimonic* person, and her work here is to guide humans to the divine form and, ultimately, to a relationship with the gods (212a6).[39] Diotima's characterisation helps to substantiate the 'commands' communicated back from the gods (202e5). If Diotima is a *daimonic* intermediary, then at least one way in which these are manifested is in the questions posed to the one making the ascent; for example, "What is 'one and the same' in this class of beautiful things?" (210b2–3). That is surely the guiding question of the ascent, which is one in which the pursuit of the *eidos* is explicitly connected to the pursuit of what is 'one and the same' in the class under consideration (210b3) and which leads ultimately to the divine (form). The characterisation of Diotima as a *daimonic* intermediary who operates in this particular way might also

---

39   Diotima's Mantinean origins and her postponement of the plague suggest a connection to the seer's art, described as part of the *daimonic* art (*Symposium* 202e–203a). Her name might also have significance since it means honouring, or honoured by, Zeus.

be taken to suggest, given the nature of this work, that the dialectical activity of the ascent is a gift from the gods. Compare the way in which the dialectical activity of collection and division – searching for one form for every many – is characterised in terms of 'binding' in the *Philebus*, in a context where it is explicitly characterised as a gift from the gods (16b).

Alcibiades' account of Socrates as a *daimonic* man (219c1) is also instructive here. Socrates reveals "those who stand in need of the god and their initiation rites." The mention of 'rites' here again recalls the *daimon* passage and the language of the ascent (*teletai*, 215c). It becomes clear from Alcibiades' discussion that he is referring to Socrates' habitual elenctic talk, which makes Alcibiades feel ashamed for neglecting things of the greatest importance and reveals those who are in need of the mysteries of philosophy (216a5–b3; 217b6). It may be significant that this is the part of *erōs' daimonic* work highlighted as the particular work of Socrates. Though Alcibiades evidently does think that Socrates has some relationship to the divine (he has inside him divine and beautiful images, 217a1), he does not also go on to say that Socrates shows him how to engage in the rites that lead to the divine, something which may reflect Alcibiades' failure to get this far or Plato's desire to distance Socratic philosophising from the hierophantic Diotima.

The philosophical interpretation of *erōs' daimonic* work suggests that the 'petitions' made by mortals in this context (202e4) would be requests for assistance in the pursuit of wisdom, for these are the needs of the particular agent making the ascent. Socrates asks for such help from Diotima (201d, 204a, 206b, 207c, 208c), and in many other places in the dialogues he also asks for such assistance from the gods. There are, in fact, many such requests or prayers in the dialogues that Socrates makes to the gods.[40] What we have here, then, is

---

40  See, for example, *Euthyphro* 275d, where Socrates prays to the Muses and Memory so that he can remember a conversation; see *Phaedrus* 237a, where Socrates asks for divine assistance in the construction of his first speech, with 278b and 279b-c; at *Republic* 432c Socrates prays for success in discovering the nature of justice; at *Timaeus* 27b–d he invokes the gods before the discussion begins (see also 48d-e); at *Philebus* 25b Socrates pauses to pray to the gods for help in argument (see also 61b–c).' Compare also *Laws* IV 712b, where the Athenian prays to god for help in his argument, and at X 893b, where he prays for assistance in proving the existence of gods. There are many other prayers to the gods as well, although these are not as explicit in requesting wisdom or assistance in relation to that specific end (e.g., *Phaedo* 117c, where Socrates prays to the gods as he takes the hemlock; *Republic* 327a where Socrates says he prayed at the festival of Bendis; and in *Phaedrus* the prayer to Pan at the end of the work). See B.D. Jackson ("The Prayers of Socrates," *Phronesis* 16 no. 1 [1971]: 14–37), who counts twelve prayers of this kind.

a radical refiguring of our relationship to the gods, whereby it is not 'prayers and sacrifices' that dominate our end of the transaction, but requests for guidance in the pursuit of wisdom, and the benefits sent by the gods via *daimonic* intermediaries such as Diotima pertain specifically to guidance in the pursuit of wisdom.

Appreciating how the activity in the highest mysteries of the ascent fulfils *erōs*' function as a *daimonic* mediator suggests that philosophical activity 'binds together' the mortal and the immortal into a unified whole in the following senses: Our characteristically mortal lack of wisdom is brought together with our resourceful attempts to understand the world whenever we provide something (become full of divine *poros*) relevant to the pursuit of wisdom. The mortal realm of sensible particulars is brought together with the divine form and, as a result, we are brought closer to a divine state of understanding. We become like the gods – implied, I take it, by our becoming dear to them – when we engage in this specific activity. One might wonder how this understanding of the form is related to the productive activity of *erōs*, which is its characteristic activity in relation to beauty (206c).[41] Cognitive engagement with the form of beauty is, I take it, how we come to be in the creative environment of the genuinely beautiful, and, given the nature of the object in question, contemplation of that object is how we come 'to have intercourse with it'. Again, given the nature of the object, 'delivering' *logoi* and, finally, understanding is how we strive to capture that value for ourselves in our productive work. The epistemological work in the ascent, then, is a particular manifestation of the productive work of *erōs*, one whose purpose is 'to bind the whole' realm of the mortal and immortal together with itself.

If this is the way in which philosophical *erōs* binds the two realms together and so fulfils its function as a *daimonic* mediator, then how might this contribute to the work of the gods? Since the gods are engaged in maintaining this whole (shown by their transportations via *daimonic* intermediaries for the sake of this end), it is not unreasonable to suppose that our contribution to this whole contributes to their work, whose 'chief product' here (to recall the language of the *Euthyphro*) seems to be the maintenance of this whole.[42] If so, this is the kind of 'service to the gods' whose specification might help the

---

41   I thank Gail Fine for pressing me on the possible tension between the epistemological and productive operations of *erōs*.

42   My thesis here fits with McPherran's claim with reference to the *Euthyphro* that "the chief product of the gods is much more likely to be something on this last sort of cosmic, overarching scale," by which he means "producing an orderly universe," and he cites the evidence of Xenophon to support the attribution of a teleological theology to Socrates

end of the *Euthyphro*. Though this activity is not characterised as a 'service' to the god in the *Symposium* (something which may, however, be intimated by the mystery terminology, whose rites were "a service to the deity... a sign of a pious disposition," on which see Edmonds),[43] the fact that we contribute to some work in which the gods are involved, and which is clearly of concern to them, indicates that our work serves some end in which they are also invested.

Clearly we are not improving the gods by this work; rather, we are improving ourselves, and in that way improving the unity of the whole of which we are a part and which is evidently of concern to the gods.[44] But how exactly does the dialectical work of binding together the divine form with sensible particulars in our own state of understanding assist the gods? In the *Timaeus* the god binds forms to sensible reality by ordering sensible reality in accordance with forms.[45] But where the philosopher understands how the form of beauty structures reality, he does not himself structure that reality. So how does his contemplation contribute to the ordering and maintenance of the whole? Much depends here on how one specifies the mortal and immortal parts of this whole – the realm of the mortal and the immortal (whatever that includes). It may be that the gods engage in binding together the elements of the cosmos, and that is their particular role in bringing together the mortal and the immortal; on this the *Symposium* is silent, whereas the *Timaeus* sings clearly. But the philosopher's role in this enterprise, in the *Symposium* at least, is to bind the mortal and immortal together in his nature (his characteristically mortal lack of wisdom, inherited from Penia, with his more-than-human resourcefulness, inherited from Poros) and engage in dialectical work, which

---

(*Memorabilia* 1.4.2–18, 4.3.3–8, with M. McPherran, "Socratic Piety: In Response to Scott Calef," *Oxford Studies in Ancient Philosophy* 13 (1995): 27–36 at 33 n. 2. Compare other works in which Plato describes god's concern for ordered wholes. As Rowe ("Socrates and His Gods," 328) argues, the *Phaedo, Republic, Timaeus,* and the end of the *Apology* display "the same kind of fundamental belief in the world as a locus of goodness and order." In the *Laws* (Book x), the nature of divine activity is discussed in terms of the ordering and preservation of the cosmos (903b–d).

43 Edmonds, "Alcibiades the Profane," forthcoming.
44 Compare the *Timaeus* (90c), mortals are said to tend to (*therapeuein*) *to theion*, where *nous* inside the mortal agent is the subject of the care. In this way, the *Timaeus* can be seen to reintroduce the *Euthyphro*'s notion of caring for divinity, but in a way that bypasses the concern that we improve the gods because the care is to the divinity within, namely, *nous*. I thank David Sedley for this comment.
45 Compare the *Timaeus* on the activity of god putting together the components of the body of the *cosmos*: "the finest of bonds is whatever makes both itself and the things being bound together as one as possible" (31b8–32a7).

binds together the sensible particulars with the divine form in his state of understanding. Since the prize for the successful achievement of this end is to become 'dear to the gods', it is also suggested that he is bound closer together to the gods. If the gods are concerned with binding together the whole realm of the mortal and the immortal, then the philosopher contributes to that work by concerning himself with a specific part of that work.

## 5 Philosophy, Piety, and Justice

Though piety is not a term employed in Socrates' speech, the religious language in which the entire account is embedded invites us to consider philosophy as a religious experience, which is to say, something that is guided by the gods through an intermediary whose very name means to 'honour god' and whose activity allows one to become closer to the gods. The philosopher becomes dear to the gods at the end of the ascent and, according to the *Euthyphro* (9e–11b, 15b–c), it is the pious and only the pious who are loved by the gods.[46] Now, if this god-beloved state is achieved in contemplation, then piety must reside in that intellectual activity which makes the agent in question god-beloved. And notice that we engage in contemplation not because this is dear to the gods (a specification which invites problems familiar from the *Euthyphro*, 10a1–3); we engage in contemplation because we recognise this to be of supreme value, the arguments for which are based on the ability of contemplation to satisfy the desire for happiness, arguments which are, in turn, grounded in the metaphysics of forms and particulars (212a5–6). The value of the activity that makes us 'dear to the gods', in other words, does not derive from the gods, that is from their loving.[47]

The role of the gods is not only to act as models for emulation (as possessors of all good and beautiful things and paradigms of *eudaimonia*, 202c7), but

---

[46] Note the contrast here with the ascent described in Aristophanes' speech, which resulted in impiety (190b5). Aristophanes' circle men thought so much of themselves that they made an ascent to attack the gods. On Socrates' ascent, by contrast, we are not aspiring to be the equal of the gods, but to become like them to the extent possible (note the guarded formulation at 212a6–7 and 208b3: 'have a share of immortality').

[47] Compare Broadie on the import of the *theophilestatos* argument in Aristotle ("Aristotelian Piety," 67): "an account saying what the gods love about the nature of the pious will be an account of the nature of piety… So Aristotle is saying that piety towards god is, in its truest form, the disposition for intellectual activity engaged in as by the *sophos*," i.e. purely for love of the activity itself.

to make the ascent known to us through transportations via such *daimonic* agents as Socrates and Diotima, though the text leaves open the question of whether this happens via divine signs or through answering prayers or inspiration.[48] We respond in the proper way to that concern by improving ourselves in accordance with their commands and instructions. Insofar as this is the appropriate repayment for their concern, we can also appreciate a sense in which philosophical practice is just, for we are giving to the gods what we owe them (and in a way which implies no deficiency on their part) when we improve ourselves in accordance with their guidance via *daimonic* intermediaries. In this way, philosophical practice can be seen as a just and proportionate return for their benevolence.[49] If so, the *Symposium's* suggested account of piety might also accommodate the *Euthyphro's* claim that piety is a part of justice (11e–12a, 12d).[50]

---

48  Compare the role of Socrates as a divinely appointed midwife in the *Theaetetus* (150b–d; 151c–d). Note also *Lysis* 204c1, where Socrates says: "this much has been given to me – I don't know how (or 'somehow or other' – *pōs*)– from god, the capacity to recognise quickly a lover and an object of love."

49  Compare R. Bodeus (*Aristotle and the Theology of the Living Immortals* [New York: SUNY Press, 2000], 155–57), who makes a similar claim with reference to the repayment of divine benevolence in Aristotle.

50  There is, perhaps, a broader sense in which this philosophical work is related to justice, too. The idea that a properly bounded whole manifested a just order is a notion that can be traced in a number of pre-Socratic thinkers, and it was also a Pythagorean view, endorsed by Plato himself in the dialogues. The Pythagoreans saw a relationship between proportion and the principle of justice, in which 'each part of the whole receives its proper due'. Harmony and justice are the result of good proportion made manifest, and the *kosmos* itself is a harmony in which all of the parts are proportionally bound together. See G. Vlastos, "Equality and Justice in Early Greek Cosmologies," *Classical Philology* 42 (1947): 156–78. This view can be seen in the *Gorgias* (508a1–8): "The wise men say, Callicles, that heaven and earth and gods and men are bound by community and friendship and order and temperance and justice; and that is why they call this whole an order (*kosmos*), not disorder or intemperance, my friend. But I think you do not heed them though you are wise yourself. You have not noticed that geometrical equality has great power among gods and men; you think you should practice taking more because you are heedless of geometry." In the *Laws*, proportionate equality – ('adjusting what you give to take account of the real nature of each') actually constitutes justice (757b–c). If we take it that philosophical activity establishes the right relations between the mortal and the immortal realms (particulars and forms, our own selves, and our relationship to the gods), by "adjusting what [one] give[s] to take account of the real nature of each" (*Laws* 757b–c), then philosophical activity is expressive of justice insofar as it contributes to the maintenance of a harmonious and just – rightly proportioned – order between the mortal and the immortal.

## 6   Putting Humpty Dumpty Together Again? Piety and Virtue

Socrates' speech refers only to true virtue, as opposed to images of virtue (212a1–6), and not to specific parts of virtue, such as 'piety' and 'justice'. Whatever stand one takes on the question of the unity of virtue for Plato, it seems clear here that any such specifications at the very least share the same basis (in wisdom), though they may have different expressions: virtue is achieved by grasping the truth (212a4–6).[51] Whatever stand one takes on that question, in relation to current debates about piety one may well ask whether this account of our relationship to divinity speaks in favour of an intellectualist account of piety, given that the agent in question becomes god-beloved when contemplating, or the view for which Vlastos argued with respect to the *Apology*, according to which piety is or involves moral virtue – that is, care and concern for others.

On the one hand, the fact that the proper relationship of *erōs* to the divine is contemplation relates this text to those in which the ethical ideal is to become like god through contemplation (cf. *Timaeus* 90a–d). But contemplation is only part of *erōs*' proper work here: *erōs* is a mediator who goes back again and interprets and transports from gods to men (202e). This might be taken to suggest that the ideal is both to become like the gods by engaging in intellectual activity of a specific kind and then to interpret and communicate that divine order to the mortal realm. This is a way in which the whole is 'bound closely together'. Caution is required here, however. There is nothing in these lines themselves to warrant the claim that other-directed service, to one's fellow men, is required for the fulfillment of *erōs*' *daimonic* work. Given the many ways in which the mortal and the immortal contrast can be borne out here, it may be that the agent in question is interpreting the mortal realm of sensible particulars in light of his understanding of the divine form in his own soul. The characterisation of Socrates and Diotima is strongly suggestive

---

51    The issue of the unity of virtue, for which Socrates argues elsewhere (*Protagoras* 329c–d, 332a–333b, *Laches* 198b–199e, and *Meno* 87e–88c), is outside the scope of this paper. For a strong formulation of the unity of virtue thesis, according to which the virtues are strictly identical, see T. Penner, "The Unity of the Virtues," *Philosophical Review* 82 (1973): 35–68. This might be suggested at the end of the ascent, where we learn that the philosopher begets true virtue by grasping the truth (212a). There is no distinction between parts of virtue or different virtues made here; it is virtue as such that he begets, and this is grounded in a grasp of the truth. But whether that means that all the virtues are identical to wisdom or grounded in it remains a controversial question. For a discussion of this issue in relation to piety and virtue in the *Euthyphro*, see Calef, "Piety and the Unity of Virtue."

of an account that integrates other-directed service in accord with Vlastos' suggestions on the *Apology*, however.[52] Part of Diotima's work is to persuade others, as she has persuaded Socrates, of proper erotic practice (212b). And Socrates explains that he has been persuaded of the mysteries of the ascent and now tries to persuade "everyone else too" (212b–c). It may be significant that the other-directed work associated with Socrates in this dialogue, through the description of Alcibiades in particular, is explored in terms of elenctic practice, which is familiar from the *Apology* and which serves god: the *daimonic* Socrates (219b7–c1, *daimoniōi hōs alēthōs*) reveals "those who stand in need of the god and his rites" (219c). The description of Socrates' *logoi* in terms of exposing the needs of himself and others, and the shame that follows that practice, resonates well with Socrates' habitual elenctic talk. In this respect he exemplifies the characteristically mortal – aporetic – aspect of *erōs* (derived in the story from Penia), the importance of which suggests that, in relation to the gods as well as the beautiful and good things whose possession defines them, we must first realise that we are worth little or nothing. But this is only part of *erōs*' characterisation here. The *daimonic* Diotima manifests the resourcefulness of someone who knows how to lead others to the contemplation of the divine form and to a state where they become as immortal as it is possible for any man to be (212a5–6). Proper relations with the gods, it is suggested, must contain both features; hence their exemplification by Socrates and his alter-ego Diotima here. Perhaps the *Symposium* is a transitional text in which we can see both strands of Plato's thinking about piety come together in the dual character of Eros, something exemplified beautifully by the elenctic Socrates, who reveals the needs of himself and others, and the mantic Diotima, who reveals the mysteries of contemplation, working together. But whatever the division of labor here, it is clear from the work of both Socrates and Diotima that part of this work is indeed other-directed. If this manifests their work as *daimonic* intermediaries, as their characterisation in this dialogue strongly suggests, then this indicates, as Vlastos rightly surmised, that the gods are concerned with human souls and their improvement.[53] Piety is, in this way and as Vlastos argued, "a release from that form of egocentricity which is endemic in Socratic *eudaimonism*."[54] The true practice of *erōs* suggests that the work of

---

52   Vlastos, *Socrates*, 175. Compare Taylor, "The End of the *Euthyphro*," 113. For a critical response, see M. McPherran, *The Religion of Socrates* (University Park: Pennsylvania State University Press, 1996), 68–9.

53   Note the claim in the *Phaedrus*' palinode that the gods guide anyone who wants to follow and is able, without jealously (247a).

54   Vlastos, *Socrates*, 175.

binding the whole realm of the mortal and the immortal together has broader scope than one's own development.[55]

## 7 Eros, Forms, and God

My aim in reading the *Symposium* alongside the *Euthyphro* has been to highlight the religious dimension of the former work and to show how much it can contribute to an understanding of Plato's thinking about our relationship with the divine. How central this text is for such an understanding will depend ultimately on how committed we think Plato was to the idea that *erōs* structures our relationship with divine ends – the forms and, ultimately, god. Lest we suppose that the absence of *erōs* in the two foundational passages for the 'becoming like god' ideal (*Theaetetus* 176a5–6; *Timaeus* 90b–c) indicates that *erōs* becomes irrelevant to divine emulation, it may be worth noting the following: If becoming like god is to contemplate and to embody the forms in one's own character and life, the question becomes whether other dialogues also articulate our relationship to these divine ends in terms of *erōs*. *Erōs* is, in fact, dominant in those dialogues in which the forms play a central role: the *Phaedo*, the *Symposium*, the *Phaedrus*, and the *Republic*.[56] In the *Phaedo* *erōs* is used repeatedly, though not exclusively, to characterise the philosopher (66e2–4, 67e5–68a2, 68a7–b6). In the *Republic erōs* plays a role in the account of the proper philosopher and his fitness for rule (485b, 490, 501d2). In the *Timaeus,* too, though *erōs* is less dominant, it is also connected to *nous* and the search for primary causes (46d7–e2: *nous* and *erōs*).[57] And even in the *Laws*, *erōs* plays a central role in education: children are encouraged to develop *erōs* for the ideal of perfect citizenship (643c8–d3, 643e4–5).

---

55  One should also include the *Phaedrus* (250bff., esp. 252d–253c), noted by Armstrong ("Becoming like God," 173); correct *erōs* is not just about becoming like god oneself, but also involves fashioning that image in another.

56  There is also *erōs* terminology use to characterise the pursuit of wisdom in a number of other dialogues that do not mention forms, e.g., *Lysis* 204b1–2; *Euthydemus* 282; and *Theaetetus* 66d.

57  "Anyone who is a lover of understanding and knowledge must of necessity pursue as primary causes those things that belong to intelligent nature, and as secondary all those belonging to things that are moved by others and that set still others in motion by necessity." It is interesting to note here that *erōs* appears in a context that draws a contrast between moved and unmoved movers – first causes; *erōs* relates to the latter. Given the structure of this desire (see above section two), we can appreciate why *erōs* might be appropriate here.

*Erōs* is used consistently, though not exclusively, to characterise the orientation we are urged to cultivate towards the highest values: forms, *nous*, and political ideals in the *Laws*. Though different objects take centre stage in different works, they are all ultimately ideals with which we are urged to become enraptured, as values central to the pursuit of *eudaimonia*, and, as such, values we are encouraged to embody in our own character and lives. And this is the unique import of the language of *erōs*. *Erōs* is an orientation of a certain kind, which follows from the appraisal of the object as something without which, more than anything else, life is not worth living; the object is considered to be so superior to anything one embodies oneself that the apparent asymmetry is unbearable without a generative response, one whose purpose is to attempt to embody the value of the desired object in the agent himself. This specific mode of valuation, its structural asymmetry, and its characteristic generative response in the agent are the distinctive hallmarks of erotic agency, ones uniquely suited to action for a divine end, as Plato, Aristotle, and the Neo-Platonists all appreciated in different ways; hence, I submit, the continued use of *erōs* in relation to the objects that underpin the various accounts of how we 'become like god'.

## 8   Conclusion

The centrality of forms may explain why Plato did not make his account of our relationship to wisdom and the divine in the *Symposium* more explicit as an account of piety. For we are not, properly speaking, becoming like god, unless we appreciate why contemplation is valuable; if so, the explanatory weight of the account is always going to fall on our relationship to wisdom and its objects.[58] Compare Socrates and his devotees at the start of the *Symposium*: they try to achieve the happiness they think Socrates manifests (173d6), and they try to become like Socrates by imitating his words and deeds. They radically misunderstand the nature of the enterprise.[59] To be like Socrates is to appreciate why these are the best *logoi* to produce and to recognise that wisdom is one of the most beautiful things. And this is to have *erōs* for wisdom. If one engages in philosophy for the sake of becoming dear to the gods, or because

---

58  Compare Broadie ("Aristotelian Piety," 69), who argues that Aristotle's account of piety is so intimately related to the arguments for the superiority of the contemplative life that "the latter seems the only possible locus for explaining the former."

59  Cf. *Euthydemus* (307b6–8): "Pay no attention to the practitioners of philosophy, whether good or bad. Rather, test thoroughly the genuineness of the thing itself."

this is what the gods want from us, then one is, in a sense, back in a dilemma familiar from the *Euthyphro*: one has not really understood what it is about the action that is dear to the gods in the first instance. And to understand *that* is to understand why "wisdom is one of the most beautiful things," and this is to have *erōs* for wisdom (204b2–5). The substance of piety comes from knowing what and how to love.

# The Real *Euthyphro* Problem, Solved

*Nicholas Denyer*

Let us suppose that God commands all and only those actions that are obligatory, and prohibits all and only those actions that are wrong. We then face questions. Does God command the obligatory because it is obligatory? If so, then why pay attention to God's commands? Why not look rather to the real source of obligatoriness? Or is it instead that the obligatory is obligatory because commanded by God? If so, then would something else have been obligatory if God had commanded otherwise? And why bother with putative obligations created and variable at whim? Or again, are wrong actions wrong because God prohibits them, or does God prohibit them because they are wrong? Whether God prohibits things for some reason or for no reason, either way, how can his prohibition have, in itself, any weight at all? Such questions are often referred to as "the Euthyphro Problem," or even "the Euthyphro Dilemma".[1]

Such names are mistaken on two counts. In the first place, questions like "Is the obligatory obligatory because God commands it, or does God command

---

[1] Some examples include: R. G. Swinburne, "Duty and the Will of God," *Canadian Journal of Philosophy* 4 no. 2 (1974): 213–27, esp. 213 n. 2: "For a theist, a man's duty is to conform to the announced will of God. Yet a theist who makes this claim about duty is faced with a traditional dilemma first stated in Plato's *Euthyphro* [Footnote: *Euthyphro* 9e]—are actions which are obligatory, obligatory because God makes them so (e.g. by commanding men to do them), or does God urge us to do them because they are obligatory anyway?"; Michael Levin, "Understanding the Euthyphro Problem," *International Journal for Philosophy of Religion* 25 no. 2 (1989): 83–97, esp. 83 n. 1: "But why is God's handiwork good, and obedience to his commands obligatory? Only two answers seem possible. Either what God wills is right because he wills it, or God wills what he wills because it is right. The rightness of what God wills is a consquence of his willing it, or his willing it is a consequence of its rightness. [Footnote: I follow standard philosophical usage in calling this the Euthyphro problem.]"; Murray Macbeath, "The Euthyphro Dilemma," *Mind*, New Series 91 no. 364 (1982): 565–71, esp. 565: "Either right actions are right because God commands their performance, or God commands the performance of right actions because they are right."; Geoff Sayre-McCord, "Metaethics," *The Stanford Encyclopedia of Philosophy* (ed. Edward N. Zalta, Spring 2012 ed), http://plato.stanford.edu/archives/spr2012/entries/metaethics/, accessed 30 April 2014: "Whatever problems one might have making sense of eternal transcendent standards re-emerge when trying to make sense of an eternal transcendent being who might issue commands. And, as Plato emphasised in *Euthyphro*, one is also left with the difficulty of explaining why God's commands are authoritative."

the obligatory because it is obligatory?" are scarcely taxing enough to be called problems or dilemmas. There are, it is true, dainty questions about how commands, prohibitions, and permissions can alter our obligations.[2] It is entirely evident how I make it wrong for you to send your children to play in a field if I plant mines there, or how I stop it being wrong by removing the mines: it is wrong to send your children to play where they risk being blown apart, and what I do with the mines makes a difference to the risk. Things are oddly different if I own the field (if it is a field of mine, not a mine field) and thereby can say with authority that you may or may not send your children to play there. My words, oddly enough, can change your obligations, but not because they change the risk. For how could mere symbols change risks? You might object that my words change the risk that if your children play in my field, they will be trespassing. If you do, then I reply that this is an odd sort of risk to take into account. Indeed, that we should be worried by the risk of trespass is exactly the same oddity as there is in the power of mere words to change obligations.

Still, the fact is that obligations can be changed by merely symbolic acts, such as words and gestures, as well as by acts that make a concrete difference, such as planting or removing mines. Think of how my betting you £5 that Cambridge will win the boat race creates an obligation for me to pay you £5 when Cambridge lose. When the time comes for me to pay up, I can hardly argue, "This alleged obligation of mine to pay you £5: Do you say that I am under this obligation because I bet you? If so, then you will have to accept that my obligations would be different if my bets had been different, and then you will have to explain why we should take seriously obligations that can be varied at whim. Or do you say instead that I bet you because I am under this obligation? If so, then you must tell me what this obligation is based on, other than the bet. Either way, the bet is irrelevant."

Because symbolic acts can change obligations, a command can also give us reason to do the thing commanded independently of its own merits. Think of soldiers whose commanding officer orders them to advance. The advance might be militarily astute; the order might even be evidence of its military astuteness. But the order is more than just evidence that the advance is militarily astute. It adds a special reason of its own for advancing. Indeed, the order can provide a reason for advancing even if, prior to and independent of the order, there was no military reason for those soldiers to advance. This is why a soldier charged with disobeying the order to advance cannot defend himself by

---

2 There are beautiful treatments of these questions by David Hume in *A Treatise of Human Nature: Book III Of Morals* (London: 1740), Part II "Of justice and injustice," and *Essays Moral, Political and Literary Part II* (London: 1742), Essay 12 "Of the Original Contract."

pointing out, for example, "But there was no good military reason for it to be my unit that advanced while the other unit remained in reserve" – however true that may be.

People who might be prepared to accept that bets can change obligations sometimes refuse to accept that the same can be so of commands. Their concern is with autonomy.[3] We are autonomous beings, they say; as such, we can perhaps bind ourselves, but we can never be bound by others. In consequence, there are strict limits to the sorts of authority we can rightly acknowledge. We can rightly defer to the authority of experts; thus, if your doctor prescribes medicine, then the prescription is a good sign that you need the medicine prescribed. As an autonomous being, you can therefore decide to take the medicine that you need; but if you take it autonomously, then you take it because you need it, not because you imagine that the doctor's – or anyone else's – mere say-so can itself constitute a reason for you to act. The nearest that another's say-so can come to being itself a reason for you to act is when you have autonomously bound yourself to treat it as a reason. Thus, in particular, if the Queen has any authority over her subjects, and we are bound to obey her laws and keep her peace, then that can only be because we are parties to a social contract in which we have autonomously agreed to give the Queen such authority.

Or so they say. And, at least to those of us who have not grown out of adolescent rebellion, it all sounds very high-minded. In my low-minded way, I consider the implications of this argument for rape. It implies that if a woman says "No," that can in itself have weight with others only if they have autonomously agreed to let it have weight with them; otherwise, it can matter only as a sign that there is something independent of her saying "No" to make sexual intercourse with her wrong. She might, for instance, be an expert on matters of sex, and delivering her expert advice, as a doctor might give you expert advice on matters of medicine. Or perhaps her "No" threatens trouble, in the way that a dog's growl might warn you not to pat. But that is all the force her "No" can have, if commands and prohibitions cannot of themselves make obligations.

The names "the Euthyphro Problem" and "the Euthyphro Dilemma" are mistaken on a second count as well. Our questions about divine commands have little to do with the dilemma that Socrates presses upon Euthyphro in Plato's dialogue, the *Euthyphro*. Socrates' dilemma takes its start not from any supposed equivalence between being obligatory and being commanded by God,

---

3 Robert Paul Wolff, *In Defense of Anarchism* (New York: Harper & Row, 1970), is a classic defence of autonomy.

but rather from the very different supposition that all the gods love all and only what is pious and hate all and only what is impious. For the dilemma is, "Is the pious loved by the gods because it is pious? Or is it pious because it is loved?" (10a2–3).[4] Of course, if there is only one god, then the difference between God in the singular with a capital G and all the gods in the plural dwindles to nothing. But that still leaves a world of difference between the impious and the wrong, for the existence of the one God would hardly abolish the unjust, the impolite, the cowardly, the unchaste, and the myriad other ways (apart from the impious) of being wrong. Morever, even if there is only one God, there is still a world of difference between loving and commanding. For one thing, loving is a mental attitude, while commanding is a linguistic act, and a mental attitude is not a linguistic act. This is why the verb "to like" has come to be ambiguous, now that the Facebook generation use it both for finding something congenial and for clicking the "thumbs up" icon. For another thing, you can love things that you cannot command. I love it when people are amused by my jokes. But I don't command people to be amused. Indeed, amusement can hardly be commanded, except as a joke, even by a sovereign legislator.

One horn of the dilemma is straightforward enough. Euthyphro agrees without argument that the pious is loved by the gods for no other reason than that it is pious (10d1–5). And in this, Euthyphro is surely right. As we will be reminded later in the dialogue (14e10–15a5), gods don't need anything from us. If they like sacrifices, that is not because they rely on sacrifices for nutrition. If they find an offering of food endearing, then this is in the way that I find it endearing when my cat brings me dead mice. To one who enjoys the nectar and ambrosia of High Table, a gift of dead mice can have no charm other than the devotion it shows. Likewise, there is nothing for a god to love in a pious sacrifice apart from the fact that it is pious.

Less straightforward is the other horn of the dilemma. Socrates has to give some argument before Euthyphro also agrees that the pious is pious because the gods love it. Let us review this argument.

The first step of the argument is that, as Euthyphro himself has recently affirmed, the pious may be defined as whatever all the gods love (ὃ ἂν πάντες

---

4  According to Philip L. Quinn in "The Recent Revival of Divine Command Ethics," *Philosophy and Phenomenological Research* 50, supplement (1990): 345–65, esp. 345: "Plato's Socrates famously asks 'Is what is holy holy because the gods approve it, or do they approve it because it is holy?'" But "holy" is not the best rendering for the word that Plato's Socrates uses here: ὅσιος. For "holy" is primarily a word for a quality of the divine, while ὅσιος is primarily a word for a quality that we have when take the proper attitude to the holy. The Greek word best rendered by "holy" is ἅγιος.

οἱ θεοὶ φιλῶσιν, 9e1–2) or as the god-loved (τὸ θεοφιλές, 10e10–11). Nothing is made to rest on the difference between these two labels. They are taken as alternative expressions of the same definition, two interchangeable labels for some one thing in common to all that is pious, some one thing that makes all that is pious be pious.

The second step of the argument is to draw a dainty distinction (10a5–c13). I will render the distinction in English as the distinction between being in a loved condition and being the object of an act of loving. Being in a loved condition is expressed in Greek by a passive participle combined with a copula: the indicative φιλούμενόν ἐστίν and its infinitive φιλούμενον εἶναι. Being the object of an act of loving is expressed in Greek by the less prolix indicative φιλεῖται and its infinitive φιλεῖσθαι. Let me say a few words about these Greek phrases and my renderings of them.

My renderings are certainly not literal. A literal rendering might turn the first into "it is being loved" (rather than my "it is in a loved condition") and the second into the less prolix "it is loved" (rather than my "it is the object of an act of loving"). But the literal rendering would be wrong. English idiom uses the difference between the longer "it is being loved" and the shorter "it is loved" to express a difference of aspect: the difference between "the process of getting the thing loved is currently in hand but not yet completed" and "in a general sort of way people succeed in loving the thing". But such a difference of aspect is not the point of the difference between the two Greek phrases, for it is evident that the two Greek phrases are presumed to apply to exactly the same things—which is simply not so of their literal English renderings.

Moreover, my renderings are not suggested by any regular difference in nuance detectable from Greek usage elsewhere. The nearest thing to a parallel passage is the comment in Aristotle's *Metaphysics* (1017a27–30) that there is no difference in the active voice between constructions with participles and copulas (ἄνθρωπος ὑγιαίνων ἐστίν, ἄνθρωπος βαδίζων ἐστίν, ἄνθρωπος τέμνων ἐστίν) and constructions with a plain indicative (ἄνθρωπος ὑγιαίνει, ἄνθρωπος βαδίζει, ἄνθρωπος τέμνει). Of course, philosophers sometimes misreport their mother tongue; and of course, what applies to the active voice might not also apply to the passive. Still, the obvious conclusion to draw from Aristotle's comment is that Plato is eliciting from φιλούμενόν ἐστίν and φιλεῖται contrasting meanings that they do not automatically and immediately convey. And this conclusion is perhaps confirmed by the very elaboration of the passage in which, at 10a5–c13, Socrates attempts to bring home the contrast.

If neither a literal nor an idiomatic translation requires my renderings, why then do I propose them? The reason is simply that with these renderings, it is easy to see why Euthyphro responds as he does; for it does seem pretty obvious that if something is in a loved condition, then that is because it is the object of an act of loving, rather than the other way round.

There is perhaps some argument against this obvious response. We can love people—that is, we can have people be the objects of our acts of loving—without producing any effects at all in those people. We do not affect Socrates by loving him; indeed, given his dates and ours, we could not affect him in any way without indulging in time-travel or backwards causation or something equally outlandish. In consequence, Socrates' loved condition is not an effect, caused by our acts of loving him. How then can Socrates be in a loved condition because he is the object of acts of loving? In reply to this argument, it should be enough to point out two things. First, "because" does not always require a relationship of cause-and-effect: you get to be a grandparent because a child is born to a child of yours, however little you are affected by the birth. Second, the generalisation at 10c1–4 offers not only the cause-and-effect language of πάσχειν ("to be acted on, to be affected"), but also, as an alternative, the less definitely causal language of γίγνεσθαι ("to get to be"): it is enough for Socrates' argument if we agree that a thing gets to be some way because it is got to be that way, rather than that it is got to be that way because it gets to be that way (οὐχ ὅτι γιγνόμενόν ἐστι γίγνεται, ἀλλ᾽ ὅτι γίγνεται γιγνόμενόν ἐστιν, 10c2–3).

We now come to the third step of the argument. In defining the pious as that which is god-loved, or loved by all the gods, Euthyphro has agreed that the pious is pious because it is in a rather special loved condition, the condition of being loved by all the gods. In accepting that a thing is in a loved condition because it is the object of acts of loving, Euthyphro has also agreed that if a thing's condition is that of being loved by all gods, then it is in that condition because it is the object of acts of loving on the part of all the gods or, less pompously, because all the gods love it. The third step is simply that if a thing is pious because it is in a condition, and it is in that condition because all the gods love it, then it is pious because all the gods love it. Once this is accepted (and it is hard to deny), we can immediately conclude that pious things are pious because the gods love them.

With this conclusion, we can now present the real dilemma of the *Euthyphro*. How can it be that pious things are pious because the gods love them, when, as we saw earlier, the gods love pious things because those things are pious? Which is it to be: pious because loved, or loved because pious? It seems that we cannot have it both ways. Water is the stuff which we drink and wash in; we drink and wash in that stuff because it is water; it is not that the stuff is water because we drink and wash in it; indeed, how could the stuff be water because we drink and wash in it, when we drink and wash in that stuff because it is water? An easy assumption is that the same goes for piety, too. Once we make this assumption, we have our dilemma: we are required to choose between pious because loved and loved because pious.

Euthyphro solves his dilemma by rejecting his definition of the pious as what is god-loved. I propose a different solution. Instead of rejecting the definition, we should reject the assumption that we cannot have it both ways. Natural kinds, such as water, are different from social kinds, such as the pious. A natural kind has what we may call a reality or an essence, and what Socrates in 11a8 calls an οὐσία. We spell out this essence when we define the kind, as when we define water as H$_2$O. What belongs to a natural kind does so because it shares that essence. How something of a natural kind gets treated (any πάθος of it, to use the word that Socrates contrasts with οὐσία in 11a8) does not belong in the thing's essence, as it is no part of the essence of water that it is the stuff we drink and wash in. With social kinds, however, there is no such difference between πάθος and οὐσία. The nearest that a social kind ever comes to having an essence is that what belongs to it gets treated in a certain way and gets treated in that way because it belongs to that kind.[5]

Consider, for example, money. What is common to tobacco in Her Majesty's prisons, Bank of England notes in some other parts of her realms, cowry shells in nineteenth-century Kano, and bitcoins in the wilder parts of the World Wide Web? What makes them all money? Evidently, they are all money because and inasmuch as they are all readily accepted in exchange for goods and services. But why are they so accepted? Some of them have some independent worth: they might be smoked, or worn as jewellery. But to accept them because of such independent worth is not to accept them as money. And in any case, some of them have no such independent worth: you cannot smoke or wear a bitcoin. These things are all accepted in exchange for goods and services simply because they are all money; we accept them in exchange for goods and services because we expect that we will be able to exchange them yet once more, for yet other goods and services. There is a circularity here: money because accepted, and accepted because money. We can, and do, have it both ways.

Another example: the left side of the road in Japan is the proper side on which to drive; so is the right side of the road in Canada. What makes each of these the proper side on which to drive? People in Japan take the left to be the

---

5 For an elaborate exploration of the ways in which, for social reality, thinking makes it so, see John R. Searle, *The Construction of Social Reality* (London: Harmondsworth, 1995) and *Making the Social World: The Structure of Human Civilization* (Oxford: Oxford University Press, 2010).

proper side; because of that, they drive on the left. Because people in Japan drive on the left, that is the safe and therefore proper side on which to drive in Japan; and because the left is the proper side on which to drive in Japan, people in Japan take it to be the proper side; and so on round in a circle. Likewise with driving on the right in Canada: the right is the proper side because people take it to be the proper side, and people take it to be the proper side because the proper side is what it is. And in parts of the world with no consensus on the matter, there simply is no such thing as the proper side on which to drive.

If we conceive of the pious along the lines of social kinds such as these, rather than as a natural kind, then we need not be intimidated by the dilemma that Socrates put to Euthyphro. We can happily maintain that the only οὐσία of the pious is a πάθος – that the pious is pious only because of an attitude that gods take to the pious, and that they take to it only because it is pious.

How would such a conception work in detail? The best model, I suggest, is the way in which people value tokens of politeness, respect, esteem, and honour. "Politeness costs nothing," I was taught as a boy. It would be more accurate to say that politeness costs a little. It is at least an extra syllable to say "please". It takes even the youngest and healthiest a little effort to stand up when someone comes into the room; and if age or infirmity make it take more than a little effort, then the gesture is all the more respectful. It is courteous to take the trouble to send an email of thanks, and more courteous, because more trouble, to write a thank-you letter by hand and send it by post. Ounce for ounce, gold costs more than silver, which in turn costs more than bronze; in keeping with that fact, medals of gold, silver, and bronze are awarded for coming first, second, and third. And so on. There are complications, of course. In particular, tokens of the very greatest honour are sometimes quite humdrum; for example, the Victoria Cross is made of bronze, yet it outranks all other medals, including some made of silver and gold.[6] Or again, victors in lesser contests might win lavish quantities of olive oil, but the victors at Olympia won only garlands made from olive leaves.[7] In such cases, I take it, the humdrum token suggests that the honorand has transcended any ordinary scale of values. Such, then, are the costs of respect for those who bestow it. What about its benefits for those on whom it is bestowed? Well, when one of the costs is the transfer of some good, then one of the benefits is of course the receipt of such a good.

---

[6] See "Medals, Awards, and Insignia," British Army Website, https://www.army.mod.uk/structure/32322.aspx, accessed 30 April 2014.

[7] See Aristophanes, *Wealth* 582–6 for prizes at the Olympic games; and Aristotle *Constitution of Athens* 60.3 and *Inscriptiones Graecae* II.ii.2311.23–70 for prizes at the Panathenaic games.

But sometimes no good is transferred; for example, when you stand up until I am seated, I do not gain the comfort that you lose. And even when some good is transferred, the receipt of the good is not exactly the benefit. I have plenty of fine ties and can easily afford plenty more. So when my pupils give me a fine tie, the improvement to my wardrobe and the savings to my pocket are negligible. Even so, I am delighted by their gift, for such a gift is a mark of esteem. But what makes it so apt a mark of esteem is the delight that it causes – delight in the recognition that my pupils have expended thought, time, and money in order to bring me delight. It is in precisely such a way that gods can like pious offerings.

This talk of marks of esteem that please because they are intended to please might suggest that such intentions to please are easily fulfilled. There can be easy fulfilment of some intentions to perform symbolic acts. For example, I may attempt to do something to tell you that I love you, and if you notice that I'm doing it with that intention, then my attempt succeeds.[8] Whether my declaration of love be welcome or unwelcome, believed or disbelieved, I have certainly succeeded in making the declaration if you notice what I am about. Nothing quite like this is true of the intention to please with a mark of esteem, for sometimes the intention to please can be there, and be noticed, and yet result in displeasure. Imagine a slacking pupil who, instead of changing his ways, tries to ingratiate himself by offering me a bottle of wine. This would displease me. And the more expensive the wine, the greater my displeasure. I am not to be bought like that. There is an obvious parallel with what the prophets tell us about the God of Israel:

> Wherewith shall I come before the Lord, and bow myself before the high God? Shall I come before him with burnt offerings, with calves of a year old? Will the Lord be pleased with thousands of rams, or with ten thousands of rivers of oil? Shall I give my firstborn for my transgression, the fruit of my body for the sin of my soul? He hath shewed thee, O man, what is good; and what doth the Lord require of thee, but to do justly, and to love mercy, and to walk humbly with thy God? (Micah 6:6–8; cf. Isaiah 1:10–17, Amos 5:21–24)

That the same would be true of the gods of the Greeks is, one hopes, a safe inference, though it is drawn only in rare texts such as Plato's (or pseudo-

---

8 The classic exposition of how such intentions work remains H.P. Grice, "Meaning," published first in *Philosophical Review* 66 no. 3 (1957): 377–88, and since reprinted in his *Studies in the Way of Words* (Cambridge, MA: Harvard University Press, 1989), 213–23.

Plato's) *Lesser Alcibiades* 149e: "The divine is not the sort of thing that can be manipulated by gifts, like some ignoble moneylender."

As these reflections should remind us, gods like and are pleased not only by symbolic marks of esteem, but also by things with other merits, such as doing justice (Homer, *Odyssey*, 14.83–84) and honouring one's father and mother (Euripides, fragment 852 TGF). How are these other things, and the liking that gods have for them, connected with piety? My pupils please me not only by their gifts and their thanks, but also, and more importantly, by their industrious application to their studies. They know this, and consequently, in addition to all the other motives they have for applying themselves, they can apply themselves also in order to please me. This in turn means that I can take additional pleasure. And thus their industrious application to their studies has an additional merit, over and above its original industry. Or again, if a pupil were to slack, I would be displeased. And if the slacking indicated that the pupil did not care about displeasing me, then that lack of care itself would add to my displeasure, and the slacking would display an additional fault, over and above laziness. In exactly the same way, I suggest, an action that the gods dislike for other reasons – for instance, because it is unjust – they can dislike also because it shows disdain for them. Such an action will be not only unjust, but also impious. Or again, even if the gods like a just action because it is just, they can like it also for the further reason that it shows them esteem. When the gods like a just action for this further reason, then they like it because it is pious. And it will be pious because they have this special liking for it. We have, in short, the same circularity here – where there is more for gods to like about an action than its piety – that we first saw in actions whose piety was their only merit. Quite generally, the pious is what gods like, and gods like it because it is pious.

We may therefore draw a moral: Euthyphro was wrong to reject his definition of the pious as the god-loved; for even though his definition leads to a circle, the circle to which it leads is wholly innocent. What, however, is the moral that Plato wishes us to draw? Not long after rejecting his definition, Euthyphro is brought to accept it once more (15b1–6) through an interrogation in which he seems to make not the slightest slip. Perhaps, then, the *Euthyphro* not only presents us with a problem quite different from what is usually supposed, but also gives us a hint at the solution.[9]

---

9  This paper has been improved by helpful remarks from Sarah Broadie, Timothy Chappell, and the participants in the Ancient Philosophy and Religion Colloquium, Cambridge, 14–16 May 2014.

# Religion, Philosophy, and the Demons in Between

Lars Albinus

For quite some time, there has been a widespread, and perhaps even growing, tendency in classical studies to dismiss the traditional notion of a Greek miracle.[1] One senses a sort of dismay, ranging from fatigue to scepticism, concerning the triumphant self-reassurance of an undisrupted ascent of modern reason from the Greek *logos*. In support of this critical attitude, one might assume that part of the inclination to detach Greek science and philosophy from a religious background was rooted in a view of polytheism as having no bearing on the later alliance between Greek philosophy and Jewish religion. In retrospect, therefore, polytheism – in myth and ritual – might have seemed inessential for understanding the nature of Greek thinking. This view informs the main thesis of Søren Skovgaard Jensen's study of ancient demonology, to which I shall return below.

It is highly problematic, however, to take a sharp distinction between religion and philosophy in ancient Greece for granted. It is true that Greek polytheism did not have the same lasting impact on future European culture as Greek philosophy and science did. Whereas the tradition of the Greek pantheon became almost obsolete in antiquity and was only reborn, much later, by way of aesthetic representations, the tradition of 'rational thought' admittedly fertilised the soil for patristic theology and sowed nutritional seeds which, though lying in wait for centuries, would later bear the fruits of Western science. As historians, however, I think we should withstand the suggestive power of a belief in history as having unfolded according to some internal necessity.[2]

---

1  Cf., for instance, Richard Buxton, ed., *From Myth to Reason? Studies in the Development of Greek Thought* (Oxford: Clarendon Press, 2001); D. Papenfuss and V.M. Strocka, *Gab es das Griechische Wunder? Griechenland zwischen dem Ende des 6. und der Mitte des 5. Jahrhunderts v. Chr.* (Tagungsbeiträge April 1999, Freiburg im Breisgau; Mainz: Philipp von Zabern Verlag, 2001); and Helmut Heit, *Der Ursprungsmythos der Vernunft: Zur philosophiehistorischen Genealogie des griechischen Wunders* (Königshausen, 2007), 34, for specific references.

2  I thus find myself in line with Foucault's Nietzschean view of history in terms of a genealogy opposed to "[a]n entire historical tradition (theological or rationalistic) [which] aims at dissolving the singular event into an ideal continuity – as a theological movement or a natural process;" Michel Foucault, *Language, Counter-memory, Practice: Selected Essays and Interviews* (ed. Donald F. Bouchard; Ithaca, NY: Cornell University Press, 1977), 154. The view that Foucault distances himself from is, for instance, the dialectic understanding of the Greek

To be sure, I share the wish to dissolve the old, die-hard stereotypes and endorse the view that the nature of discursive interrelations in antiquity has not been fully appreciated in all of its complexity. In this chapter, I shall thus offer my own examples, concentrating on the concept of the *daemon*. I am fully aware that we are dealing with a linguistic entity whose various shapes and forms make it an extremely slippery object of study. However, I shall restrict myself to focus specifically on its ambiguous, not to say ambivalent, adaption in the newborn tradition of academic philosophy.

## 1   Setting the Parameters

The concept of philosophy, probably not in general circulation until the fifth century BCE, seems to have been coined in opposition to *sophia*, the possession of wisdom among the sages (*sophoi*),[3] and developed stylistically in critical opposition to sophism, the later rhetoric art of argumentative persuasion that included no serious interest in knowledge.[4] Thus, Socrates, who may have appeared to engage in the same kind of discourse as the sophists, definitely did not regard himself as either a sage (*sophos*) or a sophist, but rather as a philosopher, who was driven by a desire to gain wisdom while admitting to knowing nothing in advance. Contrary to the sophist, the philosopher regarded argumentative monologues with reserve and invited instead the exchange of arguments in dialogue (*dialogos*) – that is, *logos* in exchange. The inclusion and transformation of the listener into an active participant in discourse made this kind of *logos* a novel one, but being a dialectics – that is, a verbal play of give-and-take – it was still anchored, as it seems, in the traditional inclination towards *agōn* (contest), which ranged from sporting combats to rhapsodic competitions. Yet, at the same time, the principle of mutuality counteracted the agonistic attitude. The goal was no longer to win the game by defeating the

---

gods as representations which, despite their still nature-bound lack of absolute freedom, heralds the realisation in Spirit (*Geist*) of self-conscious subjectivity; cf. G.W.F. Hegel, *Vorlesungen über die Philosophie der Religion, II* (Werek 17; Frankfurt a.M.: Suhrkamp, 1986), 11:105. Foucault in part formed his own view of a history of ideas in opposition to Hegel, whom he studied and wrote about as a student.

3   Cf. Walter Burkert, "Platon oder Pythagoras, Zum Ursprung des Wortes 'Philosophia,'" *Hermes* 88 (1960): 159–77, 172.

4   See, for instance, W.K.C. Guthrie, *A History of Greek Philosophy, Volume III: The Fifth-Century* (Cambridge: Cambridge University Press, 1971); M. Detienne, *The Masters of Truth in Archaic Greece* (trans. Janet Lloyd; New York: Zone Books, 1996), 118ff.

opponent, but to acquire the prize of truth by overcoming the lack of knowledge (*mathēsis*) in oneself, abiding by the ascetic principle of *gnōthi seauton*.[5] That something innovative was definitely taking place, although in rather restricted circles at first, did not mean, however, that the traditional complex of myths and cults was sidetracked. Indeed, Socrates largely seems to have met the prescribed cultic obligations, and nothing suggests that Plato did not honour their civic function as well. Formally, the latter established his own school in honour of the Muses and located it physically in the grove of the eponymous hero, Academus, sacred to Athene and a site for long-standing cult traditions, including processions and funeral games. Plato's own attachment to the local gymnasium further testifies to the uncontroversial way in which his school was tailored to the framework of the polis cults.

But new voices were also heard. By the end of the fourth century BCE, Theophrastus (371–287), Aristotle's successor in the peripathetic school of the Lyceon, was openly hostile to polytheism, derogatorily calling it *deisidaimonia* – literally 'fear of the gods', but actually close to synonymous with 'superstition'. Surely there is no denying that, at this point, times were changing, and we might speak of an overall shift from *mythos* to *logos*, provided that we use the concepts in an etic sense.[6] The problem is that it tells us very little about the finer nature of things. Homing in on the meanings associated with the concept of the *daemon*, I shall offer two theses with which I intend to problematise the notion of a clear break between the old and the new: on the one hand, I shall argue for a counter-movement in Plato's work from *logos* to *mythos*; on the other hand, I shall claim, paradoxical though it might seem, that *dialectics* – the genre of dialogue and the *logon didonai*[7] contained in it – introduced a criterion of irreversibility according to which *mythos* could never again be disrobed of *logos*.

---

5 Cf. Foucault, The Hermeneutics of the Subject: Lectures at the Collège de France, 1981–82 (ed. Graham Burchell; New York: Picador, 2005), 65ff.).

6 I endorse G.E.R. Lloyd's view that the very concepts of *mythos* and *logos* were entangled in a polemic "forged to defend a territory, repel boarders, put down rivals" (Lloyd, *Demystifying Mentalities* [Cambridge: Cambridge University Press, 1990], 23), but it doesn't change the fact that a new kind of polemic saw the light of day, and although the adoption of a distinction between *mythos* and *logos* may be part of that polemic, it is still reasonable to speak of it as changing the parameters of communication. That both *mythos* and *logos* were used with other connotations before the onset of dialogical rivalry is another matter (and rather a question about whether we speak about actor's categories or observer's categories, to use Lloyd's own terms).

7 *Logon didonai* means 'giving reasons' or 'accounting for one's own statement'.

However, it requires an introductory clarification of basic concepts to approach this topic intelligibly. Instead of speaking of *mythos*, which invites us to think more or less exclusively about a poetic institution, I suggest we talk about the interrelated complex of myth and ritual – that is, a tradition of verbally and bodily narrative practices that take place in name of, or for the sake of communicating with, trans-empirical beings. It is, however, strained to speak of one religious tradition as such in ancient Greece, considering the cultural differences between the various tribes. Still, the formation of the famous city-states in ancient times did a lot with respect to creating a panhellenic (common Greek) horizon. Local traditions – which were already comparable, at least with respect to a roughly shared language – became associated with panhellenic gods or even reformed along the lines of the new polis ideology.[8] For this reason, it is possible, with some necessary caution, to speak about ancient Greek religion in the singular. The standing question is, however, what makes a tradition religious? The criterion I should like to appeal to here is the discursive strategy of referring to a transcendent source of legitimation, whether this took place in the verbal contests of the *symposioi*, in rhapsodic recitations, in theatrical plays, or in the body-engaging sacrifices, calendar festivals, sporting games, and initiations. Together they made up a multifarious network of cult practices in recognition of a shared need for divine benevolence. What makes the epic traditions of Homer and Hesiod religious in this sense is thus not merely their semantic reference to supernatural beings or the ritual pragmatics concerning their recitation, but rather their ultimate appeal to the authority of being inspired by the Muses, the daughters of Apollo.[9] The invocation of non-empirical entities in various other kinds of rituals, such as prayers and sacrifices, can be seen along the same lines. The crucial distinction, pertaining to the pragmatic as well as semantic aspects of tradition, is the division between the world of men and the world of gods, which was expressed unequivocally in Greek as the difference between mortals (*thnētoi*) and immortals (*athanatoi*). However, clear-cut as the distinction appears in panhellenic poetry, oriented primarily towards the reign of the Olympian gods, it often seems blurred in local traditions, as expressed, for instance, in the lyric genres, which in their reflection on local affairs were closer to chthonian traditions. In the cult of the dead, moreover, including oracular hero shrines, we get a glimpse of spiritual activity and chthonian beings that have very little to

---

8   On the latter aspects, see L.B. Zaidmann and P. Schmitt Pantel, *Religion in the Ancient Greek City* (trans. Paul Cartledge; Cambridge: Cambridge University Press, 1992).

9   Cf., *The Masters of Truth*, 41.

do with the shadowy images of Hades, presented in the Homeric epics (e.g., *Odyssey* 11). This is a long and complex story,[10] but what I am driving at here is that the concept of *daemon* served in many respects as a mediator between the two worlds, not only in the semantic sense of being a mythical entity of mediation, spelled out as a *metaxy* in Plato's *Symposium* (202e), but also by indicating the ritual role of a ritual instructor, a *mystagogue* (from the Greek *mystagogus*), as well as the initiated (*mystēs*). The latter can be seen, for instance, among the Pythagorean *acousmatic*.[11] Roughly speaking, although the particular arguments are beyond the scope of this chapter, the Olympian powers only approached the human world in the disguise of *daemons*, whereas the mortals and the chthonian powers, including the dead, were in mutual contact within the confines of a ritual context, and in this context human beings could act as *daemons*.[12] Scarce as these remarks may be, they will have to do by way of delineating the background for the focus of this chapter, namely the way in which the *daemons* entered the academic discourse of Platonism as a linguistic but pragmatically significant phenomenon with detectable traces of esoteric initiation.[13]

## 2 The *Daimonion* of Socrates

Let us begin by looking at the way in which Plato spoke about the *daemonic* in relation to Socrates. The 'Socrates' of the dialogues is, of course, a Platonic Socrates rather than the real-life person who died in 399 BCE. Still, the development of Plato's dialogues seems to show a gradual divergence from the direct influence of his teacher. Thus, in the dialogues from the early and the

---

10   Cf. Lars Albinus, *The House of Hades: Studies in Ancient Greek Eschatology* (Aarhus: Aarhus Universitetsforlag, 2000).
11   Cf. Walter Burkert, *Lore and Science in Ancient Pythagoreanism* (Cambridge, MA: Harvard University Press, 1972) 73f.
12   Albinus, "The Greek δαίμων between Mythos and Logos," in *Die Dämonen/Demons* (ed. Armin Lange et al.; Tübingen: Mohr Siebeck, 2003), 425–46.
13   I should perhaps stress that by academic Platonism I am not merely referring to the dialogues written by Plato himself, but to the whole discourse of the Academy, including pseudo-Platonic dialogues, authored – religiously, as it were – in his name (thus, the contributions of Xenocrates, to which I shall return below, count as well). What I am interested in here is a certain institutionalised discourse of philosophy rather than the work of a single person. Again, I find myself in line with Foucault ("Orders of discourse," *Social Science Information* 10 no. 2 [1971]: 7–30, 14f.) on this point.

middle period, including the *Apology*, to which I will return below, we are presented with Socrates as a person who insists on the mutual search for truth by means of the dialogue and who disavows positive knowledge. Hence, the dialogues from the early to the middle phase are traditionally labeled as aporetic, owing to the apparent lack of clear results. In the later dialogues, customarily called dogmatic, ranging from parts of *The Republic* to *The Laws*, the discourse increasingly assumes the form of a monologue, casting its secondary interlocutors in the role of saying essentially yes or no to rhetorical questions. This may be seen as a result of the aging Plato insisting on a more positive philosophy than in his earlier years, where he was perhaps still under influence from the historical Socrates, who kept entirely to a dialogical practice. The obvious changes in philosophical style throughout Plato's dialogues might, of course, be counterbalanced by the famous seventh letter, in which he denounces the presence of any positive knowledge in the written dialogues. This does not mean, however, that he disavows true knowledge; he merely claims that it cannot transmit to a soul who has not, for a long time and in many ways, been in association (*synousia*) with the matter (*pragma*) itself (Plato, *Epinomis* 7.341c), guided, if necessary, by philosophical instruction (341e). There is very little doubt that Plato maintained the ideal of philosophy as an open-ended dialectics of truth, but in actual practice he came to acknowledge the ability to know the truth as something one either had or not. It goes without saying that there may be more to the change of style in Platonic discourse. Another issue worth considering is the significance of religious influence. In order to estimate the unacknowledged forces of tradition and the die-hard inertia of religious discourse, however, we will have to look beyond Plato's self-interpretation, and even beyond the authenticity of authorship. What we are aiming at is rather a level of discursive interaction that enables us to estimate when and where Platonic authority spoke with a religious voice and on what occasion it allowed itself to speak non-religiously.

If we stick to the suggested understanding of a religious discourse as a strategy of speaking in the name of a divine power that guarantees the legitimacy of the discursive content, it appears that even Socrates speaks with a religious voice in the *Apology*. In this dialogue, which is customarily regarded as written soon after the execution of the historical Socrates, Plato lets his protagonist admit to something *daemonic* (*daemonion*) which has accompanied him from early childhood (cf. *Apology* 31d; *Theages* 128d). It appears to him from time to time, typically as a *daemonic* sign or voice or just something nonspecifically *daemonic* (*Republic* 496c; *Euthyphro* 272e; *Phaedrus* 242b; *Theaetetus* 129b8). The important thing, however, is that it merely communicates with him in a negative sense, namely by holding him back from doing something he intended to do upon insufficient reflection (*Apology* 31d).[14] Contrary to a common view, Socrates is nowhere – by Plato at least – mentioned to have anything to do with a *daemon*, but only with something *daemonic* (ranging from an adjectival sense to a substantiation of the adjective itself), and it is worth emphasising that he does not attribute any positive content of truth to this *daemonic* influence. Rather, when he defends himself against Meletus' charge of perverting the young and introducing new *daemonic* beings at the expense of neglecting the city gods (Plato, *Apology* 24c), he speaks in his own name and justifies his speech by accounting for it (cf. *logon didonai*) with reasons (27e). It is true that Socrates refers to the authority of the Delphic god for having called him the wisest among men (*Apology* 20e; 21b), but the irony with which he speaks about this wisdom as a prudence of not-knowing serves a double strategy of presenting him as an actual authority and undermining any personal authority that cannot speak for itself by the use of arguments. In other words, the *daemonic* influence on Socrates, as well as the oracular pronouncement of his wisdom (20e), can only be defined negatively. I find this very important by way of introducing a new discursive principle with an irreversible impact on future thinking, even though the older Plato seems to fall back on a more authoritarian note. Nevertheless, the premises for dictating a positive truth were profoundly unsettled as a matter of principle,[15] a circumstance that underlies the condition of possibility as well as, paradoxically, the dogmatising development of Platonic discourse itself.

Returning to the Socrates of the *Apology*, the question is whether it is important that he relates to something *daemonic* but not, strictly speaking, the voice of a *daemon*? I think it is. By repeatedly pointing out the adjective aspect, Plato emphasises a relational meaning that is in accordance with the mediating role ascribed to *daemons* elsewhere – as, for instance, in the *Symposium* (202e). But there is more to it than that.

The Socrates of the early and middle dialogues is generally disinclined to take any traditional truth for granted. He pays his respects, if perhaps only superficially, to the authority of the cult obligations of the polis, and he declares it inconceivable that he should be guilty of neglecting gods who can only be thought of as parents to the *daemons* he is accused of introducing (*Apology* 24c). It might have been quite obvious to the intended reader, though, that

---

14  Thus, in Xenophon, Socrates dissociates his own experience of a *daemonic* voice from the *phōnē*, which is said to inspire the oracular pronouncements in Delphi, x. *Apology* 5.1; 13.7; see also Gregory Vlastos, *Socrates. Ironist and Moral Philosopher* (Cambridge: Cambridge University Press, 1991), 11–13, who argues for the same disconnection.

15  Cf. H.G. Gadamer, *Platos dialektische Ethik* (Hambrug: Felix Meiner Verlag, 1983), 40.

Socrates here only pays lip service to his accuser Meletus by ironically deconstructing his charge. In other words, he turns the traditional frame of conceptions into a play of words, which serves to alter the connotations of divine wisdom. An intriguing strategy takes place, as I am going to argue, which allows the ascription of meaning to turn both ways – that is, towards a traditional context of meaning seen in the light of the new style of discourse as well as towards new meanings in the light of the old context. I should like to call this deployment of meaning potentials, which is ambiguous rather than unintelligible, metaphorical. I do not hereby speak of metaphor in Aristotle's sense, though it was him who actually coined the term.[16] Against Aristotle's own point in speaking about *metaphora* as the transference of meaning from a primary semantic domain to a secondary one, I shall draw attention to the new dialogical interchange of words which rather opened the way for a semantic traffic that went both ways. Rather than utilising a play of words in which something simply meant something else, it seems that revolutionary rules of crisscross associations were in the making.

## 3   *Daemonie*: The Ambiguous Apostrophe

In one of the middle dialogues, the interlocutor Phaedrus asks Socrates whether the speech of Lysias was to his satisfaction. Socrates answers that

---

16   In the *Poetics*, Aristotle introduces the meaning of *metaphora* as "the application of a foreign term" (*onomatos allotriou epiphora*, 1457b6ff.). This obviously implies a hierarchical order between two ways of using the same term – that is, a dominating (*kurios*) or appropriate (*oikeiōs*, also meaning 'at home') one, which strives for lucidity in meaning, and an inappropriate (or 'foreign') one, which is called metaphorical; cf. Lloyd, *Aristotelian Explorations* (Cambridge: Cambridge University Press, 1999), 207. I agree with Lloyd, however, that Aristotle's own definition of *metaphora* lacks this prescribed lucidity itself by already making use of *metaphora*, inasmuch as the strict meaning (*kurios*) of the very term, *metaphora*, namely "the transport of physical objects," here denotes "the 'strange' *allotrion* context of terms" (*Aristotelian Explorations*, 211). I also favour Lloyd's view that Aristotle, contrary to his own attack on metaphorical expressions as being unclear (139b34f.), makes a heavy use of them inasmuch as they serve his rhetorical style (214ff.). I am more reluctant to buy into Lloyd's argument that we should abstain altogether from speaking about a metaphorical use of words in the first place. We might agree that Aristotle's coinage of the term is somewhat polemically directed against a *poetic* use of words that pretends to carry philosophical insight (as, for instance, in *Metaphysics* 357a24ff.; cf. Lloyd, *Aristotelian Explorations*, 209), but when Lloyd turns Aristotle's definition of *metaphora* against itself, it merely points to a lack of intended clarity, not that there is not any interchange of meaning potentials.

he found it *daemonic* (*Phaedrus* 243d1), which, in this context, seems to mean that it was overwhelming and immediately convincing, but for all the wrong reasons (234e). It is noteworthy that the conventional apostrophe, *daemonie*, is used shortly afterwards, seemingly related to the subject matter of seductive speech. The counter-speech Socrates is persuaded to give is thus announced to stem not from himself, but from a source beyond his own wits, and he introduces it by addressing Phaedrus with *daemonie*. To cut it short, *daemonie* is indeed a conventional but not a random form of address. As can be seen from its use by Homer and Hesiod, it generally appeals to the willingness to bow to the divine will or to the inevitability of fate.[17] In the discourse of Herodotus' *Histories* it changes into reminding a person of his or her submission to the will of human superiors instead (4.126; 7.48). In Plato, *daemonie* also seems to imply an appeal to give in to the strongest will, yet instead of stemming from divine or human individuals, the will is now transformed into a shared search for truth and the argumentative commitment following from this enterprise (*Laches* 199d4; *Republic* 344d6; 522b3; *Cratylus* 415a). It may not always look that way at first glance, however. In *Phaedrus*, Socrates' interlocutor is told to submit to the influence of the divine tale he is going to hear, but in the light of Socrates' subsequent self-renouncement of the 'inspired' speech as being terrible and impious (*asebē*, 242d7), this appeal becomes hollow. Hence, Socrates here takes an ironical distance to *daemonie* as being associated with the unreasoned impression of the seductive tale.[18]

In general, *daemonie* was frequently used from the fifth century and onwards for emphasising praise as well as blame. Plato is no exception. In *Laches*, for instance, Nicias is addressed with *daemonie* as an expression of appreciation of his willingness to respect the power of the argument, whereas Phaedrus and Criton are examples of being addressed with *daemonie* as a means of reproach (although, as indicated above, Socrates might be intentionally ambiguous). Apparently, *daemonios* is generally used by Plato as indicative of legitimate intuition, yet of a merely negative, withholding kind, whereas the weaker

---

[17] This meaning potential of *daemonie* pertains to *Iliad* 1.561–2; 2.190, 200; 4.31; 6.326, 407, 486, 521; 9.40; 13.448, 810; 24.194; *Odyssey* 4.274; 10.472; 14.443–45; 18.15, 406; 19.71; Hesiod, *Theogonia* 655; *Opera et dies* 207. See also the study of E. Brunius-Nilsson (*ΔAIMONIE – An Inquiry into a Mode of Apostrophe in Old Greek Literature* [Uppsala: Almquist & Wiksell, 1955], 19–32), who, for instance, relates the use of the apostrophe in Hesiod with a combination of admonition and reproach, which seems to have become conventional from around the fifth century BCE.

[18] The same applies to the dialogue *Euthydemus* (290e–291a), in which Socrates ironically addresses Criton with *daemonie*, inasmuch as he bows to something 'stronger' than reasoned argumentation.

*daemonie* is used to denote (and appeal to) the willingness to let oneself be convinced – by whatever it is. Only the precise context discloses whether the person has been a passive victim of persuasion or an active participant in the search for truth. In both cases, however, the apostrophe fits – exactly because of its double edge, as it were. Thus, whereas *daemonios* indicates external truth conditions beyond the reach of the mortal mind, *daemonie* seems to address and indicate the internal state of the mind in its attitude towards the former. Derivatives of the *daemon* have opened up the distinction between mortality and immortality from each side of the gap.

When Socrates, who is never addressed with *daemonie*, gives in to something *daemonic*, it is not because it indicates some positive truth, but because he senses that it hints at something he is not yet fully aware of. His receptiveness may rather be seen to follow from the fact that he disavows any positive knowledge to begin with. Inversely, those who believe they have superhuman knowledge, as addressed in the *Apology* (20d–e), have been trapped by the *daemonic*. In fact, they don't know what they claim to know (21d), and consequently they have no real authority. Later on in Plato's work, however, the protagonist of *Timaeus* acknowledges that we will have to trust those who claim to be descendants of the gods and accordingly are in possession of knowledge (*eidosin*) about their own ancestors (*Timaeus* 40d–e). Even though their statements cannot be proved to be either likely or necessary, it is obligatory for everyone to acknowledge them. It goes without saying that Plato is not Timaeus, and even Timaeus admits to offer nothing but a 'likely story' (*eikos mythos*) about the genesis of the changeable world (*Timaeus* 29d). Nonetheless, something has changed between the *Apology* and the *Timaeus*. Roughly speaking, while Socrates in the earlier dialogues is only willing to believe what can be acknowledged by the dialectic use of reason, protagonists of the later dialogues (including Socrates, Timaeus, and the Stranger from Athens) seem to acknowledge the sheer importance of tradition. Seen from an overall perspective of Platonic discourse, the *daemonic* points in two directions: it is associated with a tradition which has to be respected, comprising a hierarchy with mortals at the bottom, gods at the top, and heroes and daemons in between; but it also becomes associated with the Socratic deconstruction of this tradition, conjoining divine reality with the faculty of reason alone.

While this metaphorical double seems present throughout Plato's work, he nevertheless appears to slide from using it in the philosophical spirit of his teacher to using it more in line with the institutional customs around him. After all, his newly established academy was itself part of this institutional network, as indicated above. The open agora and the city streets were being exchanged for the secluded walls and the air of esoteric knowledge that may have surrounded the academy (whether intentionally or not). How esoteric the Platonic school actually was is an unsettled matter that I shall not take up here, but it should be uncontroversial, in any case, to point out the increased importance that Plato attributed to the institutional role of philosophers for the ideal administration of the city.

## 4  Against the Thesis of Søren Skovgaard Jensen

I should like, in this respect, to address a very interesting thesis about dualism and demonology in Greek philosophy launched by the late Danish scholar Søren Skovgaard Jensen. Skovgaard Jensen's thesis is that Greek demonology was entirely a philosophical invention that developed from relative to absolute dualism owing to the universal duality between sense experience and reason.[19] These developments took place twice. First ritual experiences of human contact with divine reality among the early Pythagoreans, the so-called *acousmatics*, changed to the focus on abstract reasoning among the *mathēmaticoi*. This development led to an absolute dualism between the earthly conditions of mortal being and the divine realm of immortal being. Secondly, a similar process took place in Platonism from a relative dualism found in Plato's authentic dialogues to the absolute dualism of his academic successors, including the author of the *Epinomis* as well as the post-Platonic thoughts of Xenocrates.

The argument is that Plato submits to a relative dualism on behalf of Socrates, following the general *homoion homoio* principle, meaning here that 'like understands like'. Thus the *daemon* is identified with the soul as the real mediator between this world and the other, the reason being that the non composite part of the soul partakes in transcendent being – that is, being as such.[20] Later, in the context of the academy, the mediating principle of the soul is, in Skovgaard Jensen's view, abandoned, inasmuch as the evil principle of matter (*sōma*) explicitly, and contrary to Plato himself, holds the human soul captive in irrationality.[21] Although the rational part of the soul is able to sense the reality of a higher order, it must, at the same time, admit the limitation of bodily existence. "The activity of the living beings [...] is limited to

---

[19]  S. Skovgaard Jensen, *Dualism and Demonology* (Munksgaard, Kbh, 1966), 31ff. It is because of this view that Skovgaard Jensen wants to speak, in general terms, of a *demonology*, rather than the use of terms related to *daemon*, which, contrary to Skovgaard Jensen, informs the pragmatic view of the present chapter.

[20]  Skovgaard Jensen, *Dualism and Demonology*, 84–90.

[21]  Skovgaard Jensen, *Dualism and Demonology*, 95f.

the sphere of the element out of which they are made and that consequently direct communication between the human being and the higher existence is precluded."[22] The *daemons*, related to man by being passionate creatures and to the gods by having "a greater intelligence and a better memory" (cf. *Epinomis* 984e–985a), are thus reintroduced as static mediators between human and divine knowledge, resulting in the reaffirmation of an absolute dualism which, at the same time, establishes a cosmological hierarchy of being. "Between the stars and the human beings there are the creatures called demons made of ether, air and water respectively."[23] This dualism will in due course be succeeded by monism, which, according to Skovgaard Jensen, is the only tenable principle of absolute knowledge. This intriguing (though not original) suggestion shall not occupy us here. What I should like to comment on is to what degree Skovgaard Jensen is justified in regarding the construction of demonology as well as its development from relative to absolute dualism as a process of rational necessity.

First of all, I will have to lay out some of the flaws that may call into question the solidity of his argument. By way of introducing his thesis, Skovgaard Jensen finds it necessary to make clear that "[i]t obviously is to misinterpret the nature of dualism to construct a theory of its origin that relates it to the essentially different, though accidentally connected sphere of religion, but does not primarily rest upon the simple fact that a human being is supposed to have been endowed with extended perception [experience] as well as with reason."[24] And further on, he writes, "Dualism as a philosophical phenomenon exists solely in virtue of the ascendancy of experience, conceived purely as a basic psychological phenomenon, over reason."[25] I think this view reflects a certain tendency to draw a sharp line between religion and philosophy for the sake of defending a linear shift from *mythos* to *logos*. I strongly believe that it is a mistake to conceive of rational reflection as an activity that, contrary to a religious way of thinking, is fostered by what Skovgaard Jensen understands as a logical reflection on the simple facts of human being. By associating philosophical thinking with universal conditions, in this case the distinction between experience and reason, religious practice is regarded as a cultural variable that can be dispensed with in the reconstruction of a process of ra-

---

22  Skovgaard Jensen, *Dualism and Demonology*, 97f.
23  Skovgaard Jensen, *Dualism and Demonology*, 97f. Skovgaard Jensen refers to *Epinomis* 980d–983d; 988d, in comparison with *Phaedo* 81c, as sources for the reformed view of absolute dualism.
24  Skovgaard Jensen, *Dualism and Demonology*, 31.
25  Ibid.

tionalisation. But this looks very much like building the conclusion into the premises. Of course, it would take an unreasonably long detour to do justice to the matter here, so let it suffice to say that approaching any given process of rationalisation as anything but situated historically and dependent on cultural conditions has to answer to the objections raised against classical metaphysics and the alleged *a priori* conditions of thought associated with that tradition.

Be that as it may, my own research into the various forms of the *daemon*-concept in ancient Greece[26] does not support Skovgaard Jensen's suggestion that the symbolic content associated with these forms is of purely philosophical (meaning 'logical') significance. I grant that the systematic exposition of a rather abstract religious hierarchy, in which *daemons* are assigned a place in the middle, may be a rather late phenomenon heavily influenced by the categorical interests of philosophical theology,[27] but the semantic structure is much older and can be traced deep into a pre-philosophical cultural tradition.[28]

Another problematic implication in Skovgaard Jensen's argument is that his view of consistency in Plato's thinking appears to rest basically on the idea of relative dualism being constitutive for the genuinely Platonic work.[29] As we have already seen, the figure of Socrates as it is presented in the early and middle dialogues is indeed associated with allocating some divine power to the soul. Yet, at the same time, this power is only assigned a negative influence on the intellect, guarding it against impulses that are less than rational. No positive content of truth can be legitimated by referring to a divine source of inspiration. Later in Plato's work, however, human souls who have led a just life and obtained philosophical insight may be regarded *post mortem* as *daemons* (*Republic* 469a; 540b); even in this life, *daemonic* beings were once

---

26  Albinus, "Greek Demons and the Ambivalence of Clemens Alexandrinus," *Temenos* 31 (1995): 7–17; Albinus, "Ancient Greek Demonology from Mythos to Logos," in *Doctorates and PhDs 1998* (ed. I. Christensen and B.S. Jensen; Vol. LXXIV 3; Aarhus: Jutlandia, 1998), 357–60; Albinus, "The Greek δαίμων."

27  Such as is found, for instance, in Xenocrates and Plutarch; cf. Plutarch *Moralia* 415b; 416c; 417b; 591d–952d; R. Heinze, *Xenocrates – Darstellung der Lehre und Sammlung der Fragmente* (Leipzig, 1892).

28  Hesiod's *Work and Days* (*Opera et dies* 109ff.), where a hierarchy of human races, including *daemons* of the Golden Age, is introduced, may serve as an obvious example. Although the poem may be seen as belonging to a tradition of wisdom literature that shows a highly reflected, non-archaic stance of the author, it still houses obvious elements of an ancient collective tradition, including the 'genealogy of the 5 races'; cf. Jean-Pierre Vernant, *Mythe et pensée chez les grecs* (Paris: Éditions La Découverte, 1990), 48ff.

29  Skovgaard Jensen, *Dualism and Demonology*, 95–99.

elected to lead the city, as the Stranger proclaims in *The Laws* (*Laws* 713e–714a). Skovgaard Jensen is thus right in noting that we can trace a tendency towards absolute dualism, but his argument for associating this penchant with Plato's pupils rather than Plato himself is circular, apart from the limited value of making these distinctions in the first place. Crudely put, his argument is that if the dualism found in the dialogue *Epinomis* can be conceived of as absolute, the dialogue can be determined as pseudo-Platonic; and if, for other reasons, it can be argued to be pseudo-Platonic, we have reasons to believe that it should be interpreted along the lines of absolute dualism.[30] But this argument is, of course, also circular.

Owing to the pragmatic stance of this chapter, I find it more fruitful to regard the complex of discursive interaction as responsible for new forms of thinking and communication. It goes without saying that the reconstruction of discursive criteria is also reductive, the difference being, however, that it deals with empirically accessible points of reference. Setting out from this premise, we can pick out the introduction of a dialectic type of discourse, and doing so is different from insisting on a universal logic in the process of rationalisation. Instead of breaking down a discursive formation, such as Platonism, into mentally intrinsic stages of rational thought, it is in line with what is often called 'the linguistic turn' in philosophy to focus on an actual discursive formation as it stands, authored and authorised by tradition, rather than by any given author.[31] Moreover, the discernible consequences of discursive interaction, such as that between different truth-making genres,[32] deserve our attention and may, for that matter, counter any prefigured distinction between new thoughts and old habits. Thus my aim, in the context of this chapter, is to dislodge the discussion of the intrinsic development in demonology from the point of view of an absolute dissociation between religion and philosophy as well as from what can conceivably be thought by one and the same person.

---

30   Skovgaard Jensen, *Dualism and Demonology*, 93ff.
31   Cf. Foucault, *Language, Counter-memory, Practice*, 116.
32   One might refer, for instance, to Plato's dialogue *Ion*, in which Socrates ironically praises the Homeric rhapsode for his recitative skills while, at the same time, challenging him, in vain, to account for his knowledge about the actual content of the epics (533e–534e; a similar point is made already by Pindar, *Olympian Odes* 2.86f.). Yet, in the *Clouds* by Aristophanes, it is Socrates who is made a laughing stock because of his lofty thoughts. Another example of interacting 'genres of truth' would be ancient philosophy as against its modern re-interpretation (as, for instance, in Gadamer, *Platos dialektische Ethik*, and the present chapter). The point is that the interpretation plays out on an intertextual stage, rather than on a privileged scene of the eternal spirit.

## 5 Against the Thesis of Marcel Detienne

One thing that can be determined from a discursive point of view, though not without in-depth analysis, is the metaphorical use of concepts, by which I am bound to repeat that I do not essentially refer to a transference of meaning from normal predications to exceptional ones. What I have in mind is rather a strategic navigation between associative networks that partly overlap and interact.[33] Here, however, I am at odds with the French historian of religions Marcel Detienne, who has suggested that the transition from *mythos* to *logos* is distinguished by a shift from the equivocal to the unequivocal use of words – that is, from a principle of ambiguity to a principle of contradiction.[34] When the magicoreligious use of efficacious words for various reasons gave way to a secularisation of speech,[35] the use of complementary contraries was exchanged for contradictory contraries,[36] setting rational deliberation apart from the old system of thought.[37] Although Detienne also describes the evolving "political sphere" as "the particular world of ambiguity," and "sophistry and rhetoric" as "forms of thought founded on ambiguity,"[38] he nonetheless refers to a "gap between two systems of thought, one of which obeys a logic of ambiguity, the other a logic of contradiction."[39] This gap thus effectually reflects Detienne's view of a shift from *mythos* to *logos*.[40] Skovgaard Jensen, who refers to Detienne with approval,[41] seems to follow this criterion when speaking of the Platonic *daemon* as an unequivocal reference to the divine nature of *nous*, as explicitly stated in the *Timaeus*, where the *daemon* is allotted to man as the

---

33 I thus largely endorse Janet Soskice's definition of metaphor as "that figure of speech whereby we speak about one thing in terms which are seen to be suggestive of another," Soskice, *Metaphor and Religious Language* (Oxford: Clarendon Press, 1985), 15. She thereby distances herself from what she calls 'the Substitution theory' of metaphor – pertaining to Aristotle and Quintillian, for instance – which holds "that metaphor is another way of saying what can be said literally" (24).
34 Cf. Detienne, *De la pensée religieuse à la pensée philosophique. La notion de Daïmon dans le Pythagorisme ancient* (Bibliotèque de la Faculté de Philosophie et Lettres de l'Université de Liège, fasc. CLXV, Paris, 1963); Detienne, *The Masters of Truth*, 119, 135–37.
35 Detienne, *The Masters of Truth*, 137.
36 Detienne, *The Masters of Truth*, 119.
37 Detienne, *The Masters of Truth*, 104 –6.
38 Detienne, *The Masters of Truth*, 116.
39 Detienne, *The Masters of Truth*, 136.
40 Cf. Detienne, *The Masters of Truth*, 104.
41 Skovgaard Jensen, *Dualism and Demonology*, 65.

upper part (*kyriōtatos*) of the soul.⁴² Against this, the *Symposium* is regarded as still containing a Pythagorean influence, which shows itself in the absolute dualism with which the *daemon* Eros functions as a mediator (*metaxy*) between gods and men.⁴³ Insofar as this concept of the *daemon* is manifestly equivocal, being simultaneously outside and inside the individual (*à la fois extérieur et intérieur à l'individu*), as Detienne puts it,⁴⁴ it betrays – in the eyes of Skovgaard Jensen and Detienne – a religious background not yet fully rationalised.

"What Plato does, then," according to Skovgaard Jensen, "is to leave the mythological form by degrees, transforming first the divinity into a demon, then the demon into a μεταξύ, the static μεταξύ into a dynamic, and finally identifying the dynamic μεταξύ with a πάθος of the human soul."⁴⁵ What I find problematic in this interpretation, however, is that Skovgaard Jensen tries to explain away an apparent inconsistency – if not, perhaps, ambiguity – in Plato between the *Symposium* and the *Timaeus* by speaking about a Pythagorean influence in the former while regarding the latter as an authentic expression of Plato's 'own' thoughts. Moreover, it is difficult to see on what premises, other than a commitment to an internal logic of rationalisation, Skovgaard Jensen justifies his view of a linear transformation from a religious notion to a philosophical conceptualisation. Rather, I would agree with I.G. Kidd, who, in his paper "Some Philosophical Demons," states on the one hand (in agreement with Skovgaard Jensen) that "[w]hat [Plato] is referring to is not some kind of intermediary being, but a functional aspect of the human mind," while on the other hand adding that Plato "has to use imagery for this, the image of daimon which his readers would understand."⁴⁶ Yet this presupposes the ability to understand the metaphorical use of the word, not least when Plato continues to use it as indicating "a guiding force... that is somehow both part of us, and yet apart from us," as Kidd phrases it.⁴⁷ I find Kidd's remark ingenious, and it implies that no absolute development takes place from the equivocal to the unequivocal use of words. I might also add that it is in no way uncontroversial to regard Pythagoreanism as being of a receding influence on Platonism throughout the fourth century, although it is true that Plato took exception to the ritual inclinations of Orphism, as to any sectarian cult

---

42  Skovgaard Jensen, *Dualism and Demonology*, 81; cf. *Timaeus* 90a.
43  Skovgaard Jensen, *Dualism and Demonology*, 77ff.
44  Detienne, *De la pensée religieuse*, 89.
45  Skovgaard Jensen, *Dualism and Demonology*, 90f.
46  I.G. Kidd, "Some Philosophical Demons," in *Bulletin, Institute of Classical Studies*, University of London, 221 (1995); cf. *Timaeus* 90a.
47  Ibid.

practice. However, since there is no allusion to any esoteric initiation in the *Symposium*, we should more likely regard the voice of Diotima, both a divine and human, as a metaphorically constructed form of legitimation[48] associated with Pythagorean ideas, which, through the mouth of Socrates, communicates a double-edged, metaphorical truth to readers who are able to grasp it.[49] In other words, I firmly disagree with identifying the invention of philosophical discourse with a shift from ambiguity to an unremitting principle of conceptual clarity when speaking, for instance, about *daemonic* mediation.[50] On the contrary, ambiguity remains closely connected with the recurrent uses of mythical concepts in dialectics, and the philosophical point rather lies in the implicit appeal to the capacity of the intellect, *nous*, to grasp the intended metaphorical meaning, while at the same time paying tradition its due according to the conventional meanings of terms (depending, of course, on context). This also seems to be the strategy Socrates utilises to full effect in the *Apology*. That it didn't impress his accusers is merely part of the dramatic effect of the dialogue, which, surely, has more sophisticated addressees in mind.

Still, as I have mentioned already, I find strong indications of an actual development in Plato's work, which is not explainable as a compulsory process of internal rationalisation, but rather as a kind of strategic recourse to the respectability of tradition. The use of *daemon* thus shows its real metaphorical and pragmatic value in its capacity to turn the direction of association both ways. Having said this, I do not wish to exclude the possibility that the older Plato's apparent retreat from Socratic irony and frankness could also be motivated by more philosophical concerns, and I shall return to these in the last section of this chapter.

---

48  Diotima literally means 'the honour of Zeus', but insofar as this meaning played out, as it were, in the context of Socrates' monologue, it is clear that it was just as much the argument of the narrative that made it representative of divine truth as *vice versa*.

49  I thus endorse Soskice's pragmatic point that metaphor is not a property of sentences, but a function of their use; *Metaphor and Religious Language*, 136.

50  I agree with Detienne and Skovgaard Jensen, however, that 'contradiction' was indeed introduced as an important principle of discourse. The fact is, though, that we already find it in the sixth century, clearly implicated in the discourse of Hecataeus (fragment 1), in which the traditional narratives are rebuked as untrustworthy and ludicrous because of the many local differences. If we regard the notion of contradiction as the principle of transition from *mythos* to *logos*, however, we will have to restrict our definition of both these terms to very confined genres as well as types of argument, which existed together side-by-side for several centuries. The principle of dialogue and dialectics, on the other hand, which in no way exclusively invites to a principle of contradiction (or rather non-contradiction, as in Aristotle), can be located quite narrowly to the Classical period.

## 6 Daemons in *The Laws*

As for the late dialogues, I shall restrict myself to dealing superficially with *The Laws* and the tenth and last book of the *Republic*. Overall, my point is that, contrary to the earlier dialogues, Plato no longer attempts to let the philosophical quest for truth substitute for or sidetrack traditional *doxa*. Rather, he tries to dominate a mythical and ritual tradition by representing them, respectfully as it seems, within a conceptual hierarchy.[51] In *The Laws* Plato speaks through the mouth of an Athenian Stranger who, among other things, prescribes an order of sacrificial obligations, thereby authorising a hierarchical explication of relations between gods, *daemons*, heroes and mortals (*Laws* 717a–b). Although such an order can be reconstructed from earlier sources, including Hesiod and various stone inscriptions as early as the fifth century BCE, Plato seems to be the first who actually explicates their significance as manifesting relations in the necessary order of things.[52]

Represented within this explicit order, for instance, is the standing conflict between the beliefs and practices of the city-state, on the one hand, and the rural cults, on the other, reflecting, among other things, sacrificial differences between Olympian and Chthonian divinities. The Platonic legislator thus assigns an obligatory place for Chthonian worship that comes next to the honours – in song and sacrifice – bestowed upon the Olympian gods (*Laws* 717a). If we include the probably pseudo-Platonic *Epinomis*, insofar as it contributes to building the Platonic discourse of the academy, the oracular tradition is also incorporated in the hierarchical system (*Epinomis* 985c). Yet it would be strange to think of any of these dialogues as the proper place for announcing public obligations. Rather, the prescriptions belong to the academic discourse, which, along the lines of the *Republic*, aims to ideally reconceive a concrete practice, i.e., by bringing it into accordance with principles of the ideal state. Whether or not the latter part of the part of the *Republic* belongs to Plato's middle or late period depends on the chosen criteria of discrimination (though several years probably lay between the genesis and the final accomplishment of the work), but the idea of dividing the civic obligations between the philosophers as rulers of the state, the warriors

---

51  Cf. A.W. Nightingale, *Genres in Dialogue – Plato and the Construct of Philosophy* (Cambridge: Cambridge University Press, 1995).

52  Herbert Nowak, *Zur Entwicklungsgeschichte des Begriffes Daimon – Eine Untersuchung epigraphischer Zeugnisse vom 5. Jh.v.Chr. bis zum 5 Jh.n.Chr.* (Ph.D. dissertation; Bonn, 1960), 38f.

as its protectors, and the farmers, craftsmen, and men of trade as its progenitors points in the direction of the later phase of Platonic discourse, not least in the almost dogmatic form through which it borders on a Socratic monologue. Considering the fact that the tripartite division reflects, at the same time, the division of the soul into the immortal intellect (*nous*), bravery (*andreia*), and the bodily appetites (*epithymeia*), one gets the impression that Plato, perhaps disillusioned by his second journey to Sicily, no longer believed in a search for truth that was directed towards each and every individual (cf. *Epinomis* 7). The street-wandering Socrates who was anxious to make anyone he met realise the importance of tending to one's own education, gave way to a Socrates who was concerned with the issues of an ideal state and the general order of things. This Socrates – taking shape already in the middle phase – represented the extraordinary status of the philosopher, envisaged in the myth of the cave, as the only one capable of releasing himself from the chains 'of illusion' and approaching the light of truth, the pure "area of thinking" (*topos noētos*) outside the cave (*Republic* 517b). Ordinary people may also learn part of this truth by way of a "noble lie" (*gennaion pseudos, Republic* 414e–15c),[53] or even perhaps through some basic education, but in general most people are best served by accepting their lot and leaving political decision-making to the philosophers. After all, the cave, *alias* the world, *alias* society, has to be attended to, even if it is barely more than a realm of shadows. Respecting this world for what it is – and it is good, inasmuch as it is modelled on the ultimate reality of ideas – Plato more or less abandons the aporetic style of the early dialogues and thereby also the Socratic disavowal of knowledge. In fact, he exchanges it, at least from *Timaeus* onwards, with a strategic intervention in the representation of traditional lore. Instead of condoning and repeating the legitimisation of authorial reference as, for instance, at work in Homeric, Hesiodic, Pythagorean, and Orphic discourse, the aging Plato wants to secure the legitimacy of tradition by representing it as *the* ideal order, *the* structuring principle in a world of changes.

It is not for everyone to grasp the transformation of traditional concepts inevitably following from this idealisation, but to those who are initiated into philosophical discourse, it stands to reason that when the Stranger refers to philosophers who become *daemons post mortem*, he speaks metaphorically –

---

53   In the immediate context, this 'deception of noble birth', which is the literal meaning of *gennaion pseudos*, may also, more specifically, imply ambiguity concerning the meaning of mythical descent.

that is, the way in which he represents a traditional cult of the dead simultaneously shows immortality to be a matter of philosophical self-realisation, which is exactly the point made later on in *The Laws* (818b–c). On the other hand, part of this self-realisation is to acknowledge the earthly and social conditions of mortal existence, represented by the traditional, mythical as well as ritual distinction between mortality and *daemonic* immortality. What he intimates, by way of a philosophical eschatology, is therefore that a soul who has gained sufficient philosophical insight and lived a pure and righteous life through several generations (cf. *metemphsychosis*) will eventually be released from the cycle of births (*cyclōn geneseōn*). For such souls alone the temporary necessity of a hierarchical structure will dissolve into pure, undifferentiated being. And it is, at the same time, the comprehension of the nature of pure being which makes them able to understand the double meaning of the hierarchy consisting of gods, *daemons*, heroes, and mortals.

Plato may very well be one of the rhetorical authors in the Classical period who most eloquently packs double messages into his discourse, but the practice of utilising the equivocal content of mythical references is by no means his invention. Vernant and Vidal-Naquet, for instance, state with regard to Athenian drama, "the tragic message, when understood, is precisely that there are zones of opacity and incommunicability in the words that we exchange."[54] However, the strategic distinction between various levels of reception, combined with a specific appeal to certain intended readers, may belong more specifically to philosophical discourse. Socrates holds in the *Phaedrus*, for example, that a discourse "can defend itself, and it knows to whom it should speak, and with whom it should remain silent" (*Phaedrus* 276a). Only the philosopher who has purified his soul through a "meditation on death" (*meletē thanatou, Phaedrus* 81a)[55] will realise that he is an alien to earthly life and understand what is meant by the words put in the mouth of the Stranger, namely that "Cronus was aware of the fact that no human being... is capable of having irresponsible control of all human affairs without becoming filled with pride and injustice; so, pondering this fact, he then appointed as kings and rulers

---

54  Jean-Pierre Vernant and Pierre Vidal-Naquet, *Myth and Tragedy in Ancient Greece* (trans. Janet Lloyd; New York: Zone Books, 1988), 43.

55  Literally, *meletē thanatou* means a 'practice in death', and although it obviously carries contemplative connotations in Plato, there is, in fact, plenty of evidence suggesting that the expression was also associated with Pythagorean and Orphic rites of death-imitation (*imitatio mortis*; cf. Albinus, *The House of Hades*, 141ff.). Again, it is therefore likely that Plato speaks metaphorically in a bidirectional sense.

for our cities, not men, but beings of a race that was nobler and more divine, namely, *daemons*" (*Laws* 713c–d).

The legitimising force of referring to the past, which makes this paragraph look like a religiously authorised piece of *mythos*, only follows from divine authority in the sense that it includes wisdom and righteousness. In the broader textual context, it is clear that the authority Cronus represents stems from the establishment of a selfless and righteous form of government in the Golden Age. In other words, it reflects an ideal order. The sheer presence of divine powers in the Homeric sense guarantees nothing in itself. In Plato, on the other hand, the gods are not idols of justice merely because they are gods, but they are supreme beings and thus divine because and only insofar as they represent justice.

Hence, in Platonic discourse, traditional storytelling was probably used, among other things, to illustrate principles which, at least in the earlier part of his authorship, were too difficult or too offensive to present in plain argument. Then by the use of mythical references as well as the cultic references that came to take over in the later dialogues, Plato on the one hand addresses those who merely get an inkling of the real matter, and on the other hand he speaks to those who have learned to grasp the subtext, being aware of the fact that both the form and the content of discourse belongs to the derived world of composite forms. Having obtained the capability of philosophical thinking, they might come to understand that the mythical as well as mystical concept of immortality rather indicates the realisation of pure being reflecting the non-composite nature of *nous* itself. In this way, Plato subtly uses elements of tradition in a complicated network of continuity and discontinuity, the unravelling of which requires dialectic training. What is learned is ultimately that there is no source of knowledge that does not stem from divine wisdom – rightly understood – that is, from a philosophical path towards truth.[56]

On the face of it, the human and divine conditions, mortality and immortality, refer to one another and therefore seem to represent interdependent levels of being. However, the conceptual relation between them is, in Platonic philosophy (heavily inspired by Parmenides in this respect), turned into an abstract distinction between beings (*ta onta*) and being (*to on*), i.e., between the

---

56  The journey which takes Parmenides beyond the gates of day and night (i.e., beyond earthly oppositions) may also be interpreted in this same light (fragment 1), although here the theme is not presented within the frames of dialectic discourse, but within the poetic form (using verses in hexameter style) of a traditional mythical discourse. This is but one example, however, of the intertwinement of new and old elements, *mythos* and *logos*, in a convoluted discursive process.

changeable world and the immutable level of ideas. Consequently, the necessity (*ananke*) of order attains a new meaning, turning world order into civic order and the inevitability of fate into a requirement of rules. It goes without saying that it is tempting to speak of a change from *mythos* to *logos* in this respect. Yet no clean break can be discerned in any social-historical sense, which does not mean, of course, that it did not take place. Located first and foremost in the game of ongoing discursive interaction, new ways of thinking were, in the long run, as consequential as any social, political, or martial upheaval. But, of course, the one was intimately associated with the other.

However, the means Plato uses in order to reach this point have pertinent structures in common with the esoteric practice of ritual of initiation. Socrates can be said to play the *daemonic* role of a ritual instructor, a mystagogue, in this respect, but insofar as it is acknowledged that practice and *pathos* (experience) in the philosophical form of life is intimately reflected in – and represented by – *theoria* and *mathos* (learning), the mediating role of the *daemon* dissolves into thin air, just as the ladder one has to climb in Wittgenstein's *Tractatus Logico-Philosophicus* (6.54). Plato's discourse, both early and late, uses the means of dialogical understanding to full effect. The development from an aporetic orientation to a more dogmatic position – that is, from negative to positive knowledge – does not change this fact, though veiled references to matters of noetic significance are gradually exchanged for more forthright intimations. Nevertheless, it remains somehow ironic that a discursive formation which disavows (what I have allowed myself to call) the religious principle of automatic authorisation eventually allows it to creep back in when the dialogues of Plato become part of an academic, and to some extent pseudepigraphic, tradition authorised in his name.

## 7 The Relational Significance of the *Daemonic*

Skovgaard Jensen is not alone in ascribing a relative dualism to Plato, though scholarly views vary on the matter. It is true that Plato refers to a participation of sensual objects in the world of ideas, as well as vice versa, but this is no real indication of a relative dualism as long as the concept of participation remains purely abstract. Although the notion of a world of ideas bears no ultimate mark of truth in Plato's work, either early or late, it still stands as a constant invitation to distinguish between the impermanence of sensual being and the purity of immutable being, which constitutes an absolute rather than a relative dualism. The concepts of the *daemon* and the *daemonic* signify a mediating role inasmuch as a *daemonic* being is imperfect (as Eros, for instance, who longs for truth and beauty) and therefore part of the changeable world, even though it may not share the same conditions of mortality as human beings. However, the *daemon* also identifies the non-composite, unchangeable part of the human soul, which recognises 'like by like' (*homoion homoiōi*) – that is, the truth of unchangeable being. Hence, the *daemon* is presented with a double nature, which is only conceivable on a mythical level as undergoing a metaphorical transformation. Consequently, Plato does not hesitate to offer myths, when argumentative reasoning reaches an apparent standstill. It is difficult to say whether he is embarrassed by an inability to express the theory of ideas in positive terms, or whether he is intentionally tactical and pedagogical in dishing up something less than pure insight in a more agreeable, imaginative form, but it hardly matters. To dress up philosophical points in a more popular form may serve at least two purposes: to address those with the congenital ability of true insight as well as those who are capable of apprehending only an already digested half-truth, which is, at any rate, better than nothing. But then again, making this apparent distinction may in fact distort the actual, and delicate, workings of discursive interaction. Let me put the point differently: True insight involves the recognition of limitation; the truth of pure being is gleaned only from immersion in matter; connoting this double participation, the traditional concept of the *daemon* may actively have influenced philosophical thought rather than being merely a convenient element for abstract conceptualisation.

My point is that the concept of the *daemon* continues to function as an image with mythical as well as practical connotations while also beginning to incorporate the double nature of man in a dynamic sense – that is, the propensity of the immortal part of the soul to reach beyond the confines of mortal being. In *Symposium*, *daemonic dynamis*, the central theme of Socrates' speech, is clearly dissociated from a ritual process (Orphic initiation, for instance) and presented solely in terms of a passionate search for truth.[57] The imagery is not part of a philosophical conceptualisation, however, but rather a pedagogical way of hinting at truth or, to be more precise, the possibility of truth. Unchangeable being is only grasped by *nous* in *logos*, whereas the world of changes, to which the *daemonic* belongs, is available through the insecure flux of sensation and is only representable by means of a "likely story" (*eikos mythos*, *Timaeus* 29d). This seems to imply an appeal to understand the narratives allegorically, not in the sense that they could have been translated

---

57  A comparison between *Symposium* 202a–e and *Epinomis* 984e–985a may thus prove more prospective than Skovgaard Jensen would care to think.

into the unequivocal language of *logos*, but in the sense of the production of meaning stemming from interactive frames of reference. My point is that although philosophical discourse certainly did, in many respects, strive for non-contradictory consistency, it also employed rhetorical tactics containing imprecise expressions, as Lloyd, for instance, has shown in relation to Aristotle.[58] Occasionally, the whole point of Socratic discourse is to appear committed to a traditional framework of meaning while, at the same time, to avoid being philosophically captured by it (as, for instance, in the *Apology*). The difference between a religious and a philosophical discourse is, in this context, the awareness of the genealogy of gods as being merely symbolic (and therefore, in a certain sense, insincere). Different strands of meanings are brought together (as in the original meaning of the Greek *symballein*) from whence something new arises, yet only gradually and probably not as intentionally as it may appear *post festum*.

The very thought that mortal beings cannot be in possession of positive knowledge was at least as old as Xenophanes of the sixth century,[59] but the dialogical principle which makes it a condition of philosophy was not developed effectively until the Classical period. My suggestion is that any description of a change from *mythos* to *logos* should take the latter rather than the former point of reference.

## 8   *Daemons* in *The Republic*

I should like to provide my overall argument with one final example, namely from the tenth book of the *Republic*, which shows the simplifying metaphorical strategy characteristic of late Platonic discourse, using the imagery and technique of mythical language (*mimēsis*) but appealing ultimately to prudence and knowledge (*epistēmē*). As mentioned above, the immortal part of the tripartite human soul is, in *Timaeus*, designated by god as a *daemon* – that is, a guiding spirit that leads the soul back to its divine origin. In the final part of the *Republic*, however, the souls of the departed gather on a meadow, an

---

58   Lloyd, *Aristotelian Explorations*, 216ff.

59   Cf. fragment 34 in J.H. Lesher, *Xenophanes of Colophon: Fragments* (Toronto/Buffalo/London: University of Toronto Press, 1992). Xenophanes actually challenged the religious principle of discursive authorisation by voicing the opinion: "Indeed not from the beginning did gods intimate all things to mortals, but as they search in time they discover better;" fragment 18. According to the traditional view of a Greek miracle, such an utterance would probably be seen as an example of an innate Greek mentality.

unmistakable reference to the ritual scene of mystery initiation among the Orphics.[60] The souls who are about to return to corporeal being for a new lifespan have to choose the kind of life they want to live and are, accordingly, allocated a *daemon* to watch over them by Lachesis, the goddess of fate (*Republic* 620d; cf. *Phaedo* 107d; 108b). Er, the pamphylian who has returned from the dead with remembrance (*mnēmosynē*) of the chthonian meadow, tells of a prophet who has told the souls that "no *daemon* shall make choices for you" (*ouch hymas daimōn lēxetai*), "but you shall chose a *daemon* for yourselves" (*all' hymeis daimona hairēsesthe*, *Republic* 617e). Thus it is up to each and every individual soul to make sure that, in the coming incarnation, it will benefit from the influence of a 'good *daemon*' (*eudaimon*), literally synonymous, in the Classical period, with 'a happy fate' or simply 'happiness' (*eudaimonia*). Whereas some of the souls, who are tempted to choose a pleasant but unjust life, will remain in the cycle of births, others will make their choice with insight and justice and finally become *eudaemonioi* with the effect of escaping the cycle of births altogether. Er's vision is bursting with references to initiation cults. The eschatological 'meadow' is described as a *topos daemonios* (*Republic* 614c1), and the presence of Lachesis clearly suggests the role of a *mystagogue* – that is, a divine nurse (*kourotrophos*) reminiscent of the goddess of truth, who addresses Parmenides with *koure* (the apostrophised form of *kouros*) in his *peri physeōs* (Fr. 1, 24; cf. Plutarch, *De virtute morali* 417a; 566b; Plato, *Republic* 617b–e).[61] Hence, when Er is said to have returned from the dead, it probably implies a return from a ritual *imitatio mortis*, which is not surprising insofar as a similar veiled reference to an Orphic 'ritual for the dead' is given earlier in the *Republic* (362d–364e). There Socrates takes exception to the Orphic attempt to purify the sins of the fathers by means of ritual cleansing and holds the justice of the soul to be the only route to 'salvation', i.e., a release from the cycle of births. In Er's vision the realisation of justice also constitutes a criterion for the soul to become fully divine. Admittedly, divine powers of fate are also at work, and their disguised representation of esoteric initiation may even, to some extent, be seen as an unexpected approval of a ritual framework. But eventually it all comes down to the choice made by the individual soul. If the soul chooses with insight to lead a just life, it takes fate into its own hands. The metaphorical use of traditional imagery, though more salient than ever, seems to wear out. In Er's vision, the recognition of individual responsibility has become explicit and turns the mythical and mystical

---

60  Albinus, *The House of Hades*, 131ff.
61  See also T.H. Price, *KOUROTROPHOS – Cults and Representations of Greek Nursing Deities* (Leiden: E.J. Brill, 1978), for an in-depth analysis of the ritual role of Greek 'nursing deities'.

framework into just another word for the power of *nous*, the *daemon* to end all *daemons*.

## 9   Conclusion

The transition from *mythos* to *logos* follows an intricate path, which might be viewed from various angles. Looking at it from the point of view of discursive interaction, the narrative form of myth and ritual does not merely stand in contrast to the dialogical exchange of arguments (evolving in interaction with the 'hoplite reform' and the emerging institutional confines of the city-state), but is also recognisable as an influential element of philosophical discourse itself. This discourse, which over a long period of time becomes recognised over and above its elite authority, actually departs from its original, horizontal dialectics by appropriating elements of cultic tradition in a way that reflects a hierarchical organisation of society – that is, a vertical differentiating between various kinds of people. This recourse to a mythical structure, including the religious inclination towards trans-empirical authority, is counterbalanced, however, with a dogmatic explicitness accompanied by the increasing legitimacy of abstracting notions. Thus, I agree with Detienne that the principle of contradiction, *mutatis mutandis* of conceptual univocity, clearly informs philosophical discourse at some point. But to see its introduction as the crucial distinction between *mythos* and *logos* is to overstep the complicated tactics of discursive changes that involve various interacting frames of reference. Whereas the legitimising principle of contradiction is present already in the sixth century BCE, the use of mythical imagery is still significant in the philosophy of the third century. In the fifth century, when dialectics had secured a place for itself, it makes use of the *daemonic* (i.e., the relational meaning of *daemon*) as a principle of having it both ways, while struggling to seize hegemony. It may be that a philosopher such as Plato actually believed in an unequivocal transport of meaning from *myth* to *logos* – in line with the concept of *metaphora* coined by his pupil – but in actual fact, the development of Platonic discourse displays a convoluted relationship that opens the way for various interpretations in both directions. Therefore I strongly disagree with Detienne that the field of conceptual ambiguity takes us back into the exotic garden of myth and esoteric rituals.[62] What constitutes the evolving field of *logos* is rather the recognition of ambiguity as significant ambiguity, as

---

62   Detienne, *The Masters of Truth*, 83f.

brought out by new discursive rules.[63] At the same time, a dialogical field of interpretation opened up that had very little to do with the reception of myth and the execution of ritual obligations (though eminently present in relation to the Delphic Oracle, cf. *Herodotus* 7.140–144).[64] But when- and wherever an interpretation of the complex of tradition took place in ancient Greece, it is wrongheaded to speak of "an accidentally connected sphere of religion" as Skovgaard Jensen does.[65] Ancient philosophy was not born *sui generis* in the mind of the Greeks, like Athene from the forehead of Zeus, but took insecure steps in various directions before a 'general inclination of the people' (borrowing an expression from Wittgenstein) made it realise that it could suddenly walk upright and self-consciously. As long as Greek religion was practiced, the poets spoke about the general difference between mortals and immortals and alluded, more or less explicitly, to *daemons* who took up a position in the middle. In this religious world, the intervening position – that is, the very place and concept of the *daemon* – was occupied by gods who, in the disguise of mortals, entered the worlds of humans and humans who, under the restrictions of ritual practice, entered the world of the gods. Yet, being at large between various genres and orders of discourse, the *daemon*, as well as its derivatives *daemonios* and *daemonie*, opened up the distinction between mortality and immortality from each side of the gap, resulting in the abstract notion of pure being over and against the changeable conditions of earthly existence. My point is that this abstracting thought could not evolve, however, without the explicit belief in the intellectual soul's *daemonic* participation in truth. And perhaps the same *daemonic* participation can be gleaned from the way in which the name of Plato attained an absolute authority in the academy.

---

[63] In fact, Detienne seems to be in line with this view when he speaks of sophistry and rhetoric "as instruments that formulated the theory of logic and ambiguity" (*The Masters of Truth*, 116). Nonetheless, he insists on a fundamental division between a logic of ambiguity and a logic of contradiction (136).

[64] The famous case of Themistocles' imaginative interpretation of Pythia's oracle not only tells a story about how a discouraging reading was – and could be – exchanged for a more promising one, but also discloses the significance of debate as a means of tactical, political consultation. In the Delphic Oracle we behold a noticeable case of the intertwinement of *mythos* and *logos* in the fifth century.

[65] Skovgaard Jensen, *Dualism and Demonology*, 31.

## PART 2

*Explorations in an Emerging Common Discourse*

∴

# Philosophical Traces in the *Sibylline Oracles*

*Helen Van Noorden*

Apocalyptic discourse, in the broad sense of a concern with the revelation of collective destiny, is an obvious arena for investigation of the ancient intermingling of 'philosophy' and 'religion'. Since the literature of Greece and Rome, unlike that of other ancient cultures, does not foreground a mythology of the end of days and contains very few 'systematic' statements of belief, doxographical surveys of apocalyptic beliefs through time have tended to represent the Classical period only through paraphrase of unusual material taken out of context.[1] However, one strand of ancient philosophy with obvious potential for 'apocalyptic' applications is Stoicism, in the sense that it explicitly envisages the destruction of the material cosmos in close connection with a concept of divine providence. In this essay, I shall investigate the potential for interactions between Stoic ideas and a corpus of material deserving more attention by classicists today: the late antique collection of *Sibylline Oracles*.

The extant *Sibylline Oracles* are prophecies attributed to the pagan prophetess Sibyl; we find her mentioned first in the sixth century BCE, and later she becomes the most authoritative and popular prophet in the Roman world. The 'Sibylline Books' of legendary origin were consulted in Rome at times of crisis by a select group of officials. After that collection was accidentally burned in 83 BCE, replacement oracles were gathered from all over the Roman Empire.[2] It is possible that Jewish material entered the tradition at that point.[3] Still, what survives as the collection of *Sibylline Oracles* bears little relation to the few fragments of the pagan Sibylline prophecies preserved in Phlegon's *Book of Wonders* (second century CE). Rather, the extant collection of twelve books consists mainly of composite Jewish/Christian redactions of pagan oracles, in Homeric/Hellenistic Greek hexameters, dated to different periods

---

1   For example N. Campion, *The Great Year: Astrology, Millenarianism and History in the Western Tradition* (London: Arkana, 1994), who cites Plato *Timaeus* 22bff., in which Egyptian priests mock Solon for the Greeks' being 'young', their civilisation, unlike that of Egypt, having had to begin again from scratch after the last widespread destruction of the area by fire and water.
2   See H. Parke, *Sibyls and Sibylline Prophecy in Classical Antiquity* (London: Routledge, 1988), 138–40 on the likely spread of source locations.
3   So speculates M.D. Usher, "*Teste Galba cum Sibylla*: Oracles, *Octavia*, and the East," *Classical Philology* 108 (2013): 21–40, 23.

between the second century BCE and the sixth century CE. In content, the extant *Sibylline Oracles* offer a mix of ethics and eschatology, reviews of world history, prophecies for and against various nations, and, in particular, reassurance for the Jews that they will not be oppressed forever. Debates about the date and location of various strata identified in each book are ongoing,[4] but Book 3 (ca. 800 verses) is agreed to be the oldest; its core, usually dated to the second century BCE, seems to have influenced the 'Messianic' Fourth *Eclogue* of Virgil as well as other Augustan poets.[5] Books 1–2 form a unit; they present a world history divided into ten generations, most recently understood as a systematic expansion of the mythical history of humankind near the start of Book 3. Books 4 and 5 are (roughly) Neronian in date; Book 6 is a 28-line hymn to Christ, and so on.

The temptation to see philosophical traces in these 'Sibylline' homilies is understandable, given that their concerns and pedigree parallel those of philosophical discourse: long-range speculative thinking about society and ethics which draws topics for debate out of the Greek hexameter tradition. What I want to emphasise at the outset, before evaluating the claims of philosophical influence on the *Sibylline Oracles*, is that the extant collection is a candidate for the closest blend of pagan, Jewish, and other traditions that we possess from antiquity.[6] One positive argument for finding Stoic echoes in this text is the authority thereby connoted for pagan audiences and the possibility of common ground between the Sibylline authority and philosophic harmonisers.[7] Given that the intended or core audience of these Greek hexameters is still a matter of debate, it is worth noting that evaluating philosophical traces in the *Sibylline Oracles* may offer another lens through which to evaluate the 'register' of the collection that we possess.[8]

---

4   For a review of the literature, see M. Neujahr, *Predicting the Past in the Ancient Near East: Mantic Historiography in Ancient Mesopotamia, Judah, and the Mediterranean World* (Providence: Brown Judaic Studies, 2012), 211–21.

5   See for example C.W. Macleod, "Horace and the Sibyl (Epode 16.2)," *Classical Quarterly* 29 (1979): 220–21.

6   On other such fusions and their ancient foundations, see for example R. Feldmeier, "'Göttliche Philosophie': Die Interaktion von Weisheit und Religion in der späteren Antike," in *Religiöse Philosophie und philosophische Religion der frühen Kaiserzeit* (ed. M.v. Albrecht, H. Görgemanns, R. Hirsch-Luipold; Tübingen: Mohr Siebeck, 2009), 99–116.

7   So J.L. Lightfoot, *The Sibylline Oracles. With Introduction, Translation, & Commentary on the First and Second Books* (Oxford: Oxford University Press, 2007), for example, 38.

8   For such an approach to determining the audience of a text, see G.E. Sterling, "Philosophy as the Handmaid of Wisdom: Philosophy in the Exegetical Traditions of Alexandrian Jews," in *Religiöse Philosophie*, 67–98 on Philo.

## 1 Philosophical or Stoic Ideas and Idioms Identified in the *Sibylline Oracles*

A review of the literature and commentaries on the *Sibylline Oracles* reveals four main ways in which loosely Stoic forms of discourse and ideas (or perhaps better terms would be emphases, motifs, or interests) have been traced in this corpus. The following list, giving examples of each point, will suggest that it is perhaps overstating the case to assert that 'the Sibyl... shows little philosophical interest of any kind'.[9]

### 1.1 Forms of Argument

The ethical urgency of the Sibyl has been linked to the diatribe, associated with both Stoic and Cynic movements in Hellenistic philosophy.[10] On the topic of God, in particular (see section 1.2 below), it was long ago argued that the Sibyl's Jewish exposition works with a classical inheritance of 'missionary preaching' adopted by, among others, the Hellenistic Stoics.[11] Within this framework, a passage on rewards for the virtuous, in *Sibylline Oracles* 2.34–55, resonates with Stoic depictions of the ascent to Virtue, in its extended 'agonistic metaphor' of a crown displayed in heaven for which the virtuous compete. The notion of Virtue almost out of reach was taken up enthusiastically by Stoic writers from the famous Hesiodic image of the difficult 'path to Virtue' (*Works and Days* 289–92), but the application of agonistic vocabulary in an eschatological dimension seems to have been confined to Jewish apocalyptic texts.[12]

A second 'philosophical' aspect of the Sibylline approach is the 'do this and do not do that' form of ethical instruction. Such a style has found its way into the collection in the form of a block of sentences of Pseudo-Phocylides, including the line σωφροσύνην ἀσκεῖν, αἰσχρῶν δ' ἔργων ἀπέχεσθαι ("Exercise moderation, and hold off from shameful deeds," *Sibylline Oracles* 2.145). The words in bold may be considered Stoic technical terms,

---

9    Lightfoot, *The Sibylline Oracles*. 338.
10   Lightfoot, *The Sibylline Oracles*. 25ff., and Lang, chapter eight in this volume.
11   As Lightfoot (*The Sibylline Oracles*) reports (24–5), Eduard Norden in *Agnostos Theos* (1913) argued that 'missionary preaching' of the kind found in *Acts* has its roots in the speech style of archaic philosophers, having been adopted into diatribe, and thereafter passing from Hellenistic Stoicism into Jewish preaching.
12   Lightfoot, *The Sibylline Oracles*. 449–52, especially 451, where she distinguishes Christian from Greek philosophical uses of the image. The notion of athletes in virtue competing for a crown finds Stoic application also in Philo, *On Rewards and Punishments* 409.

for they echo the language and style of Epictetus' most famous exhortations.¹³

### 1.2 Thought About God

In the fragments of the *Sibylline Oracles* cited by the bishop Theophilus, God is presented in terms vaguely reminiscent of early philosophical critique of traditional pagan religion, such as Xenophanes' criticisms of Homer's divinities, or otherwise reflecting pagan cultural debates about the nature of the divine:

> Now if all that is born must also perish,
> It is not possible for God to be
> Formed from the thighs of man and from a womb…¹⁴

However, in the main, such sentiments are too widespread to identify with a specific strand of philosophical thinking, and there are in the Sibyl very few idioms of expression that may be strongly identified with particular philosophical schools. One exception is the description of God as the 'sole ruler' (μόναρχος, *Sibylline Oracles* 3.11, 3.704 and, in connection with polemics against idolatry, in the 'atypical'¹⁵ fragment 1; cf. also fragment 1.7, μόνος ἄρχει). The concept of God as solely in charge of all the cosmos (a city writ large) was a Stoic tenet;¹⁶ other pagan conceptions of divinity imagine Zeus delegating to a host of lesser divinities the less elevated details of the universe.¹⁷ However, as Jane Lightfoot notes, the Sibyl does not refer to any other aspects of the

---

13   The verb ἀσκεῖν appears with similar vocabulary in *Euripides* Bacchae 641 but otherwise mostly in morally exhortative contexts, ranging from Isocrates, Xenophon, and Philo to Diogenes Laertius and many other Stoic sources. Epictetus' dictum ἀνέχου καὶ ἀπέχου ('bear and forbear') is quoted by Aulus Gellius, *Attic Nights* XVII.19, a text well known in antiquity. I am grateful to Aldo Dinucci for alerting me to these resonances.

14   *Sibylline Oracles* fragment 3.1–3. However, J.J. Collins ("Sibylline Oracles: A New Translation and Introduction," in *The Old Testament Pseudepigrapha 1: Apocalyptic Literature and Testaments* [ed. J.H. Charlesworth; London: Darton, Longman and Todd, 1983], 317–472, 360) finds the closest analogues in Philo and in Jewish Orphic material of the second century BCE.

15   Collins, *Between Athens and Jerusalem: Jewish identity in the Hellenistic Diaspora* (Grand Rapids, MI: William B Eerdmans, 2000), 167, cited by Lightfoot, *The Sibylline Oracles*, 28.

16   It features, for example, in the proem of Cleanthes' *Hymn to Zeus* (vv. 7–8).

17   See T. Bénatouïl, "How Industrious Can Zeus Be? The Extent and Objects of Divine Activity in Stoicism," in *God and Cosmos in Stoicism* (ed. R. Salles; Oxford: Oxford University Press, 2009), 23–45. A single reference in the Sibylline corpus to the 'Begetter of gods' (3.278) recalls this hierarchy, too.

Stoic God, such as his permeability throughout the cosmos. Her monotheism is likely to be of Jewish origin (the epithet is found in *Maccabees*, for example). A parallel example of apparently 'Stoic' terminology with a Jewish footprint is the Sibyl's unique reference to ἄτρεπτον... θεόν (*Sibylline Oracles* 1.157–8); this epithet is applied by the Stoics to Zeus, identified with fate, but it was applied to the Jewish God by Philo, who often adopted Stoicising language.[18]

## 1.3  Ethical and Political Theory

The climax of *Sibylline Oracles* 3 contains a vision of the eschatological kingdom founded on a "common law" (κοινὸν...νόμον, 3.757) "throughout the whole earth." This phrase, found for example in Cleanthes' *Hymn to Zeus* (v. 39), has been termed an "incontrovertibly Stoic idea and expression;"[19] Plutarch and others credit the *Republic* of Zeno, founder of the Stoic school, for the idea of a society which contains no distinction between mortals, but rather one way of life and order.[20] However, it has been argued that such "cosmopolitanism" is a later extension of Zeno's ideal city of the *wise*, based on a "common law" in the sense of the "natural law" of human reason.[21] This Stoic notion is also possibly present in the *Sibylline Oracles*, adapted to a context celebrating Judaism, as the Sibyl envisions a resurgent community of Greeks no longer opposed to Jewish law, but "having a mind in their breasts which is in harmony with the right" (ὁμόθεσμον, *Sibylline Oracles* 5.265; cf. in a similar context καθαρὸν νοῦν / ἀνθρώπων, 7.144–5).

A more debateable case concerns the degree of Stoic influence on details of the world restored for the righteous, as described at the end of *Sibylline Oracles* 2. The earth will yield its wealth spontaneously (αὐτομάτη), and there will be κοινοί...βίοι (2.321), which Lightfoot translates as "common produce."

---

18   D. Sedley, *Lucretius and the Transformation of Greek Wisdom* (Cambridge: Cambridge University Press, 1998), 167.

19   M. Schofield, *The Stoic Idea of the City* (Cambridge: Cambridge University Press, 1991), 110, noting that the Stoics cited Heraclitus as a source for this idea (fragment 114 DK). See also J. Bremmer, "Paradise in the Oracula Sibyllina," in *Ultima Aetas: Time, Tense and Transience in the Ancient World* (ed. C. Kroon and D. den Hengst; Amsterdam: VU University Press, 2000), 83–94, 87 on the common law notion as probably coming from the Stoics.

20   Plutarch, *On the fortune and virtue of Alexander the Great* 329a–d (νόμῳ κοινῷ); Cicero, *On the Nature of the Gods* 1 36; Lactantius, *Divine Institutes* 1 5. Diogenes Laertius 7.32–3 records that some of the more extreme features of Zeno's 'communist' vision came in for criticism.

21   R.W. Sharples, *Stoics, Epicureans and Sceptics: An Introduction to Hellenistic Philosophy* (London: Routledge, 1996), 125, citing Schofield. Clement SVF 1.180 (Von Arnim 1, 552) preserves Cleanthes on the subject of reason.

Combined with restoration of the "earth equal for all, not divided by walls or fences" (γαῖα δ' ἴση πάντων οὐ τείχεσιν οὐ περιφραγμοῖς / διαμεριζομένη, 2.319–20),[22] the most popular context in which to put this thought is the communism of the Golden Age tradition, as expounded in the work of Roman writers such as Ovid's *Metamorphoses*.[23] The notion of the return of such an era was expounded most memorably by Virgil, and Karin Neutel posits a significant exchange of ideas between the Sibyl and Virgil as the extant origin of the notion that the Golden Age will return.[24] Virgil's cyclical turn in *Eclogue* 4 has, however, recently been differently explained as coming from the framework of the Stoicising Hellenistic poet Aratus, combined with the myth of the reversed cosmos in Plato's *Statesman*.[25] At the same time, a Jewish background perhaps better explains for the Sibyl; as Lightfoot notes with reference to 2.322–9, the context of the line in Book 2 is a return to an elemental, undivided state, in which time is also undivided, a feature not found in paradise descriptions, but rather in Jewish descriptions of the days of judgement, perhaps derived from commentary on the creation story in Genesis. The extent and form of the interface between Stoic and Sibylline thought in relation to ethical and political ideals, then, remains open to debate.

### 1.4   *Physics*

By far the most popular focus for discussion of philosophical traces in the *Sibylline Oracles* is the language of cosmic catastrophe in its eschatological sections. Such themes have been connected to the Stoic notion that the world is periodically reduced to its dominant element, fire, in a kind of purification before it is renewed. Certainly this is the ancient philosophical doctrine whose vision most closely resonates with Judaeo-Christian 'end of days' mythology. Echoes of the Stoic doctrine of universal conflagration have been found particularly in the climactic depiction of the final judgement which closes *Sibylline Oracles* 2 and in the details in Book 4 of a world restored after judgement. However, it is really quite far down the stream of evidence that the Stoic fusion of ethics and physics is comparable to the Sibylline spin on eschatology.

---

22   Compare a world 'common for all' asserted as the original intention for *this* world at *Sibylline Oracles* 3.247.

23   Bremmer ("Paradise in the Oracula Sibyllina," 89) notes that the 'communal ownership of land' notion is found only in Roman literature.

24   K.B. Neutel, *A Cosmopolitan Ideal: Paul's Declaration 'Neither Jew Nor Greek, Neither Slave Nor Free, Nor Male and Female' in the Context of First-Century Thought* (London/New York: Bloomsbury, 2015), 63–4.

25   E. Gee, *Aratus and the Astronomical Tradition* (Oxford: Oxford University Press, 2013), 41–4.

In section two below I shall review the evidence for these Stoic ideas and their possible relationship to the Sibylline lines.

The bulk of my discussion will focus on eschatological visions of destruction and paradise, drawing evidence from across the corpus. I will argue in four stages for caution regarding 'Stoic influence': in section two, against survey work on early Jewish material which asserts Greek influence on Jewish eschatology,[26] I emphasise that the presence of Stoic 'buzzwords' in the *Sibylline Oracles* can be no more than suggestive, given the complexity of the Stoic contexts. Next (in section three), I note the possibility that Sibylline material itself influenced the rather late testimonia for 'Stoic' ideas; in section four I discuss the likelihood that these apparently 'Stoic' echoes had become 'common currency' in this period. I argue that we should look further back to more foundational 'common currency', especially to Plato and to the archaic Greek poets. Finally (in section five), I look more closely at the Sibylline development of potentially eschatological elements in Homer and Hesiod. My conclusion is that while the Sibyl draws from the cosmic scope of archaic epic the core fuel for her approach and shares with 'philosophy' an interest in debates about human civilisation, no single idea is thought through in a manner we may consider 'philosophical'.

## 2  The Sibylline Idiom and the Complexity of 'Stoic Sources'

For those aiming to judge how far the *Sibylline Oracles* engage with Stoic 'eschatological' thought, their treatment of the notion of cosmic conflagration is an obvious starting point. Pieter van der Horst, who focuses on Jewish and Christian adaptations of this Stoic theme, identifies *Sibylline Oracles* 3.80–92, a section which he dates to the end of the first century BCE,[27] as one of the first surviving Jewish examples of reference to a universal conflagration, which he does not doubt emerged under Stoic influence:[28]

---

26  T.F. Glasson, *Greek Influence in Jewish Eschatology. With Special Reference to the Apocalypses and Pseudepigraphs* (London: SPCK, 1961).

27  Manuscript evidence suggests that this section does not belong to the rest of Book 3. On grounds for the dating, see for example Collins, *Seers, Sibyls and Sages in Hellenistic Judaism* (Leiden: Brill, 1997), 201, who holds that the passage reflects the perspective of Egyptian Jews after the battle of Actium in 31 BCE.

28  P. van der Horst, "'The Elements Will Be Dissolved With Fire'. The Idea of Cosmic Conflagration in Hellenism, Ancient Judaism, and Early Christianity," in *Hellenism-Judaism-Christianity: Essays on Their Interaction* (Leuven: Peeters, 1994), 227–51, 237–8, discounting other candidates, such as the Jewish Ps. Sophocles fragment 2.

..................τότε δὴ ***στοιχεῖα*** πρόπαντα
***χηρεύσει κόσμου***, ὁπόταν θεὸς αἰθέρι ναίων
οὐρανὸν εἰλίξῃ, καθ' ἅπερ βιβλίον εἰλεῖται·
καὶ πέσεται πολύμορφος ὅλος πόλος ἐν χθονὶ δίῃ
καὶ πελάγει· ῥεύσει δὲ πυρὸς μαλεροῦ ***καταράκτης***
ἀκάματος, φλέξει δὲ γαῖαν, φλέξει δὲ θάλασσαν,
καὶ πόλον οὐράνιον καὶ ἤματα καὶ κτίσιν αὐτὴν
***εἰς ἓν χωνεύσει καὶ εἰς καθαρὸν διαλέξει.***
κοὐκέτι φωστήρων σφαιρώματα καγχαλόωντα,
οὐ νύξ, οὐκ ἠώς, οὐκ ἤματα πολλὰ μερίμνης,
οὐκ ἔαρ, οὐχὶ θέρος, οὐ χειμών', οὐ μετόπωρον.
καὶ τότε δὴ μεγάλοιο θεοῦ κρίσις εἰς μέσον ἥξει
***αἰῶνος μεγάλοιο***, ὅταν τάδε πάντα γένηται.

And then all the ***elements*** of the world
***will be widowed***, when the god who dwells in the ether
rolls up heaven, just as a scroll is rolled:
and the entire manifold heavenly vault will fall on the marvellous earth
and ocean: and an unwearied ***cataract*** of raging fire will flow,
and will burn the land, and will burn the sea,
and the heavenly sky and days and creation itself
***will it smelt into one and separate each into its pure state.***
and there will no longer be the exulting spheres of luminaries,
Not night, not dawn, nor the many days of anxiety,
not spring, not summer, not winter, not autumn.
And then will the judgement of the great God come into the midst
***of the great eon***, when these things come to pass.

One passage comparable to this in its envisaging of a truly universal conflagration is *Sibylline Oracles* 2.196–213, generally dated to the first century CE and sometimes taken to be a Christian interpolation:[29]

................................ἀτὰρ οὐράνιοι φωστῆρες
εἰς ἓν συρρήξουσι καὶ εἰς μορφὴν πανέρημον.
ἄστρα γὰρ οὐρανόθεν τε θαλάσσῃ πάντα πεσεῖται...
καὶ τότε ***χηρεύσει στοιχεῖα*** πρόπαντα τὰ κόσμου
ἀὴρ γαῖα θάλασσα φάος πόλος ἤματα νύκτες...

---

[29] See Lightfoot, *The Sibylline Oracles*, ad loc.

...........................................ἅμα πάντα
εἰς ἓν χωνεύσει καὶ εἰς καθαρὸν διαλέξει.

......................while heavèn's fiery stars
Shall melt into one desolated form.
All stars from heaven will fall into the sea...
The cosmos' *elements* shall *widowed* be –
Air, earth, the sea, light, sky, the days and nights...
...........................................everything
***Will melt into a single, smelted mass.***
(*Sibylline Oracles* 2.200–2, 206–7, 212–3, trans. Lightfoot)[30]

Such critical strictness about the degree of fiery destruction envisaged (van der Horst admits only two other Sibylline passages as 'cosmic' in scope)[31] cannot be matched on the level of vocabulary.[32] In neither of these passages do we find ἐκπύρωσις, the Stoic term for the conflagration; the Sibyl envisages rather a 'cataract' (καταράκτης, 3.84) or 'river' (ποταμός, 2.196) of fire. Jane Lightfoot acknowledges the possibility of Stoic influence here, but rather emphasises the passage's echoes of Isaiah 34:4 (stars falling into the sea) and systematic undoing of the creation narrative in Genesis 8:22.[33] Although both passages refer to στοιχεῖα, the standard term for 'elements' or 'atoms' discussed at length by Chrysippus,[34] the term in *Sibylline Oracles* 3.80 may refer to 'heavenly

---

30    Lightfoot, *The Sibylline Oracles*.
31    *Sibylline Oracles* 4.171–92 (on the fates of the good and bad) and 5.155–61 (a star will destroy the sea and the land of Italy), both datable towards the end of the first century CE; he dismisses, as envisaging only partial destruction, 5.206–13 (on Ethiopia) and 512–31 (the battle of the stars), both often cited as 'Stoic' in content: see below p. 113.
32    Sibylline terminology has been subject to a number of studies (G. Panayiotou, "Addenda to the *LSJ* Greek-English Lexicon: Lexicographical Notes on the Vocabulary of the *Oracula Sibyllina*," *Hellenica* 38 (1987): 46–66, 296–317; Lightfoot, *The Sibylline Oracles*, 170–79, 535–51), but specifically Stoic terms for the conflagration have not been in question.
33    See Lightfoot, *The Sibylline Oracles*, 483–6, suggesting that the 'river' and 'cataract' substitute for the flood in Genesis; see also V. Nikiprowetzky, *La Troisième Sibylle* (Paris: Mouton, (1970), 160–6, distinguishing both 'punitive fire' and 'testing fire' [a Zoroastrian concept] from the Stoic concept of 'noetic fire' into which the sun is resolved at the conflagration. It is worth noting that at *Sibylline Oracles* 4.161, anticipating one other possibly 'cosmic' description of fire as the expression of divine wrath, and at 5.211 (addressing the Ethiopians), we find ἐμπρησμός, a term for destructive burning found in medical and mythical as well as Stoic contexts.
34    *Apud* Stobaeus 1.129.2–130.13.

bodies';[35] still, in 2.206 it must indeed mean 'elements' of the universe, which are specified in the following line. Note, however, that the Sibyl retains her own idiom, too – the language in each passage of 'widowed' elements is a uniquely sibylline metaphor in eschatology.[36]

Another point of argument about Stoic reminiscence in this passage concerns the combination of melting 'into one' and the emphasis on purification (3.87; 2.213). Stoic physics holds that during the conflagration, everything is reduced to fire, which is the original dominant element and a manifestation of divine activity in matter.[37] The conflagration is for Stoics a wholly positive event, not a 'destruction' but a natural transformation of the cosmos.[38] The characterisation of this process as a 'punishment' for human degeneracy or a 'purification' of the world's evils is not found before Seneca.[39] I doubt that the notion goes back to Chrysippus (as von Arnim argued regarding Origen *Contra Celsum* 4.64 = SVF II 1174). It may be an *interpretatio christiana*,[40] or even a Zoroastrian import,[41] but Origen (*Against Celsus* 5.15) refers to πῦρ καθάρσιον ('purifying fire') as a notion borrowed from the Hebrews.

For van der Horst, the absence of a notion of cyclical recurrence is the main marker of the Sibyl's difference from Stoic belief. There is indeed no παλιγγενεσία (exact recurrence of events) anticipated here.[42] The Sibyl often speaks of "another world" (ἄλλος πάλι κόσμος ὁρᾶται, 7.139), a "new heaven and new earth," or a temple or mortal race renewed "as it was before" (ὡς πάρος,

---

35   This is deduced from the Sibyl's use of Isaiah 34 filtered through Petrine literature (2 Peter 3 and the Apocalypse of Peter); see van der Horst, "'The Elements Will Be Dissolved With Fire,'" and Lightfoot, *The Sibylline Oracles*, 487.

36   Lightfoot, *The Sibylline Oracles*, 487 ad loc.

37   See for example A.A. Long, "The Stoics on World-Conflagration and Everlasting Recurrence," in, *From Epicurus to Epictetus* (Oxford: Clarendon, 2006), 256–82.

38   The harmony of the event is emphasised by Dio Chrysostom, *Oration* 40.37 (= SVF 2.601).

39   See G. Mader, "Some Observations on the Senecan Götterdämmerung," *Acta Classica* 26 (1983): 61–71, 62, on Seneca, *Natural Questions* 3.30.7–8.

40   See for example van der Horst, "'The Elements Will Be Dissolved With Fire,'" 234, on Hippolytus, *Refutation of all Heresies* IX 22, but noting Seneca as a possible pagan exception.

41   The source most often cited is Dio Chrystostom, *Oration* 36.47–50, but J. Mansfield, "Providence and the Destruction of the Universe in Early Stoic Thought," in *Studies in Hellenistic Religions* (ed. M.J. Vermaseren; Leiden: Brill, 1979), 129–88, notes that the 'hymns of the Magi' in *Oration* 36.47–49 describe, in their more Platonising part, alternating partial destruction by fire and water, sharply distinguished from total conflagration only in the more Stoicising section, 51–54.

42   See Philo, *On the eternity of the world* 47.1, 76.5 for commentary on Stoics, and Matthew 19.28 as the earliest extant Christian use of the term in discussion of the world to come.

3.294; 7.145; 4.182; 8.319; πάλι is also the standard term for restored races in 3.180, 194 and elsewhere), but her terminology is too general to encourage reference to specifically Stoic notions, pointing rather to Jewish and Christian sources.[43]

One more suggestive term, that of a 'great eon' or 'century', occurs at 3.92 (cited above), but the notion of the judgement of God in the midst of the αἰῶνος μεγάλοιο is, as Nikiprowetzky observes, not the 'Great Year' concept which is later cited in conjunction with the Stoic theory of periodic conflagration (see section three below) but a vision of the eternal kingdom of God.[44] Evidently, even if Stoic ideas are incorporated among others in the Oracles, they are adapted to the Sibyl's own theme of eschatological judgement. Whether intended or not, the utilisation of Stoic motifs gives the Sibyllist's expectation 'a quasi-scientific base'.[45]

Attempting, however, to establish the degree of contact with 'Stoic' thought in the Sibyl's fusion of sources and development of her own idiom in eschatological utterances may in fact be a misplaced exercise, to the extent that the conflagration was not a doctrine universally or constantly accepted among major Stoics from the late third century BCE onwards. Cleanthes and Chrysippus, who succeeded him as head of the Stoic school in 232, differed as to whether the world is destroyed in the conflagration,[46] and Philo (*On the Eternity of the World* 76–7) reports that Boethus of Sidon and Panaetius (second century BCE) denied the regeneration doctrine, while Diogenes came to doubt it.

We should also be wary of referring to certain details of the Sibyl's eschatological visions as 'Stoic' ideas, based on parallel images in the consolatory or poetic work of later Stoic or Stoicising writers. The detailed vision in *Sibylline Oracles* 5.512–31 of an astral battle and stars falling into the sea, while not one of the passages admitted as a truly universal image of upheaval, has been much discussed with reference to passages in Seneca's *Consolation for Marcia* (26.6), the Senecan tragedies, and Lucan's *Bellum Ciuile* (1.75–6 and 1.655–8; see also Cato's comparison of the civil war to a falling sky, at 2.289–92).[47] James Harrill's

---

43  For example, the phrase 'new heaven and new earth' is found in Isaiah 65:17 and 66:22 as well as 2 Peter 3:13.
44  Nikiprowetzky, *La Troisième Sibylle*, 110.
45  This is one of the argumentative lines in E. Adams, *The Stars Will Fall from Heaven: Cosmic Catastrophe in the New Testament and its World* (London: T & T Clark, 2007), 91.
46  See R. Salles, "Chrysippus on Conflagration and the Indestructibility of the Cosmos," in *God and Cosmos in Stoicism* (ed. R. Salles; New York: Oxford University Press, 2009), 118–34, for full details of Chrysippus' point of difference with Cleanthes.
47  Discussed especially by Adams, *The Stars Will Fall*.

discussion of the adaptation of Stoic ethical and eschatological ideas in the Apocalypse of Peter provides a model for caution; he points out that such passages, taken as Stoic 'witnesses' to the doctrine of cosmic conflagration, are neither technically complete nor required to be so.[48] Rather, each Latin author is adapting, omitting, or expanding selected aspects of the Stoic notion for the purposes of his own rhetorical project. Seneca, for his part, manipulates a picture of the conflagration to suit his consolatory project for Marcia. In the very different context of the *Thyestes*, the chorus' view of an eclipse as a natural event (835–84) contrasts with other characters' perspective on it as a disruption of the cosmic order; Seneca here exploits an ambiguity within Stoic thought to characterise the distance between the tyrant Atreus and his subjects.[49] Lucan, by contrast, may be seen to allude in abbreviated fashion to the notion of universal conflagration at the start and end of Book 1, but he omits the possibility of renewal; he seeks rather to amplify the horror in Rome's state of civil war.[50] In a similar vein, his use of Stoic metaphors such as that of cosmic 'bonds' (*uincula*) has perceptively been described as "having little to do with doctrinaire Stoicism."[51] These texts are therefore not to be taken as doxographical statements by which to measure the Stoic content of the *Sibylline Oracles*.

## 3   'Stoic Sources' Influenced by the *Sibylline Oracles*?

Another reason for caution about the value of these texts as Stoic *comparanda* comes from a suggestion that the *Sibylline Oracles* themselves may have contributed to new emphases in at least one later presentation of world-renewal attributed to Seneca. The character 'Seneca' in the Roman historical tragedy *Octavia*, a play which used to be attributed to Seneca himself, offers a soliloquy on world history and periodic renewal (vv. 377–434), a passage identified by Mark Usher as remarkably 'Sibylline' in its division of time into four (or

---

48   J.A. Harrill, "Stoic Physics, the Universal Conflagration, and the Eschatological Destruction of 'the Ignorant and Unstable' in 2 Peter," in *Stoicism in Early Christianity* (ed. T. Rasimus, T. Engberg-Pedersen, and I. Dunderberg; Grand Rapids, MI: Baker Academic, 2010), 115–40.

49   K. Volk, "Cosmic Disruption in Seneca's *Thyestes*: Two Ways of Looking at an Eclipse," in *Seeing Seneca Whole: Perspectives on Philosophy, Poetry and Politics* (ed. K. Volk and G.D. Williams; Leiden/Boston: Brill, 2006), 183–200.

50   P. Roche, "Righting the Reader: Conflagration and Civil War in Lucan's *De Bello Civili*," *Scholia* 14 (2005): 52–71.

51   M. Lapidge, "Lucan's Imagery of Cosmic Dissolution," *Hermes* 107 (1979): 344–70.

five) ages and the "stark moralistic colouring"[52] of its presentation of cosmic collapse, with an apocalyptic focus on 'that day'. Usher argues that this outlook could well have been influenced by unofficial oral circulation of Sibylline Oracles in the late first century CE.

While details of his interpretation may be questioned, Usher's suggestion prompts consideration of aspects in which the circulation of Sibylline Oracles could help to explain the thrust of Seneca's own *Natural Questions* 3.27–30, a very unusual apocalyptic passage concluding a discussion of terrestrial waters, in which Seneca strikingly envisages the 'fated day' of a deluge as comparable to the conflagration as a form of 'destruction' (*exitium*) decided (*placuit*) by God and Nature (3.28.7). The parallelism of a destructive flood and a fire goes back at least as far as Plato's *Timaeus* (22c–e) and is quite common in Greek and Latin literature,[53] but the Senecan passage is novel among pagan 'philosophical' sources in its intentionalist phrasing of the cataclysm as punishment for human behaviour (3.29.5). Such a moralising spin on large-scale physical events distinguishes Seneca from the earlier Stoics, for whom the conflagration was a purely physical event.[54] Seneca builds up this line of argument to suggest that the human race will deliberately be wiped out, after which the earth will be repopulated by humanity "ignorant of sin" (*inscius scelerum*, 3.30.8).

There is a non-pagan parallel for such a "two-calamity scheme" combined with an emphasis on divine punishment in *Sibylline Oracles* 1–2, in which a historical review of ten generations of humanity tells of a flood after the fifth generation and anticipates destruction by fire at the end of the sequence.[55] Matthew Neujahr has recently pointed out that even the classical reputation of the Sibyl (judging by the reference which Plutarch attributes to Heraclitus) associates her voice both with a historical review and with gloomy prediction.[56] It is worth considering, then, whether the *Sibylline Oracles* could have been a source for Seneca.

The sources and influences behind Seneca's focus in the *Natural Questions* are disputed. Modern scholars are sceptical of Seneca's citation of the Baby-

---

52  Usher, "'*Teste Galba cum Sibylla*'," 29.
53  See the references in *Brill's New Jacoby* s.v. Berossus 680 F21.
54  Mader, "Some Observations on the Senecan Götterdämmerung," 62; G. Downing ("Cosmic Eschatology in the First Century: 'Pagan', Jewish and Christian," *L'Antiquité classique* 64 [1995]: 99–109) is wrong to assert (108) that notions of physical and moral decline "often" went together in pagan sources.
55  The phrase is that of Lightfoot, *The Sibylline Oracles*, 129, who also suggests (70–77, 112, 146) that it may be influenced by the prophetic sections of the book of Enoch.
56  Neujahr, *Predicting the Past*, 197.

Ionian Berossus for a link between these cosmic catastrophes and the movements of the planets, yielding a conflagration when they are aligned (if this is what *conuenit* means) in the constellation Cancer, and an inundation when they 'coincide' in Capricorn (*Natural Questions* 3.29.1). Many theories, both ancient and modern, find classical sources for related ideas. For example, a cosmic cycle with an inundation in 'winter' and a conflagration in 'summer' is attributed to Aristotle (*apud* Censorinus, *On the Natal Day* 18.11 [third century CE], who also refers to different opinions on the length of such a 'Great Year'). Van der Sluijs, by contrast, finds the source of the 'Great Year' tradition in a combination of Plato's *Timaeus* 22c–d (on the periodic demise of civilisations) with *Timaeus* 39c–e.[57] Meanwhile, Lucretius (an important source for Seneca's treatise) makes use of the idea of a universe periodically consumed and reborn (e.g., *On the Nature of Things* 5.235ff.), but this is more likely derived from a theory of alternating periods of dominance of fire and water attributed to Empedocles (Philo, *On Providence* II 61 = 31 A 66.15–18 DK) than from Berossus. We should probably therefore follow Momigliano in supposing that Berossus the astrologer was cited by the Greeks as an appropriate mouthpiece for the revelations they wanted to emphasise.[58]

I find this process strikingly analogous to the Jewish and Christian uses of the 'Sibyl' for their own oracles, and perhaps it is no coincidence that Pausanias (10.12) describes Sibyl as the daughter of Berossus – surely an expression of their 'relatedness' as traditional sources of wisdom for the Greeks. Given that the neat derivations of the 'Great Year' theory from classical authors alone are so late and so patchy, it is more plausible to imagine that for the moralising tendency in Seneca's *Natural Questions*, the influence of Sibylline Oracles was a transformative element.

However, we might also choose to take this process back a step, for at least one scholar has also seen the pagan Sibyl behind the text which is an explicit provocation for this passage of the *Natural Questions* – Ovid's account of the Flood in *Metamorphoses* 1, in which Jupiter, wanting to punish humankind for Lycaon's impiety, recalls that the universe is fated to be destroyed by fire, and so chooses destruction of the current human race by a flood.[59] In Ovid's

---

57   M.A. van der Sluijs, "Phaethon and the Great Year," *Apeiron* 39 (2006): 57–90.

58   A. Momigliano, *Alien Wisdom: The Limits of Hellenization* (Cambridge: Cambridge University Press, 1975), 148.

59   *Metamorphoses* 1.235–61 – from Seneca's ensuing flood description, *Metamorphoses* 1.285, 290, 304 are cited at *Natural Questions* 3.27.13. Nikiprowetzky (*La Troisième Sibylle*, 93) notes in passing that we may look for the 'intermediary link' between Stoicism and Ovid in the doctrine of the pagan Sibyl.

description of the flood and in the context of the narrative in Book 1, it has long been observed that there are striking structural parallelisms with the account in the book of Genesis;[60] for Lightfoot, such "traces" must have been mediated by Hellenistic Judaism.[61] The extant *Sibylline Oracles* are just such a source.

It is at least plausible that the circulation of Sibylline texts of this kind actually contributed to the development of the 'Stoic' tradition of conflagration in Roman texts with both philosophical and tragic agendas. However, as we will see in more detail below, the *Sibylline Oracles* are nothing if not a remarkable fusion of a variety of classical and Jewish sources, some of which had likely become common currency.

## 4 'Common Currency'

A third point of caution against the idea that the *Sibylline Oracles* draw on sources consciously considered 'Stoic' is that by the first century CE, notions such as the Stoic 'Great Year' are better considered as "common property."[62] Such popularisation may have been due to the Sibylline prophecy (if it is genuine), which Virgil cites at the start of his Fourth *Eclogue*; Servius (*ad* Virgil, *Eclogue* 4.4) explains that the Cumaean Sibyl predicted a cycle of ages divided into metals, with Apollo ruling over the ninth age (referred to in the poem) that would renew itself when all the constellations returned to their proper places, a concept which Servius identifies as the 'Great Year' of the philosophers. Indeed, the 'long view' of history as a sequence of ages is a stream crucial to the Sibylline literature in a way that the 'Great Year' concept cannot claim to be, except insofar as it is linearised and hence robbed of its Stoic/philosophical identity. Alternatively, we may prefer to think that Virgil himself, in fusing the concept of the Great Year with notions from other systems of time-reckoning at the start of his Fourth *Eclogue*, may, as a high-profile author, have helped this process along. Certainly, this *Eclogue* was fed back into later traditions of 'Sibylline' prophecies.

There are contemporary parallels for wider diffusions in 'non-philosophical' texts of what seem to have been originally Stoic and Epicurean ideas. Gerald

---

60   W. Speyer, "Spuren der 'Genesis' in Ovids Metamorphosen?" in *Kontinuität und Wandel. Lateinische Poesie von Naevius bis Baudelaire* (ed. U.J. Stache, W. Maaz, and F. Wagner; Hildesheim: Weidmann, 1986), 90–9.
61   Lightfoot, *The Sibylline Oracles*, 418.
62   Lightfoot, *The Sibylline Oracles*, 219, noting that, by contrast, the Sibyl is resistant to other pagan philosophical notions, such as the Epicurean idea of *natura creatrix*.

Downing, in particular, has argued that in this period the notion of cosmic catastrophe was common to pagans, Jews, and Christians. In pagan texts, he finds echoes of the Epicurean belief in the world's senescence (for which our main source is Lucretius; see below) both in the Elder Pliny's reference to *exustio* (fiery consumption) of the world's fertility (*Natural History* 7.73) and in the Younger Pliny's account of the eruption of Vesuvius (*Letter* 6.20.17), from which he derived "consolation in my mortal lot from the belief that the whole world was dying with me and I with it."[63] Downing also exposes various blends of philosophical ideas and perhaps reflections of pagan cosmological debates in early Christian texts,[64] and we may compare the 'popular philosophy' in 4 Maccabees.[65]

Conversely, and worth highlighting in this context, our most famous ancient 'philosophical' sources draw on a mixture of 'philosophical' and other ingredients. The prime example is Lucretius, writing in the first century BCE, who combines notions of the world's senescence (e.g., *On the Nature of Things* 2.1150–2) and destructibility, perhaps from Theophrastus,[66] with that of a final flood/fire (5.380–415), which does not belong to 'Epicureanism' proper.[67] While Downing seems to be arguing that "deliberate" assimilation of different sources is a distinctive feature of the Sibylline writings,[68] classicists would disagree; novel reconstructions and fusions of traditions are key to the texture of ancient writings aiming to convert their readers to new ways of thinking. This is found throughout Greek and Roman literature, not merely in the obviously cross-cultural philosophical fusions by authors at the Judaeo-Hellenic interface, such as Philo.

Scholars considering the Sibyl's adaptations of 'common currency' understandably turn to contemporary philosophical sources with clear 'theological' potential. However, it is worth broadening our notions of 'common currency' to embrace those sources used both by the Stoics and Epicureans themselves

---

63 Downing "Cosmic Eschatology," 104. Downing also finds a reminiscence of the Stoic conflagration theory in the Younger Pliny's record of the panicked crowds believing "there were no gods" any more (6.20.15) as a 'popular version' of the Stoic belief that all gods were absorbed into one in the divine fire. I find this latter echo less persuasive.

64 Downing, "Cosmic Eschatology," 107–8; see also Downing, "Common Strands in Pagan, Jewish and Christian Eschatologies in the First Century," *Theologische Zeitschrift* 51 (1995): 196–211, 203 on 2 Peter 3:5–7, 10–13, and further Adams, *The Stars Will Fall*.

65 See Klostergaard Petersen, chapter six in this volume.

66 Sedley, *Lucretius*, 166–85.

67 Downing, "Common Strands," 200–3.

68 Downing, "Cosmic Eschatology," 108: "Of course the clearest echoes are the deliberate ones in the Sibylline books."

and by the Sibyl. For while the *Sibylline Oracles* themselves may not offer much in the way of serious philosophical interest, their rapprochement with the general aims and approaches of philosophical pagan traditions is signalled by the fact that the extant collection incorporates whole swathes of pagan material, such as vv. 5–79 of the ethical exhortations attributed to Phocylides adapted in *Sibylline Oracles* 2 to resemble the Noachide laws for Gentiles.[69] We are therefore justified in considering more closely the 'common currency' of Graeco-Roman culture exploited both by contemporary pagan philosophical texts and by the *Sibylline Oracles*.

One example of such 'common currency' is Plato, in particular the eschatological myths, which offer climactic moments in the dialogues. The Stoics' depth of interest in Platonic dialogues such as the *Timaeus* is well known; their broader and subtler references to Plato, including both thematic and structural references to the great Platonic myths (such as that of the *Gorgias*) have recently received elaboration.[70] Works contemporary with the developing Sibylline tradition include Plutarch's dialogue *On the Face of the Moon*, which draws on the 'likely story' of Plato's *Timaeus*.

By contrast, Plato's influence on the *Sibylline Oracles* has barely been considered.[71] The focus of attention so far, however, has been the eschatological climax of Book 2 of the *Sibylline Oracles*, which describes at great length sinners' punishments in hell, followed by the restored paradise for the righteous and those they choose to rescue from punishment "by the waves of the ever-flowing, deep Acherousian lake" (2.337–8). In her study of *Sibylline Oracles* 1–2, Lightfoot observes that accounts of divine dispensation for the dead in the underworld form a tradition going back to the concluding myth of Plato's *Phaedo*, with its famous description of the geography of the underworld. Distinctive features in the *Phaedo* include sinners escaping from the cycle of punishments into the 'Acherousian lake', also found in the Sibylline passage (noted above);[72] the Sibyl also shares with the *Phaedo* a curious emphasis on the waves across

---

69 On this section of the Oracles as evidence of the 'Sibylline' willingness to find common ground with pagans, see Lightfoot, *The Sibylline Oracles*, 456–67.

70 See D. Sedley, "The School, from Zeno to Arius Didymus," in *The Cambridge Companion to the Stoics* (ed. B. Inwood; Cambridge: Cambridge University Press, 2003): 7–32, 20–24, and for recent literature, https://ndpr.nd.edu/news/50643-plato-and-the-stoics/.

71 Plato refers to the Sibyl only at *Phaedrus* 244b, in reference to a sibyl as a soothsayer, prophesying about the future in heaven-inspired divination. R. Buitenwerf, *Book III of the Sibylline Oracles and its Social Setting* (Leiden: Brill, 2003), 93 notes the spurious *Theages* 124d.

72 Lightfoot, *The Sibylline Oracles*, 523.

the lake (*Phaedo* 112b, 114a–b), which could be a direct borrowing or an indirect one via Hermesianax or even Virgil *Aeneid* 6 (a text also recalled by the thematic way in which the Sibyl divides groups of sinners). For Lightfoot, the Sibyl's main, immediate reference point for this section is the Apocalypse of Peter; she argues that the Sibylline text is best seen as "classicising" images taken from 2 Peter, whose geography likewise combines Acheron with Elysium, and where the theme of the righteous interceding on behalf of sinners makes more sense.[73]

Extensive and serious Sibylline intertextuality with the *Phaedo* is indeed difficult to maintain; the Sibyl makes no mention of the different underworld rivers Oceanos, Pyriphlegethon, and Cocytus, although she quite often uses the classical 'Tartarus'. In terms of the blend of pagan and Christian sources, however, I find telling disagreement in the secondary literature; while Collins regards the fiery character of the netherworld as a distinctively Jewish development, Lightfoot finds this classical,[74] perhaps because she also argues that the Platonic geography of the underworld ultimately influenced Christian thought on this realm.

It has also been observed that the Platonic myths of post-mortem souls in *Republic* 10.614–21 and *Gorgias* 523 have likely influenced this passage of the *Sibylline Oracles*. However, nothing has been said in detail about these texts, beyond positing the influence of Orphism,[75] and this is *prima facie* surprising, since there is much more about post-mortem judgement in these myths than in that of the *Phaedo*. Significant for me is the fact that we find in *Gorgias* 525b–c the notion that the suffering souls of sinners undergoing punishment should be an example to the rest and help them ethically; the exemplarity of punishments is an important didactic notion in the *Sibylline Oracles* (e.g., 3.528; 8.130). Other distinctive features of the *Gorgias* myth are absent from the Sibyl's image of Tartarus. It is, however, striking to find in *Gorgias* 526e the notion of life as a contest or struggle (ἀγών), which was discussed above as a possible Stoic motif in *Sibylline Oracles* 2. And one version of the afterlife of the Sibyl herself seems to be modelled on the Myth of Er from *Republic* 10 (see the postscript in section six below).

We come much closer to the 'common currency' exploited by the Sibyl herself, however, when we go back a step to Homer and Hesiod. The archaic poets

---

73   Lightfoot, *The Sibylline Oracles*, 528.
74   Collins, "Sibylline Oracles," 334; Lightfoot, *The Sibylline Oracles*, 141; however, it is odd that she describes the *lack* of mud in the Sibylline underworld as a classical feature of the geography of hell, when mud features distinctively in the *Phaedo*'s underworld (113a–b).
75   Collins, "Sibylline Oracles," 334.

were available both to the Sibyl and to all the contemporary philosophical traditions going back to Plato. Archaic Greek hexameter epic was the common fuel for Epicurean and Stoic cosmology and even ethics, as when Lucretius concludes Book 3 of *On the Nature of Things* with a rationalising reinterpretation of the mythical sinners in the underworld of Homer's *Odyssey*. Meanwhile, the Stoics found in Homer sources for their own ideas, especially in the realm of theology/cosmology. Above all, Cleanthes interpreted isolated Homeric words in relation to Stoic physical and ethical doctrines;[76] we learn from Philodemus (*On Piety*, col. vi) that Chrysippus likewise tried to harmonise 'things in Homer' with Stoic ideas, while the Stoic philosopher Cornutus (first century CE) uses etymology to find germs of Stoic cosmogony (e.g., in the story from *Iliad* 1.396–406 of how Thetis defended Zeus from rebellious gods).[77] As for Hesiod, Zeno is said to have demythologised the genealogies of the *Theogony* through etymology (Cicero, *On the Nature of the Gods* 1.36 = SVF 1.162); he interpreted χάος as 'primal water', deriving the word from χέεσθαι ('pouring') (Valerius Probus on Virgil, *Eclogue* 6.31 = SVF 1.103–4) and through etymology identified the Titans as cosmic powers. In Plutarch's *Obsolescence of Oracles* (415f.), one character cites Hesiod's account of the finite lifetime of nymphs (= fragment 304M–W) as a veiled allusion to the Stoic theory of ἐκπύρωσις, and his interlocutor takes it as unremarkable that this theory exploits ideas from Hesiod, among other sources.[78]

The *Sibylline Oracles*, of course, do not take the same approach as the Stoics to Homer's account of the fall of Troy or Hesiod's images of the destruction of the Titans. It is striking to see, however, how closely the Sibyl engages with the archaic origins of such canonical myths of Graeco-Roman culture. Above all, the notion of a sequence of human races or ages, whose first expression in Greek is found in Hesiod's *Works and Days* (106–201), forms an unprecedented structural and material backbone of *Sibylline Oracles* 1–2,[79] in combination

---

[76] See A.A. Long, "Stoic Readings of Homer," in *Homer's Ancient Readers* (ed. R. Lamberton and J.J. Keaney, Princeton: Princeton University Press, 1992), 41–66, 63.

[77] See Long, "Stoic Readings," 55.

[78] Heraclitus, author of a work entitled *Homeric Problems* in the first century CE, alludes (no. 53) to "some people's" view of the battle of the gods in *Iliad* 21 as a war between natural elements and heavenly bodies, an allegorical vision of the destruction of the universe [σύγχυσιν... τοῦ παντός]. See the classic treatment of Long, "Stoic Readings," refuting Heraclitus as evidence that Stoics themselves interpreted Homer as an allegorist.

[79] For a detailed list of Hesiodic and Homeric parallels in the Sibylline descriptions of the metallic races, see A. Kurfess, "Homer und Hesiod im 1 Buch der Oracula Sibyllina," *Philologus* 100 (1956): 147–53.

with echoes of Genesis.[80] By the first century BCE, this Hesiodic story has long been taken up for 'philosophical' purposes in Greek and Roman literature. For example, a debate over whether the history of culture is an 'ascent' or 'descent'[81] is variously reflected in Lucretius' history of culture (*On the Nature of Things* 5.925ff.) and Seneca's denial of the reality of the Golden Age in *Letter* 90.[82] Plato, in his *Statesman* myth and elsewhere, had already challenged Hesiod's vision of the life of the first human race, the 'golden men' ruled by Cronus, as an image of paradise by alluding to Hesiod's degenerate metallic races in his account of that era (*Statesman* 269ff.).[83] The Sibyl, like Plato, is provocative in redeploying echoes of Hesiod's narrative, but her aim seems to be to prompt theological reflection in Judaeo-Christian terms; for example, as Lightfoot suggests, the presence of Hesiodic Iron Age topoi already in the Sibylline narration of the first age (intrafamilial hatred, *Sibylline Oracles* 1.73–6) reinforces interpretation of the foregoing Adam and Eve story as a fall into sin.[84]

## 5     The Sibyl on Homer and Hesiod

Before concluding, it is worth looking more closely at how the *Sibylline Oracles* build on Homeric and Hesiodic foundations to bring out the apocalyptic potential of these authoritative Greek texts. Essentially, Homeric and Hesiodic phrases are resituated in the story that the Sibyl wants to tell.[85] For example, Hesiod, noting how the Muses sing of the "great sun and bright moon" (*Theogony* 19), is recast as a prophecy of the day of destruction in *Sibylline Oracles* 3.65. Homer's *Odyssey* 9.14, in which Odysseus wonders, "What shall I tell you first, what last?" as he launches into the narrative of his adventures, is taken up by the Sibyl at *Sibylline Oracles* 3.197 as doubt about how to recount the disasters to come. She also expands on memorable Homeric lines

---

80   On the tension in the blend in these books, see Lightfoot, *The Sibylline Oracles*, 123–5.

81   A debate acknowledged in Downing, "Common Strands," 204ff.

82   On these texts see, respectively, M. Gale, *Myth and Poetry in Lucretius* (Cambridge: Cambridge University Press, 1994); and P. Van Nuffelen and L. Van Hoof, "Posidonius and the Golden Age: A Note on Seneca, *Epistulae Morales* 90," *Latomus* 72 (2013): 186–95.

83   For a detailed interpretation, see H. Van Noorden, *Playing Hesiod: The "Myth of the Races" in Classical Antiquity* (Cambridge: Cambridge University Press, 2014), 149–50.

84   Lightfoot, *The Sibylline Oracles*, 125.

85   Some of the following parallels are noted (without interpretation) in the appendix of A. Rzach, *ΧΡΗΣΜΟΙ ΣΙΒΥΛΛΙΑΚΟΙ = Oracula Sibyllina* (Vindobonae: F. Tempsky, 1891).

predicting doom for an individual, turning them into global threats. For example, Hephaestus' warning to Hera in *Iliad* 1.579 to obey Zeus in case he should upset (ταράξη) their feast is echoed at *Sibylline Oracles* 3.187 in a prophecy of Rome's violent conquest of the world: "it will throw everything into confusion." It is no surprise to find the Sibyl echoing the cry of Thetis as she prophetically laments Achilles's doom (ὤ μοι ἐγὼ δειλή, *Iliad* 18.54), applying it both to the Sibyl's own situation (*Sibylline Oracles* 2.339) and to the coming doom of humankind at large (3.55). Thematic rather than verbal echoes of Hector's fears for Andromache's fate at the hands of the Greeks after his death (*Iliad* 6.454–63) may be felt in the Sibyl's warning about slavery for the *Greek* nation ("they will be seen in fetters suffering at the hand of strange-speaking enemies every terrible outrage, and they will have no one to ward off war a little or be a helper in life," *Sibylline Oracles* 3.528–30).

If this last example deliberately recalls Homer, it seems distinctly ironic (in the vein of Cassandra predicting woes for the Greeks in Euripides' *Trojan Women*). Following up this thread, we can see that phrases in several images of collective destruction and paradise in the *Sibylline Oracles* likewise seem to overturn their Homeric contexts. For example, the Sibyl at *Sibylline Oracles* 3.647 uses ἄσπαρτος καὶ ἀνήροτος ('unsown and unploughed') in the same metrical *sedes* as that in which the phrase is found in Homer's description of the isle of the Cyclopes (*Odyssey* 9.123), whose spontaneous prosperity, given that the Cyclopes are described as 'lawless' (ἀθέμιστες, e.g., 9.106), has always seemed to commentators undeserved. In the *Sibylline Oracles*, however, this collocation is used as an emblem of human neglect of the earth; it describes the nightmare of widespread death in the end time as a 'lack of sowing and ploughing'. Likewise, Homer's denial of seasons, an expression of the miraculous fertility on Phaeacia (*Odyssey* 7.118), is in *Sibylline Oracles* 3.90 (cited above in section two) made over into a prophecy of doom in a context of cosmic dissolution. Conversely, with the description of harmony between 'lion and lamb', no longer predator and prey in the paradise of *Sibylline Oracles* 3.788, the Sibyl marks its difference from the world in which Achilles refuses parley with Hector because 'lions and lambs' do not converse (*Iliad* 22.263).

The discovery of such irony in the Sibyl's re-use of Homeric expressions is unsurprising in the context of her rivalry with this traditional Greek authority; the Sibyl of Book 3 asserts that Homer copied her books, telling of the Trojan War "not truthfully but cleverly" (*Sibylline Oracles* 3.419–25). This phrasing may be taken as a sort of twist on the allegorising traditions of finding hidden philosophy in Homer (the Sibyl told the truth, which Homer then covered up),[86]

---

86   I owe this formulation to Karla Pollmann.

but any anti-Homeric spirit we detect here is not 'philosophically' thought through in this text. While it is not in the Sibyl's interest to support the traditional picture of divine wilfulness and arbitrary punishment, for which Homer was pilloried among philosophers, she does not systematically explore alternative ideas of God or questions of cause and effect in natural events, as did Plato, the Epicureans, and the Stoics.

The most we can safely say is that across all the strata of the *Sibylline Oracles*, the universe has a moral logic. Catastrophes may be described as acts of God or as purely natural events, but they always reflect collective human behaviour. Such a moral dimension is found in Homer only in one extended simile – the roar of the Trojan chariots fleeing before Patroclus in *Iliad* 16.384–93 is compared to that of torrents sent by Zeus to sweep away the works of men, in anger at their crooked judgements in the assembly. We may consider such responsive nature loosely Stoic in origin, or else consider that the Sibylline view of the divine more closely resembles the Hesiodic Zeus, concerned above all with justice (foregrounded, for example, in the proem to *Works and Days*; see also *Works and Days* 327–34 on his punishment of sinners). My point is that in the case of the *Sibylline Oracles*, we do not have to choose between sources or definitively pin down influences; rather, this text is best viewed as a harmonising fossil of a developing discourse between ancient traditions of thought about collective reward and destruction, whether we classify those traditions today as 'literary', 'philosophical', or 'theological'.

## 6  Conclusion

I have sought to downplay the simple idea that the Sibyl consciously draws on 'Stoic' ideas; it is indeed much more likely that she was drawing on various forms of 'common currency' in the late BCE/early CE period. What we possess is not internally coherent, in the manner of a philosophical system or school, and the multiply-redacted text means we cannot securely trace doxography or logic through the collection; this Sibyl should rather be characterised as a magpie, latching on to a wide range of sources, provided they offer her the phrases and ideas with which to run. Yet, even in comparison to the sophisticated pagan authors in the multicultural environments of the Hellenistic period, this Sibyl is not unthinking; she has her own take not only on biblical ideas but also on Hesiodic traditions about human progress and on allegorical readings of Homeric/Hesiodic stories, with their long-range vision and cosmic scope. One angle on the *Sibylline Oracles* is to find here the end-points of traditions as core fuel for her own concerns; she can show us what became of Homer, Hesiod, and Plato (if not others) in antiquity, as far as 'apocalyptic' readings are concerned. In turn, however, the Sibyl's interest in debates about the place of humans in the universe contributes new material to these developing subjects for philosophical-theological discussion (witness, for a start, the influence of the *Sibylline Oracles* on the early Christian apologists).

By way of postscript to this discussion, it is intriguing to note that contemporary pagan images of the Sibyl may themselves have been composed under Stoic influence. Plutarch, in his dialogue *On the Oracles at Delphi No Longer Given in Verse*, has his character Sarapion, a poet with Stoic leanings, paraphrase a fragment of Phlegon about the fate of the Sibyl: she prophesied that at her death she would become the face of the moon, while her breath mingled with the air and her body with the land would enable the divination of omens by various means (*Moralia* 398c). Parke[87] has suggested that the emphasis on universal sympathy in this legend would fit well with a Stoic source, which perhaps explains Plutarch's choice of speaker in his dialogue. As Parke notes, however, it is equally important that Plutarch's speaker is someone who elsewhere cites poetry as evidence. It would not be surprising if contemporary literary accounts of the Sibyl's death, like the biographies of other ancient poets, display the same blend of loosely philosophical influences and poetic legacies as do the oracles transmitted under her name.[88]

---

[87] Parke, *Sibyls and Sibylline Prophecy*, 114–7.
[88] On this trend in ancient biography, see M. Kivilo, *Early Greek Poets' Lives: The Shaping of the Tradition* (Leiden/Boston: Brill, 2010).

# Philosophy and Religion and Their Interactions in 4 Maccabees

*Anders Klostergaard Petersen*

> Wie Alles sich zum Ganzen webt, eins in dem Anderen wirkt und lebt
> GOETHE, *Faust*

⁂

In a recent essay, "Finding a Basis for Interpreting New Testament Texts from a Graeco-Roman Philosophical Perspective," I examined to what extent the ethical tradition of various forms of Graeco-Roman philosophy could be helpful in achieving a better understanding of matters pertaining to ethos in the New Testament writings.[1] Since there has been a time-honoured tradition in classics, ancient philosophy, history of religion, and in New Testament scholarship of arguing that philosophy and religious discourses belong to two categorically different and mutually antagonistic realms, it has been difficult to truly acknowledge the affinities between the ethical traditions found in Graeco-Roman moral philosophy and those testified to by the New Testament texts. In recent years, however, the traditional picture of an irreconcilable relationship between ancient philosophical and religious discourses has increasingly been dissolved, with a growing number of scholars acknowledging the close resemblances and similarities that exist between the moral inculcations and values of the post-Aristotelian philosophical schools and those subscribed to by New Testament authors – not least in relation to Paul.[2]

---

1   Anders Klostergaard Petersen, "Finding a Basis for Interpreting New Testament Ethos from a Greco-Roman Perspective," in *Early Christian Ethics in Interaction with Jewish and Greco-Roman Contexts* (ed. Jan Willem van Henten and J. Verheyden; STAR 17; Leiden: Brill, 2013), 53–81. Since there is no discussion of moral values in the New Testament writings in terms of proper second-order language, I refrain from using the term ethics in that context. Needless to say, this is different in the context of the Graeco-Roman moral philosophical tradition.

2   See, for instance, the work produced by Malherbe and the trajectory of scholarship he initiated. Abraham J. Malherbe, *Paul and the Popular Philosophers* (Minneapolis: Fortress Press, 1989); Stanley K. Stowers, *A Re-Reading of Romans. Justice, Jews, and Gentiles* (New Haven:

In the essay mentioned above, I argued that there is every good reason to use the Graeco-Roman philosophical traditions as one suitable frame of reference – among others – to shed light on matters pertinent to ethos in the New Testament writings. At the same time, however, it is equally important to develop a model of culture that will enable us to acknowledge similarities (and differences of course) between diverse cultural traditions without having to select particular ones at the expense of others. Rather than turning the interpretation of the texts of the early Christ-movement into a zero-sum game in which one has to make a choice for either Judaism or the Graeco-Roman world as exclusive cultural contexts for the emergence of formative Christ-religion, one should recognise that they constitute different horizons which – when seen at separate analytical levels and with respect to particular structures, topics, and motifs – may each contribute to a deeper understanding of the emergence of diverse forms of ethos in early Christ-religion. Years ago in another essay I made a more fundamental plea for abandoning our manner of conceptualising the relationships between different cultural entities in the ancient world on the basis of a homogenised concept of culture.

In the light of such a homogenised understanding of culture, we shall never come to appreciate the fluid and overlapping nature of diverse cultural entities.[3] In terms of actual cultural connections, I consider it advantageous to think of the ancient world on the basis of a Venn diagram, characterised by the acknowledgement of cultural criss-crossings and perpetual interchanges as the norm rather than the exception. Such a model is also superior to an essentialised *Stillleben-Bild* of culture by virtue of the fact that within an overall set (eventually designated a cultural κοινή), it is possible simultaneously to point to identical, similar, or overlapping sets (*per genus proximum*) and to emphasise traditions specific to the particular cultural entities under scrutiny (*per differentiam specificam*).[4]

The New Testament writings differ markedly from each other in their degree of intertwinement with Graeco-Roman philosophical traditions. Whereas

---

Yale UP, 1997); John T. Fitzgerald, *Cracks in an Earthen Vessel: An Examination of the Catalogues of Hardships in the Corinthian Correspondence* (SBL DS 99; Atlanta: Scholars Press, 1988); Troels Engberg-Pedersen, *Paul and the Stoics* (Edinburgh: T&T Clark, 2000).

3 See Anders Klostergaard Petersen, "Reconstructing Past (Jewish) Cultures," in *With Wisdom as a Robe: Qumran and Other Jewish Studies in Honour of Ida Fröhlich* (ed. Károly Dániel Dobos and Miklós Kőszeghy; Sheffield: Sheffield Phoenix Press, 2009), 367–83, esp. 375–82. See also Anders Klostergaard Petersen, "Alexandrian Judaism: Rethinking a Pproblematic Cultural Category," in *Alexandria: A Cultural and Religious Melting Pot* (ed. George Hinge and Jens A. Krasilnikoff; ASMA IX; Aarhus: Aarhus UP 2009), 115–43, esp. 119–28.

4 Cf. Petersen, "Basis," 66–67.

Paul is ostensibly among the most suitable candidates for a comparison with the philosophical traditions and the ethics in particular characteristic of Stoicism, Platonism, and Graeco-Roman popular moral philosophy, it may be more difficult to see the rationale for a comparison between, for instance, the Gospel of Mark and this tradition. Despite this obvious difference, it may nevertheless also be illuminating to instantiate a dialogue with Mark and the Graeco-Roman philosophical moral traditions, as long as we acknowledge that the comparison is situated at a more general level of analysis than, say, the comparison between Paul and the same philosophical traditions. Some of the elements which have been highlighted in Paul as originating in the Graeco-Roman philosophical traditions could also be found in Mark, but here they are, in contrast to Paul, located at a higher level of abstraction in terms of influence pertaining to moral enjoinments in general.

Not only do the different New Testament texts at a general level of analysis belong to the same cultural κοινή, but they also bear witness to similar important changes which a number of both philosophical and religious currents underwent during the Classical and subsequent Hellenistic periods. If the moral philosophy of the four major Hellenistic post-Aristotelian schools (in its admittedly very different manifestations) is understood – as has been especially argued by André-Jean Voelke, Pierre Hadot, and Martha Nussbaum – in terms of a 'therapy of desire' that enables men to live a life more in accordance with their true nature,[5] it is both tempting and reasonable to compare this dimension with the aspect of ethos found in the New Testament writings. After all, an important point – permeating all New Testament texts – is that Christ-adherents, on account of the Christ-event, have been incorporated into a new world in which they have been liberated to act in accordance with their new worldview. Whatever else Christ-adherence may consist of, it is also conceived of as a matter of attaining a new mode of thinking from which a purportedly compliant set of actions freely flow. Such an idea evidently constitutes a conspicuously close parallel to one of the main features of the Graeco-Roman

---

5   Cynic philosophy constitutes a problem on its own. It is obvious also to include it in the discussion, but for lack of proper sources Martha Nussbaum, for instance, left this branch of philosophy out of her examination. See Martha Nussbaum, *The Therapy of Desire. Theory and Practice in Hellenistic Ethics* (Princeton: Princeton University Press, 1994), 8. See, however, Pierre Hadot, *Qu'est-ce que la philosophie antique?* (Paris: Gallimard, 1995), 102. For the importance of philosophy in conjunction with therapy, see the sagacious work of André-Jean Voelke, *La philosophie comme thérapie de l'âme. Étude de philosophie hellénistique* (Vestigia. Pensée antique et médiévale 12; Fribourg: Éditions universitaires, and Paris: Éditions du CERF, 1993) and in particular his *Remarques Préliminaires*.

philosophical virtue system. Content-wise, of course, there are important differences, but when it comes to the overall structure, there may not after all be that much of a difference between the disciple of Greece and that of heaven, between the Academy and the Church.

1    Four Targets

In this chapter, I shall move one step backwards in order to shed light on the relationship between Graeco-Roman philosophical writings and those of a specific literary specimen of Judaism of the late Second Temple period, namely that of the Maccabean trajectory. My aim is fourfold. First, in line with my most recent work on the topic of the relation between philosophy and religion in antiquity, I shall push the argument even further in order to dissolve the habitual penchant to conceptualise the two as not only distinct but also categorically different discourses. Although I certainly acknowledge the dissimilarities that exist between the two types of discourse, I shall contend that from a modern etic perspective on religion, religious and philosophical discourses constituted two sub-classes of the wider category religion, and that there may indeed be a point in acknowledging this (this point is even more accentuated in the first chapter of this book on Platonic philosophy as religion). It is not only a matter of the nomenclature we are using but also of recognising the ultimately religious nature of philosophical discourses in antiquity. Of course, it should come as no surprise that ancient philosophical discourses contain a number of features also to be found in religious discourses 'proper', but my point here is more radical in nature. I endorse the view that from its very inception onwards, philosophical discourses of antiquity constituted what we, from the etic perspective, shall in fact dub religious discourse. However, much of this discussion also hinges on what exactly is meant by 'religion' and 'religious discourse'. In fact, it is not least confusion in this regard that has led us to think of philosophy as something definitively different from religion.

Independent of the long history of reception (both with respect to *Wirkungs-* and *Rezeptionsgeschichte*) which has conceptualised philosophy and religion as opposing realms of thinking, it is also difficult to acknowledge the religious nature of philosophical discourses when measured against tribal and archaic forms of religion (cf. my fourth point below). This has been fittingly formulated by Glenn Most, who also espouses the view that Greek philosophy be conceived of as a religious type of discourse from the third-order perspective, although he does not use the latter terminology:

> It is the discontinuity between ancient and modern religion that makes it difficult for us to understand ancient religion, but it is the very continuity between ancient and modern philosophy that poses traps for understanding ancient philosophy, for, as we shall see later, the ways in which philosophy was practiced in antiquity shared many of the most prominent features of religion.[6]

Most has a clear perception of the anachronism that pertains to the time-honoured tradition of conceiving religion and philosophy in the ancient world as contrary to each other. He rightly emphasises how, "[a]t least since the Enlightenment, if not since the Reformation and Counter-Reformation, we have come to expect an adversarial relation between philosophy and religion: reason conflicting with faith unmasked as superstition, philosophers persecuted as heretics."[7] Unlike Most, however, I am prepared to retroject this binary propensity to think of the relationship between philosophy and religion in antagonistic categories as far back as to prominent Christian thinkers of the late second and third centuries CE, with Tertullian as presumably the most renowned paragon of the scheme.

Second, by including a different type of Jewish text belonging to the era of the late Second Temple period (such as 4 Maccabees) in the discussion, I intend to continue my work on the dissolution of the Hellenism-Judaism dichotomy, the misleading effects of which – despite three decades of intense problematisation – linger on. In spite of the work of Martin Hengel, who once and for all showed that no Judaism of the Hellenistic era existed which was not simultaneously part and parcel of the Hellenistic world (cf. George van Kooten's and my introduction to the present book), many scholars continue to conceptualise the ancient Mediterranean world as if it were constituted by the two focal points of Athens and Jerusalem. Although this might make partial sense from the perspective of the subsequent history of reception in the Western world, it never constituted a cultural and social reality in the ancient Mediterranean world. Additionally, the use of this dualism, verging on a dichotomy, in much current scholarship continues to constitute a problem. The insight of Hengel, however, that no Judaism of the post-Alexander epoch existed that was not also intrinsically part of Hellenism remains moot and apparently difficult to grasp the full consequences of. The perception – even in the work of my former teacher and mentor – often becomes a zero-sum game

---

6  Glenn W. Most, "Philosophy and Religion," in *The Cambridge Companion to Greek and Roman Philosophy* (ed. D. Sedley; Cambridge: Cambridge University Press, 2003), 300–22, esp. 301.

7  Most, "Philosophy," 305–6.

according to which one can only think of the one at the cost of the other.[8] However much one thinks of the one as being innate to the other, they are not conceived of in terms of a Venn diagram but along the sharp lines of two at the outset incongruent entities. I concur on the subtle comment made by Erich Gruen in relation to the Judaism-Hellenism debate, when he advocates for the view that:

> "Judaism" and "Hellenism" were neither competing systems nor incompatible concepts. It would be erroneous to assume that Hellenization entailed encroachment upon Jewish traditions and erosion to Jewish beliefs. Jews did not face a choice of either annihilation or resistance to Greek culture. A different premise serves as a starting point here. We avoid the notion of a zero-sum contest in which every gain for Hellenism was seen as a loss for Judaism or vice-versa. The prevailing culture for the Mediterranean culture hardly be ignored or dismissed. But adaptation to it needs not require compromise of Jewish precepts or practices.[9]

These problems, which do not only have a bearing at the macro-level of the relationships between cultures but also at the micro-level of groups and even at the level of selves, should force us to embark on renewed work on developing models more suitable for an adequate understanding of the ancient Mediterranean world in general and for the relationship between Judaism and Hellenism in particular.

It may at first perhaps appear slightly abstruse to include this debate in the context of this chapter, but it is, in fact, germane to incorporate the discussion here as well. Over the past hundreds of years of scholarship, the Hellenism-Judaism dualism has proved extremely elastic and versatile in the sense that it – depending on the particular context – could be assigned mutually contradictory values. In as much as one wanted to place emphasis on the difference between Graeco-Roman philosophy and formative Christ-religion, one could point to the Jewish nature of the pristine Christ-movement and, thereby, underline its alleged character as a religion of revelation. If, conversely, one had a wish to underscore the purportedly vast differences between early 'Christianity' and Judaism – undergirded by the belief that the two constituted different religions – one would typically point to the Hellenised nature of Christ-

---

8  Cf. the criticism put forward by John J. Collins, "Judaism as *Praeparatio Evangelica* in the Work of Martin Hengel," *Religious Studies Review* 15 (1989): 226–28.
9  Erich Gruen, *Heritage and Hellenism: The Reinvention of Jewish Tradition* (Berkeley/Los Angeles/London: University of California Press, 1998), xiv.

religion, often with an emphasis on purported Jewish forerunners such as Philo, who would then be seen to have paved the way for the emergence of Christianity.[10] Ultimately, I think that the tendency to conceive of philosophy and religion as representative of two different types of discourses is a reverberation of this old Hellenism-Judaism debate in which the two sets of arguments come to enforce each other.

Third, and related to the previous point, I believe that much of the previous scholarly discussion pertaining to the relationship between philosophy and religion in the ancient world has suffered from the use of a slightly problematic comparative model. Although one may and should discuss similarity and resemblance in terms of historical influence between different entities, the adoption of a genealogical model as the predominant or (most often) exclusive manner of conceptualising parallelism and relationships between different cultural entities is one-sided. There are other ways of conceiving historical relationships without having recourse to a model that implies an understanding of similarity in terms of an 'x' which has exerted direct influence on a 'y'. In fact, we may gain new insight by subscribing to different models, which is what I shall advocate here.

Already my initial point on the difference between Paul and Mark in terms of their respective embeddedness with regard to different levels of familiarity with the Graeco-Roman philosophical moral tradition underlines the importance of the argument. Similarly, the idea of using the Venn diagram as the underlying model for conceptualising relations between different cultural entities of the ancient world points to the need for finer gradations than a monolithic notion of historical influence. Although Søren Kierkegaard has been read by only a relatively small number of contemporary Danes, much of his thinking has, by virtue of different processes of cultural sifting, been absorbed by the current Danish culture. I surmise that the same argument pertains to, for instance, the familiarity one can expect from numerous Jewish texts with Graeco-Roman elite thinking. Ostensibly they show no evidence of any direct acquaintance with the higher levels of rhetorical training of the Graeco-Roman tradition of antiquity (cf. the emphasis van Kooten and I place on the notion of common cultural currency in the introduction to this book).

---

10   For the Judaism-Hellenism binary as floating signifiers in the history of scholarship susceptible to being invested with all kinds of value dependent upon the particular nature of the argument, see Dale B. Martin, "Paul and the Judaism/Hellenism Dichotomy: Toward a Social History of the Question," in *Paul Beyond the Judaism/Hellenism Divide* (ed. T. Engberg-Pedersen; Louisville/London/Leiden: Westminster John Knox Press, 2001), 29–61, esp. 30–32.

Yet, it would be fallacious thereby to reject any form of familiarity with this thinking.

Fourth, and in continuity of the previous point, by focusing on 4 Maccabees I want to cast further light on the religious transformations that took place in the centuries of what has sometimes, in the wake of Karl Jaspers (ultimately dating back to Ernst von Lassaulx of the 1860s and presumably originating in Hegel's notion, in continuity with Anquetil du Perron, of an *angel der Zeit*), has been dubbed the Axial Age.[11] Although this terminology may be moot (see the first chapter of this book), I think the recent reformulation of a cultural evolutionary perspective on the history of religion/culture by the late Robert Bellah provides us with an extraordinary opportunity to rethink also the question of the relationship between philosophy and religion in the ancient world. This is a point to which I shall return below and which I already discussed in some detail in chapter one on Platonic philosophy or religion.

Since 4 Maccabees is a distinctly Jewish work that simultaneously vacillates between what, from a modern perspective, may be designated philosophical and religious discourse, it is a particularly suitable candidate for scrutinising the relationship between philosophy and religion and their interactions in the Graeco-Roman world of antiquity. The more so, since commentators have often had severe difficulties in grasping the exact nature of 4 Maccabees, a matter which may be seen as a repercussion of the underlying (and in my view flawed) conceptualisation of the relationship between Judaism and Hellenism and the concomitant dualism between religion and philosophy. When, for instance, a majority of scholars characterise 4 Maccabees as being of a genuinely religious nature with a superficial philosophical veneer, such an assessment epitomises the problem.[12] In other words, the book is considered to be a poor philosophical work cloaked in a religious garment. Others have been voicing

---

[11] For the historical background of the notion, see Hans Joas, "The Axial Age Debate as Religious Discourse," in *The Axial Age and Its Consequences* (ed. R. N. Bellah and H. Joas: Cambridge, MA/London: The Belknap Press of Harvard University Press, 2012), 9–29, esp. 10–19.

[12] See, for instance, the harsh remark of Emil Schürer (*The History of the Jewish People in the Age of Jesus Christ* [rev. and ed. Geza Vermes, Fergus Millar, and Martin Goodman; Edinburgh: T&T Clark, 1986], vol. III.1, 590) that: "It would be misleading, however, to designate him an eclectic philosopher (sc. the author of 4 Macc.) in his own right. Whether or not he worked within an existing philosophical school, he was only a dilettante *in philosophicis*, somewhat like Josephus, who also knew how to give his Judaism a philosophical veneer. The philosophy of the book is by no means consistent and it is quite probable that the author simply used ideas from all sources, in the fashion of contemporary rhetoric, to support his case wherever appropriate." Similar sentiments are found across the schol-

the opposite view, holding that 4 Maccabees is 'sacrificing' genuine Judaism at the altar of Hellenism or Greek philosophy, but regardless of the specific viewpoint, the general understanding is that 4 Maccabees is constituted by two worldviews and discourses that are incompatible in terms of intellectual history and aspirations.

As indicated by my previous reference to Bellah, I think it advantageous to resume and relocate the old discussion of the relationship between philosophical and religious discourse in antiquity in light of a cultural evolutionary perspective. As is well known, evolutionary questions had their heyday in the late nineteenth and early twentieth centuries but came to a halt in terms of intellectual history subsequent to the devastating catastrophe of World War I. From around this time it became intellectually impossible to retain a view that understood Western culture as the zenith of cultural history and Christianity as the pinnacle of the history of religion superior to all other religions, given that the alleged apex of human civilisation had succeeded in nearly annihilating itself in an outburst of barbarism which, in terms of extent, had hitherto been unknown or, perhaps more appropriately, not technologically possible. Needless to say, in the context of political thinking, there was the horrendous aftermath of evolutionary thinking in Nazi and fascist movements of the 1930s, but in terms of intellectual history, this trajectory of thinking had come to an end around 1920. But does that not make it ludicrous to reassume such a perspective? I do not think so.

## 2  A Cultural Evolutionary Context for the Discussion

Firstly, it is crucial to make it patently clear that the current discussion of cultural evolution takes place within the domain of aesthetic complexity and

---

arly literature; see, for instance, Urs Breitenstein (*Beobachtungen zu Sprache, Stil und Gedankengut des Vierten Makkabäerbuches* [Basel/Stuttgart: Schwabe Verlag, 1976], 179), who writes that the philsophy of 4 Macc. shows the author to be representative of a "nicht nur als unselbständigen, sondern auch als recht verständnislosen Kopf;" Moses Hadas, *The Third and Fourth Books of the Maccabees* (New York: Harper & Brothers, 1953), 123; Niels Hyldahl, "Fjerde Makkabæerbog. Indledning," in *De gammeltestamentlige Pseudepigrafer. I oversættelse med indledning og noter ved E. Hammershaimb, Johannes Munck, Bent Noack, Paul Seidelin* (2nd ed, Bodil Ejrnæs and Benedikt Otzen; Copenhagen: Det Danske Bibelselskab, 2001), 625–31, esp. 628; and John M.G. Barclay, *Jews in the Mediterranean Diaspora: From Alexander to Trajan (323 BCE – 117 CE)* (Edinburgh: T&T Clark, 1996), 371, 379. The scholarly literature abounds with such statements placing emphasis on the veneer or scaffolding of philosophy in a basically Jewish religious work.

does not have any bearing on the domains of truth and ethics. Nobody in the current debate is posing cultural evolutionary questions in a manner that implies the superiority of one cultural entity over and against another with respect to either truth or the good. To this we may add the important point that there never was one generalised story of human progress. There have been different patterns of evolution, as the pluriform nature of contemporary cultures across the globe amply demonstrates.[13] In that sense, the contemporary discussion is not a resuscitation of the former debate. But in my view it would be scholarly credulous and scientifically unsatisfactory if one could no longer make distinctions between different forms of culture in terms of complexity, i.e., the aesthetic perspective. The emergence of philosophical discourse in ancient Greece with the Pre-Socratic philosophers, for instance, introduced a form of thinking which, compared to previous types of religiosity, was more complex by virtue of the fact that it added to the previous cultural traditions and was unthinkable without them.[14] Similarly, the appearance of various types of Judaism subsequent to older and more archaic forms of Israelite religion is unthinkable without the existence of the former ones, which they, in a simultaneous process, both presupposed and polemicised against. This is the manner in which I think of aesthetic complexity in relation to the question of cultural evolution.

Secondly, ongoing and vibrant research in the field of cognitive science has made it imperative for the humanities to reflect upon the relationship between nature and culture, and not least upon their interactions. Ultimately, I think that – also in the context in which we speak of culture – we need to acknowledge that there is no culture that, in terms of agency, is not an ingrained part of biology. In that sense, it may also be artificial to speak of a cultural evolutionary perspective. It is more adequate to designate it – as I have done in

---

13   Cf. Colin Renfrew, *Prehistory: The Making of the Human Mind* (London: Phoenix, 2007), 129.

14   In that sense I absolutely concur on the point compellingly made by George Boys-Stones in an excellent and thought-provoking essay in which he espouses the view that: "In general, then, there is no evidence at all that philosophy began with a movement opposed to 'religious' ways of thinking: none that it was, at least through the sixth and fifth centuries BCE, even an option. The continuity of language, on the other hand – and, one might add, of topic (the Milesians thematized the 'origin,' *archē*, of things and their *generation* just as much as Hesiod or the Orphic cosmogonies; cf. West 1983: chs 3–4; Clay 2003: 2–3) – suggests that there might be a way of understanding the new cosmology as a *development* of religious expression." See George Boys-Stone, "Ancient Philosophy of Religion," in *The History of Western Philosophy of Religion. Volume 1. Ancient Philosophy of Religion* (ed. G. Oppy and N. Trakakis; Oxford: Oxford Univeristy Press, 2009), 1–22, esp. 5, cf. also 13.

some recent publications – as a biocultural evolutionary approach, since even in those contexts in which we engage with the most complex forms of culture, such as attending an opera or making use of the Internet, we are still *totaliter et aliter* part of nature. We have reached a point which has enabled us – to an extent never seen before in cultural history – to make use of extraordinary, complex forms of external memory storage, but again that does not make us less biological in terms of our nature.[15] It is a prerogative of human biology that natural selection has acted on our genes in such a way that our psychology has developed "by means of *nongenetic evolutionary processes* capable of producing cultural adaptations" (italics retained from Henrich's text).[16] Like Bellah, I base my understanding of the evolution of humankind along the lines of theorisation developed by the Canadian cognitive neuroscientist Merlin Donald.[17]

Donald has become famous for dividing human cultural history into a three-stage theory, with each novel phase characterised by radical transitions as compared to the former one. Donald is also keen to emphasise that his theory – with both onto- and phylogenetic bearing[18] – allows for gradual transitions to have occurred between four phases. The first took place when our bipedal but apelike ancestors acquired the ability to communicate via voluntary motor acts approximately two million years ago and possibly even further

---

15  For the importance of the Internet in this development, see Nicholas Carr, *The Shallows: How the Internet Is Changing the Way We Think, Read and Remember* (London/New York: W. W. Norton, 2010).

16  On the basis of such a view, "[c]ulture, and cultural evolution, are then a consequence of genetically evolved psychological adaptations for learning from other people." See Joseph Henrich, *The Secret of Our Species: How Culture Is Driving Human Evolution Domesticating Our Species and Making Us Smarter* (Princeton: Princeton University Press, 2016), 34–35, cf. 259–77.

17  I base my brief summary of main tenets of Donald's work in particular on Merlin Donald, *Origins of the Modern Mind: Three Stages in the Evolution of Culture and Cognition* (Cambridge, MA/London: Harvard University Press, 1991); and *A Mind So Rare: The Evolution of Human Consciousness* (London/New York: W. W. Norton, 2001). In addition, I have benefitted over the last several years from numerous conversations with Donald, to whom I am most grateful.

18  See in particular Merlin Donald, "The Central Role of Culture in Cognitive Evolution: A Reflection on the Myth of the 'Isolated Mind,'" in *Culture, Thought, and Development* (ed. Larry Nucci, Geoffrey B. Saxe, and Elliot Turiel; Mahwah, NJ/London: Lawrence Erlbaum Associates Publishers, 2000), 19–38; and "The Mind Considered from a Historical Perspective: Human Cognitive Phylogenesis and the Possibility of Continuing Cognitive Evolution," in *The Future of the Cognitive Revolution* (ed. David Martell Johnson and Christina E. Erneling; Oxford: Oxford University Press, 1997), 478–92.

back in prehistory – that is, mimetic culture. The next decisive change took place with the emergence of mythic culture approximately 150,000 years ago, when predecessors of our specific lineage, homo sapiens sapiens, acquired the ability to communicate by means of linguistic signs – that is, what ultimately became spoken language[19] – and thereby the capacity to interact in communal story-telling; hence the name: mythic.

According to Donald, the final crucial evolutionary transition occurred with the appearance of literate or symbolic culture, which increased the possibilities of external memory storage considerably – that is, theoretical culture. Once again, the precise appearance of this phenomenon is contested. On a more narrow account, it may be dated back to around 2000 BCE, but from a slightly wider perspective, which would allow us to include, for instance, cave paintings and portable sculptures from France and Spain, we are taken as far back as the upper Paleolithic culture, dating from approximately 50,000 to 12,000 BCE.[20] This is characterised by the appearance of three novel representational devices: (1) visuo-symbolic competence, as testified in cave paintings, which eventually led to the invention of numerical counting and writing systems; (2) external memory, which enabled humans to make use of their surroundings in order to store their knowledge and eventually led to external memory becoming a governing factor for human cognition; (3) and, finally, large externally intertwined thinking in the form of theories.[21] However, as

---

19  The dating of the precise inception of each of the phases constitutes a considerable debate, and the uncertainty pertaining to the precise emergence of the stages may also be seen in Donald's work, which he frankly emphasises at different places. An obvious vagueness with respect to the dating pertains to the appearance of language understood in the narrow Peircian sense of symbolic communication. Although language capacity may be dated as far back as to around half a million years ago, since it is from around this time that the first provisional abilities to communicate by means of linguistic signs is likely to have occurred, there is nothing to indicate a more precise mastery of language, in the sense resembling modern languages, prior to the emergence of our specific predecessors, i.e., *homo sapiens sapiens*. In that sense, one may argue, as Donald has also done in several contexts, that the emergence of mythic culture goes back to around 500,000 BCE with the arrival of archaic *homo sapiens*, but that the more sophisticated use of language did not emerge until the appearance of *homo sapiens sapiens* around 125,000 years ago, and even more so around 40,000–30,000 years ago. See Donald, *Mind*, 260–62, and even more so *Origins*, 210–68.

20  At the same time as I say this, it is also crucial to point to the special nature of these phenomena, which cannot be taken to constitute general features of human cultural evolution. See Renfrew, *Prehistory*, 100.

21  See in particular Merlin Donald, "Précis of *Origins of the Modern Mind: Three Stages in the Culture and Evolution*," *Behavioral and Brain Sciences* 16 no. 4 (1993): 719–48, esp. 745.

Donald has also been continuously keen to emphasise, this whole development has been a process of increasing acceleration which has not yet come to an end – at the current point in time, for instance, nobody can predict the impact of the Internet on our biology.[22]

One of the things this new research in the field of cognitive studies forces us to do is to rethink the relationship between culture and nature, especially those intermediary layers with regard to which it is difficult to ascertain the precise influence of biological and cultural components. The more so, since there is a perpetual interaction between the two, to an extent to which even this way of formulating the reciprocal relations become skewed. Even when we are engaging in the most complex forms of culture – such as, for instance, writing an opera or producing manuals for large-scale advanced machinery such as space shuttles – we are intrinsically relying on our biology; but this is a biology that has reached a level of evolution whereby it is not only capable of making impressively grand use of its environment, but also of changing it on a massive scale. Additionally, and very importantly on the basis of Donald's theory, there is the insight that the modern mind comes forward as a hybrid structure built from vestiges of earlier biological stages as well as new external symbolic memory devices which have radically altered its organisation. Bellah's and Donald's basic assumption, with which I fully concur, implies that all human culture should be conceived of in relation to and built upon older cultural layers of memory. "Nothing is ever lost," as Bellah programmatically formulated the insight – that is, nothing decisive is ever lost.[23] Implied in their view is also the fact that biocultural evolution is not of a peremptory, irreversible nature. Any cultural phenomenon may, by virtue of being built on older strata, be rolled back, just as the biocultural evolutionary development they envision is based on the Durkheimian idea that symbolic or theoretical culture can only persist by means of the underlying biocultural layers.

But what does this have to do with the question of the relationship between philosophy and religion and their interactions in the ancient world? Much indeed, I argue. If one places this discussion in the wider context of Axial Age culture, the difference between philosophy and religion fades away

---

22  Cf. Carr, *Shallows*.
23  Robert N. Bellah, "What Is Axial about the Axial Age?" *Archives Européennes de Sociologie* 46 no. 1 (2005): 69–89, esp. 72; and "Nothing Is ever Lost: An Interview with Robert Bellah," interview with Robert N. Bellah by Nathan Schneider, posted on the *Immanent Frame: Secularism, Religion, and the Public Sphere*, 14 September 2011, accessed 1 November 2015. Cf. Hans Joas, *Was ist die Achsenzeit? Eine wissenschaftliche Debatte als Diskurs über Transzendenz* (Basel: Schwabe Verlag, 2014), 19–20, 59–60.

in the sense that the question cannot be reduced to a difference between Greek philosophy, on the one hand, and Jewish religion/Christianity, on the other. The developments in ancient Greece and Israel should preferably be seen as embedded in larger and far more comprehensive processes of transitions, which took place in a number of Eurasian cultures sometime during the mid-sixth century BCE and subsequent centuries, from China in the far East over India to the Near Oriental world – with ancient Israel as a prominent example – to ancient Greece in the West. In China the change was personified by renouncers and thinkers like Lao-tse (whether he was an actual historical figure is without importance in this regard, since we have the traditions ascribed to him), Confucius, and, slightly later, Mencius, Xunzi, and the subsequent philosophical tradition. In India the development was embodied by Gautama Siddharta, the Buddha-to-be, and the later trichotomisation of the three grand trajectories of Indian religion: Buddhism, Hinduism,[24] and Jainism. In Israel the prophets and the emergence of Deuteronomian theology were important stepping-stones for a history of development, which, in terms of Axial Age thinking, became even more prominent in the Hebrew Bible with wisdom books such as Job and Ecclesiastes. In Greece the development was characterised by the arrival of the Pre-Socratic or nature philosophers and, obviously, by the later development culminating in figures such as Socrates, Plato, Aristotle, and the subsequent development of the four post-Aristotelian, Hellenistic schools of philosophy.

There are a number of prevalent features across these different Eurasian cultures which make it meaningful to compare them.[25] First, we find the hitherto most complex form of theoretic culture in the form of a 'thinking about thinking'. In contrast to previous forms of religion, the Axial Age religions were characterised by increasing self-reflexivity, often formulated in second-order concepts and manifested in the ability to understand one's own think-

---

24   Obviously there is a problem in talking about Hinduism as a major religion, since it is constituted by a variety of individually very different traditions and groups. Yet, in as much as these different groups do share certain clusters of signs, it is meaningful to designate them as representative of Hinduism.

25   See Robert N. Bellah, "Religious Evolution," *American Sociological Review* 29 no. 3 (1964): 358–74, esp. 366–68; "What Is Axial," 74–81; and *Religion in Human Evolution: From the Paleolithic to the Axial Age* (Cambridge, MA/London: The Belknap Press of Harvard University Press, 2011), 265–82; Shmuel N. Eisenstadt, "Introduction. The Axial Age Breakthroughs," in *The Origins and Diversity of Axial Age Civilizations* (ed. S. N. Eisenstadt; Albany, NY: State University of New York Press, 1986), 1–25, esp. 2–15; and Yehuda Elkana, "The Emergence of Second-order Thinking in Classical Greece," in *The Origins and Diversity of Axial Age Civilizations*, 40–64, esp. 63–64.

ing and practice from an ostensibly external perspective. Second, this form of self-reflexivity, amounting to a foundational epistemology, is often voiced in spatial categories whereby differences between opposing views become projected onto a vertical axis, manifested as a contrast between the heavenly over and against the earthly perspective. This dualistic spatial staging is frequently projected onto an axis of depth, whereby the contrast becomes extended to a difference between interiority and exteriority, soul and body. Sometimes the attribution of values to these two axes is further developed to include a horizontal, temporal axis whereby the difference becomes instantiated as a contrast between past and present.[26] Third, the transition is commonly characterised by the development towards heno- or monotheism – that is, a reduction of the divine pantheon of archaic types of religion to one supreme or even exclusive deity. Fourth, Axial Age religions are typified by a strong awareness of the existence of rival worldviews that, in terms of representing competing claims to truth, need to be denigrated in order to substantiate one's own truth. Fifth, these religions are distinguished from archaic ones by their call to adherents to emulate the godhead to such an extent that they eventually may be understood to transcend the ontological differentiation between divine and human. Thereby they become transformed into the same material as the deity and, in some cases, were even held to enter the divine abode.[27] Sixth, Axial Age forms of religion place considerable emphasis on the element of ἄσκησις, understood in the basic Greek sense of training. By engaging in self-disciplinary exercises and spiritual training-programs as one may see, for instance, in Stoicism, the adherents of the different axial worldviews undergo various forms of privation relating to what they consider false values. Together with their abandonment of previous values, the adherents strive to internalise the principles of their new worldview in order to embody them. Seventh, axial types of religion are exemplary of a change in accent from the ritual observance of traditional religion to various forms of inner disposition as a prerequisite for proper cultic observance. This is sometimes called a displacement of importance from a ritual to a moral stance. Yet such an understanding is deficient,

---

[26] For an illustration of this, see my chapter "The Use of Historiography in Paul: A Case-Study of the Instrumentalisation of the Past in the Context of Late Second Temple Judaism," in *History and Religion. Narrating a Religious Past* (ed. B.-C. Otto, S. Rau, and J. Rüpke; RVV 68; Berlin/Boston: De Gruyter, 2015), 63–92, esp. 71–76, 89.

[27] Anders Klostergaard Petersen, "Attaining Divine Perfection through Different Forms of Imitation," *Numen* LX no. 1 (2013): 7–38, esp. 23–34; and David M. Litwa, *We are Being Transformed: Deification in Paul's Soteriology* (BZNW 187; Berlin/New York: De Gruyter 2012), 58–116.

since it is not the traditional cult *per se* that is criticised. What is called for is a moral attitude that reflects the new worldview as a presupposition for observing rituals. Eighth, the emergence of Axial Age religion typically takes place in a situation of considerable social competition involving religious entrepeneurs' dissociation from the ruling elite – whether political or religious or both – and defiance of traditional kinship structures and political power.[28]

Needless to say, this development was not of a purely intellectual nature. As Jared Diamond and others have argued, there were good reasons why this development took place in precisely this geographical area. Natural predispositions contributed to social processes such as enhanced density of populations and increased urbanisation, which led to scientific inventions and better exploitation of natural resources that simultaneously and reciprocally gave rise to new forms of thinking. Although these various intellectual manifestations were individually very different from each other, there were also noticeable similarities. They all marked an important transition in terms of thinking with respect to previous forms of religion, which continued, but at the same time were supplied by new types of discourses, which in turn led to continuous interchange between the two in both positive and (frequently) negative manners. In this way, the whole question of the relationship between philosophy and religion in the ancient world should not be confined to Greece and Israel. We need to situate the two in the wider context of Axial Age types of religion, just as it is crucial to take the dependence of this type of religion on previous forms of cultural evolution into consideration. Thereby we shall be able to see how the classical dualism between philosophy and religion evaporates. Philosophical discourses may preferably be understood as constituting an alternative form of cultural-evolutionary development, but the important point is that it took place within the context of ancient religion.

In focusing on 4 Maccabees, I want to discuss four issues of key importance. First, there is the particular question of the relationship between philosophical and religious discourses and their interactions in Graeco-Roman antiquity. Second, there appears the related question of the Hellenism-Judaism debate

---

28   This is a point that has been especially underscored by Seth Abrutyn, "Religious Autonomy and Religious Entrepeneurship: An Evolutionary-Institutionalist's Take on the Axial Age," *Comparative Sociology* 13 no. 2 (2014): 105–34, esp. 113: "But, what is of central importance was that Axiality came in the form of a new institutional sphere becoming autonomous for the first time in human history; and, as opposed to kinship which is always provincial and polity which is always delimited by physical boundaries, this sphere was capable of stretching its boundaries much further because it extended the criteria for membership beyond old local, tribal, or purely ethnic definitions."

and how the two cultural and social entities should be conceived of in terms of their relation to each other. Third, I suggest that we supply our traditional model of conceptualising similarity as predominantly a question of direct historical influence with other models, such as, for instance, one that discusses parallelism in terms of convergent evolution. Fourth, I advocate the view that the question of the relationship between philosophy and religion in the ancient world in terms of cultural evolution may have a particular bearing on the transition from archaic forms of religion to utopian or Axial Age types of religion.

## 3   4 Maccabees in Its Historical Context: Genre and Cultural Origin

4 Maccabees may advantageously be conceived of as a piece of rewritten scripture from 2 Maccabees.[29] In terms of dating and place of origin, however, it constitutes a floating signifier, since we do not know much about the historical context in which it arose. The text dates presumably to the first half of the first century CE, but could have been written anytime from 50 BCE to 100 CE.[30] It was possibly written somewhere in Asia Minor, possibly in Cilicia, or in Syria, but we do not know exactly. Unlike its predecessor, however, which dates to sometime between one and two centuries earlier, 4 Maccabees does not constitute a piece of history writing. As is evident from the opening of the text, the exordium, 4 Maccabees presents itself as a philosophical work:

> Highly philosophical is the subject (φιλοσοφώτατος λόγος) I propose to discuss, namely, whether devout reason (ὁ εὐσεβὴς λογισμός) is ab-

---

29  Strangely enough, such an approach has not yet been applied to 4 Maccabees. Scholars working on the text have exclusively been concentrating on the relationship between 2 and 4 Maccabees in terms on textual dependence, whether 4 Maccabees does, in fact, depend on 2 Maccabees or not. To the best of my knowledge, nobody has understood 4 Maccabees as a philosophical rewriting of 2 Maccabees. For such an approach, see my article "From Morse to Matthew: Sons Dethroning or Embracing Fathers," in *Contextualising Rewritten Scripture: Different Approaches to the Rewriting of Scripture and the Attribution of Authority to Rewritings* (ed. A. K. Petersen and L. Wijnia; Leiden: Brill, forthcoming).

30  See Jan Willem van Henten, *The Maccabean Martyrs as Saviours of the Jewish People. A Study of 2 and 4 Maccabees* (JSJ SS 57; Leiden/New York/Köln: Brill, 1997), 73–82; and the famous article by Elias Bickermann "The Date of Fourth Maccabees," *Louis Ginzberg Jubilee Volume*, English Section (New York: The American Academy for Jewish Research, 1943), 105–22.

solute master of the passions (αὐτοδέσποτός τῶν παθῶν), and I would strictly counsel you to give earnest attention to my philosophical exposition (προσέχετε προθύμως τῇ φιλοσοφίᾳ). The subject is an indispensable branch of knowledge but it also includes a eulogy of the greatest of virtues (ἄλλως τῆς μεγίστης ἀρετῆς περιέχει ἔπαινον) by which I mean of course prudence (φρονήσις). (1:1–2)[31]

This tenet of devout reason as a master over the passions permeates the entire text and could have been the original title of the book. Although Eusebius erroneously assigns 4 Maccabees to Josephus, he may, in fact, render the original title of the work correctly as *On the Supremacy of the Spirit* (Περὶ αὐτοκράτορος λογισμοῦ, see *Historia ecclesiastica* 3.10.6; cf. also Jerome, *De Viris Illustribus* 13). In 1:13–14, for instance, the opening of the text is recapitulated: "The subject of discussion then is whether reason is absolute master of the passions. But we have to define what reason is and what passion is, how many forms of passion there are, and whether reason is lord over them all" (cf. 1:7, 30; 2:6, 7, 9; 6:31–55; 13:1–5; 16:1; 18:2). In continuity with the classical rhetorical genres, the text is most appropriately designated as an epideictic piece of work. However, there is a rejoinder with respect to the Aristotelian differentiation between the temporal aspects pertaining to each of the three main rhetorical genres. Often too much emphasis is placed on the relationship between the epideictic genre and the presence envisaged to constitute the temporal location of the intended audience. Parallel with the deliberative genre, however, there is also an important aspect pertinent to the epideictic genre pertaining to the future, which has to do with the fact that the epideictic genre in particular was conceived of as the type of speech that does not aim at a particular course of action, but aims to exert influence on the values and representations of the audience. George Kennedy rightly argues that "[t]he basic function of epideictic oratory is to enhance belief in certain moral and civic values and thus to increase social bonding and the solidarity of the cultural group."[32]

Such an understanding implies that there is a crucial ideological aspect at play in the epideictic genre pertaining to its role in forging social cohesion and contributing to the formation of group identity, since it aims to enhance and to strengthen the universe of values and concepts of the audience. This is evident from the end of 4 Maccabees, in which there is a notable leap from

---

31   I use the translation of Hugh Anderson in *The Old Testament Pseudepigrapha. Volume 2* (ed. J. H. Charlesworth; New York: Doubleday, 1985).

32   George A. Kennedy *A New History of Classical Rhetoric* (Princeton: Princeton University Press, 1994), 22.

the narrated world to the level of discourse in order for the authorial voice to direct itself appealingly to the audience: "O offspring of the seed of Abraham, children of Israel, obey this Law and be altogether true to your religion (καὶ πάντα τρόπον εὐσεβεῖτε) knowing that devout reason is master over the passions, and not only over pains from within but also from outside ourselves" (18:1–2).[33] It is evident that the text aims to encourage, exhort, inculcate, and to move its audience to understand and to acknowledge that reason shall prevail over the passions, and that the reason called for in the combat over against the passions is not only available in the Torah but is, in fact, the Jewish law. Obedience of the Torah is the means to ensure that reason will triumph over and domesticate the passions. In this manner, 4 Maccabees is a philosophical text intended to strengthen and consolidate the self-understanding of the intended audience that the insight to be gained from philosophy that reason shall prevail over the passions consists in obedience of the Torah.

The ascription of 4 Maccabees to the epideictic genre, however, is complicated by virtue of the fact that the book simultaneously constitutes panegyrics, a eulogy or *encomium* of the ideal life of the martyrs – a fact already seen from the opening verses of the book, in which the author emphatically underscores how he will praise (ἔπαινον) insight as the greatest virtue. The book is divided into two clearly distinct parts, of which the first philosophical part comprises 1:1–3:18, whereas the other is a comprehensive narrative substantiation of the philosophical main thesis of the first part, illustrated by the narrative of the martyrs in 3:19–18:24.[34] However one decides on the genre designation of the

---

[33] I generally appreciate the translation of Anderson, but when it comes to his rendering of εὐσεβεῖα as religion, I am not particularly fond of the choice. I do not think that our third order category is a suitable translation of εὐσεβεῖα and lexemes of the same stem. It should rather be rendered 'piety' or 'seemly reverence to the god(s)'. This applies to renderings of εὐσεβεῖα and cognate terms in the book.

[34] The intimate relation between the two parts intonated in the exordium of the book is ignored by scholars who, like Jürgen Lebram, argued that 4 Maccabees is divided into two parts possibly deriving from separate sources. See Jürgen H.C. Lebram, "Die literarische Form des vierten Makkabäerbuches," VC 28 (1974): 81–96. Similarly, André Dupont-Sommer, *Le quatrième livre des Maccabées: Introduction, traduction et notes* (Bibliotèque de l'École des Hautes Études 274; Paris: Honoré Champion, 1939), 19, also underlines the loose relationship between the two parts and suggests different authorships for them. Apart from the fact that the opening of the books is emphatically aimed to unite the two parts, Urs Breitenstein has amply documented how the vocabulary and style of the two sections do not differ very much at all, although he is also keen to emphasise the elusive nature of the two parts of the work to each other. See Breitenstein, *Beobachtungen*, 148–51. For the consistency in language and limited degree of variation, see ibid., 91–130.

second main part of the book, it is indisputable that it also belongs to the wider category of the epideictic genre.

As has been pointed out by Jan Willem van Henten, a number of similarities exist between this part and the subgenre of the *genus demonstrativum* designated the ἐπιτάφιος λόγος or the burial speech. I tend to emphasise caution when it comes to a closer genre specification of 4 Maccabees, since it witnesses to several sub-genres belonging to the epideictic main genre. In the burial speech, for instance, we find both the ἀγών, and the *encomium*. The important thing is that the second main part of the book may be understood as a narrative amplification of the main philosophical thesis of the first part of the work, and also that the second main part falls within the parameters of the epideictic genre.[35]

Be that as it may, unlike its scriptural predecessor 2 Maccabees, 4 Maccabees does not testify to an apologetic form of history writing. As literature, 4 Maccabees is related to Aristeas, Philo of Alexandria, and partly to Aristobulus. David deSilva aptly encapsulates the purpose of the work as consisting in the rhetorical effort "to strengthen the commitment of Jews to the Jewish way of life, making that way of life credible, reasonable and honourable through the double presentation of argument and example."[36] Although not apologetic in either genre or tone, the book does contain an apologetic element well integrated into the purpose of the text. Bernhard Heininger endorses the view that the philosophical questions raised in 4 Maccabees are intertwined with a concrete social purpose. They refer to a difficult form of balancing between 'assimilation' and what Heininger anachronistically designates 'ghettoisation' – that is, on the one hand, the abandonment of a specific identity and, on the other hand, the commitment to a particular tradition conceived by the author to be either threatened or in danger of disappearance.[37] It is this particular threat – real or imagined – that prompts the writing of 4 Maccabees.

Once again, I shall underscore the point that the text should not be considered exemplary of a discrepancy between Judaism and Hellenism, such as has frequently been done and is evident in Heiniger's manner of phrasing the overall aim of the text. In that regard I also disagree with recent scholarly work on the book, which tends to see it as being involved in an ambiguous and dif-

---

35   Cf. Hans Josef Klauck, *4 Makkabäerbuch* (JSHRZ 3.6; Gütersloh: Mohn Verlag, 1989), 659; Henten, *Martyrs*, 63; David A. deSilva, *4 Maccabees* (Guides to Apocrypha and Pseudepigrapha; Sheffield: Sheffield Academic Press, 1998), 47; Bernhard Heiniger, "Der böse Antiochus. Eine Studie zur Erzähltechnik des 4. Makkabäerbuches," BZ NS 33 (1989): 43–59, esp. 44.

36   deSilva, *4 Maccabees*, 28.

37   Heiniger, "Antiochus," 55.

ficult negotiation between a fundamentally Jewish identity over and against a Hellenistic or Graeco-Roman one. It should come as no surprise at this point that this binary or digital manner of conceputalising the text – highly germane to the topic of this essay – often comes out as a mediation between Greek philosophy and Jewish religion.[38] In dire contrast to such an understanding, which turns the author of 4 Maccabees into an omniscient Olympic individual in possession of a cultural overview that enabled him to pick and choose between different cultural traditions, I do not think that Greek philosophy constituted a 'foreign' element to him. Intellectually, he saw it not only as an ingrained part of Judaism, but he also understood his Judaism to exemplify a philosophy superior to rival forms of philosophy which did not identify true philosophy with the Torah. Although we may, from an etic perspective, conceptualise the author's endeavour as amounting to an amalgam of 'Judaism' and 'Hellenism' by which he reconciles the two on the basis of a cannibalisation of the latter in his version of the former, we cannot or should not extend this understanding to the emic level of analysis. In fact, it is crucial that we do not conflate such a model with what took place at the indigenous level and, additionally, that in our rendering of the author's enterprise at the emic level of analysis we do not confuse the two with each other. Rather, we should understand 4 Maccabees as being involved in a discursive fight among Jews about the right to define true Judaism – a Judaism which the author conceives of as being threatened by the failure among Jews to acknowledge the Torah as the means to overcoming passion and, in addition, to exhibit an uncompromising preparedness to die as (the Maccabean) martyrs for this conviction. This is an internal Jewish discussion that does not have much to do with an attempt to reconcile Jewish religion with Greek philosophy. It only has to do with the non-Jewish world in as much as Judaism has been and could be accused of not promoting philosophical values. In that regard, I think deSilva is basically correct in his assessment that 4 Maccabees should be seen in connection with the apologetic tenor of writers like Aristeas, Josephus, and Philo.[39] The textual em-

---

38  See, among the most noticeable representatives of such an approach, Barclay, *Jews*, 371, 378–80; John J. Collins, *Between Athens and Jerusalem: Jewish Identity in the Hellenistic Diaspora* (Grand Rapids, MI: Eerdmans, 2000), 208f.; deSilva, *4 Maccabees*, 33, 44–46.

39  I strongly underline the notion of apologetic tenor, by which I do not mean to say that the text constituted an apology. For typological gradations between different forms of apologetic discourse, see Anders Klostergaard Petersen, "The Diversity of Apologetics: From Genre to a Mode of Thinking," in *Critique and Apologetics: Jews, Christians and Pagans in Antiquity* (ECCA 4; ed. A.-C. Jacobsen, J. Ulrich, and D. Brakke; Frankfurt am Main: Peter Lang, 2009), 15–41, 23–41; and "Heaven-borne in the World: A Study of the Letter to Dio-

phasis placed on the Torah in 4 Maccabees as the promoter of humanitarian behaviour with respect to all people, friend or enemy, Jew and non-Jew, should be interpreted as eliciting a defence over and against accusations against Jews from different sides. The work reacts to allegations voiced over and against Judaism, such as that which reverberated in Diodorus of Sicily's claim that the Torah is representative of a xenophobic collection of laws (34/35.1.4).

4 Maccabees is not apologetic *per se*,[40] but is a philosophical encomial tractate intended to keep the attention of its envisioned audience on what the author conceives to be the true Jewish way of life. The aim is to strengthen and to enhance their commitment to this understanding and practice. Simultaneously, it aims to prove to the intended audience how accusations voiced from a Graeco-Roman, non-Jewish public against Judaism rest on false foundations. Although it is sometimes claimed from the Graeco-Roman, non-Jewish side that Judaism is and cannot be congruent with philosophy, the author amply demonstrates that this cannot be true. On the contrary, according to the author, Judaism constitutes the truest form of philosophy and is, in fact, the means for fulfilling and enacting a philosophical life (a point to which I shall return below, since this correlates with the core idea of the post-Aristotelian trajectories of philosophy). When the author of 4 Maccabees, addressing his intended audience, presents the martyrs' refusal to consume pork as the epitome of true Jewish behaviour, this should be seen as a narrative defence over and against the accusations raised against Judaism as being credulous superstition rather than noble philosophy (Plutarch, *Moralia* 169c), for ridiculously and reprehensibly prohibiting the consumption of pork (Plutarch, *Moralia* 669e–f; Tacitus, *Histories* 5.4.3; Juvenal, *Satires* 14:98–99; Josephus, *Contra Apionem* 2:137; cf. Aristeas 128–130). Yet the importance of such accusations as a background does not warrant an overall understanding of the text as apologetic. On the contrary, it is a highly adamant and self-conscious attempt to engage in a rhetorical ἀγών against rival philosophies in order to palpably substantiate how Judaism surpasses them all. In that sense, the book is considerably less apologetic than it is a self-laudatory affirmation of (the author's) Judaism as the supreme philosophy.

But are such self-affirmative panegyrics of Judaism as philosophically superior to all other forms of philosophy, enough to substantiate a reading of

---

gnetus," in *In Defence of Christianity: Early Christian Apologists* (ECCA 15; ed. J. Engberg, A.-C. Jacobsen, and J. Ulrich; Frankfurt am Main: Peter Lang, 2014), 125–38, esp. 131–35.

40   In that regard I disagree with Collins (*Athens*, 206–08), who in my view overemphasises the importance of this apologetic motive underlying the book.

the work as exhibiting a philosophical discourse? After all, we do not find any comprehensive argumentation along the lines of the previous Greek elenchic tradition. Nor does the book testify to the comprehensive and subtle allegorical exegesis of Philo. In other words, what is it that legitimises an interpretation of 4 Maccabees as philosophy, and how may this particular work open our eyes to problematising the time-honoured proclivity to think of philosophy and religion as constituting contradictory forms of discourses representing two incompatible worldviews?

## 4 An Appraisal of the Central Points in 4 Maccabees that Relate It to Other Philosophical Traditions

So how should we conceive of 4 Maccabees? Is it philosophy, religion, or something in between? Is it a Jewish encroachment on or usurpation of something intrinsically foreign to Judaism? In what sense is it representative of a discourse that may be said to testify to the transition from μῦθος to λόγος? As I have indicated in my argument so far, I think we are off track by posing questions in such a manner, since they not only presuppose an underlying concept of culture that is moot, but also a manner of conceptualising the relationship between religious and philosophical discourse which is dubious. Additionally, such a way of formulating the problem is likely to reflect a skewed manner of conceiving the relationship between Judaism and Hellenism.

Unlike its literary antecedent, 4 Maccabees is no longer history writing in the classical sense. It is a text engaged in a philosophically excessive form of rewriting the martyr narratives of 2 Maccabees. It does so to exemplify its own particular philosophical project aimed at proving that reason is lord over the passions and that reason shall be sought in, or rather is identical with, the Torah.[41] As several scholars have noted over the years, the author of 4 Maccabees does not belong to one particular philosophical school. In terms of intellectual milieu, the text is most appropriately contextualised in what we, for lack of more precise terminology, shall designate Graeco-Roman popular philosophy or a philosophical κοινή with a strong penchant towards Platonism and (partly) Stoicism.[42]

The book is an exquisite example of how a Jewish author, presumably dating to the first part of the first century CE, was as much at home in Graeco-

---

41  Henten, *Martyrs*, 270–90.
42  Cf. deSilva, *4 Maccabees*, 13, 51. For a general assessment of the philosophical reliance of the book, see Moses Hadas, *Books*, 116–18; and Klauck, *4 Makkabäerbuch*, 666.

Roman philosophical and literary traditions as he was in Jewish scriptural traditions without acknowledging or showing awareness of the differences between what to us are ostensibly different cultural frameworks. In this manner, the text calls for renewed reflection on the analytical value of excessively finely drawn lines between Jewish and Graeco-Roman cultural and religious traditions in a cultural and social context in which these trajectories of traditions not only intersected, but in which cultural amalgamation and social hybridisation was the rule rather than the exception.

There are three key points of importance for the assessment of 4 Maccabees with respect to philosophy. First, through the first three chapters of the book it is obvious that 4 Maccabees engages in a philosophical enterprise aimed at demonstrating the truth of a particular tenet – namely, how devout reason is the absolute master over the passions (αὐτοδέσποτός ἐστιν τῶν παθῶν ὁ εὐσεβὴς λογισμός, 1:1b). Although the book does not exemplify philosophy in the sense of substantial second-order thinking, i.e., a form of thinking about thinking, it clearly evokes a philosophical argument stemming from Graeco-Roman popular moral philosophy in order to make its message obvious to the intended audience. One may add to this that the central thesis of the book corresponds well with a core idea of all the philosophical schools of the post-Aristotelian era in the sense of seeing not only (devout) reason as the remedy for curing passion, but also in understanding passion to constitute the vice *par excellence* that needs to be overcome in order to obtain a true human life. In this sense, philosophy identified with the Torah becomes the 'Jewish' response to the therapy of desire. By extirpating passion, it is the Torah that enables human beings to live a life in accordance with what is required by the divine world.

Second, the book – similarly to the emergence and development of Greek philosophy – is representative of a utopian or an axial form of religiosity. In the context of ancient Israel, Axial Age types of Judaism marked an important break with archaic forms of Israelite religion. In dire contrast to a worldview in which humans were to acknowledge the ontological difference between god and humans in order for the perpetual flow of divine gifts to stream into the world of humans, Axial Age forms of religion evoked an understanding whereby humans were called not only to imitate the gods but to become like them. In order to do that, humans had to detach themselves from the fetters which bound them to this world, a world considered to be helplessly succumbed to passion, decay, carnality and other elements considered adversarial to the celestial realm. We see this in the martyr deaths of the mother and the seven sons. Through their martyr deaths they join the chorus of the fathers who have received pure and immortal souls from God. Although this may sound conspicuously remote from Plato, I think what we see in, for instance, the passage in the *Theaetetus* 176a–b on the need to imitate the god as much as possible similarly exemplifies this type of religiosity – that is, an Axial Age form of religion.[43] In the same manner, 4 Maccabees exemplifies a type of religion that is not far from the teaching on the nature of the soul in the *Phaedrus* (246a–249e, as part of the longer speech on the character of the soul comprising the entire section 243e–257b). The emphasis 4 Maccabees places on the immortality of the soul (cf. 9:22–25; 13:13–15; 14:5–6; 17:12; 18:23) correlates well with a basic Platonic tenet as well as that of Axial Age religion – namely, that only the divine part of humans – the soul – shall be saved.[44]

Third, by virtue of its narrative exemplification of the lives of the martyrs as an embodiment of the fundamental thesis of 4 Maccabees, the text shares with all Hellenistic philosophical schools the idea highlighted by Pierre Hadot that philosophy should be conceived of as a way of life, *une manière de vivre*.[45] The principle that devout reason is an absolute master over the passions should be exhibited in an excessive practice that implies self-immolation for the sake of the Jewish law as a martyr. In the wake of Hadot's groundbreaking work, the German philosopher and sociologist Peter Sloterdijk has pointed to the Axial Age transition as one that has been conducive to a manner of conceiving life in terms of programs of training; hence the title of Sloterdijk's book, *Du mußt dein Leben ändern*.[46] Thereby Sloterdijk, in continuity with Hadot, underscores the importance of the Greek term ἄσκησις, the basic meaning of which is exercise,

---

43   See also the unequivocal statement of Most ("Philosophy," 313) that: "For Aristotle, as for Plato, one of the fundamental purposes of engaging in philosophy is, by studying god, to become as godlike as possible," as well as George van Kooten's grand monograph *Paul's Anthropology in Context: The Image of God, Assimilation to God, and Tripartite Man in Ancient Judaism, Ancient Philosophy and Early Christianity* (WUNT 232; Tübingen: Mohr-Siebeck, 2008), in which he makes the idea of the ὁμοίωσις θεῷ a key point in Paul's anthropology.

44   It is conspicuous that 4 Maccabees, in its rewriting of 2 Maccabees, omits those passages in which 2 Maccabees explicitly refers to a resurrection of the dead; see 2 Maccabees 7:9, 11, 14, 22–23.

45   See Hadot, *philosophie*, 161–62, 168; and his additional important works *La philosophie comme manière de vivre. Entretiens avec Jeannie Carlier et Arnold I. Davidson* (Paris: Albin Michel, 2001), 159; and *Exercises spirituels et philosophie antique. Préface d'Arnold I. Davidson. Nouvelle édition revue et augmentée* (Paris: Albin Michel, 2002), 47, 290–91, 293, 296. Similar emphasis on philosophy as a way of life, but without reference to Hadot, is found in Most, "Philosophy," 305.

46   Peter Sloterdijk, *Du mußt dein Leben ändern. Über Anthropotechnik* (Frankfurt am Main: Suhrkamp, 2009).

practice, or training, not to be confused with the later second- and third-order use of asceticism as renunciation or forsaking.[47] The latter is representative of the subsequent Christian 'takeover' of the concept and, not least, the inclination of the later tradition, based on Christian ascetic practices, to constrain the idea of asceticism to different forms of renunciation detached from the wider frame of exercise or training.[48]

Be that as it may, 4 Maccabees similarly places emphasis on self-mastery, as expressed in the individual call to each member of the intended audience to emulate the martyrs and, thereby, attain a manner of living that enables them to control their passions (cf., for instance, 1:19, 31; 2:6; 3:1). As part of the farewell speech of the youngest brother, the narrator has him address the tyrant Antiochus: "Impious man, of all the wicked ones you most ungodly tyrant, are you not ashamed to receive your kingdom with all its blessings from the hand of God and then to kill those who serve him and torture those who practice piety" (καὶ τοὺς τῆς εὐσεβείας ἀσκητὰς στρεβλῶσαι, 12:11d). Similarly, we find the use of ἄσκησις in the sense of Hadot and Sloterdijk in the speech of the narrator of 4 Maccabees which sums up the teaching to be learned from

---

47   Sloterdijk, *Leben*, 448–50, 470–72. Cf. Hadot, *Exercises*, 78.

48   This is my primary point of criticism against Hadot's otherwise brilliant and truly thought-provoking work on asceticism, that he inserts a robust caesura between the philosophical and the Christian asceticism. See, for instance, Hadot, *Exercises*, 77–78: "Avant de commencer cette étude, if faut bien préciser la notion d'exercise spirituel. «Exercise» correspond en grec à *askesis* ou à *meletè*. Il nous faut donc bien souligner et déterminer les limites de notre enquête. Nous ne parlerons pas d'«ascèse» au sens moderne du mot, tel qu'il est défini par exemple par K. Heussi: «abstinence complète ou restriction dans l'usage de la nourriture, de la boisson, du sommeil, de l'habillement, de la propriété, tout spécialement continence dans le domaine sexuel.» Il faut en effet soigneusement distinguer cet emploi chrétien, puis moderne du mot «ascèse» de l'emploi du mot *askesis* dans la philosophie antique. Chez les philosophes de l'Antiquité, le mot *askesis* désigne uniquement les exercises spirituels dont nous avons parlé, c'est-à-dire une activité intérieure de la pensée et la volonté. Qu'il existe chez certains philosophes antiques, par exemple chez les cyniques our les néoplatoniciens, des practiques alimentaires, ou sexuelles, analogues à l'ascèse chrétienne, c'est une autre question." Hadot, however, is also capable of including parts of the Christ-movement in his reflections, but in this context he pays attention to those currents which, like that of the Christian Apologetes, converge with Hadot's 'Greek' understanding *askēsis*. I consider this understanding to constitute a twofold problem. First, Hadot does not satisfactorily acknowledge the relationship between the different types of asceticism. Second, he does not recognise how the transition in terms of ascetic practice needs to be understood against the background of a development within the history of religion, which is not narrowly confined to the Greek philosophical schools, but is part of a wider axial development.

the death of the seven brothers (13:1–14:10). At this point, the narrator instantiates a joint chorus of the martyrs in which he has them speak directly to the intended audience (13:16–18). As a conclusion to this panegyric speech, he emphasises the importance of φιλαδελφία or brotherly love:

> You cannot be ignorant of the charm of brotherhood which the divine and all-wise providence has allotted through fathers to their offspring, implanting it, in fact, in their mother's womb. There brothers dwell for the same period and are formed over the same duration of time; they are nurtured from the same blood and are brought to maturity through the same source of life. They are brought to birth through the same span and draw milk from the same fountains, and through being embraced at the same breast, fraternal souls are nourished, and they grow from strength to strength through a common nurture and daily companionship as well as in the training imposed by our discipline in the Law (καὶ τῆς ἄλλης παιδείας καὶ τῆς ἡμετέρας ἐν νόμῳ θεοῦ ἀσκήσεως).[49] The ties of brotherly love, it is clear, are firmly set and never more firmly than among the seven brothers; for having been trained in the same Law and having disciplined themselves in the same virtues (νόμῳ γὰρ τῷ αὐτῷ παιδευθέντες ἐξασκήσαντες ἀρετάς), and having been reared together in the life of righteousness, they loved one another all the more. (13:19–24)

## 5  4 Maccabees as a Manifestation of Axial Age Religion

Apart from these three key points, which clearly demonstrate the religio-philosophical nature of 4 Maccabees, we also see how the book testifies specifically to an Axial Age type of religion with respect to the eight points I previously emphasised as particularly pertinent to Axial Age forms of religion over and against archaic ones. Let us briefly rehearse them in relation to 4 Maccabees.

First, we have noted how the book pays witness to theoretic culture in the form of a 'thinking about thinking'. This is evident already from the beginning of 4 Maccabees, which smoothly and at ease with the conceptual world of philosophy presents its argument in the form of second-order language in order to bring its message through. Philosophy is the preferred discourse called upon to document the veracity of the author's worldview and his specific les-

---

49  I find this translation slightly strange. I would prefer: "as well as in other teaching and in our training by God's law."

son to his audience – namely that the cure for overcoming vice in the form of passion is found in the Torah. Second, this form of self-reflexivity amounting to a foundational epistemology is staged in spatial categories, whereby differences between opposing views are projected onto a vertical axis and, thereby, manifested as the contrast between the heavenly over and against the earthly perspective. This dualistic instantiation has its counterpart in an axis of depth, which expresses the same contrast in the form of a difference between interiority and exteriority, soul and body. Third, the transition that commonly characterises the change from archaic to Axial age forms of religion – that is, the development towards heno- or monotheism – is emphatically at play in 4 Maccabees. The continuous emphasis placed on God as the exclusive god not only of Israel but also of the world exhibits this tendency (cf. 4:11–12; 5:24–25; 9:8–9, 15; 10:18–21; 11:7–8; 12:11; 15:3). Fourth, Axial Age religions are typified by a strong awareness of the existence of rival intellectual worldviews that, in terms of thinking, need to be denigrated in order to substantiate one's own truth. We have observed how 4 Maccabees exhibits a form of theoretical thinking used in order to criticise the existing world and, in particular, the political systems opposed to the Israel heralded by 4 Maccabees. The text amply demonstrates an awareness of other worldviews that are considered threats to the one advocated and inculcated by 4 Maccabees. Fifth, we have found abundant evidence that demonstrates how 4 Maccabees, like other manifestations of Axial Age forms of religion and contrary to archaic ones, fervently calls upon its adherents to emulate the godhead to such an extent that they eventually can claim to have transcended the ontological differentiation between divine and human. Thereby they are transformed into the same material as the deity and are held to enter the divine abode. Obviously, the martyrs are not by their martyrdom imitating the godhead and, thereby, setting a divine ideal to be emulated. Unlike the hero of another contemporaneous form of Judaism, the god of 4 Maccabees does not engage in actions of self-immolation. Yet the martyrdom of Eleazar and the seven sons and their mother is set up as the ideal for the intended audience. The acknowledgement of and trust placed in the Jewish Torah, held to represent the truest form of philosophy, should also entail preparedness to sacrifice oneself for the god of Israel. This marks another important feature which characterises the transition from archaic to Axial Age types of religion – that is, the transfer from transitive to reflexive forms of sacrifice, by which the adherents are not called to sacrifice something on behalf of themselves, but are, in fact, summoned to immolate themselves. Sixth, and in conjunction with the previous point, we have noted how 4 Maccabees places emphasis on ἄσκησις, understood in the basic Greek sense of training. The intended addressees of the book are called to emulate the martyrs by pursuing their ἄσκησις, even if it involves death. Seventh, in passing we have also observed how 4 Maccabees exemplifies the change in accent from the ritual observance of traditional religion to the emphasis placed on inner disposition as a prerequisite for proper cultic observance. With respect to the martyrs and the injunction to emulate them, one may think of this transition in terms of a change from a transitive type of sacrifice to a reflexive one by which one is called to sacrifice oneself. Eighth, although it may not be that conspicuous in 4 Maccabees that Axial Age religion typically takes place in a situation of considerable social competition involving religious entrepeneurs' dissociation from the ruling elite and defiance of traditional kinship structures and political power, this point is pertinent as well. In the focus on the martyrs and the call to imitate them, there is a shift in religious accent from the priesthoods of traditional archaic religions to the individual adherent who, on the basis of his or her ἄσκησις, should exhibit in life the meaning of the religion in question. In 4 Maccabees this emphasis on religious determination and sincerity is, as we have seen, even taken to the point of suffering martyrdom.

Prior to summing up my argument, it is reasonable to take a closer look at that major part of 4 Maccabees which is not considered by a majority of scholars to constitute anything of particular philosophical interest. This view, in my understanding, exemplifies a gross misunderstanding, since by the same logic we would be forced to ignore those parts of alleged philosophical texts that have recourse to other sub-genres than the elenchic mode *per se*.

## 6   The Exemplary Part of 4 Maccabees 3:20–18:23

Apart from the philosophical discourse exhibited by 4 Maccabees in the first three chapters (1:1–3:19), we are moving into a melodramatic narrative world full of *pathos* – in terms of genre characterised by the *encomium* and the burial speech – which comes to full expression in the rhetorical staging of a number of ἀγῶνες.[50] Yet it would be awkward to assign these chapters a non-philosophical character, since this part of 4 Maccabees is also permeated with motifs and clusters of ideas well known from philosophical literature. Additionally, they are meant to convey a narrative amplification of the preceding philosophical tenet. Through the narrative ἀγῶνες, the author orches-

---

50   For the importance of the *agōn*-motif in Graeco-Roman popular philosophy (including Philo), see Victor C. Pfitzner, *Paul and the Agon Motif: Traditional Athletic Imagery in the Pauline Literature* (NovT Sup 16; Leiden: Brill, 1967), 23–47. Cf. also Fitzgerald, *Cracks*, 97–100.

trates his understanding of the relationship between Judaism and paganism, which, in the symbolic world of the text, correlates with the overall philosophical principle. The narrative of the martyrs overcoming the tyrant exemplifies how devout reason is absolute master over the passions, since the martyrs embody devout reason and Judaism. Conversely, Antiochus metonymically incarnates paganism at the mercy of passion. Two examples will suffice to illustrate the permeating motif of the ἀγών. Shortly before his martyr death, the oldest of the brothers exhorts his younger brothers, "Imitate me (Μιμήσασθέ με), my brothers; do not become deserters in my trial nor forswear our brotherhood in nobility. Fight the sacred and noble fight for true religion (ἱερὰν καὶ εὐγενῆ στρατείαν στρατεύσασθε περὶ τῆς εὐσεβείας) and through it may the just providence that protected our fathers become merciful to our people and take vengeance on the accursed tyrant" (9:23–24). In the same fashion, the sixth of the brothers challenges the tyrant by scorning him for being at the mercy of his feelings (11:13–16). At the same time as he is excruciatingly tortured, he calmly retorts, "How sacred and seemly is the agony (Ὦ ἱεροπρεποῦς ἀγῶνος) to which so many of my brothers and I have summoned as to a contest in sufferings for piety's sake (διὰ τὴν εὐσεβείαν εἰς γυμνασίαν πόνων), and yet, we have not vanquished (οὐκ ἐνικήθημεν)" (11:20). The martyrs embody the immovability of devout reason in dire contrast to the tyrant, who, in his attempts to persuade the martyrs to refrain from their endeavour, is shown to vacillate continuously between different feelings:

> For religious knowledge (ἡ εὐσεβὴς ἐπιστήμη), tyrant, is unconquerable (ἀνίκετος). Fully armed with goodness I, too, shall die along with my brothers, and I myself, too, shall confront you with one great avenger more, you deviser of new tortures, you enemy of men of true religion (πολέμιε τῶν ἀληθῶς εὐσεβούντων). Six of us, lads though we are, have destroyed your tyranny. For your inability to sway our reason (ὁ λογισμός ἡμῶν) or to force us to eat unclean food, is not that your ruin (κατάλυσίς)? Your fire is cool for us and your catapults painless and your violence powerless. No tyrant's guards, but the guardians of the divine Law (θείου νόμου οἱ δορυφόροι) have been our protectors, and that is why our reason remains undefeated (διὰ τοῦτο ἀνίκετον ἔχομεν τὸν λογισμον). (11:21–27)

The narrative orchestration of the ἀγών motif serves to inculcate and consolidate those virtues which the author considers to be the true encapsulation of the Torah; needless to say, the very same virtues are attributed similar significance in Graeco-Roman moral philosophy. They are, among others, piety (εὐσέβεια), manliness (ἀνδρεία), endurance (ὑπομονή), righteousness (δικαιοσύνη), knowledge (φρόνησις), prudence (σωφροσύνη), temperance (ἐγκράτεια), and self-mastery (ἐπικράτεια). Antiochus' dialogues with the martyrs are an instrumentation of a rhetorical ἀγών, where he and they metonymically represent paganism and Judaism respectively. The rhetorical contests are apologetically interesting because the refutations and accusations put by the author in the mouth of Antiochus most likely correspond to those points of criticism the dominating culture of the era directed against Judaism. In this manner, 4 Maccabees is an apologetic text in the form of a narrative in defence of that Judaism which the author conceived to be the true one and which he considered threatened by internal, dissenting voices and especially by the criticism directed against it from the non-Jewish, Graeco-Roman world. In its basic tone the text is apologetic, as it reacts against an imagined threat to Jewish culture and religion. In terms of voice and melody, however, the text does not come forward as particularly defensive. Rather it may, through its subordination and its inscription of the dominating culture of the epoch into the conceptual world and value system of the author, be seen as representative of an active usurpation and absorption of the universe of the values of this culture. However, such an interpretation does not imply that the text is 'more' Jewish and concomitantly 'less' Hellenistic than a number of contemporaneous texts. On the contrary, the book is an exquisite testimony to the fact that different cultural and religious elements were intrinsically related. For instance, in those passages in which the martyrs emerge as most Jewish, they use terms and concepts closely aligned with thoughts and traditions that we know of from Greek tragedy. In the same fashion, as we find in the Greek tradition of burial speeches – most famously known from Thucydides' staging of Pericles' speech over the dead – in 4 Maccabees an appeal is made to the living to follow the example of the dead by imitating them.

The noble death of the martyrs for virtue (ἀρετή), for the good and true (καλοκἀγαθία), has a close parallel in Graeco-Roman moral philosophy, not least in Plato's use of the figure of Socrates. As Socrates manfully – and in imitation of the virtue to which he, in the philosophical theatre of Plato, devoted his life – went to death for the sake of his conviction, the martyrs in 4 Maccabees die for the sake of their trust in God. 4 Maccabees echoes the well-known maxim of Graeco-Roman moral philosophy pertaining to the figure of Socrates: "Anytus and Meletus may kill me, but they are incapable of harming me" (cf. *Apol.* 30c–d).[51] It is not entirely unfair to take the ending of

---

51   For the prevalence of this statement in subsequent Graeco-Roman popular philosophical literature, see Klaus Dörring, *Socratis. Studien zur Sokratesnachwirkung in der kynisch-stoischen Popularphilosophie der früheren Kaiserzeit und im frühen Christentum* (Hermes 42; Wiesbaden: Franz Steiner Verlag, 1979).

*Gorgias* and turn it into the overall aim of 4 Maccabees: "Let us, then, take the argument as our guide, which has revealed to us that the best way of life is to practice justice and every virtue in life and death. This way, let us go; and in this exhort all men to follow, not in the way to which you trust and in which you exhort me to follow you; for that way, Callicles, is nothing worth!", or Antiochus, I venture to say (*Gorgias* 527e; Epictetus, *Discourses* 4.1.123; Seneca, *De Constantia* 16:4). It is certainly not coincidental that in 4 Maccabees we find a number of encouragements and exhortations in the form of the ship and ocean metaphors of Graeco-Roman moral philosophy to have reason, as an outstanding captain, steer the vessel of piety on the sea of passion (7:1–5; 13:6–7).

## 7 Conclusion: *Wie Alles sich zum Ganzen webt, eins in dem Anderen wirkt und lebt*

David deSilva may be quite right when, with respect to 4 Maccabees, he asserts that the best description of the book is to understand it as "a sort of 'protreptic' discourse similar to Epictetus' discourse on the true Cynic (*Discourses* 3.22) – an oration which mingles philosophical argumentation and vivid examples of the philosophy at work, all for the purpose of making that philosophy more credible (4 *Macc*. 7.9), appealing and worth wholehearted commitment."[52]

4 Maccabees is a Jewish manifestation of Graeco-Roman moral philosophy. Through his protreptic discourse, the author of the book apologetically aims to retain the Torah as the embodiment of the truest form of philosophy, an assertion made in a discursive argument unfolded in a melodramatic narrative, but definitely not as something to be ascribed to a non-argumentative, divine, authorial instance. The author's use of the burial speech and the *encomium* in the narrative world of the text bears witness to the fact that he sees his Jewish world as being threatened by failing zeal for and lack of uncompromising fidelity towards the Jewish law. In this particular situation, the author, by virtue of his textual creation, aims to strengthen and to consolidate the commitment of his intended audience to the Torah. He does this, firstly, by philosophically substantiating that the Torah is the means to overcome and rule over the passions and, secondly, by elevating the martyrs as an *exemplum* for the intended audience to imitate.

So, ultimately, do philosophy and religion constitute two different discourses, as testified by this particular text? No, I do not think so. In fact, I

---

52  deSilva, *4 Maccabees*, 28.

hold that 4 Maccabees bears witness to an understanding of the relationship between philosophy and religion and their interactions in the ancient Graeco-Roman world in which they – formulated in the words from *Faust* – may be seen as deeply entangled with each other: *Wie Alles sich zum Ganzen webt, eins in dem Anderen wirkt und lebt!* (Faust 1, 447–48).

4 Maccabees is not only representative of an Axial Age type of religiosity in terms of cultural evolution, but the book also exhibits a Jewish text deeply enmeshed in the traditions of Graeco-Roman popular philosophy of the first century CE with a particularly strong penchant towards a Platonic worldview and, in terms of ethos, with a propensity towards Stoicism. To dissolve the work into 'Jewish' and 'Graeco-Roman' elements or 'religious' and 'philosophical' elements would do violence to the interwoven nature of traditions that appear different from each other only by virtue of our time-honoured perceptual filters.

# The Rapprochement of Religion and Philosophy in Ancient Consolation: Seneca, Paul, and Beyond

*Christoph Jedan*

Over the last century, the interpretation of ancient philosophy has been dominated by approaches attempting to separate philosophy from religion. In the present chapter I take issue with this trend and argue that we should strive for a rapprochement between religion and philosophy in antiquity (see section one below).

The pursuit of new historiographies is by no means an easy task. Many of the conceptual tools used in the interpretation of ancient philosophical texts carry with them the baggage of being dismissive of anything that smells even faintly of religion. To develop better conceptual tools as well as to demonstrate the potential of 'historiographies of rapprochement', I use as a source of promising case studies the ancient practice of consoling by means of persuasive speech acts ('arguments'). My initial focus is Seneca's *Ad Marciam* (see section two below). I discuss the case study in some detail in order to demonstrate how concepts stemming from recent social scientific research on grieving can sharpen our perception of what is going on in the text (e.g., 'assumptive worlds', 'continuing bonds', and 'symbolic immortality'), and I suggest new conceptual tools (e.g., 'theo-philosophy' and 'integrative concepts') that can help us account for the impossibility of disentangling religion from philosophy in Graeco-Roman antiquity (and, I hope, far beyond).

I then offer suggestions as to how we could gradually broaden the focus from the *Ad Marciam* to discuss other consolatory texts, *inter alia* the consolatory passages in Paul's epistles (see section three). From the perspective established by the interpretation of Seneca's *Ad Marciam*, these letters show a high degree of continuity with ancient 'philosophical' modes of consolation.

In the conclusion (section four), I draw together the strands of the discussion. If the number and extent of the commonalities between Paul and 'philosophical' argumentative consolation make it impossible to convincingly differentiate 'philosophy' from 'religion' or 'theology', it seems better to avoid such labels for the wide array of texts that are clearly somewhere between the poles of 'religion' and 'philosophy'.

## 1 Overcoming Historiographies of Separation

There can be little doubt that we observe a strong secularist tendency in those Western societies which seek to marginalise the import of religion. Even historical and philosophical research have succumbed to this tendency. In the area of Stoic studies, a good example is John Sellars' dismissal of Victorian interpretations in his – otherwise excellent – introduction to Stoicism. Sellars writes,

> This Victorian interest in Stoic authors, like many aspects of Victorian culture, ignored the developments of the Enlightenment and harked back to an earlier period. Marcus and Epictetus were read again as friends of Christianity, just as the Neostoics had read them some three hundred years earlier. Diderot's judgment in the *Encyclopédie* was seemingly forgotten. Within this context a number of books were written about the late Stoics, including F.W. Farrar's *Seekers After God* (1868) and Alston's *Stoic and Christian in the Second Century* (1906). These presentations of the late Stoics as quasi-religious thinkers no doubt did as much damage to the development of serious Stoic scholarship as the unfavourable judgments of the German classicists earlier in the century.[1]

It is hard not to be struck by the unfairness of this critique. Neither Farrar nor Alston was able to profit from Johannes von Arnim's collection of Stoic fragments and testimonies (1903–1924), which inaugurated modern research on the earlier phases of Stoicism.[2] In the absence of this scholarly tool, research was inevitably directed at the later Stoics (Seneca, Epictetus, and Marcus Aurelius), of whom we have extensive written records. In effect, an objective reader of, for instance, Epictetus would find it difficult to explain how his philosophy could be separated from religion. Moreover, the claim that the Victorians interpreted the Stoics simply as 'friends of Christianity' is blatantly false. In fact, the Victorians had a good eye for the ambivalence of the relationship between Stoics and Christians. Farrar, for instance, writes, "The Christians disliked the Stoics, the Stoics despised and persecuted the Christians."[3] And indeed, Farrar

---

[1] John Sellars, *Stoicism* (Berkeley/Los Angeles: University of California Press, 2006), 153.
[2] Leonard Alston, *Stoic and Christian in the Second Century: A Comparison of the Ethical Teaching of Marcus Aurelius with that of Contemporary and Antecedent Christianity* (London/New York: Longmans, Green & Company, 1906); Johannes von Arnim, *Stoicorum veterum fragmenta* (4 vols; Stuttgart: Teubner, 1903–27).
[3] Fredric William Farrar, *Seekers after God* (London: Macmillan, 1868), 103.

in particular has a keen eye for the social and cultural gap between the Stoics and the early Christians and the contingencies of the cultural developments ever since. He evokes in a Pythonesque manner how Paul might have appeared to the haughty, wealthy, eloquent, prosperous, powerful philosopher Seneca: as "a poor, accused, and wandering Jew... whom, if he had heard of him, he would have regarded as a poor wretch, half fanatic and half barbarian."[4]

What Sellars' critique comes down to, in the end, is the claim that scholarship which highlights religion in philosophical texts is not to be taken seriously simply because it highlights religion in philosophical texts. Religion and serious philosophy have always been, and must be in principle, two different things. In this chapter, I argue that instead of pursuing such historiographies of separation, we should build historiographies of rapprochement.

One can pursue the goal of an historiographical rapprochement between religion and philosophy in two ways. The first way is weaker: it aims to show that philosophers use religious ideas, and that religious authors use philosophical ideas, while maintaining that religion and philosophy are separate realms. Thus, since religion and philosophy remain separate realms, we can – and indeed must – ask why religious authors were taking over philosophical ideas and why philosophers were taking over religious ideas.[5]

While this would be a perfectly feasible strategy as a default option, I suggest we should aim for a stronger historiographical approach. To illustrate the stronger approach, I propose the notion of a continuum between religion and philosophy. While at one extremity there are 'religious' authors who would have little to do with the persuasive strategies and tactics employed by 'the philosophers', and at the other extremity there are philosophers whose interest in religion is slight or even negative, we find an extended central area in which the crossovers between what we might be tempted to describe as 'the religious' and what we might be inclined to characterise as 'the philosophical' are so pervasive that it remains difficult to maintain any hard-and-fast distinctions between religion and philosophy. Perhaps we ought to continue to employ the terms 'religion' and 'philosophy' in order to respond to a deeply rooted intuition that a corpus of texts or an approach is either philosophical or religious, but it is with the understanding that we would be hard-pressed to find any convincing criteria that match and support such an intuition.

---

4 Ibid.
5 The publications of Troels Engberg-Pedersen (for example, *Paul and the Stoics* [Edinburgh: T & T Clark, 2000]) on the interaction of Stoicism and Pauline theology are, in my view, an exemplar of this approach.

I suggest that Stoicism is a prime candidate, situated indisputably in the extended middle of this continuum. Where the crossovers between religion and philosophy become so pervasive, one could say that quantity translates into quality. We have what we could call a 'religious' movement in the sense that it is a 'philosophical religion' or, if you will, a 'religious philosophy' which is being practised. But perhaps, I suggest, it is better to discard such assemblages that still bear witness to a history of antagonism and to reach for a new label. For this purpose, I suggest 'theo-philosophy' as a term to identify the extended centre of overlap between philosophy and religion.

To support and illustrate my historiographical approach, I analyse argumentative consolation for death as a cultural phenomenon *par excellence*, transcending the boundaries between the two supposedly separate realms of philosophy and religion. The central case study, from which I develop this perspective, is Seneca's *Ad Marciam*.[6]

## 2 A Case Study: Seneca's *Ad Marciam* as Category-Defying Enterprise

### 2.1 *Argumentative Consolation*

While I take my cue from an extended consolatory text, I should like to stress that my approach is not intended to contribute to a history of 'the genre' of the *consolatio*. Dictionary definitions, such as the OED's ("A consolatory treatise, letter, or poem (sometimes an alternation of prose and verse) in Greek, Latin, or a vernacular tongue, setting forth philosophical or religious themes as comfort for the misfortunes of life"), convey the impression that there is a well-delineated genre of the *consolatio*. In the same vein, older studies in the field have focused on consolatory texts as exemplars of that genre; they thus aim at writing its history.[7] The genre approach, however, is highly problematic

---

6 This is an attractive choice, given Seneca's prominence in the Western consolatory tradition and his being a contemporary of Paul, another mainstay of Western consolation, thus inviting comparison between the two. The *Ad Marciam* is the earliest of Seneca's three extended consolations (*Ad Marciam*, *Ad Helviam*, and *Ad Polybium*) and is the earliest extant large-scale consolatory letter in Latin.

7 For general overviews, see for example F.-B. Stammkötter, "Trost," *Historisches Wörterbuch der Philosophie* 10 (1998): 1523–7; Günter Stemberger and E. Kohler, "Trost" (I-III), *TRE* 34 (2002): 143–53. Ancient philosophical and early Christian consolation is *inter alia* analysed in Carolus [= Karl] Buresch, "Consolationum a Graecis Romanisque scriptarum historia critica," *Leipziger Studien zur Classischen Philologie* 9 (1887): 1–170; Charles Favez, *La consolation latine chrétienne* (Paris: J. Vrin, 1937); Rudolf Kassel, *Untersuchungen zur griechis-*

on two counts. First, it tends to lump together different sorts of texts that have different literary functions and follow different literary conventions. Looking back to the OED definition, we might identify those texts as letters that are often directed at identifiable individuals or groups of people, treatises that display a more abstract approach to loss, and poems.[8]

Second, the genre approach lends credence to what I propose to call the 'siren of unity', which has marred much scholarship on consolation. It is propped up by two interconnected assumptions: (1) that texts have only a single purpose, and (2) that in order to qualify as consolatory, the whole text must be shown to be 'a consolation'. Both assumptions, however, are highly implausible. If it could be shown that consolatory texts had, for instance, a political 'subtext' or another, additional meaning,[9] this would abrogate the status of the text in question as consolatory. Moreover, I would argue that it is often implausible to consider an entire text as consolatory. For instance, it is highly unlikely that any Pauline letter as a whole is a consolation.[10] It is far more plausible to attribute a consolatory purport to certain passages in the Pauline letters, just as it is far more plausible to assume that texts can have more than one mean-

---

*chen und römischen Konsolationsliteratur* (Munich: Beck, 1958); Horst-Theodor Johann, *Trauer und Trost: Eine quellen- und strukturanalytische Untersuchung der philosophischen Trostschriften über den Tod* (Munich: Fink, 1968); Robert C. Gregg, *Consolation Philosophy: Greek and Christian Paideia in Basil and the Two Gregories* (Cambridge, MA: Philadelphia Patristic Foundation, 1975); Paul A. Holloway, *Consolation in Philippians. Philosophical Sources and Rhetorical Strategy* (Cambridge: Cambridge University Press, 2001); Concepción Alonso del Real, ed., *Consolatio. Nueve estudios* (Pamplona: Ediciones de la Universidad de Navarra, 2001); and Fernando Lillo Redonet, *Palabras contra el dolor. La consolación filosófica latina de Cicerón a Frontón* (Madrid: Ediciones Clásicas, 2001). The collection by Han Baltussen, ed., *Greek and Roman Consolations. Eight Studies of a Tradition and Its Afterlife* (Swansea: The Classical Press of Wales, 2013) is a powerful voice against the genre approach critiqued above (see Christoph Jedan, "Cruciale teksten: De Grieks-Romeinse consolatio," *Nederlands Theologisch Tijdschrift* 68 nos. 1 and 2 (2014): 165–73).

8   For this reason, David Scourfield ("Towards a Genre of Consolation," in *Greek and Roman Consolations: Eight Studies of a Tradition and its Afterlife* (ed. Hans Baltussen; Swansea: The Classical Press of Wales, 2013), 1–36) has suggested a new map of consolatory writing that centres on the social practice of offering comfort. In the middle are texts that convey consolation for specific individuals in an 'address mode'; at the margins are texts that operate in a 'reflective mode', which one could label 'metaconsolatory'. The latter texts operate much in the style of a philosophical treatise (e.g., Cicero's *Tusculan Disputations*).
9   See Marcus Wilson, "Seneca the Consoler? A New Reading of his Consolatory Writings," in *Greek and Roman Consolations*, 93–121, for Seneca's consolations.
10  *Pace* Holloway (*Consolation in Philippians*), who makes a case for Philippians as consolation.

ing. Surely a letter can be a serious, heartfelt consolation while at the same time containing a sneer against dictatorship? In short, if we want to conduct meaningful comparisons between ancient philosophical and early Christian modes of consolation (and then show that differentiation between the modes is problematic), we should not pay heed to the siren's call.

I suggest that instead of considering questions of genre, we ought to focus on the social practice of offering consolation by means of arguments ('argumentative consolation'). This practice (1) allows specific comparisons with respect to argumentative content, (2) is sufficiently widespread to be instantiated across different cultural traditions, and (3) displays a surprising degree of durability over time and thus offers the possibility of diachronic comparisons.

Of course, I have to explicate in more detail what I mean by 'argument'. The label 'argument' identifies persuasive speech acts aimed at putting loss into perspective and thus at attenuating or overcoming grief. By using the terminology of persuasive speech acts, it becomes clear that I wish to avoid an overly limited understanding of the word 'argument'. Arguments in the required sense are not merely forms of reasoning one comes across in textbooks on logic; they include a wide array of images and stratagems that offer an interpretation of the loss and of wider reality. Such arguments structure reality in different ways (alethically, deontically, etc.) and propose what the sender sees as constructive and helpful ways of coping with the loss. Seneca's detailing in *Ad Marciam* of the afterlife that might await Marcia's son Metilius and his admonishing her is a case in point (25.3): "Do you therefore, Marcia, always act as if you knew that the eyes of your father and your son were set upon you—not such as you once knew them, but far loftier beings, dwelling in the highest heaven. Blush to have a low or common thought, and to weep for those dear ones who have changed for the better!"[11] The passage can fruitfully be compared to Paul's admonition in 1 Thessalonians 4:13 (REB): "You should not grieve like the rest of mankind, who have no hope," which is conjoined with his expression of hope in an afterlife that is given to the believers and with the fact that "Jesus died and rose again" (1 Thessalonians 4:14).

The cultural phenomenon of argumentative consolation has received little attention in philosophical and theological scholarship.[12] This is not wholly sur-

---

11 Here and in what follows I use the edition and translation of John W. Basore, ed./trans., *Seneca, Moral Essays, Volume II* (Cambridge, MA/London: Harvard University Press, 1932).

12 See Jedan, "Troost door argumenten: Herwaardering van een filosofische en christelijke traditie," *Nederlands Theologisch Tijdschrift* 68 nos. 1 and 2 (2014): 7–22.

prising, given today's heavy emphasis on non-intervening, non-judgemental empathy as a standard route in grief counselling. Seen from this perspective, ancient argumentative consolation might appear insensitive and crucially lacking in much-needed empathy.

I contend that the contrast between reason and argument on the one hand and the emotions on the other is not only alien to the ancient moral psychologies that undergird argumentative consolation; it is also shown to be parochial by recent trends towards interpreting the emotions as cognitive phenomena, which are to a large extent re-appreciations of ancient theories of the emotions.[13]

### 2.2  Context and Argumentative Strategy

It is most likely that Seneca wrote his consolation for Marcia in or shortly after 40 CE. Marcia, a friend of the Empress Livia, suffered from what we nowadays might call 'complicated grief', which was due to an accumulation of traumatic losses.[14] She had lost her father, Aulus Cremutius Cordus, who was forced to commit suicide under Tiberius in 25 CE, and her oldest son, one of four children (two sons, two daughters), and she had borne these losses admirably. In the case of her father, she had acted as his literary executor as soon as political circumstances permitted. But then her second son, Metilius, to whom she was particularly close, also died. Marcia collapsed. She failed to re-engage with life. For three years, she led a secluded life and even neglected Metilius' children (her own grandchildren). In response to this situation, Seneca wrote his letter.

It is necessary to take a step back in order to appreciate the doctrines that inevitably underpin argumentative consolation. First and foremost, grief is considered a destabilising and undesirable emotion. As Cicero's schematic differentiation of the therapeutic tasks (*officia*) of consolers makes clear, such activities must be directed at the grief, either by eradicating it, or at least by reducing the hold it exerts over the life of the bereaved.[15] In the same vein,

---

13    See for example Martha C. Nussbaum, *Upheavals of Thought: The Intelligence of the Emotions* (Cambridge: Cambridge University Press, 2001); David Konstan, *The Emotions of the Ancient Greeks: Studies in Aristotle and Classical Literature* (Toronto/Buffalo/London: University of Toronto Press, 2006); Sabine A. Döring, ed., *Philosophie der Gefühle* (Frankfurt: Suhrkamp, 2009). For more on the theory underpinning ancient consolation that grief is a cognitive phenomenon, see below.

14    See for example Linda Machin, *Working with Loss and Grief: A New Model for Practitioners* (London/Thousand Oaks, CA: SAGE, 2009), 45–7.

15    *Tusculan Disputations* 3.75.

Seneca lays down in the first sentence of his letter that he is about to assail Marcia's grief (*obviam ire dolori tuo*, 1.1).[16]

Second, in order for consolation to be possible at all, grief (like other emotions) must to some extent be under the control of the bereaved. For the ancient consolers, this doctrine was underpinned by a third, closely connected conviction: grief (like other emotions) has what we might call, for want of better terminology, a 'cognitive component'. Grief depends on an evaluative perception of or a judgement about reality, and in particular about the loss that has been experienced. This explains why there is agency on the part of the bereaved: their grief depends on a value judgement of this kind, namely that 'something dreadful has happened'. The ancient argumentative consolers were convinced that such value judgements are consistently wrong. This is why the argumentative intervention of the consolers is warranted. The consoland has formed a mistaken judgement(s), and now the therapy aims to set straight the consoland's perspective. Again, in the very first sentence of his letter, Seneca identifies Marcia's mistaken judgement by stating his hope that Marcia will drop her bitter charges against Fortune (*ut fortunam tuam absolveres*, 1.1).

I suggest that the three philosophical doctrines that underpin argumentative consolation help us to understand the structure and content of argumentative consolatory texts far better than previous scholarship, which focused on identifying structures derived from ancient rhetoric. Seneca is not so much concerned to give his letter the right *prooemium*, stating in a detached style that the time is ripe for his letter,[17] but he attempts right from the outset to strike a delicate balance. On the one hand, he acknowledges the full extent of Marcia's losses; on the other hand, he wants to rekindle in her an appreciation of her capacity for resilience. Again, this is not – or at least not primarily – to tick the boxes of a rhetorical handbook. Seneca needs to strike this delicate

---

[16] To us today, this might at first sight seem alien, steeped as we are in a rhetoric that 'grief must run its course'. This widespread conviction might be understood as expressive of a fear of insensitively policing another person's grief and laying down schedules of recovery for them. We should note, however, that stage theories of grieving are a modern invention (see for example Elisabeth Kübler-Ross, *On Death and Dying: What the Dying Have to Teach Doctors, Nurses, Clergy, and Their Own Families* [New York: Macmillan, 1969]); Seneca's letter – in line with much other argumentative consolation – is extremely careful in establishing that a therapeutic, argumentative intervention is timely. Arguably, Marcia's protracted and intense grieving is of a nature that justifies intervention in the form of a letter.

[17] Cf. Constantine C. Grollios, *Seneca's Ad Marciam: Tradition and Originality* (Athens: G. S. Christou, 1956).

balance because it is a necessary condition of all argumentative consolation. For argumentative consolation to be effective, the consoland needs to retain or regain a sense of their own agency in the face of adversity. In other words, argumentative consolation is crucially about an empowerment of the consoland. This is why Seneca, in parallel with acknowledging Marcia's losses, reiterates how strong she really is: she is "as far removed from womanish weakness of mind as from all other vices;" her "virtue was looked upon as a model of ancient virtue;" she coped admirably with the loss of her beloved father and even acted with great personal courage as his literary executor; and so forth (1.1–4). However, in no way does this abrogate Seneca's sensitivity to Marcia's losses and his empathy for her.

## 2.3  Keeping Together Consolation and Argument

We have seen that in order to fully understand Seneca's text, we have to take it seriously as an attempt to console by means of arguments rather than as an attempt to fit the agenda of a fixed literary genre and fixed rhetorical forms.

However, the failure to take Seneca's text seriously as argumentative consolation has marred much modern scholarship in another way, as scholars have been much troubled by the perception that Seneca's text exhibits a certain eclecticism. As a Stoic, or so runs the assumption of modern scholars, Seneca ought to adhere to a Stoic moral psychology pure and simple. The problem is closely connected to the third principle underpinning argumentative consolation. I wrote above that the ancient argumentative consolers were convinced that value judgements leading to grief 'are regularly wrong'. Now it is time to refine this statement in order to appreciate how Stoic moral psychology differed from the moral psychologies of other ancient schools. Whereas some consolers were convinced that moderate grief is acceptable and so aimed their therapy at pruning excessive grief (*metriopatheia*), others saw grief as an unwanted emotion *tout court* and attempted to rid the consoland of it completely (*apatheia*). The first stance can roughly be associated with the moral psychology of the Academy and the Peripatos, the second with the Stoa. However, in *Ad Marciam* as well as in other consolatory texts, Seneca seems to show considerable sympathy for the theory of *metriopatheia*.[18] Recently, Marcus Wilson has critically elaborated on this line of interpretation. In his view, "[i]t is an underestimation of the strength of Seneca's position to describe it as an acceptance of *metriopatheia*, for that is to convert into a positive doctrine what for

---

18   C.E. Manning, "The Consolatory Tradition and Seneca's Attitude to the Emotions," *Greece and Rome* 21 (1974): 71–81; Manning, *On Seneca's 'Ad Marciam'* (Leiden: Brill, 1981).

Seneca is quintessentially a negative action in disowning the ideal of *apatheia*. The rejection is not only of a specific Stoic ideal but also of the fitness of any philosophical doctrinal framework to the practical work of defeating grief."[19]

In my view, Wilson's stance fails as an interpretation of Seneca's consolatory texts. In line with the widespread neglect of argumentative consolation in today's culture, Wilson plays out consolation against reason-giving, or against what he terms 'philosophy'. To support his claim, he comes up with a problematic picture of philosophy, arguing that Seneca goes out of his way so as not to "specify the doctrinal source of his consolatory arguments... Rightly so, because where the apparent aim is to console, this kind of academic 'footnoting' would be wholly counterproductive and likely to do little more than annoy the grief-stricken recipient. Seneca is only sometimes a philosopher."[20] If we measured philosophy against the criterion of careful academic referencing of sources and allegiances, I fear that little of ancient philosophy would qualify. The conflation of philosophy with writing for academic journals results in Wilson's contention that "one of the most remarkable feature of Seneca's consolations is the almost complete absence of philosophy."[21]

This entails, however, losing sight of our task in interpreting the *Ad Marciam* as well as other consolatory texts, which is to appreciate them as argumentative consolations, efforts at combatting grief that do not warrant a contrast between argument and consolation. It is crucial to understand those texts as instances of engaged thinking, truly argumentative and truly directed towards the support of embodied human beings at the same time. For want of better descriptors, we could call them instances of 'pastoral thinking' or – anticipating the results of our discussion – instances of 'pastoral theo-philosophy'.

### 2.4  *Defining Intellectual Space: The 'Socratic Alternative'*

Contrary to what Wilson suggests, Seneca's pastoral theo-philosophy is not characterised by sloppiness. He pinpoints *Ad Marciam* 19.4 (in his translation: "Consider that the dead are affected by no evils, and that those things that instil in us fear of the underworld are fictitious") and argues, "In the conso-

---

19   Wilson, "Seneca the Consoler?" 108. Wilson even goes on to deny that defeating grief was the purport of Seneca's consolations: "It is more important to contend with grief than to be free of it" (109). Unfortunately the passages Wilson quotes ("It is better, says Seneca, to defeat sorrow than to try to trick it," *Ad Helviam matrem* 17.2) do not support his claim, and the passages quoted above (*Ad Marciam* 1.1: assailing Marcia's grief; 25.3: do not weep) contradict it. There is more on *metriopatheia* and *apatheia* in Seneca's *Ad Marciam* below.
20   Wilson, "Seneca the Consoler?" 105.
21   Ibid.

lation, Marcia is not encouraged to notice that this argument clashes logically with the picture of her son's life after death that will be drawn in the last sentences."[22] What he overlooks, however, is that Seneca's consolation is modelled on the template of Plato's *Apology*.[23] At 40c–41d, Plato has Socrates explain why his death sentence is no evil to him. Socrates distinguishes two scenarios: either death is the absolute end of human existence and thus the end of human perception, or it is like a relocation to another place.[24] In the first case, death must be likened to a profound, dreamless sleep, which would be supremely worthwhile;[25] in the second case, Socrates expects that he, a just and innocently executed man, will find himself in the company of poets and heroes of the past, to be and to converse with whom would constitute indescribable happiness.[26] Socrates sums up his discussion as follows: "You too must be of good hope as regards death, gentlemen of the jury, and keep this one truth in mind, that the good man (ἀνδρὶ ἀγαθῷ) cannot be harmed either in life or in death, and that his affairs are not neglected by the gods."[27]

I have proposed elsewhere to call the above argumentative structure the 'Socratic alternative': death is either the end of human existence or the transition to a postmortal existence, but in neither case is it an evil.[28] Important in the Socratic alternative is the emphasis on goodness, on virtue. Virtue rounds off a life and makes it complete. If you have acquired virtue, you have achieved the single most important thing in this life, or perhaps the only important thing; if you have virtue, your life cannot be said to be incomplete. The possession of virtue effectively insulates a life against loss. Needless to say, this is a highly revisionist conception of the good life (εὐδαιμονία). Why is that? Because talk of virtue shifts the focus from what someone has achieved (if you will, a list of plans, attachments, and projects) to how someone has lived.[29] This is a clever

---

22  Wilson, "Seneca the Consoler?" 100.
23  See Jedan, "Troost door argumenten."
24  Plato, *Apology* 40c5–9: δυοῖν γὰρ θάτερόν ἐστιν τὸ τεθνάναι· ἢ γὰρ οἷον μηδὲν εἶναι μηδὲ αἴσθησιν μηδεμίαν μηδενὸς ἔχειν τὸν τεθνεῶτα, ἢ κατὰ τὰ λεγόμενα μεταβολή τις τυγχάνει οὖσα καὶ μετοίκησις τῇ ψυχῇ τοῦ τόπου τοῦ ἐνθένδε εἰς ἄλλον τόπον.
25  Plato, *Apology* 40e2–3: εἰ οὖν τοιοῦτον ὁ θάνατός ἐστιν, κέρδος ἔγωγε λέγω.
26  Plato, *Apology* 40e4–41c4: οἷς ἐκεῖ διαλέγεσθαι καὶ συνεῖναι καὶ ἐξετάζειν ἀμήχανον ἂν εἴη εὐδαιμονίας.
27  Plato, *Apology* 41c8–d2, trans. Grube.
28  See Jedan, "Troost door argumenten."
29  For the differentiation between *what* and *how* in Stoicism, see Jedan, *Stoic Virtues: Chrysippus and the Religious Character of Stoic Ethics* (London/New York: Continuum, 2009), esp. ch. 11; for its application to ancient consolation, see Jedan, "Troost door argumenten."

move indeed: a list of plans, attachments, and projects – which we all, in our normal mode, find extremely important – is in principle endless, and death would always curtail something important. So for consolation to be possible, one has to change one's perspective. Virtue is exemplified in whatever you do; virtue brings about the necessary biographical closure. What Socrates does here is to ask his audience to rethink their perspective on what is supremely important in life.

I suggest that the Socratic alternative defines the intellectual space in which ancient consolation is played out, in two ways at least. First, I show how Seneca's *Ad Marciam*, together with many other ancient 'philosophical' consolations, engages with the two options of the Socratic alternative. Second, I suggest that ancient consolations – including Christian consolations – revolve around the virtue-ethical core of the Socratic alternative sketched above: consolation is sought in the completeness of the life of the deceased, and this completeness is envisaged as the acquisition and possession of virtue. I argue that the common virtue-ethical core allows us to explain the continuity between philosophical and theological modes of argumentative consolation. I will return to the latter claim in the next section. In the remainder of the present section, I develop my claim that the options of the Socratic alternative provide a structure both for the *Ad Marciam* and for other ancient philosophical consolations.

Epicurean authors, for instance, chose the first part of the alternative and radicalised it, explicitly shunning the rhetoric of 'death as sleep' as conveying a mistaken sense of the continuity of human experience beyond death.[30] Cicero argues on the basis of the Epicurean interpretation when he uses the mould of the Socratic alternative in his discussion of death and the afterlife in *Tusculan Disputations* 1. That the Socratic alternative was felt to be a structuring feature of ancient consolation is confirmed by its explicit use in the Pseudo-Plutarchian *Consolatio ad Apollonium*, a treatise pre-occupied with offering a survey of ancient consolatory material.[31]

The Socratic alternative plays the same role as a structuring device in Seneca's *Ad Marciam*. Seneca first suggests (19.4–21.1) that Metilius' death, although early, brought him no evil. In accord with the Socratic alternative, he interprets death both as the complete end of Metilius' existence and also as a rest, providing liberation from mundane afflictions and offering well-deserved peace: "Death is a release from all suffering (*Mors dolorum omnium exsolutio est et finis*), a boundary beyond which our ills cannot pass – it restores us

---

30  On Epicurean consolation, see section three.
31  See in particular Pseudo-Plutarch, *Consolatio ad Apollonium* 107d–109f and 119e *ad finem*.

to that peaceful state (*tranquillitatem* ... *reponit*) in which we lay before we were born" (19.5), which is also described as "a great and everlasting peace" (*magna et aeterna pax*, 19.6). A little later in the text (23.1), Seneca turns to the second part of the Socratic alternative. Having died young, Metilius' soul is unlikely to be overly attached to mundane things and will have travelled easily to the heavenly sphere (*facillimum ad superos iter est animis cito ab humana conversatione dimissis*, 23.1). Metilius' soul had early reached the perfection of virtue (23.3; 24.1), and, stripped by death of all exterior limitations, he strives towards a heavenly place where he is welcomed by his grandfather and other heroes of the past (*Excepit illum coetus sacer, Scipiones Catonesque, interque contemptores vitae et veneficio liberos parens tuus, Marcia*, 25.1). The afterlife awaiting Metilius is one of cognitive fulfilment; he is initiated into Nature's secrets (*arcana naturae*). He beholds with pleasure the things he left behind (*Et in profunda terrarum permittere aciem iubet; iuvat enim ex alto relicta respicere*, 25.2). With this imagery of Metilius' afterlife, Seneca counsels Marcia to abandon her grief with an admonition that by no means reads as an endorsement of *metriopatheia* or a "disowning of the ideal of *apatheia*" (25.3): "Do you therefore, Marcia, always act as if you knew that the eyes of your father and your son were set upon you—not such as you once knew them, but far loftier beings, dwelling in the highest heaven. Blush to have a low or common thought, and to weep for those dear ones who have changed for the better."

So Seneca follows the Socratic alternative and, what is more, he employs it purposefully. He uses the two options of the Socratic alternative to refute different accusations made by Marcia against Fate. In a carefully developed argument, he uses the first, more limited and defensive option to refute the weaker accusation and the more expansive, second option to refute the weightier accusation. The two charges against Fate are: (1) that Metilius' death is an evil, and (2) that his having died prematurely is an evil.[32] Seneca corrects the misapprehension underlying the first charge by pointing out *inter alia* that mortality is the common lot of all human beings. In this context, he uses the first option of the Socratic alternative as showing that even if death were no more than annihilation of the person, it would be no evil. When he turns to the second, weightier charge, he starts out by building on the limited and defensive option of the Socratic paradox: he shows the insignificance of the human lifespan when compared to the universe, so that on a cosmic scale any additional

---

32  *Ad Marciam* 19.3: "What, then, Marcia, is it that troubles you?—the fact that your son has died, or that he did not live long?" (*Quid igitur te, Marcia, movet? Utrum quod filius tuus decessit, an quod non diu vixit?*)

life-time remains insignificant. Seneca reinforces the sense of insignificance by showing that even the world as a whole is transitory, since it "renews itself over and over within the bounds of time" (*cum ille* [*sc. mundus*] *se intra huius spatium totiens remetiatur*, 21.2). With this, Seneca alludes to the Stoic doctrine of cyclic conflagration of the world: the divine element consumes the other elements and remains alone until a new world-cycle begins. The doctrine of cyclic conflagration functions as a connector between the first and second option of the Socratic alternative. The Stoics were convinced that human souls could survive death, but that conflagration is the ultimate endpoint of the souls' existence.[33] Seneca makes use of the second option of the Socratic alternative from the perspective of the Stoic doctrine of conflagration. Metilius does enjoy a *post mortem* existence, in which he is welcomed by a community of saints and is initiated into Nature's secrets (see above). At the same time, it is important to note that what Seneca presents as the supreme insight gained during *post mortem* existence is precisely the transitoriness of the world: ultimately the world as we know it will swallowed up in a conflagration, to be recreated by God.[34] In addition, the souls who have enjoyed a *post mortem* existence will undergo conflagration and be dissolved into their former elements. The prospect of conflagration, however, is far from being a threatening scenario; it should be considered supreme fulfilment to be implicated in this grand cosmic process. Seneca concludes: "Happy, Marcia, is your son, who already knows all this" (*Felicem filium tuum, Marcia, qui ista iam novit!* 26.7, trans. Basore, modified).

Seneca thus skilfully adapts the Socratic alternative to Stoic doctrine. He does not produce a contradiction that "Marcia is not encouraged to notice," as Wilson has claimed (see above). Instead, he formulates what could be described as an 'ascent', starting out with the limited option that Metilius' death is his extinction and revisiting this scenario on a higher level. Marcia is assured

---

33  See Jedan, *Stoic Virtues*, 14–17. Among the early Stoics there seems to have been a debate in which Cleanthes held that all souls last until conflagration, whereas Chrysippus held the more restrictive view that only the soul of the sage does. With his emphasis on Metilius' virtue and phrases such as 'great souls' (*magnis ingenis*: 23.2; *felices animae*: 26.7), Seneca seems to incline towards the Chrysippean stance, without claiming sagehood for Metilius.

34  *Ad Marciam* 26.6–7: *Et cum tempus advenerit, quo se mundus renovaturus extinguat, viribus ista se suis caedent et sidera sideribus incurrent et omni flagrante materia uno igni quicquid nunc ex disposito lucet ardebit. Nos quoque felices animae et aeterna sortitae, cum deo visum erit iterum ista moliri, labentibus cuncties et ipsae parva ruinae ingentis accessio in antiqua elementa vertemur.*

of a highly attractive afterlife for Metilius, but even so, the lifespan of his soul is limited by cosmic conflagration. The difference in outlook produced by the ascent is the realisation that the souls who enjoy a *post mortem* existence not only acquiesce in the limitation of human life but positively embrace it. They have already learnt the lesson that Seneca puts into Cremutius Cordus' mouth for Marcia's sake: the ultimate destruction of the souls is part and parcel of their being implicated in the grand cosmic process under divine administration. Their joyful assent must teach Marcia to be reconciled with the finitude of Metilius' life. This is the ultimate consolation that Seneca can offer.

## 2.5  Cutting Across Categories

What defines the specific profile of Seneca's consolation and, at the same time, makes it difficult for us to appreciate is the fact that it cuts across categories that many scholars today strive to keep apart. Let me discuss three instances.

First, at the most general level, Seneca's consolation cuts across the distinction between 'consolation' and 'argument' that seems to have become a cultural orthodoxy for us today (see section one above).

Second, Seneca's use (and, indeed, adaptation) of the Socratic alternative transcends the opposition between what I propose to term 'real' immortality and psychologist Robert Jay Lifton's concept of a merely 'symbolic' immortality. If 'real' immortality is thought of as unlimited continuance of the individual soul, it is clear that this is not what Seneca has to offer: he uses the term immortality (*aeterna sortitae*, 26.7) to refer to a limited, although possibly long, period of existence. Lifton's concept of a symbolic immortality, by contrast, epitomises the widespread cultural backlash against real immortality. He follows Freud in stating,

> The danger with religious images of immortality is that they can quickly lose their symbolic quality and result in the assertion that people don't really die. ...Such images as heaven, hell, reincarnation, and the resurrection of the body are often understood in the same sense as scientific observations of nature. Thus, the concept of the 'immortal soul' – a part of man that escapes death – was seen by Freud as a characteristic example of the human capacity for self-delusion through religion. We believe that Freud was justified in his attack upon literalized doctrines that deny death.[35]

---

35  Robert Jay Lifton and Eric Olsen, *Living and Dying* (New York: Praeger, 1974), 79; see also Lifton, *The Life of the Self: Toward a New Psychology* (New York: Simon and Schuster, 1976).

Against the background of the unquestioned identification of belief in 'real' immortality and 'self-delusion through religion', Lifton formulates five modes of a sanitised, merely symbolic immortality. These are: (i) biosocial immortality (to live on in one's family, tribe, nation, species, etc.); (ii) the creative mode (surviving in one's works); (iii) the theological mode (not a literal immortality but expressions of one's "spiritual death and rebirth which may occur many times during one's earthly existence"); (iv) continuity with nature; and (v) experiential transcendence ("the feeling of being beyond the limits and confines of ordinary daily life").[36]

Seneca's descriptions of immortality defy the contrast implicit in Lifton's classification between a real or literal sense of immortality and a symbolic one. Seneca certainly offers ideas that fit four of Lifton's five modes of symbolic immortality. For instance, when he calls on Marcia to think of Metilius' children, we can interpret this as an instance of biosocial immortality; we interpret Cremutius Cordus' historical work and Marcia's involvement as an instance of the creative mode; being part of nature is an important consolatory moment in Seneca, and feeling 'beyond the limits and confines of ordinary daily life' is exactly what Seneca seeks with his description of the elevated viewpoint of the community of saints to which Metilius now belongs. There is a marked absence, however, of any thought resembling Lifton's sanitised 'theological mode', which indicates that Seneca does not play out a 'symbolic' immortality against a 'real' or 'literal' one.

Thus, Seneca's description of immortality is crucially about what today's grief researchers have called 'continuing bonds' with the deceased.[37] Seen in this light, Seneca manages again to strike a delicate balance: a purely symbolic immortality could hardly satisfy Marcia, but Seneca does not have to formulate a 'real', unending immortality in order to offer her a correlate for her continuing bonds with Metilius.

A third instance of Seneca's cutting across categories merits our attention. In Seneca's text, the heavy argumentative work is done by what I propose to call 'integrative concepts'. Such concepts bundle ideas that many scholars to-

---

36   Lifton and Olsen, *Living and Dying*, 76–82.
37   The continuing bonds theory combats Freudian calls for a radical severing of the bonds with the deceased ('decathexis'). See for example Dannis Klass, Phyllis R. Silberman, and Steven L. Nickman, eds., *Continuing Bonds: New Understandings of Grief* (London/New York: Taylor & Francis, 1996). To Freudians, attachment to the deceased appears quite simply irrational, since the deceased has ceased to exist. Lifton's theory of symbolic immortality is notable for searching beyond Freudian orthodoxy, but arguably remains too close to Freudianism.

day might prefer to keep separate: 'philosophical' and 'scientific' ideas on one side, and 'religious' or 'theological' ideas on the other. A prime example of such an integrative concept in Seneca's *Ad Marciam* is the concept of 'nature'. This concept is expressive of regularities in the visible world around us, the concatenation of cause and effect, and it connects these regularities with the idea of nature being a unified whole that is organised purposefully. It includes ideas of divine agency, God-willed order, and the beauty of the cosmos.

Owing to the trajectory of Western culture over previous centuries, there is nowadays a widespread intuition that these ideas properly belong to separate realms. I have some misgivings as to whether the ideas aggregated in integrative concepts can be 'disentangled' satisfactorily, even in present-day culture. To give an example: the natural burials that are gaining prominence in highly industrialised European countries can fulfil a consolatory function only if 'nature' is divinised and represented as a unitary whole encompassing and transcending individual life-stories.[38] But whatever our stance on the matter in respect of today's culture, it is clear that integrative concepts, both in Seneca's *Ad Marciam* and in ancient thought more generally, do their work precisely because they are intended to form a whole and cannot be disentangled.[39]

---

38   On natural burials see for example Tineke Nugteren, "Troost en 'troosteloosheid' op natuurbegraafplaatsen," *Nederlands Theologisch Tijdschrift* 68 no. 1 and 2 (2014): 83–100.

39   The question might arise of how 'integrative concepts' relate to 'thick concepts', a construct that has gained considerable prominence also in the study of religion. My succinct answer is that the notion of 'integrative concepts' is designed to undercut the construct of 'thick concepts'. To begin with, the construct of 'thick concepts' or 'thick descriptions' can be traced back to Gilbert Ryle's famous 1968 lecture, "The Thinking of Thoughts: What is 'Le Penseur' Doing?". In this lecture, Ryle explores the sense in which different strata of meaning could be prised apart. Ryle comes up with the simile of a sandwich: "thick description is a many-layered sandwich, of which only the bottom slice is catered for by [the] thinnest description" (Ryle, "The Thinking of Thoughts: What Is 'le Penseur' Doing?" *University Lectures* 18 [University of Saskatchewan, 1968]; reprinted in Ryle, *Collected Essays 1929–1968* [London/New York: Routledge, 1968/2009], 494–510, 497). The notion of 'thick concepts' has given rise to two only marginally related research traditions. Harking back to Ryle, Clifford Geertz (*The Interpretation of Cultures: Selected Essays* [New York: Basic Books, 1973]) formulated a research programme of 'thick descriptions', emphasising the importance of context in anthropological fieldwork. This research tradition is not relevant to our present concerns. The second research tradition developed in the field of philosophy. Building on the rediscovery of ancient virtue ethics in the works of Elizabeth Anscombe and Philippa Foot, Bernard Williams popularised the use of 'thick concepts', indicating how concepts such as treachery, promise, brutality, or courage "seem to express a union of fact and value" (Williams, *Ethics and the Limits of Philosophy* [Cambridge,

Nonetheless, attempts at disentanglement are regularly undertaken, and Sellars' critique of Victorian interpretations of Stoicism (see section one above) taps into this source. We can see at once that this strategy has its attractions, as it renders Stoic philosophy more palatable to 'secular' readers. We must nevertheless raise the question of what is lost in such attempts. When we retroject onto a Stoic text such as the *Ad Marciam* the intuition that religion belongs to a different realm from philosophical or scientific analyses of the world around us, the similes employed in the text become unintelligible, the arguments lose much of their persuasive force, and we are left with little more than an assortment of highly-problematic generalisations.

In the *Ad Marciam*, however, initiation into nature's secrets is supremely attractive precisely because of the divine status of nature, which also imparts a quasi-divine status to the communion of saints, which is similarly privileged.[40] The fact that nature functions as an integrative concept, combining regularity with notions of purpose and authorship, allows Seneca to present 'nature' as a normative guideline: Marcia is invited to accept the lessons of nature evident in the grieving of animals (which is intense but short) and in the observation that passions derived from nature are invariant. The variety of human grieving can be explained only by its dependence upon mistaken opinion superimposed by human activity (7.4). Nature, by contrast, is represented as a divine benevolent power, giving human beings the correct cues, which we regularly fail to heed.

Marcia's bitter charge against Fortune shows that she, too, has formed a mistaken view of her own situation – and, indeed, of human circumstance. She brings her frustrated expectations of a sheltered existence for herself and her loved ones to bear against the belief that the cosmos is ordered providentially, but Seneca attempts to show that fulfilment of such desires is not what nature is about (17.1–6). He underscores the lesson that life means being a co-dweller in a cosmic city of gods and men (18.1–2) and that life in this city remains supremely worthwhile, even if fortune seems to strike at random and we inevitably experience loss.

All this is Stoic doctrine, and instead of philosophy being hidden away, as Wilson claims (see above), Stoic theo-philosophy is brought to Marcia's attention and underpins the consolatory project of the *Ad Marciam*, which is at one

---

MA: Harvard University Press, 1985]), 129). However, the Humean distinction between 'is' and 'ought' that 'thick concepts' are meant to bridge could arise only after the view of nature had changed from a purposefully-structured whole to a purpose-free, arbitrary process. The notion of 'integrative concepts' thus points to the intellectual transformation that made a gap between 'is' and 'ought' plausible in the first place.

40   Cf. 25.3: *tanto excelsiorum*.

and the same time both genuine argument and genuine consolation. For our present purposes, it is particularly important to note that 'religion' and 'philosophy' are inseparable in the *Ad Marciam*. The inseparability is visible right from the opening sentence, in which Seneca identifies what he perceives as the root cause of Marcia's unabated grief. This is that Marcia's beliefs about Fortune, about the world as divinely ordained, have been shattered, and with their loss she struggles to make sense of the situation that she is in.[41] This is the problem that Marcia faces. Seneca offers consolation by showing that, after all, nature is divinely ordained. He invokes God as the structuring force and creator of the universe. Metilius' afterlife, presented as a cognitive fulfilment in the communion of saints, will be limited in duration by the arrival of cosmic conflagration. Seneca calls on Marcia to accept and even embrace the limitation of human existence in view of the attractiveness of Stoic eschatology.

If we still wanted to play out the labels 'philosophy' and 'theology' against each other, we would have to say that Seneca addresses a 'theological' disorientation in a 'theological' way, but then Seneca is a philosopher, who uses arguments stemming from what we perceive as the history of philosophy. In short, in the case of Seneca's *Ad Marciam*, it is impossible to draw a persuasive dividing line between religion and philosophy. The *Ad Marciam* is an excellent example of a text in the extended centre of the spectrum between philosophy and religion. It is what I propose to call 'theo-philosophy'.

## 3   Enlarging the Focus

So far, we have concentrated on Seneca's *Ad Marciam*. It is time to offer suggestions as to how we can proceed. How can we expand our scope to include

---

41   In the terminology of modern bereavement theories, Marcia has experienced the loss of what has been called her 'assumptive world', the fundamental "ordering principle for the psychological or psychosocial construction of the human world" (Jeffrey Kauffman, ed., *Loss of the Assumptive World: A Theory of Traumatic Loss* [London/New York: Brunner-Routledge, 2002], 2). In the literature, it is suggested that the loss of the assumptive world plays out at different levels, from the need to 'rediscover the world' at a ground level and learn new attitudes and routines allowing a fruitful continuation of life after the loss (Thomas Attig, "Questionable Assumptions About Assumptive Worlds," in *Loss of the Assumptive World*, 55–68); Attig, *How We Grieve* [rev. ed.; Oxford: Oxford University Press, 2011]) to the loss of highly general religious and philosophical beliefs about the world and our place in it (Kenneth Doka, "How Could God? Loss and the Spiritual Assumptive World," in *Loss of the Assumptive World*, 49–54). However, Seneca does not play out concrete problems against abstract principles; instead, he is convinced that (mistaken) fundamental beliefs lie at the root of Marcia's more concrete problems.

other consolatory texts, and what light can they shed on the interconnections between religion and philosophy in antiquity?

I suggest that ultimately our goal should be an interpretation of human flourishing (εὐδαιμονία) as an integrative concept. If, as I am convinced, it is true that practically all ancient ethical theories are not only virtue-centred but also describe the importance of the virtues in terms of their contribution to human flourishing (i.e., are *eudaimonistic* ethical theories), and if, moreover, early Christian ethics exhibit the same characteristics,[42] then it will be rewarding to analyse how religious features are present in the different ideas of human flourishing. I claim that they are: wherever ancient authors offer their ideas of what *eudaimonia* consists in, they consistently return to their ideas about the life of (the) god(s). This holds even for the Epicureans, who are – to say the least – not usually credited with offering an overly religious ethic.

While an analysis of *eudaimonia* as integrative concept should be our ultimate goal, the scope of such a project lies beyond the limitations of the present chapter. What I shall discuss here, instead, is an important stepping-stone towards that goal. I want to suggest that there is an underexplored common consolatory theme that allows us to consider ancient argumentative consolations as members of an extended family. This common theme lies in the virtue-ethical core at the centre of ancient argumentative consolation, which is—as we have seen above—already evident in the Socratic alternative. When ancient argumentative consolations confront the challenge that death has tragically cut short a life and that there is, therefore, ample reason to grieve, the consolers point to the importance of the virtues: virtue makes life complete in the sense that death cannot tragically disrupt it and destroy its shape. Indeed, the virtues' pathway to what we might call, for want of better labels, 'biographical closure' is an important but underappreciated aspect in the attractiveness

---

42   Recent attention to Christian ethics as virtue-centred has been stimulated by Alasdair MacIntyre, *After Virtue* (Notre Dame, IN: University of Notre Dame Press, 1981) and Stanley Hauerwas, *The Peaceable Kingdom: A Primer in Christian Ethics* (Notre Dame, IN: University of Notre Dame Press, 1983). Studies include Stanley Hauerwas and Charles Pinches, *Christians among the Virtues: Theological Conversations with Ancient and Modern Ethics* (Notre Dame, IN: University of Notre Dame Press, 1997); David S. Cunningham, *Christian Ethics: The End of Law* (London/New York: Routledge, 2008); Romanus Cessario, *The Moral Virtues and Theological Ethics* (2d ed.; Notre Dame, IN: University of Notre Dame Press, 2009); Daniel J. Harrington and James F. Keenan, *Paul and Virtue Ethics: Building Bridges between New Testament Studies and Moral Theology* (Lanham, MD: Rowman and Littlefield, 2010).

of the ideal of *eudaimonia*: the possession of virtue shields mortal beings from the disruptive effects of death.

The association between the virtues and biographical closure, I contend, is found throughout ancient argumentative consolation. Again, Plato's *Apology*, with its Socratic alternative, is the *Urtext*, but we find the link also in Seneca's *Ad Marciam*, where Seneca extolls the virtues of Metilius and connects them to the notions of maturity and perfection that convey the completion of Metilius' life:

> Tell me, Marcia, when you saw in your son, youth that he was, the wisdom of an old man, a mind victorious over all sensual pleasures, unblemished, faultless, seeking riches without greed, honours without ostentation, pleasures without excess, did you think that you could long have the good fortune to keep him safe and unharmed? Whatever has reached perfection, is near its end. Ideal virtue hurries away and is snatched from our eyes, and the fruits that ripen in their first days do not wait long for their last. (23.3)

Seneca proceeds to admonish Marcia: "Undertake to estimate him by his virtues, not by his years, and you will see he lived long enough" (24.1), expressing once more the idea of biographical closure through virtue. The same point is made again a little later (25.1); Seneca skilfully uses the word *integer* ('complete'), which expresses in this context two things: first, that the body vacated by Metilius' soul is unimportant – the soul is all that matters, and this is the core of his personhood; second, that Metilius' life had completed the shape of his soul, so that his soul and life are not fragmentary. "He is complete and has left nothing of himself behind, he has fled away and wholly departed from earth" (*Integer ille nihilque in terris relinquens sui fugit et totus excessit*, 25.1).

Of course, I cannot prove in a direct way my claim that the link between virtue and biographical closure is a common theme in ancient argumentative consolation. No discussion of any subset of ancient consolatory texts could suffice. However, I can support my claim by analysing a small number of characteristic cases that might seem to pose problems for my interpretation.

The first of these cases is Plutarch's *Consolatio ad uxorem*, written to his wife on the occasion of the death of their two-year old daughter Philoxena. Ancient philosophers, who connected virtue and intellect and assumed that the level of reason necessary for virtue develops gradually and rather late in life, had to be reluctant to attribute virtue to a very young child, and hence could not offer consolation in such cases by recourse to virtue. However, even though ancient consolers were unable to attribute fully-fledged virtue to a very young child, they could invoke character traits as gifts from nature. This is exactly the strategy to which Plutarch resorts when he describes Philoxena's character: "She had herself, moreover, a surprising gift of mildness and good temper, and her way of responding to friendship and of bestowing favours gave us pleasure while it afforded an insight into her kindness" (608d, trans. Midgley).

The second case that might pose interpretive problems is Epicurean consolation. Many interpretations set Epicureanism apart from other currents of ancient philosophy, so much so that the rediscovery of Epicureanism and its forerunners, the Greek atomists, has been credited with being a driving force of (early) modern secularisation processes.[43] In our present context, it is noteworthy that the Epicureans denied any form of experiential continuity after death. Instead, they believed that human beings are constellations of atoms and that these constellations are irrevocably dissolved by death. Death is the absolute end of human existence, and the Epicureans saw in the finitude of life a liberating, consoling truth: "So death, the most frightening of bad things, is nothing to us; since when we exist, death is not yet present, and when death is present, then we do not exist."[44] Of course this is a far cry from affirmations of the afterlife such as those we have encountered in Seneca, but, importantly, Epicurean consolation still follows the template of the Socratic alternative, playing out the first option against the second. Following the Socratic template, Epicurean consolation is premised on a shift away from what someone has achieved in terms of attachments, plans, and projects towards a virtue ethical emphasis on how someone has lived and locates biographical closure in the possession of the virtues. This becomes evident once we ask how our extract from Epicurus' *Epistula ad Menoeceum* could be convincing. Plans, projects, and attachments are inherently future-directed and will regularly involve a period of time after our death. By thwarting those plans, projects, and attachments, death would normally be an evil. Death can be indifferent if and only if we have transformed our outlook so that the completeness of a life does not rest on what we have achieved in terms of plans and projects, but on how we have lived. As for Socrates, just so for the Epicureans; this shift is connected to the possession of virtues. Arguably the best expression of the shift is provided by Philodemus, a first-century BCE Epicurean: "The one who understands, having grasped that he is capable of achieving everything sufficient for the good life, immediately and for the rest of his life walks about already

---

43  See for example Jonathan Irvine Israel, *Radical Enlightenment: Philosophy and the Making of Modernity, 1650–1750* (Oxford: Oxford University Press, 2001).

44  *Epistula ad Menoeceum* = DL 10.125, trans. Inwood and Gerson.

ready for burial, and enjoys the single day as if it were eternity" (Philodemus, *De morte* 38.14–19 Kuiper, trans. Warren). The sage, the model human who possesses all the virtues, here understatedly referred to as 'the one who understands' (ὁ δὲ νοῦν ἔχων), has a life that is complete at any point.

The third and final case – or rather area of case studies – that I discuss is early Christian consolation. In the present context, I focus on a few passages in Paul's letters. This is a sensible choice, not only because of Paul's importance for the later history of Christianity in general, but also because of the centrality of his texts in later Christian consolation. Moreover, Paul's letters were written in a remarkable chronological vicinity to Seneca's consolatory letters, postdating Seneca's letters by only a decade. Again, the few cursory remarks and suggestions that I can offer here are a far cry from the detailed engagement that Paul's texts merit, not least in view of the wide extent and high level of scholarly discussion.[45] I suggest that Paul's letters offer consolatory strategies that are surprisingly similar to those found, for instance, in Plato's *Apology* and Seneca's *Ad Marciam*. This suggestion holds despite the unquestionable emphasis on the Christ event as central to Paul's consolation, which is not replicated in the surrounding culture of non-Christian consolations. A good example of the emphasis upon the Christ event is 1 Thessalonians 4:13–18 (REB):

> We wish you not to remain in ignorance, friends, about those who sleep in death; you should not grieve like the rest of mankind, who have no hope. We believe that Jesus died and rose again; so too will God bring those who died as Christians to be with Jesus. ...first the Christian dead will rise, then we who are still alive shall join them, caught up in clouds to meet the Lord in the air. Thus we shall always be with the Lord. Console one another, then, with these words.

However, as in the 'philosophical' consolations examined above, Paul deems central to his consolatory project the message that the well-lived life is at any

---

45  However, considering the wealth of literature on Paul, analyses of his consolatory strategy are surprisingly rare. They include R. Scott Sullender, "Saint Paul's Approach to Grief: Clarifying the Ambiguity," *Journal of Religion and Health* 20 no. 1 (1981): 63–74; Abraham J. Malherbe, "Exhortation in First Thessalonians," *Novum Testamentum* 25 no. 3 (1983): 238–56 (exhortation); James L. Jaquette, "Life and Death, *Adiaphora*, and Paul's Rhetorical Strategies" *Novum Testamentum* 38 no. 1 (1996): 30–54; Holloway, *Consolation in Philippians*; and Richard S. Ascough, "A Question of Death: Paul's Community-Building Language in 1 Thessalonians 4:13–18," *Journal of Biblical Literature* 123 no. 3 (2004): 509–30.

time complete. In the passage that follows, Paul evokes biographical closure with the simile "the day of the Lord comes like a thief in the night," wherein the followers of Jesus will not be wrong-footed (1 Thessalonians 5:1–5): "About dates and times, my friends, there is no need to write to you, for you yourselves know perfectly well that the day of the Lord comes like a thief in the night. ...But you, friends, are not in the dark; the day will not come upon you like a thief. You are all children of light, children of day." The claim that biographical closure is produced by the virtues is endorsed by the list of virtues offered just before the passages already quoted, in 1 Thessalonians 4.

From the perspective of biographical closure, Paul can view the length of his own life, and the question of whether it is preferable to live or die, with a degree of detachment comparable to the detachment exhibited by Stoic philosophers (Philippians 2:20–24):

> It is my confident hope that nothing will daunt me or prevent me from speaking boldly; and that now as always Christ will display his greatness in me, whether the verdict be life or death. For to me life is Christ, and death is gain. If I am to go on living in the body there is fruitful work for me to do. Which then am I to choose? I cannot tell. I am pulled two ways: my own desire is to depart and be with Christ – that is better by far; but for your sake the greater need is for me to remain in the body.

It is noteworthy that in the passage from Philippians, Paul does not talk of his hope in the form of a plan or project. He does not use a phrase that would indicate the expectation of a set goal to be achieved by his action (for instance, "I shall convert my audience in Rome"). Instead, the phrase 'speaking boldly' is expressive of an emphasis on how he wants to act when given the opportunity to speak in Rome.

Finally, the well-worn passage 1 Corinthians 13:12–13 shows that Paul's conception of the afterlife dignifies fundamental life-choices: "At present we see only puzzling reflections in a mirror, but one day we shall see face to face. My knowledge now is partial; then it will be whole, like God's knowledge of me. There are three things that last forever: faith, hope, and love; and the greatest of the three is love." The virtues that have become known as 'the theological virtues' ought not only to structure the lives of the followers of Christ but to remain important for all time, even in the afterlife. And this afterlife is understood as cognitive fulfilment, expressed in the visual metaphor of seeing 'face to face'.

## 4  Conclusion: Appreciating Theo-Philosophy

Where does this leave us? I have argued that a common framework undergirds argumentative consolation in antiquity and that this framework is first visible in the Socratic alternative explored by Plato's *Apology*. Following the lead of the Socratic alternative, ancient consolations seek to achieve a cognitive transformation. They prompt their audiences to rethink what they find important in life and what brings about biographical closure. Ancient consolations steer away from the view that plans, attachments, and projects are central to biographical closure. By being future-directed, those plans, attachments, and projects are vulnerable to curtailment by death. Instead, ancient consolations emphasise the importance of virtue. Virtue makes a life complete, so that death does not tragically interrupt and destroy what was important in life. From this perspective, ancient consolations affirmed that, for a well-lived life, death is at no point an evil. Conceptions of the afterlife can – but need not – play a role in this larger framework; they do play a central role, *inter alia*, in Plato, Cicero, Plutarch, Seneca, and Paul. Where they are employed, they serve primarily to dignify fundamental life-choices, and that means in the consolatory context the individual's striving for virtue. The afterlife is regularly cast in terms of a cognitive fulfilment. Even the Epicureans – who play out the first option of the Socratic alternative against the second, i.e., by denying the possibility of an afterlife – share the larger, virtue-ethical argumentative consolatory framework with the aforementioned group of Plato, Cicero, Plutarch, Seneca, and Paul.

All of this shows that there is no fundamental difference between philosophical and theological modes of consolation. Paul's consolatory arguments fit into the larger framework, and they share this framework even with remote and apparently opposed thinkers such as Epicurus. Paul differs from Epicurus in his affirmation of an afterlife; but, again, Paul's invocation of the afterlife fits into a tradition of afterlife-affirming conceptions that occupy a central spot in ancient consolation.

This supports my claim that there are far-reaching commonalities between 'religion' and 'philosophy' in antiquity. We should thus envisage ancient philosophy and theology as located on a continuum, with authors such as Paul and the Stoics at its extended centre. At this centre, it is impossible to come up with convincing criteria which would allow us to distinguish philosophy from religion; we have seen how Seneca exhibits a form of 'pastoral thinking' that is irreducibly premised on 'religious' motifs through 'integrative concepts', and we have seen how Paul employs consolatory ideas that place him in continuity with the 'philosophical' tradition of ancient consolation.

To conclude, we should abandon attempts to find criteria for separating philosophy from theology, at least for the extended centre of the continuum. What we find in authors such as Seneca and Paul is neither philosophy nor theology; it is something in between. Perhaps in such cases we should discard the differentiating labels of 'philosophy' and 'religion' or 'theology'. Nevertheless, we need a label to delimit the territory and to fence off reductive interpretations based on historiographies of separation. 'Theo-philosophy' might serve as that label.

**PART 3**

*Placing Jesus among the Philosophers*

# Jesus among the Philosophers: The Cynic Connection Explored and Affirmed, with a Note on Philo's Jewish-Cynic Philosophy

*Bernhard Lang*

> …the case of the vagrant philosopher Yeshua.
> MIKHAIL BULGAKOV, *The Master and Margarita*[1]

• • •

> No doubt of it, then, as in the first, so in the twenty-first, century A.D., Christian Cynicism is the place to be. …Of all the ancient pagan philosophies, Cynicism is the one most nearly endorsed by God.
> JOHN MOLES[2]

⁝

The Cynic philosophers constituted an ancient Greek school of philosophy.[3] It originated around 400 BCE in Athens as a decidedly scandalous and countercultural movement. Its founder, Antisthenes, one of the students of Socrates, radicalised the Socratic call to a simple lifestyle, for only a life unencumbered

---

1  Mikhail Bulgakov, *The Master and Margarita* (trans. D. Burgin and K. O'Connor; London: Vintage, 2003), 37.
2  John Moles, "Cynic Influence upon First-Century Judaism and Early Christianity," in *The Limits of Ancient Biography* (ed. B. McGing and J. Mossman; Swansea: The Classical Press of Wales, 2006), 89–116, 104.
3  The complete set of ancient sources on the Cynics is available in Gabriele Giannantoni (ed.), *Socratis et Socraticorum Reliquiae* (4 vols.; Naples: Bibliopolis, 1990), vol. 2. Two convenient collections translate the bulk of this material: Robert Dobbin (ed.), *The Cynic Philosophers from Diogenes to Julian* (London: Penguin, 2012); Robin Hard (ed.), *Diogenes the Cynic: Sayings and Anecdotes, with Other Popular Moralists* (Oxford: Oxford University Press, 2012). For similar collections in French and German, see Léonce Paquet, *Les Cyniques grecs: fragments et témoignages* (Paris: Librairie générale française, 1992); Georg Luck, *Die Weisheit der Hunde: Texte der antiken Kyniker in deutscher Übersetzung* (Stuttgart: Kröner, 1997).

by family, wealth, and regular work would guarantee the freedom needed for critical thought and enquiry.

We know about the Cynics mainly from a late-ancient book entitled *The Lives and Teachings of the Philosophers*, compiled by Diogenes Laertius in the third century CE This work offers biographic information in the form of anecdotes about practically all ancient Greek philosophers, including figures such as Socrates, Plato, Aristotle, Diogenes, and many others. Although dealing with individual thinkers, Diogenes Laertius always tells us to which 'school' or movement a thinker belongs, whether to the school of Plato, Aristotle, or some other school of thought. One category of philosophers who were particularly dear to him comprise the Cynics, and among these, his namesake Diogenes is the most prominent figure. The anecdotes told about Diogenes take up much space, and they are retold with pleasure. They tell of an eccentric; dispensing with all material possessions, he lives by begging in the cities of Athens and Corinth. At night, having no other home, he reportedly retires into a huge barrel or storage-jar that offers adequate protection. Diogenes is a historical figure whose dates we know (ca. 403–323 BCE). Known as "the Dog" (κύων), he is the emblematic founding figure of the Cynic school of philosophy.

In *The Lives and Teachings of the Philosophers*, Cynic philosophy is summed up as follows:[4] the Cynics did not deal with disciplines such as logic, natural philosophy (i.e., physics), geometry, and music; their interest lay exclusively in ethics. For them, a life of virtue is the foremost aim of man. Virtue can be learned and, once it is acquired, it cannot be lost. The wise man must be amiable, without fault, and a friend to all who are wise. Cynics lead a simple, modest life. They wear only one garment. They despise wealth, fame, and noble birth. They are happy with a frugal meal, some being vegetarian; they drink only water and are satisfied with the most simple of shelters, such as Diogenes' barrel. Finally, they are almost god-like in their desire for nothing. The attentive reader of *The Lives and Teachings of the Philosophers* will not miss the author's nostalgia for this noble philosophy.

---

4 Diogenes Laertius, *Lives of Eminent Philosophers* 6.104. The editions used are idem, *Lives of Eminent Philosophers* (trans. R.D. Hicks; LCL; New York: Putnam, 1925), vol. 2, and *Lives of Eminent Philosophers* (ed. T. Dorandi; CCTC 50; Cambridge: Cambridge University Press, 2013). – For recent introductions to the philosophy of the ancient Cynics, see R. Bracht Branham and Marie-Odile Goulet-Cazé (eds.), *The Cynics: The Cynic Movement in Antiquity and Its Legacy* (Berkeley: University of California Press, 1996); William D. Desmond, *The Greek Praise of Poverty: Origins of Anceint Cynicism* (Notre Dame, Ind.: University of Notre Dame Prss, 2006); William D. Desmond, *Cynics* (Ancient Philosophies; Berkeley: University of California Press, 2008).

Cynicism developed in a manner quite unlike all the other ancient schools of philosophy. Schools such as Stoicism or the Academy of Plato professionalised philosophy. They transformed their schools into well-established institutions, recommended their doctrines as something an educated person should be familiar with, and offered lecture courses that transmitted this doctrine to large numbers of students. This development was consciously resisted by the Cynics. The members of their movement remained loners. They did not value the regular, systematic transmission of their teaching to students; instead, they acted as popular preachers of morality, trying to influence the masses and elevate the moral climate of ancient society through their public speeches. Their own lifestyle was meant to provide others with an example of the virtuous life. In the Hellenistic and Roman worlds they were very successful as moralists and moral exemplars, though not many converts could be made to the philosophical lifestyle of Diogenes.

In what follows, we will sketch seven observations that provide evidence of the impact Cynic philosophy made on ancient Judaism in general and, more specifically, on Jesus and the early tradition associated with him.

## 1    First Observation: How Cynic Philosophy Entered the Jewish World

Isaak Heinemann, author of *Philons jüdische und griechische Bildung*, was the first scholar to point out the substantial reception of Cynic philosophy in Hellenistic Judaism, in particular the contribution made by Philo.[5] To Heinemann, the great expert on Alexandrian Judaism, we owe the reconstruction of a lost book that circulated in first-century Alexandria among the Jewish intellectual elite.[6] We may call this work "The Book of the Ten Festivals." Written from a Cynic cosmopolitan perspective, it offered a new and rather radical reinterpretation of the major Jewish festivals, all of which provided Jewish farmers with the opportunity to celebrate and to enjoy the fruits of their own labours. It exhorts them to stay in their villages, away from the corrupt world of the city – an ideal reminiscent of the Cynic utopia of creating a community of people who practice some agriculture but are otherwise committed to the philosoph-

---

5   Isaak Heinemann, *Philons jüdische und griechische Bildung* (1932; repr., Darmstadt: Wissenschaftliche Buchgesellschaft, 1962). Some of Heinemann's ideas were anticipated in Paul Wendland, "Philo und die kynisch-stoische Diatribe," in idem and Otto Kern, *Beiträge zur Geschichte der griechischen Philosophie und Religion* (Berlin: Reimer, 1895), 1–75.
6   Heinemann, *Philons jüdische und griechische Bildung*, 97–154. The relevant source analysed by Heinemann is Philo, *De specialibus legibus* 2.41–261.

ical life.⁷ According to the "Book of the Ten Festivals," the Jewish festivals also serve to teach the people about the one and only God in his true temple, but "the highest and truest temple of God" is the universe, and not a building made by human hands.⁸ This bold reinterpretation plays down what is specifically Jewish about Jewish thought and practice, thus giving the impression of a universal religion meant for all humanity.

Although Philo in his own writing seems to avoid Cynic radicalism, he does appreciate and even celebrate the Cynic ideal of voluntary poverty. In his treatise "That Every Good Person Is Free" (*Quod omnis probus liber sit*), he relates anecdotes about Diogenes with relish, portraying him and other Cynic philosophers as exemplars of individuals who have acquired true freedom – freedom from the burden of possessions and freedom of speech even before the high and mighty. This work includes only a few biblical references; the dominant note is Cynic, and it would be wrong to exclude it from the corpus of original Cynic literature.⁹

Philo, who lived in the early first century CE, was not the first Jewish thinker to be impressed with the Cynic way of life and thinking. A first trace of Jewish Cynicism can be found in the biblical book of Ecclesiastes or Koheleth (ca. 200 BCE). Koheleth is the name of this Jewish author but it is also a title, apparently translating the Greek συναγωγεύς – "leader of a philosophical club" – into Hebrew. Absolutely essential for Koheleth is the abandonment of wealth, because riches cannot lead to happiness – a common subject of Cynic preaching. Echoing his Greek models, he famously states that "a living dog is better than a dead lion" (Ecclesiastes 9:4). Another aspect of Koheleth's philosophy can be traced to its Cynic origins: his admonition to enjoy life and possessions as long as fate permits. "It was a kind of opportunistic attitude to life, taking with both hands when there were things to take, yet not complaining when times were lean, enjoying life when it could be enjoyed, but accepting the whims of fortune with a shrug of the shoulder."¹⁰ It is with these words that Bertrand

---

7   See the poem on the invented Cynic city of "Pera" by Crates, quoted in Diogenes Laertius, *Lives of Eminent Philosophers* 6.85. On the Cynics and daily work, see the discussion in Suzanne Husson, *La République de Diogène: une cité en quête de la nature* (Paris: Vrin, 2010), 114–17.

8   Philo, *De specialibus legibus* 1.66.

9   See below, "Appendix: References to Cynic Philosophy in the Works of Philo of Alexandria."

10  Bertrand Russell, *Wisdom of the West: A Historical Survey of Western Philosophy* (New York: Doubleday, 1959), 106. The theme of enjoyment of life, presumably missing from the earliest layer of the Cynic tradition, is well established by the first century C.E., when Aristippus of Cyrene was reckoned among the Cynics; see Philo, *De plantatione* 151; Giannantoni,

Russell characterises the attitude of the Cynic philosophers, but in fact, the best example of such a view is the biblical book of Ecclesiastes/ Koheleth.

A hidden portrait or caricature of the Cynic beggar-like existence can be found in the book of Sirach, an early-Jewish writing contemporaneous with, or slightly later than, Koheleth. It reads as follows:

> It is a poor life going from house to house, keeping your mouth shut because you are a visitor. You receive the guests (of the patron) and hand the drinks without being thanked for it, and into the bargain must listen to words that rankle: "Come here, stranger, and lay the table; whatever you have there, hand it to me." – "Be off, stranger! Make way for a more important guest; my brother has come to stay, and I need the guestroom." (Sirach 29:24–27, NEB)

Cynic philosophers, as we shall see in the next section, depended on being guests, and Sirach describes the bleak reality rather than the theory. It must have been a tough experience for Cynics not to be allowed to talk, because they considered the giving of moral advice their special competence. The toughest experience of all was of course to be sent away. Sirach, whom we take to be a wealthy aristocrat-philosopher, is not completely unsympathetic to the poor,[11] though in the passage quoted he confines himself to describing the plight of the Cynic philosophers, whom he does not seem to like.

Not only in the books of Koheleth and Sirach, but also in the gospels, Cynic ideas and attitudes appear. Without much difficulty, Jesus and John the Baptist can be understood as men who were intent on realising Cynic ideals. Some of the evidence for this assertion will be presented below. We will begin with the most visible side of Cynicism – the Cynic way of life.

## 2   Second Observation: Cynic Poverty – Hellenistic and Jesuanic

Voluntary poverty, as practiced by Jesus and some of his early disciples, matches the Cynic way of life. As soon as someone has decided to adopt the Cynic way of life, he must abandon his possessions – a challenge not easily met

---

*Socratis et Socraticorum Reliquiae* 4:152–53; Bernhard Lang, *Jesus der Hund: Leben und Lehre eines jüdischen Kynikers* (Munich: Beck, 2010), 59–61. See also below, "Appendix," no. 6.

11   Bradley C. Gregory, *Like an Everlasting Signet Ring: Generosity in the Book of Sirach* (Deuterocanonical and Cognate Literature Studies 2; Berlin: de Gruyter, 2010).

by many. When meeting and talking with a wealthy young man, Jesus recommends that he should get rid of his possessions in a radical act of conversion to the philosophical life: "If you want to be perfect, off you go and sell all you have and give the proceeds to the poor, and you will have treasure in heaven. Then come and follow me" (Matthew 19:21). The young man is surprised. Unable to change his life as radically as Jesus suggests, he goes away in distress. We do not know exactly how the young man felt after having been confronted with the suggestion made by Jesus, but let me have a guess. The young man may have anticipated the advice generally given to rich young men in the Hellenistic and Roman worlds:[12] take some of your money to your hometown and build something of real, enduring value for the community: a public bath, a sports field – a 'gymnasium' – or a synagogue. Then you will be held in great honour by your fellow citizens. They may mention your name in an inscription, or erect a statue in your honour. But Jesus did not give this advice. He did not recommend the career of a public benefactor. Instead, he wanted the young man to cut off his social roots, to abandon his former life, and to embark on the career of a philosopher.

Did Koheleth, the Cynic philosopher of the Old Testament, abandon any riches he might have inherited or accumulated in his early life? The chapters about King Solomon's dissatisfaction with his wealth may have just this implication, though one cannot be sure. Neither can we be sure whether Jesus owned and subsequently abandoned substantial possessions. At least one scholar considers this possibility, invoking the Pauline dictum, "Though he was rich, yet for your sake he became poor" (2 Corinthians 8:9).[13] According to recent research on first-century Galilee, the inhabitants of this region were neither as poor, nor as heavily indebted, nor as lacking in cultural life as has been traditionally alleged.[14] At any rate, the advice Jesus gives to the rich man

---

12   See the advice Cicero gives to his son Marcus: Cicero, *De officiis* 2.60 and 64. Benefactors are regularly honoured in inscriptions; first-century examples belong among the inscriptions most often referred to in biblical studies: the Latin inscription that honours Erastus for laying the pavement near the theatre of Corinth at his own expense, and the Greek inscription that commemorates the extension of a synagogue in Jerusalem by one Theodotus. The Erastus inscription is still *in situ* in Corinth; the Theodotus inscription is in the Rockefeller Museum, Jerusalem; see Clyde E. Fant and Mitchell G. Reddish, *A Guide to Biblical Sites in Greece and Turkey* (Oxford: Oxford University Press, 2003), 59.

13   George W. Buchanan, "Jesus and the Upper Class," *NovT* 8 (1964): 195–209.

14   David A. Fiensy and Ralph K. Hawkins (eds.), *The Galilean Economy in the Time of Jesus* (Early Christianity and Its Literature 11; Atlanta, GA: SBL, 2013); Bradley W. Root, *First Century Galilee: A Fresh Examination of the Sources* (WUNT II.378; Tübingen: Mohr Siebeck, 2014).

would make sense in the mouth of someone who has actually taken the step himself.

Very few can meet and live up to the challenge of the saying: "You cannot serve God and mammon" (Matthew 6:24), or, in paraphrase, you cannot be a slave to both God and wealth. But some actually succeed in shedding the fetters of mammon. They can be recognised by their very simple clothing. John the Baptist, like Jesus, under the influence of Diogenes, wears "a garment of camel's hair and a leather belt round his waist" (Matthew 3:4; Mark 1:6). What our translations render as "leather belt" may actually be a kind of loincloth, not a belt.[15] What John wears echoes both the dress of the Old Testament prophet Elijah (2 Kings 1:8) and the costume of the philosophers. John and his likes do not wish to be identified as individuals "dressed in soft clothing" (Matthew 11:8). The dress code of the Cynic philosophers is reflected in the rule that Jesus gives to his closest disciples: "He charges them to take nothing for their journey except a staff – no bread, no bag, no money in their belts – but to wear sandals and not to put on two tunics" (Mark 6:8–9). Even stricter is the rule in an alternative version of the same passage: "Acquire no gold nor silver nor copper for your belts, no bag for your journey, nor two tunics nor sandals nor a staff" (Matt 10:9–10). No bag, no sandals – this reminds us of a statue in the Naples Museum of Antiquities (Fig. 1): Naked and barefoot, the beggar has nothing but a staff; the accompanying dog serves to identify the beggar – this is none other than Diogenes, the dog philosopher. Despite its lack of the beauty we might expect from an ancient statue, this one creates an atmosphere of rigour and force. We are perceived by Diogenes. We are reminded of Rilke's poem "Archaic Torso of Apollo," in which the poet exchanges the roles of beholder and artefact; rather than being an object to look at, the statue actually is looking at you. Rilke's poem ends with these famous lines:

> ...for here there is no place
> that does not see you. You must change your life.[16]

The statue preaches modesty in one's needs and contempt for the body, for beauty, and for urban conventions.

---

15   A leather loincloth can be seen in the Egyptian department of the British Museum (item no. 2564); see Gillian Vogelsang-Eastwood, *Pharaonic-Egyptian Clothing* (Leiden: Brill, 1993), 19, 208.

16   Trans. Mary D. Herter-Norton, in Rainer Maria Rilke, *Translations from the Poetry of Rainer Maria Rilke* (New York: Norton, 1962), 181. The poem may be read as Rilke's response to the sculptural work of Auguste Rodin, with whom he was associated in Paris.

FIGURE 1    *Diogenes as naked beggar.* This is how an ancient artist, supported by an eighteenth-century restorer, envisaged the philosopher. The accompanying dog is not the philosopher's pet but an attribute that defines the man portrayed as a member of the Cynic school, the "dog" philosophy. His nakedness refers to poverty, but also to heroism, because heroes such as the demi-god Heracles were always depicted in the nude. Philosophical poverty shades into heroic beauty. – The sculpture is in the Museo Archeologico Nazionale, Naples, the drawing from J.J. Winkelmann, *Monumenti antichi inediti* (Rome, 1767), vol. 2, fig. 172.

What do the Cynics live on? As a rule, they refuse to engage in regular work, begging for their bread – or eating what they find in nature. Anecdotes and incidental information tell us how the Cynics live. "He had no other food than what grew of its own accord," reports Josephus about Bannus, a Cynic practitioner whom he often visited and whom he calls his teacher.[17] A hungry and

---

17    Josephus, *Life* 11. For a full discussion of Bannus, see Lang, *Jesus der Hund*, 67–68 and 153.

indeed famished Jesus examines a fig tree; he is disappointed to find no fruits and pronounces a curse (Matthew 21:18–19). The disciples of Jesus go through the grain fields, and as they make their way, they pluck heads of grain, thus appeasing their hunger (Mark 2:23; Matthew 12:2). In keeping with ancient custom, travellers are allowed to help themselves in the fields; the relevant rule can be found in the Old Testament: "If you go into your neighbour's vineyard, you may eat your fill of grapes, as many as you wish, but you shall not put any in a bag. If you go into your neighbour's standing grain, you may pluck the ears with your hand, but you shall not put a sickle to your neighbour's standing grain" (Deuteronomy 23:24–25). Without such rules, no one in the ancient world could have travelled.

But even though nature offers its fruits, it cannot feed the Cynics completely. The Cynics are always in need of more provisions. These they get from those who honour the philosophic vocation by supporting its representatives with material goods. Diogenes reports: "Some gave money, others things worth money, and many invited me to dinner."[18] Jesus also was often invited; he must have been a popular guest. He frequented the house of Simon, a well-to-do Pharisee, as well as the home of Martha, an apparently no less wealthy woman (Luke 7:36; 10:38). Wealthy women, the gospels report, followed Jesus and "served" him (Mark 15:41); "they provided for him out of their means" (Luke 8:3). One of the disciples, the tax collector Levi, owned a house, in which he entertained Jesus and his friends (Mark 2:15; Luke 5:29). Being cared for by others may seem to us precarious and undesirable, but a true Cynic philosopher would in no way be bothered. The Cynic way of life may be characterised as eccentric, parasitical, and unconcerned about economic activity.

Let us conclude this section with a brief consideration of Jesus' famous blessing μακάριοι οἱ πτωχοί (Luke 6:20), generally rendered "blessed are the poor." As David Balch has shown, this translation, though not incorrect, is actually misleading.[19] If the saying had been intended to refer to poverty in very general terms, one would expect the use of the word πένεις, "the poor." The word πτωχοί, however, has a more specific meaning: it refers to those who live by begging. While the πένεις worked for their living – however modest –, the πτωχοί did not. They were beggars. As Balch explains, ancient philosophical discourse had a technical term for the poverty of the Cynics. Distinguishing

---

18  *Cynic Epistles: Letters of Diogenes* 38.3; see Abraham J. Malherbe, *The Cynic Epistles: A Study Edition* (Missoula, MT: Scholars Press, 1977), 160–61 (Greek and English).

19  David L. Balch, "Philodemus, 'On Wealth' and 'On Household Management': Naturally Wealthy Epicureans against Poor Cynics," in *Philodemus and the New Testament World* (ed. J. Fitzgerald, D. Obbink, and G. Holland; NovTSup 111; Leiden: Brill, 2004), 177–96.

between πενία and πτωχεία, the first means "poverty," while the second refers to "Cynic poverty," i.e., mendicancy. Thus when Jesus pronounced his famous blessing, he was actually blessing the Cynic way of life: "blessed are they that beg."

Next, we will turn to a well-known saying of Jesus that both illustrates and defends voluntary poverty.

## 3 Third Observation: "Consider the Birds" – Animals in Cynic and Jesuanic Thought

Diogenes – according to an anecdote transmitted by Plutarch[20] – once saw a mouse. He noticed the carefree attitude with which the little animal moved about, only paying attention to breadcrumbs. Impressed by its wisdom, he drew the lesson: animals are superior to most humans, and it falls to the philosopher to imitate them – to be equally carefree.

A conspicuous feature of the Cynic worldview is its new appreciation of animals. Traditional Greek thought believed in a clear hierarchy of all living beings: at the bottom of the scale are the animals, followed by man as a higher being, who is again followed by demi-gods such as Heracles; at the upper end of the scale, forming its apex, are the gods. This sequence of 'animal – man – demi-god – god', seemingly entirely natural, is an upwards-rising scale of power and intelligence: each step up on the ladder means an increase in intellectual and physical abilities. The order of the scale is rearranged by the Cynics because, according to them, it is not power and intelligence one should consider, but happiness. Humans are the least happy beings; animals are happier, and the gods are happiest. This description invokes a call to change one's life: humans must return to their animality, a state that has been corrupted by civilisation. Accordingly, in the same measure as we imitate animals, we can succeed in becoming happy again. As a matter of fact, the doctrine of the happiness of animals belongs among the oldest and most basic convictions of the Cynic philosophers.[21] To acquire happiness is not easy; you must give up typically human institutions – especially property, but also marriage. Only those who renounce these can gain the great good of happiness: freedom from cares, which means, quite simply, freedom.

---

20  Plutarch, *Quomodo quis suos in virtute sentiat profectus* 77E, trans. in Luck, *Die Weisheit der Hunde*, 129–30.
21  Marie-Odile Goulet-Cazé, "Religion and the Early Cynics," in Bracht-Branham and Goulet-Cazé, *The Cynics*, 47–80, 61.

Accordingly, in the teaching of the Cynics, animals play an important role as models one should imitate. One example already invoked is the anecdote about Diogenes and the mouse. Another example comes from Dio Chrysostom of Prusa's speech about the Cynics as people who are very different from others. Just consider the troubles that are associated with anything we own, including slaves. Animals, by comparison, are much wiser:

> Consider the beasts yonder and the birds, how much more freely from trouble they live than men, and how much more happily also, how much healthier and stronger they are, and how each of them lives the longest life possible, although they have neither hands nor human intelligence. And yet, to counter-balance these and their other limitations, they have one very great blessing – they own no property.[22]

Health, strength, long life – all that most people aspire to – can be found in animals, not despite their lack of property, but precisely because of this lack. Animals, in other words, are happy – happier than property-owning men and women.

Jesus, too, comments on the happiness of the animals. This has its roots in their freedom from cares and in their exemplary sense of liberty. "Do not be anxious about your life, what you will eat or what you will drink, nor about your body, what you will put on. Is not life more than food, and the body more than clothing? Look at the birds of the air: they neither sow nor reap nor gather into barns, and yet your heavenly father feeds them. Are you not of more value than they? And which of you by being anxious can add a single hour to his span of life?" (Matthew 6:25–27). The close parallelism between the saying of Jesus and that of Dio Chrysostom, both speaking about the carefree birds in the same context – that of the expectations of human life –, is worthy of note. Obviously, this is a topic of Cynic concern that has reached the Jewish Cynics. Within Jewish wisdom – that of the Old Testament and that of later rabbinic tradition – we find not a single parallel of this saying of Jesus; its derivation from the Cynic philosophical tradition is therefore highly plausible.[23] The emphasis on being free from cares and on trust in a benign god makes us aware of the thorough optimism of the Cynic philosophy, both Greek and Jewish.

---

22   Dio Chrysostom of Prusa, *Discourses* 10.16; see idem, *Discourses 1–11* (trans. J.W. Cohoon; LCL; Cambridge, MA: Harvard University Press, 1961), 429, slightly edited.
23   F. Gerald Downing, "Deeper Reflections on the Jewish Cynic Jesus," *JBL* 117 (1998): 97–104, 103.

Tranquillity and inner peace are its hallmark; perhaps contentment is the best English word to describe this state of mind.

When the Cynics recommended voluntary poverty and celebrated the freedom and happiness of animals, they did so in a particular form of speech for which they are rightly famous: the diatribe. This will be our next subject.

## 4    Fourth Observation: Cynic Diatribes in the Gospels

The Cynics are well known for their 'diatribe'. This form of public speech can be defined as the instruction of laypeople and social criticism couched in an entertaining form. As a rule, it does not aim at recruiting people for the philosophical life, but at the moral advancement of everyone – the audience or the readership. The diatribe is meant to speak personally to everyone, and everyone is meant to learn something.

The diatribe often adopts an urgent, serious tone of exhortation, but despite its pedagogical aim, it equally often creates a conversational atmosphere in which themes and perspectives are only loosely connected. Diatribes may be quite chatty. In this vein, the speaker resorts to similes and comparisons and is eager to use witty quotations from established authors. Typical subjects include: the comparison of wealth and poverty (which consistently extolls poverty, for wealth is inevitably associated with trouble); the recommendation of self-sufficiency as the ideal rule of life; the battle against the passions that make life so difficult; reconciliation to being banned from one's hometown by political adversaries; and warnings against the seeking of pleasure that some consider the highest good humans can achieve. Advice is given for dealing with the difficulties of human interaction and one's acceptance of illness, old age, and death. The general objective is to teach "a helpful view of life that minimises affliction and sadness."[24] Later, popular Christian preachers came to adopt the same range of subjects, which is why they sound so familiar to us.

The Jewish Cynics also use the rhetorical form of the diatribe. John the Baptist gave a sermon calling for social solidarity:

> And the crowds asked him, "What shall we do?" And he answered them: "Whoever has two tunics is to share with him who has none, and whoever has food is to do likewise." Tax collectors also came to be baptised

---

[24] Thomas Schmeller, *Paulus und die "Diatribe". Eine vergleichende Stilinterpretation* (NTA NF 19; Münster: Aschendorff, 1987), 206 (my translation).

and said to him: "Teacher, what shall we do?" And he said to them: "Collect no more than you are authorised to do." Soldiers also asked him, "And we, what shall we do?" And he said to them, "Do not extort money from anyone by threats or by false accusation, and be content with your wages." (Luke 3:10–14)

The exhortation aims at an ethos of sharing, of self-sufficiency, of not engaging in acts of greed. The same rhetoric of the diatribe is characteristic of the manner in which Jesus taught. This is particularly evident in his use of parables, stories he made up ad-hoc, and the use of quotations from the Bible and allusions to scriptural passages. In the ancient world, the similarity of the manner in which Jesus and the Cynic diatribe communicated was well known and commented upon. The church father Origen, for instance, states what Jesus has in common with Epictetus: both use simple language that can be understood by everyone. By contrast, the esoteric idiom used by the Platonic philosophers is only of use to a very few people. "Many have received advantage from those who wrote and taught in a simple and practical manner, and with a view to the wants of the multitude" (*Contra Celsum* 6.2). Such teachers, says Origen, are Jesus and Epictetus, the Stoic-Cynic philosopher.

The Jesuanic parable of the rich man and poor Lazarus is a particularly fine piece from the repertoire of the diatribe: the rich man does not give away a single morsel from his opulent dinner; he has no sympathy for the poor and famished man. When the two die, their fortunes are reversed. Lazarus now takes his rest in heaven, whereas the rich man suffers in hell, being unable to quench his terrible thirst (Luke 16:19–31). This story finds its closest equivalent in the tale of the wealthy tyrant Megapenthes and the poor shoemaker Mikyllos. Transmitted by Lucian, this story belongs to Menippan satire, a literary type devised by the Cynic philosopher Menippus.[25] The story, set in the netherworld, tells of the arrival of three men who had just died: the philosopher Cyniscus, the tyrant Megapenthes, and the shoemaker Mikyllos. The three stand before the judge of the dead. The judge sends the shoemaker and the Cynic philosopher to the Isles of the Blest. As for the rich man, the judge is undecided: shall he be thrown into the lake of fire or left to Cerberos, to be devoured by the beast that guards the entrance to Hades? Cyniscus suggests

---

25  Lucian, "The Downward Journey of the Tyrant," in *Lucian in Eight Volumes* (trans. A.M. Harmon; LCL; Cambridge, MA: Harvard University Press, 2009), vol. 2. For a recent discussion of this text and its relationship with Luke 16, see Nils Neumann, *Armut und Reichtum im Lukasevangelium und in der kynischen Philosophie* (SBS 220; Stuttgart: Katholisches Bibelwerk, 2010).

a different kind of punishment: he shall stand in chains next to Tantalus, to suffer eternally from thirst, and remember his former life. No reader of this story will miss its Cynic provenance. The shoemaker (in the Hellenistic story) and the beggar (of the New Testament parable) represent the poor philosopher whose misfortune will be reversed in the afterlife.

The actual point made in the story of the poor Cynic and the rich man is not to teach about the afterlife; the point has to do with the present life: the well-to-do are exhorted to be generous toward the Cynic philosophers and welcome them as guests. This is clear from a feature of the New Testament parable that is overlooked by modern interpreters: Lazarus is placed in Abraham's bosom. Read with Greek culture in mind, this means that he is Abraham's guest. Abraham is someone known for his generous entertainment of guests, as can be seen from Genesis chapter 18, where Abraham receives guests and entertains them well. So much for a Jesuanic piece straight from the repertoire of the Cynics!

The next piece of evidence for Cynic influence in the gospels has to do with popular reactions to the diatribe.

## 5 Fifth Observation: "Love Your Enemies" – A Cynic and Jesuanic Commandment

Those who adopt the philosophical way of life are often ridiculed and made fun of; in fact, they may even be insulted and driven away. This happens all the more to those who are begging or seek to instruct others through their public speeches. Those who meddle with other people's affairs are rarely welcome. How shall the philosopher react?[26]

The answer belongs to the very core of Cynic teaching: maltreatment is to be borne with patience; the Cynic philosopher must under all circumstances avoid pointless debates and must never strike back or let himself provoke fights and brawls. The philosopher, steadfast in character, must be utterly immune to insults. The endurance of maltreatment ranks as a kind of initiation trial for those who take up the Cynic life. According to Epictetus, everyone who prepares for the Cynic profession has to expect many beatings. "A very pretty thread, woven into the Cynic way of life, is this: he must be thrashed like a donkey, and while being thrashed, he must love those who beat him, as

---

26 For a survey of philosophical answers, see John P. Meier, *A Marginal Jew: A New Perspective on the Historical Jesus* (vol. 1ff.; London: Yale University Press, 1991–), 4:544–48.

though he were the father or brother of them all" (Epictetus, *Discourses* 3.22, 54).[27] Despite such maltreatment, the Cynic has to stay true to the role that he has adopted: that of the father or brother, who is bound always to show forbearance and even love.

In the Roman Imperial Period at least, the Cynics recommend love of the enemy to their followers. An example can be found in Seneca's treatise *De clementia* (*On Clemency*, 55/56 CE), which is dedicated to the boisterous Nero on the occasion of his eighteenth birthday. Clemency and humanity are recommended on the basis of an impressive, though historically doubtful example: after a failed attempt on his life, the Emperor Augustus summons his opponent Cinna. On the advice of his wife Livia, the emperor offers Cinna friendship and a government position. "From this very day, our friendship shall once again begin" (*ex hodierna die inter nos iterum amicitia incipiat*, Seneca, *De clementia* 3.7.11). The enemy is to be made into a friend. There is no truly philosophical life without love of the enemy! With this rule, the old aristocratic ethos is abandoned, which was based upon a contrary rule: there is no truly heroic life without revenge on the enemy! Odysseus, upon his return home, slaughters the suitors of his wife Penelope, as was expected of him. But the philosophers no longer subscribe to the ethos of revenge: Odysseus is bound to take revenge, but Augustus must show clemency. Such clemency finds its model in the gods who bestow their benefits irrespective of the worthiness of the recipients: "If you wish to imitate the gods, then bestow benefits upon the ungrateful as well as the grateful; for the sun rises upon the wicked as well as the good, the seas are open even to pirates" (Seneca, *De beneficiis* 4.26.1). Let me quote one final passage: "But the genuine Cynic has no enemy, even though men strike his feeble body or drag his name in the mire, or slander and speak ill of him, because enmity is felt only towards an opponent, but that which is above personal rivalry is usually loved and respected" (Julian, *Against the Cynic Herakleios* 214d). With these words, the Emperor Julian recommends love of the enemy, the hallmark of the Cynic ethics.

The Jewish Cynic teaches: "Love your enemies, pray for those who persecute you, so that you may become sons of your father," because God also loves his enemies, for "he makes his sun rise on the evil and on the good, and sends rain on the just and on the unjust."[28] This is what Jesus teaches, and it sounds

---

27  All translations are adapted from Epictetus, *Discourses, Fragments, Handbook* (trans. Robin Hard; Oxford World's Classics; Oxford: Oxford University Press, 2014).

28  Q 6:27; this is a passage in the Sayings Source, reconstructed from Matthew 5:44–45 and Luke 6:27, see James M. Robinson et al. (eds.), *The Critical Edition of Q: Synopsis* (Leuven: Peeters, 2000), 56–58.

like the abstract of a diatribe whose pattern would require an elaboration that develops arguments and commentary on ethical teaching. Transmitted only in the gospels of Luke and Matthew, the relevant saying comes from the Sayings Source, the oldest collection of the sayings of Jesus. The 'love of the enemy' theme is absent from the Old Testament, and it can be found nowhere else in the New Testament; it is also absent from the Judaeo-Hellenistic authors such as Philo of Alexandria and Josephus. Only where the Cynic spirit reigns can the love of enemies be taught and practiced.[29]

Thus far, we have neglected a subject of much importance: that of religion. How do the Cynics feel about this subject?

## 6 Sixth Observation: The God of the Cynics – and That of Jesus

It seems that the Cynics were generally sympathetic to the monotheistic notion of God. From Antisthenes, historically the very first Cynic philosopher, we have the following quotation: "Many gods exist by convention, but only one in reality."[30] But whether the early Cynics actually believed in God is a controversial question debated among specialists. Only the sources dating from the time of the Roman emperors attest to Cynic belief in a living god with personal characteristics. "All things are full of God" (πάντα γάρ ἐστιν αὐτοῦ πλήρη) is a saying Diogenes reportedly quoted, though – characteristically – he uses it in a satirical context (Diogenes Laertius, *Lives of Eminent Philosophers* 6.37). Another dictum, also attributed to Diogenes, reads as follows: "All things belong to the gods. The wise are friends of the gods, and friends hold everything in common. Therefore all things belong to the wise," i.e., to the Cynic philosophers (Diogenes Laertius, *Lives of Eminent Philosophers* 6.37). In the *Cynic Epistles*, an epistolary novel about the early Cynics, Diogenes describes his way of life as "going about the whole earth a free man under father Zeus, afraid of none of the great lords."[31] If we wish to resort to the language of the Chris-

---

29  Lang, *Jesus der Hund*, 132–34; see also Walter Radl, "Feindesliebe in der Umwelt des Neuen Testaments," in idem, *Das Evangelium nach Lukas* (vol. 1ff.; Freiburg: Herder, 2003–), 1:400–403.

30  Λέγεται... τὸ κατὰ νόμον εἶναι πολλούς, κατὰ δὲ φύσιν ἕνα: Philodemus, *On Piety* (ed. Dirk Obbink; Oxford: Clarendon Press, 1996), 88. The same dictum is transmitted by Cicero, *De natura deorum* 1.32: "There are many gods believed in by the people, but only one that is known to nature."

31  *Cynic Epistles: Letters of Diogenes* 34.3; see Malherbe, *The Cynic Epistles*, 144–45 (Greek and Engl.): περιέλθω δὲ ἐλεύθερος ὑπὸ τὸν Δία πατέρα ἐπὶ ὅλης τῆς γῆς, μηδένα φοβούμενος τῶν μεγάλων δεσπότων.

tian tradition – and we have no other language – we may speak of a feeling of friendship with God or of being children of God. In this context, the Cynics generally speak of god in the singular, of one god, i.e., Zeus.

This monotheistic kind of belief was particularly developed by Epictetus; he may be considered the main representative of the pious Cynicism of the Roman Imperial Period, a period in which Greek philosophy, including Cynicism, had long since gained general acceptance. Gone were the days of Socrates during which philosophy had to fight for recognition.[32] Homer had already called Zeus "the father of gods and men" (*Odyssey* 1.28), and Epictetus could start from there. For him, Zeus is the good father; he practices benevolence to everyone. "No human being is an orphan; but all have a father who takes care of them – constantly and for ever" (Epictetus, *Discourses* 3.24.15). Zeus, deeply concerned about humanity, entrusts the Cynics with the task of serving humankind as teachers. Epictetus has no doubt about this mission: the true Cynic "must know that he has been sent to men by Zeus as a messenger, to show them that they are wholly mistaken with regard to what is good and bad, and are seeking the nature of the good and the bad where it is not to be found, and never think to look for where it is" (*Discourses* 3.22.23). In other words, the philosopher feels himself to be called and commissioned by Zeus – a proud and altogether noteworthy self-assessment of the Cynics.

One special feature of Epictetus' version of Cynic philosophy is the way in which he refers to Heracles, the demi-god whom Cynics had always considered their model. Epictetus extols the almost excessive personal piety of Heracles, who felt that he was a privileged child of God: "To him [Heracles] it was not merely a matter of hearsay that Zeus is the father of men, but he truly regarded him as his own father, and called him so. He looked to him in all that he did. That is why he was able to live happily wherever he was" (*Discourses* 3.24.16). Epictetus addresses young men, and he exhorts them to leave the protection of the parental home in order to entrust themselves to God, in imitation of Heracles:

> If Hercules had sat around at home with his family, what would he have been? ...Come now, as he travelled through the world, how many com-

---

32  Two recent works by Jan Dressler offer an update on the fifth-century BCE Athenian controversies about philosophy and religion and the court case of Socrates: *Philosophie vs. Religion? Die Asebie-Verfahren gegen Anaxagoras, Protagoras und Sokrates im Athen des fünften Jahrhunderts v. Chr.* (Norderstedt: Books on Demand, 2010); *Wortverdreher, Sonderlinge, Gottlose: Kritik an Philosophie und Rhetorik im klassischen Athen* (Beiträge zur Altertumskunde 331; Berlin: De Gruyter, 2014).

> rades did he have with him, and how many friends? But he had no dearer friend than God. For this reason he was believed to be a son of God, and indeed he was. Accordingly, it was in obedience to God that he travelled around the world, purging it of injustice and lawlessness. (*Discourses* 2.16.44)

Heracles is deemed the model philosopher who regards himself as being under the special care and protection of his divine father.

The variety of Jewish Cynicism found in the New Testament is closely related to the pious Cynicism of Epictetus. Its key idea is the fatherhood of God. Just think of Jesus' advice: "Pray to your Father" (Matthew 6:6); "I thank you, Father, Lord of heaven and earth, that you have hidden these things from the wise and understanding, and revealed them to little children" (Matthew 11:25). Very much like some of the Greek Cynics, their Jewish counterparts thought of themselves as the privileged children of the divine father. The title "messenger of God" given to the Jewish Cynic is well attested; John the Baptist, for instance, is portrayed as "a man sent from God" (John 1:6), and our sources include similar statements about Jesus and Paul (Luke 4:18; Galatians 1:1).

The underlying notion of God merits a closer look. The Bible and ancient Jewish sources speak about God in many ways, and it contributes to our understanding when we see how the view of Jesus differs from other views. Two main trajectories within the biblical tradition can be discerned: according to one, God is in the first place the lord of the Jewish people, the god of the nation and its history – for instance in the prophet Hosea and in the traditions associated with the name of Moses; according to the other trajectory, represented by wisdom writings such as the book of Job and the book of Proverbs, God is the God of all of humankind, and the notion of a specially privileged nation is absent. The notion of God we find with Jesus is of the latter kind: the individual is seen as being confronted with God as his creator and caretaker. Accordingly, Jesus says, God "makes the sun rise on the evil and on the good" (Matthew 5:45). In the words of Ernest Renan: "The God of Jesus is not a narrow-minded despot who elected the Israelites to be his people and specially protects them. He is the God of humanity – *c'est le Dieu de l'humanité*."[33] Jesus' notion of God stands closer to philosophical ideas than to a specifically national theology. God, for Jesus, is a universal god rather than an ethnic deity.

---

33   "Le dieu de Jésus n'est pas le despote partial qui a choisi Israël pour son people et le protégé envers et contre tout. C'est le Dieu de l'humanité." Ernest Renan, *Vie de Jésus* (Paris: Lévy, 1863), 78 (ch. 5).

A particularly prominent feature in the New Testament portrait of God is his caring love. "Your Father knows what you need before you ask him" (Matthew 6:8), says Jesus in the Sermon on the Mount. This notion derives from the Old Testament, where it is particularly well expressed in the book of Psalms, especially in Psalms 145 and 146. The Psalmist praises God's beneficence: "The eyes of all look to you, and you give them their food in due season. You open your hand, you satisfy the desire of every living thing" (Psalm 145:15–16).

But we must not misinterpret these statements. The Jewish Cynic portrays God as father, but he does not offer any precise description. While God "used to speak to Moses face to face, as a man speaks to his friend" (Exodus 33:11) and Isaiah saw God (Isaiah 6:1), we hear of no comparable contact between Jesus and God. Whereas the prophets of old, such as Isaiah and Jeremiah, transmit divine messages literally, i.e., in the form of divine speech in the first person, Jesus never quotes God. Jesus is indebted to the worldview of Elijah, the prophet who is not allowed to see God. When Elijah comes into immediate contact with the divine realm, he has to do with an angel. Although called father, God somehow remains transcendent. God's appearance is not visualised, neither are his words quoted, nor do we hear (strange as it may seem) of any personal contact between Jesus and the deity.

His positive, yet restricted view of the deity is closely related to how the Cynics felt about ritual acts.

## 7 Seventh Observation: Ritual Acts, Critically Assessed – By the Cynics and by Jesus

As is well known, ancient culture was shaped by, and indeed based upon, its religion – i.e., cultic observances, rituals, and associated beliefs. Sacrificial offerings, festivals, temples, and respect for purity customs lay at the heart of religious life. The ancient Greek *polis* thought of itself as a ritual community that acknowledged its gods through ritual acts. But Greek religion was exposed to the criticism of philosophers, and in Hellenistic-Roman times, some Jewish philosophers also expressed their critical opinion of the religious traditions of their culture.

The first figure to consider is Socrates, because the Cynics regarded him as their master and their model. As is well known, Socrates was accused of not acknowledging the gods of Athens, and his defence against this charge was not accepted by the Athenian jury. Socrates was sentenced to death and died in 399 BCE, at the age of seventy. Modern authors do not agree with the Athenian jury; Socrates, they assure us, shared his contemporaries' belief in the gods.³⁴ According to Xenophon, who deplored the death sentence, Socrates often offered sacrifices, both in public and in his home (Xenophon, *Memorabilia* 1.2.1). In reality, this may not be true. He either never or very rarely took part in public acts of worship. The same reserved attitude toward public worship can be seen in Diogenes, the emblematic representative of the Cynic way of life. As late as the fourth century CE, the Emperor Julian – known as Julian the Apostate (from Christianity) – eloquently defended Diogenes:

> Let not the Cynic be like Oenomaus shameless or impudent, or a scorner of everything human and divine, but reverent towards sacred things, like Diogenes who obeyed the Pythian oracle, and did not repent of his obedience. But if anyone supposes that because he did not visit the temples or worship statues or altars this is a sign of impiety, he does not think rightly. For Diogenes possessed nothing that is usually offered, incense or libations or money to buy them with. He held right opinions about the gods, and that alone was sufficient. He worshipped them with his whole soul, thus offering them as, I think, the most precious of his possessions – the dedication of his soul through his thoughts.³⁵

Diogenes is portrayed here as a philosopher who dispenses with outward religious acts; this he can legitimately do, because he cultivates what is essential in religion: correct thinking about the gods. This well-known argument has often been made, generally in the following manner: simple folk need outward acts of worship, including liturgical splendour, but the educated prefer to venerate God spiritually. The deists of the eighteenth century believed they could do without all outward ceremonies. For them, ritual acts were only meaningful if they reminded people of their moral duties – thus Immanuel Kant in his book *Religion within the Limits of Reason Alone* (1793).

Greek Cynics not only distanced themselves from sacrificial worship; they also did not think very highly of the mystery cults. According to Greek belief, initiation into the mysteries of Eleusis secured a better life after death. Those who were initiated were sure to spend life after death on the Isles of the

---

34 For an excellent statement of the case, see Mark L. McPherran, "Socratic Theology and Piety," in *The Bloomsbury Companion to Socrates* (ed. J. Bussanich and N.D. Smith; London: Bloomsbury Academic, 2013), 257–75.

35 Julian, *To the Uneducated Cynics* (362 CE) 199 B, in *The Works of Emperor Julian* (3 vols.; trans. Emily Wilmer Cave Wright; LCL; Cambridge, Mass.: Harvard University Press, 1913), 2:53 (slightly edited).

Blest in the company of the gods. A fragment of Sophocles explains: "Thrice blessed are those mortals who have seen these rites before they come to Hades, for to them alone is granted true life. Everything evil awaits the rest."[36] After Sophocles' poem had become known, thousands of people – the uninitiated – were driven to despair. In Athens, poets were taken as seriously as the belief in the power of the mysteries. Yet Diogenes made fun of the mysteries. Should one's happiness in Hades really depend upon initiation into the mysteries rather than upon one's morality? When the Athenians urged Diogenes to become initiated, he was quick to point out the paradox: people of no distinction would enjoy all the privileges in Hades, while some of the great men of Greek history – King Agesilaos of Sparta and Epameinondas of Thebes – would "dwell in mire" (*Lives of Eminent Philosophers* 6.39). The response of Diogenes implies – and in part conceals – three paradoxes: first, the paradox of the unearned, post-mortem privilege of common folk; second, the paradox of the non-admission of non-Athenians to the mysteries; and third, the paradox of a possible privilege for distinguished personalities who would be united on the Isles of the Blest despite their having been enemies. Ancient thought was generally predisposed to believing in post-mortem privileges for the great men of political life. By associating Epameinondas and Agesilaos in a pleasant afterlife, Diogenes paradoxically united two enemies: Agesilaos, the leader of Sparta, and Epameinondas, the military commander of the city of Thebes. The two military leaders had actually fought against each other – and one can only speculate why Diogenes linked them in life after death. Would they become friends? Or did the philosopher simply mean to discredit the notion of afterlife privileges, or the notion of life after death altogether? These questions can be raised, but we do not have enough evidence to provide the answers. At any rate, Diogenes rejected belief in the power of the Eleusinian mysteries.

Let us pause here for a moment. Thus far, we have dealt with participation in public worship and the mystery cults. Both animal sacrifice (which epitomises public worship) and mystery initiation were rejected by the Cynics. Interestingly, the only complete biography of an ancient Cynic, *The Life of Demonax* by Lucian (ca. 160 CE), explicitly refers to both. Like Socrates before him, Demonax was accused in Athens of the double crime of not sacrificing to the gods and of not having himself initiated in the Eleusinian mysteries. Lucian tells how Demonax publicly defended himself: the gods need no sacrifices, and the prohibition of speaking about the details of the initiation seems

---

36  Sophocles, as quoted by Plutarch, *Quomodo adolescens poetas audire debeat* 21F.

to him irrational – it is surely irrational to prevent people from speaking about something that is good and valuable.[37]

Like its Greek model and inspiration, Jewish Cynicism was critical of traditional religious practice. Koheleth, the Cynic philosopher of the Old Testament, rejects the practice of sacrifice: "Guard your steps when you go to the house of God. To draw near to listen is better than to offer the sacrifice of fools, for they do not know that they are doing evil" (Ecclesiastes 4:17). Koheleth teaches a clear hierarchy of acts: the intellectual ritual (i.e., the explanatory interpretation of scripture, the sermon) ranks higher than sacrificial worship; the latter is of lesser relevance or, to be exact, is a sign of foolishness.[38] In his magisterial *Judaism and Hellenism,* Martin Hengel asks whether, under the increasing influence of the Greek spirit, the criticism introduced by Koheleth was not extended to become the "sharp criticism of the temple cult and the ritual law" voiced by the – eventually unsuccessful – Hellenistic reform party in Jerusalem of the 170s and 160s BCE.[39]

Like all Cynic philosophers, Jesus has a critical attitude towards the religious customs of his people. He infringes the Sabbath legislation and defends himself: "The Sabbath was made for man, not man for the Sabbath" (Mark 2:27). The human person therefore is the measure, not custom or law. Bold as they are, the Jewish Cynics are far from accepting the irritating and cumbersome complexities of traditional religious practice; instead, they simplify or abandon them. One particularly prominent case is the abolition of the rules of purity that prohibit the eating of certain foods: "Hear me, all of you, and understand: there is nothing outside a person that by going into him can defile him, but the things that come out of a person are what defile him" (Mark

---

37  Lucian, *Life of Demonax* 11; see *The Works of Lucian* (4 vols.; trans. H.W. Fowler and F.G. Fowler; Oxford: Clarendon Press, 1905), 3:4 or Dobbin (ed.), *The Cynic Philosophers from Diogenes to Julian*, 138. See also Daniel E. Ullicci, *The Christian Rejection of Animal Sacrifice* (New York: Oxford University Press, 2012), 62–63, who comments on the Cynics' outright rejection of animal sacrifice.

38  This is the conventional interpretation of Ecclesiastes 4:17. A thorough analysis of the syntactical and interpretive challenges of this verse is offered by Aron Pinker, "Intrusion of Ptolemaic Reality on Cultic Practices in Qoh 4:17," *Perspectives Hebrew Scriptures* (ed. E. Ben Zvi; Piscataway, NJ: Gorgias, 2010), 6:455–87. According to Pinker, Koheleth warns against the making of huge sacrifices. Pinker summarises his own suggestion as follows: "In the Ptolemaic reality those who make exorbitant gifts are fools. They would be observed and more severely taxed, and might lose all their possessions when unable to meet the demand of the tax collector" (478).

39  Martin Hengel, *Judaism and Hellenism: Studies in Their Encounter in Palestine During the Early Hellenistic Period* (2 vols.; Eugene, Oreg.: Wipf & Stock, 2003), 1:128.

7:14–15) – a stark statement whose scatological reference cannot be missed. Defecation defiles, not the eating of pork. The biblical commentator glosses the statement as follows: "Thus he declared all foods clean" (Mark 7:19). It may well be justifiable to call this saying "the most radical statement in the whole of the Jesus tradition."[40] The saying has a remarkable parallel in an anecdote about Diogenes: "Seeing someone perform religious purification, he said: 'Unhappy man, don't you know that you can no more get rid of errors of conduct by sprinklings than you can of mistakes of grammar?'" (*Lives of Eminent Philosophers* 6.42).

In his handling of ritual that lay people practice at the temple, Jesus demonstrates a similar sense of freedom. In this case, his critique of ritual acts develops into the founding of a new type of worship. In the circle of Jesus, the complex ritual with its animal sacrifice, priestly participation, temple, and altar with eternally burning fire is replaced by a rather simple ritual act: that of the offering of a piece of bread and a cup of wine, as practiced to this day in the churches. The details need not be considered here; they can be found elsewhere.[41]

## 8      The Inevitable Conclusion: Jesus Belongs among the Philosophers

After having offered a comparative study of the practice and thought of Cynics and the Jesuanic tradition and compiled observation upon observation, we must come to the conclusion.

---

40   Norman Perrin, *Rediscovering the Teaching of Jesus* (London: SCM, 1967), 150. According to some historians, Christian non-observance of food laws does not actually reflect the practice of Jesus himself, but dates only from after his death, i.e., from the 40s, and was introduced into the Jesus anecdotes of the gospels. Jesus may actually have followed Jewish purity customs. He may have been arguing against Pharisaic innovations, not against kosher regulations *per se*. He may have rejected the notion that impurity was transferred from unclean hands to food. See Yair Furstenberg, "Defilement Penetrating the Body: A New Understanding of Contamination in Mark 7.15," NTS 54 (2008): 176–200; James E. Crossley, "From Jesus Observing Food and Purity Laws to Some Christians Not Bothering: A Socio-Historical Explanation," in *Jesus in Continuum* (ed. T. Holmén; Tübingen: Mohr Siebeck, 2012), 87–113. A review of recent and traditional interpretations of the issue is offered by Wolfgang Stegemann, "Hat Jesus die Speisegesetze der Tora aufgehoben? Zur neuesten kontroversen Einschätzung des sog. 'Reinheitslogions' Mk 7,15," in *Jesus – Gestalt und Gestaltungen* (ed. P. von Gemünden et al.; Göttingen: Vandenhoeck & Ruprecht, 2013), 29–50.

41   Bernhard Lang, *Sacred Games: A History of Christian Worship* (London: Yale University Press, 1997), 215–33; idem, *Jesus der Hund*, 114–19.

It has become a commonplace to say that Jesus was a Jew (and not a Christian, for Christianity developed only after the life and work of Jesus). What often fails to be sufficiently considered, however, is the reality of Hellenistic Judaism or, as Stanley Porter prefers, "Judaism within Hellenism."[42] Appreciation for the Hellenistic context in which Jesus lived, Porter explains, "has been brought to the fore over the last thirty to forty years, as scholars have explored the post-classical world and come to terms with the spread of Hellenism to the furthest reaches of the Roman empire."[43] Hellenism implies the presence of some Greeks as well as contact between Greeks and non-Greeks, some knowledge and use of the Greek language, and the development of "rational philosophies" that were often sceptical of traditional religion.[44] "It is within this context that the question of Jesus' relation to Judaism and Hellenism must be asked and answered."[45]

Since the fourth century BCE, Judaism both in Palestine and in the Mediterranean Diaspora had come under the influence of Greek culture – its literature, its thinking, its philosophy, and, not least, its language. Judaism in the time of Jesus was thoroughly hellenised, even among those who sought to cultivate traditional Jewish ways. In the gospel, we read of a woman as "Greek, of Syro-Phoenician descent" (Mark 7:26), i.e., a hellenised Syrian. One wonders how this woman would have defined Jesus: possibly as "Greek, Jewish by descent." We know of several first-century individuals of whom this would be a good description – Herod the Great and his sons, Paul of Tarsus, Philo of Alexandria, Titus Flavius Josephus, and Justus of Tiberias. Jesus, I argue, belongs not just to Judaism but to Hellenistic Judaism. In Hellenistic Judaism, traditional Israelite and new Greek ways met and formed new, hybrid cultural formations – such as Christianity, which I take to be the main form in which Hellenistic Judaism survived.

Jewish Cynicism is the product of the encounter between Judaism and Greek culture in the Hellenistic period. Its existence is first attested in the book of Koheleth, dating from around 200 BCE. In the first century CE, we find another productive encounter between Judaism and Cynic philosophy, now leading to a social movement that attracted many people – Jewish Cynicism. It is to this movement that Jesus belongs. As a matter of fact, he absorbed Cynicism more fully than earlier Jewish Cynics.

---

42  Stanley E. Porter, "The Context of Jesus: Jewish and/or Hellenistic?," in *Handbook for the Study of the Historical Jesus* (ed. T. Holmén and S.E. Porter; 4 vols.; Leiden: Brill, 2011), 2:1441–63, 1461.

43  Porter, "The Context of Jesus," 1463.

44  Porter, "The Context of Jesus," 1456.

45  Porter, "The Context of Jesus," 1463.

Among the many subjects we have considered, three facts in particular lend strong support to the thesis of "Jesus the Cynic philosopher" and indeed make it inevitable:

- First, we know nothing about itinerant Jewish preachers in the time of Jesus; however, Cynic popular preachers travelled through the entire Mediterranean world. Jesus himself was one of them.
- Second, the encounter with a Cynic philosopher led many individuals to change their lives spontaneously, for instance by giving up all of their possessions. Stories about such conversions abound; they are also echoed in the New Testament – but not elsewhere in ancient Jewish sources.
- Third, the exhortations to love one's enemies and to "consider the birds" are typical of both Cynicism and Jesus, but not of traditional Judaism.

Where did Jesus come into contact with the philosophy of Diogenes? In the strongly hellenised milieu of Galilee, where he grew up. His activity as a skilled manual woodworker, the trade he abandoned, required a certain familiarity with the Greek language. Sepphoris, then the most important city of Galilee, boasted a mixed population of Jews and Gentiles. Its Roman theatre, apparently built in the early first century, existed until late antiquity. "Why should Jesus, who grew up in the vicinity of Sepphoris, not have heard some of the sayings told by itinerant Cynic preachers? The assumption that Jesus understood some Greek makes this even more likely," argues Martin Hengel in a study of the extent of the hellenisation of first-century Palestine.[46] Without his having had some knowledge of Greek and contact with Cynic thought, and without the Greek culture of Galilee, neither Jesus nor his followers can be understood. Although we have no means of measuring the competence Jesus had in speaking and understanding Greek, it is hardly likely that he only understood Aramaic. Too much points to his being bilingual in Greek and Aramaic, the main two languages spoken in first-century Galilee.[47] Tom Wright, to quote

---

46   Martin Hengel, "Zum Problem der 'Hellenisierung' Judäas," in idem, *Judaica et Hellenistica. Kleine Schriften I* (WUNT 90; Tübingen: Mohr Siebeck, 1996), 1–9 and 72 (my translation).

47   The main proponents of Jesus' competence in Greek are Stanley Porter and his student H.T. Ong; see Stanley E. Porter, "Did Jesus ever Teach in Greek?" *Tyndale Bulletin* 44 (1993): 199–235; idem, "Jesus and the Use of Greek in Galilee," in *Studying the Historical Jesus* (ed. B. Chilton and C.A. Evans; NTTS 19; Leiden: Brill, 1994), 123–54; idem, "The Language(s) Jesus Spoke," in *Handbook for the Study of the Historical Jesus* (ed. T. Holmén and S.E. Porter; 4 vols.; Leiden: Brill, 2011), 3:2455–71; Hughson T. Ong, *The Multilingual Jesus and the Sociolinguistic World of the New Testament* (Linguistic Biblical Studies 12; Leiden: Brill, 2016).

one more specialist, is convinced that Jesus knew more than one language. In an article, he supports this idea with reference to the matter-of-fact knowledge of several languages among many, even simple people in the Middle East today. Without difficulty, they get along in Arabic, Greek, and English.[48] For many people today and in ancient times, multilingualism was the rule rather than the exception.

We may therefore think of Jesus and John the Baptist as young men who, after having come into contact with Cynic ideas, enthusiastically adopted them and even infected others with their enthusiasm. We may consider Jesus a Diogenes-like figure. He merits a place among the philosophers.[49]

## Appendix: References to Cynic Philosophy in the Works of Philo of Alexandria

Philo's knowledge of, and indebtedness to, ancient philosophical authors is well known and well documented in recent scholarship. Philo is generally and correctly credited with a penchant for Platonism, but other schools of philosophy also figure in his writings. Occasionally, he refers to Cynic philosophers and uses their sayings or anecdotes for making a point or illustrating one. This annotated list is in three parts: the first part lists explicit references, the second one possible echoes, and the third one longer, Philonic texts that may be read as, or reflect, Cynic treatises.

### *Explicit References*

No. 1. "It is that which Antisthenes had in view when he said: 'A virtuous man is a burden hard to be borne.' For as want of sense is a light thing easily tossed about, so,

---

[48] Tom Wright, "In Israel's Scriptures," *Times Literary Supplement* 5672 (16 December 2011): 10–12, 12.

[49] While believing in Cynic influence on Jesus, I do not overstate the case: Jesus apparently relies on *two* sources of inspiration – one Greek and Cynic, and another one Jewish and prophetic, as explained in Lang, *Jesus der Hund*. While "Jesus the philosopher" still lacks general acceptance among biblical scholars, he does receive scholarly attention. The relevant research was pioneered by F. Gerald Downing; for a summary of this scholar's views, see Downing, "Jesus and Cynicism," in *Handbook for the Study of the Historical Jesus* (ed. T. Holmén and S.E. Porter; 4 vols.; Leiden: Brill, 2011), 2:1105–36. Recent studies include Bernhard Lang, *Jesus der Hund: Leben und Lehre eines jüdischen Kynikers* (Munich: Beck, 2010); Leif E. Vaage, "Q and Cynicism: On Comparison and Social Identity," in idem, *Columbus, Q and Rome: Reframing Interpretation of the Christian Bible* (SBAB 52; Stuttgart: Katholisches Bibelwerk, 2011), 143–69.

on the contrary, wisdom is a well-established and immovable thing so heavy that is not easily agitated." Philo, *Quod omnis probus liber sit* 28. – Antisthenes (ca. 445–365 BCE) is generally taken to be the founder of Cynic philosophy. It is not known from which of his lost works the quotation comes.

No. 2. Philo tells the story of how Diogenes did not despair when he was taken prisoner by robbers and sold into slavery; see Philo, *Quod omnis probus liber sit* 121–24. – The account belongs to the stock of well-known anecdotes associated with the emblematic figure of Cynic philosophy; a shorter version than Philo's can be found in an independent, post-Philonic source: Diogenes Laertius, *Lives of Eminent Philosophers* 6.29–30. According to Goulet-Cazé,[50] Philo may have actually read *The Sale of Diogenes* by the Cynic philosopher Menippus.

No. 3. "Diogenes, seeing one of the so-called freedmen preening himself, and a great many others who congratulated him, marvelled at their want of reason and judgment. 'It is just as if someone were to proclaim that one of his servants, from this day forth, should be accounted a grammarian, geometrician, or musician, without having the very slightest idea of the art.' Just as the proclamation would not make men learned, neither would it make them free (for then it would be a blessed thing). All that it could do would be to make them no longer slaves." Philo, *Quod omnis probus liber sit* 157. – This anecdote is not known from any other ancient source.

No. 4. "His [i.e. Diogenes'] freedom of speech (παρρησία) was emulated by Chaereas, a man of culture. When he was living in Alexandria by Egypt, he once incurred the anger of [king] Ptolemy who threatened him in no mild terms. Chaereas, considering that his own natural freedom was not a whit inferior to the other's kingship, replied: 'Rule your Egyptian slaves; but as for me, I neither care for you, nor fear your wrath and angry threats' [parody on Homer, *Iliad* 1.180–81]." Philo, *Quod omnis probus liber sit* 125. – Philo, who lived in Alexandria, must have heard the anecdote there. But we cannot determine which Ptolemy is meant, and we cannot date Chaereas. This philosopher or philosophically-minded individual does not figure in the standard list of Cynic philosophers,[51] but Goulet-Cazé acknowledges that Chaereas "could have been" a Cynic.[52]

No. 5. "For he indeed is the true man, and it was of him that one of the ancients [i.e. Diogenes the Cynic] spoke, when he lit a lamp at midday and told those who asked

---

50  Marie-Odile Goulet-Cazé, *Cynisme et christianisme dans l'Antiquité* (Paris: Vrin, 2014), 108.
51  Marie-Odile Goulet-Cazé, "A Comprehensive Catalogue of Known Cynic Philosophers," in *The Cynics: The Cynic Movement in Antiquity and Its Legacy* (ed. R. Bacht Branham and O. Goulet-Cazé; Berkeley: University of California Press, 1996), 389–413; eadem, "Répertoire des philosophes cyniques connus," in eadem, *L'ascèse cynique* (2nd ed; Paris: Vrin, 2001), 231–49.
52  Goulet-Cazé, *Cynisme et christianisme dans l'Antiquité*, 107.

what he meant that he was seeking – a man." Philo, *De gigantibus* 33 [in LCL, 34]. – This is a well-known Diogenes anecdote, also found in Diogenes Laertius, *Lives of Eminent Philosophers* 6.41.

No. 6. Commenting on the many meanings of the Greek word for 'dog', Philo also refers to the Cynic or dog-philosophers Diogenes and Aristippus, adding that "an incalculable number of men" practice these philosophers' way of life; see Philo, *De plantatione* 151. – The names 'Diogenes' and 'Aristippus' seem to stand for two alternatives within the Cynic school of thought: Diogenes represents the austere, ascetic approach, whereas Aristippus the hedonistic one. It may well be that Philo himself sided with Aristippus, who held that riches and pleasures were compatible with the Cynic way; this is also what the Cynic Demonax (second century CE) thought.[53] Philo's own view is this: "The bad man considers the acquisition of riches as the most perfect good possible; but the good man looks upon riches only as a necessary and useful thing" (Philo, *Legum allegoriae* 2.17).[54]

No. 7. There are two opinions regarding the future of the world: according to one, the world is periodically conflagrated and subsequently regenerated; according to the other, it is indestructible and preserved for all time. Diogenes, when he was very young, agreed with the latter opinion; see Philo, *De aeternitate mundi* 77.

## *Possible Echoes – Individual Passages*

No. 8. According to Philo, someone of lower rank should not be submissive when talking to someone of higher rank; instead, he should demonstrate boldness by speaking frankly (Philo, *Quis rerum divinarum heres* 5). Moses made use of this approach when speaking with God (Philo, *De sacrificiis Abelis et Caini* 12). In *De Iosepho*, Philo has two humble individuals address a dignitary with frankness: "Joseph, nothing awed by the high dignity of the speaker (i.e., the king of Egypt), spoke to him with frankness (παρρησία) combined with modesty, rather as a king to a subject than as a subject to the king" (*De Iosepho* 107). One of Joseph's brothers demonstrates the same virtue when speaking to the vice-regent of Egypt: "the fourth in age, who combined boldness and courage with modesty and practiced frankness of speech (παρρησία) without effrontery, approached him (i.e., the vice-regent) and said..." (*De Iosepho* 222). – The Cynics valued 'frankness of speech' (παρρησία) and are well known for it; see above,

---

53  Lucian, *Life of Demonax* 52 and 62, in *The Cynic Philosophers from Diogenes to Julian* (trans. R. Dobbin; London: Penguin, 2012), 144–45.

54  On the debate between austere and hedonistic Cynics, see Troy W. Martin, *By Philosophy and Empty Deceit: Colossians as Response to a Cynic Critique* (JSNT.S 118; Sheffield: Sheffield Academic Press, 1996), 64, 70, and 98; Bernhard Lang, *Jesus der Hund: Leben und Lehre eines jüdischen Kynikers* (Munich: Beck, 2010), 61 and 66. The validity of the distinction is questioned by Goulet-Cazé, *Cynisme et christianisme dans l'Antiquité*, 56–65.

no. 4. In particular, the passage that refers to Joseph, the slave who speaks like a king, definitely sounds like an echo of the Diogenes tradition.[55]

No. 9. The Greeks would identify themselves as citizens of a particular *polis*, such as Athens or Corinth. The Cynics, by contrast, identified their *polis* with the whole world. To express this notion, they coined the word κοσμοπολίτης, 'citizen of the world'. Diogenes is reported to have used it when he was asked where he was from; see Lucianus, *Vitarum auctio* 8; Diogenes Laertius, *Lives of Eminent Philosophers* 6.63. – Philo, the first author in whose work the word 'cosmopolitan' can be found, uses it nine times: Philo, *De opificio mundi* 3 (the man who is obedient to the law is a 'citizen of the world'), 142 and 143; *De gigantibus* 61; *De confusione linguarum* 106 (Moses is a 'citizen of the world'); *De migratione Abrahami* 59; *De vita Mosis* 1.157; *De specialibus legibus* 2.45; *De somniis* 1.243 (here in the feminine form, 'the cosmopolitan souls').[56] The opposite is μικροπολίτης, 'citizen of a petty state', a word coined to denote parochialism (Philo, *De somniis* 1.39).

No. 10. "The law" – meaning the Jewish law – "sets down every day as a festival." Philo, *De specialibus legibus* 2.42. – In Greek sources, the notion of every day being a festival appears only in association with the Cynics Diogenes and Crates. When Diogenes "saw his host in Sparta preparing with much ado for a certain festival," he said, "Does not a good man consider every day a festival?" (Plutarch, *De tranquilitate animi* 20, 477c). "Crates, though he had but a wallet and a threadbare cloak, passed his whole life jesting and laughing as though at a festival" (Plutarch, *De tranquilitate animi* 4, 466e). No Jewish law considers every day to be a festival, though it has been argued that Philo derived the idea from the biblical prescription of daily sacrifices at the temple (Numbers 28:1–8) and not from a Cynic dictum.[57]

No. 11. It happens rather frequently, reports Philo, that robbers, pirates, and women of questionable behaviour become initiated into the mystery cults, whereas some men of noble virtue avoid the mysteries; see Philo, *De specialibus legibus* 1.323. – This critique of the practice of mystery cults is also attributed to Diogenes the Cynic; see Plutarch, *Quomodo adolescens poetas audire debeat* 21f; Diogenes Laertius, *Lives of Eminent Philosophers* 6.39.

No. 12. For drinking, no cup is needed; use your two hands and form them into a cup; see Philo, *De somniis* 2.60. – The Philonic diatribe that includes this advice echoes many Cynic themes. This particular item may reflect the well-known anecdote

---

55  On the Cynic as philosopher-king, see Lang, *Jesus der Hund*, 93–95.
56  On Philo's use of the word, see Philo of Alexandria, *On the Creation of the Cosmos according to Moses. Introduction, Translation and Commentary by David T. Runia* (Philo of Alexandria Commentary Series 1; Leiden: Brill, 2001), 103.
57  Jutta Leonhardt, *Jewish Worship in Philo of Alexandria* (TSAJ 84; Tübingen: Mohr Siebeck, 2001), 25–28.

according to which Diogenes, upon seeing a child drinking out of his hands, threw away his cup; see Diogenes Laertius, *Lives of Eminent Philosophers* 6.37. In Islamic tradition, the same anecdote is told of Jesus.[58]

### Longer Philonic Texts

No. 13. There is a notable density of explicit references to Cynic anecdotes in Philo, *Quod omnis probus liber sit*; see above, nos. 1–4. – In this treatise on freedom, Philo used and exploited a written source that we may identify as a collection of anecdotes about Diogenes and some of his followers (nos. 2–4). This source may have been more comprehensive; the evidence warrants the assumption that it included other material, such as the saying of Diogenes' teacher Antisthenes (no. 1). Accordingly, one may assume that most, if not all, of Philo's references to and echoes of the Cynic tradition derive from a single written source. Philo exploited this source for compiling *Quod omnis probus liber sit*. But he added material of his own – a few scattered references to the Bible and, notably, the sketch of the life of the Essenes (*Quod omnis probus liber sit*, 75–87). Essene antipathy toward luxury and refinement, their refusal to own weapons and engage in warfare, refusal of slavery, and preference for practical ethics over philosophical speculation and physics all correspond closely to Cynic ideas and ideals.[59] Accordingly, historians should include Philo's treatise in the Cynic literary corpus.

No. 14. Many, if not most, people act according to the 'pleasure principle', which tells them to seek pleasure at all costs. The moralising sections of Philo, *Legum allegoriae* II and III understand pleasure (ἡδονή) as the root of all evil, which is a Cynic idea. Accordingly, fighting against the 'pleasure principle' is one of the essential tasks of the Cynic; see for instance Dio of Prusa, *Orations* 8.20–26 (*The Cynic Philosophers from Diogenes to Julian*, 106–107). – Émile Bréhier called the moralising sections of *Legum allegoriae* II and III "un veritable traité de morale cynique" – a treatise on Cynic ethics.[60]

No. 15. In writing about the Hebrew festivals in his *De specialibus legibus* 2.41–261, Philo may have used a Jewish-Cynic treatise that one may call "The Book of the Ten Festivals." – This idea was suggested by Isaak Heinemann.[61] This suggestion has received support from at least one more scholar, Richard Goulet. A better understanding

---

58  Tarif Khalidi, *The Muslim Jesus: Sayings and Stories in Islamic Literature* (Cambridge, MA: Harvard University Press, 2001), 94 (no. 222).

59  Goulet-Cazé, *Cynisme et christianisme dans l'Antiquité*, 108.

60  Émile Bréhier, *Les idées philosophiques et religieuses de Philon d'Alexandrie* (Paris: Picard, 1907), 262.

61  Isaak Heinemann, *Philons griechische und jüdische Bildung* (1932; repr. Darmstadt: Wissenschaftliche Buchgesellschaft 1962), 97–154; see esp. Heinemann's tentative reconstruction of the contents of this source, 142–44.

of Philo's exegetical writing can be gained, argues Goulet, through insight into his indebtedness to and reworking of earlier and philosophically more radical work on the books of the Pentateuch written by anonymous Alexandrian intellectuals, who may have belonged to the Jewish fraternity of the Therapeutae, a group of philosophically-minded ascetics.[62] Accordingly, the notion of Philo as a redactor may well be the key to understanding much of Philo's literary production. In the case of the "Book of the Ten Festivals," one may also consider the possibility that it represents an early work written by Philo himself, a work that he revised in the light of his later, more pietistic approach to the Jewish heritage.

No. 16. In *De Iosepho* 28–32, 35–36, 58–60, 125, Philo may have used a Jewish-Cynic treatise that included an interpretation of the biblical Joseph figure. – Heinemann,[63] who suggested the idea, offers a paraphrase of the possible source. This source followed the Cynic notion of the state and its laws as being essentially superfluous in its biblical interpretation. The biblical laws that God established for Israel were seen as 'additions' to the natural law, the latter alone being deemed universal and binding for the Cynics, who lived according to nature. The name of Joseph, the Jewish statesman who became viceroy in Egypt, was understood to mean "addition to the Lord" and taken to be a reference to the additional nature of the laws that God gave to the Jews. The source portrayed the statesman as a ridiculous figure who depends on and constantly seeks the support and admiration of the mob.

No. 17. Philo finds fault with "those who without full consideration give up the business and financial side of a citizen's life, saying that they have conceived contempt for fame and pleasure. For they do not despise these things, they are practicing an imposture. Their dirty bodies and gloomy faces, the rigour and squalor of their pinched life, are so many baits to lead others to regard them as lovers of orderliness, temperance, and endurance. But they are unable to deceive the more far-sighted" (*De fuga et inventione* 33–34). Although Philo does not actually refer to Cynics in this passage, he seems to think of them, or rather of pseudo-Cynics whose shabbiness he abhors. With these, Philo has no patience. A similar description can be found in *Quod deterius potiori insidiari soleat* 19.

## Conclusion

The list above may be incomplete, but despite its defects, it clearly demonstrates Philo's indebtedness to and reception of the Cynic tradition. At least occasionally, Philo appears as a follower of Diogenes and his like. Although Philo did not espouse

---

62   Richard Goulet, *La philosophie de Moïse: essai de reconstitution d'un commentaire philosophique préphilonien du Pentateuque* (Paris: Vrin, 1987).
63   Heinemann, *Philons griechische und jüdische Bildung*, 449–50.

the Cynic life of utter poverty himself, he was in favour of Cynical ethics. The Cynics never meant to convert everyone to their lifestyle, but they wanted to make people think and give up a life in pursuit of mere pleasures. In Philo, they certainly found a friend or, in more modern parlance, appointed him an honorary member of their trade. If speculation were allowed, we could think of *Quod omnis probus liber sit* as a Cynic treatise that the young Philo composed when going through a phase of positive association with the philosophy of the Cynics. This could have been some time around 25 CE,[64] i.e., during the lifetime of Jesus. Later, possibly after some sort of conversion, he adopted a more explicitly Jewish identity.[65] But even then he maintained his Cynic leanings, because the Cynic critique of mainstream Hellenistic-Roman culture supported his critical view of pagan Hellenism.[66]

---

64   As suggested by Joan E. Taylor, *The Essenes, the Scrolls, and the Dead Sea* (Oxford: Oxford University Press, 2012), 24.
65   Goulet, *La philosophie de Moïse*, 562 and 566.
66   For a statement of Philo's nuanced attitude, see Maren Niehoff, *Philo on Jewish Identity and Culture* (TSAJ 86; Tübingen: Mohr Siebeck, 2001), esp. 62–69.

# The Last Days of Socrates and Christ: *Euthyphro, Apology, Crito*, and *Phaedo* Read in Counterpoint with John's Gospel

*George van Kooten*

This paper will explore similarities between John's Gospel and the dialogues of Plato's *The Last Days of Socrates* in their portrayal of the figures of Socrates and Christ. What I intend to make plausible is that the author of John's Gospel was acquainted with these Platonic dialogues and found them useful for casting the biography of Jesus in terms recognisable for the Greek audience for which he wrote. Certainly, the figures of Christ and Socrates were amalgamated in later early Christian writings, as has been well researched by both Michael Frede and Mark Edwards.[1] What I will argue is that this amalgamation has already taken place in the first-century CE Gospel of John. It is noteworthy that, also from a pagan perspective, the compatibility of the figures of Socrates and Christ was recognised at an early stage, if indeed – as scholars such as Sebastian Brock, Fergus Millar, Craig A. Evans, and Ilaria Ramelli have argued – the letter from the Syrian Stoic philosopher Mara bar Serapion from Antioch, the manuscript of which is in the British Library, is written by a pagan and can be dated to the end of the first century CE.[2] In this letter Mara draws a comparison between the execution of particular philosophers by their own people and the subsequent divine punishment these people receive. According to Mara,

> What else can we say, when the wise are forcibly dragged off by tyrants, their wisdom is captured by insults, and their minds are oppressed and

---

1 Michael Frede, "The Early Christian Reception of Socrates," in *Remembering Socrates: Philosophical Essays* (ed. Lindsay Judson & V. Karasmanēs; Oxford: Oxford University Press, 2006), 188–202; Mark Edwards, "Socrates and the Early Church," in *Socrates from Antiquity to the Enlightenment* (ed. M. Trapp; Aldershot: Ashgate, 2007), 1:125–42.
2 See Sebastian Brock in *The Cambridge Ancient History* (Vol. 13; Cambridge: Cambridge University Press, 1998), 709; Fergus Millar, *The Roman Near East 31 BC – AD 337* (Cambridge, MA: Harvard University Press, 1993), 507; Craig A. Evans, "Jesus: Sources and Self-Understanding," in *Jesus and Philosophy: New Essays* (ed. Paul K. Moser; Cambridge: Cambridge University Press, 2008), 27–40, esp. 32–33; and Ilaria Ramelli, *Hierocles the Stoic: Elements of Ethics, Fragments, and Excerpts* (Atlanta, GA: Society of Biblical Literature, 2009), xx–xxi, with a full bibliography on recent scholarship on Mara bar Serapion.

without defense? What advantage did the Athenians gain by murdering Socrates, for which they were repaid with famine and pestilence? Or the people of Samos by the burning of Pythagoras, because their country was completely covered in sand in just one hour? Or the Jews [by killing] their wise king, because their kingdom was taken away at that very time? God justly repaid the wisdom of these three men: the Athenians died of famine; the Samians were completely overwhelmed by the sea; and the Jews, desolate and driven from their own kingdom, are scattered through every nation. Socrates is not dead, because of Plato; neither is Pythagoras, because of the statue of Juno; nor is the wise king, because of the new laws he laid down. (*Letter of Mara bar Serapion*; trans. Van Voorst)[3]

Of course, this comparison of the fate of Socrates with other historic figures is already undertaken in Plato's *Apology*, where Socrates expresses the delightful prospect of meeting other victims of unjust judgement in heaven: "I am willing to die many times over, if these things [i.e., concerning the soul's migration to heaven] are true; for I personally should find the life there wonderful, when I met Palamedes or Ajax, the son of Telamon, or any other men of old who lost their lives through an unjust judgement (καὶ εἴ τις ἄλλος τῶν παλαιῶν διὰ κρίσιν ἄδικον τέθνηκεν), and compared my experience with theirs" (41a–b).[4] And he likewise connects his own prospective death with the likelihood of divine vengeance on his opponents, although this retribution is not conceived of as physical punishment, but consists of spiritual, intellectual self-harm (*Apology* 30c–31b) and the blame and reproach they receive from others (*Apology* 38c; 39c–d), although the tone is no less threatening: "if you kill me, I being such a man as I say I am, you will not injure me so much as yourselves" (30c); "[a]nd now I wish to prophesy to you, O ye who have condemned me… And I say to you, ye men who have slain me, that punishment will come upon you straightway after my death, far more grievous in sooth than the punishment of death which you have meted out to me" (39c). It seems likely that Mara, who starts his list of wise men killed by tyrants with Socrates, has taken these threats into account and elaborates them in a physical sense.

---

3  Robert E. Van Voorst, *Jesus Outside the New Testament: An Introduction to the Ancient Evidence* (Grand Rapids, MI: Eerdmans, 2000), 53–58, 54.

4  As regards translations, classical authors are normally quoted from the Loeb Classical Library, the New Testament writings from the New Revised Standard Version, and early Christian authors from the Ante-Nicene Fathers, the Nicene and Post-Nicene Fathers, and the Early Church Fathers series, with adaptations where necessary or useful.

It seems also probable that Mara's reference to the "wise king" of the Jews,[5] who laid down "new laws" and whose death was avenged by the destruction of Jerusalem (although described in a somewhat imprecise way[6]), concerns Jesus. There is even reason to assume that Mara is dependent here on John's Gospel; first, the phraseology of the kingdom of the Jews having been taken away mirrors John's reference to the Romans "taking away" the place and ethnicity of the Jews (John 11:48),[7] and second, the explicit mention of Christ issuing new laws or new commands occurs within the New Testament corpus only in the Johannine literature (John 13:34; 1 John 2:7–8).[8] But regardless of whether Mara's comparison between Socrates and Christ was inspired by John's Gospel or not, it is highly relevant to note that such an early comparison was drawn by a pagan philosopher at the end of the first century.

This also accords very well with the high respect for Socrates' pupil and biographer Plato evident in early Christianity. According to Irenaeus, writing in the second half of the second century, some Christian circles in Rome – the Christian sect of Carpocrates – even possessed images of Jesus and of philosophers such as Pythagoras, Plato, and Aristotle (*Against Heresies* 1.25.6), and slightly later, both Tertullian and Hippolytus regard Valentinus, the leader of the Christian sect of the Valentinians, as a Platonist. According to Tertullian, he "was of Plato's school" (*The Prescription Against Heretics* 7), and he calls him "Valentinus… the disciple of Platonism" (*The Prescription Against Heretics* 30)

---

5 Cf. the trial before Pilate in #336 and the inscription on the cross in all gospels, ##344–345, although with some additional emphasis in John's Gospel, #336. References are to the section numbering in Kurt Aland's *Synopsis of the Four Gospels* (Stuttgart: Deutsche Bibelgesellschaft, 2007, 13th ed.).

6 The kingdom in the sense of political independence had already been taken away, and the Jews had long since been "'scattered through every nation." But of course, after the destruction of Jerusalem even more Jews fled abroad, were taken prisoner and sold as slaves, and hence scattered throughout the world.

7 Mara's "their kingdom was taken away at that very time" resembles John 11:48 (καὶ ἐλεύσονται οἱ Ῥωμαῖοι καὶ ἀροῦσιν [LSJ s.v. αἴρω *lift and take away, remove*; III.2 *make away with, destroy*] ἡμῶν καὶ τὸν τόπον καὶ τὸ ἔθνος) rather than Matthew. Although there are explicit references to the punishment of the Jews in Matthew 21:43 and Matthew 22:7 ("The king was angry, and he sent his troops and destroyed those murderers and burned their city"), the wording of John 11:48 seems to be closer to Mara's "taken away" than Matthew 22:7.

8 So acquaintance with John is more probable than with Matthew, where Jesus' Sermon on the Mount is only implicitly presented as "new law;" despite some criticism of "the ancients" in 5:21 and 33, and despite the advancement of "what is new" alongside "what is old" in 13:52 and the positive promulgation of "new wine" in "new skins" in 9:17, the explicit terminology of "new laws" is absent from Matthew's Gospel; see Matthew 5:17–19, 7:12, 15:3, 19:17, 22:40.

and "Valentinus... the Platonist" (*On the Flesh of Christ* 20; cf. Hippolytus, *The Refutation of All Heresies* 6.16, 24, 32).

Interestingly, in his *Against Celsus* (from the middle of the third century), Origen criticises Celsus' polemical contrast a 'non-miraculous,' 'philosophical' Plato and a 'miraculous,' 'religious' Christ by reminding Celsus of the various Platonic accounts of Plato's superhuman generation by Apollo and of Socrates' dream about Plato coming to him as his pupil. According to Origen, Celsus does not differ from those who all too easily criticise the upper class of notable men, such as Socrates and Christ, who distinguish themselves from the masses: "But occasion for slanderous accusations will never be wanting to those who are ill-disposed, and who wish to speak evil of what has happened to such as are raised above the multitude. Such persons will deride as a fiction even the demon of Socrates. We do not, then, relate marvels when we narrate the history of Jesus, nor have his genuine disciples recorded any such stories of him" (*Against Celsus* 6.8). In this way, Origen criticises Celsus' non-miraculous portrayal of Socrates and even defends the non-fictitious nature of Socrates' *daimonion*. In terms of Plutarch's discussion of Socrates' demon in the first of his *Platonic Questions*, one could say that Origen opposes a reductive interpretation of Socrates' demon and indeed believes that "some truly divine and spiritual cause (did) guide Socrates" (Plutarch, *Platonic Questions* 1, 999d–e). Origen is clearly willing to grant the same degree of combined historicity and divine inspiration to both Socrates and Christ. Something similar seems to be the case in John's Gospel, as I will suggest shortly.

Origen's positive appreciation of Plato is echoed in Eusebius of Caesarea's *Preparation for the Gospel*, in which he, incorporating a fragment from Atticus, describes Plato as "a man newly initiated in the mysteries of nature and of surpassing excellence, as one verily sent down from heaven in order that the philosophy taught by him might be seen in its full proportions" (Πλάτων, ἀνὴρ ἐκ φύσεως ἀρτιτελὴς καὶ πολὺ διενεγκών, οἷα κατάπεμπτος ὡς ἀληθῶς ἐκ θεῶν, ἵν' ὁλόκληρος ὀφθῇ ἡ δι' αὐτοῦ φιλοσοφία, *Preparation for the Gospel* 11.2.4; Atticus, fragment 2.4 [ed. Baudry]).

Furthermore, Augustine, although remarking that "It is, forsooth, a degradation for learned men to pass from the school of Plato to the discipleship of Christ," also mentions that he himself had heard from Simplicianus, the later bishop of Milan, that "a certain Platonist was in the habit of saying that [the] opening passage of the holy gospel entitled 'According to John' [about the divine Logos] should be written in letters of gold, and hung up in all churches in the most conspicuous place," although there is no Platonic appreciation, he notices, for John's subsequent description of the Logos' incarnation (*The*

*City of God* 10.29; cf. Ilinca Tanaseanu-Döbler's contribution to this volume in chapter 14).

Particularly relevant for our purposes is also the following issue. In one of his letters, Augustine expresses his wish that, of all the books of Ambrose, he may see "those which, with much care and at great length, he has written against some most ignorant and pretentious men, who affirm that our Lord was instructed by the writings of Plato" (Augustine, *Letters* 31: *Letter to Paulinus and Therasia*). Regrettably, these books of Ambrose are considered lost. Augustine also refers to these views in his *On Christian Doctrine*, when he mentions Ambrose's refutation of "the readers and admirers of Plato" who "dared calumniously to assert that our Lord Jesus Christ learnt all those sayings of his, which they are compelled to admire and praise, from the books of Plato" (*On Christian Doctrine* 2.28; cf. *Retractations* 2.4). Unfortunately, it is no longer possible to see on which arguments these "readers and admirers of Plato" based their assumption of Christ's acquaintance with the books of Plato. Were they pagans who polemicised against Christianity by showing that Christ himself was dependent upon Plato? If so, they were not like Celsus, who believed the miraculous Christ to be rather different from the non-miraculous Socrates. Or did they also include Christians who, although not necessarily to the same extent as Carpocrates, who placed images of Jesus and Plato alongside each other, still emphasised the resemblance between Socrates and Christ, a correspondence which could also be noted by pagan philosophers such as Mara bar Serapion?

What I intend to explore in this chapter is whether this correspondence between Socrates and Christ is indeed already envisioned in John's Gospel. It would be interesting to see whether John's vision is so radically different from the view of Origen, who, against Celsus, defended the figure of Christ by comparing him to Socrates, if the latter is properly understood. This approach of comparing Christ and Socrates in the Gospel of John is now greatly helped by the emergence of a paradigm in the study of the Gospels that argues that the Gospels are not a distinctive literary genre, but are best understood as ancient biographies. This view has been particularly argued by C.H. Talbert and Richard Burridge and has recently been further strengthened in Tomas Hägg's *The Art of Biography in Antiquity*, which includes an entire chapter on the Gospels (chapter four).[9] With regard to John's Gospel, Talbert's treatment of the Gospels as ancient biographies has implied that John's Gospel can be

---

9   C.H. Talbert, "Biography, ancient," *Anchor Bible Dictionary* (1992), 1:745–49; R.A. Burridge, *What Are the Gospels? A Comparison with Graeco–Roman Biography* (2d ed.; Grand Rapids, MI: Eerdmans, 2004); Tomas Hägg, *The Art of Biography in Antiquity* (Cambridge: Cambridge University Press, 2012). See further also Richard A. Burridge, "Reading the Gospels as

read formally as a fusion of ancient biography and Platonic dialogues (as exemplified in the cases of Satyrus' *Life of Euripides*, Palladius' *Dialogue on the Life of Chrysostom*, and Sulpicius Severus' *Dialogues on the Life of St. Martin*), without explicitly applying this insight to John's Gospel. Picking up on this suggestion, there is reason to believe that John found Plato's *Symposium* and his *Last Days of Socrates* particularly useful for his recasting of Jesus' biography because, among the Platonic dialogues, these dialogues contain the most vivid of all Plato's portrayals of Socrates as the ideal philosopher and are also concerned with discipleship.[10]

First of all, Plato's *Symposium* is very useful for John in providing him with the format and content to recast the Last Supper into a symposium with farewell speeches and also to apply such a sympotic setting to many other episodes of his narrative. The application of the sympotic setting throughout his narrative is twofold. As Kathryn Topper has recently argued in her *The Imagery of the Athenian Symposium*, it is possible to differentiate between symposia of the primitive, where the symposiasts recline on the ground outside, and the familiar luxurious symposia, where people recline on furniture.[11] Such a differentiation between primitive and luxurious symposia is also present in Plato's *Republic* (*Republic* 2.372b–d and 2.372d–373a). Both types of symposia can also be distinguished in John's Gospel. Jesus' encounter with the Samaritan woman at the well in John 4; his feeding of the five thousand, who recline on the ground, in John 6; and the meal after Jesus' resurrection on the shores of the Sea of Tiberias in John 21 all bear the features of the primitive symposia, whereas the wedding feast at Cana in John 2, with an ἀρχιτρίκλινος (a president of a reclining banquet) in charge of the festive meeting and an abundant supply of wine; the luxurious symposium at the house of Lazarus, with the provision of expensive perfume, in John 12; and the Last Symposium in John 13–17, with foot-washing and Jesus' extensive speech, are examples of the formal, luxurious symposium. Moreover, the speeches and dialogues of many of these sympotic events, whether primitive or luxurious, are, similarly to Plato's *Symposium*, about love, whether marital love at the wedding in Cana;

---

Biography," in *The Limits of Ancient Biography* (ed. J. Mossman and B. McGing; Swansea: The Classical Press of Wales, 2006), 31–49; Aage Pilgaard, "The Classical Biography as Model for the Gospels," in *Beyond Reception: Mutual Influences Between Antique Religion, Judaism and Early Christianity* (ed. David Brakke, Anders-Christian Jacobsen, and Jörg Ulrich; Frankfurt am Main: Peter Lang, 2006), 209–26.

10   I owe this characterisation to a very profitable discussion with Frisbee Sheffield.
11   See Kathryn Topper, *The Imagery of the Athenian Symposium* (Cambridge: Cambridge University Press, 2013), chap. 2: "Symposia of the Primitive."

insatiable love at the Samaritan well; spiritual, abiding love at the table of the Last Symposium; or the mending of unfaithful, unrequited love at the shores of the Sea of Tiberias; with hints of erotic love – the desires of which are then transformed and transcended – throughout several of these sympotic settings, whether from one of the female hostesses pouring perfume over Jesus' feet and drying them with her hair or from the beloved disciple who reclines at Jesus' bosom. The Christian reception of Plato's *Symposium* has been pointed out by Richard Hunter and studied in John Rist's *Eros and Psyche* and Catherine Osborne's *Eros Unveiled*, with particular attention to Origen.[12] I have explored the application of Plato's *Symposium* in John's Gospel on the occasion of the first Aarhus–Groningen colloquium in 2012 (this paper will be published elsewhere) and was encouraged to look also at the possibility of using Plato's *Last Days of Socrates*.

Second, Plato's *Last Days of Socrates* indeed seems to be equally useful for John. Whereas Plato's *Symposium* helped him to reconfigure the Last Supper, to restructure the Gospel's entire narrative (at least partially) with the aid of multiple sympotic settings, and to address the issue of divine love (and generation), so the several dialogues of *The Last Days of Socrates* – the *Euthyphro*, the *Apology*, the *Crito*, and the *Phaedo* – offered him a perspective through which he could retell the story of Jesus' trial, execution, and immortality.

How fruitful it is to regard John's Gospel as a mixture of biography and Platonic dialogue is immediately apparent when comparing it with Plato's *Phaedo*. At the beginning of the *Phaedo*, one of the interlocutors asks Phaedo, who was present at Socrates' death, "Then what did he say before his death? And how did he die?" (57a). This is subsequently followed by the questions, "What took place at his death, Phaedo? What was said and done? And which of his friends were with him?" (58c), and "Well then, what was the conversation?" (Τί οὖν δή; τίνες φῂς ἦσαν οἱ λόγοι;, 59c). These are also the questions which determine much of the structure of John's description of the last days of Christ; "what he said before his death" is especially captured in his extensive farewell speech during the Last Symposium. Plato allocates Socrates' final words to the long interval Socrates needs to spend in prison between his judgement and his execution. As Socrates cannot be executed during the Festival of Apollo, which had just commenced at the time of his trial, he needs to wait

---

12   Richard Hunter, *Plato's Symposium* (Oxford: Oxford University Press, 2004), 129, 132–35; J.M. Rist, *Eros and Psyche: Studies in Plato, Plotinus, and Origen* (Toronto: University of Toronto Press, 1964); Catherine Osborne, *Eros Unveiled: Plato and the God of Love* (Oxford: Oxford University Press, 1994); cf. also Mark Edwards, "The Figure of Love in Augustine and in Proclus the Neoplatonist," *Downside Review* 127 (2009): 197–214.

until the festival has ended. John, however, attributes Jesus' final words to the event of the Last Symposium in John 13–17, immediately preceding Jesus' arrest, as the short timeframe between trial and immediate execution, before the Jewish festival of Passover begins, leaves no time for final words. Just as Plato's *Phaedo* describes Socrates' final λόγοι (59c), so in his account of Jesus' Last Symposium, John describes how Jesus says, "'Those who love me will keep my word (τὸν λόγον μου τηρήσει)... Whoever does not love me does not keep my words (τοὺς λόγους μου οὐ τηρεῖ)'" (14:23–24). Whereas this relates to "what he said," "how he died" is then related in John 18–19 in the description of Jesus' arrest, trial, and execution.

Before exploring the similarities between Plato's and John's accounts of the last days of their respective protagonists, I will make three short preliminary remarks of a more methodological nature. First, it is important to be aware of John's literary capacities and strategies. It seems that John is rather independent and sovereign in the literary reworking of and allusions to his sources. This was emphasised by Richard Hays in his 2014 Hulsean Lectures at Cambridge in his comments on John's use of the Jewish writings. Drawing attention to a particular case (the allusion in John 3:14 to Moses and the bronze serpent from Numbers 21:8–9), Hays argued that, despite a clearly demonstrable intertextuality between John and a particular book from Moses' Pentateuch, the verbatim similarities are limited to a few keywords.[13] This means that John's literary reworking of a source he is acquainted with is rather pervasive. This seems also to be the case with John's reworking of Plato's dialogues, if it is granted that he is indeed familiar with them. The analogy with John's extensive reworking of the passages in the Jewish scriptures he alludes to suggests that his intention is not to hide his dependence upon the Platonic writings; rather, his pervasive rewriting seems to be part of his literary technique, just as Plutarch in his *Amatorius* is clearly dependent on Plato's *Symposium* but frames his dialogue differently. This implies, however, that it will be difficult to develop a balanced view of John's use of Plato's *Last Days of Socrates* between the two possibilities of a minimalist and a maximalist reading of John's Gospel in terms of these Platonic dialogues.

Second, however, such a balanced view will greatly benefit from the following: I will only base my overview of similarities between Plato's *Last Days of Socrates* and John's Gospel on those features of John's Gospel which are distinctive for this gospel and do not occur in the other, Synoptic Gospels. For instance, I will draw no attention to the metaphorical cup which Jesus drinks

---

13   See Richard Hays, *Reading Backwards: Figural Christology and the Fourfold Gospel Witness* (London: SPCK, 2015), 78.

(John 18:11) and will not suggest that there are literary similarities with the cup of Socrates (*Phaedo* 117a–c), as Jesus' cup is also mentioned in the Synoptic Gospels (Mark 10:38–39, 14:36; Matthew 26:39, 42; Luke 22:42), whose authors cannot be demonstrated to be acquainted with Plato's dialogues and with whom John shares these traditions. Hence, the parallels I will list concern distinctively Johannine features, unparalleled in the Synoptic Gospels.

Finally, in my exploration I will follow the chronological order implied in the sequence of Plato's *Euthyphro*, *Apology*, *Crito*, and *Phaedo*. Whereas the *Euthyphro* contains the charges against Socrates, the *Apology* focuses on Socrates' trial, during which he answers these charges, whereas the *Crito* deals with Socrates' determination not to escape his judgement but to respect the laws despite their unjust application, and the *Phaedo* reports on Socrates' final words. I will structure my comparison along the lines of these dialogues, taking them as a starting point.

## 1    Plato's *Euthyphro*

First of all, then, I take Plato's *Euthyphro*, in which the charges that a certain Meletus of Pitthus brings against Socrates are discussed in a dialogue between Socrates and Euthyphro, who meet while they both have dealings with the Athenian court. The one, Socrates, is being indicted; the other, Euthyphro, is prosecuting an independent case, although both cases have a bearing on what 'piety' is (cf. the contributions by Frisbee Sheffield and Nicholas Denyer to this volume, chapters two and three, respectively). Aspects of the charges against Socrates are: (1) that he makes new gods and does not believe in the old ones; (2) that his so-called personal "*daimonion*" is such a new god; and (3) that making such innovations in religion is considered sinning. In their explorations what piety is, Euthyphro is concerned about "how to say and do what is gratifying to the gods, in praying and sacrificing" (14b), whereas Socrates suggests that the pious is part of, and hence determined by, the righteous. These various features of Plato's *Euthyphro* compare to John's Gospel as follows.

Firstly, according to Socrates, his opponent, Meletus of Pitthus, "says I am a maker of gods; and because I make new gods and do not believe in the old ones, he indicted me for the sake of these old ones, as he says" (φησὶ γάρ με ποιητὴν εἶναι θεῶν, καὶ ὡς καινοὺς ποιοῦντα θεοὺς τοὺς δ' ἀρχαίους οὐ νομίζοντα ἐγράψατο τούτων αὐτῶν ἕνεκα, ὥς φησιν, 3b). This charge is paralleled in John's Gospel, where the charges against Jesus also concern his making of gods – in this case his making himself god – in the very same wording of ποιεῖν θεούς, the only difference being that the repetitive charge against Jesus by his opponents in John's Gospel is that he makes *himself* god. According to John 5:18, the Jews seek to kill him because he was "calling God his own Father, thereby making himself equal to God" (πατέρα ἴδιον ἔλεγεν τὸν θεόν, ἴσον ἑαυτὸν ποιῶν τῷ θεῷ, John 5:18). And again in John 10:33, his opponents state, "It is not for a good work that we are going to stone you, but for blasphemy, because you, though only a human being, are making yourself God" (ὅτι σὺ ἄνθρωπος ὢν ποιεῖς σεαυτὸν θεόν, John 10:33), and the same charge is finally repeated by the Jews in front of Pilate at Jesus' trial (John 19:7).[14] Hence the charges against both Socrates and Christ are that they are "makers of gods."

John's geographical and temporal setting of the second, repeated charge in John 10:33 is particularly interesting, because this charge is levelled against Jesus during the Feast of τὰ ἐγκαίνια, the so-called Feast of Renovation, while he walks up and down in the Stoa of Solomon in the Jerusalem temple (10:22–23).[15] Two things are noteworthy about this topographical and temporal setting.

Firstly, the Stoa of Solomon in Jerusalem is the place where Jesus' opponents charge him with making himself god. This reminds us of the opening of Plato's *Euthyphro*, where Euthyphro and Socrates meet near the Stoa of the King in Athens, where Socrates has been indicted and charged with making new gods (2a). While Jesus is engaged in the act of walking up and down in the Stoa of Solomon (περιπατεῖν ἐν τῇ στοᾷ τοῦ Σολομῶνος), Socrates is similarly occupied in the act of passing all his time around the Stoa of the King (διατρίβειν περὶ τὴν τοῦ βασιλέως στοάν). It seems that John consciously evokes the atmosphere of the Athenian Royal Stoa and transfers it to Jerusalem, to the Stoa of King Solomon.[16]

---

14  The charge in John 19:7 seems slightly different: "We have a law, and according to that law he ought to die because he has claimed to be the Son of God" (ὅτι υἱὸν θεοῦ ἑαυτὸν ἐποίησεν), but for John, claiming to be the Son of God is the same as making oneself equal to God (5:18) and making oneself God (10:33), because being a son of God means being begotten from God, and what God – in the Greek mode of thinking – begets, are gods; hence "the only-begotten son of God" (3:16, 18) is synonymous in John's Gospel with "the only-begotten god" (1:18). This is also implied in the charge of John 5:18, where the charges that he was "calling God his own Father" and that he was "making himself equal to God" are combined and causally connected (πατέρα ἴδιον ἔλεγεν τὸν θεόν, ἴσον ἑαυτὸν ποιῶν τῷ θεῷ). This understanding of a son of God as being by definition a god himself is different from the Jewish metaphorical application of the title "son of God" to the messiahs.

15  John 10:22–23: Ἐγένετο τότε τὰ ἐγκαίνια ἐν τοῖς Ἱεροσολύμοις· χειμὼν ἦν, καὶ περιεπάτει ὁ Ἰησοῦς ἐν τῷ ἱερῷ ἐν τῇ στοᾷ τοῦ Σολομῶνος.

16  References to the Stoa of Solomon are absent from the Synoptic Gospels, but cf. Acts 3:11 and 5:12, although not in connection with Jesus.

Secondly, the temporal setting of this charge against Jesus is remarkable because it is the Feast of τὰ ἐγκαίνια, the Feast of Renovation of the Jerusalem temple, the feast differently known as Hanukkah – the festive commemoration of the renewal of the Jerusalem temple by the Maccabees after its desecration by the Hellenistic-Seleucid King Antiochus IV Epiphanes, who depicted himself as a manifest god and installed – through the intermediary of an Athenian (!) senator – a cult for Zeus Olympios in the Jerusalem temple in 168/167 BCE (2 Maccabees 6:1–5). He also inaugurated such festivals as the Festival of Dionysus (2 Maccabees 6:7; cf. 2 Maccabees 14:33) after having previously already allowed the erection of a gymnasium at the foot of the temple mountain (2 Maccabees 4:7–15), thus sparking the Maccabean Revolt (2 Maccabees 8–9), which led to the reconsecration of the temple and the instalment of its annual commemoration (2 Maccabees 10:1–8). John evokes this sensitive Hellenistic episode as the background against which the Jews charge Jesus with making himself a god. Moreover, John's evocation of the temple's Feast of Renovation (ἐγκαίνια; cf. 2 Esdras 6:16–17 LXX) is also provocative, because John's claim is essentially that the Jerusalem temple complex is not God's temple, but that Jesus' body, in which the divine Logos has become incarnate, is God's temple (John 2:20–21, without Synoptic parallels); it is Jesus himself, not the temple, who is consecrated (10:36).[17] In this sense, John is 'renewing' the temple in a far more radical way than the renewal commemorated at the Feast of τὰ ἐγκαίνια.[18] The reference to this feast of τὰ ἐγκαίνια also seems to allow him to link up with the very terminology of the repetitive charges in Plato's *Euthyphro* against Socrates "making new gods" (καινοὺς ποιῶν θεούς, 3b) and "making innovations in religion" (καινοτομῶν περὶ τὰ θεῖα, 3b; cf. καινοτομῶν περὶ τῶν θείων, 5a).

Hence, the topographical and temporal setting of the Jews' charges against Jesus in John 10 seems aptly chosen to resonate both with Judaism's still-remembered, traumatic, almost archetypal encounter with Hellenism and

---

17  This view resembles Philo's view that the Logos is the high priest in the temple of the universe, whereas "the real man" is priest in the temple of the soul (*De somniis* 1.215); cf. Graeco-Roman views of human beings as temples of God, bearing in the inner shrine of their mind the image of God. See George van Kooten, *Paul's Anthropology in Context: The Image of God, Assimilation to God, and Tripartite Man in Ancient Judaism, Ancient Philosophy and Early Christianity* (Tübingen: Mohr Siebeck, 2008), 389–90. The real temple is where the divine Logos is; cf. Romans 12:1–2. In John's Gospel Jesus is both the divine Logos and the exemplary human being, see 19:5.

18  Probably also with the suggestion that it is Jesus' body which is eventually renewed at his resurrection; see John 2:19–22.

with the charges of the same nature against Socrates in Athens' Royal Stoa. Both Jews and Greeks would have been triggered by John's passage, and it seems that we need to seek John's intended audience between these two poles.

We will learn about Socrates' response to these charges of making new gods and making innovations in religion in Plato's *Apology*. John's strategy of responding to the charges against Jesus making himself god seems to contain at least three elements. Firstly, John affirms that Jesus is indeed the incarnation of the only-begotten son of God, just as Athena is the only-begotten daughter of Zeus (*Orphic Hymns* 32.1; Aelius Aristides, *Orations* 37 (*Athena*).2 [ed. Behr; ed. Jebb 9.9]), and that, like Hermes, he is the (hermeneutical and cosmological) Logos of God (Heraclitus, *Homeric Problems* 28.2, 55.1, 72.4–5; and Porphyry, *On Images* 8.103–06). This kind of assertion is not paralleled in Plato's dialogues about Socrates, although Platonic traditions about Plato's own generation by Apollo come close, and although, as we shall see later, the implication of the talk of Socrates' *daimonion* is also, in the wording of A.A. Long, that "its most likely source for Socrates would be the god Apollo whose oracles initiated his interpretation of his mission to the citizens of Athens."[19]

Secondly, if the charges against Socrates of innovation in religion are in the background, it is noteworthy that John concedes that there is something new about Jesus, but this is his "new command." During his final symposium, Jesus tells his disciples, "I give you a new commandment, that you love one another. Just as I have loved you, you also should love one another" (John 13:34), something on which John further reflects explicitly in his letters (see 1 John 2:7–8 and 2 John 5). In this sense, John is willing and even keen to acknowledge that Christ made innovations in religion by issuing a new command, something which we saw recognised in Mara bar Serapion's reference to "the new laws" which "the wise king" of the Jews laid down. Besides, as we have seen, John also seems to connect Christ's teaching in the temple's Stoa of Solomon with the Feast of τὰ ἐγκαίνια, suggesting that he himself performs an even more far-reaching renewal of the temple than that undertaken at its reconsecration after the Hellenistic desecration.

Thirdly, although John confirms that Jesus is divine and admits the innovations Jesus made in matters of religion, at the same time he emphasises that there are no grounds for a charge such as Meletus of Pitthus brought against Socrates, who, as Socrates states in Plato's *Euthyphro*, "says I am a maker of gods; and because I make new gods and do not believe in the old ones, he indicted me for the sake of these old ones, as he says" (φησὶ γάρ με ποιητὴν εἶναι

---

19   A.A. Long, "Daimôn," in *Continuum Companion to Plato* (ed. G.A. Press, F. Gonzalez, D. Nails, and H. Tarrant; London: Continuum, 2012), 152–54 at 154.

θεῶν, καὶ ὡς καινοὺς ποιοῦντα θεοὺς τοὺς δ' ἀρχαίους οὐ νομίζοντα ἐγράψατο τούτων αὐτῶν ἕνεκα, ὥς φησιν, 3b). According to John, there is, to retain Socrates' terminology, no contrast between "new gods" (καινοὶ θεοί) and "the old ones" (οἱ ἀρχαῖοι). It seems that, for that reason, John's Gospel opens with the statement "In the beginning was the Logos, and the Logos was with God, and the Logos was God. He was in the beginning with God" (Ἐν ἀρχῇ ἦν ὁ λόγος, καὶ ὁ λόγος ἦν πρὸς τὸν θεόν, καὶ θεὸς ἦν ὁ λόγος. οὗτος ἦν ἐν ἀρχῇ πρὸς τὸν θεόν, John 1:1–2). Of course, this is an allusion to the beginning of the book of Genesis, Ἐν ἀρχῇ ἐποίησεν ὁ θεὸς τὸν οὐρανὸν καὶ τὴν γῆν (Genesis 1:1), yet the repetition of the phrase ἐν ἀρχῇ in the opening of John's Gospel (Ἐν ἀρχῇ ἦν ὁ λόγος...οὗτος ἦν ἐν ἀρχῇ πρὸς τὸν θεόν) and the exclusive attention paid to the pre-creational status of the Logos in John 1:1–2 before proceeding to the narration of its participation in creation in John 1:3–4, shows that the emphasis is slightly different than in Genesis and serves to highlight the 'archaic', pre-creational status of the Logos and its proximity to, or even its identity with, God. The Logos is no new god, even if he became incarnate in Jesus. Something similar is found in Jesus' statement to the Jews that he existed even prior to their founding father Abraham (John 8:33–58; πρὶν Ἀβραὰμ γενέσθαι ἐγὼ εἰμί, 8:57).

In this way, John seems to develop a comprehensive response to the charges against Jesus, arguing that, although he is divine, there is no antithesis between the new god and the old god. Precisely because he is the Logos of God, this new god is not really new, but was already in the beginning with God, and hence he was earlier than Abraham. This strategy is not dissimilar to Socrates' strategy in Plato's *Apology*, as we shall see in due course, although in Socrates' case this is argued on the basis of his possession of a divine *daimonion*.

Returning to the charges against Socrates mentioned in Plato's *Euthyphro*, there are three further aspects I wish to mention briefly. Firstly, the well-known allegation that Socrates corrupts the youth (2c), whereas Euthyphro is playfully said to corrupt the old (5b), is not directly repeated in John's Gospel, although there may be an echo in the accusation that Jesus "is deceiving the crowd" (πλανᾷ τὸν ὄχλον, 7:12), and that even the attendants who have been sent out by the chief priests and Pharisees to arrest him (7:32) while he was teaching in the temple during one of the festivals (7:14, 28) have been deceived by him (7:47), and for that reason have failed to arrest him (7:44–46).[20]

---

20 It may be considered whether the term 'attendants' (ὑπηρέται) is not an allusion to ὁ τῶν ἕνδεκα ὑπηρέτης (Plato, *Phaedo* 116b), the assistant of the Eleven at Athens, employed in executions of state criminals, as LSJ s.v. ὑπηρέτης indicates. Indeed, οἱ ὑπηρέται (7:32, 45–46) are the ones who also assist at the final successful arrest of Jesus and at his trial,

Secondly, it is noteworthy that in the *Euthyphro* the charge of Socrates making innovations in religion with the introduction of new gods is also associated, at least by Euthyphro, with Socrates' possession of a *daimonion* (3b-c). Hearing from Socrates that he has been indicted by Meletus for making new gods, Euthyphro immediately responds as follows: "I understand, Socrates; it is because you say the *daimonion* keeps coming to you (ὅτι δὴ σὺ τὸ δαιμόνιον φῂς σαυτῷ ἑκάστοτε γίγνεσθαι). So he [i.e, Meletus] has brought the indictment against you for making innovations in religion" (3b). Euthyphro instantly finds an ally in Socrates, because, as Euthyphro says, *hoi polloi* "even laugh at me and say I am crazy (καταγελῶσιν ὡς μαινομένου) when I say anything in the civic assembly about divine things and foretell the future to them" (3b–c). The combined allegation against Socrates and Euthyphro of possessing a *daimonion* and of being crazy (μαινόμενος) is also made against Christ. The charge that he possesses a *daimonion* is frequently repeated (7:20; 8:48, 52; 10:20; and is different from the isolated case of Mark 3:22–26 and the synoptic parallels in ##117 and 188 in Aland's *Synopsis of the Four Gospels*, where the charge is phrased differently and indirectly) and in the final instance is combined with an accusation of madness which is absent from the Synoptic Gospels: "He has a *daimonion* and is out of his mind (Δαιμόνιον ἔχει καὶ μαίνεται)," many of the Jews say in response to one of Jesus' figures of speech (παροιμία, 10:6), although others contest this (10:20–21). In contrast to Socrates, however, Jesus denies the charge that he possesses a *daimonion* (8:49). This is unsurprising, because in Jewish ears *daimonion* has a negative sense, and also in pagan Greek sources it has a potentially negative meaning, as several references to δαιμόνια φαῦλα in the writings of philosophers demonstrate.[21] So it would be difficult for John to acknowledge that Jesus has a *daimonion*. Instead, Jesus is closely connected with a *pneuma* (πνεῦμα), the so-called πνεῦμα of truth (14:16–17; 15:26; 16:13–14; see further 1:33; 6:63; 7:39; 14:26; 20:22; cf. 4:24). The notion of *pneuma* comes close to that of *daimonion*; the frequent equation of δαιμόνιον with πνεῦμα πονηρόν or πνεῦμα πλάνον, or the combined phraseology of πνεῦμα δαιμονίου in the Septuagint and the New Testament writings, indicates that δαιμόνιον and πνεῦμα are near-synonyms in Jewish and Christian sources (cf. also δαιμόνιον πνεῦμα in Dionysius of Halicarnassus, *Antiquitates Romanae* 1.31.1), although

---

and who call for his crucifixion (18:3, 12, 18, 22; 19:6), yet the term is also employed in the Synoptic Gospels (Mark 14:54, 65 and synoptic parallels), although their role is considerably increased in John's Gospel, and they are already introduced here in John 7.

21  See SVF 2.1178 apud Plutarch, *De Stoicorum repugnantiis* 1051C; further Plutarch, *Dion* 2.6 and *Aetia Romana et Graeca* 276–277A; Origen, *Contra Celsum* 1.31, 5.5; and Iamblichus, *De mysteriis* 3.13.

the Jewish-Christian use of δαιμόνιον seems always negative, whereas that of πνεῦμα, if not further qualified in a negative sense, can be positive. Hence it seems that the allegations of possessing a *daimonion* and being mad in Plato's *Euthyphro* are mirrored in John's Gospel.

Thirdly, there is the noteworthy view in the *Euthyphro* that making innovations in religions is considered erroneous or sinful. According to Socrates, Meletus "says I am doing wrong (ἐξαμαρτάνειν) by acting carelessly and making innovations in matters of religion" (με ἐκεῖνος αὐτοσχεδιάζοντά φησι καὶ καινοτομοῦντα περὶ τῶν θείων ἐξαμαρτάνειν [LSJ s.v. ἐξαμαρτάνω A.2 *err, do wrong*], 5a). Likewise, Jesus is considered by some of the Pharisees to be sinning by healing a man blind from birth on the Sabbath; they question whether he is "from God," deny that he is God-fearing (θεοσεβής), and explicitly designate him as an ἁμαρτωλός (someone who errs, a sinner; 9:16, 24–25, 31), an allegation that is absent from the Synoptic Gospels.[22]

After the charges against Socrates have been introduced and briefly discussed in the *Euthyphro*, only to be answered in the *Apology*, the *Euthyphro* develops into a detailed exploration of what piety (τὸ ὅσιον) and impiety (τὸ ἀνόσιον) are, as both Socrates and Euthyphro are involved in legal cases concerned with allegedly impious behaviour. Their discussion about piety and impiety (4e–15e passim) is equally conceived in terms of what is τὸ θεοφιλές ("dear to the gods," "loving God") and τὸ θεομισές ("hated by the gods," "hating God;" *Euthyphro* 7a, 8a, 9c, 10d–e, 11a, 15c). Similarly, but again differently than in the Synoptic Gospels, John's Gospel indicates that Jesus' opponents doubt him to be God-fearing (θεοσεβής; 9:31), defines the relation between God and human beings in terms of loving and hating (16:27; 15:23), and connects this closely with the response of human beings to Jesus, especially in his ethical capacity as the light of the world, hated by those who do evil (cf. Xenophon, *Symposium* 4.47) but attracting those who do what is good (3:19–21).

Although there is no parallel in John's Gospel to the *Euthyphro*'s detailed discussion of what constitutes piety and impiety, the concern expressed in Euthyphro's assertion that "when one knows how to say and do what is gratifying to the gods, in praying and sacrificing, that is holiness, and such things bring salvation to individual families (οἵ ἴδιοι οἶκοι) and to states (the leagues / the governments / the public affairs of cities: τὰ κοινὰ τῶν πόλεων) (ἐὰν μὲν κεχαρισμένα τις ἐπίστηται τοῖς θεοῖς λέγειν τε καὶ πράττειν εὐχόμενός τε καὶ θύων, ταῦτ' ἔστι τὰ ὅσια, καὶ σῴζει τὰ τοιαῦτα τούς τε ἰδίους οἴκους καὶ τὰ κοινὰ τῶν

---

22   Cf. Mark 2:16 a.o. for the view that Jesus associates with sinners, but without calling Jesus himself a sinner.

πόλεων)" (14b) is reflected in the concerns of the Samaritan woman at the well, who gets confused about the difference between Samaritan and Jewish modes of worshipping God (John 4:20). Her concerns are addressed by Jesus, who offers a worship which transcends these ethnic modes of worship (4:21) and consists in a non-locative, spiritual worship which is concerned with truth: "the true worshippers will worship the Father in spirit and truth (οἱ ἀληθινοὶ προσκυνηταὶ προσκυνήσουσιν τῷ πατρὶ ἐν πνεύματι καὶ ἀληθείᾳ), for the Father seeks such as these to worship him. God is spirit, and those who worship him must worship in spirit and truth (καὶ τοὺς προσκυνοῦντας αὐτὸν ἐν πνεύματι καὶ ἀληθείᾳ δεῖ προσκυνεῖν)" (4:23–24). According to John, what constitutes proper worship is non-locative, spiritual worship "in spirit," which corresponds with God's nature as spirit and is directed towards truth (because God himself is true, as John had already stated in 3:33: ὁ θεὸς ἀληθής ἐστιν; cf. 8:26).

Just as Euthyphro states that the proper judgements of "how to say and do what is gratifying to the gods... bring salvation to individual families and to the leagues of cities" (σῴζει...τούς τε ἰδίους οἴκους καὶ τὰ κοινὰ τῶν πόλεων), so John emphasises that Jesus' stipulation of proper worship brings salvation not only to the Samaritan woman individually, but to the entire Samaritan πόλις she belongs to; after having met Jesus, she collects the inhabitants of her city and tells them how Jesus has been concerned about her individual, domestic life (4:28–30; cf. 4:16–19), after which the inhabitants of the πόλις themselves go out to meet Jesus and confirm for themselves: "we know that this is truly ὁ σωτὴρ τοῦ κόσμου, the Saviour of the world" (4:30, 39–42). With his unusually frequent use of the term πόλις (4:5, 8, 28, 30, 39) in this particular narrative to refer to this city in Samaria, together with separate single references throughout his gospel to a πόλις in Galilee (1:44), another πόλις "in the region near the wilderness" (11:54), and the πόλις of Jerusalem in Judaea (19:20), John seems to parallel *Euthyphro*'s "leagues of cities" (τὰ κοινὰ τῶν πόλεων) with a league of Galilean, Samaritan, and Judaean cities and to suggest here, in this narrative of the Samaritan woman and the fellow-inhabitants of this Samaritan city, how Jesus brings both individuals and cities salvation by revealing a supra-ethnic, universal, spiritual worship "in truth," which takes "the true worshippers" (οἱ ἀληθινοὶ προσκυνηταὶ) directly to the very nature of God himself.

John's choice of words to characterise "the true worshippers" (οἱ ἀληθινοὶ προσκυνηταὶ) is also rather Platonic, although the terminology of worshipping (προσκυνεῖν) and worshipper (προσκυνητής) does not occur in Plato's *Last Days of Socrates* (although it does occur in Plato's *Republic* 451a, 469a–b and *Laws* 887e). It could be that the terminology of προσκυνεῖν, which means "make obeisance to the gods or their images, fall down and worship" or, with regard to holy places, "do reverence to it" (LSJ I.1), has been chosen by John because of its strongly orientalising meaning of prostrating oneself before kings and superiors (LSJ s.v. προσκυνέω 1.2). Despite the different choice of wording, however, the Johannine phrase "the true worshippers" (οἱ ἀληθινοὶ προσκυνηταὶ) resonates with the frequent occurrences in Plato's *Phaedo* of οἱ ὡς ἀληθῶς φιλόσοφοι, "the true philosophers" (*Phaedo* 64b; cf., in the singular, ὁ ὡς ἀληθῶς φιλόσοφος in 64e and 83b), and οἱ ὀρθῶς φιλοσοφοῦντες, "the right, correct philosophers" (*Phaedo* 67e; cf. 67d: οἱ φιλοσοφοῦντες ὀρθῶς, and 69d: οἱ πεφιλοσοφηκότες ὀρθῶς). In the *Phaedo*, they are the ones who "desire death" (64b), despise the so-called pleasures and the cares of the body (64e), whose soul "stands aloof from pleasures and lusts and griefs and fears, so far as it can" (83b), and who are "always most eager to release the soul" (67d) and "practice dying" (67e). *Phaedo*'s "true philosophers" and John's "true worshippers" share a movement from the physical and the locative to the spiritual, the true, and the universal. John certainly seems to imply that Jesus' spiritual, true worship would appeal to the Greeks.

In John's Gospel, the use of the terminology of worshipping is highly significant, as he applies it first here, in the narrative of the Samaritan woman (4:20–24), subsequently in the highly symbolic, paradigmatic, and distinctively Johannine narrative of the healing of the man "blind from birth" (9:1), who after his healing "worships" Jesus (9:38), and finally also in the narrative of the pagan Greeks who travel to Jerusalem on the occasion of one of the festivals in Herod's magnificent temple in order to "worship" there, and then express their wish to "see" Jesus (12:20–21). The last two narratives are told to illustrate the importance of worshipping in spirit and truth and its appeal to pagan Greeks. The man blind from birth is healed by Jesus because Jesus wishes to reveal himself as "the light of the world" (9:3–5) and is the only one in John's Gospel who is said to actually worship Jesus: "He said, 'Lord, I believe.' And he worshipped him" (ὁ δὲ ἔφη, Πιστεύω, κύριε· καὶ προσεκύνησεν αὐτῷ, 9:38). Unlike Socrates' disciples Simmias and Cebes, who continue for a long time in the course of Plato's *Phaedo* to disbelieve (ἀπιστεῖν, 73b, 77a, 87a–c, 91c, 107a) Socrates' argument for the immortality of the soul, and whose disbelief also makes Phaedo's interlocutor Echecrates puzzled about what to believe (πιστεύειν, 88c–d), the man healed from his blindness proves himself to be a true disciple who worships Jesus as "the light of the world" and hence is a representative of the true worshippers, whereas Jesus' Pharisaic opponents, who reproach Jesus for healing this blind man on a Sabbath, are in fact truly blind (9:39–41). The act of worshipping is then subsequently attributed to some pagan Greeks ("Ἕλληνές τινες) who have come to Jerusalem with the intention of worshipping at the festival (ἵνα προσκυνήσωσιν ἐν τῇ ἑορτῇ), but then express their wish to "see" (ἰδεῖν) Jesus (12:20–21), implying that it is eventually Jesus whom they have come to worship, as he, according to the prologue of John's Gospel and in the exact terminology which also occurs in Plato's *Phaedo*, is τὸ φῶς τὸ ἀληθινόν, "the true light" (John 1:9; *Phaedo* 109e: τὸ ἀληθινὸν φῶς; cf. 1 John 2:8).[23]

There is thus a significant thematisation of the issue of proper worship in John's Gospel, which is described as worship "in spirit and truth" and is exemplified in the worshipping of Jesus as the light of the world by the healed blind man and anticipated in the wish of pagan Greeks to see Jesus. It is in the sketch of this anticipation that we get a glimpse of the reason why John, if my analysis is correct, drew so heavily on Plato's dialogues about *The Last Days of Socrates*; he wishes to portray Jesus not only as the aspiration of the Jews and Samaritans, as expressed in the narratives of the Samaritan woman and the Jewish man born blind, but also as the aspiration of the Greeks; they are all united through true worship. What makes this worship true, according to John, is the fact that it is not restricted in a physical, locative, or ethnic sense, but is levelled at the nature of God: God being spirit, and being true, is to be worshipped in spirit and truth.

A similar mode of thinking can also be found elsewhere in the Johannine corpus: God is not only spiritual and true, but also righteous (δίκαιος). This divine "father," whom "the true worshippers" worship "in spirit and truth" (4:23), is qualified as the "righteous father," the πατὴρ δίκαιος (17:25). This qualification of God as "righteous," which is not paralleled in the Synoptic Gospels, seems to resonate with Socrates' view in the *Euthyphro* that what is pious needs to be seen as a part of what is righteous (μόριον...τοῦ δικαίου τὸ ὅσιον...μέρος τὸ ὅσιον τοῦ δικαίου, 12d), implying that what is pious is not arbitrary and dependent on the conflicting narratives about the often-contradictory behaviour of the mythological gods, but depends on and is determined by ethical reasoning (cf. again the contributions by Frisbee Sheffield and Nicholas Denyer in chapters two and three of this volume). This is very much John's view of the God who needs to be worshiped "in truth" and who is righteous, so that – as John spells out in his letters – it is human righteousness that corresponds with God being righteous: "Everyone who does righteousness is righteous, just as he [i.e., God] is righteous" (ὁ ποιῶν τὴν δικαιοσύνην δίκαιός ἐστιν, καθὼς ἐκεῖνος δίκαιός ἐστιν, 1 John 3:7; cf. 1 John 2:29 and 1:9).

---

[23] On this topic, see George van Kooten, "The 'True Light which Enlightens Everyone' (John 1:9): John, Genesis, the Platonic Notion of the 'True, Noetic Light,' and the Allegory of the Cave in Plato's *Republic*," in *The Creation of Heaven and Earth: Reinterpretations of Genesis 1 in the Context of Judaism, Ancient Philosophy, Christianity, and Modern Physics* (ed. G.H. van Kooten; Themes in Biblical Narrative 8; Leiden/Boston: Brill, 2005), 149–94.

According to John, it is this ethical behaviour of human beings which prepares them for their future, full assimilation with God after death: "we will be like him (ὅμοιοι αὐτῷ ἐσόμεθα), for we will see him as he is. And all who have this hope in him purify themselves, just as he is pure" (καὶ πᾶς ὁ ἔχων τὴν ἐλπίδα ταύτην ἐπ' αὐτῷ ἁγνίζει ἑαυτὸν καθὼς ἐκεῖνος ἁγνός ἐστιν, 1 John 3:2–3). It is noteworthy that this way of thinking seems to reflect Plato's view of the assimilation of human beings with God, as expressed in his *Theaetetus*. This assimilation with God, according to Plato, consists in an escape from earth to the dwelling of the gods: "and to escape it to become like God, so far as this is possible; and to become like God is to become righteous and holy with wisdom" (φυγὴ δὲ ὁμοίωσις θεῷ κατὰ τὸ δυνατόν· ὁμοίωσις δὲ δίκαιον καὶ ὅσιον μετὰ φρονήσεως γενέσθαι, *Theaetetus* 176b), the reason for this pursuit of virtue being that "God is in no wise and in no manner unrighteous, but utterly and perfectly righteous, and there is nothing so like him as that one of us who in turn becomes most nearly perfect in righteousness" (θεὸς οὐδαμῇ οὐδαμῶς ἄδικος, ἀλλ' ὡς οἷόν τε δικαιότατος, καὶ οὐκ ἔστιν αὐτῷ ὁμοιότερον οὐδὲν ἢ ὃς ἂν ἡμῶν αὖ γένηται ὅτι δικαιότατος, 176c). In this passage Socrates' view from the *Euthyphro* that the pious is a part of the righteous is now phrased differently, in the sense that the pious and the righteous are taken as a pair, but it is clear that the righteous still determines what is pious, as both the righteous and the pious are clearly understood as ethical virtues. Moreover, it is that which is righteous which connects virtuous human beings with God's profoundly righteous nature. This correspondence is echoed in John's view that God is righteous and that human beings become like him by purifying themselves and by becoming righteous, just as God is pure and righteous (1 John 3:2–3, 7).

This suggests that John was not only familiar with the dialogues of Plato's *Last Days of Socrates* and with the *Symposium*, but also with his *Theaetetus*, either directly (as seems to be the case with the other dialogues just mentioned) or at least indirectly. Considering, however, that the *Theaetetus* also belongs to the same narratological setting as the dialogues now dubbed "The Last Days of Socrates," as the reported dialogue between Theaetetus and Socrates takes place on the day before Socrates' indictment (see *Theaetetus* 210d; cf. 142c), it seems that John was interested in this full set of dialogues. John's description of the anticipation of this prospective full assimilation with God after death as a "hope" (ἐλπίς) (1 John 3:3) – a term which, in the entire Johannine corpus, is used only here – seems to echo Plato's similar, repeated use of the very same term in his *Phaedo* with regard to the expectation of a heavenly afterlife for the purified and the virtuous (*Phaedo* 67b–c, 67e–68b, 70a, 114c; cf. *Apology* 40c). We'll deal with the *Phaedo*, however, in due course.

As regards John's resemblance to Plato's *Euthyphro*, we can conclude not only that the charges against Socrates about making gods and making innovations in religion seem to be echoed in John's description of the charges against Jesus, but also that the broader subject matter of the *Euthyphro* – regarding what counts as pious, what one ought to say and to do, and what is gratifying to the gods – is taken up and answered in terms of worship in spirit, truth, and righteousness, which is considered salutary both for individuals and for entire cities.

The scope of the present paper does not allow me to give similarly detailed treatments of the other three dialogues of Plato's *Last Days of Socrates*. However, I will give a very brief synopsis of other distinctive resemblances between the remaining dialogues and John's Gospel before coming to my conclusions.

## 2 The *Apology*

As regards the *Apology*, there are some similarities between Plato's *Apology* and John's Gospel that one might expect given the similar setting of a juridical trial. So we find a similar emphasis on the importance of what is true/truth (ἀλήθεια) and the same vocabulary of just and unjust judgement (κρίσις ἄδικος and δίκαια κρίσις), accusing (κατηγορεῖν), accusers (κατήγοροι) and accusation (κατηγορία), and slandering (διαβάλλειν). Furthermore, both Socrates and Jesus provoke the authorities, causing, as Socrates states, "many enmities [to] have arisen against me" (*Apology* 22e–23a), so that their words (λόγοι) are not endured (37c–d), and both explicitly distance themselves from politics (31d–e; John 18:36–37). Yet these are rather general, although still noteworthy, parallels.

Rather more specific are the following similarities. At his trial, Socrates refers his judges to his public teaching, in the same way Jesus does in front of the Jewish high priest. Socrates tells his judges: "you hear me making my defence with the same words with which I have been accustomed to speak both in the market place at the bankers' tables, where many of you have heard me, and elsewhere" (διὰ τῶν αὐτῶν λόγων ἀκούητέ μου ἀπολογουμένου δι' ὧνπερ εἴωθα λέγειν καὶ ἐν ἀγορᾷ ἐπὶ τῶν τραπεζῶν, ἵνα ὑμῶν πολλοὶ ἀκηκόασι, καὶ ἄλλοθι, 17c). John has a similar account of the engagement between the high-priestly court and Jesus: "Then the high priest questioned Jesus about his disciples and about his teaching" (ἠρώτησεν τὸν Ἰησοῦν περὶ τῶν μαθητῶν αὐτοῦ καὶ περὶ τῆς διδαχῆς αὐτοῦ). "Jesus answered, 'I have spoken openly to the world; I have always taught in synagogues and in the temple, where all the Jews come together. I have said nothing in secret'" (Ἐγὼ παρρησίᾳ λελάληκα τῷ κόσμῳ· ἐγὼ πάντοτε ἐδίδαξα ἐν συναγωγῇ καὶ ἐν τῷ ἱερῷ, ὅπου πάντες οἱ Ἰουδαῖοι συνέρχονται, καὶ ἐν κρυπτῷ ἐλάλησα οὐδέν, John 18:19–20).

Moreover, just as Socrates is at the bankers' tables in the Agora, so Christ, according to John, "was teaching in the treasury of the temple" (ἐν τῷ γαζοφυλακίῳ διδάσκων ἐν τῷ ἱερῷ, 8:20), a detail not paralleled in the Synoptic Gospels and a rather peculiar point of information which acquires significance, however, against this background in Plato's *Apology*.[24]

Even more specific, I would suggest, is Socrates' appeal to Apollo as witness to his wisdom: "For of my wisdom – if it is wisdom at all – and of its nature, I will offer you the god of Delphi as a witness (μάρτυς)" (20e), just as Jesus refers to God's witness (μαρτυρία) about him (5:31–32, 37). This connection between Apollo and Socrates in Plato's *Apology* seems to be related to Socrates' *daimonion*, the most likely source of which, according to A.A. Long, is "the god Apollo whose oracle initiated his mission to the citizens of Athens."[25] Socrates' *daimonion* is also called "the sign of the god" (τὸ τοῦ θεοῦ σημεῖον, *Apology* 40a–c). This relation between the god Apollo and Socrates seems to be echoed in John's picture of the relationship between God and Jesus, who is said to perform the signs (σημεῖα) of God (3:2; cf. 11:47–48). Implicit in both narratives, then, is the view that both the Athenian court of the Areopagus and the Jewish συνέδριον of Jerusalem silence the divine σημεῖα, either the σημεῖον of Apollo or the σημεῖα of the divine Father (John 1:12; 4:21, 23; 8:41–42; 20:17).

A further similarity between Socrates and Jesus can also be observed in the behaviour of both Jesus and the *daimonion* of Socrates. Socrates' *daimonion*, as is well known, is not protreptic ('urging him on, impelling, persuading him to do a thing') but apotreptic ('turning him away from, dissuading him from doing something'). As Socrates clearly states in *Apology* 31d, "it is a sort of voice that comes to me, and when it comes it always holds me back from what I am thinking of doing, but never urges me forward" (31d), and Socrates regards it as significant that his *daimonion* no longer holds him back during his trial,

---

24  References to the treasury of the temple do occur in Mark 12:41–44 and its parallel in Luke 21:1–4, but without the explicit statement that Jesus taught the crowds in the treasury; in Mark's Gospel, Jesus, sitting down opposite the treasury, notices how a poor widow put money into the treasury and draws his disciples' attention to her, whereas in Luke's Gospel it remains unclear whom Jesus addresses. John, however, describes Jesus as actively "teaching in the treasury of the temple" (ἐν τῷ γαζοφυλακίῳ διδάσκων ἐν τῷ ἱερῷ) (8:20).

25  Long, "daimôn," in the *Continuum Companion to Plato*, 154.

considering this as a sign that his hour has come: "the sign of the god (τὸ τοῦ θεοῦ σημεῖον) did not oppose me... and yet on other occasions it stopped me at many point in the midst of a speech; but now, in this affair, it has not opposed me in anything I was doing or saying... the accustomed sign (τὸ εἰωθὸς σημεῖον) would surely have opposed me if I had not been going to meet with something good" (40a–c; cf. 41d). This is absolutely similar to the behaviour of Jesus, who is continuously held back from performing a particular miracle (John 2:4; 11:6) or from travelling to Jerusalem (7:6) until his hour has come. And just as Socrates during his trial states, "But now the hour has come to go away (ἀλλὰ γὰρ ἤδη ὥρα ἀπιέναι...). I go to die" (42a), so the Johannine Christ likewise states, during his last public teaching, in his response to the Greeks who have come to see him, and also during the Last Symposium which precedes his trial: "Now the hour has come" (Ἐλήλυθεν ἡ ὥρα, 12:23; cf. 13:1, 17:1). This picture of Jesus, I would suggest, depends, beyond reasonable doubt, on Plato's *Apology*.

## 3   The *Crito*

I'm less certain with regard to Plato's *Crito*, in which Crito tries to convince Socrates to escape from prison, and Socrates refuses because of his radical respect for the laws, regardless of how they are applied. It is true that Jesus' disciples, in a similar although different vein, try to dissuade him from going to Judaea, lest he would be caught and killed (11:7–8; cf. 10:31, 39). Jesus similarly emphasises that what is written in the Mosaic law cannot be undone (10:34–35; cf. 7:23), and Nicodemus, his crypto-disciple within the circle of the Jewish authorities, appeals to the law to give Jesus a proper trial (7:50–51). Yet these similarities remain vague, unless they acquire more prominence when John's acquaintance with Plato's dialogues is taken for granted.

## 4   The *Phaedo*

Finally, I will give a very brief overview of possible correspondences between Plato's *Phaedo* and John's Gospel. Socrates' view that the philosophical life entails criticism of the so-called pleasures of eating, drinking, *aphrodisia*, and the body but a love for "what is most true" (τὸ ἀληθέστατον, 65d-e) and for true nurture, "beholding that which is true (τὸ ἀληθές) and divine and not a matter of opinion, and making that its only food" (καὶ ὑπ' ἐκείνου τρεφομένη, 84a–b), is paralleled, I believe, in the reference of the Johannine Christ to the true nurture of the true bread (6:32), true food (ἀληθής βρῶσις), and true drink (ἀληθής ἐστιν πόσις) (6:55) in contrast to physical nurture (4:8).[26]

Similarly, just as Socrates pictures death as a purification and initiation (67a–c; 69c–d; 118a), the very same terminology is used by Jesus during the Last Symposium (13:10–11; 15:3; 17:22–23; 19:28, 30). Moreover, the view that death is a transmigration (μετοίκησις) to another, heavenly home (*Phaedo* 117c, cf. *Apology* 40c: μετοίκησις...τοῦ τόπου τοῦ ἐνθένδε εἰς ἄλλον τόπον) seems mirrored in the assertion of the Johannine Christ, again during the Last Symposium, about his preparing place (τόπος) in the heavenly home (οἰκία; 14:1–3).

Importantly, Socrates' reference to the possibility after death of seeing τὸ φῶς τὸ ἀληθινόν, "the true light" (*Phaedo* 109e–110a) seems to be echoed in John's identification of Christ with the true light (τὸ ἀληθινὸν φῶς) in the prologue to his gospel (1:9) and in the assertion in his first letter that "the true light is already shining": τὸ φῶς τὸ ἀληθινὸν ἤδη φαίνει (1 John 2:8). Given the fact that Plato talks about seeing the true light only eschatologically, after death, it seems that John's proclamation that "the true light is already shining" is polemically addressed against and surpasses Socrates' statement in Plato's *Phaedo*.

All kinds of narratological details from Plato's *Phaedo* also seem to resonate with John's Gospel. Just as the readers of Plato's *Phaedo* are surprised to hear that Socrates actually wrote in prison, although his writings have not been preserved and the content remains necessarily unknown (60d–61b), so the readers of John's Gospel find Jesus, in equally ephemeral mode, writing in the sand (8:6, 8) and are left to guess at what he actually wrote.[27] And just as Socrates invites his disciples in prison to call for his instruction "while there is still light" (ἕως ἔτι φῶς ἐστιν, 89c), the Johannine Christ introduces his last teaching by similarly stating, "The light is with you for a little longer" (Ἔτι μικρὸν χρόνον τὸ φῶς ἐν ὑμῖν ἐστιν, 12:35–36).

There are also notable and deliberate inversions. Whereas Socrates turns his relatives away at the moment of his death (116a–b, 117b; cf. 60b), Jesus, hanging on the cross, asks his beloved disciple to look after his mother (19:25–27). And whereas Socrates' disciples state that he leaves them ὀρφανοί, "orphans" (116a), Jesus states that he will not leave his disciples orphaned: "I will not leave you

---

26  In the light of my previous remarks on John's use of the *Symposium*, it is noteworthy that John takes the above reflections on true nurture from Plato's *Phaedo* and attributes them to sympotic settings in John 4 and 6.

27  Of course, as Aland's synopsis states, "The most ancient authorities omit [John] 7.53–8.11; other authorities add the passage here or after 7.36 or after 21.25 or after Luke 21.38, with variations of text." So this episode remains text-critically uncertain, although its contents would fit John's Socratic Jesus.

orphans; I am coming to you" (Οὐκ ἀφήσω ὑμᾶς ὀρφανούς, ἔρχομαι πρὸς ὑμᾶς, 14:18). With regard to other parallels, even the rather enigmatic cloak of Jesus, which is woven in one piece "from above" and for which the soldiers cast lots at the foot of the cross (19:23–24), seems to echo the imagery of the weaver and his cloak to which one of Socrates' disciples, Cebes, alludes in their discussion about the relation between soul and body (87b, d–e; see the terms ὑφαίνω, "to weave," and ὑφαντός, "woven," in *Phaedo* 87b and John 19:23). Finally, it would be worth comparing the role of Socrates' and Jesus' disciples, as the unbelieving Simmias and Cebes, who question Socrates' view on the immortality of the soul, much resemble the unbelieving Thomas in John's Gospel (John 20:24–29), who doubts that Christ lives after his death.[28]

## 5 Concluding Reflections

So where does this leave us? I have been struck by the many similarities – verbal, conceptual, and narratological – between John's Gospel and Plato's dialogues on the last days of Socrates. But could such an acquaintance of John with Plato's dialogues be considered plausible? And what is John's motive?

Firstly, such Jewish acquaintance with Plato's dialogues is fully possible and is also abundantly attested in the writings of John's Jewish contemporaries, such as Philo of Alexandria, throughout his many treatises, and Flavius Josephus, particularly in his *Against Apion*. In addition, I also draw attention to the fascinating figure of Justus of Tiberius, a Jew from contemporary Galilee, who not only engages with Plato, but is even credited by Diogenes Laertius with the otherwise unknown story that Plato intervened during Socrates' trial. According to Diogenes Laertius, "Justus of Tiberias in his book entitled *The Wreath* says that in the course of the trial Plato mounted the platform and began: 'Though I am the youngest, men of Athens, of all who ever rose to address you'—whereupon the judges shouted out, 'Get down!' 'Get down!'" (*Lives of Eminent Philosophers* 2.41).[29] This shows that even Jews in contemporary Galilee could entertain an interest in Socrates' trial, and all that would have been needed for the Gospel of John to be written was the conversion of a kind of Justus of Tiberias.

---

28  For an exploration of the figure of Thomas from a Platonic perspective, see Glenn W. Most, *Doubting Thomas* (Cambridge, MA: Harvard University Press, 2007).

29  See also the fragments of Justus of Tiberias, edited by René Bloch, "Justus of Tiberias: Greek Text, English Translation, Commentary," in *Brill's New Jacoby* (BNJ) (ed. J. Worthington; Leiden: Brill, 2012), online ed..

Secondly, and finally, it seems that John's motive for fusing the figures of Socrates and Christ has already emerged in the course of this paper. It seems to have been his intention to show that Jesus was not only the aspiration of Jews and Samaritans, but also of Greeks. Although it would not be correct to say, as Jerome and Augustine feared, that "Jesus Christ learnt all those sayings of his... from the books of Plato" (*On Christian Doctrine* 2.28), Origen's simultaneous defence of the credibility of stories about Jesus and the *daimonion* of Socrates and his conclusion that "[w]e do not, then, relate marvels when we narrate the history of Jesus, nor have his genuine disciples recorded any such stories of him" (*Against Celsus* 6.8) seem to reveal something of John's intentions. For this purpose, Plato's *Last Days of Socrates* and *Symposium* were particularly useful because of their vivid picture of Socrates and his disciples.[30]

---

30  According to Gregory Sterling, Luke, too, in his account of Jesus' death, likens Jesus to Socrates. See Gregory E. Sterling, "Mors Philosophi: The Death of Jesus in Luke," *Harvard Theological Review* 94 (2001): 383–402. It is also noteworthy that in Acts 17 Paul's trial before the Athenian Areopagus seems to harbour some references to the trial of Socrates, notably with regards to the issue of introducing new gods into Athens (17:18, 32) and the reference to a just judgement (17:31).

# Criticism of Verbosity in Ancient Philosophical and Early Christian Writings: Jesus' Critique of the 'Polylogia' of Pagan Prayers (Matthew 6:7) in its Graeco-Roman Context

*Daniele Pevarello*

1       Jesus and the Gentile Babblers in Matthew 6:7

The prayer in Matthew 6:9b–13, known as the 'Lord's Prayer' or 'Our Father', is perhaps the most popular and most frequently recited passage of the New Testament. Liturgical use has been instrumental in promoting the diffusion of the Matthean version. The prayer, however, has been preserved in two other recensions, namely the shorter edition of Luke 11:2b–4 and the version of *Didache* 8.2, which, apart from minor linguistic details, largely agrees with the Matthean text.[1] Liturgy and piety have led to a widespread diffusion of the Lord's Prayer. Tradition and common practice, however, have attributed less importance to the context in which Matthew introduces the prayer in the gospel narrative. Luke introduces the Lord's Prayer as a direct answer to a petition of one of the disciples: "Lord, teach us to pray" (Luke 11:1).[2] The Matthean narrative does not mention any such request. Unlike Luke, Matthew introduces the Lord's Prayer as part of a larger instruction on prayer, which starts in Matthew 6:5 with a polemic against the "hypocrites" (ὑποκριταί), whose prayers are described as a form of religious exhibitionism. Since the "hypocrites" of Matthew 6:5 pray "in the synagogues," the polemic is probably directed against Jewish devotional practices.[3] In Matthew 6:7, however, Matthew shifts his polemical target from the Jews to the "Gentiles": "When you are

---

[1] Scholars do not agree on the relationship between the version of the Lord's Prayer of Matthew 6:9b–13 and *Didache* 8.2. Hans D. Betz, *The Sermon on the Mount: A Commentary on the Sermon on the Mount, Including the Sermon on the Plain (Matthew 5:3–7:27 and Luke 6:20–49)* (Hermeneia; Minneapolis, MN: Fortress, 1995), 371 n. 328, for example, suggests that the two recensions are independent from each other. Ulrich Luz, *Matthew 1–7: A Commentary* (Edinburgh: T&T Clark, 1990), 370, argues that "the author of the Didache presupposes Matthew" although their dependency is not textual but originates from the author's memory of the Matthean version.

[2] Biblical quotations in English are taken from the New Revised Standard Version.

[3] See Betz, *Sermon*, 361; and Luz, *Matthew*, 358–59.

praying, do not heap up empty phrases (μὴ βατταλογήσητε) as the Gentiles (ἐθνικοί) do; for they think that they will be heard because of their many words (ἐν τῇ πολυλογίᾳ). Do not be like them, for your Father knows what you need before you ask him. Pray then in this way: Our Father in heaven…"[4] A distinctive feature of the Matthean version is that the Lord's Prayer is presented as a response to what Matthew's Gospel describes as a pagan inclination towards lengthy and babbling prayers. According to Matthew, the Gentiles rely on the abstruse wordiness (πολυλογία) of their prayers to secure the attention of their gods and the satisfaction of their requests. Unlike the Gentiles, says Matthew, Christians should rely on God's foreknowledge of their needs and replace the wordy prayers of the pagans with the Lord's Prayer. As noted above, these characteristics are specifically Matthean. Luke does not have any polemical undertone, while the polemical component of *Didache* 8.1–2 is aimed at the "hypocrites" rather than the Gentiles.[5] Neither Luke nor the *Didache* refer to verbosity when introducing the Lord's Prayer.[6]

The vocabulary of Matthew's reference to Gentile verbosity presents some linguistic difficulties. The verb βατταλογέω ('to babble') is not attested in Greek prior to Matthew 6:7a and is a *hapax legomenon* in the New Testament. Subsequent occurrences are found in Christian texts mostly in direct connection with Matthew 6:7.[7] Apart from two occurrences in the *Pseudo-Clementines*, the noun βαττολογία is hardly used in Greek before the fourth century.[8] The cognate verb βατταρίζω ('to stammer') occurs in Plato (*Theaetetus* 175d), Strabo,

---

4  Matthew 6:7–9a.

5  The identity of the "hypocrites" in *Didache* 8.1–2 has been discussed, for example, in Jonathan A. Draper, "Christian Self-Definition against the 'Hypocrites' in Didache VIII," in *The Didache in Modern Research* (ed. Jonathan A. Draper; Leiden: Brill, 1996), 223–43; and Marcello del Verme, Didache *and Judaism: Jewish Roots of an Ancient Christian-Jewish Work* (London: T&T Clark, 2004), 167–88.

6  Instead of referring to God's foreknowledge of one's needs and the rejections of long petitions, Luke accompanies his discourse on prayer with the parable of the friend at midnight (Luke 11:5–8). As the midnight caller obtains attention thanks to his shameless persistence (ἀναίδεια), so too Christians are invited to persevere in their prayers; see Mathias Nygaard, *Prayer in the Gospel: A Theological Exegesis of the Ideal Prayer* (Biblical Interpretation Series 114; Leiden: Brill, 2012), 165.

7  In non-Christian authors, βαττολογέω occurs in the first-century CE *Life of Aesop* (*Vita Westermanniana*) 109 and in Simplicius' sixth-century *Commentary on Epictetus' Enchiridion* 37.

8  *Epistulae de virginitate* 1.8.2 and 1.12.3, which may date to the third century CE. On the dating of the Pseudo-Clementine *Epistulae de virginitate*, see Daniel Caner, *Wandering, Begging Monk: Spiritual Authority and the Promotion of Monasticism in Late Antiquity* (Berkeley, CA: University of California Press, 2002), 65–6.

and Dio Chrysostom, among others. In *Geography* 14.2.28, Strabo explains βατταρίζω as an onomatopoeic word, such as the adjective βάρβαρος and the verbs τραυλίζω ('to lisp') and ψελλίζω ('to speak inarticulately'), which refer to some form of speech impairment.⁹ In *Histories* 4.155, Herodotus says that the first king of Cyrenaica was named Battus (Βάττος) by his father because of his weak-voiced (ἰσχόφωνος) and limping (τραυλός) speech.¹⁰ The verb βατταρίζω, however, could also be used figuratively to indicate lack of clarity. Dio Chrysostom uses the verb βατταρίζω with reference to the hesitating and unclear (ἀσαφῶς) speech of those who lie knowingly, and Lucian applies it to a shy and inarticulate orator who could not make clear arguments (οὐκ ἀποσαφῶν ὅ τι βούλεται).¹¹

The term πολυλογία and the cognates πολυλογέω and πολύλογος are better attested in Greek.¹² In the New Testament, however, the term is a *hapax legomenon*. In the Septuagint, πολυλογία also occurs only once, in Proverbs 10:19 LXX: "By a multitude of words (ἐκ πολυλογίας) you shall not escape sin (ἁμαρτίαν), but if you restrain your lips you will be judicious." Here πολυλογία possibly translates the Hebrew רב דברים ('abundance of words'). The same Hebrew expression occurs elsewhere in the Hebrew Bible, for example in Job 11:2 and Ecclesiastes 5:2.¹³ In these texts, verbosity is depicted in negative terms and charged with moral overtones. In Job 11:2–3, Job's wordy accusations against God are said to be 'idle talk' or 'babbles' (Heb. בד), which shall not go unpunished. Ecclesiastes is especially close to Matthew 6:7, maintaining the inappropriateness of verbosity when speaking to God: "Do not be hasty with your mouth nor let your heart be quick to bring forth a word in the presence of God, because God is in heaven and you on earth. For this reason, let

---

9  Aristotle says that children ψελλίζουσι καὶ τραυλίζουσι until they have acquired control of their tongues; cf. *History of Animals* 536b.

10  Demosthenes' nickname βάταλος (cf. Aeschines, *In Timarchium* 126, 131 and 164; and *De falsa legatione* 98–9; cf. Demosthenes, *De corona* 180), or βάτταλος according to some manuscript traditions, does not seem to refer to Demosthenes' legendary speech impairment (cf. Cicero, *De divinatione* 2.46.96). In *Demosthenes* 4.5–7, Plutarch, who describes Demosthenes' impairment as ἀσάφεια ('lack of clarity') and τραυλότης ('lisping'), explains the nickname βάταλος as a derogatory reference to Demosthenes' sickly and pitiful appearance and derives it from an effeminate flute-player named Batalus.

11  Dio Chrysostom, *Discourses* 11.27 and Lucian, *Jupiter tragoedus* 27.

12  See for example Xenophon, *Cyropaedia* 1.4.3; Plato, *Laws* 641e; Aristotle, *Politics* 1295a; Plutarch, *De curiositate* 519c; Pseudo-Plutarch, *De liberis educandis* 6c; Cassius Dio *Roman History* 52.41.1 and 76.16.2 and Galen, *De placito Hippocratis et Platonis* 7.2.15.

13  In Job 11:2 LXX the Greek reads ὁ τὰ πολλὰ λέγων for the Hebrew הרב דברים and Ecclesiastes 5:2 LXX reads ἐν πλήθει λόγων where the Masoretic reads ברב דברים.

your words be few (ἔστωσαν οἱ λόγοι σου ὀλίγοι), for a dream comes with abundance of distractions and a foolish (ἄφρονος) voice with abundance of words (ἐν πλήθει λόγων)."[14]

The Septuagint contains numerous other passages that express a negative bias towards verbosity. In these texts, the Septuagint employs the terms ἀδολεσχία ('garrulity') and ἀδολεσχέω ('idle talking'), which are standard in philosophical discussions on talkativeness.[15] In 1 Samuel 1:15–16 LXX, Samuel's mother, mistaken for a drunken woman by the priest Eli, apologises for the ἀδολεσχία of her supplications and explains her verbosity as her being troubled and not intoxicated. Psalm 118:85 LXX also refers to verbosity in negative terms, describing how the lawless (παράνομοι) annoy the Psalmist with idle words (ἀδολεσχίας).[16]

Such Jewish examples of criticism of verbose prayers have led some commentators to read Matthew 6:7 as a problem internal to Judaism. William Davies has argued that the reference to the Gentiles in Matthew 6:7 does not alter the fact that the Lord's Prayer in Matthew is "set over against Pharisaism."[17] As mentioned above, the tradition of *Didache* 8.2 introduces the Lord's Prayer with the invitation not to imitate the "hypocrites" rather than the "Gentiles." The unexpected appearance of Gentiles in a text discussing Jewish piety seems to have been problematic in some textual traditions of Matthew 6:7. The Codex Vaticanus and the Syriac Curetonian Gospels witness to a textual tradition that reads ὑποκριταί instead of ἐθνικοί in Matthew 6:7, referring the criticism of lengthy prayers to the hypocrites worshipping "in the synagogues" mentioned in Matthew 6:2 and 5. Some commentators who read Matthew 6:7 as a debate within Judaism have explained the Greek βατταλογέω from the Aramaic root בטל ('to be futile' or 'void'), bringing the introduction to the Lord's Prayer in Matthew linguistically closer to a Palestinian

---

14  Ecclesiastes 5:2–3 LXX.
15  The Peripatetic Theophrastus, for example, dedicates the third chapter of his *Characters* to ἀδολεσχία and Plutarch devotes an entire treatise of his *Moralia*, the *De garrulitate*, to the same topic; cf. Betz, *Sermon*, 366. On Plutarch's *De garrulitate* and its relationship with texts from Jewish and Christian literature, see William A. Beardslee, "De garrulitate (Moralia 502B–515A)," in *Plutarch's Ethical Writings and Early Christian Literature* (ed. Hans D. Betz; SCHNT 4; Leiden: Brill, 1978), 264–88.
16  See also 2 Kings 9:11 LXX; Psalm 118:85 LXX; Sirach 7:14, with specific reference to prayer, and 32:9.
17  See William D. Davies, *The Setting of the Sermon on the Mount* (BJS 186; Atlanta, GA: Scholars Press, 1989), 309. On the same line, see also Matthew Black, *An Aramaic Approach to the Gospels and Acts* (3d ed.; Oxford: Oxford University Press, 1967), 176–8, who stresses the incongruity of exhorting Jews not to pray like Gentiles.

setting.¹⁸ Matthew 6:7–8 would then preferably be read alongside later rabbinic instances of Jewish arguments against verbosity and lengthy prayers, such as the condemnation of wordiness attributed to Shimon ben Gamliel and Shammai in the Mishnah.¹⁹ Although these studies have successfully drawn attention to the discussion of verbosity in rabbinic Judaism, their tendency to divorce Matthew 6:7–8 from contemporary discussions on verbosity in its Graeco-Roman context appears problematic, if not arbitrary.

The majority of modern commentators of the Gospel of Matthew seem to interpret Matthew 6:7 as a contextual and genuine polemic against pagan piety. A number of these scholars read βατταλογέω literally as a reference to the utterance of inarticulate and repetitive sounds to which pagan worshippers would have attributed supernatural virtues.²⁰ Donald Senior has suggested that "[t]he text may have in mind the incantations or magical formulae of some Greco-Roman cults in which names or phrases were repeated."²¹ The *Greek Magical Papyri* and some Graeco-Roman amulets contain numerous examples of incoherent incantations and *voces magicae* – that is, unintelligible successions of vowels and consonants sometimes penned in evocative geometrical shapes.²² In spite of the widespread diffusion of magic in Graeco-Roman society, however, the role of magic formulae and *voces magicae* in pa-

---

18  This is the suggestion of Frederick Bussby, "A Note on ρακα (Matthew v. 22) and βατταλογέω (Matthew vi. 7) in the Light of Qumran," *ExpTim* 76 (1964): 26, who considers "dubious" and "not encouraging" the hypothesis of a Greek origin of the term. See also David Hill, *The Gospel of Matthew* (NCB; London: Oliphants, 1972), 134; and Robert H. Gundry, *Matthew: A Commentary on His Literary and Theological Art* (Grand Rapids, MI: Eerdmans, 1982), 104. That the word may have been derived from Aramaic, however, is rather unlikely; cf. John Nolland, *The Gospel of Matthew: A Commentary on the Greek Text* (NIGTC; Bletchley: Paternoster, 2005), 284 n. 306; and Betz, *Sermon*, 364–65.

19  Shimon ben Gamliel depends on Proverbs 10:19 when he argues that excessive talking causes sin (דברים מביא חטא וכל המרבה) in *m. 'Abot* 1.7. In *m. 'Abot* 1.15, Shammai invites his disciples to "say little and do many things" (אמור מעט ועשה הרבה). See also *m. 'Abot* 6.6, which exhorts the wise to make a fence (סיג) around their words. In medieval times, rabbi Samuel ben Meir links Ecclesiastes 5:2–3 to an explicit prohibition to utter verbose prayers; see Ruth N. Sandberg, *Rabbinic Views of Qohelet* (Mellen Biblical Press Series 57; Lewiston, NY: Mellen, 1999), 166–68.

20  See Luz, *Matthew*, 364.

21  Donald Senior, *Matthew* (ANTC; Nashville, TN: Abingdon, 1998), 84. Daniel J. Harrington, *The Gospel of Matthew* (SP Series 1; Collegeville, MN: Liturgical Press, 1991), 94–5 focuses on the onomatopoeic character of the word and explains it as "a flood of word and formulas."

22  See for example the magical triangles of *PGM* I.15–19; V.84–90 and CXXX.6–13, or the unintelligible spells of *PGM* I.134–43 and II.1 and 5 and the love spell of *PGM* IV.1560–79.

gan religions remains unclear.²³ Commentators also link the reference to verbose prayers in Matthew 6:7 with the repetition of the numerous names and epithets of the gods in pagan worship in order to acquire a supernatural power over them. Commenting on Matthew 6:7, David Hill has argued that "[t]he idea behind the verse is that of the long prayers made by heathen people who believe that, in order to be sure of addressing the right god by the right name, all the gods and their titles have to be named."²⁴ Greek and Latin literature offer some examples of the various and sometimes mysterious names with which pagan deities were invoked in Graeco-Roman religion.²⁵ As Simon Pulleyn has argued, however, the function of the repetition of names and epithets of a deity may be aimed at honouring the deities by listing their names and titles rather than magically compelling the gods to answer the prayers of the supplicants.²⁶

---

Magic series of vowels and consonants can be seen on amulets from Hellenistic Egypt, such as Mich. 26072 and Mich. 26099; cf. Campbell Bonner, *Studies in Magical Amulets: Chiefly Graeco-Egyptian* (University of Michigan Studies Humanities Series 49; Ann Arbor, MI: University of Michigan Press, 1950), 256 n. 17 and 295 n. 254. On the function of *Vokalreihen* in ancient magic, see Franz Dornseiff, *Das Alphabet in Mystik und Magie* (ΣΤΟΙΧΕΙΑ 7; Leipzig: Teubner, 1922), 35–60. In Lucian, *Alexander* 13, the mystic Alexander tries to impress the crowd by uttering nonsensical words imitating the sounds of Hebrew or Phoenician; see Eric R. Dodds, *Pagan and Christian in an Age of Anxiety* (Cambridge: Cambridge University Press, 1965), 55 n. 1.

23   Although magicians and priests display a similar ability to communicate with the supernatural world, ancient authors have often discussed the boundaries between incantations and prayers. On the distinction between magic and religion in the ancient world, see Fritz Graf, "Theories of Magic in Antiquity," in *Magic and Ritual in the Ancient World* (ed. Paul Mirecki and Marvin Meyer; Religions in the Graeco-Roman World 141; Leiden: Brill, 2002), 92–104, esp. 92–95, where the author discusses prayers and incantations in Apuleius and Iamblichus. On the relationship between Christian glossolalia and *voces magicae* as magical prayers, see David E. Aune, "Magic in Early Christianity," *ANRW* 23 no. 2: 1507–57, esp. 1549–51.

24   Hill, *Matthew*, 134.

25   In his *Hymn to Zeus*, Cleanthes addresses Zeus as the one "with many names" (πολυώνυμος); cf. Cleanthes, fragment 537 (DK). The numerous epithets of the goddess Isis are recorded in Diodorus of Sicily, *Bibliotheca Historica* 1.27.4. Apuleius, *Metamorphoses* 11.5 has a list of the foreign names of the goddess. See also Plato, *Cratylus* 400e and Catullus, *Carmina* 34.1–12, with reference to the names of Diana; Nolland, *Matthew*, 284 argues that Matthew 6:7 refers to both "unintelligible" (magic formulae) and "intelligible" (names, formulaic sentences) expressions.

26   See Simon Pulleyn, *Prayer in Greek Religion* (Oxford Classical Monographs; Oxford: Clarendon, 1997), 96–115. Pulleyn suggests that later examples of magic attempts to compel the gods could be attributable to "post-classical syncretism" (111).

Commentators who read Matthew 6:7 as a polemic against the pagan belief that prayers could compel the gods reject the notion that Matthew may have intended to provide Christians with an instruction about the content and form of prayer. According to these scholars, Matthew 6:7 should rather be understood theologically as a reflection on the relationship between human prayer and God's response to it.[27] Matthew 6:7–8 would then exhort Christians not to expect to coerce God with their prayers. These studies refer to educated critiques of popular religion in Graeco-Roman literature and especially to the Latin notion of 'vexing' (*fatigare*) the gods with prayers.[28] Seneca's argument in the *Moral Epistles* that it is shameful for those who have achieved much to continue vexing the gods, for example, is sometimes mentioned as evidence that pagan worshippers understood prayer as a means of compelling the gods by relentlessly reiterating one's supplications.[29] Since Matthew would be interested in the theological significance of prayer rather than its length and form, some of these studies tend to soften the impact that Graeco-Roman discussions on verbosity had on the Matthean text. Matthew 6:7 would serve the sole purpose of teaching Jesus' disciples that the Christian God already knows the real needs of the worshippers (Matthew 6:8), and prayers should not be understood within the economy of 'give-and-take' which characterised pagan worship.[30] In these readings, criticism of verbosity in Matthew 6:7–8 is confined to a secondary role or even considered a slight misrepresentation of the purpose of the evangelist. John Nolland, for example, observes that "[t]he ancients frequently criticised garrulousness, but that is not what is at issue here," explaining that the meaning

---

27  Betz (*Sermon*, 363) sees in Matthew 6:7 "a theological statement of doctrine concerning prayer".

28  See for example Horace, *Carmina* 1.2 (*prece qua fatigent virgines sanctae minus audientem carmina Vestam*); Statius, *Thebaid* 2.244 (*superosque in vota fatigant*); and Phaedrus, *Fables* 4.21 (*caelum fatigas*).

29  *iam per maxima acto viro turpe est etiamnunc deos fatigare*, Seneca, *Moral Epistles* 31.5. References to the concept of vexing the gods can be found, for example, in Nolland, *Matthew*, 284 n. 307; and Frederick D. Bruner, *The Christbook: Matthew 1–12* (vol. 1 of *Matthew: A Commentary*; Dallas: Word Publishing, 1987), 235.

30  On the "give-and-take" character of the relationship between gods and humanity in ancient Greek religion, see Pulleyn, *Prayer*, 7. On prayer as a negotiation between gods and humans, see also Paul Veyne, "Inviter les dieux, sacrifier, banqueter: Quelques nuances de la religiosité gréco-romaine," *Annales (Histoire, Science Sociales)* 55 no. 1 (2000): 3–42, esp. 16–17, where Veyne mentions the example of the Emperor Galba, who keeps vexing (*fatigabat*) the gods, although their favour has already been granted to his successor; cf. Tacitus, *Histories* 1.29.

of Matthew's criticism is rather a view of "prayer as a means of pressuring God."[31]

In the following pages, I would like to argue that it is neither necessary nor advisable to consider Matthew's reflection on prayer separately from the wealth of examples of criticism of verbosity and verbose prayers in Graeco-Roman, Hellenistic Jewish, and early Christian texts. By examining some of these texts, I shall show how Graeco-Roman and early Christian authors converge into a philosophical tradition that conveys a stark bias against loquacity.

Although Matthew 6:7–8 is also certainly a theological reflection on the Christian God's response to prayer, its early Christian interpreters, and possibly its author, participated in a conceptual world profoundly influenced by philosophical discourses on verbosity. The adherents to this conceptual world deemed verbosity and the predisposition to long discourses as unsuitable for religious discourse in particular – and, more generally, for the articulation of wisdom – and often interpreted loquacity as a sign of moral degeneration.

## 2 Criticism of Verbose Prayers in Graeco-Roman Philosophical Piety

According to Hans Dieter Betz, "[a]nyone who looks for babbling pagans will find them."[32] Although some commentators have attempted to read Matthew 6:7–8 as a realistic depiction of pagan piety, the talkative and babbling prayers of the Gentiles in Matthew are an unforgiving caricature of Graeco-Roman religiosity.[33] As Betz has suggested, Jewish and early Christian caricatures of paganism, such as Matthew 6:7–8, pertain primarily to the language of "self-identity and demarcation" between opposing tendencies within the same religious tradition and are not intended as a direct polemic against pagan devotion.[34] The sporadic use of *voces magicae* and formulaic utterances as magic means of compelling the gods in Graeco-Roman popular religion does not adequately represent the complexity of the ancient discourse on prayer. Greek

---

31  Nolland, *Matthew*, 285. A notable exception is Leon Morris, *The Gospel According to Matthew* (Leicester: Inter-Varsity, 1992), 141, who ascribes a central role to the criticism of talkativeness in Matthew 6:7.

32  Betz, *Sermon*, 367.

33  On Matthew 6:7 as a caricature, see Nolland, *Matthew*, 284–5; and Betz, *Sermon*, 366, who argues that the caricature of pagan religion in Matthew 6:7 derives from Jewish traditional representations of paganism.

34  Ibid. On the Matthean caricature of the ἐθνικοί and early Christian identity, see also Judith M. Lieu, *Christian Identity in the Jewish and Graeco-Roman World* (Oxford: Oxford University Press, 2004), 132–33.

and Roman philosophers and cultivated critics of religion have frequently condemned superstitious beliefs about prayer in popular piety.[35] In the works of these authors, the devout prayers of the Graeco-Roman wise are often opposed to the trivial supplications of popular piety with arguments that very closely resemble those adduced by Matthew. Like Matthew 6:7–8, some of these texts contain a number of instructions and warnings about the function, content, and proper form of prayer.

In relation to the function of prayer, some Greek and Roman philosophical traditions dispute the popular understanding of prayer as a means of enticing the gods into a trading relationship of giving and taking. More than four centuries before Matthew, Plato had already exposed in his *Euthyphro* the weaknesses of an understanding of religion as a mercantile activity (ἐμπορικὴ τέχνη) that brings together gods and humans in a joint venture of mere bartering.[36] In the *Republic* 364b–e, Plato openly censures the Homeric tradition. The idea that the gods can be manipulated by sacrifices and prayers, as stated for example in the *Iliad* 9.497–501, says Plato, results in moral corruption, as it conveys to both individual citizens and whole cities that unjust deeds can be expiated by bribing the gods with appropriate cultic acts.[37] In the *Laws*, Plato includes the belief that the gods can be influenced by sacrifices and prayers among the most common forms of impiety. Those who hold this view, says Plato, deserve to be punished together with those who negate the existence of the gods or their interest in humankind.[38] As mentioned above, scholars have identi-

---

[35] A collection of ancient philosophical texts on prayer can be found in Heinrich Schmidt, *Veteres philosophi quomodo iudicaverint de precibus* (Religionsgeschichtliche Versuche und Vorarbeiten 4/1; Giessen: Töpelmann, 1907).

[36] See Plato, *Euthyphro* 14e. On criticism of sacrifices and prayers in the *Euthyphro*, see Mark L. McPherran, "Platonic Religion," in *A Companion to Plato* (ed. Hugh H. Benson; Oxford: Blackwell, 2006), 244–59, esp. 245–6; and Gregory Vlastos, "Socratic Piety," in *Plato 2: Ethics, Politics, Religion, and the Soul* (vol. 2 of *Plato*; ed. Gail Fine; Oxford Readings in Philosophy; Oxford: Oxford University Press, 1999), 56–77, esp. 73–4.

[37] On Plato's criticism of Homeric religion as bribing the gods, see Jon D. Mikalson, *Greek Popular Religion in Greek Philosophy* (Oxford: Oxford University Press, 2010), 45–6; and Richard J. Klonoski, "The Portico of the Archon Basileus: On the Significance of the Setting of Plato's 'Euthyphro'," *CJ* 81 no. 2 (1985–86): 130–37. Plato's disapproval of the Homeric depiction of the gods has been also analysed in Michelle Lacore, "La théologie d'Homère jugée par Platon," in *Les dieux de Platon* (ed. Jérôme Laurent; Caen: Presse Universitaire de Caen, 2003), 79–95. In Latin literature, see for example Vergil, *Aeneid* 6.376: *desine fata deum flecti sperare precando*.

[38] *Laws* 885b, see Michael L. Morgan, "Plato and Greek Religion," in *The Cambridge Companion to Plato* (ed. Richard Kraut; Cambridge: Cambridge University Press, 1992), 227–47, esp. 242–3.

fied one of the main theological realisations of Matthew 6:7–8 as the notion that the Christian God cannot be manipulated by prayer.[39] If this is the case, the criticism of the popular concept of religion as bargaining with the gods in the Platonic tradition presents remarkable similarities with the Matthean instruction.

Analogies between the philosophical piety of the Graeco-Roman philosophical tradition and Matthew 6:7–8 can also be adduced in relation to instructions about the content and form of prayer. Matthew 6:7–8 teaches Christian believers to avoid the verbosity of pagan prayers and preferably rely on God's foreknowledge of their needs (οἶδεν γὰρ ὁ πατὴρ ὑμῶν ὧν χρείαν ἔχετε, Matthew 6:8). After this instruction, Jesus recommends the Lord's Prayer to his disciples as an archetypal prayer ("pray then in this way," Matthew 6:9). Similarly, the philosophical piety of the Graeco-Roman tradition invites supplicants to purge their prayers of personal petitions and rely instead on the gods' knowledge of what is good. Although these texts do not explicitly discuss verbose prayers, they promote simple and unadorned prayers as a sign of the petitioner's confidence in the gods. Xenophon, for example, reveals that Socrates used to pray solely for "good things" (τὰ ἀγαθά) without expressing any personal wish, explaining that the gods "know best what things are good" (ὡς τοὺς θεοὺς κάλλιστα εἰδότας ὁποῖα ἀγαθά ἐστι, *Memorabilia* 1.3.2).[40] Diodorus of Sicily follows a similar tradition when he states that Pythagoras taught that one should only pray for τἀγαθά, as it is unadvisable to expect that one could suggest to the gods what good is (*Bibliotheca Historica* 10.9.8).[41] In the *Moral Epistles*, Seneca exhorts Lucilius to release the gods from answering the petitions of past prayers and pray simply for a good mind and good health of body and spirit (*Moral Epistles* 10.4). Prayers for success and fame, such as those previously offered by Lucilius' relatives, says Seneca, should be rejected; in fact, one should wish that similar prayers may remain unanswered (32.4 and 60.1).[42] As in Matthew 6:7–8, these texts invite the supplicants to express their

---

39  See Harrington, *Matthew*, 95; Luz, *Matthew*, 365; Betz, *Sermon*, 367; Morris, *Matthew*, 142; and also Georg Strecker, *Die Bergpredigt: Ein exegetischer Kommentar* (Göttingen: Vandenhoek & Ruprecht, 1984), 109; and Craig S. Keener, *A Commentary on the Gospel of Matthew* (Grand Rapids, MI: Eerdmans, 1999), 212–13.

40  See Mikalson, *Popular Religion*, 2–3.

41  See Betz, *Sermon*, 366.

42  As knowledge of the divine and human things is the greatest good (*summum bonum*), Lucilius should aim at accepting the divine decrees and being a companion of the gods rather than a petitioner (*deorum socius esse, non supplex*); cf. 31.8. When people lose sight of the good and embrace evil, their prayers necessarily reflect their confusion; cf. *pugnant vota nostra cum votis*, 45.6.

confidence in divine knowledge of their necessities, or their good, through a lessening of their petitions.

The Pythagorean tradition also seems to favour prayers that are not conceived of as a display of eloquence. In the *Life of Apollonius*, Philostratus portrays Apollonius as the archetypal Pythagorean philosopher.[43] In keeping with the emphasis on religion observable in later Pythagorean sources, Philostratus understands Apollonius as a model of piety.[44] Apollonius, says Philostratus, taught that sacrifices and offerings should be performed without exceeding the right measure (μὴ ὑπερβάλλειν τὸ μέτριον, *Life of Apollonius* 1.11.1–2).[45] Like Socrates in Xenophon's *Memorabilia*, Apollonius argued that, since the gods are just and wise and fully aware of human needs, worshippers should pray in such a way as to express their complete confidence in the gods. Petitioners should then refrain from expressing specific requests in their prayers and limit themselves to declarations of acceptance of the divine decree. Apollonius explains to the Roman consul Telesinus that, rather than praying separately for justice, observance of the laws, a simple life for the wise, and honesty for the populace, all petitions may be condensed into one prayer (ξυνείρω τὰ πάντα ἐς εὐχὴν μίαν, *Life of Apollonius* 4.40.21). As in Matthew 6:7–8, Apollonius taught that worshippers should rely on the good disposition of the gods rather than populating their prayers with a meticulous array of petitions. When approaching the gods, continues Philostratus, Apollonius adopted one short paradigmatic prayer: "o gods, may you accord me what I deserve" (ὦ θεοί, δοίητέ μοι τὰ ὀφειλόμενα), trusting that the gods would grant their favour to the worthy.[46]

---

43  On Philostratus' portrayal of Apollonius as a recapitulation of classical ideals of philosophical and heroic life, see James A. Francis, *Subversive Virtue: Asceticism and Authority in the Second-Century Pagan World* (University Park, PA: Pennsylvania State University Press, 1995), 126.

44  Maria Dzielska, *Apollonius of Tyana in Legend and History* (Problemi e ricerche di storia antica 10; Rome: Bretschneider, 1986), 142, says that Philostratus sees in Apollonius a "Pythagorean saint;" see also Charles H. Kahn, *Pythagoras and the Pythagoreans: A Brief History* (Indianapolis, IN: Hackett, 2001), 142. On religion in Apollonius and the Pythagorean apocryphal literature, see Walter Burkert, *Lore and Science in Ancient Pythagoreanism* (Cambridge, MA: Harvard University Press, 1972), 96.

45  See Betz, *Sermon*, 366.

46  Philostratus repeats this prayer twice, in *Life of Apollonius* 1.11.15–16 and 4.40.22–3. In 1.33, Philostratus mentions another short prayer of Apollonius: ὦ θεοί, δοίητε μοι μικρὰ ἔχειν καὶ δεῖσθαι μηδενός. On the centrality of prayer as the "highest form of sacrifice" in Apollonius' piety, see Dzielska, *Apollonius*, 146–7.

Later Pythagorean traditions are more explicit in linking Pythagorean piety with the rejection of verbosity. The apocryphal *Pythagorean Sentences* instruct the Pythagorean sage about prayer and sacrifice:[47]

> Knowledge of god makes concise (βραχύλογον) in the highest degree; the reason for many words (πολλῶν δὲ λόγων) about god is ignorance (ἀμαθία) of god... It is not the tongue of a sage (σοφοῦ) that is principally held in honour by god, but the works. For a sage can honour god even by remaining silent (σιγῶν). A talkative (γλώτταλγος) and ignorant (ἀμαθής) person when praying (εὐχόμενος) and making offerings defiles god; the sage is the only priest, the only one dear to god, the only one who knows how to pray (μόνος εἰδὼς εὔξασθαι). Knowledge of god makes concise (βραχύλογον).[48]

According to the *Pythagorean Sentences*, the Pythagorean sage should aim at being concise (βραχύλογος) both when talking about god and when addressing god directly in prayer. A characteristic feature of this text is that verbosity in prayer and religious discourses is explained as ignorance (ἀμαθία) of God. The petitioners' lack of theological understanding causes them to be verbose (γλώτταλογος) and makes their prayers unacceptable in the light of the profound concern for ritual purification among the Pythagoreans.[49] The philosophical piety envisaged by the *Pythagorean Sentences* sees the Pythagorean philosopher as the only person suited to address the deity in worship. The brevity of the prayers of the devout Pythagoreans demonstrates their familiarity with the deity and their deeper understanding.

---

47  The dating of the *Pythagorean Sentences* is uncertain. A slightly different version of the *Pythagorean Sentences* from the one handed down in the manuscript tradition served as a source for Porphyry's letter *To Marcella*, compiled around 300–303 CE; see Édouard des Places, ed., *Porphyre: Vie de Pythagore, Lettre à Marcella* (Collection des universités de France; Paris: Les Belles Lettres, 1982), 89–90; and George Rocca-Serra, "La lettre à Marcella de Porphyre et les Sentences des Pythagoriciens," in *Le néoplatonisme: Royaumont, 9–13 Juin 1969* (ed. Pierre Maxime Schuhul and Pierre Hadot; Colloques internationaux du Centre National de la Recherche Scientifique. Sciences humaines 535; Paris: Éditions du Centre national de la recherche scientifique, 1971), 193–202. On the text and manuscript tradition of the *Pythagorean Sentences*, see Henry Chadwick, *The Sentences of Sextus: A Contribution to the History of Early Christian Ethics* (Texts and Studies. Contributions to Biblical and Patristic Literature, Second Series 5; Cambridge: Cambridge University Press, 1959), 84–94.

48  *Pythagorean Sentences* 10 and 15–16.

49  On purification rites in early Pythagoreanism, see Kahn, *Pythagoras*, 21.

The positions expressed in the *Pythagorean Sentences* display some crucial analogies with Jesus' instruction on prayer in the Gospel of Matthew. As in Matthew 6:7–8, the *Pythagorean Sentences* postulate a stark opposition between an appropriate way of addressing god and verbose prayers. As the *Pythagorean Sentences* see brief prayers as a sign of a deeper knowledge of the divine, so Matthew 6:7–8 also bases its invitation to avoid a profusion of words when praying on a greater understanding of the Christian God and God's benevolent farsightedness.

## 3 Brief and Long Discourses in the Philosophical Tradition

When the *Pythagorean Sentences* say that the sage can honour god even by remaining silent, they probably allude to the centrality of the vow of silence in the Pythagorean initiation and ritual practice.[50] In *Life of Apollonius* 1.1, Philostratus refers to Pythagorean silence, stating that "silence also can be a form of speech" (καὶ τὸ σιωπᾶν λόγος). The spurious letters of Apollonius openly contrast Pythagorean silence with πολυλογία: "Verbosity (πολυλογία) involves many false steps (σφάλματα), but silence is steadfast."[51]

In agreement with the Pythagorean tradition, the *Epistles* of Pseudo-Apollonius also attribute great importance to silence.[52] According to Pseudo-Apollonius, the profusion of words in the discourses of verbose people increases the possibility of stumbling and error. The same notion probably

---

50   A five-year period of silence was imposed on new Pythagorean adepts; cf. Diogenes Laertius, *Vitae philosophorum* 8.10; Iamblichus, *De vita Pythagorica* 72; Philostratus, *Life of Apollonius* 6.11 and 20; see Kahn, *Pythagoras*, 8; and Leonid Zhmud, *Pythagoras and the Early Pythagoreans* (Oxford: Oxford University Press, 2012), 162–3. On the importance of the vow of silence in protecting the secrets of Pythagorean piety, see Burkert, *Lore*, 178–79. Philostratus shows Apollonius' strict adherence to the Pythagorean way of life by insisting on his observance of Pythagorean silence; cf. *Life of Apollonius* 1.14–16.

51   Pseudo-Apollonius, *Epistles* 93. I follow here the numbering and the text of Robert J. Penella, ed., *The Letters of Apollonius of Tyana: A Critical Text with Prolegomena, Translation and Commentary* (Mnemosyne Bibliotheca Classica Batava Supp. 56; Leiden: Brill, 1979); cf. Stobaeus, *Florilegium* 3.36.28. On the authenticity of the *Epistles* of Pseudo-Apollonius, see Penella, *Letters*, 23–9.

52   Although Penella (ibid., 28) is right in observing that the *Epistles* are eclectic rather than outspokenly Pythagorean and that Philostratus "over-Pythagorized" the historical figure of Apollonius, the work of Pseudo-Apollonius often refers to Pythagoras and depicts Apollonius as a follower of Pythagoras; cf. Pseudo-Apollonius, *Epistles* 16; 23; 28; 48.2; 50; 53; 55.1; 62.

prompted the *Pythagorean Sentences* to establish a direct relationship between verbosity and ignorance (ἀμαθία) in religious discourses about god. As the language of error and ignorance, verbosity is not suitable for worship. When the *Pythagorean Sentences* refer to the wise as βραχύλογος, however, they follow a tradition in Greek thought which extends beyond the boundaries of religious discourses. The disapproval of long prayers in the *Pythagorean Sentences* is rooted in a tradition that regards verbosity with suspicion and adopts brevity as the appropriate linguistic register for the transmission of wisdom.[53]

Warnings against talkative people figure in most wisdom traditions of the Mediterranean and the ancient Near East.[54] The Greek philosophical tradition, however, tends to emphasise the notion of a direct connection between brevity and the very origins of Greek thought. If verbosity exposes the speaker to ignorance and error, brevity becomes a sign of sound reasoning and a distinctive feature of a true philosopher. In some of his dialogues, Plato claims that Socrates was more inclined to use a short style (βραχυλογία) rather than a long one (μακρολογία). This preference for brevity is mentioned above all when Socrates engages in dialectical arguments with sophists and teachers of rhetoric. In *Gorgias* and *Protagoras*, for example, Socrates demands that the two sophists answer his questions only with the greatest brevity possible. Although some commentators have argued that this opposition to making a display of eloquence may have been based on the historical figure of Socrates, Socrates' use of brevity in Plato follows a specific dialectical strategy.[55] In the

---

[53] In this regard, it would have been noteworthy to consider Democritus, fragment 44 (DK): ἀληθόμυθον χρὴ εἶναι, οὐ πολύλογον; see also Betz, *Sermon*, 267. The version of Democritus' fragment preserved in Stobaeus, *Florilegium* 3.12.13, however, seems to be the better reading: ἀληθομυθέειν χρεών, ὃ πολὺ λώιον; cf. Solomon Luria, *Democrito: raccolta dei frammenti, interpretazione e commentario* (Milano: Bompiani, 2007), 1289.

[54] Bezt (*Sermon*, 366) observes that "the topic was transcultural in nature." The sixteenth-century BCE Assyrian *Counsels of Wisdom*, for example, contain a section (26–30) on improper speech and the necessity of exercising control over one's lips; see Wilfred G. Lambert, *Babylonian Wisdom Literature* (Oxford: Oxford University Press, 1960), 101. The eleventh- to eighth-century BCE Egyptian *Instruction of Ani* invites supplicants not to be garrulous, especially in the presence of the gods (cf. *ANET*, 420). See also the fifth-century BCE Aramaic papyrus of the *Words of Ahiqar* (7.96–8), which equally instructs readers to avoid chatter (cf. *ANET*, 428).

[55] See Andrew Ford, "The Beginnings of Dialogue: Socratic Discourses and Fourth-Century Prose," in *The End of Dialogue in Antiquity* (ed. Simon Goldhill; Cambridge: Cambridge University Press, 2008), 29–44, esp. 36–9. Although Aristophanes (*Clouds* 482–3) seems to depict Socrates as favouring brevity, Eupolis describes Socrates as a "poor babbler" (πτωχὸν ἀδολέσχην); cf. Eupolis, fragment 352 (Kock).

development of the argument, Socrates' request serves the purpose of weakening the rhetorical arsenal of his antagonists. Deprived of the persuasive and epideictic power of macrology, Socrates' interlocutors are forced into a position of dialectical disadvantage. Ultimately, Plato's reference to Socrates' brevity is an argumentative ploy which ironically discloses the limits of all rhetorical efforts, the long as well as the brief.[56]

In later receptions of the Platonic discourse, however, the irony of the argument seems to fade, and conciseness turns out to be part of the common attire of the philosopher, above all in philosophical biographies and in works destined for a wider audience. In these works, brachylogy is presented as the language of demonstration, dialectic conversation, focus, and philosophical thinking, while macrology is relegated to the domain of deceitful persuasion, public display, digression, and sophistry. In an ironic passage from Plato's *Protagoras*, Socrates suggests that the brevity traditionally associated with the Spartans may have been the favourite style of the legendary Seven Sages and the very origins of Greek thought:[57]

> We're talking about men like Thales of Miletus, Pittacus of Mytilene, Bias of Priene, our own Solon, Cleobulus of Lindus, Myson of Chen, and, the seventh in the list, Chilon of Sparta. All of these emulated, loved, and studied Spartan culture. You can see that distinctive kind of Spartan wisdom in their pithy (ῥήματα βραχέα), memorable sayings, which they jointly dedicated as the first fruits of their wisdom to Apollo in his temple at Delphi, inscribing there the maxims now on everyone's lips: 'Know thyself' and 'Nothing in excess'. What is my point? That the characteristic style (τρόπος) of ancient philosophy was laconic brevity (βραχυλογία τις Λακωνική).[58]

Socrates' claim that philosophy began with laconic brevity in *Protagoras* is probably intended to be nothing more than a clever witticism. Philosophy was

---

56  See Plato, *Gorgias* 449a–c; and *Protagoras* 335a–b. On the use of brachylogy as a Socratic strategy in the *Gorgias*, see Seth Benardete, *The Rhetoric of Morality and Philosophy: Plato's Gorgias and Phaedrus* (Chicago: University of Chicago Press, 1991), 12–13. On Socrates' claim not to be versed in long speeches, see for example *Protagoras* 335c.

57  On the concise (βραχύλογος) style of the Spartan as opposed to the talkative (φιλόλογος) and verbose (πολύλογος) style of the Athenians, see Plato, *Laws* 641e; cf. Stobaeus, *Florilegium* 3.35.11; and Pseudo-Plutarch, *Apophthegmata Laconica* 224c.5–7.

58  Plato, *Protagoras* 343a–b, ET Stanley Lombardo and Karen Bell, ed., "Protagoras," in *Plato: Complete Works* (ed. John M. Cooper; Indianapolis, IN: Hackett, 1997), 746–90, esp. 774.

believed not to have prospered in Sparta. Socrates' attempt to persuade Protagoras that Greek philosophy originated among the inarticulate Spartans and Cretans serves the sole purpose of ridiculing the sophists' claim to wisdom.[59] It would be misleading to equate Socrates' preference for brachylogy with an explicit criticism of verbosity. Orators were trained to express themselves both in the long and lavish style of μακρολογία and in the terse and succinct forms of βραχυλογία.[60] Ultimately, the limits of μακρολογία reside in its attempt to manipulate the listeners, making them forgetful of the topic discussed, rather than in length as such.[61]

In later reception, however, Plato's irony and his scepticism towards the long as well as the brief discourse are not always maintained. Some authors tend to receive the claim that brevity was the original form of expression of philosophy in more earnest terms than intended in Plato's *Protagoras*. In *Lycurgus*, for example, Plutarch reiterates the Socratic claim that the apophthegmatic style of the ancient Spartans revealed a predilection for philosophy: "The character of their apophthegms (τὸ μὲν οὖν τῶν ἀποφθεγμάτων εἶδος), then, was such as to justify the remark that love of wisdom (φιλοσοφεῖν) rather than love of bodily exercise was the special characteristic of a Spartan (Λακωνίζειν)."[62] The influence of *Protagoras* 343a–b on this passage is highly probable. As Socrates had interpreted Spartan brevity as the cradle of philosophical thought, Plutarch equates the brevity of the Spartans with a sign of their philosophical attitude, so that philosophy becomes the distinctive feature of Spartan life.

---

59   On the Spartans and Cretans as incognito philosophers, see Plato, *Protagoras* 342b–e. Laurence Lampert, *How Philosophy Became Socratic: A Study on Plato's* Protagoras, Charmides *and* Republic (Chicago: University of Chicago Press, 2010), 90–1, highlights the comical effect of Socrates' claim.

60   Philostratus (*Life of Apollonius* 8.2) says that Apollonius was able to defend himself in court using long discourses (μακρηγορεῖν), short discourses (βραχυλογεῖν), and even silence (σιωπᾶν), like Socrates during his own trial.

61   Long discourses could contain apologies for one's μακρολογία; see for example Isocrates, *Panathenaicus* 88 and *Busiris* 44. In *Panathenaicus* 88, Isocrates ironically ascribes his "forgetfulness and prolixity" (τῆς λήθης καὶ τῆς μακρολογίας) to old age. On Socrates' criticism of macrology as criticism of a discourse which confounds the audience and circumvents the questions asked, see Monique Dixsaut, "Macrology and Digression," in *The Platonic Art of Philosophy* (ed. George Boys-Stones, Dimitri El Murr, and Christopher Gill; Cambridge: Cambridge University Press, 2013), 10–26, esp. 12–13.

62   Plutarch, *Lycurcus* 20.6, ET Bernadotte Perrin, ed., *Plutarch's Lives* (11 vol.; LCL; Cambridge, MA: Harvard University Press, 1955–1967), 1:271.

In Greek biographies, in particular, the conciseness of philosophers and sages is often mentioned as an incontrovertible indication of wisdom. This notion applies to standard descriptions of wise philosophers and sages across different philosophical persuasions and schools. In *Alexander* 64.1, Plutarch demonstrates the philosophical demeanour of the Indian Gymnosophists by drawing attention to their cleverness (δεινούς) and conciseness (βραχυλόγους). In his philosophical biographies, Diogenes Laertius insists that the Stoic Zeno was βραχύλογος and describes the philosopher in the act of rebuking his pupil Ariston for being verbose (λαλός).[63] Whether philosophers actually adopted a brief style in their writings is of less importance, as biographers use brevity as a conventional signpost to the readers that the character said to have been concise is a real philosopher and not prone to manipulation and sophistry. In his *Life of Plotinus*, Porphyry celebrates the intellectual excellence of his former teacher by mentioning Plotinus' concise and brief style: "In writing he is concise (σύντομος) and full of thought. He puts things shortly (βραχύς) and abounds more in ideas than in words."[64] Similarly, Iamblichus ascribes the pithiness of Pythagoras' teachings to the philosopher's exceptional capacity for brachylogy: "The most divine Pythagoras hid the sparks of truth for those able to kindle them; his brevity of speech (βραχυλογία) conceals a boundless treasury of knowledge."[65]

As conciseness gradually comes to be portrayed as the language of sound reasoning, brevity and the rejection of verbosity are included in the customary repertoire of popular philosophy and philosophical vulgarisation. In the third book of the *Florilegium*, Stobaeus dedicates an entire section of his work to philosophical maxims about the use of βραχυλογία and another to talkativeness (ἀδολεσχία). Stobaeus records sentences rejecting verbosity from a number of famous philosophers of the past. In Stobaeus' *Florilegium*, for example, Apollonius observes that the most excellent people are also the most concise (βραχυλογώτατοι).[66] Stobaeus also attributes to Zeno a preference for students

---

[63] Diogenes Laertius, *Vitae philosophorum* 7.18. In 1.72, Chilon of Sparta, one of the Seven Sages, is famous for being βραχύλογος, to the point that Diogenes describes brevity as "the Chilonean style" (τὸν τρόπον Χιλώνειον).

[64] Porphyry, *Life of Plotinus* 14, ET Arthur H. Armstrong, ed., *Plotinus* (7 vol.; LCL; Cambridge, MA: Harvard University Press, 1966–1988), 1:39–41.

[65] Iamblichus, *De vita Pythagorica* 29.162, ET Gillian Clark, ed., *Iamblichus: On the Pythagorean Life* (Translated Texts for Historians 8; Liverpool: Liverpool University Press, 1989), 72–3.

[66] Stobaeus, *Florilegium* 3.36.29; cf. Pseudo-Apollonius, *Epistles* 94.

who are fond of reasoning (λογοφίλους) over students who are fond of words (φιλολόγους).[67]

The preference for brevity as a desirable philosophical trait is not limited to depictions of philosophers but extends to a wider context. As brevity defines intellectual superiority and commitment to sound thinking as opposed to sophistry, verbosity is increasingly seen as a sign of moral and cognitive weakness. From the realms of rhetoric, education, and learning to those of political and military life and any other domain where speech and thought are crucial, brevity becomes a distinctive trait of success. In *Phocion* 5.4–5, for example, Plutarch tells of the orator Phocion's inclination towards βραχυλογία and of his ability to express the most meaningful concepts "in the shortest utterance" (ἐν ἐλαχίστῃ λέξει). Although some may have found Phocion's style bossy, harsh, and bitter (προστακτικήν τινα καὶ αὐστηρὰν καὶ ἀνήδυντον), Plutarch ascribes to Phocion's brevity the reason for his success.[68] In the same way, military leaders are often celebrated for their brevity. In *Agesilaus*, Plutarch describes how Admiral Lysander stripped King Agesilaus of the loyalty of the Spartans thanks to the vehemence, severity, and brevity of his speech.[69] Plutarch describes even Caesar's famous utterance "*veni, vidi, vici*" as evidence of his outstanding propensity to brachylogy.[70]

Plutarch's remarks on the harshness of Phocion's language and the severity of Lysander's speech suggest that brevity was not universally accepted as good style.[71] Brevity, however, marks the intelligence and decisional power of political and military leaders. In Plutarch's biography of Brutus, the notion of brachylogy as the language of philosophy and that of brevity as characteristic of successful leaders converge in Plutarch's description of Brutus' writing style: "In Latin, now, Brutus was sufficiently trained for narrative or pleading; but in Greek he affected the brevity of the apophthegm and the Spartan (τὴν ἀποφθεγματικὴν καὶ Λακωνικὴν ἐπιτηδεύων βραχυλογίαν), of which he sometimes gives a striking example in his letters."[72] According to contem-

---

67  *Florilegium* 3.36.26; see also Stobaeus, *Florilegium* 2.7.11k, with a similar distinction.
68  According to Plutarch, if Demosthenes was the most excellent speaker, Phocion was the "most powerful" (δεινότατος). See also Plutarch, *Praecepta gerendae reipublicae* 803e, where Phocion's brevity is admired in spite of the harshness of his style.
69  See Plutarch, *Agesilaus* 7.2.
70  See Plutarch, *Caesar* 50.3–4.
71  Plutarch, *Conjugalia praecepta* 142b, describes the character of a taxing wife using negative expressions very close to the portrayal of Phocion's style: τις αὐστηρὰ καὶ ἄκρατος γένηται καὶ ἀνήδυντος.
72  Plutarch, *Brutus* 2.5, ET Perrin, *Plutarch's Lives*, 6:129–31.

porary sources, Brutus was known for the brevity of his letters.⁷³ Plutarch's mention of traditional Spartan brevity offers an erudite referent for Brutus' brevity and confers an educated flavour to the directness and lack of sophistication of some of Brutus' letters. The letters of Brutus which Plutarch reproduces in *Brutus* 2.4–5, however, are particularly harsh and austere. Plutarch's examples are rather surprising, considering that ancient sources witness that Brutus was rather fluent in Greek and that he wrote a moral work on duty in Greek, entitled περὶ καθήκοντος.⁷⁴ Plutarch's examples of Brutus' letters, however, are probably intended to display the same vehemence and imperiousness attributed to Lysander and other successful leaders.

In all probability, the mention of Spartan brachylogy also serves another significant purpose in Plutarch's portrayal of Brutus. As observed by Christopher Pelling, one of the main purposes of Plutarch's *Brutus* was to depict the Roman leader as "the philosopher in action."⁷⁵ Plutarch's comparison of Brutus' life with the life of Dion in the *Parallel Lives* was probably motivated by the fact that both men had cultivated Platonic philosophy. Dion had been a student of Plato, and Brutus had been educated in the teachings of the Old Academy.⁷⁶ It is significant that Plutarch mentions Brutus' βραχυλογία immediately after

---

73   Cicero, *Letters to Brutus* 1.14.1, expresses with great emphasis how brief Brutus' letters were: *breves litterae tuae – breves dico? immo nullae. Tribusne versiculis his temporibus Brutus ad me? nihil scripsisses potius*; see also 2.5.3. The use of brevity in Brutus' Greek letters is analysed in Pier L. Meucci, "Le lettere greche di Bruto," *Studi italiani di filologia classica* 19 (1942): 47–102, esp. 69 and 76–7. On the authenticity of Brutus' Greek epistolary, see Luigi Torraca, ed., *Marco Giunio Bruto: Epistole greche* (Collana di studi greci 31; Napoli: Libreria scientifica, 1959), v–xxviii; and Jürgen Deininger, "Brutus und die Bithynier: Bemerkungen zu den sog. griechischen Briefen des Brutus," *Rheinisches Museum für Philologie* 109 (1966): 356–72.

74   See for example Seneca, *Moral Epistles* 95.45.

75   Christopher Pelling, "Plutarch: Roman Heroes and Greek Culture," in *Philosophia Togata I: Essays on Philosophy and Roman Society* (ed. Miriam Griffin and Jonathan Barnes; Oxford: Oxford University Press, 1989), 199–232, 222.

76   ἣ τόν τε Βρούτου περιέχει βίον καὶ τὸν Δίωνος· ὧν ὁ μὲν αὐτῷ Πλάτωνι πλησιάσας, ὁ δὲ τοῖς λόγοις ἐντραφεὶς τοῖς Πλάτωνος, Plutarch, *Dion* 1.1. In *Brutus* 2.2, Plutarch observes that although there was not a single Greek philosopher with whom Brutus was not acquainted, he studied especially the followers of Plato (διαφερόντως δ' ἐσπουδάκει πρὸς τοὺς ἀπὸ Πλάτωνος). On Brutus' acquaintance with the philosophy of the Academy, and in particular with the Old Academy of Antiochus of Ascalon and Aristus, see Simon C. R. Swain, "Hellenic Culture and the Roman Heroes of Plutarch," *JHS* 110 (1990): 126–45, 134; and David Sedley, "The Ethics of Brutus and Cassius," *JRS* 87 (1997): 41–53; cf. Cicero, *Tusculan Disputations* 5.21; *Brutus* 120, 149 and 332; and *Letters to Atticus* 13.25.3, where Cicero says of Brutus that *est enim is quoque Antiochius*.

his notes on Brutus' philosophical education. As seen above, Plutarch derived from the Platonic tradition the idea that the apophthegms of the Spartans were the primary language of philosophy. Plutarch's reference to the apophthegmatic brevity of the Spartans in *Brutus* 2.5 reinforces the notion that Brutus was versed in philosophy. Brevity places Brutus both among resolute men of action, such as Lysander and Caesar, and also alongside the Spartans at the very origins of the philosophical tradition.

Since brevity is the language of sound reasoning, some pagan authors see the tendency to verbosity as a mark of moral decay. Talkative children, for example, were believed to grow up arrogant and self-indulgent.[77] In the spurious *De liberis educandis*, Pseudo-Plutarch warns parents and teachers of the risk of training young students to deliver public discourses pleasing to the crowds. The views of Pseudo-Plutarch probably reflect a suspicion of the educational value of public displays of eloquence similar to that observed in the Socratic tradition.[78] In *De liberis educandis* 6b–c, Pseudo-Plutarch says that young students who are encouraged to make a display of their eloquence become dissolute (ἄσωτοι) lovers of pleasures (φιλήδονοι) and tend to fall into verbosity (πολυλογία). In Pseudo-Plutarch, verbosity is seen as an inability to exercise self-control over words, which ultimately signals a deeper lack of stability on the moral level. Here πολυλογία becomes the initial station of a descent into debauchery. Plutarch expresses similar views in the treatise *De garrulitate*, which discusses idle talking (ἀδολεσχία). Plutarch presents talkativeness not only as an irritating habit, but as a veritable illness of the soul (νόσημα τῆς ψυχῆς, Plutarch, *De garrulitate* 502e.7). As in Pseudo-Plutarch's *De liberis educandis*, verbosity is described as a sign of moral failure, comparable to greed, love of fame, and φιληδονία (502e.8).[79] As William Beardslee has observed, "[t]o Plutarch ἀδολεσχία results from the separation of the λόγοι from the λόγος."[80] The cure (φάρμακον) for the illness, says Plutarch, is provided by

---

77  In *Cyropaedia* 1.4.3, Xenophon relates that at a young age Cyrus was very talkative (πολυλωγότερος). Xenophon, however, feels compelled to clarify that Cyrus' verbosity was not due to insolence but to youthfulness and eagerness to learn (τὸ φιλομαθὴς εἶναι) and that as an adult Cyrus learned to use very few words (λόγοις μανοτέροις ἐχρῆτο, ibid. 1.4.4).

78  On the role of rhetoric in Pseudo-Plutarch's *De liberis educandis*, see Martin W. Bloomer, *The School of Rome: Latin Studies and the Origins of Liberal Education* (Berkeley, CA: University of California Press, 2011) 53–7. Anastasios Maras, "The Issue of Rhetoric for Christian Apologists in the Second Century," *Aug* 50 (2010): 409–21, 417, draws attention to the moral reservations of *De liberis educandis* towards public displays of eloquence in the education of children.

79  In 504a9–b6, talkativeness is compared to drunkenness.

80  Beardslee, "De garrulitate," 267.

philosophy and consists in shifting the habit of the verbose from their excessive speaking to being able to listen to the word of reason (λόγος).[81] As in *De liberis educandis*, the discussion on talkativeness in Plutarch's *De garrulitate* is rooted in the traditional opposition between the brevity of sound philosophy and the verbosity of sophistry. As in *Lycurgus* 20.6, Plutarch is dependent here on *Protagoras* 343a–b, where Socrates presents ancient philosophical maxims such as "know thyself" as examples of old brachylogical wisdom:

> And among the men of old also sententious speakers (βραχυλόγοι) are admired, and upon the temple of the Pythian Apollo the Amphictyons inscribed, not the Iliad and the Odyssey or the paeans of Pindar, but "Know thy-self" and "Avoid extremes" and "Give a pledge and mischief is at hand," admiring, as they did, the compactness and simplicity of the expression which contains within a small compass a well-forged sentiment. And is not the god himself fond of conciseness (φιλοσύντομος) and brevity (βραχυλόγος) in his oracles, and is he not called Loxias because he avoids prolixity (ἀδολεσχίαν) rather than obscurity?[82]

In this passage, the discussion about verbosity as incompatible with philosophical utterances and the religious discourse about brevity converge. The same traits of brevity and rejection of verbosity that Plutarch, Diogenes Laertius, Porphyry, and Iamblichus ascribe to their ideal philosophers are applied directly to the deity. Because brevity is the language of wisdom and moral rectitude, even the god Apollo is concise (σύντομος), like Plotinus, and fond of brevity (βραχύλογος), like Pythagoras and the founders of the philosophical tradition.

## 4  Brevity and the Criticism of Verbosity in Philo and in Early Christianity

In spite of the examples of the use of verbose prayers and magic formulae in Graeco-Roman devotion mentioned in contemporary scholarship, the texts

---

81  See Plutarch, *De garrulitate* 502b. Beardslee ("De Garrulitate," 265) observes that "Plutarch's essay lifts the notion of ἀδολεσχία from the level of popular ethics to the level of serious philosophical ethics." On criticism of verbosity in Greek popular morality, see Kenneth J. Dover, *Popular Morality in the Time of Plato and Aristotle* (Indianapolis, IN: Hakett, 1994), 25–6; and Teresa Morgan, *Popular Morality in the Early Roman Empire* (Cambridge: Cambridge University Press, 2007), 48–9.

82  Plutarch, *De garrulitate* 511a.9–b.8, ET William C. Helmbold, ed., *Plutarch's Moralia* (15 vol.; LCL; Cambridge, MA: Harvard University Press, 1908–1969), 6:445–7.

considered so far confirm Hans Dieter Betz's observation that "babblers have also been criticized... by other 'pagans'."[83] As shown above, the criticism of religious verbosity in Greek and Roman literature derives from traditions that identify talkativeness as a philosophical and moral problem. Jewish and early Christian authors from the Graeco-Roman world display a similar tendency to favour brevity over verbosity. In *De sacrificiis Abelis et Caini*, Philo of Alexandria compiles a long list of moral vices incurred by a person devoted to living like a lover of pleasure (φιλήδονος). Among other vices and misbehaviours, observes Philo, a person given to pleasure will also speak in an inopportune (ἀκαιρολόγος) and verbose (μακρήγορος) way and be a talkative babbler (ἀδολέσχης).[84] The connection seen by Philo between verbosity and the lack of self-restraint typical of a debased moral life reproduces the same notions expounded in Pseudo-Plutarch's *De liberis educandis* in relation to the rhetorical education of children. Philo shares the view of Graeco-Roman popular morality that verbosity may result in intemperance and hedonism. Just as his pagan counterparts, Philo employs brevity as evidence of a philosophical disposition and sound reasoning.

As with Plutarch's account of Brutus' style (mentioned above), Philo also turns to brevity in order to defend the philosophical and literary reputation of texts that do not make a display of eloquence. In Philo, this excellence of brevity possesses a profound apologetic character and is central in his defence of the philosophical and literary authority of Jewish scripture. In *On Creation*, for example, Philo tries to demonstrate that Moses refers to the Platonic notion of ideas in his narrative of creation. Commenting on the creation of plants and herbs, Philo argues that, with the biblical remark that God made "the grass of the field before they sprang up,"[85] Moses meant to allude to the incorporeal and intelligible ideas (τὰς ἀσωμάτους καὶ νοητὰς ἰδέας) of Platonic philosophy.[86] As expected, the biblical text is not explicit about it, but Philo thinks that the Platonic meaning of Genesis is indisputable. Moses' silence on the matter, explains Philo, is the result of a stylistic choice: "For although he [Moses] went through everything as a whole and not in detail, being concerned like no one else about brevity (βραχυλογίας), even so the few things he says are examples of the nature of the whole" (*On creation* 130.3–5). The reference to brevity allows Philo to corroborate what would otherwise be a rather implausible interpretation of scripture. It is because of Moses' concern for brevity that scripture

---

83   Betz, *Sermon*, 367.
84   Philo, *De sacrificiis Abelis et Caini* 32. On Philo's criticism of verbose speakers, see also Philo, *Quod deterius potiori insidiari soleat* 130.
85   πάντα χόρτον ἀγροῦ πρὸ τοῦ ἀνατεῖλαι (Genesis 2:5 LXX); cf. *On creation* 129.
86   Ibid.

is not more explicit. The mention of brevity not only conveniently explains Moses' silence on the Platonic ideas, but also serves the purpose of conferring a philosophical and literary respectability to Moses and to Jewish scripture. As with Brutus' letters in Plutarch, by stating that Moses was "concerned like no one else about brevity" (φροντίζων εἰ καί τις ἄλλος βραχυλογίας), Philo depicts Moses not only as a sound thinker but as one of the brachylogical philosophers of old.

As brevity adds intellectual sophistication to Jewish scripture, Philo is also zealous in shielding biblical repetitions from any allegation of verbosity. In *De congressu eruditionis quaerendae gratia* 71–3, Philo presents an elaborated allegorical reading of Abraham's union with Sarah's maidservant Hagar (Genesis 16:1–4). Philo observes that Genesis unnecessarily repeats many times the information that Sarah was "Abraham's wife" (Genesis 11:29, 31; 12:17; 16:1, 3). Philo claims, however, that the reiteration of the concept in Genesis 16:3 is intentional. Interpreting Sarah as wisdom and Hagar as the ἐγκύκλιος παιδεία ('general education'), Philo argues that what appears to be an unnecessary repetition reminds those who embrace culture as their mistress to remain loyal to wisdom, their lawful wife. What would otherwise be stylistically inelegant is presented as an intentional effort to convey a deeper meaning: "Now it is worth considering carefully why in this place Moses again calls Sarah the wife of Abraham, when he has already stated the fact several times (πολλάκις); for Moses did not practise the worst form of prolixity (μακρολογίας τὸ φαυλότατον εἶδος), namely tautology (ταυτολογίαν)."[87] Moses' repetitions here serve a crucial purpose for Philo's allegorical exegesis of the text. The repetitions in the biblical narrative, however, could suggest that Moses had an inclination towards verbosity. By suggesting that the redundant remark that Sarah was Abraham's wife in Genesis 16:3 hides a deeper meaning, Philo casts off the suspicion that Moses may have embraced the inferior and morally questionable forms of μακρολογία. Philo's explanation is made more crucial here by the fact that repetition (ταυτολογία) was considered a particularly severe kind of verbose discourse. In *De garrulitate*, Plutarch says that verbose people wear out the ears of their listeners with their repetitions, like those who keep smudging and erasing a palimpsest.[88] According to Origen, ταυτολογία was a sufficient reason for dismissing the work of one's opponents and disengaging with their writing. In

---

87  Philo, *De congressu eruditionis quaerendae gratia* 73, ET Francis H. Colson and George H. Whitaker, ed., *Philo in Ten Volumes (and Two Supplementary Volumes)* (12 vol.; LCL; London: Heinemann, 1929–1943), 4:495.

88  οἱ δ'ἀποκναίουσι δήπου τὰ ὦτα ταῖς ταυτολογίαις ὥσπερ παλίψηστα διαμολύνοντες, Plutarch, *De garrulitate* 504d.

*Against Celsus*, Origen refuses to address the numerous ταυτολογίας found in Celsus' *True Discourse* lest he may produce a similar unfortunate sequence of repetitions.[89] Thus Philo's reassuring statement that Moses was not inclined to practise ταυτολογία authenticates the good reputation and argumentative quality of his writings.

Philo's depiction of Moses was profoundly influenced by the philosophical tradition of brevity as the language of philosophy and sound reasoning, as already attested in the Platonic criticism of rhetoric.[90] The Socratic argument about the merits of brachylogical dialectic over macrology, as attested in the *Protagoras*, seems to have equally influenced some Christian authors' positions on verbosity. The second-century CE *Sentences of Sextus* are a Christian gnomology that largely drew upon the same philosophical sources used by the compilers of a Pythagorean collection of maxims known as the *Sentences of Clitarchus* and of the *Pythagorean Sentences* mentioned above.[91] In a number of instances, Sextus combines and harmonises Greek γνῶμαι from the Pythagorean tradition with sayings of the New Testament and Jewish wisdom literature, creating a seamless collection of Christianised Hellenistic aphorisms and Hellenised biblical sayings.[92] In *Sentences of Sextus* 155–7, the Christian Sextus seems to merge the philosophical traditions of his source material about brachylogy and macrology with biblical traditions on verbosity: "Excessive speech (πολυλογία) does not escape sin. Wisdom accompanies brevity of speech (βραχυλογία). Prolonged speech (μακρολογία) is a sign of ignorance (ἀμαθίας)."[93] The last two sentences of this text belonged to Sextus' Pythagorean gnomic source, as they also figure unchanged and in the same order in Clitarchus' collection.[94] Sextus' source material here is very close to

---

89   διὸ οὐκ ἀναγκαῖον ἐπαναλαμβάνειν τὰ εἰρημένα, ἵνα μὴ πρὸς τὰς ταυτολογίας Κέλσου καὶ ἡμεῖς ταυτολογῶμεν, Origen, *Against Celsus* 2.32.

90   On Plato and rhetoric, see Laurent Pernot, *Rhetoric in Antiquity* (Washington, DC: Catholic University of America Press, 2005), 45–52.

91   On the shared traditions and the complex relationship between the sources of the *Sentences of Sextus*, the *Pythagorean Sentences*, the *Sentences of Clitarchus*, and Porphyry's letter *To Marcella*, see Chadwick, *Sextus*, 138–62; and also Walter T. Wilson, *The Sentences of Sextus* (Wisdom Literature from the Ancient World 1; Atlanta, GA: Society of Biblical Literature, 2012), 11–29.

92   On the hellenisation of biblical sources in the *Sentences of Sextus*, see Gerhard Delling, "Zur Hellenisierung des Christentums in den 'Sprüchen des Sextus'," in *Studien zum Neuen Testament und zur Patristik. Erich Klostermann zum 90. Geburtstag dargebracht* (ed. Kommission für spätantike Religionsgeschichte; TU 77; Berlin: Akademie-Verlag, 1961), 208–41.

93   *Sentences of Sextus* 155–7, ET Wilson, *Sextus*, 177.

94   Cf. *Sentences of Clitarchus* 31–2.

the content of *Pythagorean Sentences* 10 and 15–16 mentioned above, where brevity is associated with knowledge of God and long discourses with ignorance. *Sentences of Sextus* 430 (ἄνθρωπον θεοῦ γνῶσις βραχύλογον ποιεῖ) shows that Sextus was probably familiar with the tradition of *Pythagorean Sentences* 10.[95]

The same tradition also may have influenced Philo, who in *Quis rerum divinarum heres sit* 10 states that "ignorance is a very impudent and loquacious thing (θρασύτατον γὰρ καὶ λαλίστατον ἀμαθία)." The first sentence of Sextus' text, however, is a slightly modified version of Proverbs 10:19 LXX, which, as mentioned above, describes πολυλογία as an occasion for sin. Strictly speaking, the Greek words μακρολογία and πολυλογία do not express the same concept. The fact that in the second century CE Ammonius feels compelled to explain their difference in his *On the Difference of Similar Expressions*, however, suggests that in later times the two expressions could have been erroneously considered interchangeable.[96] In the understanding of the Christian compiler of the *Sentences of Sextus*, philosophical traditions about macrology and biblical traditions about verbosity converge in one notion of verbosity as the result of both ignorance and sin. The Socratic exposure of the shortcomings of rhetoric and sophistic eloquence, together with the Pythagorean tradition about brevity as the appointed language of worship, join the biblical tradition in a wide-ranging rejection of verbosity in Christian circles.

Further evidence from early Christian literature seems to link criticism of verbosity in Christian circles with the promotion of brevity as a cure for sophistic eloquence, understood as a descent into ignorance and self-indulgence. The contrast between the brevity of the ideal wise person and the verbosity of the sophists, for example, has influenced Justin's portrayal of Jesus in his *First Apology*:

> Lest we should seem to deceive (σοφίζεσθαι), we consider it right, before embarking on our promised demonstration, to cite a few of the precepts given by Christ Himself. It is for you then, as powerful rulers, to find out whether we have been taught and do teach these things truly. Short

---

95  See also πολλοὺς λόγους περὶ θεοῦ ἀπειρία ποιεῖ, *Sentences of Sextus* 341.

96  Ammonius, *On the Differences of Similar Expressions* 307, explains that μακρολόγος is someone who speaks at length on a few arguments (περὶ ὀλίγων), while the πολύλογος uses many words and touches on many different issues (περὶ πολλῶν). Ammonius, like Sextus, is believed to have lived in Egypt, probably in Alexandria. On the connection between Sextus and Egypt, see Roelof van den Broek, "Juden und Christen in Alexandrien im 2. und 3. Jahrhundert," in *Studies in Gnosticism and Alexandrian Christianity* (ed. Roelof van den Broek; Nag Hammadi and Manichean Studies 39; Leiden: Brill, 1996), 181–96, 185.

(βραχεῖς) and concise (σύντομοι) utterances come from Him, for He was no sophist (οὐ γὰρ σοφιστὴς ὑπῆρχεν), but His word was the power of God.[97]

As Judith Perkins has observed, Christian apologists often tended to contrast "Christian linguistic and rhetorical simplicity with sophistic practices."[98] In Justin's *First Apology*, the demonstration that Christ was not a sophist draws heavily on arguments used in philosophical biographies to portray thinkers such as Pythagoras, Apollonius, or Plotinus as the ideal sage. Justin also restates that Jesus taught using βραχέα λόγια in *Dialogue with Trypho* 18.1.[99] The evidence of Jesus' brevity works against the allegation that Jesus may have been a sophist or a charlatan.[100] As seen in *Protagoras* 343a, Plato had indicated in ῥήματα βραχέα the very origin of Greek philosophy, a view later adopted and developed by Plutarch. Justin then credits Jesus with the same fondness for short (βραχύς) and concise (σύντομος) discourses that Porphyry ascribes to Plotinus in *Life of Plotinus* 14 and Plutarch assigns to Apollo himself in *De garrulitate* 511b.

The connection between early Christian rejection of verbosity and philosophical criticism of sophistic rhetoric was not limited to the portrayal of Jesus as a brachylogical sage. Verbosity features, for example, in early Christian debates about Christian ministry. If Graeco-Roman moralists consider verbosity as a typical trait of charlatans and sophists, the early Christian tradition applies the same notion to its internal struggle for criteria that would allow Christians to discern between true and false prophets (ψευδοπροφῆται):[101]

---

97  Justin, *First Apology* 14.4–5, ET Leslie W. Barnard, ed., *St. Justin Martyr: The First and Second Apologies* (ACW 56; New York: Paulist, 1997), 32.

98  Judith Perkins, "Jesus Was No Sophist: Education in Christian Fiction," in *The Ancient Novel and Early Christian and Jewish Narrative: Fictional Intersections* (ed. Marília P. Futre Pinheiro, Judith Perkins, and Richard Pervo; Ancient Narrative Supplementum 16; Groningen: Barkhuis and Groningen University Library, 2012), 109–31, 114.

99  Graham N. Stanton, *Jesus and Gospel* (Cambridge: Cambridge University Press, 2004), 95–6, sees in the mention of Jesus' brevity in *Dialogue with Trypho* 18.1 an attempt to impress Trypho and a public accustomed to sophistic eloquence.

100 On the polemical allegation that Jesus was a sophist, see for example Lucian, *The Death of Peregrinus* 13, where Christians are said to worship an impaled, or crucified, sophist (τὸν δὲ ἀνεσκολοπισμένον ἐκεῖνον σοφιστὴν αὐτὸν προσκυνῶσιν). On Lucian's "crucified sophist," see Robert E. van Voorst, *Jesus Outside the New Testament: An Introduction to the Ancient Evidence* (Grand Rapids, MI: Eerdmans, 2000), 58–63.

101 The identification of false prophets is already debated in the New Testament; see for example Matthew 7:15 and 24:11, 24; Acts 13:6; 2 Peter 2:1; 1 John 4:1; and Revelation 16:13 and 19:20.

"Listen, now," he said, "concerning the earthly spirit that is empty and powerless, and also foolish. First, the person who appears to have this spirit exalts himself and wishes to be given pride of place; and he is immediately impetuous, shameless, and garrulous (πολύλαλος), and he indulges himself with many luxuries and with many other deceptions. Moreover, he receives wages for his prophecy—without them, he does not prophesy."[102]

*Didache* 11.4–12 identifies in greed, hypocrisy, and opportunistic behaviour the typical mannerisms of false prophets. The Shepherd of Hermas also lists verbosity as a characteristic attribute of false prophecy, alongside deceptive behaviour and a fondness for luxury and money.[103] There are significant analogies between early Christian discussions about talkativeness and false prophecy and the description of verbosity as a distinctive trait of those who prefer φιληδονία to virtue. Early Christian writers and Graeco-Roman moralists agree in considering talkativeness not just as a problem of style or speech, but as a moral issue. As mentioned above, in the Pythagorean tradition and in the Shepherd of Hermas the moral problem also assumes a religious significance. With their brevity, the pious Pythagoreans of the *Pythagorean Sentences* as well as the true prophets of the Shepherd of Hermas express the ritual and spiritual soundness of their piety. As Ambrose notes when commenting on Proverbs 10:19, brevity becomes a sign of spiritual health so that "the one who is sparing with words is rich in spirit (*parcus in verbis, dives in spiritu*)" (*Enarrationes in Psalmos* 36.28).[104]

Early interpretations of Matthew 6:7–8 have been equally influenced by philosophical discussions about verbosity and brevity in the Graeco-Roman world. Contrary to some modern commentators, early Christian interpreters have read the verb βατταλογέω as a reference to wordiness and idle talking rather than to the utterance of inarticulate sounds. The babbling of the Gentiles of Matthew 6:7 is thus understood as a remark on the content – that is, the things one prays for – and form – above all, length – of prayer. In the Latin-speaking church, the Vulgate treats both the verb βατταλογέω and the clause ἐν τῇ πολυλογίᾳ αὐτῶν as references to lengthy prayers, translating the former

---

102  Shepherd of Hermas, *Mandate* 11.11–12, ET Bart D. Ehrman, ed., *The Apostolic Fathers* (2 vol.; LCL; Cambridge, Mass.: Harvard University Press, 2003), 2:289.

103  See Shepherd of Hermas, *Mandate* 11.1–2,4,7. On false prophets and verbosity in the Shepherd of Hermas, see Jannes Reiling, *Hermas and Christian Prophecy: A Study of the Eleventh Mandate* (NovTSup 37; Leiden: Brill, 1973), 51.

104  In the same text, Ambrose observes *loquacitas innocentiae virtutisque naufragium*.

as *multum loqui* and the latter as *in multiloquio suo*.[105] In Syriac, the Peshitta focuses instead on content, rendering βατταλογέω with the root *pqq*, 'to talk nonsense' or 'to utter idle words'.[106]

The early Christian reception of Matthew 6:7 reflects the same traditions of the early translations. Basil of Caesarea reads βατταλογέω as a reference to the content of the supplications. The babblers, explains Basil, are those who pray for things which are transient (φθαρτά) and not worthy of the Lord (ἀνάξια τοῦ Κυρίου) (*Regulae morales* 56.2 [PG 31:785]). Similarly, the exegetical tradition of the *Catena in Matthaeum* interprets Matthew 6:7 as a prohibition against 'talking nonsense' or 'foolery' (φλυαρία) and praying for power, glory, luxuries, or prevailing against one's enemies.[107] The *Pseudo-Clementines* invite Christians not to pray using verbose compositions (μὴ ἐκ συνθέσεως πολλῶν λόγων, *Epistulae de virginitate* 1.12.2), and they call the prayers of those who make a display of eloquence φλυαρίας ('fooleries') and βαττολογίας ('babbles', 1.12.3). Commenting on the Matthean βατταλογέω, John Chrysostom emphasised the importance of avoiding lengthy prayers, suggesting that Jesus intended the Lord's Prayer to set a measure (μέτρον) for the prayers of the disciples.[108] As seen above, the same need for sacrifices and prayers not to exceed the right measure (τὸ μέτριον) is a core aspect of Apollonius' philosophical devotion

---

105 Byzantine lexicographers have considered βαττολογία and πολυλογία as synonyms; see for example the ninth-century *Etymologicum genuinum* β.68. The compiler of the *Etymologicum* derives βαττολογία from a Βάτος, perhaps the same Battos of Herodotus, *Historiae* 4.155, who is not described as a stutterer, but as the author of long and repetitive (ταυτολογίαν) lines; cf. *Suda* β.183

106 In *Lexicon* β.340, the fifth-century Alexandrian lexicographer Hesychius explains βαττολογία as ἀργολογία ('empty talk') and ἀκαιρολογία ('untimely talk'). Concerning ἀκαιρολογία, see also Philo, *The Sacrifices of Abel and Cain* 32, mentioned above.

107 See *Catena in Matthaeum* (*catena integra e cod. Paris. Coislin. gr. 23*) at p. 44 of John A. Cramer, ed., *Catenae in evangelia S. Matthaei et S. Marci* (vol. 1 of *Catenae Graecorum patrum in Novum Testamentum*; ed. John A. Cramer; Oxford: Oxford University Press, 1844), where the comment to Matthew 6:7 reads: τί δέ ἐστιν, ὅπερ εἶπε, "μὴ βαττολογήσητε"; βαττολογίαν ἐνταῦθα τὴν φλυαρίαν λέγει οἷον ὅτ' ἂν τὰ μὴ προσήκοντα αἰτῶμεν παρὰ Θεοῦ, δυναστείας καὶ δόξας, καὶ πλοῦτον, καὶ τρυφὰς, καὶ τὸ ἐχθρῶν περιγενέσθαι. In the sixth century, John Climacus describes someone who babbles (βαττολογεῖ) as a person who talks in vain (εἰς μάτην φιλολογεῖ); see *Scala paradisi* 25 (PG 88:988).

108 εἰπὼν γὰρ τοῖς μαθηταῖς, μὴ κατὰ τοὺς ἐθνικοὺς εὔχεσθαι, καὶ μὴ βαττολογεῖν, καὶ μέτρον ἡμᾶς εὐχῆς ἐδίδαξε, John Chrysostom, *De Anna* 2.2. On John Chrysostom's warning against lengthy prayers, see also Cyrille Crépey, "La prière chrétienne selon Origène, Grégoire de Nysse et Jean Chrysostome," in *La rhétorique de la prière dans l'Antiquité grecque* (ed. Johann Goeken; Recherches sur les rhétoriques religieuses 11; Turnhout: Brepols 2010), 155–74, esp. 165.

in Philostratus' *Life of Apollonius* 1.11. The early Christian interpretation of Matthew 6:7–8 envisages a reflection on the nature and length of one's petitions in the same way as the pagan sages are advised to do in Seneca's *Moral Epistles* and in Xenophon's *Memorabilia*, as mentioned above.

Some early Christian texts seem to extend the condemnation of verbosity in Matthew 6:7–8 beyond the context of cult and prayer to a general warning against any display of eloquence. In another text from the *Pseudo-Clementines*, for example, βαττολογίαι ('babbles'), πολυλογίαι ('verbose discourses'), and πλοκολογίαι ('deceitful discourses') are included in a long list of moral evils alongside the "works of the flesh" of Galatians 5:19–21 and without any reference to prayer (*Epistulae de virginitate* 1.8.2–3). Origen's *De oratione* also depicts verbosity as an expression of moral depravity and the result of poor reasoning. Like Basil and *Catena in Matthaeum*, Origen interprets Matthew's warning against the stammering of the Gentiles as a prohibition against praying for bodily and exterior things rather than for what is heavenly and honourable.[109] While the Matthean Gentiles stammer (βατταλογέω), says Origen, the faithful should aim at "speaking the things of God" (θεολογέω).[110]

In *De oratione* 21.2, however, Origen engages in a philosophical argument that recalls Plutarch's contrast between the many words of the ἀδολέσχης and the λόγος of philosophy in *De garrulitate*. Starting from a widespread philosophical convention – that is, the notion that the unity of the one is preferable to the plurality of the many –, Origen explains that, in the material world, all things of inferior rank are fragmented and divisible and of lesser rank when compared to the things that are one.[111] God's goodness, truth, righteousness, and wisdom, however, are one, explains Origen, while shameful acts, falsehoods, deceptions, and the ephemeral wisdom of this world (cf. 1 Corinthians 2:6) are many.[112] As God's λόγος is also one, continues Origen, the use of many words is inherently inadequate to express the one truth of God, hence the warning against verbosity in Matthew 6:7. Verbosity is then invariably seen

---

109   Origen, *De oratione* 21.1.8–11, observes: βαττολογοῦσι γὰρ κατὰ τὴν λέξιν τοῦ εὐαγγελίου μόνοι "οἱ ἐθνικοί", οὐδὲ φαντασίαν μεγάλων ἔχοντες ἢ ἐπουρανίων αἰτημάτων, πᾶσαν εὐχὴν <περὶ> τῶν σωματικῶν καὶ τῶν ἐκτὸς ἀναπέμποντες. On Origen's instruction to pray only for great and heavenly things in the *De oratione*, see Wilhelm Gessel, *Die Theologie des Gebetes nach "De Oratione" von Origenes* (München: Schöningh, 1975), esp. 172–78.

110   See *De oratione* 21.1.1–2.

111   On the Platonic development of the problem of parts and wholes, see Verity Harte, "Plato's Problem of Composition," in *Proceedings of the Boston Area Colloquium in Ancient Philosophy* (ed. John J. Cleary and Gary M. Gurtler; vol. 17; Leiden: Brill, 2002), 1–17.

112   On the Middle and Neo-Platonic character of Origen's argument, see Gessel, *Theologie des Gebetes*, 144.

as an indication of the speaker's failure to perceive the truth of Christ, the one Word of the Christian God.[113] In support of his argument, Origen quotes Proverbs 10:19 LXX, which, as seen above, explicitly links πολυλογία to sin.[114] Referring to Proverbs 10:19 LXX in his *Commentary on the Gospel of John*, Origen speculates whether Solomon, who composed thousands of proverbs and songs,[115] or Paul, who authored long letters, are not liable to sin because of their πολυλογία. Origen's answer to the problem opposes words and Word in a way different than but nonetheless reminiscent of Plutarch's discussion. As scripture talks about the one Word of God who was from the beginning, says Origen, scripture cannot be considered verbose as it testifies to that one Word.[116]

In Origen's understanding of Matthew 6:7–8, verbosity and the conceptual failure to grasp God's reality are two aspects of the same problem, in the same way as talkativeness is seen to be ignorance of god in the Pythagorean traditions mentioned above. According to Origen "the man who talks much speaks vain things, and the man who speaks vain things is one who talks too much (ὁ πολυλογῶν βαττολογεῖν, καὶ ὁ βαττολογῶν πολυλογεῖν)."[117] As in the philosophical traditions considered above, the reference to the stammering and verbosity of the Gentiles in Matthew is thus reinterpreted as a broader criticism of verbosity as a sign of the fallacious reasoning and moral inadequacy of the speaker.

## 5   Conclusion

According to Ulrich Luz, the early Christian interpretation that saw Jesus' caveat against the babbling Gentiles in Matthew 6:7–8 as a reflection on the

---

113   On prayer as expression of a correct notion of God in Origen's *De oratione*, see for example Lorenzo Perrone, "Il discorso protrettico di Origene sulla preghiera. Introduzione al Περὶ Εὐχῆς," in *Il dono e la sua ombra: ricerche sul Περὶ Εὐχῆς di Origene. Atti del I Convegno del Gruppo Italiano di Ricerca su 'Origene e la Tradizione Alessandrina'* (ed. Francesca Cocchini; Studia Ephemeridis Augustinianum 57; Rome: Institutum Patristicum Augustinianum, 1997), 7–32, esp. 9 n. 6.

114   See Origen, *De oratione* 21.2.9–11: διὰ τοῦτο οὐδεὶς ἐκφεύξεται "ἁμαρτίαν" "ἐκ πολυλογίας", καὶ οὐδεὶς δοκῶν "ἐκ πολυλογίας" εἰσακουσθήσεσθαι εἰσακούεσθαι δύναται.

115   Cf. 1 Kings 5:12.

116   ὁ πᾶς δὴ τοῦ θεοῦ λόγος ὁ ἐν ἀρχῇ πρὸς τὸν θεὸν οὐ πολυλογία ἐστίν· οὐ γὰρ λόγοι· λόγος γὰρ εἷς, Origen, *Commentary on the Gospel of John* 5.4.

117   Origen, *De oratione* 21.2.1–2, ET Eric George Jay, ed., *Origen's Treatise on Prayer: Translation and Notes with an Account of the Practice and Doctrine of Prayer from New Testament Times to Origen* (London: SPCK, 1954), 143.

form and content of prayer and a rejection of idle talking has obscured rather than improved the comprehension of the text. If Matthew 6:7 had simply intended to criticise verbosity, says Luz, "it would agree with many a Jewish and also many a Hellenistic statement. But it means more," namely, a theological refutation of prayers "as a means to win God's hearing."[118] Luz sees the novelty and originality of Matthew's discourse on prayer in Jesus' confident reassurance that God's caring love is bestowed on the petitioners even before they utter their prayers. Hence prayers do not need to be long. Luz is unquestionably right in identifying the theological core of the Matthean instruction.

Modern commentators have often tried to separate a conventional Graeco-Roman criticism of verbosity in Matthew 6:7–8 from its theological vision. The evidence from the Graeco-Roman traditions considered above, however, has shown a strict correlation between philosophical piety in Socratic and, above all, Pythagorean traditions on avoiding lengthy prayers and a confident reliance on the gods' ability of granting what is good to the petitioner.[119] These traditions have also shown how a philosophical reinterpretation of prayer and other cultic practices can be used for the criticism of a popular understanding of the Homeric religion, which suggested that the gods could be manipulated through acts of devotion. As in Matthew 6:7–8, the tradition of the *Pythagorean Sentences* and Philostratus' description of Apollonius' piety insist that sage worshippers who are familiar with the deity are βραχυλόγοι, while talkative petitioners are ignorant of the divine nature. From the evidence considered above, I have shown that traditions on brevity as the most suitable language for religious knowledge are rooted in ancient discussions about brevity as the archetypal language of philosophy and sound reasoning and verbosity as a display of eloquence that characterises sophistry and intellectual deceit. Greek biographers have developed this notion in their insistence that brevity and pithy wisdom are a characteristic trait of the ideal philosophical sage and of discerning political leaders. Philo and a number of early Christian documents have adopted the same view, using brevity as a way of advocating the philosophical reputation of Moses and Jesus respectively. Christian sources, in particular, single out verbosity as the language of false prophets and sinners in the same way as talkativeness is seen as a philosophical and moral problem in Plutarch's *De garrulitate* and in Pseudo-Plutarch's *De liberis educandis*.

---

118   See Luz, *Matthew*, 365.
119   Luz, ibid., n. 12, acknowledges the similarities between Matthew 6:7–8 and Socrates' prayer for τὰ ἀγαθά in Xenophon's *Memorabilia* 1.3.2, but does not develop a comparison between the two texts.

It is probably not possible to argue that Matthew 6:7–8 shows any direct knowledge of these philosophical traditions. Separating criticism of verbosity from the theological purpose of the text, however, does not allow for appreciation of the extent to which Matthew's discourse on prayer is deeply embedded in the philosophical piety of the Graeco-Roman tradition.[120] Matthew's discourse on prayer agrees in many respects with popular depictions of the piety of sages and philosophers. In denouncing long petitions as a failure to understand the nature of God's relationship with the worshipper and as manipulating God with acts of devotion, Matthew portrays Jesus as a model pious sage, not dissimilar to the example set by philosophers such as Socrates, Pythagoras, and Apollonius.[121]

---

120   Betz (*Sermon*, 363) sees in Matthew "an appropriation of the Hellenistic-Jewish critique of religion, which in turn has amalgamated ideas from Greek philosophy."

121   For a recent suggestion that Matthew's Sermon on the Mount intended to depict Jesus as a philosophical, Stoic sage, see Stanley K. Stowers, "Jesus the Teacher and Stoic Ethics in the Gospel of Matthew," in *Stoicism in Early Christianity* (ed. Tuomas Rasimus, Troels Engberg-Pedersen, and Ismo Dunderberg; Grand Rapids, MI: Baker Academic, 2010), 59–76.

# PART 4

*Reconsidering Early Pagan-Christian Relations*

∴

# Christians According to Second-Century Philosophers

*Simon Gathercole*

Who are the true philosophers? Who are the *atheoi*, the atheists? Who are guilty of *superstitio*, or its near if not exact equivalent, *deisidaimonia*? Who are guided by the true *logos*? These are some of the questions that define the interactions between Christians and pagans in antiquity. This paper jumps into the second century, *in medias res*, into a debate that had already started in the first century – as for example in Acts 17, where Luke's Paul is accused of introducing new gods and accuses the Athenians in turn of being δεισιδαιμονεστέρους.[1]

My aim here is to explore just one inning in the ongoing series of these interactions, namely the second-century verdicts from pagan philosophers upon Christians. There is a certain artificiality in this timeframe, of course, but I hope it emerges that there is some coherence to what are among the first extant pagan literary responses to Christianity. My criterion for who counts as a philosopher is also a rather pragmatic one: one might more or less say that the figures included here could reasonably find themselves read at Cambridge's Thursday evening Ancient Philosophy Seminar. There is one group, however, who are added to the category, for reasons that will be made clear. The literature on this subject is vast, but there have been surprisingly few attempts to focus specifically on philosophers and to provide a reasonably comprehensive conspectus of these figures.[2]

---

1  Acts 17:18 and 22. Cf. Colossians 2:8: Βλέπετε μή τις ὑμᾶς ἔσται ὁ συλαγωγῶν διὰ τῆς φιλοσοφίας καὶ κενῆς ἀπάτης κατὰ τὴν παράδοσιν τῶν ἀνθρώπων, κατὰ τὰ στοιχεῖα τοῦ κόσμου καὶ οὐ κατὰ Χριστόν.

2  For example, there are some broad surveys that take in all the pagan evidence from the period, such as P. de Labriolle, *La réaction païenne: Étude sur la polémique antichrétienne du Ier au VIe siècle* (Paris: L'Artisan du livre, 1942), esp. 19–169; and S. Benko, "Pagan Criticism of Christianity during the first Two Centuries A.D.," *ANRW* II 23 no. 2 (1980): 1054–1118; on the other hand, some, such as R.L. Wilken, *Christians as the Romans Saw Them* (New Haven: Yale University Press, 2003), focus on particular philosophers, in Wilken's case, on Galen and Celsus.

## 1 Epictetus[3]

Epictetus' evidence comes to us, closely transcribed by Arrian, from Nicopolis in around the year 108 CE, as Millar's clever detective work makes clear.[4] He therefore marks something of a false start in this story of second-century philosophers because he precedes most of the others discussed here by a good half-century.

In *Discourses* 4.7, "On Freedom from Fear," Epictetus begins as follows: When one comes into the presence of a tyrant, what is it that instills fear? Is it the guards with their weapons? No, a small child coming into the presence of the tyrant would not be afraid, because the child does not feel the presence of the guards (4.7.2). Nor would fear be felt by someone coming towards the tyrant with the express purpose of being killed (4.7.3). A person, then, whose goal is neither particularly to prolong their life nor to die should not be afraid either (4.7.4). Again, one should reckon material possessions – and children and wife – as nothing; one has nothing to fear from losing them (4.7.5). Let goods and kindred go, this mortal life also. They are mere counters with which one plays the game, not the game itself. This is entirely consistent with one of the main thrusts of Epictetus' philosophy – namely, that that which is not in our power (what is 'aprohairetic') does not belong to us.

He then asks the question:

> If someone can then be so disposed towards these things by madness, or by habit like the Galileans, then cannot someone learn by reason and proof that God has made all things in the world as well as the world itself, whole and unhindered and self-determining, and at the same time with its parts arranged for the needs of the whole?

> Εἶτα ὑπὸ μανίας μὲν δύναταί τις οὕτως διατεθῆναι πρὸς ταῦτα καὶ ὑπὸ ἔθους οἱ Γαλιλαῖοι· ὑπὸ λόγου δὲ καὶ ἀποδείξεως οὐδεὶς δύναται μαθεῖν, ὅτι ὁ θεὸς πάντα πεποίηκεν τὰ ἐν τῷ κόσμῳ καὶ αὐτὸν τὸν κόσμον ὅλον μὲν ἀκώλυτον καὶ αὐτοτελῆ, τὰ ἐν μέρει δ' αὐτοῦ πρὸς χρείαν τῶν ὅλων; (*Discourses* 4.7.6)

Leaving aside Epictetus' main point here, we can consider his passing remark about the Galileans. First, there cannot be much doubt that the reference is

---

3 See Labriolle, *La réaction païenne*, 45–50.
4 Millar adduces the evidence for transcription both from Arrian's claim and from the contrast in style between the *koine* of the *Discourses* and the Attic of his other compositions; see F. Millar, "Epictetus and the Imperial Court," *JRS* 55 (1965): 141–48, 142. Cf. P.A. Brunt, *Studies in Stoicism* (Oxford: Oxford University Press, 2013), 332: 'perhaps verbatim'.

to Christians. There is a scholion to this effect,[5] and it is difficult to imagine a better alternative explanation.[6] One might wonder, however, why the Christians are called Galileans, given that his contemporaries, Pliny, Tacitus, and Suetonius, call them Christians (though this latter title was not necessarily widespread either).[7]

Epictetus here again contrasts with Tacitus, who writes of the pestilence of Christianity having begun not in Galilee but in Judaea. No other second-century pagan author mentions Galilee or Galileans in connection with Christianity (not even Celsus in his large tome), though Galilee is referred to by Porphyry and extensively by Julian.[8] It is likely that Julian used the label "Galilaeans" to emphasise the obscure origins and parochial nature of Christianity.[9] Alternatively, if R.L. Wilken (as well as Beard, North, and Price) is correct that accusations of *superstitio* in Suetonius, Tacitus, and Pliny allude to the foreignness of Christianity,[10] then Epictetus might be closer to these writers in

---

5  W.A. Oldfather, *Epictetus: The Discourses* (LCL; Cambridge/London: Harvard/Heinemann, 1966–1967), 1:xxvi n. 2, and 2:362 n. 1.

6  See most recently, C. Gill and R. Hard, *Epictetus: Discourses, Fragments, Handbook* (Oxford: Oxford University Press, 2014), 341. N. Huttunen, "Stoic Law in Paul?" in *Stoicism in Early Christianity* (ed. T. Rasimus, T. Engberg-Pedersen, and I. Dunderberg; Peabody, MA: Hendrickson, 2010), 39–58, 41 n. 9, raises the question, but merely hypothetically; in his *Paul and Epictetus on Law* (LNTS; London: Bloomsbury/ T&T Clark, 2009), he maintains the Christian interpretation, in one place (87 n. 40), against Hengel's argument that the Galileans are Zealots. On this, see M. Hengel, *The Zealots: Investigations into the Jewish Freedom Movement in the Period from Herod I until 70 A.D.* (Edinburgh: T&T Clark, 1989), 58–59: Hengel's arguments against the interpretation 'Christians', however, do not lead him to assert confidently the Zealot meaning.

7  Some have thought that the Galileans mentioned by Simon bar Kochba (BK 1 Martone; Mur. 43) are Christians, but this view has not been widely received. See C. Martone, *Lettere di Bar Kokhba* (Brescia: Paideia, 2012), 43; and H. Eshel, "The Bar Kochba Revolt, 132–135," in *The Cambridge History of Judaism. Volume 4: The Late Roman-Rabbinic Period* (ed. W.D. Davies, L. Finkelstein, and S. Katz; Cambridge: Cambridge University Press, 2006), 105–27, 114.

8  *Against the Galileans* 164 l.10: τοὺς οὔτε Ἕλληνας οὔτε Ἰουδαίους, ἀλλὰ τῆς Γαλιλαίων ὄντας αἱρέσεως.

9  Cf. W.C. Wright, *The Works of the Emperor Julian* (LCL; Cambridge/London: Harvard/Heinemann, 1923), 3.313: "Julian, like Epictetus, always calls the Christians Galilaeans because he wishes to emphasise that this was a local creed, 'the creed of fishermen', and perhaps to remind his readers that 'out of Galilee ariseth no prophet'."

10  R.L. Wilken, "Christians as the Romans (and Greeks) Saw Them," in *Jewish and Christian Self-Definition. Volume 1: The Shaping of Christianity in the Second and Third Centuries* (ed. E.P. Sanders; Philadelphia: Fortress, 1980), 100–25, 106: "a religious group whose practices were at odds with those of the Romans and did not promote genuine religion." W.M.

highlighting the un-Roman character of the sect and its divergence from true *religio*. But this is not clear. Clearer is the fact that using an ethnic designation such as Γαλιλαῖοι means that Epictetus is not here treating the Christians as anything like a philosophical school.

Epictetus assumes the Christians here not only to be indifferent to death (as we will see in Marcus Aurelius), but also to property and family. Epictetus and the Christians agree that this disposition is the correct one. They disagree on how this disposition should be acquired.

Clearly it is the ingrained custom of the Christians to take this attitude. 'Custom' or 'ethos' was, according to Julian, proverbially known as 'second nature' or, in Dio Chrysostom's definition in his discourse on *ethos*: "Custom is judgement common to those who use it, an unwritten law of tribe or city, a voluntary principle of justice, acceptable to all alike with reference to the same matters, an invention made, not by any human being, but rather by life and time."[11] This is all well and good, Epictetus might say if he were feeling charitable, but it is not philosophical: the disposition is not inculcated through *logos kai apodeixis*, as Epictetus would wish. The result is, as Renan and Labriolle note, that Epictetus views these Galileans as fanatics, following blind, robotic habit.[12]

Epictetus' verdict, then, is fairly but perhaps not entirely negative. The Galileans have the right disposition, but they have not derived it from reason and proof, but from *ethos*. Epictetus is nevertheless drawing a line between a philosophical approach to these things and an unphilosophical approach – and the Galileans are on the wrong side of that line.[13]

---

Beard, J.L. North, and S.R.F. Price, *Religions of Rome. Volume 1: A History* (Cambridge: Cambridge University Press, 1998), 211–12.

11    Julian, *Misopogon* 353a, Ἔθος, φασί, δευτέρη φύσις; Dio Chrysostom, *Oration* 76, Περὶ ἔθους; cf. the more negative discussion of custom in Clement, *Protr.* 10. I am grateful to my colleague James Carleton Paget for these references.

12    Labriolle, *La réaction païenne*, 49, citing Renan.

13    Another piece of evidence which should be mentioned is a fascinating section in Book 2 which rebukes the philosopher who does not hold fast to the principles to which he assents (2.9.1–22, on the claim to be a philosopher). Such a philosopher is accused of hypocrisy, of being like a Greek acting the part of a Jew, in terms perhaps redolent of Paul's account of Peter's hypocrisy in the Antioch incident (Galatians 2:11–14). Moreover, the Jewish convert is not said to be a true one unless he is baptised – such that philosophers not acting in accord with their own reason are said to be 'parabaptists' or 'counterfeit baptists'. A reference to baptism is perhaps more suggestive of Christianity than Judaism, always assuming that Epictetus distinguished sharply between them, which he may well not have done. In any case, there is no particular 'view' of Judaism or Christian-

## 2 Crescens[14]

And so I expect to be plotted against by one of those mentioned, and impaled on a stake – or at any rate by Crescens the sillywophler, and lover of praise. For it would not be right to say the man is a philosopher – this one who indicts us for things he is ignorant of, for being atheists and impious Christians. He does this to curry favour with and entertain the ignorant crowd.

Κἀγὼ οὖν προσδοκῶ ὑπό τινος τῶν ὠνομασμένων ἐπιβουλευθῆναι καὶ ξύλῳ ἐμπαγῆναι, ἢ κἂν ὑπὸ Κρίσκεντος τοῦ φιλοψόφου καὶ φιλοκόμπου. οὐ γὰρ φιλόσοφον εἰπεῖν ἄξιον τὸν ἄνδρα, ὅς γε περὶ ἡμῶν ἃ μὴ ἐπίσταται δημοσίᾳ καταμαρτυρεῖ, ὡς ἀθέων καὶ ἀσεβῶν Χριστιανῶν ὄντων, πρὸς χάριν καὶ ἡδονὴν τῶν πολλῶν τῶν πεπλανημένων ταῦτα πράττων. (Justin, 2 *Apology* 8.1–2)

Justin reports that one of the people who may be plotting against him (either already or in the future) is Crescens, a Cynic philosopher apparently of the 150s, unknown outside of the responses to him from Justin's school and in a later report in Eusebius. According to Tatian, Crescens was an example of a philosopher who proclaimed the doctrine of contempt for death but was actually fearful of death.[15] Crescens apparently made official accusations against the Christians; this is suggested by Justin's statement that he δημοσίᾳ καταμαρτυρεῖ (2 *Apology* 8.2).[16]

---

ity, merely a mild jeer at the hesitant convert from paganism. See Oldfather, *Epictetus*, 1:xxvi, for the view that the reference is to Christians; and M. Stern, *Greek and Latin Authors on Jews and Judaism* (Jerusalem: Israel Academy of Sciences and Humanities, 1976), 1:542–44 = Stern §254, who takes them to be Jews. Among more recent mentions, N. Huttunen, *Paul and Epictetus on Law: A Comparison* (London/ New York: T&T Clark, 2009), 18, deems a Christian reference possible; and Gill and Hard, *Epictetus*, 320, similarly do not pronounce a definite view.

14  See esp. A. Malherbe, "Justin and Crescens," in *Light from the Gentiles: Hellenistic philosophy and Early Christianity. Collected Essays by Abraham J. Malherbe, 1959–2012* (ed. C.R. Holladay, J.T. Fitzgerald, J.W. Thompson, and G.E. Sterling; Leiden: Brill, 2014), 883–94, who shows up the flaws in K. Hubik, *Die Apologien des hl. Justinus des Philosophen und Märtyrers: Literarhistorische Untersuchungen* (Vienna: Mayer, 1912); see also Labriolle, *La réaction païenne*, 59–65; P. Parvis and D. Minns, *Justin, Philosopher and Martyr: Apologies* (Oxford: Oxford University Press, 2009), 42–43.

15  Tatian, *Or.* 19.1: θανάτου δὲ ὁ καταφρονῶν; or in Eusebius' citation, θανάτου δὲ ὁ καταφρονεῖν συμβουλεύων.

16  Chapter divisions follow those in Parvis and Minns, *Justin, Philosopher and Martyr: Apologies*.

In response to Crescens, Justin then engages in an interesting philosophical contest, claiming that his opponent is utterly ignorant of Christianity and lampooning Crescens as φιλοψόφος, φιλοκόμπος (8.1) and φιλόδοξος (8.6), but not worthy of the name 'philosopher'. This is because he is ignorant of the Christians, as Justin has found in discussion with him. Tatian adds the point that he himself was also the object of Crescens' plotting. All we know of the substance of Crescens' attack on Christians appears in Justin,[17] and the substance of the charge is that they were ἄθεοι and ἀσεβεῖς (8.2). Malherbe's discussion of Crescens is a helpful reminder that we do not know whether Crescens was successful, in part because the surviving account of Justin's martyrdom makes no mention of Crescens.[18] On the other hand, Mark Edwards rightly raises the possibility that Crescens may have lodged the accusation and brought the information against Justin before the trial proper.[19] This fits with the direct connection Jerome makes between Crescens and Justin's martyrdom.[20]

Crescens therefore has the distinction of being the first named individual we know to have accused the Christians of atheism.[21] Justin has already reported the accusation in general in *1 Apology* 6, and he owns up to the charge, as far as the traditional gods are concerned. Justin's description of Crescens is also roughly contemporaneous with the martyrdom of Polycarp in Smyrna (*Martyrdom of Polycarp* 19.1)[22] after his refusal to recant with the words which, according to the *Martyrdom*, were the customary mode of recantation: "Swear by the genius of Caesar; repent and say, 'Away with the atheists'" (9.2; cf. also

---

17  The main sources for our knowledge of Crescens are *2 Apolology* 8, Tatian's *Oratio* 19, and Eusebius' *Ecclesiastical History* 4.16.1–9, though Eusebius may not have any independent knowledge. Jerome mentions Crescens (*De Viris Illustribus* 23), and he seems there to have independent knowledge of Justin; cf. also the *Chronicon*, where Crescens is placed ca. 152 CE in the 233rd Olympiad.

18  See Malherbe, "Justin and Crescens."

19  M.J. Edwards, "Religion in the Age of Marcus Aurelius," in *A Companion to Marcus Aurelius* (ed. M. van Ackeren; Oxford: Wiley Blackwell, 2012), 200–16, 208.

20  Jerome, *De Viris Illustribus* 23.

21  See T. Whitmarsh, "Away with the Atheists!" in a forthcoming volume on the second century edited by J. Carleton Paget and J.M. Lieu.

22  On the date of the execution of Polycarp, see P. Hartog, ed., *Polycarp's Epistle to the Philippians and the Martyrdom of Polycarp: Introduction, Text and Commentary* (Oxford: Oxford University Press, 2013), 191–200; he places it ca. 155–161 CE. See further Hartog, *Polycarp's Epistle to the Philippians and the Martyrdom of Polycarp*, 171–86, on the date of composition, which he tentatively suggests is the third quarter of the second century (186); cf. also C.R. Moss, "On the Dating of Polycarp: Rethinking the Place of the Martyrdom of Polycarp in the History of Christianity," *Early Christianity* 1 (2010), 539–74, for a date in the early third century.

3.2). In the case of Crescens here, philosophical critique here is intermingled with, or has even given way to, a criminal charge from the standpoint of *religio*, although in this case we only have snippets of Justin to go on.

## 3   Apuleius[23]

The evidence of Apuleius is perhaps the most difficult. Debate particularly circles around the novel *The Golden Ass*, whereas the philosophical and rhetorical writings, including the *Apology* in which he defended himself against the charge of having acquired his wife by magic, contain no reference to Christianity at all.[24] Walsh in particular has pressed the view on a number of occasions that *The Golden Ass* is a veiled polemic against Christianity.[25] On Walsh's view, the book recounts autobiographically how Apuleius himself was a metaphorical ass for a time during a stint as a Christian, but latterly came to his senses and became a man, identifying the religion of Isis as the true source of salvation. Walsh seeks support for this view both in the circumstantial evidence of the rise of Christianity in North Africa in the late second century and also, more importantly, in the references in Tertullian to allegations that Christians worship the head of an ass (*Apology* 16)[26] and Tertullian's report that a man was paraded in the amphitheatre dressed as an ass and adorned with a placard labelling himself "the God of the Christians, offspring of an ass" (*Apology* 16). Furthermore, one of the characters whom the asinine protagonist encounters in the narrative is a baker's wife, who, among her many other misdemeanours, has abandoned the gods in favour of one special one and also wakes up to

---

23   On Apuleius and Christianity, see esp. Labriolle, *La réaction païenne*, 65–71; P.G. Walsh, "Lucius Madaurensis," *Phoenix* 22 (1968): 143–57; B. Baldwin, "Apuleius, Tacitus, and Christians," *Emerita* 52 (1984): 1–3; D. Tripp, "The Baker's Wife and her Confidante in Apuleius: Some Liturgiological Considerations," *Emerita* 56 (1988): 245–54; B. Baldwin, "Apuleius and the Christians," *Liverpool Classical Monthly* 14 no. 4 (1989): 55; B.L. Hijmans, "Appendix 4," in idem, ed., *Apuleius Madaurensis: Metamorphoses IX* (GCA; Groningen: Egbert Forsten, 1995), 380–82; V.L. Schmidt, "Reaktionen auf das Christentum in den Metamorphoses des Apuleius," *VC* 51 (1997): 51–71; V. Hunink, "Apuleius, Pudentilla, and Christianity," *VC* 54 (2000): 80–94; W.S. Smith, "Apuleius' *Metamorphoses* and Jewish/Christian Literature," in *Ancient Narrative* 10: 47–87, http://www.ancientnarrative.com/pdf/anvol10_03wsmith.pdf.

24   Benko raises the possibility that Aemilianus, one of Apuleius' opponents in the *Apology*, is a Christian, but without accepting the opinion himself. See S. Benko, *Pagan Rome and the Early Christians* (Bloomington, IN: Indiana University Press, 1984), 105.

25   See for example Walsh, "Lucius Madaurensis," 151–57.

26   Cf. also Minucius Felix, *Octavius* 9.

indulge in unmixed wine early in the morning, *matutino mero* (*Metamorphoses* 9.14).[27]

The potential difficulties here are several. First, *The Golden Ass* is a rewriting of an existing tale in which the ass and his transformation were already present, so the novel was not designed by Apuleius for an anti-Christian purpose, though it may in his hands have taken on such a purpose.[28] The story of the baker's wife is suggestive but does not clearly identify the wife as a Christian rather than, say, a Jew. Among her many misdemeanours, the reference to getting up early to start drinking may be invoking a stock vice (one thinks, for example, of Isaiah 5:11).[29] Additionally, there is a possible chronological difficulty: even on the later dating of the *Golden Ass*, preferred by Walsh,[30] there is a gap in time of a generation or so before Tertullian's *Apologeticum* reports the events connecting Christianity and donkeys. Harrison's conclusion, therefore, may not be overly cautious: "There is little firm evidence that Apuleius knew much of contemporary Christianity and its literature; though this has been argued, it can remain only as an interesting speculation."[31]

There is, however, one final strand of evidence which, in my judgement, tips the balance in favour of a Christian reference. Baldwin notes a few linguistic parallels between Tacitus' notice of the Christians in *Annals* 15.44 and Apuleius' description of the baker's wife, which are perhaps sufficient to indicate that he had the passage in mind: both use the words *flagitia, confluo, pudicitia/pudeo*, and other similar items of vocabulary in the two short stretches of text.[32] This, together with the combination of monotheism and drinking

---

27   "Then she spurned and scorned the divine powers, and instead of true religion presumed to worship a specious and sacrilegious deity, whom she named the 'only One'. She concocted empty rituals, misleading everyone and tricking her poor husband, and gave her body over to early-morning wine and to endless fornication" (*Tunc spretis atque calcatis diuinis numinibus in uicem certae religionis mentita sacrilega praesumptione dei, quem praedicaret unicum, confictis obseruationibus uacuis fallens omnis homines et miserum maritum decipiens matutino mero et continuo stupro corpus manciparat*, 9.14).

28   P.G. Walsh, trans., *Apuleius: The Golden Ass* (Oxford World's Classics; Oxford: Oxford University Press, 2008), xx–xxi.

29   Tripp's interesting suggestion ("The Baker's Wife and her Confidante") that there is a reference to deacons administering sacramental wine here is a little speculative, although he helpfully draws attention to the fact that the confidante also appears to join the baker's wife in her drinking in *Metamorphoses* 9.15.

30   Walsh, *Apuleius: The Golden Ass*, xx: "in or after the 160s."

31   S.J. Harrison, *Apuleius: A Latin Sophist* (Oxford: Oxford University Press, 2004), 43, though perhaps slightly more optimistic at 249; similarly also Hijmans, "Appendix 4," 382.

32   Baldwin, "Apuleius, Tacitus, and Christians," 2–3.

wine in the early morning, is strongly suggestive of a mockery of Christians by Apuleius.

## 4 Marcus Aurelius[33]

In keeping with the theme of this paper, this section will focus narrowly on the treatment of Christians by Marcus Aurelius *qua* philosopher, without reference to the question of what his policy as an emperor may have been, on which much has been written elsewhere.[34] There is one passage that refers explicitly to Christians:[35]

---

[33] On Marcus Aurelius and Christianity, see esp. Labriolle, *La réaction païenne*, 71–79; A. Birley, "Appendix IV: Marcus and the Christians," in *Marcus Aurelius* (London: Eyre & Spottiswoode, 1966), 328–31; C.R. Haines, *Marcus Aurelius* (LCL; Cambridge/London: Harvard/Heinemann, 1970), 381–89; D. Berwig, *Mark Aurel und die Christen* (Diss. Muenchen, 1979); P.A. Brunt, "Marcus Aurelius and the Christians," in C. Deroux, ed., *Studies in Latin Literature and Roman History* (Brussels: Latomus, 1979), 483–520.

[34] To take one much-cited example, see T.D. Barnes, "Legislation against the Christians," *JRS* 58 (1968): 32–50, which notes that already in 1968 the bibliography on the subject was huge. Since then, Berwig (*Mark Aurel*) has also treated the activities specifically of Marcus; see also Edwards, "Religion in the Age of Marcus Aurelius," which is also helpful on the broader context across the empire; P. Keresztes, "The Imperial Roman Government and the Christian Church I. From Nero to the Severi," *ANRW* II 23 no. 2 (1980): 247–315; and W.H.C. Frend, "Persecutions: Genesis and Legacy," in *The Cambridge History of Christianity. Volume 1: Origins to Constantine* (ed. M.M. Mitchell and F.M. Young; Cambridge: Cambridge University Press, 2006), 503–23.

[35] In the notes to his Loeb edition, Haines (*Marcus Aurelius*, 381–85) argued that there are other passages that allude to Christianity. They are as follows: *Med.* 1.6 refers to Diognetus' advice to Marcus not to believe in miracle-workers or exorcists; *Med.* 3.16 is perhaps more suggestive, with its reference to "those who do not believe in the gods and forsake their father-land and who act any which way behind closed doors" (τῶν θεοὺς μὴ νομιζόντων καὶ τῶν τὴν πατρίδα ἐγκαταλειπόντων καὶ τῶν <ὁτιοῦν> ποιούντων, ἐπειδὰν κλείσωσι τὰς θύρας) – to emphasise the possibility of a Christian reference, I have translated the three characteristics as belonging to the same group, though it could equally refer to three different classes of people; *Med.* 7.68 (cf. 8.51), with its reference to the innocent being torn by wild beasts, is another possibility, though perhaps attributes too positive an attitude towards Christians on Marcus' part. Marcus may have had Christians in mind in some of these places, but the references are too general to be certain. Haines also mentions *Med.* 8.48, but this is of little relevance except in the light it may shed on the meaning of παράταξις in 11.3.

The right sort of soul is the one which is ready if necessary to be released straight away from the body, whether that soul is to be extinguished or scattered or to abide. But this readiness must come from a specific decision, not out of sheer opposition as is the case with the Christians, but in a manner that is reasoned, and grave and – in order to persuade others – without song and dance.

Οἵα ἐστὶν ἡ ψυχὴ ἡ ἕτοιμος, ἐὰν ἤδη ἀπολυθῆναι δέῃ τοῦ σώματος, [καὶ] ἤτοι σβεσθῆναι ἢ σκεδασθῆναι ἢ συμμεῖναι. τὸ δὲ ἕτοιμον τοῦτο ἵνα ἀπὸ ἰδικῆς κρίσεως ἔρχηται, μὴ κατὰ ψιλὴν παράταξιν ὡς οἱ Χριστιανοί, ἀλλὰ λελογισμένως καὶ σεμνῶς καὶ ὥστε καὶ ἄλλον πεῖσαι, ἀτραγῳδῶς. (*Meditations*. 11.3)

### 4.1 The Text of 11.3

The first point that needs to be discussed here is the question of whether the reference to the Christians is original or a later gloss. The phrase ὡς οἱ Χριστιανοί appears in the manuscripts of the *Meditations*[36] and in the early editions beginning in the sixteenth century. The text, according to Dalfen's Teubner edition, was first called into question by Eichstaedt in 1821,[37] and now most commentators do not mention the text without observing that it is questioned by some.[38] Editors also signal the doubt: influentially, Haines' Loeb places the Greek phrase and its English translation in square brackets.[39] Dalfen's Teubner editions do the same.[40] Haines' argument on linguistic grounds has not been widely accepted, largely because, however awkward the parenthetical remark is, it is well within the bounds of Marcus' somewhat quirky Greek style.[41]

The most vigorous attack on the authenticity of the reference to Christians comes from P.A. Brunt.[42] His criteria are that the three-word phrase should be

---

36   Both the manuscript edited by Xylander: P, now lost, and the extant A. See C. Gill, ed., *Marcus Aurelius: Meditations. With Selected Correspondence* (trans. R. Hard; Oxford World's Classics; Oxford: Oxford University Press, 2011), 1.
37   Referring to H.C.A. Eichstaedt, *Exercitationes Antoninianae* (vol. 3: 1821, *non vidi*).
38   See for example R.B. Rutherford, *The Meditations of Marcus Aurelius: A Study* (Oxford: Clarendon, 1989), 188.
39   C.R. Haines, *Marcus Aurelius* (LCL; Cambridge/London: Harvard/Heinemann, 1970), 294–95, and see the comment on 384.
40   J. Dalfen, ed., *Marci Aurelii Antonini ad se ipsum Libri XII* (Leipzig: Teubner, 1979).
41   Haines, *Marcus Aurelius*, 382. Cf. Brunt, "Marcus Aurelius and the Christians," 484; R. Hard, "Note on the Text," in *Marcus Aurelius: Meditations*, xxv. On the other hand, Haines is followed and cited by Staniforth in a footnote in the Penguin Classics translation.
42   Brunt, "Marcus Aurelius and the Christians."

taken to be inauthentic "if there are good grounds for regarding it as inapposite to the sense, and if its later insertion in the text can be explained."[43] On the latter point, Brunt's argument is merely that it is "a gloss, a marginal exclamation made by a pagan reader who lived at a time when the persecutions of the Christians filled a larger part in men's thoughts than I think they did in those of Marcus... and intruded into the text by a still later copyist."[44] The further complication is that the scholiast "did not fully grasp Marcus' meaning."[45] This is of course a possible explanation, but it should probably only be an absolute last resort.

The main argument is from the sense of the passage. Brunt takes it as follows: the readiness for suicide should come from a specific decision not as sheer opposition (to God) but reflectively and gravely... and without lamenting.[46] Understood this way, Brunt concludes that a contrast with Christians would make no sense, in particular because παράταξις means a defiant opposition (to God),[47] and ἀτραγῴδως does not mean 'without histrionic display' (thus Farquharson) but, more probably, 'without lamenting'.

He has three further worries about the reference to Christians: (1) "How could the Christians have been regarded as men ready to commit suicide, though in the wrong way?"[48] (2) he observes that Marcus hardly thought about the Christians;[49] and (3) he notes that Marcus is thinking in 11.3 about his own predicament, not that of execution by the state.[50] (He further discusses the additional passages in the *Meditations*, which Haines in the Loeb edition considers, much more speculatively, to be references to Christians.) These

---

43  Brunt, "Marcus Aurelius and the Christians," 484.
44  Brunt, "Marcus Aurelius and the Christians," 498.
45  Brunt's remark that the misinterpretations of modern scholars make this plausible loses force when one considers that modern scholars have a text with ὡς οἱ Χριστιανοί, whereas the alleged ancient reader did not.
46  See Brunt, "Marcus Aurelius and the Christians," 489 (on 'specific decision'), 493–94 (on 'as sheer opposition [to God])', and 487–88 (esp. 487 n. 11) on the adverbs.
47  Brunt is confusing here, as he initially seems to want παράταξις to refer to 'battle-array', with a contrast between reasoned, reflective suicide and death in battle ("Marcus Aurelius and the Christians," 488), but then shifts to a different sense in 493–94. In the meantime, however, he seems to have used the 'battle-array' interpretation as an argument against the authenticity of the reference to Christians ("the allusion to the Christians would then be absurdly inappropriate"). But Brunt's sense is not completely clear to me.
48  Brunt, "Marcus Aurelius and the Christians," 491.
49  Brunt, "Marcus Aurelius and the Christians," 492
50  Brunt, "Marcus Aurelius and the Christians," 492.

three points merit brief consideration; we will return later to the meanings of παράταξις and ἀτραγῴδως.

In the first place, Brunt acknowledges the existence of voluntary martyrs but questions whether such people would lead Marcus Aurelius to apply his accusation to οἱ Χριστιανοί *in toto*.[51] But this shows a rather wooden approach to a text that should be read alongside similar passages where polemical remarks are made; one might compare, for example, Celsus' apparently generalised, hyperbolic statement that Christians are "mad" and "deliberately rush forward to arouse the wrath of an emperor or governor which brings... blows and tortures and even death."[52] On the same point, in connection with the "peculiarly perverse" idea that Marcus, on the "Christian" reading, would be equating his potential suicide with "the readiness of a man to undergo death by the executioner,"[53] the issue at hand in 11.3 is readiness to go to a voluntary death, and so there is sufficient common ground between voluntary martyrdoms and Marcus' hypothesised suicide.

On his second point, it is very likely that Brunt is correct that Marcus thought very little about Christians.[54] However, alongside this point, it should be borne in mind that there were considerable numbers of Christians in the empire by this time, and that Marcus' contemporary Celsus deemed the Christians a sufficiently virulent threat to write a whole book about them. Closer to home, Marcus' teacher Fronto comments on Christians, and another of his teachers, Q. Junius Rusticus, presided as prefect at the trial of Justin Martyr and his companions.[55]

Finally, some of the points relating to the first observation apply again here. Of course Marcus is contemplating his own situation, which would be different from the circumstance of execution. Nevertheless, the comparison enables him to contrast Christian voluntary death with what he theoretically considers as a possible option for himself, namely a suicide that is reasoned, solemn, and without histrionics. The Christian approach to death, which, for Marcus, is characterised by melodramatic opposition of some sort, serves as a suitable counterpoint to his own, making it appear rationally defensible. We should

---

51  Brunt, "Marcus Aurelius and the Christians," 492.
52  *Contra Celsum* 8.65 (trans. Chadwick, 501): "Ἔνθα μέντοι οὐδὲν ἐναντίον πράττομεν νόμῳ καὶ λόγῳ θεοῦ, οὐ μεμήναμεν οὐδ᾽ ὁρμῶμεν καθ᾽ ἑαυτῶν ἐγείρειν βασιλέως ἢ δυνάστου θυμόν, ἐπὶ αἰκίας καὶ βασανιστήρια ἢ καὶ θανάτους ἡμᾶς φέροντα.
53  Brunt, "Marcus Aurelius and the Christians," 492.
54  Brunt, "Marcus Aurelius and the Christians," 492.
55  See the *Martyrdom of Justin*, where Justin and his companions are brought before Rusticus; H. Musurillo, ed., *Acts of the Christian Martyrs* (Oxford: Clarendon, 1972), 42–61.

probably conclude that there is no good reason to reject the authenticity of the reference to the Christians in Marcus' text.[56]

### 4.2 Interpretation

For Marcus, life should be conducted in accordance with nature and by holding fast to the guardian-spirit within (2.13; 3.7). The goal of living is not only to cultivate the virtue of the inner spirit, however, but also to seek both civic good and the good of the universe. It is possible, however, that political circumstances can militate so strongly against nature that it is no longer possible to live correctly, and in such circumstances, suicide is the best course of action (5.29). With reference specifically to *Meditations* 11.3, when faced with suicide, the soul should be ready, but such readiness should spring from a deliberate decision and be reasoned out, serious, and (literally) without a song and dance (λελογισμένως καὶ σεμνῶς καὶ…ἀτραγῴδως).[57]

In contrast to the measured approach to suicide that Marcus contemplates, he implies that Christians too readily die as drama queens (following the implication that ἀτραγῴδως is not how Christians go about things). Brunt, as part of his argument for the non-Christian reference, prefers to take the adverb ἀτραγῴδως as 'without lamenting', but it is worth noting that Marcus' other use of this word cannot be taken in the sense in which Brunt takes it. In 1.16, Marcus states that he learned from his adoptive father that one should "look far ahead, and plan even the smallest matters in advance ἀτραγῴδως."[58] This is unlikely to refer to the planning of small matters without lamenting, but is perfectly understandable as referring to the planning of minutiae "without making a song and dance about it," as Hard nicely translates.[59]

Additionally, according to Marcus, Christians die κατὰ ψιλὴν παράταξιν. This is a difficult phrase: παράταξις usually means arrangement in a battle-line. The meaning of ψιλὴν παράταξιν now taken by a long string of interpreters is something like 'sheer obstinacy'. Already in Wolle's 1729 translation, the now-common parallel is drawn between Marcus' reference to Christians' παράταξις and Pliny's reference to their *obstinatio* and *pertinacia*. A parallel in *Meditations* 8.48, which has the verb παρατάσσω, might support this interpretation –

---

56  It is perhaps worth noting that both the context and the form of the parenthetical remark are similar to the parallel comment in Epictetus.
57  Worthy of comparison here is Marcus' insistence that death should be conducted αἰδημόνως καὶ κοσμίως, in 3.7. Or again, in 5.29, one should commit suicide if necessary.
58  Trans. R. Hard, in *Marcus Aurelius. Meditations*, 6.
59  Gill and Hard, *Marcus Aurelius. Meditations*, 6.

there the verb appears to mean 'oppose', 'attack', or 'array against'.[60] (The παρα- prefix here, then, has the sense of 'against' rather than the meaning 'along', as it usually does in combination with τάσσω.) Brunt suggests the possibility of death in the line of duty, but he seems later to reject this in favour of the sense 'opposition to God'. Supplying a reference specifically to God here seems gratuitous, however. Rutherford suggests the possibility of peer pressure among Christians such that martyrdom was pressed upon individuals, at least from Marcus' viewpoint.[61] More likely here is a view similar to what we shall see in Celsus: Christians offer themselves out of sheer opposition, blindly arraying themselves against the authorities. In my view this is the most probable solution, though given the laconic expression any interpretation must remain tentative.

## 5    Galen[62]

Galen wrote one book entitled, *The Best Doctor Is Also a Philosopher'* (OTI O ΑΡΙΣΤΟΣ ΙΑΤΡΟΣ ΚΑΙ ΦΙΛΟΣΟΦΟΣ). Since he clearly thought that he was that best doctor, it follows he must also be a philosopher, and so merits inclusion here.

There are two references to Christians in what survives of Galen in Greek, and two further in Arabic translation. He is notable among our philosophers here for seeing a close relationship between Christians and Jews, which will also be emphasised in Celsus. On the other hand, however, Walzer is perhaps incorrect to see in the references to Christians surviving in Greek a double reference to Jews and Christians; rather, the more natural sense, especially of

---

60  Μέμνησο ὅτι ἀκαταμάχητον γίνεται τὸ ἡγεμονικόν, ὅταν εἰς ἑαυτὸ συστραφὲν ἀρκεσθῇ ἑαυτῷ, μὴ ποιοῦν τι ὃ μὴ θέλει, κἂν ἀλόγως παρατάξηται ("even if it is irrationally attacked/opposed/arrayed against").

61  He sees the contrast more with ἀπὸ ἰδικῆς κρίσεως. Birley's interpretation is similar, in that he sees the meaning 'spirit of resistance' not in the sense of Pliny's accusation of obstinacy, but rather meaning that the Christians were trained to die; Birley, *Marcus Aurelius*, 210.

62  The foundational work on Galen and Christianity is R. Walzer, *Galen on Jews and Christians* (Oxford: Clarendon, 1949), who reports scholarship on Galen and Christianity existing at the time in his introduction. Walzer and most work subsequent to him, however, has not noted M. Sprengling, "Galen on the Christians," *American Journal of Theology* 21 (1917): 94–109. I owe this reference to Roger Pearse. In addition to the other works cited below, see also R. Köbert, "Das nur in arabischer Überlieferung erhaltene Urteil Galens über die Christen," *Orientalia* [Rome] 25 (1956): 404–09.

Μωϋσοῦ καὶ Χριστοῦ διατριβή in the first passage we will discuss, is a reference to a single group, namely Christians.[63]

The two Greek references both appear in *On the Differences in Pulses* (probably 176–180). In the first, he is criticising what he sees as mere assertions on the part of Archigenes about different qualities of pulse. Archigenes has failed to demonstrate (ἀποδεῖξαι) what he says. He has merely drawn his categories from authorities. This is anathema to Galen, for whom demonstration was a prime concern. (One of the great losses from Galen's oeuvre is his *On Demonstration.*) Archigenes might at least have provided some kind of "explanation, in order that one should not right at the start, as if one had come into the school of Moses and Christ, hear undemonstrated laws" (παραμυθία, ἵνα μή τις εὐθὺς κατ' ἀρχὰς, ὡς εἰς Μωϋσοῦ καὶ Χριστοῦ διατριβὴν ἀφιγμένος, νόμων ἀναποδείκτων ἀκούῃ, *On the Differences in Pulses* 2.4). The general point about Christians here has been rightly observed by the commentators to be a criticism of their lack of proof for their assertions.[64] Just as Archigenes has not given ἀπόδειξις, the same failure is found in Christian schools. The same stance is evident in one of the Arabic fragments of *On the Unmoved Prime Mover* (dated any time before 192 CE): "If I had in mind people who taught their pupils in the same way as the followers of Moses and Christ teach theirs—for they order them to accept everything on faith—I should not have given you a definition."[65]

A further important dimension that I missed in the secondary literature, though, might be the contrast between proof and appeal to past authority. An implication of Galen's picture of Christians lies in their dogmatic attachment to an individual. Galen distinctively and perhaps in all four references speaks of the school or followers of Christ.[66] The Christians' fundamental flaw is that they attach themselves to an individual, just as Archigenes here in his discussion of the pulse foregoes demonstration in favour of citing the καθάρειοι, the decent chaps, who are bound to be right.

Potentially on the positive side, it is worth noting that Galen dignifies the Christians with the label of διατριβή. One way to take this is as in line with Walzer's attribution to Galen of a very fair and positive view of the Christians, seeing him as "the first pagan author who implicitly places Greek philosophy and the Christian religion on the same footing."[67] I would qualify this a lit-

---

63  Cf. Walzer's references to Jews and Christians in his explanation of this passage; *Galen on Jews and Christians*, 47–48.
64  Walzer, *Galen on Jews and Christians*, 46–47.
65  Walzer, *Galen on Jews and Christians*, 15.
66  On the Arabic testimonium in a Plato *Epitome*, see below.
67  Walzer, *Galen on Jews and Christians*, 43.

tle, however. The most that one can say about this passage is that the school of the Christians is rather like a philosophical school, but for Galen this is by no means necessarily a ringing endorsement. In the course of his education, Galen's father insisted on his not being schooled in one particular αἵρεσις, and Galen aimed to maintain this independence of mind throughout his career: Galen is ambivalent towards sects. He has no particular interest here in policing the boundaries of what might count as a school, though he is concerned to comment that the school of the Christians is not a very good one. This leads us neatly into a second passage surviving in Greek, in which Galen is commenting on the fact that it is precisely attachment to a particular school that is inimical to proper research. It is useless engaging in *viva voce* discussion with stubborn opponents, he remarks. In fact, "one might sooner convert the followers of Moses and Christ than the physicians and philosophers who cling fast to their schools!" (θᾶττον γὰρ ἄν τις τοὺς ἀπὸ Μωϋσοῦ καὶ Χριστοῦ μεταδιδάξειεν ἢ τοὺς ταῖς αἱρέσεσι προστετηκότας ἰατρούς τε καὶ φιλοσόφους, *On the Differences in Pulses* 3.3). Here it is less clear even that the Christians belong among the schools, nor does it really seem the case that Galen takes Christians to be "less rigid" than dogmatic doctors and philosophers, as Walzer supposes.[68] This is one of several ways in which Walzer tries to view Galen's attitude to Jews and Christians in as positive a light as possible, and sometimes more positively than is possible.

Or again, a more positive view of Christians might be found in the second Arabic fragment, a quotation from Galen's lost summary of either the *Phaedo* or the *Republic*. This testimonium, however, is the least textually secure with respect to its origin (which Platonic summary it derives from),[69] its transmis-

---

68   Cf. Walzer, *Galen on Jews and Christians*, 38: "he [sc. Galen] attacks dogmatic adherence to particular schools in more general terms, comparing it with the less rigid though equally reproachable loyalty of Christians and Jews to their sects." Galen is really just juxtaposing the groups for rhetorical purposes, rather than evaluating their respective levels of rigidity.

69   In brief, Walzer proposed that the reference clearly came from the epitome of the *Republic*, because Bar Hebraeus' attribution of the extract to the *Phaedo* epitome was a bungle in the course of his use of another source, Ibn al-Qifti's *History of Learned Men*, and so does not have independent value; *Galen on Jews and Christians*, 93. G. Levi della Vida argued conversely that Bar Hebraeus has just as much claim to independent value as the converse 'Republic' tradition, because he is dependent on the earlier work of Agapius: Bar Hebraeus and Agapius on the one hand, and Ibn al-Qifti on the other, follow two distinct translations of Galen's *Epitomes*; "Two Fragments of Galen in Arabic Translation," *JAOS* 70 (1950): 182–87, 185–86. Gero, however, noted that the situation is still more complicated, showing that the reference to Galen in "Agapius" is actually a marginal gloss, per-

sion, and its contents. There is a positive view of the Christians here, at least as far as their behaviour is concerned:

> Most people are unable to follow any demonstrative argument consecutively; hence they need parables, and benefit from them... just as now we see the people called Christians [or people belonging to Christ[70]] drawing their faith from parables [and miracles], and yet sometimes acting in the same way [as those who philosophize]. For their contempt of death [and its sequel] is patent to us every day, and likewise their restraint in cohabitation. For they include not only men but also women who refrain from cohabiting all through their lives; and they also number individuals who, in self-discipline and self-control [in matters of food and drink], and in their keen pursuit of justice, have attained a pitch not inferior to that of genuine philosophers.

In short, the Christian use of *rumuz* (parable, or symbol) to elicit an emotional response can, to a degree, have the same effect as demonstration in sometimes producing virtue and, in the case of some Christians, even attaining the same level as philosophers.[71] On the other hand, however, one must reckon with the textual difficulties.[72] The content here might also suggest Arabic influence, since the theme of religion and philosophy producing the same goals through different means is a topic of interest among Islamic philosophers.[73]

Grant further proposes two interesting potential examples of actual influence of the wording of the New Testament upon Galen: the latter's "I think I will show not with persuasive words, but with clear proofs" (δοκῶ μοι δείξειν

---

haps from the fourteenth century, and in fact derives from the influence of Bar Hebraeus rather than the other way around. See S. Gero, "Galen on the Christians: A Reappraisal of the Arabic Evidence," *Orientalia Christiana Periodica* 56 (1990), 371–411.

[70] See the arguments in favour of this reading in Gero, "Galen on the Christians," 403, esp. n. 94.

[71] J. Barnes, "Galen, Christians, Logic," in *Classics in Progress: Essays on Ancient Greece and Rome* (ed. T.P. Wiseman; Oxford/London: Oxford University Press/The British Academy, 2006), 399–418, comments that Galen may implicitly be defending Christians from charges of immorality, such as that of Fronto.

[72] Having said that, Gero, who certainly reckons with the textual difficulties, is generally supportive of authenticity; "Galen on the Christians," 403–04.

[73] Cf. Alfarabi, *Philosophy of Plato and Aristotle*, e.g. §55: "In everything of which philosophy gives an account based on intellectual perception or conception, religion gives an account based on imagination." See M. Mahdi, ed. and tr., *Philosophy of Plato and Aristotle* (Ithaca, NY: Cornell University Press, 1969), 44.

οὐ λόγοις πιθανοῖς, ἀλλ' ἐναργέσιν ἀποδείξεσιν)[74] is perhaps influenced by Paul's claim, οὐκ ἐν πειθοῖς σοφίας λόγοις ἀλλ' ἐν ἀποδείξει πνεύματος καὶ δυνάμεως (1 Corinthians 2:4).[75] In addition, Grant quite sensibly attributes Galen's criticism of the possibility of God making people out of stones to the New Testament,[76] although it is not completely clear that Galen thinks himself to be citing an example from Moses; he may simply be imagining something impossible.[77] Strikingly, however, Galen immediately goes on to disagree with something else Moses allegedly thinks: πάντα γὰρ εἶναι νομίζει τῷ θεῷ δυνατά.[78] Here we have another close verbal similarity with Synoptic tradition (παρὰ δὲ θεῷ πάντα δυνατά, Matthew 19:26), but on the other hand, the sentiment is also common in Philo.[79]

Overall, it is not clear to me that Galen's view of the Christians, as expressed here, is one of sunny "tolerance"[80] or that his remarks are "friendly criticism" from "a sympathetic observer."[81] (On the other hand, one might remark that Galen perhaps did not approach his contemporaries in general with a hermeneutic of charity.) His criticism of Christians' indifference to proof is, for Galen personally, an absolutely fundamental error – especially for him, as the author of a work *On Demonstration* in fifteen volumes,[82] even more than for others, such as Celsus and Lucian, who also make this charge.[83]

---

74  *De usu partium* 14.7 (Kühn IV, 169 l. 8).

75  R.M. Grant, "Paul, Galen, and Origen," *JTS* 34 (1983): 533–36, 534.

76  Grant, "Paul, Galen, and Origen," 534.

77  Compare οὐδὲ γάρ, εἰ τὴν πέτραν ἐξαίφνης ἐθελήσειεν ἄνθρωπον ποιῆσαι, δυνατὸν αὐτῷ (*Usu Partium* 11.14; Kühn III, 905 ll. 17–18) with δύναται ὁ θεὸς ἐκ τῶν λίθων τούτων ἐγεῖραι τέκνα τῷ Ἀβραάμ (Matthew 3:9; Luke 3:8).

78  *Usu Partium* 11.14; Kühn III, 906 ll. 4–5.

79  Philo, *Opif.* 46: πάντα γὰρ θεῷ δυνατά.
    *Somn.* 1.88: πάντα γὰρ ὡς δυνατά, οὕτως καὶ γνώριμα θεῷ.
    *Abr.* 112: πάντα γὰρ ᾔδει θεῷ δυνατά.
    *Abr.* 175 πάντα δ' ἴσθι θεῷ δυνατά.
    *Spec. Leg.* 4.127: πάντα θεῷ δυνατά.
    *Virt.* 27: πάντα γὰρ θεῷ δυνατά.

80  Walzer, *Galen on Jews and Christians*, 44, on Galen exhibiting "religious tolerance." One might also contextualise Walzer's assumption of Galen's "interest" in Christians (*Galen on Jews and Christians*, 16) and in "Christian thought" (10), given the proportional amount of references in Galen's massive output. We will return to this point later.

81  Benko, "Pagan Criticism of Christianity," 1100.

82  Barnes, "Galen, Christians, Logic," 399.

83  Barnes, "Galen, Christians, Logic," 402, comments on the accusation being common to all three.

## 6 Celsus[84]

We know nothing about Celsus beyond what can be deduced from Origen's rebuttal.[85] He apparently died some considerable time before Origen wrote the *Contra Celsum* at around 250 CE (*Contra Celsum*, Preface 4); on the other hand, he is conversant with Marcion and Marcionites, who flourished in the mid-to-late second century. Celsus is usually thought to have written his *Alethes Logos* between 177–180 during the joint *imperium* of Marcus and Commodus.[86] He is committed both to traditional piety and to Platonism. With Celsus we find the first large-scale attack on Christianity, and the massive disproportion between the amount of attention Christianity receives in Celsus in comparison with the other figures we have mentioned means that only the most cursory of glances at some facets of his work is possible here.

It is notable, first, that a number of Celsus' objections are social criticisms, and these occupy prominent positions both at the beginning of the *Alethes Logos* and at the end: Christianity is first a secret society, and therefore illegal (1.1; 1.3; cf. 8.17). Celsus closes with the criticisms that Christians are ungrateful to the emperor in not swearing by him, because he gives them everything they have (8.67; cf. 65); forgetting the emperor would lead to barbarism (8.68); the God of the Jews and Christians clearly could hardly be trusted to protect Rome, because he has not done a very good job of looking after the Jews (8.69); Christians should join in the civic cult (the main theme covered in book 8), should muck in and help the emperor with all their power, fight in the army (8.73), and accept public office if needed (8.75). This is what they should do. Instead, what they get up to is a mix of ethical behaviour, which is simply philosophical ethics *réchauffé* (1.4; 7.58) and borrowed Jewish laws (2.4–5) on the one hand, and their own new barbarous practices, such as sorcery, on the other (1.6; 6.14; 6.39–40); they wall themselves off from others (8.2); they are even guilty of στάσις (8.49; cf. 8.2; 3.5). They deliberately provoke emperors and governors despite the torture and death to follow (8.65) – echoes of Marcus Aurelius. He also hints (5.63) at darker immoralities among some groups at least. In sum, "they profess nothing good, but everything for the ills of mankind" (οὐδὲν μὲν χρηστὸν ὑπισχνεῖσθαι πάντα δ' ἐπ' ἀνθρώπων βλάβαις, 6.40).

---

84  For a helpful survey of the secondary literature on Celsus, see H. Lona, *Die wahre Lehre des Kelsos* (Freiburg: Herder, 2005).

85  He is almost certainly not to be identified with the Celsus who is the addressee of Lucian's *Alexander*, who is an Epicurean.

86  H. Chadwick, *Origen: Contra Celsum* (3d ed.; Cambridge: Cambridge University Press, 1980), xxvi; Lona, *Die wahre Lehre des Kelsos*, 55.

He also has a set of historical objections. This Christianity only emerged recently, Celsus avers on several occasions (1.26; cf. 6.10; 8.12). Celsus does not have much time for Jews, but at least they have a history. The material covered in Origen's first book is mostly taken up with Celsus' use of what is probably a written Jewish text, an anti-gospel concerned to demonstrate that Jesus' claims to being the Son of God are unfounded (1.28–71), a criticism which Celsus makes his own (2.44). Jesus was no modest rabbi to start with, being convinced of his own deity (here Celsus differs from Porphyry), but the disciples invented even more extravagant claims on his behalf (2.13–20). Celsus makes it clear what he thinks Jesus ought to have done to make himself a successful Son of God. He also engages in some criticism of the book of Genesis, mocking the creation accounts and the primeval histories up to the episode of Joseph and Pharaoh (4.33–47). In the present, they undermine their claim to the truth through their internal divisions (3.10–12): Celsus seems particularly aware of the Marcionites,[87] even if he does consider there to be a *magna ecclesia* (5.59). They also squabble externally with Jews about various items of trivia (e.g., 3.1).

Celsus is no Dawkins or Hitchens, however, as a major plank in his attack is theological as well as philosophical.[88] According to the *Alethes Logos* it is impious to depict God as Moses does, as creating a weak man (4.40). God did not make anything mortal, only soul (4.54–61). God could not make man in his image because he does not have a form (6.63–64). Before the incarnation, did God not care (4.8)? A god just cannot be born from a mortal human being (3.41). Incarnation could only be a change for the worse (4.14).[89] God's concern to visit us reveals an anthropocentric sort of god (4.23, 28), and Celsus develops a lengthy argument to show that the world is by no means anthropocentric (4.74–99). No God or Son of God has ever descended (5.2). If Jesus' body had possessed a divine spirit, that body would have looked much more impressive (6.75–77). It is shameful to imagine that God defiled himself with mortal flesh and wandered around ignominiously on earth as Jesus did (7.13–15). It is not just that the resurrection did not happen; it could not have happened (2.57–58). God would not have received Jesus' spirit back once it had been defiled by flesh (6.72). All this physicality is nonsense, because God can only be known by the mind (7.36). God's desire for glory seems like a human projection (4.6). God's judgement with fire makes him a torturer (4.11) or a cook (5.14). It is blasphemous to imagine that there is a power opposed to God,

---

87   See for example the arguments directly specifically at Marcionites in 6.74; cf. 7.2.
88   Rightly emphasised in the section of Chadwick's introduction, "Celsus' Theology."
89   If it is not a real change, he says, it is a deception (4.14).

viz. the devil (4.42). Overall, Celsus has a highly developed sense that Christian claims are simply blasphemous claims about God: Τῷ δ' αἰσχρῷ καὶ κακῷ, κἂν πάντες ἄνθρωποι μαινόμενοι προλέγειν δοκῶσιν, ἀπιστητέον. Πῶς οὖν τὰ περὶ τοῦτον ὡς περὶ θεὸν πραχθέντα ἐστὶν ὅσια (7.14). The real truth for Celsus is that of the nameless First Being, who is neither mind nor intelligence (7.43, 45).

These considerations are every bit as concerning to Celsus as the fact that Christians are gullible, not following reason (1.9; 2.30),[90] and advocate blind faith (1.12–13), or that there are no good proofs that Jesus is the Son of God (2.47–48). Indeed, one might say that if Celsus had simply thought that Christianity was irrational and not susceptible to proof, he might have contented himself with the off-hand remarks on this subject that one finds in Epictetus, Galen, and Marcus Aurelius. Or if his primary concern was that Christians do not come from among the πεπαιδευμένοι, but rather from the dregs of society (where they also seek their converts), he might have merely adopted a mocking tone akin to that of Lucian. For Celsus, Christianity is much more dangerous than that. Though Celsus may occasionally laugh like Lucian (though he does not write half as well), Christianity in the *Alethes Logos* is really no joke. It is a menace.

## 7  Justin, Tatian, Theophilus of Antioch, Athenagoras, Pantaenus

One can add a further category of philosophers that serves as something of a counterweight to the foregoing observations. There were at least some philosophers whose favourable verdict on Christianity led to their conversions. Therefore the conditions these figures need to meet to be included here are (a) that they were converts from paganism and (b) that they can be regarded as πεπαιδευμένοι, having worn the *pallium* before their conversions. I will focus here on Justin and Tatian, simply mentioning the others like the drunk uses the lamppost – more for support than for illumination.

### 7.1  *Justin*
At the beginning of the *Dialogue with Trypho*, the narrator describes himself as wearing the philosophical garb and reports on his shopping trip for the best philosophical school before he finally settles on Platonism. When he goes to a field to contemplate, however, he encounters an old man who inspires in him a love for "the prophets and those who are friends of Christ" (*Dialogue with Trypho* 8.1), and this encounter with scripture leads to his conversion.

---

90  Cf. Celsus' God, who is ἀρρήτῳ τινὶ δυνάμει νοητός (7.45).

Justin gives a different emphasis in his own voice in the *Second Apology*: "I myself rejoiced in the teachings of Plato and listened to Christians being abused. But as I saw that they showed no fear in the face of death and of everything else usually thought fearful, I reflected that it was impossible that they were vicious and pleasure loving" (Καὶ γὰρ αὐτὸς ἐγώ, τοῖς Πλάτωνος χαίρων διδάγμασι, διαβαλλομένους ἀκούων Χριστιανούς, ὁρῶν δὲ ἀφόβους πρὸς θάνατον καὶ πάντα τὰ ἄλλα νομιζόμενα φοβερά, ἐνενόουν ἀδύνατον εἶναι ἐν κακίᾳ καὶ φιληδονίᾳ ὑπάρχειν αὐτούς, *2 Apology* 12.1). Justin's change of heart here is not quite his conversion, but in the following section of the *Second Apology* he implies that it was an important impulse in his turn to Christ. In the *Second Apology*, then, the focus in the conversion account is upon the fortitude of the Christians rather than on scripture directly, the reference to fearlessness at death probably specifically relating to martyrdom.[91] Justin is, either way, a prime example of a philosopher who observed roughly the same phenomena as Epictetus and Marcus Aurelius but came to quite different conclusions. Eusebius confirms the overall picture of Justin as a philosopher even after his conversion, describing Justin as "an ambassador for the divine word in philosophical dress" (ἐν φιλοσόφου σχήματι πρεσβεύων τὸν θεῖον λόγον, Eusebius, *Ecclesiastical History* 4.11.8).

### 7.2   Tatian

Tatian, a student of Justin best known for the *Diatessaron*, was born of pagan parents and, judging by his *Oration to the Greeks*, has some claim to be called a philosopher. He subsequently converted to Christianity, perhaps under the influence of Justin. He ends his *Oration* referring to himself with the epithet, ὁ κατὰ βαρβάρους φιλοσοφῶν, concluding: "All this, men of Greece, I have compiled for you – I, Tatian, a philosopher among the barbarians, born in the land of Assyrians, and educated first in your learning and secondly in what I profess to preach" (42.1). He draws a telling analogy, then, between his *paideia* in philosophy before conversion and his Christian *paideia* after it. His quotations from epic and tragedy and his allusions to the sweep of the philosophical tradition from the pre-Socratics go some way towards confirming Eusebius' judgement that he was very learned (4.16.7): "a man who in his former life philosophised in the learning of the Greeks, and who obtained no small glory in it, and has left behind abundant memorials in his writings."[92]

---

91  This is contested, but the reference to 'seeing' tilts the balance of probability towards events which Justin witnessed, which are more likely to be the deaths of martyrs.

92  Τατιανός, ἀνὴρ τὸν πρῶτον αὐτοῦ βίον σοφιστεύσας ἐν τοῖς Ἑλλήνων μαθήμασι καὶ δόξαν οὐ σμικρὰν ἐν αὐτοῖς ἀπενηνεγμένος πλεῖστά τε ἐν συγγράμμασιν αὐτοῦ καταλιπὼν μνημεῖα; it

## 7.3 Theophilus of Antioch[93]

Theophilus, Bishop of Antioch, who wrote an apology in three parts to the pagan Autolycus, is certainly a convert from paganism. He writes (*Autolycus* 1.14) of how he once himself did not believe in resurrection, but – rather like the narrator of the *Dialogue with Trypho* – encountered the scriptures and was convinced by them. The question of Theophilus' philosophical credentials is more difficult: although his writing is fairly basic in its level, he certainly cites an array of authorities, including Pythagoras, Protagoras, Plato, Diogenes, Zeno, Cleanthes, and Chrysippus,[94] though of course one might question how deeply he might have absorbed them.

## 7.4 Athenagoras

A further contender is the shadowy figure Athenagoras, author of the *Plea on Behalf of the Christians* in the late 170s during the co-regency of Marcus Aurelius and Commodus. There are four considerations here. The first line of evidence is far from secure, coming as it does in a fourteenth-century manuscript reporting the opinion of the fifth-century historian Philip of Side giving an account of the career of the second-century Athenagoras:

> Philip of Side says in his twenty-fourth book: Athenagoras was the first to head the school in Alexandria. He flourished at the time of Hadrian and Antoninus, to both of whom he addressed his *Plea on behalf of the Christians*. He became a Christian while he wore the philosopher's cloak and was at the head of the Academy. Even before Celsus he was anxious to write against the Christians. He read the sacred Scriptures in order to aim his shafts more accurately, but he was so powerfully seized by the Holy Spirit that like the great Paul he became a teacher rather than a persecutor of the faith which he was harassing. Philip says that Clement the writer of the *Stromata* was his disciple and that Pantaenus [MS. Clement] was the disciple of Clement. Pantaenus himself was also an Athenian philosopher, of the Pythagorean school. But Eusebius says the opposite: that Pantaenus was the teacher of Clement. (trans. Schoedel)[95]

---

is possible that the content of the *Oratio* is itself the source of Eusebius' judgement, in which case Eusebius would not constitute independent evidence.

93  On Theophilus, see R. Rogers, *Theophilus of Antioch: The Life and Thought of a Second-Century Bishop* (Oxford: Lexington Books, 2000).

94  For a list of authors referred to by Theophilus, see the index in R.M. Grant, ed., *Theophilus of Antioch: Ad Autolycum* (Oxford: Clarendon, 1970).

95  Cod. Bodl. Baroccianus 142, fol. 216 (PG vi.182). See the translation in W.R. Schoedel, *Athenagoras: Legatio and De Resurrectione* (Oxford: Clarendon, 1972), ix.

The blunders in the chronology and about the addressees at the beginning – the plea was addressed to Marcus Aurelius and Commodus – do not inspire confidence, nor does the stylised account of the damascene conversion. But there may be a kernel of truth in the depiction of Athenagoras as a philosopher. A connection with the Academy may be reinforced by Photius' statement that Boethus dedicated his volume *Difficult Questions in Plato* to an Athenagoras.[96]

The second line of evidence is the superscription to the *Legatio*: ΑΘΗΝΑΓΟ-ΡΟΥ ΑΘΗΝΑΙΟΥ ΦΙΛΟΣΟΦΟΥ ΧΡΙΣΤΙΑΝΟΥ ΠΡΕΣΒΕΙΑ ΠΕΡΙ ΧΡΙΣΤΙΑΝΩΝ, the *Plea on Behalf of the Christians*, by Athenagoras of Athens, the philosopher.[97]

Third, there is the content of the plea. The technical character of the *Legatio* speaks in favour of philosophical training. He seems indebted at certain points to Philo, in phraseology such as ἔνθεον πνεῦμα (*De Decalogo* 175/ Athenagoras, *Legatio* 7.3), which is only found before Athenagoras in Philo.[98] He also adopts some arguments that have parallels in pagan criticisms of Christianity, such as the ignobility of the pagan gods (*Legatio* 20.2–5), which, as we have seen, is paralleled in the other direction by Celsus. Similarly, just as some Jews and Christians are attacked by Celsus for allegorising the unallegorisable and producing interpretations even worse than the literal senses,[99] so also Athenagoras attacks (albeit in a corrupt passage) pagan theologians for theologising myths in a self-defeating way (*Legatio* 22.10).

Finally, albeit a very thin strand of evidence, it has been suggested by Jaap Mansfeld that the Pseudo-Aristotelean *De Melisso Xenophane Gorgia* refers to our Athenagoras, and while the similarities are tantalising, it is also possible that another Athenagoras is in view, or indeed that the passage is corrupt.[100]

Overall, the evidence for Athenagoras as a philosopher before his adherence to Christianity is suggestive, even if not overwhelming.

---

96   Photius, *Bibliotheca* 155; L.W. Barnard, *Athenagoras: A Study in Second Century Christian Apologetic* (Paris: Beauchesne, 1972), 16. It is not certain that the two Athenagorai are one and the same.
97   Barnard, *Athenagoras*, 16, sees this as a reliable testimony.
98   This passage has played a role in the debate over whether Athenagoras' origins lay in Athens or Alexandria, a debate which is not of relevance here. See D.I. Rankin, *Athenagoras: Philosopher and Theologian* (Farnham: Ashgate, 2009), 5–10.
99   *Contra Celsum* 4.50–51; cf. 6.29; 1.17; 4.38, 48–51, 87.
100  *MXG* 975b 13–19. See J. Mansfeld, "DE MELISSO XENOPHANE GORGIA: Pyrrhonizing Aristotelianism," *Rheinisches Museum für Philologie* 131 (1988): 239–76, 275.

## 7.5 Pantaenus[101]

Little is known of Pantaenus, and as a result he has been a convenient locus of speculation.[102] Eusebius states, however, that he was strongly influenced by Stoicism, with Eusebius making the point that he based his life on Stoic philosophy: ἀπὸ φιλοσόφου ἀγωγῆς τῶν καλουμένων Στωϊκῶν ὡρμημένον.[103]

In sum, despite the varying degrees of confidence that we can have about these different figures, we gain access here to another angle on philosophers and Christians in the second century. There are some complications, in that some of their contemporaries might have wondered whether these Christians had ever had the right to wear the *pallium*; on the other hand, for the Christians it seemed useful to emphasise conversion from the wisdom of this age to *philosophia Christi*. Nevertheless, if we exclude this part of the picture, we are in danger of getting only a partial (in both senses) account of second-century philosophers.

## 8  Conclusion

Finally, some synthetic thoughts. The results of this survey permit no neat, all-encompassing narrative. Some of the criticisms of Christians seen here are shared more widely, others are particular to the individual thinkers. Marcus Aurelius finds in Christian martyrdom a distasteful theatricality, as one might expect in someone as earnest as Marcus. Galen's criticisms of Jews and Christians as proponents of undemonstrated laws, for example, might be expected of one who places enormous weight on demonstration. Celsus' critique is not only unparalleled in its scale but is also notable as the response of a pious pagan anxious about the way in which the Christians might undermine both

---

101   See the helpful summary of what we do know about Pantaenus in A. van den Hoek, "Pantaenus," in *The Encyclopedia of Ancient History* (ed. R.S. Bagnall, K. Brodersen, C.B. Champion, A. Erskine, and S.R. Huebner; Oxford: Wiley Blackwell, 2012), 5030–31.

102   See for example G. Schenke Robinson, ed., *Berliner 'Koptische Buch' (P20915). Eine wiederhergestellte frühchristlich-theologische Abhandlung* (Louvain: Peeters, 2004), 2:xiv, noting that he frequently has anonymous works attributed to him.

103   Eusebius, *Ecclesiastical History* 5.10.1. The use of ὁρμάω in this context does not simply refer to "making a start in philosophy," as the parallel in Athenagoras, *Leg.* 2.3 makes clear. Cf. also Philodemus, *On Rhetoric* I, 357: "I pass over the fact that one could point to some with philosophical training who are guilty of, or accessory to, the crimes just mentioned" (ἐῶ γὰρ ὅτι καὶ ἀπὸ φιλοσοφίας ὡρμημένους ἔχοι ἂν ἐπιδεικνύειν τινὰς αἰτίους κα(ὶ συ)ναιτίους τῶν εἰρημένων).

*religio* towards the traditional gods and the appropriate attitude towards the emperor and the empire.

Moving beyond this sort of unsatisfactory *tot homines, tot sententiae* conclusion, some commonalities can also be discerned. Although it might be impossible to construct an all-encompassing narrative of these figures, one can perhaps tell three short stories.

The first of these is made up of the strand of authors who more or less ignore the Christians. There are second-century philosophers, such as Sextus Empiricus, who make no mention of Christians, either because they are not aware of them or because they have no reason to talk of them. But even Epictetus, Apuleius, Marcus Aurelius, and Galen are really not far from this category. In the cases of Epictetus and Marcus Aurelius, they make merely parenthetical remarks about Christians; in Marcus' case, the aside is usually in square brackets. If Apuleius does mock Christians, he does so very much less clearly and at considerably less length than does his contemporary Lucian. Again, even if Walzer could write a short, 100-page monograph entitled *Galen on Jews and Christians*, the evidence is really very slight, considering Galen's massive overall output; it is questionable whether one can really talk, as Walzer does, of Galen's "interest in Christian thought" or – with Labriolle – of Galen having "studied" Christians.[104]

The second group are those for whom Christianity is a threat. Here we see some continuation of what is found in the Pliny-Trajan correspondence, and a fuller discussion of those regarding Christianity as a threat would also have to take in the legislation of the period against Christians. Crescens fits into this category of those who want to bring Christians to trial, although we know nothing about him outside of Justin's response to his machinations, whether actual or potential. Celsus is the prime example of a philosopher who is genuinely concerned about the impact made by Christianity and so is not content merely to argue against its indifference to proof and irrationality, but argues that its understanding of God is blasphemous and – perhaps above all – that this is a seditious secret society which is dangerous.

The third group consists of those philosophers who not only come to see Christianity as a real option, but as an attractive and compelling one. Justin, Tatian, and others need to be factored into this discussion in order to gain a more variegated picture of philosophical responses to Christianity.

One tantalising final piece of evidence is instructive. According to Origen's *Contra Celsum* (IV 51), Numenius of Apamea gives in his work *Concerning the*

---

104  Walzer, *Galen on Jews and Christians*, 10; Labriolle, *La réaction païenne*, 94–97.

*Good* an allegorical interpretation of a narrative about Jesus, though without mentioning him by name.[105] We do not know which narrative it was, or even whether Origen was right to see it as coming from the Gospels, because Numenius' *Concerning the Good* is not extant. This is a sobering reminder of how the passages we have examined in this paper are mere fragments, like pieces of a jigsaw puzzle found underneath the sofa after the box with the other pieces has long been lost.[106]

---

105   Numenius, *Concerning the Good* (= fragment §10 in E. des Places, *Numénius: Fragments*) (Paris: Les Belles Lettres, 1973). See further M.J. Edwards, "Atticizing Moses? Numenius, the Fathers and the Jews," *VC* 44 (1990): 64–75.
106   I am grateful to the members of the highly stimulating and enjoyable seminar in Cambridge, organised by Prof. George van Kooten, for their feedback on the oral version of this paper. My colleague Dr. James Carleton Paget also provided invaluable comments on an earlier draft, for which I am extremely thankful.

# Epictetus' Views on Christians: A Closed Case Revisited

*Niko Huttunen*

The earliest Roman sources on Christians are dated to the beginning of the second century. Tacitus (*Annales* 15.44), Suetonius (*Nero* 16.2), and Pliny the Younger (*Epistulae ad Trajanum* 10.96) are the sources that are quoted time and again. Their contemporary, the Stoic Epictetus, has won less consideration. He never unambiguously speaks of Christians, but I am going to show that two passages actually refer to them (*Discourses* 2.9.19–21 and 4.7.6). Both instances are easily confused with Judaism, which has led some scholars astray. There are also philological difficulties that require profound consideration. I will show that Epictetus gives us quite a moderate assessment of Christians, in contrast to Tacitus, Suetonius, and Pliny the Younger. I suggest that this is due to the philosophical elements in Christian teachings.

Epictetus lived around 50–130 CE. He was born as a slave and was brought early on to serve in Rome in close contact with Nero's court.[1] Later he was freed, then banished from Rome during the reign of Domitian. Thereafter Epictetus founded a school in Nicopolis, today in Northern Greece, close to the Albanian border. As he became famous for his teaching, the school attracted students from the Roman well-to-do families. Among those students was Arrian of Nicomedia, who attended Epictetus' lectures for some years in the first decades of the second century. His notes are our primary source of Epictetus' teaching. Nicopolis is mentioned in the Epistle to Titus (3:12), though it is not clear whether there was a Christian community in Epictetus' lifetime. The city, however, was an important harbour on the route to Rome, and it surely did not avoid Christian influences.[2] We also know that Epictetus was in Rome during Nero's persecution of Christians.

Epictetus' neutral or even moderately positive view of Christians is quite interesting in comparison to Tacitus, Suetonius, and Pliny, who counted Chris-

---

1 For these contacts, see F. Millar, "Epictetus and the Imperial Court," *JRS* 55 (1965): 141–48. The following presentation of Epictetus' career and his *Discourses* is based on N. Huttunen, *Paul and Epictetus on Law: A Comparison* (LNTS 405; London: T&T Clark, 2009), 4–5.
2 For Nicopolis' character as a city, see for example J.D. Quinn, *The Letter to Titus: A New Translation with Notes and Commentary and an Introduction to Titus, I and II Timothy, the Pastoral Epistles* (AB 35; New York: Doubleday, 1990), 255.

tianity as being among the criminal superstitions. Scholars have often taken these three sources as representatives of the Roman view of Christians. For example, John Granger Cook analyses these three and some other Roman texts on Christians in his book *Roman Attitudes Toward the Christians: From Claudius to Hadrian*. The result is that the Roman picture of Christianity is nothing but negative:

> Probably the Roman intellectuals and governors like Tacitus and Pliny were so disgusted at the phenomenon of Christianity that they lacked the inclination to make any profound explorations into the nature of early Christian faith, morality, and ritual practice. What I have sought to do during this project is develop a sympathy for the Romans' shock when they had to deal with this 'other' – these Christians who were so difficult to conceive using the categories they were familiar with.[3]

Cook's profound study on the texts of Tacitus, Suetonius, and Pliny adds considerably to our understanding. However, it is an overestimation to understand their shock as an overall Roman view. One would get another picture when reading two of Epictetus' texts, *Discourses* 2.9.19–21 and 4.7.6. Cook passes over the latter briefly,[4] while he does not mention the former at all. His procedure is indicative of a more general tendency in scholarship on the subject. This scholarly negligence is surely due to Adolf Bonhöffer's classic *Epiktet und das Neue Testament*, which deals with parallel texts in depth but delivers only a short discussion on *Discourses* 4.7.6; furthermore, it passes over the other passage with superficial references.[5] Scholars routinely refer to Bonhöffer's classic text.[6]

A recent example of Bonhöffer's authority is A.A. Long's magnificent monograph on Epictetus. Long's subject is not Epictetus' relationship towards Christians, and it is understandable that he passes over the theme with brief remarks. Long supposes that Epictetus mentions Christians,[7] but he shares

---

3  J.G. Cook, *Roman Attitudes Toward the Christians: From Claudius to Hadrian* (WUNT 261; Tübingen: Mohr Siebeck, 2010), 2.
4  Cook, *Roman Attitudes Toward the Christians*, 173.
5  A. Bonhöffer, *Epiktet und das Neue Testament* (Religionsgeschichtliche Versuche und Vorarbeiten 10; Gießen: Verlag von Alfred Töpelmann (vormals J. Ricker), 1911), 41–44, 72, 273.
6  For the significance of Bonhöffer's view on the subsequent study, see J. Hershbell, "The Stoicism of Epictetus: Twentieth Century Perspectives," in ANRW II.36.3 (ed. W. Haase and H. Temporini; Berlin: Walter de Gruyter, 1989), 2150–63, 2161.
7  A.A. Long, *Epictetus: A Stoic and Socratic Guide to Life* (Oxford: Clarendon Press, 2002), 17, 110.

Bonhöffer's view of the very remote relationship between Epictetus' thinking and the New Testament: "Notwithstanding striking verbal parallels, there is no strong reason to think that one has directly influenced the other."[8] As we see here, the discussion on Epictetus' view of Christians is strongly steered by Bonhöffer even today.

Without questioning Bonhöffer's great merits, one should be more careful with his works. In a response to Rudolf Bultmann's article, in which he has questioned Epictetus' Stoic orthodoxy, Bonhöffer claims in an offended tone that his own scholarly life's work was dedicated to proving that Epictetus presents "the pure, the genuine and the coherent theory of the old Stoicism."[9] Here we see a tendency in Bonhöffer which is later questioned. Long points out that, despite the fact that Bonhöffer's works are "indispensable for close study of Epictetus relation to the Stoic tradition," "they tend to overemphasize his doctrinal orthodoxy."[10]

I claim that Bonhöffer's tendency also affects his assessment of the passages on Christians. The most eye-catching example is the word πάθος in its positive meaning (*Discourses* 2.9.20). I will return to this term below. At this moment, it is enough to note that the Stoics usually understood it in the negative sense. Bonhöffer generally claims that "Epictetus' conception of the essence and the origin of the πάθη is compeletely similar to the old and the genuine Stoicism."[11] Surprisingly, he does not discuss *Discourses* 2.9.20 in his lengthy chapter on the passions. I cannot avoid the impression that a profound discussion on Epictetus' references to the Christians would have contributed to ruining this rigid view of Stoic orthodoxy. As this view is relativised today, one can be open to a more relaxed assessment of Epictetus' relationship to early Christianity.

In his *Epiktet und das Neue Testament*, Bonhöffer shot down all attempts to find Christian influences in Epictetus' texts. His main object of attack was

---

8   Long, *Epictetus*, 35.
9   "Ich darf wolhl darauf hinweisen, daß meine wissenschaftliche Lebensarbeit hauptsächlich dem Nachweis gewidmet ist, daß wir dem kostbaren Vermächtnis, das uns Arrian von seinem Lehrer hinterlassen hat, im wesentlichen die reine, unverfälschte und konsequente Lehre der alten Stoa, deren ursprüngiche Zeugnisse uns fast ganz verloren gegangen sind, vor uns haben" (Bonhöffer, "Epiktet und das Neue Testament," ZNW 13 (1912): 281–92, 282; my English translation).
10  Long, *Epictetus*, 36.
11  "Epictets Ansicht über das Wesen und den Ursprung der πάθη entspricht vollständig den Anschauungen der Alten, echten Stoa" (Bonhöffer, *Epictet und die Stoa. Untersuchungen zur stoischen Philosophie* (Stuttgart: Verlag von Ferdinand Enke, 1890), 278; my English translation).

Theodor Zahn's inaugural speech as a vice-principal of the University of Erlangen.[12] In this speech, Zahn proposed that Epictetus had known the New Testament writings and embraced ideas from it "as long as they are not in contrast to his dogma."[13] Thus Zahn did not question Epictetus' philosophical orthodoxy. He emphasises that Epictetus differed from Christians on many points and that "he did not become a Christian, because he was a Stoic and wished to die as a Stoic." He was not even a friend of Christianity or Christians.[14] This was a moderate statement, but it was too much for Bonhöffer. Zahn claimed that Epictetus' views were not fully coherent, which is basically due to inconsistencies in old Stoic theory but is strengthened by non-Stoic influences.[15] Bonhöffer defends Epictetus' consistency and in a detailed analysis – partly based on an article by Franz Mörth,[16] who had already criticised Zahn – shoots down every sporadic parallel Zahn presented as proof of Christian influence on Epictetus.[17]

A few years after Bonhöffer's *Epiktet und das Neue Testament,* Douglas S. Sharp published his *Epictetus and the New Testament.* Sharp concluded that "it is doubtful whether Epictetus was acquainted with the New Testament." The linguistic similarities are mostly due to the fact that both are written in the *koine* of their time.[18] The case was closed, and Bonhöffer has become the

---

12  T. Zahn, *Der Stoiker Epiktet und sein Verhältnis zum Christentum. Rede beim Eintritt des Prorektorats der Königlich Bayerischen Friedrich-Alexanders-Universität Erlangen am 3. November 1894 gehalten* (Erlangen: Deichert'sche Verlagsbuchhandlung Nachf, 1895). Since the king of Bavaria was the honorary principal, whom Zahn blesses at the end of this speech, the office of the vice-principal meant in practice that he handled the tasks of the principal.

13  "Aber auch religiöse Ideen und Lebensregeln des Neuen Testaments konnten den Epiktet ansprechen und, soweit sie seinem Dogma nicht geradezu widersprachen, von ihm angeeignet warden" (Zahn, *Der Stoiker Epiktet,* 29; my English translation).

14  Zahn *Der Stoiker Epiktet,* 33–34.

15  Zahn *Der Stoiker Epiktet,* 10.

16  F. Mörth, "Epiktet und sein Verhältnis zum Christentum," in *Jahresbericht des mit hohem Ministerial-Erlaß vom 20. Jänner 1895, Z 29,755, mit dem Öffentlichkeitsrecht beliehenen fürstbischöflichen Gymnasiums am Seckauer Diözesan-Knabenseminar Carolinum-Augustineum in Graz am Schlusse des Schuljahres 1908/1909* (Graz: Selbstverlag des f.-b. Knabenseminars, 1909), 1–22.

17  Zahn, *Der Stoiker Epiktet,* 29–34; Mörth "Epiktet;" Bonhöffer, *Epiktet,* 30–42.

18  D.S. Sharp, *Epictetus and the New Testament* (London: Charles H. Kelly, 1914), 135, 137. One may also note that even a larger common background produces parallels, which at first sight are striking. A good example is Ζήτει καὶ εὑρήσεις (*Discourses* 4.1.51), which closely resembles ζητεῖτε καὶ εὑρήσετε (Matthew 7:7; Luke 11:9). Mörth ("Epiktet," 22) al-

main authority on the consensus since then. However, there is one caveat in Bonhöffer's profound work, which has yet to be investigated in detail: the two passages, *Discourses* 2.9.19–21 and 4.7.6, which more or less clearly speak of Christians. Quite surprisingly, they have been left without further consideration.

A close reading of these two passages will show against all doubt that they speak of Christians and that Epictetus knew something about Christians and their teachings. He even borrowed some expressions from them, which is the most interesting result for further study. As Epictetus cited Christian expressions, there may be more of them in the *Discourses*. This reopens a discussion that Bonhöffer and some others had closed a hundred years ago. Moreover, a close reading of these passages also shows that the Roman attitude towards Christians was not only hostile, but that there was room for a more relaxed assessments than what Tacitus, Suetonius, or Pliny had provided. It is possibly no coincidence that it is a philosopher in the end who loosens the discussion. This situation is certainly due to the philosophical components in Christian teachings. In what follows I analyse first *Discourses* 4.7.6, as it is the clearer case; then I proceed to *Discourses* 2.9.19–21, before arriving at a conclusion with suggestions for further study.

## 1  Galileans (*Discourses* 4.7.6)

In the beginning of *Discourses* 4.7, Epictetus speaks of children and lunatics who do not fear the tyrant, his guards, and their swords. Because of their lack of understanding, children and lunatics can be fearless before such threats (sections 1–5). From lunatics Epictetus proceeds to the Galileans, who are also fearless: "Therefore, if madness can produce this attitude of mind toward the things which have just been mentioned, and also habit, as with the Galileans, cannot reason and demonstration teach a man that God has made all things in the universe?" (εἶτα ὑπὸ μανίας μὲν δύναταί τις οὕτως διατεθῆναι πρὸς ταῦτα καὶ ὑπὸ ἔθους οἱ Γαλιλαῖοι· ὑπὸ λόγου δὲ καὶ ἀποδείξεως οὐδεὶς δύναται μαθεῖν ὅτι ὁ θεὸς πάντα πεποίηκεν τὰ ἐν τῷ κόσμῳ, *Discourses* 4.7.6; trans. W. A. Oldfather, LCL).

---

ready notes that even Plato uses a similar phrase. L. Willms (*Epiktets Diatribe* Über die Freiheit [4.1]. *Einleitung, Übersetzung, Kommentar.* Band 1–2 [Wissenschaftliche Kommentare zu Griechischen und lateinischen Schriftstellern; Heidelberg: Universitätverlag Winter, 2011], 263–65) sees numerous parallels for this saying in philosophical texts. Thus, on closer analysis this striking parallel does not provide any ground for the theory that Epictetus was influenced by the New Testament.

The reference to God as a creator is the beginning of an extensive argumentation that one can attain fearlessness through philosophical demonstration (sections 6–11). Children, lunatics, and Galileans are just a starting point for this argumentation; as they do not fear the tyrant, the guards, and the swords, the fear does not automatically follow from certain outer circumstances. Fear or fearlessness is rather up to the person who feels or does not feel the fear. Epictetus concludes that this fact makes it meaningful to seek philosophical reasons for fearlessness.

Thus Epictetus uses children, lunatics, and Galileans to introduce the audience to the philosophical discussion. They are not the center of his focus; therefore the reference to them is just a passing one. Does Epictetus really mean 'Christians' when he speaks of Galileans? Most scholars have held this identification as a self-evident fact. Bonhöffer is among them.[19] Martin Hengel, however, presented an alternative interpretation: the Galileans are Zealots. He referred to the fact that during the Jewish War Epictetus lived in Rome, where it was possible to learn the details of the war in Palestine. Hengel also notes that, according to Josephus, the Jewish resistance movement *sicarii* – which he lumps together with the Zealots – became very famous (*Jewish War* 7.409–421, 433–450).[20]

The German historian Eduard Meyer already tackled the hypothesis of the Galileans as Zealots in the beginning of the twentieth century. He denied it,

---

19 Bonhöffer *Epiktet*, 41–43. Similarly, for example, Zahn *Der Stoiker Epiktet*, 26–27; K. Hartmann, "Arrian und Epiktet," *Njahrb* 8 (1905): 248–75, 267; Mörth "Epiktet," 21; H. Karpp, "Christennamen," in RAC 2 (ed. T. Klauser et al.; Stuttgart: Anton Hiersemann, 1954), 1114–38, 1131; M. Spanneut, "Epiktet," in RAC V (ed. T. Klauser et al.; Stuttgart: Anton Hiersemann, 1962), 599–681, 628; J.N. Sevenster, "Education or Conversion: Epictetus and the Gospels," *NovT* 8 (1966): 247–62, 254–55; S. Benko, "Pagan Criticism of Christianity During the First Two Centuries A.D.," in ANRW II.23.2 (ed. W. Haase and H. Temporini; Berlin: Walter de Gruyter, 1980), 1055–118, 1077; Benko, *Pagan Rome and the Early Christians* (London: B.T. Batsford, 1985), 40; Hershbell "The Stoicism of Epictetus," 2161; T. Engberg-Pedersen, *Cosmology and Self in the Apostle Paul. The Material Spirit* (Oxford: Oxford University Press, 2010), 132–33.

20 M. Hengel, *Die Zeloten. Untersuchungen zur Jüdischen Freiheitsbewegung in der Zeit von Herodes I bis 70 n.Chr.* 2. (2d rev. ed.; AGJU 1; Leiden: E.J. Brill, 1976), 60–61. Hengel, however, makes a distinction between the *sicarii* and the Zealots in another place (*Die Zeloten*, 49). S. Applebaum ("The Zealots: the Case for Revaluation," *JRS* 61 [1971]: 155–70, 164) had identified Galileans with Zealots before Hengel. It is also unreliable to think that Galileans refer to some other resistance movement during the Jewish war (for such a hypothesis, see S. Zeitlin, "Who were the Galileans? New Light on Josephus' Activities in Galilee," *JQR* 64 [1974]:189–203).

as one cannot reliably explain how Epictetus could incidentally refer to a group that had been defeated several decades earlier. Meyer suggested that "Galileans" must refer to the Christians.[21] This is a reasonable suggestion, as the group must be known to the students being lectured to without further explication. Christians are the clearest candidate for such a group.

This being the case, some scholars have seen the words οἱ Γαλιλαῖοι as a later addition, since Epictetus must have seen the Christian grounds for fearlessness as being negative rather than as just a habit. Alternatively, the word "habit" is emended to some more negative term.[22] However, all the emendations of the text are highly hypothetical and unnecessary. The manuscript reading is understandable, and it does not appreciate Christians in such a way that one should doubt its non-Christian origin.[23] Syntactically (μέν – δέ) Christians are

---

21   E. Meyer, *Ursprung und Anfänge des Christentums in drei Bänden* III: Die Apostelgeschichte und die Anfänge des Christentums (Stuttgart: J.G. Cotta'sche Buchhandlung Nachfolger, 1923), 530 n. 1. There was also a quite unknown Jewish group called Galileans in the second century (Justin Martyr, *Dialogue with Trypho* 80; Eusebius, *Ecclesiastical History* 4.22.7). Though this group seems to be somewhat critical towards the state authorities (*mishnah Yadayim* 4:8), as Epictetus' fearless Galileans before the tyrant, it is still unreliable to assume that Epictetus would incidentally refer to this kind of minor group.

22   I. Schweighäuser (See sources: Epictetus [1799a–d/1800], 1799c, 913–915) and J. Barnes (*Logic and the Imperial Stoa* [Philosophia Antiqua: A Series of Studies on Ancient Philosophy 75; Leiden: Brill, 1997], 63 n. 157) have seen οἱ Γαλιλαῖοι as an emendation. Several scholars have been inclined to change the word ἔθους to a more negative one. See the textual apparatus in Schenkl's edition; K. Meiser, "Zu Epiktet IV 7,6," *Hermes* 45 (1910): 160; P. Corssen, "Zu Epiktet, Διατριβαί IV 7,6," *BphWS* 30 (1910): 832; A.J. Kronenberg, "Zu Epiktet IV 7,6," *BphWS* 30 (1910): 1623.

23   Cf. the account of Christ in Josephus' *Jewish Antiquities*, which is surely a Christian addition or – if Josephus himself wrote something about Jesus – fully rewritten by some Christian. The tone is unmistakably that of a Christian: "About this time there lived Jesus, a wise man, if indeed one ought to call him a man. For he was one who wrought surprising feats and was a teacher of such people as accept the truth gladly. He won over many Jews and many of the Greeks. He was the Messiah. When Pilate, upon hearing him accused by men of the highest standing amongst us had condemned him to be crucified, those who had at first come to love him did not give up their affection for him. On the third day he appeared to them restored to life, for the prophets of God had prophesied these and countless other marvelous things about him. And the tribe of the Christians, so called after him, has still to this day not disappeared" (Josephus, *Jewish Antiquities* 18.63–64; trans. L. H. Feldman, LCL). Ulrich Victor ("Das *Testimonium Flavianum*. Ein authentischer Text des Josephus," *NovT* 52 (2010): 72–82) has recently defended the authenticity of this passage. While he argues with certain success that the words "if indeed one ought to call

on the side of the lunatics against those whose fearlessness is based on reason and demonstration. Thus, Christians are as unphilosophical as lunatics. There is, however, a difference between the lunatics and the Christians: the latter are not mad, but rather habit is the apparent reason for their fearlessness.[24]

What, then, is the ἔθος, the habit? According to Troels Engberg-Pedersen, Epictetus perhaps "means that the Christians were brought up more or less blindly, that is, without 'reason and demonstration', to have their strange beliefs."[25] This is true, but one can be more precise. Zahn saw this clearly when he noted that "the habit to good – and the question is about this here – is something which Epictetus holds in no little reverence."[26] The word ἔθος and its cognate ἐθίζω are technical terms in Epictetus' philosophy.[27] Habit emerges in thinking and acting without elaborated consideration. Habits are developed from birth, and as they are strongly rooted, it is difficult to change them. Epictetus says, "In the course of years we have acquired the habit (εἰθίσμεθα) of doing the opposite of what we learn and have in use opinions which are the opposite of the correct ones" (*Discourses* 2.9.14; trans. W. A. Oldfather, LCL. Cf. 3.19.4–6).

To fight bad habits one can use contrary habits (*Discourses* 1.27.4–6), which are activated with short sentences or "canons" (κανόνες).[28] One should memorise them in order to have them at hand in practical situations; for example, "When death appears to be an evil, we must have ready at hand [the canons] 'It is a duty to avoid evils' and 'Death is an inevitable thing'" (*Discourses* 1.27.7; trans. W. A. Oldfather, LCL, revised). The short canons recall the deeper philosophical truths and thus help the person to maintain his or her philosophical character.

---

him a man" are a fixed *topos* in antiquity and that "the Messiah" should be understood as a proper name "Christ," he does not explain how a Jew would admit that prophets were speaking of Christ. This idea sounds too Christian to have come from Josephus' pen.

24  Zahn, *Der Stoiker Epiktet*, 27.
25  Engberg-Pedersen, *Cosmology and Self*, 133.
26  "Die Gewöhnung zum Guten – und um ein solches handelt es sich hier – schätzt Epiktet nicht gering" (Zahn, *Der Stoiker Epiktet*, 41 n. 27; my English translation).
27  It may be added that Epictetus also uses the word ἕξις as an equivalent of ἔθος. For habit in Epictetus, see B.L. Hijmans, Jr., ἌΣΚΗΣΙΣ. *Notes on Epictetus' Educational System* (WTS 2; Assen: Van Gorcum, 1959), 64–65; and Huttunen, *Paul and Epictetus*, 127–28.
28  For the canons in Epictetus, see R.J. Newman, "Cotidie Meditare: Theory and Practice of the Meditatio in Imperial Stoicism," in *Aufstieg und Niedergang der römischen Welt: Geschichte und Kultur Roms im Spiegel der neueren Forschung* II.36.3 (ed. W. Haase and H. Temporini; Berlin: Walter de Gruyter, 1989), 1473–1517, esp. 1496–1502.

As Epictetus speaks about the habit of the Galileans, he possibly presupposes that Christians had canons of their own. And they really had.[29] For example, the sentence "[n]either circumcision nor uncircumcision is anything; but a new creation is everything!" is called a canon by Paul (Galatians 6:15–16; NRSV; cf. 1 Corinthians 7:19).[30] Epictetus acknowledged that Christian canons are not pure madness, though they were surely strange beliefs to him. In Epictetus' ranking, Christian fearlessness is an admirable result derived from the wrong reasons. His words do not reflect the prejudices Tacitus or Suetonius expressed.

There is no reason to think that Epictetus would have known Christians or Christianity very deeply. However, he seems to know more than he says and to expect the same knowledge from his audience. Otherwise a passing reference could not be understandable. Zahn has rightly noted this point.[31] It becomes very clear that Epictetus and his audience had some contacts with Christianity when we turn our attention to the passage in *Discourses* 2.9.

## 2  Christians as Baptised Jews

In *Discourses* 2.9 Epictetus claims that a Stoic philosopher should not only speak of philosophy, but also do according to its doctrines.[32] He compares a Stoic to a Jew:

> (19) Why, then, do you call yourself a Stoic, why do you deceive the multitude, why do you being a Jew act the parts of Greeks? (20) Do you not see in what sense men are severally called Jew, Syrian, or Egyptian? For example, whenever we see a man halting between two faiths, we are in the habit of saying, "He is not Jew, he is only acting the part." But when he adopts the *pathos*[33] of the man who has been baptized and has made his choice, then he both is a Jew in fact and is also called one. (21) So we are also counterfeit "baptists," Jews in words, but in deeds something else,

---

29  For the use of the word κανών in Christian writings, see for example H.W. Beyer, "Κανών," in *TDNT* 3 (ed. Gerhard Kittel; trans. G. W. Bromiley; Grand Rapids, MI: Wm. B. Eerdmans, 1974), 596–602.

30  Fourth Maccabees says, in the good Stoic way, that vicious emotions (πάθη) are ruled by those, who "philosophise the whole canon of the philosophy" (πρός ὅλον τὸν τῆς φιλοσοφίας κανόνα φιλοσοφῶν) (4 Maccabees 7:21–22; my translation).

31  Zahn, *Der Stoiker Epiktet*, 27.

32  See also Bonhöffer, *Epictet und die Stoa*, 11–13; Long, *Epictetus*, 107–12.

33  Possible translations of this Greek word are discussed below.

not in sympathy with our own words,[34] far from applying the principles which we profess, yet priding ourselves upon them as being men who know them.

(19) τί οὖν Στωικὸν λέγεις σεαυτόν, τί ἐξαπατᾷς τοὺς πολλούς, τί ὑποκρίνῃ Ἰουδαῖος ὢν Ἕλληνας; (20) οὐχ ὁρᾷς, πῶς ἕκαστος λέγεται Ἰουδαῖος, πῶς Σύρος, πῶς Αἰγύπτιος; καὶ ὅταν τινὰ ἐπαμφοτερίζοντα ἴδωμεν, εἰώθαμεν λέγειν 'οὐκ ἔστιν Ἰουδαῖος, ἀλλ' ὑποκρίνεται'. ὅταν δ' ἀναλάβῃ τὸ πάθος τὸ τοῦ βεβαμμένου καὶ ᾑρημένου, τότε καὶ ἔστι τῷ ὄντι καὶ καλεῖται Ἰουδαῖος. (21) οὕτως καὶ ἡμεῖς παραβαπτισταί, λόγῳ μὲν Ἰουδαῖοι, ἔργῳ δ' ἄλλο τι, ἀσυμπαθεῖς πρὸς τὸν λόγον, μακρὰν ἀπὸ τοῦ χρῆσθαι τούτοις ἃ λέγομεν, ἐφ' οἷς ὡς εἰδότες αὐτὰ ἐπαιρόμεθα. (*Discourses* 2.9.19–21; trans. W. A. Oldfather, LCL, slightly revised)

Epictetus speaks of two kinds of Jews. First, there are Jews whose deeds do not follow their words. Second, there are real Jews whose deeds follow their words after baptism and choice. I claim that the latter group actually refers to Christians. In order to demonstrate this, I first go through some text-critical problems and then proceed to a close reading of the text.

The text-critical problems are not due to the manuscript, but rather to the emendations. The metaphoric use of the Jews is somewhat confusing in the manuscript text. In section 19 the basic identity is that of a Jew who does not practice. In section 20, however, there is a non-Jew who is playing the part of a Jew. Finally, in section 21 Epictetus speaks of persons who are Jews with respect to their words while they are non-Jews with respect to their deeds. So the question is: Did Epictetus deliver a metaphor in which the basic identity is that of a Jew or that of a non-Jew?

Section 21 can be seen in either way. Thus the real tension is between sections 19 and 20. An editor of Epictetus' *Discourses*, Heinrich Schenkl, solved this tension with an emendation in section 19.[35] Instead of reading with the manuscript that "you" are a Jew acting the part of Greeks (Ἰουδαῖος ὢν Ἕλληνας), he emended the text to say that "you" are a Greek acting the part of a Jew (Ἰουδαῖον ὢν Ἕλλην). Schenkl's emendation was then accepted by W. A. Oldfather in his edition, published in the Loeb Classical Library (1925–1928, with several reprints).

According to the emended text, Epictetus is speaking of Greeks who in some respect play the part of Jews, but who should become Jews in every respect. Scholars reading the emended text have usually presented it as a ref-

---

34   An alternative translation for the 'words' is 'reason', but the context prefers the former.
35   For the earlier emendations, see Schenkl's text critical notes.

erence to the Gentile God-fearers who are assumed to become proselytes.[36] This had created the odd feature that the conversion to Judaism was based on proselyte baptism, without a word about circumcision. Scholars have been at pains to explain this, either by finding a covert reference to circumcision or claiming that there were uncircumcised proselytes.[37] The problem, however, is not in the manuscript text, but rather in Schenkl's and Oldfather's editions.

The manuscript reading is admittedly difficult but nevertheless understandable. It is clear that the Jew is a metaphor for the Stoic. As Epictetus assumes that his audience consists of Stoics, the basic identity in the metaphor is that of "being a Jew" (section 19). This is Epictetus' own understanding. As these "Jews" are non-practicing ones, they deceive the multitude (οἱ πολλοί). In section 20 Epictetus presents the understanding of the multitude: when words and deeds are in tension with each other, the common people base their understanding on deeds and, consequently, see the basic identity as that of a non-Jew (section 20). In section 21, Epictetus admits that a Jew becomes a real Jew when his or her deeds are concomitant with Jewish words.

The manuscript text does not speak of non-Jews becoming Jews. Therefore the common view that Epictetus is speaking of proselytes is wrong. Epictetus is speaking of two kinds of Jews. The manuscript provides a situation where Jews who are not following their faith are supposed to make a change in their conduct after baptism and choice. I claim that the baptised Jews are actually Christians. The word βεβαμμένου is in the perfect tense, denoting "a completed action the effects of which still continue in the present."[38] The perfect tense rules out renewed purification rites and indicates a single baptism which has an ongoing effect.[39] As Epictetus is not speaking of non-Jews becoming Jews,

---

36    See, for example J.G. Gager, *The Origins of Anti-Semitism: Attitudes Toward Judaism in Pagan and Christian Antiquity* (New York: Oxford University Press, 1983), 77.

37    J. Ysebaert (*Greek Baptismal Terminology: Its Origins and Early Development* [Græcitas Christianorum Primæva 1; Nijmegen: Dekker & van de Vegt N.V., 1962], 20 n. 2) proposes that *pathos* denotes the circumcision and Sharp (*Epictetus*, 134–35) that the participle ᾑρημένου means that. Conversion without circumcision is proposed by N. McEleney ("Conversion, Circumcision and the Law," *NTS* 20 (1974): 319–41, 332) but rejected by J. Nolland ("Uncircumcised Proselytes?" *JSJ* 12 (1981): 173–94; 179–82).

38    H.W. Smyth, *Greek Grammar* (Harvard: Harvard University Press, 1984), 434 (§ 1945). This is the basic meaning of the perfect tense. Smyth also lists other meanings, but the context of Epictetus' passage does not indicate any of them. It is safest and most natural to keep the basic meaning here.

39    On the purification rites, see for example J. Thomas, "Baptistes," in *RAC* I (ed. T. Klauser et al.; Stuttgart: Anton Hiersemann, 1950), 1167–1172; E.P. Sanders, *Judaism: Practice and Belief 63 BCE – 66 CE* (London: SCM Press, 1992), 222–30.

there is no question of a proselyte baptism. One cannot avoid the thought that he is referring to Christian baptism.

However, there is not only one baptism. In section 21 Epictetus says, "we are also counterfeit 'baptists (παραβαπτισταί)', Jews in words, but in deeds something else" (trans. Oldfather, LCL). As there is no mention of baptists earlier, we should assume that the counterfeit baptists are negative counterparts for the Jews who have adopted the πάθος of the baptised person. This comparison also presumes that the word βαπτιστής means a baptised person. Although we usually tend to think that this word denotes the person who baptises in contrast to the baptised one, this kind of differentiation is not necessary. The word can also denote persons who practice self-immersion.[40] In theory, it could denote both the one who takes the proselyte baptism and the one who practices the repeated ablutions of mainstream Judaism (see, e.g., Leviticus 15; Numbers 19). The latter is the probable alternative, as the passage by no means refers to the proselyte baptism.

The prefix παρα- denotes that there is something wrong in these baptisms. The counterfeit baptists, so to say, "misbaptise" and, thus, their baptism is somehow invalid.[41] This seems to reflect disputes over baptism: all the Jews have invalid baptisms (section 21), while real Jews have a valid baptism (section 20). As the valid baptism is the Christian baptism, Epictetus reproduces the Christian and anti-Jewish view. Justin Martyr makes plain that Christians do not accept Jewish ablutions but prefer the Christian baptism (*Dialogue with Trypho* 14.1; 19.2). There is something similar going on in Epictetus' metaphorical contrast between the counterfeit Jews and the real Jews.[42] Epictetus' words for Christians, who are the real Jews, undoubtedly reflect a Christian self-understanding. This self-understanding is seen in the New Testament (Romans 9:6–8), not to speak of later Christian literature.[43]

---

40   See the names of certain Jewish sects; K. Rudolph, "The Baptist Sects," in *The Cambridge History of Judaism* 3 (ed. W. Horbury, W.D. Davies, and J. Sturdy; Cambridge: Cambridge University Press, 1999), 471–500).

41   This is the earliest occurrence of the word παραβαπτιστής. Later we encounter it in the church fathers, who use it to refer to the persons who commit schismatic baptisms; G.H.W. Lampe, *A Patristic Greek Lexicon* (Oxford: Clarendon Press, 1961): παραβαπτιστής.

42   Rudolph ("The Baptist Sects," 482) speaks of a rivalry between Christian and proselyte baptism.

43   L.H. Feldman, *Jew and Gentile in the Ancient World: Attitudes and Interactions From Alexander to Justinian* (Princeton: Princeton University Press, 1993), 196–200; S.G. Wilson, *Related Strangers: Jews and Christians 70–170 C.E.* (Minneapolis: Fortress Press, 1995): 295–96.

## 3 Loan Words

I have already mentioned that the word πάθος is one that instantly catches the eye of the one who knows Epictetus' philosophy or Stoic philosophy in general. In Stoic philosophy it denotes the morally questionable passions. Epictetus also uses it in this negative sense – except here.[44] Keeping this general background in mind, it is odd that Epictetus makes a moral example of a Jew with the πάθος. One can suppose that πάθος is a loan word from some source.

Epictetus' use of a loan word is visible in the fact that it creates tensions in the passage. The πάθος is qualified as the πάθος of the person who is baptised and who has made the choice. This expression assumes that the person has the πάθος after the baptism and the choice. Surprisingly, Epictetus adds that a person should also adopt the πάθος that he or she has already received as a baptised person and as a person who has made the choice. The baptism and the choice, which qualify the πάθος, do not fit with the requirement to adopt the πάθος.

The πάθος acquired through baptism and choice is certainly considered too ritualistic by Epictetus, who tends to prefer rational operations. For example, it is not enough to attend the Eleusinian mysteries. He says that one should also understand "that all these things were established by men of old time for the purpose of education and for the amendment of our life" (*Discourses* 3.21.15; trans. W. A. Oldfather, LCL).[45] A similar moral emphasis is visible when he speaks about baptism. One does not get the πάθος through the ritual of baptism, but through conscious adoption. Thus the baptism and the choice have lost their significance in Epictetus' thinking. Therefore I am inclined to suppose that the Greek expression τὸ πάθος τὸ τοῦ βεβαμμένου καὶ ᾑρημένου is best understood as a loan expression. The word πάθος has a deviant meaning here; βάπτω and the perfect tense of ᾑρημένου are *hapax legomena* in the Epictetan

---

44   Other occurrences include: *Discourses* 1.4.26; 1.27.10; 2.18.11; 3.1.8; 3.2.3 (two times); 4.1.57; 4.8.28; fr. 20. For the Stoic definition of πάθος, see M. Forschner, *Die stoische Ethik. Über den Zusammenhang von Natur-, Sprach- und Moralphilosophie im altstoischen System* (Darmstadt: Wissenschaftliche Buchgesellschaft, 1995), 114–23; and T. Brennan, "The Old Stoic Theory of Emotions," in *The Emotions in Hellenistic Philosophy* (ed. T. Engberg-Pedersen and J. Sihvola; The New Synthese Historical Library 46; Dordrecht: Kluwer Academic Publishers, 1998), 21–70, esp. 21–39. Bonhöffer (*Epictet und die Stoa*, 276–84) has analysed Epictetus' use of the Stoic philosophy on πάθος rather than the use of the word itself.

45   H.-J. Klauck, *The Religious Context of Early Christianity: A Guide to Graeco-Roman Religions* (London: T&T Clark, 2003), 103–05.

corpus. The other expression related to the baptism, the substantive "counterfeit baptist" (παραβαπτιστής), is rare in Greek. It should also be counted among the loan expressions.

Unfortunately, we cannot show any exact source for these loan words. Generally speaking, they fit well within the Christian usage. The word βαπτιστής and its derivates are philologically a Christian phenomenon, as they occur only in Christian texts, with two exceptions. Those two are Epictetus and Josephus. In Epictetus it seems to be a Christian loan word, and Josephus uses it when speaking of "John called the Baptist" (*Jewish Antiquities* 18.116). Thus the word 'baptist' occurs even in Josephus' usage in a theme closely related to the Christians.

When it comes to choice, one can note that Justin Martyr speaks of it in the context of baptism. It is possible that Justin is dependent on earlier tradition, which also influenced Epictetus, who was older than Justin. According to Justin, the converts are baptised so that they become children of free choice (προαιρέσεως) and knowledge. They have chosen (ἑλομένῳ) the rebirth (*First Apology* 61.10.). Justin speaks of Christ's πάθος, meaning his suffering (e.g., *Dialogue with Trypho* 74.3; 97.3), but not in the context of a baptised Christian. In this respect, better analogies are found in the epistles of Ignatius of Antioch, a contemporary of Epictetus.

For Ignatius the πάθος is an important concept, and its root is in Christ's πάθος – that is, Christ's suffering.[46] Christ's πάθος is the constituent for the Christian communities (see, e.g., the introductory salutations in Ignatius, *To the Ephesians* and *To the Trallians*). It also ensures the effect of baptism, as Christ was baptised so that he could cleanse water through his suffering (Ignatius, *To the Ephesians* 18.2).[47] Ignatius also speaks of choice and πάθος in the same context. He says that Christians should freely choose (αὐθαιρέτως) death and thus join in Christ's suffering (Ignatius, *To the Magnesians* 5.2). Ignatius presents no clear source for Epictetus' loan words. However, it helps us to reconstruct the enigmatic meaning of the πάθος in Epictetus' text. Epictetus may refer to Christians who are ready for suffering because of their beliefs. This interpretation fits in well with what Epictetus says of the Galileans' fearlessness in the face of violence.

---

[46] W. Bauer and H. Paulsen, *Die Briefe des Ignatius von Antiochia und der Polykarpbrief* (Die Apostolischen Väter II; Handbuch zum Neuen Testament 18; Tübingen: J.C.B. Mohr (Paul Siebeck), 1985), 21; W.R. Schoedel, *Ignatius of Antioch: A Commentary on the Letters of Ignatius Of Antioch* (Hermeneia; Philadelphia: Fortress Press, 1985), 85–86.

[47] Bauer and Paulsen, *Die Briefe des Ignatius*, 42.

## 4 Conclusions and Further Paths for Study

*Discourses* 4.7.6 shows quite clearly that Epictetus knew Christians and their use of canons in habituation. The passage on Jews and real Jews (*Discourses* 2.9.19–21) utilises Christian views. Epictetus even borrows expressions from some unknown Christian source, whether textual or not. What is interesting in these two passages is the fact that Epictetus mentions Christians in passing. Granted that these passages do not betray any interest in Christianity *per se*, but they do betray a self-evident knowledge of Christians, even among the audience. Epictetus does not explain who the Christians are or what their beliefs are. He seems to expect that his audience knows enough to understand his points. He even expects that the audience knows the Christian suprasessionist theology, which proclaims Christians as the real heirs of Judaism. Thus the passing references to Christians indicate a more profound knowledge of Christians.

This fact reopens the discussion of Epictetus' relationship to Christians, which Adolf Bonhöffer closed over a century ago. The discussion, however, should be framed anew. Bonhöffer is right when he supposes that Epictetus would not have supplemented his philosophical system with Christian thought.[48] His *Discourses*, however, shows that Epictetus used different motifs from everyday life to illustrate his Stoic philosophy. Christians were presented as examples of fearless people whose words and deeds were in harmony. As Epictetus even uses some expressions from Christian sources, one can legitimately ask whether there might be even more in the *Discourses*. The case closed by Bonhöffer should be opened again, but in a reframed version.

First, it is unnecessary to limit the study to Epictetus' relationship with the New Testament. There is much more early Christian literature, which is relevant for the comparison. Epictetus' πάθος has a good equivalent in Ignatius' epistles. Second, after Mörth's, Bonhöffer's, and Sharp's evaluations, one should not simply pick up parallels and make claims of dependences in a parallelomanic way. This was Zahn's deficiency. In many cases the similarities can be explained with reference to a common cultural and linguistic background, without forgetting the philosophical elements in Christian literature. On the other hand, the fact that Epictetus cites Christian expressions increases the probability that some similarities are due to Epictetus' contact with Christians.

In order not to fall into the trap of parallelomania, one should concentrate on those Epictetan passages that include a special hint – for example, that of

---

48  Bonhöffer, *Epiktet*, 72–81.

quietly waiting for the cross in *Discourses* 2.2.19–20. In that context, Epictetus blames those who incite the judges in court. This procedure will ruin the case. On the other hand, if one likes and wants to provoke the judges, why not keep quiet? "Why do you mount the platform at all, why answer the summons? For if you wish to be crucified, wait and the cross will come" (εἰ γὰρ σταυρωθῆναι θέλεις, ἔκδεξαι καὶ ἥξει ὁ σταυρός). There are two points here which attract interest. First, one should wait for the cross without answering the summons, like Jesus, who did not "answer, not even to a single charge, so that the governor was greatly amazed" (Matthew 27:14). Second, the students were from well-to-do families, presumably Roman citizens who were practically never punished with the cross.[49] To be sentenced to death on the cross is just a theoretical or symbolic idea for them. Does Epictetus hint to Jesus as an example, as he openly refers to Socrates' example just before the reference to the cross? A further analysis of this and possibly other passages may show whether or not one can find more contacts between Epictetus and early Christians, in addition to *Discourses* 2.9.19–21 and 4.7.6.

John Granger Cook tried to develop sympathy for the Romans' shock in the face of the otherness of Christianity. His profound and excellent book tells us how Tacitus, Suetonius, and Pliny beheld Christians with disgust. However, Epictetus shows that the Romans did not only feel pure disgust when observing Christians. While Pliny thought that Christianity was madness (*amentia*, *Epistulae ad Trajanum* 10.96.4), Epictetus held a different view. Epictetus thought that Christians and madmen had similarly inadequate philosophical grounds for fearlessness, but he did not lump these groups together. He admits that the Galileans bravely attained virtuous conduct through habituation. In this respect, Christians are braver than the common people, who are not trained for a fearless encounter with threats. Thus Epictetus' statement is quite a laudable one.

This raises the question of the relationship between early Christian religion and ancient philosophy. In a way, Epictetus counted Christians as above-average people, close to the category of philosophy. Christians are not madmen, but they are not fully philosophers either. They do not belong to the multitude, but rather to the Jews who practice what they preach and who can be compared to real Stoics with their blameless conduct. That Epictetus sees Christians in proximity to philosophy may be a mirror effect of the philosophical elements in Christianity. Christians had been acquainted with philosoph-

---

49   On the rare exceptions, see M. Hengel, *Crucifixion in the Ancient World and the Folly of the Message of the Cross* (London: SCM Press, 1977), 39–45.

ical themes since Paul,[50] and in the second century there are clear examples of Christian philosophers, Justin Martyr being the main one.[51] There are also other examples of moderate accounts of Christians among the pagan philosophers during the late second century.[52] It is possible that the philosophical elements in Christian teachings induced different philosophical assessments due to the shock of otherness, as experienced by Tacitus, Suetonius, and Pliny. Epictetus is the earliest representative of the moderate view.

---

50   For Paul and philosophy, see for example A.J. Malherbe, *Paul and the Popular Philosophers* (Minneapolis: Fortress Press, 1989); T. Engberg-Pedersen, *Paul and the Stoics* (Louisville: Westminster John Knox Press, 2000); and Engberg-Pedersen, *Cosmology and Self*; G.H. van Kooten, *Paul's Anthropology in Context: The Image of God, Assimilation to God, and Tripartite Man in Ancient Judaism, Ancient Philosphy and Early Christianity* (Wissenschaftliche Untersuchungen zum Neuen Testament 232; Tübingen: Mohr Siebeck, 2008); E. Wasserman, *The Death of the Soul in Romans 7. Sin, Death, and the Law in Light of Hellenistic Moral Psychology* (Wissenschaftliche Untersuchungen zum Neuen Testament 2. Reihe 256; Tübingen: Mohr Siebeck, 2008); Huttunen, *Paul and Epictetus*; R.M. Thorsteinsson, *Roman Christianity and Roman Stoicism: A Comparative Study of Ancient Morality* (Oxford: Oxford University Press, 2010).

51   On Justin's Christian philosophy, see Thorsteinsson, "By Philosophy Alone: Reassessing Justin's Christianity and His Turn from Platonism," *Early Christianity* 3 (2012): 492–517. See also Simon Gathercole's contribution to this volume.

52   Huttunen, "In the Category of Philosophy? Christians in Early pagan Accounts," in *Others and the Construction of Early Christian Identities* (ed. Raimo Hakola, Nina Nikki, and Ulla Tervahauta; Publications of the Finnish Exegetical Society 106; Helsinki, 2013), 239–81.

# Plotinus, Origenes, and Ammonius on the 'King'

*Harold Tarrant*

1    Introduction

In the early Roman Empire the theology of Platonist philosophers became increasingly concerned with a number of Platonic texts that appeared to offer some hope of settling debate over the kind of god(s) that Plato had postulated. Most of these seemingly authoritative texts were drawn from what we refer to as the 'middle' and 'late' dialogues, sometimes but not always considered in context. Small snippets of relevant texts could be quoted for a variety of purposes, not least in order to underline the erudition, authority, and perhaps orthodoxy of the teacher himself. In this regard it had much in common with emerging early Christian theology, with which it shared some interesting traits. These traits enabled some of the early Christian writers to find a surprising pre-Christian ally in Plato, while the similarities sharpened the need felt by others, both Christians and Platonists alike, to distance themselves from their rivals.

The particular problem of Plato's dialogues was that that they did not, in any straightforward manner, declare Plato's beliefs; sometimes these seemed to emerge in question-and-answer materials, while at other times they appeared in myth, or when 'Socrates' adopted some unusual voice in response to a given source of inspiration. In all of these cases, hermeneutic disputes could easily arise. Since some seemed to have felt a deep need to penetrate to the true depths of Plato's system and to require some lead from him concerning what was really important in the debated passages, material from the *Seventh*, *Second*, and *Sixth Epistles* seemed to offer the direct insights into Plato's mind and into the reasons why the dialogues did not disclose the theological heart of his system more openly.

In this paper I shall concentrate on Platonist authors of the third century CE and try to respond to a number of ongoing problems:

1. How is it that Plotinus, regarding the interpretation of the hypotheses of the *Parmenides* and the esoteric passage of the spurious *Epistle II*, can represent himself as a simple follower of Plato, when he would today normally be regarded as highly innovative?

2. How is it that Origenes the Platonist (as opposed to the prolific Christian author of that name)[1] seems to have become a regular part of the exegetical tradition of the *Parmenides* when he normally did not write, and when the titles of the two known exceptions do not suggest any relation to that dialogue?
3. Why did Proclus expect Origenes to have learned enough to avoid his 'errors' of interpretation from Ammonius Saccas, with whom he studied alongside Plotinus? Did Proclus think that Plotinus' interpretation of Plato also went back to studies in Alexandria with Ammonius?

In trying to answer these problems, I hope to be able to offer some insight into the authorship of the anonymous commentary on Plato's *Parmenides*, once preserved in a Turin palimpsest, though of course without settling this question.

## 2 The Works of Origenes

It is probable that most of our information about Origenes derives from Porphyry and that his contributions to Platonic exegesis came to us through Porphyry's lost commentaries on Plato's dialogues. He had studied under Ammonius with Plotinus and was known to Porphyry's original teacher Longinus as the author of a treatise on *daimones*; it is from this treatise that his interpretation of the Atlantis story as a war between *daimones* (= fragment 12) is likely to have been derived. Of the thirteen named references to Origenes in Proclus, twelve occur in the first book of the *In Timaeum*, and they all concern what precedes Timaeus' monologue. The details of material unrelated to the Atlantis story relate to matters of documented controversy between Longinus and Origenes (1.31.18–27; 1.59.31–60.4; 1.63.24–64.7; 1.68.3–15), which is shown by the third of these passages to have been at least partly oral. Porphyry him-

---

1 The fragments of Origenes were collected in a monograph by Karl-Otto Weber, *Origenes der Neuplatoniker: Versuch einer Interpretation* (München: Beck, 1962 = *Zetemata* 27). The fragment numbers below refer to this edition. Also of importance is the treatment of Origenes' first principle and the commentary tradition in H.-D. Saffrey and L.G. Westerink, eds., Proclus: *Théologie Platonicienne*, tome ii (Paris: Les Belles Lettres, 1974), x–xx. While it is methodologically correct to separate this Origenes from the Christian, it is not certain that they are distinct.

self (*Vita Plotini* 3 = Origenes, fragment 2)[2] knew of a later treatise with the title *That Only the King Is Creator*, written under Gallienus (253–68), and there is little doubt that this is behind the only other passage where Proclus names Origenes, namely *Theologia Platonica* 2.4.31.4–22 (= Origenes fragment 7):[3]

> Through this I believe that it has been made obvious that the One is the origin and first cause of all and that all else is second (δεύτερα) to the One. I personally am surprised at all other interpreters of Plato who granted the kingdom of intellect (τὴν νοερὰν βασιλείαν) among beings, but failed to revere the ineffable transcendence of the One (τὴν ... τοῦ ἑνὸς ἄρρητον ὑπεροχὴν) and its subsistence beyond the universe (τῶν ὅλων ἐκβεβηκυῖαν ὕπαρξιν), and particularly at Origenes who shared the same education as Plotinus (τὸν τῷ Πλωτίνῳ τῆς αὐτῆς μετασχόντα παιδείας). For he too ends up with Intellect and the very first Being, and he lets go of the One that is over-and-above all Intellect and the whole of Being. And if he means that it is superior to all cognition, all reasoning, and all perception (ὡς κρεῖττον ἀπάσης γνώσεως καὶ παντὸς λόγου καὶ πάσης ἐπιβολῆς, cf. *Parmenides* 142a3–6), then we should not say that he is out of tune with Plato or with the nature of reality. Whereas if he means that the One is entirely without foundation or substance (παντελῶς ἀνύπαρκτον τὸ ἓν καὶ ἀνυπόστατον), that the supreme good is Intellect (τὸ ἄριστον ὁ νοῦς), and that the first Being and the first One are the same (ταὐτόν ἐστι τὸ πρώτως ὂν καὶ τὸ πρώτως ἕν), we should not agree with him on this, nor would Plato accept him among the number of his disciples.

---

2  "Herennius first contravened the agreement (sc. not to disclose their teacher Ammonius' doctrine), Origenes followed Herennius' lead, but he wrote nothing other than the treatise *On Daimones* and under Galienus *That the King alone is Creator*": Ἑρεννίου δὲ πρώτου τὰς συνθήκας παραβάντος, Ὠριγένης μὲν ἠκολούθει τῷ φθάσαντι Ἑρεννίῳ. Ἔγραψε δὲ οὐδὲν πλὴν τὸ «Περὶ τῶν δαιμόνων» σύγγραμμα καὶ ἐπὶ Γαλιήνου «Ὅτι μόνος ποιητὴς ὁ βασιλεύς».

3  Since the names of interpreters are not routinely mentioned by Proclus in his later commentaries, the absence of any explicit mention of Origenes in the *Parmenides* commentary is much less surprising than the fact that he disappears in the *Timaeus* commentary before the cosmology is reached; given the fact that the *Theology* is also a commentary-style work, it is somewhat surprising that he is mentioned here at all. Allusions to Origenes are found by the OCT editors at four points in Book VI of the *in Parmenidem* and at book VII 515.4. Dillon (in the introduction to Book 1 of Glenn R. Morrow and John M. Dillon (trans.), *Proclus' Commentary on Plato's Parmenides*, Princeton: Princeton University Press, 1987) suspected Origenes' influence at Book I 635–8, but what is said there could probably apply to several interpreters.

Proclus here announces that he is surprised by various Platonic interpreters who "have freely admitted the kingdom of intellect among things that are, but have not revered the ineffable transcendence of the One and its subsistence beyond the universe," but he is particularly surprised at Origenes, who had shared the same education as Plotinus, obviously referring to their status as pupils of Ammonius Saccas at Alexandria. The term βασιλεία seems to make allusion to Origenes' treatise *That Only the King Is Creator*. According to Proclus, whom we shall suppose to be following Porphyry, "even this man himself ends up with intellect and the very first being (καὶ γὰρ αὖ καὶ αὐτὸς εἰς τὸν νοῦν τελευτᾷ καὶ τὸ πρώτιστον ὄν), and rejects the One that is over and above all Intellect and the whole of Being."

## 3    Education with Ammonius

In what sense should Origenes' education with Ammonius have prepared him for the rigid separation of a transcendent One from a level below this belonging to Intellect? Was Ammonius supposed to have prepared him for a metaphysical doctrine (some variation on the three Plotinian hypostases), or did he rather prepare him for a particular interpretation of Plato? Proclus' response to what he fears is Origenes' position directly concerns the interpretation of Plato, and he takes first *Republic* VI 508b–509c (mentioning particularly the sun-King, 32.7), then *Sophist* 243d–250d, then various passages from the *Philebus* before concluding with his own target dialogue, the *Parmenides*, primarily the first and second hypotheses. Plato's authority is clearly crucial, though this does not entail that Proclus' quarrel with Origenes is ultimately one of doctrine. Origenes' title also suggests a debate about Platonic interpretation; indeed, the picture of Origenes debating philological details with Longinus early in the *Timaeus*-commentary suggests that hermeneutic detail was of real concern to Origenes.[4]

The 'King' of the title recalls several passages of Plato, including the Sun-analogy of *Republic* VI 509d2 that Proclus goes on to interpret, and *Philebus* 27b–30d. Here the "cause of the mixture" is introduced as "that which acts as demiurge" (τὸ δημιουργοῦν, 27b1), and later it inspires the remark that the wise agree upon Intellect being our King of heaven and earth (βασιλεὺς ἡμῖν οὐρανοῦ τε καὶ γῆς, 28c7–8); indeed, 30d affirms that soul is what is queenly and intellect what is kingly (βασιλικὴν μὲν ψυχὴν βασιλικὸν δὲ νοῦν) in the nature of

---

[4]  Compare also fragment 17 from Nemesius, *De Natura Hominis* 13, which also concerns interpretation.

Zeus, again with reference to the "cause." A third dialogue that may have been relevant is the *Statesman*, given that its ancient subtitle was *On Kingship* (περὶ βασιλείας, Diogenes Laertius, *Lives of the Philosophers* 3.57) and that it speaks of a god who has engendered the cosmos and endowed it with many blessed gifts (269d8–9).[5] Finally there is the cryptic passage at *Epistle II* 312e, a passage that made no mark on the interpretation of Plato until a century or so before Plotinus, but then rapidly came to the fore and accounts for most of Plotinus' use of the *Epistles*.[6]

## 4  Plotinus' Denial of Innovation

It is primarily with regard to *Epistle II*, *Republic VI*, and *Parmenides* 137c–155e (with help from *Epistle VI* 323d and *Timaeus* 34b–41d) that Plotinus makes his bold claim that his theory of the three hypotheses is neither recent nor of the present,[7] but implicit in ancient discourse,[8] as confirmed in the very writings of Plato:

> Hence Plato's [levels of divinity?] are three: "All concern the King of All" (for he speaks of the "first" [*Epistle* II 312d7?]) and a second concerns the

---

[5] πολλῶν μὲν καὶ μακαρίων παρὰ τοῦ γεννήσαντος μετείληφεν, cf. τὴν ἀνακύκλησιν εἴληχεν, e3–4. If one tries to correlate this passage with the *Timaeus*, then it is hard to resist identifying this figure (responsible not only for the Kronos-phase of the world, but for its very being) with the Demiurge; but shortly before (269c1–2), it had been declared relevant for revealing the King (cf. 274c1 3). Hence it could encourage the identification of the King and the Demiurge. I shall pursue this question further elsewhere.

[6] It is widely believed that this *Epistle* had its origins in the shadowy 'Neo-Pythagoreans' who flourished around the break-up of the Roman Republic and the commencement of the Imperial Period; see John M. Rist, "Neopythagoreanism and Plato's Second Letter," *Phronesis* 10 (1965): 78–81; Paul Keyser, "Orreries, the Date of [Plato] Letter ii, and Eudorus of Alexandria," *Archiv für Geschichte der Philosophie* 80 (1998): 241–67; Saffrey and Westerink, (eds), Proclus, xx–xxvi.

[7] καὶ εἶναι τοὺς λόγους τούσδε μὴ καινοὺς μηδὲ νῦν, 5.1.8.10–11.

[8] 'Ancient discourse' is not of course limited to Plato and his followers, but includes at the very least Parmenides, who is then quoted (5.1.8.14–23); as 5.1.9 claims, many other Pre-Socratics had a share in it, especially those in the same camp as Pythagoras, the Pythagoreans, or Pherecydes, while Aristotle at least is seen as going somewhat astray in differing from Plato and failing to postulate a One entirely removed from the realm of intellect. However, as 5.1.9.30–32 shows, Plotinus does not believe that the early figures whom he regards as allies always recorded their doctrines of principles, as opposed to communicating them orally or leaving them aside altogether.

second and a third concerns the third. And he speaks also of a "Father of the Cause" [*Epistle* VI 323d4], meaning Intellect by "cause," for Intellect is Demiurge for him. And he says that it creates the soul in that mixing bowl of his. And of this cause, which is Intellect, he says that its "Father" is the Good, both over-and-above Intellect and over-and-above Being. And in many places he speaks of Being and the Intellect as the Idea. Hence Plato knew that Intellect was from the Good, and Soul from Intellect. And these explanations are not new nor of the present, but have been set out long ago in a covert fashion, and our present explanations were their interpreters using Plato's own writings as evidence that those views were ancient.[9]

Plato was the figure in whom the separation of the hypostases was supposed to be most easily documented, so that Platonic interpretation is central to the metaphysical debate in which Plotinus engages. If one can trust the denial of novelty, it is very likely that Plotinus had at least one forerunner who anticipated this kind of interpretation, affording him a degree of confidence that his reading of Plato had a more solid foundation than that of his rivals, many of whom were more scholarly in their writings than he. Plotinus' confidence in his own Platonic interpretation, esoteric though it is, is hard to match in ancient Platonism other than in Proclus, and we know very well that the essence of Proclus' interpretation had already been thought out by his revered teacher Syrianus. The interpretation that one grows up with, because it facilitates one's own philosophic development, is the hardest to abandon. Hence it is likely that Plotinus' interpretation of Plato had been developed under Ammonius' guidance and that Plotinus would have taken this to be the meaning of Ammonius also. Deviations from his own reading would therefore be regarded, perhaps unfairly, as deviating also from his teacher and perhaps from the whole Platonic tradition. Thus it is not surprising that the later Neo-Platonist tradition, with its reverence for Plotinus and Porphyry, should have looked upon Origenes as one who betrayed the true Ammonian heritage. But was he really the traitor depicted, or did he simply understand Ammonius differently?

---

9  Καὶ διὰ τοῦτο καὶ τὰ Πλάτωνος [sc. θεῖα?] τριττά· τὰ πάντα περὶ τὸν πάντων βασιλέα—φησὶ γὰρ πρῶτα—καὶ δεύτερον περὶ τὰ δεύτερα καὶ περὶ τὰ τρίτα τρίτον. Λέγει δὲ καὶ τοῦ αἰτίου εἶναι πατέρα αἴτιον μὲν τὸν νοῦν λέγων· δημιουργὸς γὰρ ὁ νοῦς αὐτῷ· τοῦτον δέ φησι τὴν ψυχὴν ποιεῖν ἐν τῷ κρατῆρι ἐκείνῳ. Τοῦ αἰτίου δὲ νοῦ ὄντος πατέρα φησὶ τἀγαθὸν καὶ τὸ ἐπέκεινα νοῦ καὶ ἐπέκεινα οὐσίας. Πολλαχοῦ δὲ τὸ ὂν καὶ τὸν νοῦν τὴν ἰδέαν λέγει· ὥστε Πλάτωνα εἰδέναι ἐκ μὲν τἀγαθοῦ τὸν νοῦν, ἐκ δὲ τοῦ νοῦ τὴν ψυχήν. Καὶ εἶναι τοὺς λόγους τούσδε μὴ καινοὺς μηδὲ νῦν, ἀλλὰ πάλαι μὲν εἰρῆσθαι μὴ ἀναπεπταμένως, τοὺς δὲ νῦν λόγους ἐξηγητὰς ἐκείνων γεγονέναι μαρτυρίοις πιστωσαμένους τὰς δόξας ταύτας παλαιὰς εἶναι τοῖς αὐτοῦ τοῦ Πλάτωνος γράμμασιν.

## 5 The Background to the Treatise on the 'King'

Porphyry regarded Origenes as a reluctant writer (*Vita Plotini* 3 = Origenes fragment 2), while Eunapius (*Vitae Sophistarum* 4.2.1–4 = Origenes fragment 4) reports that he was among those whose style had suffered from lack of charm.[10] Hence it is likely that he had only taken up his pen to reject any Creator other than the King in order to counter serious perceived flaws in contemporary discourse. On the one hand there were the Gnostics, with whom Plotinus engaged in 2.9 and elsewhere and whose activities were reported by Porphyry in *Vita Plotini* 16. Their treatises, which included Greek versions of the Nag Hammadi treatises *Zostrianus* and *Allogenes*, were of such concern that Amelius and Porphyry wrote extensive polemical works against them. It seems that such "Christians" (as Porphyry calls them) were in direct competition with Plotinus' circle and presumably with Origenes too, who would certainly have been mentioned here by Porphyry had he had been one of them. The Gnostics are accused by Plotinus of mixing Plato with their own characteristic innovations (2.9.6.10–12). Gnostic views on the evils of the created world necessarily had implications for the origin of that evil and for the status of the creator himself, and Plotinus draws attention to his opponents' misuse of *Timaeus* 39e7–9 in their ignorance of who Plato's Demiurge really is (2.9.6.14–24). They do violence to Platonic doctrines, particularly with regard to matters of creation, thinking their own insights superior to those of Plato and other revered men (2.9.6.24–28). They blame the soul for its association with the body, find fault with the universe's governor, and in general put the creator on the same level as the soul (2.9.6.59–62). So the Gnostics were a plausible target for a polemical work by Origenes involving the nature of the Creator, and as in the case of Plotinus, any disagreements with Gnostic doctrines regarding the Creator were likely to have been especially concerned with matters of the interpretation of Plato, specifically *Timaeus* 39e.[11]

One interpreter at least partly responsible for contemporary controversy over *Timaeus* 39e was Numenius of Apamea, who wrote perhaps a century or more beforehand. As one might expect of an avowed Pythagorean who aimed to revive the kind of doctrine that would not have been openly broadcast by his early predecessors, Numenius interpreted a wide variety of early poetic

---

10   The term used is the rare ἀκύθηρος, derived from the name of Aphrodite, and it further explains why he repeatedly rejected explanations of the details of the *Timaeus* in terms of the charms of Plato's style (see fragments 9, 13, 14).

11   This passage is also tackled at some length by Plotinus in 3.9.1.

and philosophic texts somewhat allegorically (fragments 30–38), and his interpretation of Plato, while rigorous in its way, nonetheless introduced a new freedom into Platonic exegesis. By the time of Plotinus, the widespread interest in, and at times suspicion of, Numenius is attested by the regularity with which his name occurs in Porphyry's *Life of Plotinus* (3, 14, 17, 18, 20, 21), in the course of which Amelius' special concern for Numenius, his presence among authors discussed in Plotinus' school, and the degree of Plotinus' debt to Numenius are all discussed. Numenius and his ally Cronius were also Porphyry's chief inspiration for his short work *On the Cave of the Nymphs*.

Now Numenius detected three gods behind the *Timaeus*, and among the passages where he found them are *Timaeus* 39e (Numenius fragment 22). Fortunately the exact interpretation of this controversial passage does not concern us here,[12] only the fact that it pioneered the distinction between the intellect (νοῦς) that sees the Ideas, the Living-Being-Itself (τὸ ὅ ἐστι ζῷον) in which they are to be found, and the power that plans the creation of the world (τὸ διανοούμενον). The important factor is that what can here look like a single Demiurge to modern readers (as indeed it had done to Plutarch) is split by Numenius into three. Likewise the famous reference to the Demiurge as "Maker and Father" at 30b is seen (fragment 21) as a reference to two separate gods, implying that Numenius saw (Plato's) Demiurge as a hybrid figure, part Good and part Creative Intellect.[13] Proclus adds that what is created is the third god, referring either to the universe or to its governing soul in particular, but the main point is that Numenius drew a distinction that gave the Good a separate, higher existence, allowing subsequent divinities a lesser degree of excellence and so sanctioning the possibility of a worldly creation whose goodness is not assured by any unerring goodness on the part of its maker and/or governor.

This Numenian digression is necessary because there can be little doubt that Origenes' work *That Only the King Is Creator* was written partly in response to the Numenian idea that more than one god must be detected behind Plato's Demiurge in the *Timaeus*. Origenes was identifying a single Creator with a 'King', presumably that of the *Second Epistle*, of whom the author says

---

12  Quite apart from the interpretation of what Proclus is saying about Numenius, he may reasonably be suspected of dependence on Porphyry at this point, and discussion of Numenius is secondary to his discussion of a parallel interpretation ascribed to Amelius. For a discussion of Proclus' knowledge of Numenius, see Harold Tarrant, "Must Commentators Know Their Sources? Proclus *In Timaeum* and Numenius," in *Philosophy, Science and Exegesis in Greek, Arabic and Latin Commentaries* (ed. P. Adamson, H. Baltussen, and M.W.F. Stone; ICS BICS Suppl.; London: 2004), 1:175–90.

13  "So that the Demiurge according to him is double (διττός), the first god and the second."

something like the following at 312e1–4:[14] "All is concerned with the King of All, and all is for his sake, and that is the cause of all that is fine, while a second is concerned with the second things and a third with the third things" (περὶ τὸν πάντων βασιλέα πάντ' ἐστὶ καὶ ἐκείνου ἕνεκα πάντα, καὶ ἐκεῖνο αἴτιον ἁπάντων καλῶν, δεύτερον δὲ περὶ τὰ δεύτερα καὶ τρίτον περὶ τὰ τρίτα).[15] Numenius seems to be the first documented mainstream philosopher to have employed the concept of the 'King' from this *Epistle*,[16] and he lays down the principle "that the first god is inert, free from any works whatever, and is King, while the Demiurgic god is in control as he passes through the heaven" (fragment 12.12–14).[17] The first "must not even create, and the first god should be considered Father of the Demiurgic god" (fragment 12.1–3). Numenius does not only split the Demiurge in two, but he also assigns the creative role to the lesser of the two only, the first being the Good itself (fragment 20.11; cf. 16.2–5). This agrees with the fact that everything is "for the sake of" the King in *Epistle II*, and Numenius also attributes a causal role to this first god, as is also required by the *Epistle*: he sows the seed of all soul into all things together (fragment 13.4–5).[18]

Origenes takes the 'King', whom Numenius identified with his first god, and identifies it with the Creator, whom Numenius identifies rather with his second; hence he would seem to be either demoting the King or promoting the

---

14  Did Origenes know approximately the same texts as we do? Plotinus has variants that indicate a willingness to quote from memory and, in turn, show where he has thought through the details with less precision. At 1.8.2.28–32 two phrases are inverted, and the word ἕνεκα is omitted: περὶ τὸν πάντων βασιλέα πάντα ἐστί, καὶ ἐκεῖνο αἴτιον πάντων καλῶν, καὶ πάντα ἐστὶν ἐκείνου, καὶ δεύτερον περὶ τὰ δεύτερα καὶ τρίτον περὶ τὰ τρίτα. However, these errors are corrected at 6.7.42.9–10: περὶ τὸν πάντων βασιλέα πάντα ἐστὶ κἀκείνου ἕνεκα πάντα.

15  It is my contention that περί should be taken as a preposition and accented thus, unless there is good reason to prefer it to be taken postpositively. It seems that the original author must have been willing for readers to take it in the more natural way, and it could easily be claimed that where X has to do with Y, then Y has to do with X as well.

16  Saffrey and Westerink (Proclus, xxi–xxvi) deal with some circumstantial evidence that would make the *Epistle* Neo-Pythagorean, and I am not entirely convinced by the claim made at xxvi that Moderatus was the first to use the theological sentence quoted. If this is the case, as they go on to argue in detail, then he must have been widely influential, given the rapidity with which it then becomes a canonical passage.

17  ...τὸν μὲν πρῶτον θεὸν ἀργὸν εἶναι ἔργων συμπάντων καὶ βασιλέα, τὸν δημιουργικὸν δὲ θεὸν ἡγεμονεῖν δι' οὐρανοῦ ἰόντα. ...that the First God is inert, free of absolutely all works, and King, while the Demiurgic god leads as he goes through the heaven.

18  Numenius' σύμπαντα seems to echo the ἁπάντων (e3) that concludes the series of four universal quantifiers at e1–3.

Demiurge. However, we should not forget what Proclus claimed in fragment 21: that Numenius made the Demiurge double, the first god and the second; his report is credible only if it were Plato's Demiurge that Numenius was discussing. Plato's Demiurge masks Numenius' Good plus Numenius' Creator. In an intellectual world that had become obsessed with Numenian ideas, Origenes is most likely to have been saying that Plato's King, i.e., Plato's first god and first cause, is the only entity required to explain the figure of the Demiurge in the *Timaeus*, a claim perhaps made primarily because of contemporary Gnostic use of Numenian ideas, while at the same time questioning Numenius' passion for discovering multiple entities behind a single figure.

## 6       Origenes and the *Parmenides*

As we have already seen, the interpretation of one Platonic dialogue or one passage of special interest was frequently discussed alongside that of another dialogue or passage in the authors whom we have been treating. They treated the Platonic corpus and sometimes other works as well as scriptural passages as revealing a single truth – much as early Christian theologians treated their own collection of scriptural texts. How far the *Parmenides* had already become involved in Numenius' theory is unclear, though fragment 11.12–16 has a little to say about the simplicity of the first god and the original unity and subsequent separation of the second and third.[19] However, somehow Origenes' views on the King became entangled with the interpretation of the first and second hypotheses of that dialogue, and the critical passage seems to have been the claim at the end of the first hypothesis that the One (according to the present line of inquiry) cannot be named, discussed, opined, known, or perceived (*Parmenides* 142a3–8), consequences that are then declared impossible. Proclus, in the passage quoted above (*Theol.* 2.4.31.12–19 = fragment 7), seems to acknowledge that there is a lack of clarity about Origenes' stance here and allows two alternatives. The first possibility is that Origenes thinks that the One under discussion is superior to all knowledge, discussion, and recogni-

---

19    It might be argued that Numenius had no documented influence upon the interpretation of the *Parmenides*, as opposed to the *Timaeus*, *Republic*, and *Phaedo*, but there is perhaps no text in which one might have expected his name to be mentioned, given that Proclus' *Commentary on the Parmenides* avoids mentioning interpreter's names, unlike that on the *Timaeus* and parts of that on the *Republic*. It could plausibly be claimed that Syrianus (*in Met.* 109.12–14 = fragment 46b) is discussing technical matters concerning Ideas that might have been discussed by Numenius in a passage interpreting the *Parmenides*.

tion (κρεῖττον ἁπάσης γνώσεως καὶ παντὸς λόγου καὶ πάσης ἐπιβολῆς), so that the conclusions at *Parmenides* 142a are too negatively expressed rather than wrong. This would meet with Proclus' approval. The other possibility is that he is claiming that this One is *anhyparkton* and *anhypostaton*, i.e., that there is nothing that transcends Being and Intellect, so that the Good becomes simply intellect. In this case Proclus would see the position as Peripatetic rather than Platonic. We hear of this position in Proclus' *Parmenides* commentary, using the otherwise rare term *anhypostaton* (VI, 1065.3, 1079.14, 1110.9, and VII 515.4), and the last of these passages directly concerns 142a. Yet one is not obliged to take these passages to refer to Origenes, given the indecision about his exact position in the *Platonic Theology*, the only passage to name him in such a context. Proclus may indeed suspect that Origenes held that position, but it is a position that he needs to eliminate regardless of whether Origenes or anybody else had openly embraced it.

## 7 Comparison with Porphyry and Anon. in *Parmenidem*

If Origenes had trouble expressing his position on just what was going on in the first hypothesis, he was not alone. John Dillon has recently resumed his discussion of the ambiguous evidence for Porphyry's position. In his words, Porphyry sometimes inclines "at least to some extent, to 'telescope'... the first two Plotinian hypostases," adopting a position that involves "the assertion that the subjects of the first two hypotheses of the *Parmenides* are substantially the same—the One in two different aspects."[20] Yet Dillon goes on to try to show that Porphyry still postulated, like Plotinus and other predecessors, presumably including Ammonius, a One above Intellect and Being. That he postulated something above both of these is a lot clearer than is his willingness to call it 'One' himself,[21] as Dillon admits.[22] So is the 'One' of the first hypothesis a transcendent entity, or is it just a convenient way of illustrating the transcendent? And if so, is the transcendent that it illustrates wholly separate from what

---

20  See John Dillon, "Intellect and the One in Porphyry's *Sententiae*," *International Journal of the Platonic Tradition* 4 (2010): 27–35, 28.

21  *Sententiae* 38 speaks of the 'One' of the ancients

22  Dillon, "Intellect and the One," 34: if the rather unconvincing reference to such a One at Sentence 43 (πολλὰ γάρ ἐστιν ὁ νοῦς, πρὸ δὲ τῶν πολλῶν ἀνάγκη εἶναι τὸ ἕν) is accepted (and here 'one' certainly does not have to be a name for what precedes intellect) this would be "the only occasion on which he mentions the One by name, rather than referring to it as τὸ ἐπέκεινα, or τὸ πρῶτον, or God."

follows, or is it the transcendent aspect of an entity that reappears in what follows? Within the *Parmenides* the key question would be: Are the 'impossible' conclusions at 142a, that the One is non-existent, and thus inaccessible to sensation, thought, and reasoning, accepted as true conclusions about the transcendent entity or not?

The difficulties in Origenes are even better paralleled in the anonymous *Commentary on Plato's Parmenides*,[23] which does of course deal directly with the Platonic text concerned. The first hypothesis is about an entity, an entity that for many reasons cannot be described or named, but this entity is called "the god who is above everything" (τοῦ ἐπὶ πᾶσιν ὄντος θεοῦ, 1.4–5). Yet this is not due to any deficiency in its nature, just like[24] the concept of the One (ἡ τοῦ ἑνὸς ἔννοια, 1.6). That notion does exclude plurality, composition, and variety and allows one to conceive of its simplicity, its having nothing prior to it, and its being in some sense the principle (ἀρχή, 1.9) of the others, which could not exist without it. Hence, out of all possible descriptions, this 'one' is suited to the 'god above all', just as long as we do not conceive of it as an indivisible minimum, as Speusippus was supposed to have done,[25] in which case one's conception of the god will be wholly alien to him. In what follows, it is at least clear that the divinity is the entity behind the first hypothesis and that the One is being treated as a concept (ἐπίνοια, 1.25, 30; 2.13; cf. 1.6) rather than as an independent object of inquiry. The divinity can therefore be approached as something analogous to the One, but it does not properly admit

---

23   The loss of the palimpsest means that texts have not been able to be updated in any secure fashion; I try to avoid building hypotheses on the more controversial lines and make free use of the editions of Pierre Hadot, *Porphyre et Victorine*, tome II (Paris: Études Augustiniennes, 1968); Antonio Linguiti, "Commentarium in Platonis 'Parmenidem'," in *Corpus dei Papiri Filosofici Greci e Latini. Part 3: Commentari* IFirenze: L.S. Olschki, 1995), 63–202; and Gerard Bechtle, *The Anonymous Commentary on Plato's Parmenides* (Berner Reihephilosophischer Studien, 22; Bern: Paul Haupt, 1999). Opinion is divided on Hadot's thesis that the commentary is actually Porphyry's, many of the arguments for such an identity having been weakened, especially by evidence from the Nag Hammadi scrolls.

24   It is hard to be sure whether this God's non-deficient nature is like or unlike the notion of the One, but since the comparison is supposed to be apt (1.17–20), I have assumed likeness; the text seems less than natural and causes Bechtle (*The Anonymous Commentary*, 39 n. 10) some concerns.

25   If the fourth chapter of Iamblichus' *De Communi Mathematica Scientia* draws on Speusippus, as many scholars believe (see particularly John Dillon, "Speusippus in Iamblichus," *Phronesis* 29 [1984]: 328–32, revisited in *The Heirs of Plato* [Oxford: Oxford University Press, 2003]), then it is clear that the primary arithmetical manifestation of his One is the unit, and its primary geometrical manifestation is the point.

of any predicates, not even such predicates as 'simple' or 'one' (1.29–30, 34–35; 2.10–14). The reduction of the 'one' of the first hypothesis to a concept with value for the understanding of the transcendent god, which breaks down in the final instance, *qua* concept might well be said to be "without foundation or substance" (cf. Origenes fragment 7, quoted above). Because of Porphyry's regard for Plotinus and his respect for Plotinus' willingness to call his first principle and the subject of the first hypothesis 'the One' even while acknowledging the problems of such terminology and being willing to vary it, I assume that he would not have reduced 'the One' as nominal subject of the first hypothesis to a concept.[26]

If Origenes had an approach to the *Parmenides* like that of the anonymous commentator, then it is no wonder that Proclus and his source (perhaps Porphyry himself) are confused. It would indeed be correct that the supreme divinity transcends all normal cognition and discussion, but there is nothing to indicate that the One, considered in the abstract in the manner of the first hypothesis, is anything but a concept, without any grounding in existence. It can therefore be called *anhyparkton* and *anhypostaton* without difficulty, whereas the supreme divinity is rather an inconceivable hypostasis (1.32). Is this god then intellect and the pinnacle of being, as Proclus suspects of Origenes' substitute for the Plotinian One? It would seem not, for this god is the cause of all beings (1.25–26) and is super-substantial in relation to all that exists on its account (πάντων ὑπερούσιος τῶν δι' αὐτὸν ὄντων, 2.11–12); he is without intellection (1.34), and he is unlike intellect, not by failing to participate in intellect, but by not being intellect – or he would be, if only it were permissible to say that he were like or unlike anything else (3.1–9). But this god is above all (1.4); he alone has his being inseparable and above all (ἀχώριστον ἔχει τὸ εἶναι καὶ ὑπὲρ τὸ πᾶν, 4.7–9), and he is what alone is truly real (τὸ μόνον ὄντως ὄν, 4.27) compared to all that comes after him. He also has, in a sense, a knowledge that is outside knowledge and ignorance (γνῶσιν ἔξω γνώσεως καὶ ἀγνοίας, 5.10–11).

The supreme god of this commentary defies any ordinary attempt to fix his relation to Being and to Intellect in the way that Proclus requires. He is so defiant of our attempts to discover him that any language normally applied to our world fails (6.23); we have no faculty for discovering him (9.20–10.35). Hence any Platonic theory that tries obliquely to reveal him will be extremely difficult for others to interpret in key respects – even for those who feel comfortable interpreting Plotinus. In the columns (11–14) that go on to interpret the more familiar world of the second hypothesis, god disappears from view,

---

26 Note that Sentence 10 has all things present in the Beyond (ἀνεννοήτως), which would appear to take it right out of the realm of concepts (ἔννοιαι).

a one-made-existent is postulated (12.9), and it is only in this context that one receives talk of what is purely one (11.8, 22, 32, 33).

I do not find it difficult to suppose that the anonymous commentary may emanate from a source closer to Origenes than to Plotinus. Admittedly there is no reference to the 'King', and thus no suggestion that the *Parmenides* is being interpreted in relation to *Epistle II*. However, there is a rare case of an allusion to another work of Plato at 10.16–23, where we are reminded of *Epistle VII* 343b8–e1, a passage that, in its original context, refers to a plurality of higher entities that defy knowledge. A related passage at *Epistle II* 312e4–313a6 deals specifically with the 'King' (313a1) and related entities, and it may well be that 312e was not so very far from the author's mind. The 'King' and his own 'god above all' at least had in common a supreme causal role (312e2–3; 1.25–26). I do not think that the anonymous commentary is itself likely to be part of Origenes' work on the 'King', but it may well have been written by him or somebody close to him as an attempt to clarify his position after an attack on the treatise from the Plotinian school.

## 8  Conclusion

Origenes was not ordinarily a writer of philosophy. The issues that mattered to him were indeed not easily communicated in writing. As the first book on Proclus' *Commentary on the Timaeus* showed (= Origenes fragments 9, 13–14), he did not appreciate the aesthetic pleasure that reading or writing philosophy could give. Proclus and others perhaps misread him, thinking that, whatever he was trying to do, he had ended up abandoning the One in favour of Being and Intellect. Proclus believed that Origenes would have learned something of the interpretation of the *Parmenides* from Ammonius, probably mistaking what had been important for Ammonius. This was the notion that the first hypothesis was unveiling an impredicable divine entity superior to Being and Mind as ordinarily conceived. Origenes accepted this doctrine but chose not to simply name it 'the One', causing confusion among those who followed Plotinus' version of Ammonius' teachings, for whom the entity behind the first hypothesis was simply 'the One'. For them, to relegate 'the One' of the first hypothesis to the status of a conception, and to imagine that it was only discussed for the insights it provided into something else, was to resign oneself to beginning at the level of Being and Intellect. The anonymous commentary shows that this is not so.

I have argued that what Proclus regards as a huge gulf between the position of Origenes and that of Plotinus on the first hypothesis is in fact the kind of hermeneutic quibble that grows over time into something far bigger. Early Christianity experienced just the same phenomenon, as circumstances suddenly made it necessary to use this form of expression rather than that one and to find politically correct terminology for the relationships involved in the Trinity. Both philosophies and religions have a surprising power to forget what had once seemed important and to quibble over new hermeneutic issues that were once not even anticipated.

Of all the Platonising authors whom I have been able to test from late antiquity, only one regularly displays a working vocabulary close to that of the anonymous commentary, and that author is not Porphyry (though the *Sententiae* do at least come close) but Plotinus himself, who is otherwise *sui generis*. The basis of one's regular vocabulary generally remains fairly constant over one's adult years. Thus Plotinus' working vocabulary for philosophic discussion was formed back in Alexandria, probably alongside Ammonius. It makes sense then that the similar working vocabulary of the anonymous commentator should also have been learnt at the feet of Ammonius. Plotinus and Origenes were among his pupils. This is not Plotinus' commentary. But in my view, it could have been written by Origenes, or by some other pupil of Ammonius.

# Neo-Platonic Readings of Embodied Divine Presence: Iamblichus and Julian

*Ilinca Tanaseanu-Döbler*

In his famous account of his encounter with the *libri Platonicorum*, Augustine draws heavily on the prologue of John's Gospel to emphasise the figure of Christ as the divine Logos incarnate as the key difference between Platonism and Catholic Christianity:

> and there I read, certainly not in the same words, but nevertheless this very same idea made plausible by many and manifold reasons, that "in the beginning was the Word, and the Word was with God and God was the Word" ... But that "He came into His own and His own did not receive him; but to all, who did receive Him, He granted the power to become children of God, to those who believed in Him," that I did not read. And I also read there that "the Word, God," was born "not from the flesh nor from blood nor from the desire of man nor from the desire of flesh, but from God"; but that "the Word became flesh and lived among us," that I did not read there.[1]

This passage, which establishes a partial compatibility of the prologue with Neo-Platonic metaphysics, is matched by other pieces of evidence from late antiquity. Augustine himself states that an anonymous philosopher considered the first verse a fit adornment for every Christian church;[2] more than a century earlier, the prologue is quoted favourably, alongside Heraclitus, by

---

[1] *Confessiones* VII 13f.: *et ibi legi non quidem his verbis, sed hoc idem omnino multis et multiplicibus suaderi rationibus, quod in principio erat verbum et verbum erat apud deum et deus erat verbum... Quia vero in sua propria venit et sui eum non receperunt, quotquot autem receperunt eum, dedit eis potestatem filios dei fieri credentibus in nomine eius, non ibi legi. Item legi ibi, quia verbum, deus, non ex carne, non ex sanguine non ex voluntate viri neque ex voluntate carnis sed ex deo natus est; sed quia verbum caro factum est et habitavit in nobis, non ibi legi.* Cf. Samuel Vollenweider, "Der Logos als Brücke vom Evangelium zur Philosophie: Der Johannesprolog in der Relektüre des Neuplatonikers Amelios," in *Studien zu Matthäus und Johannes: Festschrift für Jean Zumstein zu seinem 65. Geburtstag* (ed. A. Dettwiler and U. Poplutz; Zürich: Zumstein, 2009), 377–97, 377.

[2] Augustine, *De civitate Dei* X 29. Cf. Vollenweider, "Der Logos als Brücke," 377.

Plotinus' student Amelius.[3] Other Neo-Platonists also engage with it, albeit in a negative manner, in order to underline its logical fallacies, as did Amelius' colleague Porphyry[4] or, later, the Emperor Julian.

The issue of the Christian idea of incarnation ultimately touches upon a larger problem: How should matter be regarded, and to what extent can the divine manifest itself tangibly within a material body? This issue was hotly debated in Neo-Platonic circles, with a focus on cultic practices: Can gods or other higher entities be present in statues, circumscribed holy spaces, or in human bodies in real time and space, apart from the realm of mythical stories about gods on earth?[5] From this angle, it appears worthwhile to read Neo-Platonic reactions to the incarnation not only as an instance of Christian-pagan polemics, but by placing them in the larger context of philosophical discourse on materiality and the divine. I will explore this reading by presenting two examples from the late third and fourth centuries: Iamblichus of Chalcis and the Emperor Julian. With these two authors we grasp Neo-Platonic discourse about the divine and its relationship to material bodies around the time of the Arian controversy and the formulation of the Nicaeno-Constantinopolitanum. In his *De mysteriis*, Iamblichus offers an apology for material rituals, which builds on the notion of the pervasive presence of the divine in all reality. His discussion of the various modes of divine presence

---

[3] For this "Relektüre" (Vollenweider, "Der Logos als Brücke," 377), which has been at the centre of a number of studies, see the discussion and bibliography in Vollenweider, "Der Logos als Brücke."

[4] Cf. Richard Goulet, "Cinq nouveaux fragments nominaux du traité de Porphyre 'Contre les chrétiens,'" *Vigiliae Christianae* 64 (2010): 140–59, esp. 141–48, Luc Brisson, "Le Christ comme Lógos suivant Porphyre dans *Contre les chrétiens* (fragment 86 von Harnack = Théophylacte, Enarr. in Joh., PG 123, col. 1141)," in *Le traité de Porphyre contre les chrétiens: Un siècle de recherches, nouvelles questions* (ed. S. Morlet; Paris: Institut d'Études Augustiniennes, 2011): 277–90, and Matthias Becker, *Porphyrios, 'Contra Christianos': Neue Sammlung der Fragmente, Testimonien und Dubia mit Einleitung, Übersetzung und Anmerkungen* (Berlin: de Gruyter, 2016), 78f. and 371–80.

[5] For the mythical parallels of incarnation theology cf. Samuel Vollenweider, "Die Metamorphose des Gottessohns: Zum epiphanialen Motivfeld in Phil 2,6–8," in id., *Horizonte neutestamentlicher Christologie: Studien zu Paulus und zur frühchristlichen Theologie* (Tübingen: Mohr Siebeck, 2002), 285–306, who analyses the presence of epiphanial motifs and terminology in the New Testament, comparing the representation of Jesus in Philippians 2 with Hellenistic mythical tales of manifest deities; he views a transposition of these myths to the epiphanies of angels in a Hellenistic Jewish setting as the "missing link" between Greek myth and this early Christological statement. A larger work on epiphanial imagery in the New Testament is announced.

during rituals is the most detailed extant Neo-Platonic statement on the matter before the works of Proclus in the fifth century. In his *Life of Pythagoras*, which may be read as a conscious engagement with the Gospel of John,[6] he presents Pythagoras' nature by drawing on patterns that evoke the Christian incarnation. The emperor Julian, who converted from Christianity to pagan Neo-Platonism after his studies with Iamblichus' successors, holds Iamblichus' theology in great esteem. In *Against the Galilaeans*, Julian attacks quite openly the Christian idea of incarnation and its scriptural basis; his other works allow us to see to what extent he adopted Iamblichus' ideas about the possibility of embodied divine presence.

In an important paper on Julian's presentation of Asclepius, John Finamore has compared Iamblichus' and Julian's ideas about "divine descent," arguing that both authors share a basic conception about the impossibility of gods descending into matter, which restricts that possibility to lesser entities, such as *daimones* and pure souls.[7] Gods may communicate with the material realm, but without descending into it.[8] The ambiguous passages where both authors may seem to contemplate or leave open the possibility of divine descent are either reduced to the Neo-Platonic exegesis of the *Phaedrus* myth – the descent of souls or other beings belonging to the retinue of a god can be regarded as a manifestation of the god himself[9] – or they are explained in terms of rhetorical emphasis that obscures the basic adherence to the Neo-Platonic theory of divine descent.[10] Thus, for Finamore, both Julian and Iamblichus are "perfectly clear about their own philosophical categories," but "both can and do couch their conclusions in terms stronger than they should."[11] This may appear like a modern attempt at reducing complexity and imposing perhaps a greater degree of systematicity and coherence on the two authors than the texts warrant.

---

6   E.g., John Dillon, "Die Vita Pythagorica – ein Evangelium?" in *Jamblich: Pythagoras: Legende – Lehre – Lebensgestaltung* (ed. Michael von Albrecht et al.; Darmstadt: WBG, 2002), 295–301, esp. 295 or 301. Cf. also Irmgard Männlein-Robert, "Zwischen Polemik und Hagiographie: Jamblichs *De vita pythagorica* im Vergleich mit Porphyrios' *Vita Plotini*," in *Bios Philosophos: Philosophy in Ancient Greek Biography* (ed. M. Bonazzi and S. Schorn; Turnhout: Brepols, 2016), 197–220, 199.

7   John Finamore, "Julian and the Descent of Asclepius," *Journal of Neoplatonic Studies* 7 (1999): 63–86.

8   Finamore, "Julian," 64–66 (for Iamblichus).

9   Finamore, "Julian," 69–71 (for Iamblichus' Pythagoras). The idea that *daimones* and souls follow one particular god as his retinue is developed in Plato's *Phaedrus* 246e–247a; 250b; 252c–253c.

10  Finamore, "Julian," 81 (for Julian).

11  Finamore, "Julian," 81.

Taking up a suggestion voiced in another context by Samuel Vollenweider,[12] I propose to look anew at the two authors by focusing not only on the notion of an active divine descent, but also on the notion of divine presence in material settings.[13] As Gregory Shaw has shown, Iamblichus can be regarded as a major theorist of divine presence in the material world, who strongly emphasises and theorises the distinctive value of embodiment in a Neo-Platonic metaphysical system.[14] I propose to bring together the issues of divine presence and ritual on the one hand, and divine incarnation and the figure of Christ on the other hand, and inquire whether we can detect behind them a common discursive framework regarding materiality and the divine.

As the focus will lie on divine embodiment and presence in material settings and not on the soul's ascent or ritual perception of or communication with the divine, I will not include in my discussion the subject of the luminous body or vehicle of the soul and its role in communication with the gods or the soul's ascent.[15] Another thematic complex, which will only be considered insofar as it becomes intertwined in Iamblichus and Julian with actual divine pres-

---

12   Cf. Vollenweider, "Der Logos als Brücke," 397, arguing for the closeness of patterns of thought in John and Neo-Platonism: "In einem ganz anderen Kontext [sc. than the Gospel of John] bildet die Dialektik von Präsenz und Absenz, von Immanenz und Transzendenz des Göttlichen eine der zentralen Figuren der neuplatonischen Philosophie, die sich von der subtilen Reflexion über die mystische Erhebung bis zur theurgischen Praxis erstreckt." On divine presence and absence in general in Neo-Platonic metaphysics, see also the historical sketch of Lloyd P. Gerson ("The Presence and the Absence of the Divine in the Platonic Tradition," in *Metaphysik und Religion: Zur Signatur des spätantiken Denkens* [ed. Michael Erler and Theo Kobusch; München/Leipzig: K.G. Saur, 2002], 365–86), who focuses on divine personhood and participability.

13   A good description of divine presence and its mediation through material objects in Iamblichus is given by Gregory Shaw, *Theurgy and the Soul: The Neoplatonism of Iamblichus* (University Park, PA: Pennsylvania State University Press, 1995), although one may disagree with his reconstruction of theurgy; see esp. 48–51.

14   This is the keynote of his book on theurgy (Shaw, *Theurgy and the Soul*), which – notwithstanding possible reservations about his actual reconstruction of theurgic ritual – still remains one of the most poignant contributions to the role of matter in Iamblichus' thought.

15   Iamblichus' conception of material rites, the human body, and the relationship with the divine has inspired many studies, not least John Finamore's study on the luminous vehicle or body of the soul (*ochēma*) as a medium between the gods and the human being (*Iamblichus and the Theory of the Vehicle of the Soul* [Chico, CA: 1985]) or Gregory Shaw's *Theurgy and the Soul*. One aspect of Shaw's analysis, namely that the human soul and its luminous body may undergo a divinisation during ritual and also serve as a medium for divine revelation (51–57) was developed recently further in Gregory Shaw, "The Role

ence in material bodies, is the larger field of divine epiphanies, which has been increasingly recognised in modern scholarship as central to Greek and Roman culture.[16] Epiphany is certainly a key mode of thought for conceptualising divine presence and communication with the divine, both in non-Christian and in Christian settings, and it also targets the sense perceptions and imagination of the human recipients, making the divine sensorily perceptible,[17] as we will see in Iamblichus. However, epiphany looks on the communication with the divine from a distinct angle: the emphasis lies on manifestation, encounter, and perception, while the notion of an actual embodiment of the divine, which forms the focus of the present inquiry, is of secondary or no importance.[18] From Petridou's historical survey of Greek epiphany, epiphany

of *aesthesis* in Theurgy," in *Iamblichus and the Foundations of Late Platonism* (ed. Eugene Afonasin, John Dillon, and John Finamore; Leiden/Boston: Brill, 2012), 91–112, where he explores the role of perception and the human body in theurgy (102). According to Shaw, gods use human bodies, and especially the vehicle or luminous body of every soul, in order to reveal themselves to human beings (96, 102). In the formulation of Shaw, *Theurgy and the Soul*, 57: "The perfect theurgist became an embodied Demiurge whose presence was enough to create harmony out of discord and drive away evil." This, however, especially the use of the capital D, is taking Iamblichus one step farther than he goes himself explicitly in his text: the practitioner may be in communion with the divine or possessed by it, but nowhere in *De mysteriis* does Iamblichus actually develop the idea that the human being is anything other than a medium or a communication partner of the gods and higher beings. Moreover, however stimulating his contributions for the emphasis on Iamblichus' positive valuation of the material world, Shaw does not draw a clear distinction between the different forms of revelation and presence of the divine in the material world; especially the category of presence remains under-defined. For further bibliography on Iamblichus and his theory of theurgy, see Crystal Addey, *Divination and Theurgy in Neoplatonism: Oracles of the Gods* (Farnham/Burlington: Ashgate 2014); Ilinca Tanaseanu-Döbler, *Theurgy in Late Antiquity: The Invention of a Ritual Tradition* (Göttingen: Vandenhoeck und Ruprecht, 2013), 95–135.

16   See, for example, from recent research, Verity Platt, *Facing the Gods: Epiphany and Representation in Graeco-Roman Art, Literature, and Religion* (Cambridge: Cambridge University Press, 2011); Georgia Petridou, *Divine Epiphany in Greek Literature and Culture* (Oxford: Oxford University Press, 2015); cf. already H. S. Versnel, "What Did Ancient Man See when He Saw a God? Some Reflections on Greco-Roman Epiphany," in *Effigies Dei: Essays on the History of Religion* (ed. Dirk van der Plas; Leiden: Brill, 1987), 42–55.

17   Cf. Petridou, *Divine Epiphany*, 23: "Divine epiphanies take place in the eyes, the ears, the nostrils, and, above all, in the minds of their witnesses."

18   Cf. already Versnel, "What Did Ancient Man See," who, in his overview of Greek epiphanies, also points to statues as media of divine presence (46f.), among a wide and ambiguous spectrum of manifestations; see also the classification of Greek epiphanies in

emerges as a a basic concept of Greek thought and religion and as a broad and open category that subsumes a whole range of modes of divine presence. As we will see in Iamblichus and especially in Julian, epiphanial terminology may actually be used as a conceptual alternative to incarnation; we may inquire whether it is not precisely this openness and under-determination of the term that may make it attractive for pagan Neo-Platonists.

## 1 Iamblichus

### 1.1 *Iamblichus on the Embodied Experience of the Divine:* De Mysteriis

The debates about whether and how material objects, especially cult images and temples, are related to the actual presence of deities can be traced back at least to Heraclitus. Do they merely symbolise and represent the divine, or can they actually contain and mediate its presence?[19] Even Plotinus, otherwise so detached from material rituals, records in one isolated passage the idea that the ancient sages fashioned statues as receptacles akin to the gods, able to draw into themselves a portion of the divine soul; the verb he uses is *pareinai*, "to be present."[20] His student Porphyry shows himself quite familiar with a broad range of practices that establish a form of divine presence at least during rituals. In his *Philosophy from Oracles*, he records that gods can be brought to enter a clearly circumscribed spatial environment.[21] In the same work, he

---

Petridou, *Divine Epiphany*, 29–105. Petridou rightly repeatedly underlines the ambiguity of divine manifestation in the Greek conceptual universe, which makes e.g. the distinction between her categories of anthropomorphic-bodily epiphanies and *phasmata* of the gods a "matter of degree" (67).

19  Heraclitus, fragment DK 22 B 5. On the interpretations of statues and their relationship to the gods they represented in Greek thought, see Platt, *Facing the Gods*; Tanja Scheer, *Die Gottheit und ihr Bild: Untersuchungen zur Funktion griechischer Kultbilder in Religion und Politik* (München: Beck, 2000), Peter Eich, *Gottesbild und Wahrnehmung: Studien zu Ambivalenzen früher griechischer Götterdarstellungen (ca. 800 v.Chr. – ca. 400 v.Chr.)* (Stuttgart: Steiner, 2011).

20  Plotinus, *Enn.* IV 3, 11: Καί μοι δοκοῦσιν οἱ πάλαι σοφοί, ὅσοι ἐβουλήθησαν θεοὺς αὑτοῖς παρεῖναι ἱερὰ καὶ ἀγάλματα ποιησάμενοι, εἰς τὴν τοῦ παντὸς φύσιν ἀπιδόντες, ἐν νῷ λαβεῖν ὡς πανταχοῦ μὲν εὐάγωγον ψυχῆς φύσις, δέξασθαί γε μὴν ῥᾷστον ἂν εἴη ἁπάντων, εἴ τις προσπαθές τι τεκτήναιτο ὑποδέξασθαι δυνάμενον μοῖράν τινα αὐτῆς. Προσπαθὲς δὲ τὸ ὁπωσοῦν μιμηθέν, ὥσπερ κάτοπτρον ἁρπάσαι εἶδός τι δυνάμενον. See Tanaseanu-Döbler, *Theurgy*, 50f.; and Maria Carmen de Vita, *Giuliano Imperatore filosofo neoplatonico* (Milano: Vita e pensiero, 2011), 242f.

21  Fragment 321F Smith.

describes how gods can be summoned to enter a human medium, how they fatigue the medium, and how they can be released.[22] In his *Letter to Anebo*, directed at a probably fictitious Egyptian priest and only preserved in fragments, he seems to take a more critical stance, inquiring into the philosophical possibility of ritual and presenting rituals such as those described in the *Philosophy from Oracles* as ultimately incompatible with philosophy.[23]

It is to this *Letter to Anebo* that Iamblichus replies in the text now known as *De mysteriis*, taking up the *persona* of Anebo's teacher Abammon. This text has been at the core of studies of Neo-Platonic ritual – theurgy – for decades.[24] As Gregory Shaw rightly noted, Iamblichus develops a positive conception of matter and embodied existence, viewing it as the only means for humans to achieve union with the divine.[25] Pursuing this path, we will inquire into the relationship between the divine and matter in *De mysteriis*. In doing so, we need to keep in mind that *De mysteriis* represents the answer to Porphyry's text and is thus a *Gelegenheitsschrift* which takes its structure and subject matter from Iamblichus' opponent.[26]

The relationship between the divine and matter is introduced at the beginning of Iamblichus' answers soon after the prologue, when Iamblichus engages with Porphyry's endeavour to distinguish between gods, *daimones*, heroes, and souls. Porphyry, who aims especially at distinguishing between gods and *daimones*, seems to have proposed a variety of criteria, *inter alia* the assignment of different divine classes to distinct regions of the cosmos and to distinct bodies, passibility versus impassibility, the understanding of gods as pure intellects and of the *daimones* as a compound of intellect and soul, or the possibility that gods are free from bodies whereas *daimones* have bodies.

Iamblichus is emphatic: all classes of higher beings (*kreittona genē*) are free from bodies and from any influence deriving from bodies, and exercise their rule and beneficence towards bodies in perfect freedom, "from the outside" (*exōthen*).[27] Whereas divided souls can be said to enter a body, higher beings

---

22 Fragment 306F, 339F, 349F, 350F Smith.

23 See Tanaseanu-Döbler, *Theurgy*, 74–81.

24 The most recent study of theurgy in *De mysteriis* is Nicholas Marshall's dissertation (*The Meaning of Theurgy: A Minimalistic Approach to Theurgy and Previous Understandings of the Term in the Study of Late Antique Religion*; PhD dissertation; Aarhus Universitet, 2016).

25 Shaw, *Theurgy and the Soul*; and Shaw, "The Role of *aesthesis*."

26 I retain the impression that the *Letter to Anebo* and *De mysteriis* represent a polemical engagement (see my discussion in Tanaseanu-Döbler, *Theurgy*, 97, with the bibliography in n. 249). A similar position is taken by Marshall, *The Meaning of Theurgy*, 65–7; 131; 157. For another, irenic, view see Addey, *Divination and Theurgy*, 127–69.

27 *De mysteriis* I 8, 23f. Parthey, 18 Saffrey/Segonds (names of editors abbreviated in all subsequent citations).

envelop in themselves the lesser beings, all down to the level of materiality, without being in any way affected by them.[28] The imagery of boundaries and containers, with the implicit opposition between external (free) and internal (constrained) spheres, is thus employed to underline that the higher beings are not constrained by a body. This is further emphasised by a series of impossible consequences arising from the idea that the gods are confined to special bodies and places within the universe:

> How should the substance which is not present to bodies in a spatial manner be distinguished by the corporeal spaces, and the substance which is not held back by divided circumscriptions of the objects underlying it be held in a divided manner by the parts of the universe? What should be that which keeps the gods from going forth everywhere and that holds their power back so that it may reach not farther than the heavenly vault? That would indeed be the work of a more powerful cause that would lock them in and circumscribe them within certain parts... Why, I do not see how the things here could be created and endowed with form, if no divine creation and participation in the divine forms reaches throughout the whole cosmos.[29]

Iamblichus' next point is that the localisation of the gods in a specific class of bodies, and thus a specific region of the cosmos, also destroys the rationale of ritual: "But this opinion amounts to a complete abolishment of the sacred cult and the theurgic communion of gods towards men, because it banishes the presence of the higher beings outside the earth. For it does not say anything else but that the divine has taken its abode far away from the matters on earth and that it does not mix with men and that the place here is without gods."[30] The presence (*parousia*, the same term as in Plotinus' explanation of

---

28   *De mysteriis* I 8, 25f. P., 19f. S./S. Cf. I 16, 50 P./38 S./S.; I 17, 51 P., 38 S./S.
29   *De mysteriis* I 8, 27 P., 20f. S/S.: πῶς δὲ δὴ ἡ μὴ τοπικῶς παροῦσα τοῖς σώμασι τοῖς σωματικοῖς τόποις διακρίνεται, καὶ ἡ μὴ διειργομένη μεριστοῖς περιγραφαῖς ὑποκειμένων κατέχεται μεριστῶς ὑπὸ τῶν μερῶν τοῦ κόσμου; Τί δὲ δὴ καὶ τὸ διακωλῦόν ἐστι τοὺς θεοὺς προϊέναι πανταχοῦ καὶ τὸ ἀνεῖργον αὐτῶν τὴν δύναμιν ὥστε ἰέναι μέχρι τῆς οὐρανίας ἁψῖδος; Ἰσχυροτέρας γὰρ ἂν εἴη τοῦτο αἰτίας ἔργον, τῆς κατακλειούσης αὐτοὺς καὶ περιγραφούσης ἔν τισι μέρεσιν. ...Οὐχ ὁρῶ δὲ ἔγωγε καὶ τίνα τρόπον δημιουργεῖται τὰ τῇδε καὶ εἰδοποιεῖται, εἴ γε μηδεμία θεία δημιουργία καὶ τῶν θείων εἰδῶν μετουσία διατείνει διὰ παντὸς τοῦ κόσμου.
30   *De mysteriis* I 8, 28 P., 21 S./S.: Ὅλως δὲ τῆς ἱερᾶς ἁγιστείας καὶ τῆς θεουργικῆς κοινωνίας θεῶν πρὸς ἀνθρώπους ἀναίρεσίς ἐστιν αὕτη ἡ δόξα, τὴν τῶν κρειττόνων παρουσίαν ἔξω τῆς γῆς ἐξορίζουσα. Οὐδὲν γὰρ ἄλλο λέγει ἢ ὅτι ἀπῴκισται τῶν περὶ γῆν τὰ θεῖα καὶ ὅτι ἀνθρώποις οὐ συμμίγνυται καὶ ὡς ἔρημος αὐτῶν ἐστιν ὁ τῇδε τόπος.

the reason behind the invention of cult statues) of gods on earth is therefore required both by the idea of demiurgy and by ritual, which can only function if there be a form of communion between gods and men also on earth, "here." This communion, handed down by priestly lore, does not entail closing off the gods into bodies:

> Neither are the gods held fast in some parts of the cosmos, nor are the matters on earth without a share in them. Rather, the higher beings in the cosmos contain everything in themselves, as they are not contained by anything. The things on earth have their being in the fullnesses of the gods, and whenever they become suitable for participation in the divine, they immediately possess the gods as preexisting in their very own substance, [even] before [they possess] that [substance].[31]

The solution to ensure divine presence to the material cosmos works by way of the theory that higher beings are not contained by bodies but instead contain them, so that the very existence of material things is prefigured and "included" in the gods. Whenever this pre-existing ontological connection of material objects with the divine is activated by achieving the required suitability, they display the gods in themselves. Thus Iamblichus can quote Thales' dictum that "everything is full of gods"[32] and proceed to a discussion of the allotment of cosmic regions, bodies, or cultic spaces to specific gods in the light of divine ubiquity and pervasiveness:

> This [the divine allotment], whether it receive certain regions of the universe, such as heaven or earth, or sacred cities and countrysides, or again certain sacred enclosures or sacred statues, illuminates all from the outside [*exōthen*], just as the sun illuminates everything from the outside [*exōthen*] with its rays. Therefore, just as the light envelops that which is illuminated, in that very manner the power of the gods, too, encompasses from the outside [*exōthen*] everything that partakes of it. And just as light

---

31   *De mysteriis* I 8, 28f. P., 21f. S./S.: οὔτε γὰρ οἱ θεοὶ κρατοῦνται ἔν τισι τοῦ κόσμου μέρεσιν, οὔτε τὰ περὶ γῆν ἄμοιρα αὐτῶν καθέστηκεν. Ἀλλ' οἱ μὲν κρείττονες ἐν αὐτῷ, ὡς ὑπὸ μηδενὸς περιέχονται, περιέχουσι πάντα ἐν ἑαυτοῖς· τὰ δ' ἐπὶ γῆς ἐν τοῖς πληρώμασι τῶν θεῶν ἔχοντα τὸ εἶναι, ὁπόταν ἐπιτήδεια πρὸς τὴν θείαν μετοχὴν γένηται, εὐθὺς ἔχει πρὸ τῆς οἰκείας ἑαυτῶν οὐσίας προϋπάρχοντας ἐν αὐτῇ τοὺς θεούς. Cf. I 15, 48f. P., 37 S./S. (the same idea of divine presence immediately attaching itself to whatever material objects are akin to them). See Finamore, "Julian," 65f.

32   *De mysteriis* I 8, 30 P., 22 S./S.

is present [*paresti*] to the air without mixing with it... just so does the light of the gods illuminate in a separated manner, and while remaining in a stable way in itself it goes forth through all beings.... This [the light of the gods] is one and the same, everywhere complete, and it is present [*paresti*] in an undivided way to everything that can partake of it.[33]

The imagery of external/internal (note the emphatic repeated use of *exōthen* to describe the unconstrained agency of the divine[34]) is reinforced through an elaborate comparison with the Platonic image of the sun and its rays and light, used here to describe the paradoxical separation and yet relationship and mutual presence of gods and bodies.[35] Interestingly, the notion of a descent of the divine does not play any role in these passages,[36] whereas the terminology of divine presence (*parousia, pareinai*) is prominent, linked also with the more traditionally Platonic idea of participation.

33  *De mysteriis* I 9, 30f. P., 23f. S./S.: Αὕτη τοίνυν ἐάν τε μοίρας τινὰς τοῦ παντός, οἷον οὐρανὸν ἢ γῆν, ἐάν τε πόλεις ἱερὰς καὶ χώρας, ἐάν τε καὶ τεμένη τινὰ ἢ ἱερὰ ἀγάλματα διαλαγχάνῃ, πάντα ἔξωθεν ἐπιλάμπει, καθάπερ ὁ ἥλιος ἔξωθεν φωτίζει πάντα ταῖς ἀκτῖσιν. Ὥσπερ οὖν τὸ φῶς περιέχει τὰ φωτιζόμενα, οὑτωσὶ καὶ τῶν θεῶν ἡ δύναμις τὰ μεταλαμβάνοντα αὐτῆς ἔξωθεν περιείληφεν. Καὶ ὥσπερ ἀμιγῶς πάρεστι τῷ ἀέρι τὸ φῶς... οὕτω καὶ τῶν θεῶν τὸ φῶς ἐλλάμπει χωριστῶς, ἐν αὐτῷ τε μονίμως ἱδρυμένον προχωρεῖ διὰ τῶν ὄντων ὅλων. ...Τὸ δ' ἔστιν ἓν καὶ αὐτὸ πανταχοῦ ὅλον, ἀμερίστως τε πάρεστι πᾶσι τοῖς δυναμένοις αὐτοῦ μετέχειν... Cf. also *De mysteriis* V 24, 233f. P., 174f. S./S. See also Shaw, *Theurgy and the Soul*, 134f. and 148; Sarah Iles Johnston, "Fiat Lux, Fiat Ritus: Divine Light and the Late Antique Defense of Ritual," in *The Presence of Light: Divine Radiance and Religious Experience* (ed. Matthew T. Kapstein; Chicago/London: Chicago University Press, 2004), 5–24, 9f.; or Lutz Bergemann, *Kraftmetaphysik und Mysterienkult im Neuplatonismus: ein Aspekt neuplatonischer Philosophie* (München/Leipzig: Saur, 2004), 347–55 for a detailed analysis of the passage and its conception of light and divine presence.

34  The importance of *exōthen* for Iamblichean thought is also noted by Shaw, *Theurgy and the Soul*, e.g., 236, 240.

35  For this function of light see, for example, John Finamore ("Iamblichus on Light and the Transparent," in *The Divine Iamblichus: Philosopher and Man of Gods* [ed. H.J. Blumenthal and E.G. Clark; London: Bristol Classical Press, 1993], 55–64), who argues that Iamblichus develops a conception of light as a continuum, ranging from the incorporeal divine light down to more corporeal forms, foreshadowing Proclus' theory of light. See also Johnston, "Fiat Lux," 9f., and the detailed discussion of light in Iamblichean metaphysics and its historical roots and context by Bergemann (*Kraftmetaphysik*, esp. 345–410), who both emphasise how light with its visible properties, oscillating between the corporeal and the incorporeal, lends itself to the role of such a connector.

36  Finamore, "Julian," 65f. includes *De mysteriis* I 8–9 into a comprehensive synthetic discussion of divine descent in *De mysteriis*, which starts from later passages (64f.), without considering their actual context.

The divine presence depends on the capability of a given object to partake of it, on an ontological compatibility, termed variously *epitēdeiotēs*, *oikeiotēs*, or *syngeneia*.[37] For the human being, Iamblichus later speaks of "the Divine and Intelligent and One in us, or, if you prefer to call it Intelligible,"[38] which is roused by prayers to a yearning after its divine kin and to connection with the gods (*synhaphē*). This optimistic idea is one aspect of Iamblichus' portrayal of the human soul in *De mysteriis*: it belongs to the divine kinds of beings, albeit as the last class. The other side of the coin is the realisation of human lowliness or nothingness (*oudeneia*) compared to the gods as the apex of the hierarchy of the divine. This requires the practice of supplications as a means to gradually accustom oneself to the divine.[39] While the *aithēr* of the heavenly bodies is considered along Aristotelian lines as quite close to the incorporeal *ousia* of the gods,[40] the inherent imperfection and weakness (*astheneia*) of the other material compounds and regions is emphasised.[41] This idea also appears in *De anima*, where Iamblichus establishes a hierarchy of souls, from divine souls down to human souls, from universally active souls to particular souls connected with one individual body. This hierarchy correlates with their degree of involvement in matter[42] and also with the exact type of body and the relationship of the respective entity to it: while higher souls have pneumatic bodies, which they direct at will, particular souls sink into solid bodies and are affected by them.[43]

Thus Iamblichus establishes the existence of a continuum[44] of divine power and radiance, which renders the gods actually present also "here" on

---

37  Cf., e.g., *De mysteriis* I 15, 48f. P., 37 S./S; see also Shaw, *Theurgy and the Soul*, 86f.
38  *De mysteriis* I 15, 46 P., 35 S./S.: τὸ γὰρ θεῖον ἐν ἡμῖν καὶ νοερὸν καὶ ἕν, ἢ εἰ νοητὸν αὐτὸ καλεῖν ἐθέλοις.
39  I 15, 47f. P., 36 S./S. For *oudeneia*, S./S. refer the reader to their note in the edition of Marinus' *Vita Procli* (p. 56, n. 10 to VP 1; however, there they emphasise mainly the rhetorical topos of modesty).
40  *De mysteriis* I 17, 51f. P., 39 S./S.
41  *De mysteriis* I 18, 54 P., 41 S./S., 55f. P., 42 S./S. Cf. also *De mysteriis* V 2, 200f. P., 149f. S./S.: while the universal soul and the celestial gods "ride upon" the heavenly bodies without being affected or hampered by them, the divided human soul experiences a "heaviness and pollution" from contact with the corporeal; or *De mysteriis* V 4, 204P., 152 S./S. (*astheneia* of human beings). Cf. also Sara Stöcklin-Kaldewey, *Kaiser Julians Gottesverehrung im Kontext der Spätantike* (Tübingen: Mohr Siebeck, 2014), 56–9.
42  Cf. *De anima* 18 and 20–21, 44–47 F./D.
43  *De anima* 21, 46f. F./D.; see also 28, 56f. F./D.
44  For the importance of continuity for Iamblichean ritual, see Shaw, *Theurgy and the Soul*, 40f., 46f.

earth, while at the same time acknowledging the gulf between them and the material world. This perception of the hierarchical structure of the divine leads him to state, in the context of sacrifice, that only material gods handle earthly matters directly. The immaterial gods envelop and contain these lesser gods and may thus be considered as the source of their benefactions; however, "nobody must be allowed to say that they do these things themselves directly (*prosechōs*) by laying hands on the matters of human life."[45] The material gods entertain a paradoxical relationship to matter, entailing both separation and presence: "Even if they are separated from it [sc. matter] to the greatest extent possible, they nevertheless are present to it".[46]

Divine presence in material settings is especially important during ritual, which is a central topic of Porphyry's letter and Iamblichus' answer. A large section is devoted to the *discretio spirituum*: Iamblichus discusses the various signs of divine epiphanies, which enable the practitioner to discern the exact status of the beings who appear. The Porphyrian question, in its Iamblichean phrasing, points to divine presence: "What is the sign of the presence [*parousia*] of a god or an archangel or an angel or a *daimon* or of an *archōn* or of a soul?"[47] Iamblichus' general principle is that of a correspondence between the "essence, powers, and energies" of the entities who appear and the *epiphaneiai*.[48] Aesthetic qualities such as the intensity, shape, or colour of light and fire emanating from the apparitions[49] or the way they transform the air around them, making it easier or more difficult to breathe, as well as the psychological impact on the practitioners are enumerated following this principle of correspondence.[50] However, an exact ontological discussion of the actual status of the *epiphaneiai* is not given; Iamblichus employs a variety of terms: *autophanē agalmata, autopsiai* of the gods,[51] *ta tōn theōn agalmata*[52]

---

45  *De mysteriis* V 17, 222 P., 165f. S./S: ὡς δὲ αὐτοὶ ταῦτα δρῶσι προσεχῶς ἐφαπτόμενοι τῶν τοῦ ἀνθρωπίνου βίου πράξεων, οὐδενὶ συγχωρητέον λέγειν.

46  *De mysteriis* V 14, 218 P., 163 S./S.: Εἰ γὰρ καὶ ὅτι μάλιστα χωριστοί εἰσιν ἀπ᾽ αὐτῆς, ἀλλ᾽ ὅμως αὐτῇ πάρεισι·

47  *De mysteriis* II 3, 70P., 52f. S./S.: ἐπιζητεῖς γὰρ τί τὸ γνώρισμα θεοῦ παρουσίας ἢ ἀγγέλου ἢ ἀρχαγγέλου ἢ δαίμονος ἤ τινος ἄρχοντος ἢ ψυχῆς.

48  *De mysteriis* II 3, 70 P., 53 S./S.: ταῖς οὐσίαις αὐτῶν καὶ δυνάμεσι καὶ ἐνεργείαις τὰς ἐπιφανείας ἀφορίζομαι εἶναι ὁμολογουμένας. See also Shaw, "The Role of *aesthesis*," 99.

49  Cf. Johnston, "Fiat Lux," 16 (for the correspondence of the light and the ontological status of the apparition).

50  Cf. *De mysteriis* II 3–9, 70–90 P., 53–68 S./S.

51  Both terms in *De mysteriis* II 4, 76 P., 57 S./S.

52  *De mysteriis* II 4, 77 P., 58 S./S.

or the *phainomenē eikōn*.⁵³ The closest he comes to capturing the connection is in II 6, 81f. P., 61 S./S.: "the presence [*parousia*] of the gods… shines forth the light of the intelligible harmony and shows that which is not a body as a body to the eyes of the soul through those of the body;"⁵⁴ here, although divine presence is effected, the vision itself is only a means to show the incorporeal to the incorporeal eyes of the soul. The *epiphaneiai* seem therefore not to entail an ontological physical presence of the gods in themselves, but to function as an effective and efficacious means of representation.⁵⁵

An important instance of divine presence effected during ritual is divination. Iamblichus emphatically insists that true divination stems from the gods.⁵⁶ In his presentation of inspired divination, Iamblichus extensively employs the imagery of light and fire, connected with that of a divine *pneuma*, which enters the human media.⁵⁷ He explains the workings of public oracular sanctuaries such as Delphi, Colophon, and Branchidae by rigorously maintaining that the material substances and objects involved, such as water or exhalations from the Delphic chasm, play a secondary part in evoking the divine presence: they are filled by a prophetic *pneuma*, but only pave the way for the actual presence (*parousia*) of the god. To quote the description of the Delphic oracle:

> The prophetess in Delphi… gives herself thus entirely over to the divine *pneuma* and she is thoroughly illuminated by the ray of the divine fire. And when the fire which springs up from the chasm envelops her all around, cumulated and abundant, she is filled by it with a divine blaze. When she then takes her seat on the seat of the god, she is harmoniously attuned to the steady divinatory power of the god. By both these two preparatory acts she becomes entirely the property of the god. And then certainly the god becomes present (*parestin*) to her in a separated

---

53   *De mysteriis* II 5, 79 P., 60 S./S.
54   ἡ μὲν τῶν θεῶν παρουσία... νοητῆς τε ἁρμονίας τὸ φῶς ἐλλάμπει, καὶ τὸ μὴ ὂν σῶμα ὡς σῶμα τοῖς τῆς ψυχῆς ὀφθαλμοῖς διὰ τῶν τοῦ σώματος ἐπιδείκνυσιν·
55   This is blurred and somewhat downplayed by Shaw, "The Role of *aesthesis*," 99.
56   *De mysteriis* III 1, 100 P., 76 S./S.
57   Πνεῦμα/ἐπίπνοια/ἐπιπνεῖν: *De mysteriis* III 2, 103 P., 78 S./S. (dream divination), *De mysteriis* III 4–6, 109–112 P., 82–85 S./S. (possession; cf. esp. III 6, 112f. P., 84f. S./S., where the *pneuma* is said to be visible to the medium before entering; the idea of *pneuma* is combined with the "presence of the fire of the gods," coming ἔξωθεν and illuminating and taking possession of the medium); *De mysteriis* III 7, 114 P./86 S./S., III 9, 117 P., 88 S./S. (*pneumata* and lights).

manner, illuminating her, being different from the fire, the *pneuma*, his own seat and every physical and sacred visible preparation related to the place.⁵⁸

The divine is present and works through material objects and through a human being illuminated by the divine fire – however, it remains completely distinct and "separated" from all of them.⁵⁹ As Iamblichus repeatedly states in his discussion of sacrifices (book V), the divine and the human, or the divine and the realm of *physis*, have nothing in common (μηδὲν κοινόν).⁶⁰ Nevertheless, in this particular context he at times departs from the static terminology of separation and illumination and goes so far as to speak of "moving" (κινεῖν) the whole chain of causes, including the gods; to judge from the elaboration of the daimonic and divine principles moved through sacrifice in V 9, the "causes" or gods that can be thus moved seem to reach up to the demiurgic causes.⁶¹ A similar passage is found in V 21:

> ...before the advent and presence [*parousia*] of the gods all the powers which are subordinated to them are set in motion before them and, whenever they [sc. the gods], are going to move towards the earth, they walk first and proceed before them as their retinue.⁶²

The image employed here implies an actual movement of the gods towards the earth. Iamblichus does not qualify the image but expands it further, connecting it with the image of descent: only the theurgists, the expert ritual practitioners know the vast "multitude of powers which is raised when the gods descend and are moved".⁶³ The correct worship of all powers involved is essen-

---

58  *De mysteriis* III 11, 126f. P., 94f. S./S.: Ἡ δ' ἐν Δελφοῖς προφῆτις...πανταχῇ οὕτω δίδωσιν ἑαυτὴν τῷ θείῳ πνεύματι, ἀπό τε τῆς τοῦ θείου πυρὸς ἀκτῖνος καταυγάζεται. Καὶ ὅταν μὲν ἁθρόον καὶ πολὺ τὸ ἀναφερόμενον ἀπὸ τοῦ στομίου πῦρ κύκλῳ πανταχόθεν αὐτὴν περιέχῃ, πληροῦται ἀπ' αὐτοῦ θείας αὐγῆς· ὅταν δ' εἰς ἕδραν ἐνιδρυθῇ τοῦ θεοῦ, τῇ σταθερᾷ τοῦ θεοῦ μαντικῇ δυνάμει συναρμόζεται· ἐξ ἀμφοτέρων δὲ τῶν τοιούτων παρασκευῶν ὅλη γίγνεται τοῦ θεοῦ. Καὶ τότε δὴ πάρεστιν αὐτῇ χωριστῶς ὁ θεὸς ἐπιλάμπων, ἕτερος ὢν καὶ τοῦ πυρὸς καὶ τοῦ πνεύματος καὶ τῆς ἰδίας ἕδρας καὶ πάσης τῆς περὶ τὸν τόπον φυσικῆς καὶ ἱερᾶς φαινομένης κατασκευῆς.
59  Cf. Finamore, *Iamblichus*, 58f.
60  *De mysteriis* V 4, 204 P., 152 S./S.; V 7, 208 P., 155 S./S.
61  *De mysteriis* V 9f., 209–211 P., 156f. S./S.
62  *De mysteriis* V 21, 228 P., 170 S./S.: πρὸ τῆς παρουσίας τῶν θεῶν προκινοῦνται πᾶσαι δυνάμεις ὅσαι αὐτοῖς προϋπόκεινται, καὶ ὅταν μέλλωσι κινεῖσθαι ἐπὶ γῆν προηγοῦνται αὐτῶν καὶ προπομπεύουσιν. Here, παρουσία also has a dynamic dimension, in the sense of *adventus*.
63  *De mysteriis* V 21, 229 P., 171 S./S.: πλῆθος δυνάμεων ἐν τῷ κατιέναι καὶ κινεῖσθαι τοὺς θεούς.

tial for the success of ritual, whether in the "visible descents of the gods" or in the "invisible presence during sacrifices."[64]

The spatial imagery of motion and descent is also connected with the theory that the earth itself receives a "divine lot, able to accomodate the gods;"[65] the demiurge creates a kind of pure matter, which can be used in ritual to create material receptacles for the divine presence which form the basis of ritual:

> For one must not reject matter as a whole, but only that which is alien to the gods, and that which is akin to them needs to be sought out, because it can be suitable for building temples for the gods and establishing cult statues and also for the sacred rites of the sacrifices. For in no other way could the places on earth or the humans who live here partake in receiving the higher beings, had not a certain first groundwork of this kind been previously established.[66]

While in these passages, taken from *De mysteriis* V 21 and 23, Iamblichus thus plays with the idea of divine descent, this remains a singular instance in *De mysteriis* and is intertwined, as seen above, with the imagery of light as an illustration of divine transcendence and presence, or elsewhere with the more unspecific notion of beneficial gifts descending from the gods.[67] The fact that the theme of motion, arrival and descent of the gods surfaces this explicitly only in the context of sacrifice, may be connected to the different conceptual frames behind the various rituals: while for divination, the notion of *pneuma* as a medium between the divine and the human is established, for sacrifice, the idea that the divine recipient is present at the sacrifice (whether by actually coming to the scene or via the representation in the cult image) is attested.[68]

---

64   *De mysteriis* V 21, 230 P., 171 S./S.: ἐπὶ τῶν φανερῶν θείων καθόδων…ἐπὶ τῆς ἀφανοῦς αὐτῶν παρουσίας ἐν ταῖς θυσίαις.

65   *De mysteriis* V 23, 233 P., 173 S./S.: ἐδέξατό τινα ἀπ' αὐτῆς θείαν μοῖραν καὶ ἡ γῆ, ἱκανὴν οὖσαν χωρῆσαι τοὺς θεούς.

66   *De mysteriis* V 23, 232f. P., 173f. S./S.; direct quotation 233f. P./174S./S.: Οὐ γὰρ δὴ δεῖ δυσχεραίνειν πᾶσαν ὕλην, ἀλλὰ μόνην τὴν ἀλλοτρίαν τῶν θεῶν, τὴν δὲ οἰκείαν πρὸς αὐτοὺς ἐκλέγεσθαι ὡς συμφωνεῖν δυναμένην εἴς τε θεῶν οἰκοδομήσεις καὶ καθιδρύσεις ἀγαλμάτων καὶ δὴ καὶ εἰς τὰς τῶν θυσιῶν ἱερουργίας. Οὐδὲ γὰρ ἂν ἄλλως τοῖς ἐπὶ γῆς τόποις ἢ τοῖς δεῦρο κατοικοῦσιν ἀνθρώποις μετουσία ἂν γένοιτο τῆς τῶν κρειττόνων λήψεως, εἰ μή τις τοιαύτη καταβολὴ πρώτη προενιδρυθείη· See Shaw, *Theurgy and the Soul*, 47f. and 167.

67   *De mysteriis* V 10, 211 P., 157 S./S. (demiurgic and lower entities); V 26, 238 P., 177 S./S. (generic) and 240 P., 178 S./S. (demiurgic gods); cf. also V 17, 222 P., 165f. S./S. (we may speak of a divine gift from the immaterial gods insofar they envelop and contain the material gods which effect the beneficial actions).

68   Cf. Petridou, *Divine Epiphany*, 282–87.

From the passages above, a largely consistent, but variously nuanced, theory of divine presence in material settings emerges. *Parousia* is the key word, denoting actual presence. Iamblichus employs the images of containers or envelopes, of light and fire, as well as the conception of a divine *pneuma* to graphically describe and make plausible this presence, albeit maintaining the hierarchy of the divine and the gulf separating the lower classes from the higher. Gods can entertain close relationships with material bodies, whether human or other. They can be rendered present in specified material settings, whether temples or statues. These receptacles are made of special matter, created as such by the demiurge. The gods use these receptacles to mediate their presence to human beings, but they do so from a privileged position, never actually 'becoming' them – they remain separate (*chōristos*), illuminate from the outside (*exōthen*), or are said to be present in an immaterial manner to material objects.[69] The basis of divine presence stems from the divine demiurgic activity, which produces the pure kind of matter and establishes the preexisting affinities between certain objects and certain gods, which can be activated during ritual. However, this presence is mostly temporary and located in a clearly delimited cultic setting – divination, sacrifice, evocation of divine apparitions; it does not occur permanently or in everyday life. The imagery he employs allows Iamblichus furthermore to foster a permanent ambiguity as to the immediacy of divine presence: although it is emphatically asserted, the metaphors of light and illumination or the idea of a *pneuma* introduce implicitly an intermediate level between the gods themselves and the material bodies in which they become graspable.

### 1.2   Pythagoras, Epiphany, and Incarnation

While pagan cult plays a prominent role in Iamblichus, Christianity or the Christians are almost entirely ignored in his extant works. One isolated reference presents them obliquely as ignorant and deserving to be ignored: "For they do not even deserve to be mentioned in our treatment of the gods; and these people are both uneducated concerning the discernment of what is true and false because they have been brought up from the very beginning in dark-

---

69   Cf. *De mysteriis* V 23, 232 P., 173 S./S. Cf. also Stöcklin-Kaldewey, *Kaiser Julians Gottesverehrung*, 60f., who reads Iamblichean divine *parousia* as being not the result of divine activity, but as an eternal presence into which human beings can enter. This interpretation rightly emphasises the eternal and cosmic basis of divine *parousia*, but may not do full justice to the account of *De mysteriis* and the passages analysed above, which partly present the gods as engaged in eternal, but conscious and beneficial action or even in motion.

ness, and they are forever unable to discern the principles from which these things [sc. divination] stem."⁷⁰

Although Iamblichus remains true to this attitude and does not explicitly engage the Christians, his presentation of Pythagoras in his *Pythagorean Life* can be read as a subtle answer to the Christian incarnate Logos.⁷¹ Such a reading has been considered, e.g., by John Dillon;⁷² it would have likely suggested itself also to Iamblichus' ancient readers, confronted as they were with an increasing Christian presence.⁷³ Pythagoras is described in various ways as a super-human saviour who mediates between the divine and the human by revealing philosophy. An exact interpretation of his essence is eschewed; this parallels the studiously created ambiguity about the precise manner of divine presence in *De mysteriis*. One key strategy for presenting Pythagoras is developed in *De vita pythagorica* 8f., where, after rejecting a particular miraculous birth story that has Apollo have sexual intercourse with Pythagoras' mother, Iamblichus takes up the *Phaedrus* myth to present Pythagoras' soul

---

70    *De mysteriis* III 31, 179 P., 134 S./S.: οὔτε γὰρ ἄξιον αὐτῶν μνημονεύειν ἐν ταῖς περὶ θεῶν ἐπιστάσεσι, καὶ ἅμα ἀμαθεῖς εἰσιν οὗτοι τῆς τοῦ ἀληθοῦς τε καὶ ψευδοῦς διακρίσεως διὰ τὸ ἐν σκότῳ τὴν ἀρχὴν τεθράφθαι, τάς τε ἀρχάς, ἀφ' ὧν παραγίγνονται ταῦτα, οὐδέποτε δύνανται διαγιγνώσκειν. Saffrey/Segonds, p. 300, n. 6 point to the further development of the topos that Christians are theological ignoramuses, which was detected and analysed by Philippe Hoffmann ("Un grief antichrétien chez Proclus: l'ignorance en théologie," in *Les chrétiens et l'hellenisme: identités religieuses et culture grecque dans l'Antiquité tardive* [ed. Arnaud Perrot; Paris, 2012]: 161–97) in a passage in Proclus. Cf. also De Vita (*Giuliano Imperatore*, 49f.), who points to Christian influences in pagan philosophical contexts, as visible, for example, in the iconography of the Apamean mosaic with Socrates and the Seven Sages, which might have been located near Iamblichus' philosophical school.

71    For Iamblichus' *Pythagorean Life* and its relationship to Porphyry's *Life of Pythagoras*, see Ilinca Tanaseanu-Döbler, "Neoplatonic Lives of Pythagoras – Media of Religious Paideia?," *Zeitschrift für Religionswissenschaft* 20 (2012): 70–93, with detailed bibliography; see also Heidi Marx-Wolf, "Pythagoras the Theurgist: Porphyry and Iamblichus on the Role of Ritual in the Philosophical Life," in *Religious Competition in the Third Century C.E.: Jews, Christians, and the Greco-Roman World* (ed. Jordan D. Rosenblum, Lily C. Vuong, and Nathaniel P. DesRosiers; Göttingen: Vandenhoeck und Ruprecht, 2014), 32–38; Männlein-Robert, "Zwischen Polemik und Hagiographie".

72    See Dillon, "Die Vita Pythagorica," esp. 295 and 301; he assumes a more or less covert reaction against the Gospel of John. For Iamblichus, Pythagoras, and the Christians see also Mark Edwards, "Two Images of Pythagoras: Porphyry and Iamblichus," in *The Divine Iamblichus: Philosopher and Man of Gods* (ed. H. J. Blumenthal and G. Clark; Bristol: Bristol Classical Press, 1993), 159–72, 168f.

73    See Männlein-Robert, "Zwischen Polemik und Hagiographie," 199.

as belonging to the retinue of Apollo:[74] "For this [i.e. the story about Apollo's intercourse] we must not accept under any circumstances. That the soul of Pythagoras was sent down from the realm of Apollo to mankind, whether it was a follower or else was even closer related with this god, certainly no one would doubt, reckoning from this birth itself and the manifold wisdom of his soul."[75] As John Dillon has suggested, we might consider this rejection of a physical conception of divine fatherhood as "ein Stück antichristlicher Übertrumpfungsstrategie"[76] and could read the theory about Pythagoras as a soul close to Apollo as a correction of the theologically ignorant Christian conception of the incarnate Son of God. The theory outlined here has other parallels in the Iamblichean corpus: in the fragments of his *De anima*, Iamblichus develops the idea of pure souls descending to earth and condescending to a corporeal life out of sheer generosity, in order to benefit mankind – as Dillon puts it, "a kind of bodhisattva."[77] In the *Pythagorean Life*, the result of the descent is something *sui generis*. Pythagoras is not like the other men. He is pre-

---

[74] This strategy was highlighted by Dominic O'Meara, *Pythagoras Revived: Mathematics and Philosophy in Late Antiquity* (Oxford: Clarendon Press, 1989), 36–9; it is also underscored as the philosophical key of Iamblichus' portrayal of Pythagoras by Finamore, "Julian," 68–71. See also Männlein-Robert, "Zwischen Polemik und Hagiographie," 212 and 215.

[75] *De vita pythagorica* 7f.: τοῦτο μὲν οὖν οὐδαμῶς δεῖ προσίεσθαι. τὸ μέντοι τὴν Πυθαγόρου ψυχὴν ἀπὸ τῆς Ἀπόλλωνος ἡγεμονίας, εἴτε συνοπαδὸν οὖσαν εἴτε καὶ ἄλλως οἰκειότερον ἔτι πρὸς τὸν θεὸν τοῦτον συντεταγμένην, καταπεπέμφθαι εἰς ἀνθρώπους οὐδεὶς ἂν ἀμφισβητήσειε τεκμαιρόμενος αὐτῇ τε τῇ γενέσει ταύτῃ καὶ τῇ σοφίᾳ τῆς ψυχῆς αὐτοῦ τῇ παντοδαπῇ. I quote the text of M. Albrecht, in M. Albrecht et al., eds., *Jamblich: Pythagoras. Legende, Lehre, Lebensgestaltung* (Darmstadt: Wissenschaftliche Buchgesellschaft, 2002). Cf. also *De vita pythagorica* 222. See O'Meara, *Pythagoras Revived*, 37–39; David S. du Toit, "Heilsbringer im Vergleich: Soteriologische Aspekte im Lukasevangelium und Jamblichs *De vita Pythagorica*," in *Jamblich: Pythagoras. Legende, Lehre, Lebensgestaltung* (ed. M. von Albrecht et al; Darmstadt: Wissenschaftliche Buchgesellschaft, 2002), 275–94, 288f. The formulation πρὸς τὸν θεὸν might even suggest an ironical engagement of Iamblichus with John 1:1f.

[76] Dillon, "Die Vita Pythagorica," 29, n. 11.

[77] Dillon, "Die Vita Pythagorica," 298; cf. also John Dillon and Jackson P. Hershbell, eds., *On the Pythagorean Way of Life* (Atlanta, GA: SBL, 1991), 27; John Finamore and John Dillon, eds., *Iamblichus: De anima* (Leiden/Boston: Brill, 2002), fragment 29, p. 57. For the descent of the pure souls, see also Finamore (*Iamblichus*, 96–114), who already points to Iamblichus' favourable reception of Taurus' view that some pure souls descend as a divinely willed means of revelation of the gods (99f. and 102f.). This is also taken up by Shaw, *Theurgy and the Soul*, 143–45, who goes so far as to speak *en passant* of "this doctrine of divine incarnation: the belief that angelic souls took on human bodies for the salvation of the race" (145). However, this stretches the concept of incarnation too far,

sented as explaining the particular acuteness of his sense organs, which allows him to perceive the music of the spheres, as a singular result of "the daimonic essence that had fathered him;" ordinary men, in contrast, can never aspire to become quite like Pythagoras, but must content themselves with his mediation.[78] This, too, although perhaps evoking a biological fatherhood model, can be accommodated within the reading of the *Life* as a Neo-Platonic sneer at the Johannine incarnation, showing off superior knowledge of how divine presence really works – only lesser beings descend into matter, not the gods themselves, and 'son of a god' implies simply an ontological relationship in a chain of being with gradually decreasing divinity. But Iamblichus remains vague and also includes an interpretation of his hero that comes much closer to Christian ideas: Abaris, the priest of the Hyperborean Apollo, encounters Pythagoras, considers him to be the god himself due to certain secret signs, and hands his sacred arrow over to him.[79] Pythagoras' reaction is narrated as follows:

> Pythagoras, however, accepted the arrow and did neither show any bewilderment to this nor did he ask for the reason why he gave it to him. Rather, as if he were indeed the god himself, he drew in his turn Abaris aside and showed him his golden thigh, providing a sign that he had not been wrong, and he also enumerated to him every single item that lay in the sanctuary [sc. of the Hyperborean Apollo] and provided sufficient proof that he [Abaris] had not been wrong in his surmise. He added that he had come to cure and benefit mankind, and that he had come in human guise so that they would not be troubled out of bewilderment at his excellence and shy away from his teaching.[80]

---

extending it to the embodiment of the soul and blurring the boundaries between the conception of a soul in a body and a god in a body. Cf. also Shaw, *Theurgy and the Soul*, 151; Du Toit, "Heilsbringer," 289f.

78  *De vita pythagorica* 65f.
79  *De vita pythagorica* 91.
80  *De vita pythagorica* 92: δεξάμενος δὲ Πυθαγόρας τὸν ὀιστὸν καὶ μὴ ξενισθεὶς πρὸς τοῦτο, μηδὲ τὴν αἰτίαν ἐπερωτήσας δι' ἣν ἐπέδωκεν, ἀλλ' ὡς ἂν ὄντως ὁ θεὸς αὐτὸς ὤν, ἰδίᾳ καὶ αὐτὸς ἀποσπάσας τὸν Ἄβαριν τόν τε μηρὸν τὸν ἑαυτοῦ ἐπέδειξε χρύσεον, γνώρισμα παρέχων τοῦ μὴ διεψεῦσθαι, καὶ τὰ καθ' ἕκαστα τῶν ἐν τῷ ἱερῷ κειμένων ἐξαριθμησάμενος αὐτῷ καὶ πίστιν ἱκανὴν παρασχών, ὡς οὐκ εἴη κακῶς εἰκάσας, προσθείς τε ὅτι ἐπὶ θεραπείᾳ καὶ εὐεργεσίᾳ τῶν ἀνθρώπων ἥκοι, καὶ διὰ τοῦτο ἀνθρωπόμορφος, ἵνα μὴ ξενιζόμενοι πρὸς τὸ ὑπερέχον ταράσσωνται καὶ τὴν παρ' αὐτῷ μάθησιν ἀποφεύγωσιν.

Here we get at least the possibility of Apollo incarnate; this possibility is also recorded as one of the interpretations of Pythagoras' status given by some of his followers – and not expressly rejected or corrected:[81]

> and they counted Pythagoras from then on among the gods as some kind of good and most man-loving *daimon*; some said he was the Pythian Apollo, others the Hyperborean Apollo, others Paian, others one of the *daimones* who have their abode on the moon, others another of the Olympian gods, who had appeared to the men of that age in a human form for the benefit and correction of the mortal life, in order to present the mortal nature with the salvific spark of blessedness and philosophy, no higher good than which had ever or would ever come as a gift from the gods through this very Pythagoras.[82]

In the following passage, Iamblichus presents the saying that Pythagoras is a third rational essence between god and man and goes on from here to commend the early Pythagoreans' deep awe towards Pythagoras in view of the benefits arising from his philosophy.[83] This appears like a rationalising account of this awe – but it encompasses and commends also the various interpretations of Pythagoras as a divine epiphany whose exact nature remains elusive.

Given the evidence, it appears safest to conclude that Iamblichus intentionally plays with various interpretations of Pythagoras in his protreptic narrative, without explicitly voicing a clear-cut decision in favour of the one or the other. Thus he may simply exploit the greater freedom the narrative genre of biography allows him; this *modus procedendi* may be compared to the narrative construction of the aura around the person of Jesus in the gospels. A rationalisation in terms of a reduction to one strategy and the interpretation of all the others in its light, as proposed by Finamore,[84] might amount *mutatis mutandis* to a dogmatic reading of a gospel narrative in the light of systematic theology – it is certainly possible, but not necessarily intended by the author.

---

81  *De vita pythagorica* 30f., 140.
82  *De vita pythagorica* 30: καὶ μετὰ τῶν θεῶν τὸν Πυθαγόραν λοιπὸν κατηρίθμουν ὡς ἀγαθόν τινα δαίμονα καὶ φιλανθρωπότατον, οἱ μὲν τὸν Πύθιον, οἱ δὲ τὸν ἐξ Ὑπερβορέων Ἀπόλλωνα, οἱ δὲ τὸν Παιᾶνα, οἱ δὲ τῶν τὴν σελήνην κατοικούντων δαιμόνων ἕνα, ἄλλοι δὲ ἄλλον τῶν Ὀλυμπίων θεῶν φημίζοντες εἰς ὠφέλειαν καὶ ἐπανόρθωσιν τοῦ θνητοῦ βίου [λέγοντες] ἐν ἀνθρωπίνῃ μορφῇ φανῆναι τοῖς τότε, ἵνα τὸ τῆς εὐδαιμονίας τε καὶ φιλοσοφίας σωτήριον ἔναυσμα χαρίσηται τῇ θνητῇ φύσει, οὗ μεῖζον ἀγαθὸν οὔτε ἦλθεν οὔτε ἥξει ποτὲ δωρηθὲν ἐκ θεῶν διὰ τούτου τοῦ Πυθαγόρου.
83  *De vita pythagorica* 31.
84  Finamore, "Julian," 70f.

We can conclude that in his *Pythagorean Life*, Iamblichus comes close to identifying a historical person with a divine epiphany. For this, he can draw on the myths of gods appearing in human shape. This narrative fits the general principles outlined in *De mysteriis*: the gods can be present and efficacious in the whole cosmos and not confined to the celestial realm. The ambiguity of Pythagoras as an exceptional human being matches the ambiguity of immediate and mediated divine presence in the realm of matter articulated and implied by the metaphors of light, *pneuma*, or successive containers or envelopes in *De mysteriis*. The emphasis on the benefit of mankind, on the communication of the σωτήριον ἔναυσμα of philosophy,[85] and on the revelation of necessary and benefic teachings as the reasons for the descent of Pythagoras into the human world would have necessarily triggered in a reader familiar with the Christian story comparisons between one and the other. The aura of secrecy surrounding Pythagoras and the ambiguity of his exact status might have called to mind the similar ambiguity surrounding the figure of Jesus in John as well as the Synoptic Gospels. However, unlike Jesus, Pythagoras is a figure who belongs to the *illud tempus* of the history of philosophy, safely removed from normal, everyday life.

## 2    Julian

After Iamblichus, the panorama of fourth-century Neo-Platonism remains shrouded in mystery. Our main sources do not include professional philosophers, but what we may term 'lay philosophers'. Eusebius of Caesarea shows that Neo-Platonists such as Plotinus, Amelius, or Porphyry are read in Christian circles; he does not mention Iamblichus. Our knowledge about the aftermath and afterlife of Iamblichus depends heavily on Eunapius' *Vitae sophistarum*, written at the end of the fourth century. Eunapius, who had studied with Chrysanthius, a student of Iamblichus' student Aidesius, describes two outstanding students of Iamblichus, of which one, Sopatrus, chooses to pursue a career at the imperial court, while the other, Aidesius, sets up a school in Pergamum. It is in this milieu that the young nephew of Constantine, Julian, studies with Aidesius' students Eusebius of Myndus, Chrysanthius, and Maximus of Ephesus. Another source writing at the turn of the fourth century is Synesius of Cyrene. Besides these two late authors and a number of letters to

---

85   For the importance of salvation as a common theme of *Vita Pythagorae* and Luke, see Du Toit, "Heilsbringer," 276 and 285.

Iamblichus, probably dating from the early fourth century and maybe written by an official at Licinius' court,[86] the only extant larger corpus of Neo-Platonic writings from the fourth century is that of the Emperor Julian, whom Eunapius links to the tradition of Iamblichus. This link is confirmed by Julian's enthusiastic praise of Iamblichus, whom he regards as his model or idol in philosophy.[87] It does not come as a surprise that the encomiastic letters to Iamblichus were – anachronistically – ascribed to him during their transmission. Given Eunapius' perspective and Julian's enthusiasm, there has been a tendency in scholarship to regard Iamblichus as basically the key philosophical inspiration for Julian, and Julian conversely as a source of Iamblichean Neo-Platonism. This view has been rightly questioned and nuanced in recent years, e.g., by Maria Carmen De Vita.[88] We have, then, a more complex case of Iamblichean reception.

For the inquiry into Neo-Platonic and Christian discourses on divine embodiment and incarnation, Julian represents a rare type of felicitous evidence: raised a Christian, he is well-versed in the Christian scriptures from an emic perspective, while sharing with pagan Neo-Platonists the same emic perspective on their writings. In *Against the Galileans*, he sets forth to a larger public "the causes which convinced me that the fraud the Galileans contrived is a man-made fiction put together by evil machination."[89] The fragments that

---

[86] See, e.g., T. D. Barnes, "A Correspondent of Iamblichus," in *Greek, Roman, and Byzantine Studies* 19 (1978): 99–106; John Dillon, "The Letters of Iamblichus: Popular Philosophy in a Neoplatonic Mode," in *Iamblichus and the Foundations of Late Platonism* (ed. E. Afonasin, J. Dillon and J. Finamore; Leiden/Boston: Brill, 2012), 51–62, 54.

[87] Ep. 12 Bidez.

[88] De Vita, *Giuliano Imperatore*, 103–05, with an overview of the recent state of the art. She discusses Iamblichean influence on Julian throughout her book: Julian's theory of myth, 109–16; the theology of Julian's two prose hymns, 139–66; his demonology, 185–95; his theory of the soul, esp. 213–24; and theurgy, 225–52. She sums up her findings on 317–20 and arrives at a balanced conclusion: Julian either inherits the Iamblichus of his teachers or himself develops "una versione alternativa del neoplatonismo giamblicheo" (319f.). See also Tanaseanu-Döbler, *Theurgy*, 144f. and 146, for differences between Julian and Iamblichus regarding the status of cultic objects and the conception of priesthood.

[89] Fragment 1 (Cyrill, *Contra Iulianum* 2, 39A) Masaracchia: τὰς αἰτίας...ὑφ' ὧν ἐπείσθην, ὅτι τῶν Γαλιλαίων ἡ σκευωρία πλάσμα ἐστὶν ἀνθρώπων ὑπὸ κακουργίας συντεθέν. For recent discussions of *Contra Galilaeos* and its possible structure and sources see de Vita, *Giuliano Imperatore*, 166–98; and Christoph Riedweg, "Allgemeine Einleitung: 5. Julian – Contra Galilaeos," in *Kyrill von Alexandrien, Werke*. Vol. I: "Gegen Julian;" Part 1: Buch 1–5 (Berlin/New York: De Gruyter, 2016), LXXXV–CVIII. For Julian's critique of the New Testament, see John Granger Cook, *The Interpretation of the New Testament in Greco-Roman Paganism* (Tübingen: Mohr Siebeck, 2000), 286–334.

have survived give an important place to biblical texts. These are, on the one hand, presented as inferior in comparison with the Hellenic tradition; on the other, their exegesis is brought to support his point that the Christians depart from their Jewish roots, especially with their conception of Christ as a divine being. The critique of the incarnation is therefore a key piece in Julian's argumentation.[90]

Julian's attack on the divinity of Christ has two angles. On the one hand, he asserts that the veneration of Christ blatantly contradicts the strict monotheism of the Old Testament.[91] The Old Testament God does not acknowledge Christ as his proper son, which renders Christ a νοθὸς υἱός.[92] The Christians' interpretations of Old Testament passages as announcing Christ are wrong: Moses enjoins the exclusive worship of one god, although he freely speaks of other beings, such as angels or even gods in the plural. Even if the announcement of a new prophet in Deuteronomy 18:15ff. is taken to refer to Jesus, he would be similar to Moses, not to God.[93] The same treatment is applied to the interpretation of Genesis 49:10, Numbers 24:17, and Isaiah 7:14ff. as referring to Christ: on the one hand, they refer to other persons and historical situations, and on the other hand, even if the reference to Christ were granted, the Christian interpretations are contradictory and the Old Testament passages do not fit the Christian conceptions of Christ as a being pre-existing and transcending the human condition:[94]

> But let us grant even the "prince from Judah" – that is not "God from God," as you say, nor is it "everything came into being through him and without him not even one thing came into being." …As you try to prove it from these [scriptures], please show me one verse derived from the same store

---

[90]  Cook, *Interpretation*, 334, sees Christology as "the primary focus of Julian's attack." Cf. also Giancarlo Rinaldi, *La Bibbia dei pagani*, vol. 1: *Quadro Storico*, vol. 2: *Testi e documenti* (Bologna: Dehoniane, 1998); here vol. 1, 201, and David Hunt, "The Christian Context of Julian's *Against the Galilaeans*," in *Emperor and Author: The Writings of Julian the Apostate* (ed. N. Baker-Brian and S. Tougher; Swansea: Classical Press of Wales, 2012), 251–61, 254–59.

[91]  Cf. Rinaldi, *Bibbia*, vol. 2, 164f.; cf. also Rowland Smith, *Julian's Gods: Religion and Philosophy in the Thought and Action of Julian the Apostate* (London and New York: Routledge, 1995), 201–3.

[92]  Fragment 31 (Cyrill, *Contra Iulianum* 5, 159C) Masaracchia.

[93]  Fragment 62 Masaracchia (Cyrill, *Contra Iulianum* 8, 252B); cf. Rinaldi, *Bibbia*, vol. 2, 168, with a reference to the Arian controversy.

[94]  Fragment 62 and 64 Masaracchia (Cyrill, *Contra Iulianum* 8, 253D–E; 261E–262E).

from which I draw plenty. That [Moses] thought that God was the one, the god of Israel, he says in Deuteronomy: "so that thou mayst know that the Lord your God is one, and that there is no other beside him." ...Thus far Moses, who asserts at length that there is only one God. But maybe our fine fellows will say: "neither do we assert two or three." But then I will show that they certainly say this also, calling John to witness, who says: "In the beginning was the Logos, and the Logos was with God, and God was the Logos." Do you notice how it says that the Logos was with God – whether it be he who was born of Mary or someone else, so that I may answer also Photeinos at the same time – it makes no difference for now. I leave the dispute to you. It suffices as testimony that he says "in the beginning" and "with God." Now how does that concord with Moses' assertions?[95]

Julian refers to the Nicene formulation of the Son as "God from God" and rightly focuses on John's prologue as a key text behind this conception, all the while showing his awareness of the Trinitarian controversies.[96] The follow-up has the Christians breaking off the argument about Moses and adducing Isaiah 7:14. Julian's answer targets precisely the problem of the relation between the human being born of Mary and the divine, only-begotten Son, foreshadowing the controversies about the nature of Christ: "Let it be granted that this, too, were said about Jesus – although it is in no way referring to him.... Does he say that a god will be born from the virgin? And yet you go on calling Mary

---

95   Fragment 64, p. 159f. Masaracchia (Cyrill, *Contra Iulianum* 8, 261E–262C): συγκεχωρήσθω δὲ καὶ ἄρχων ἐξ Ἰούδα, οὐ "θεὸς ἐκ θεοῦ" κατὰ τὰ παρ' ὑμῶν λεγόμενα οὐδὲ "τὰ πάντα δι' αὐτοῦ ἐγένετο καὶ χωρὶς αὐτοῦ ἐγένετο οὐδὲ ἕν." ... ὥσπερ οὖν ἐκ τούτων ἐπιχειρεῖτε συμβιβάζειν, ἐπιδείξατε μίαν ἐκεῖθεν ἑλκύσαντες ῥῆσιν, ὅποι ἐγὼ πολλὰς πάνυ. ὅτι δὲ θεὸν τὸν ἕνα τὸν τοῦ Ἰσραὴλ νενόμικεν, ἐν τῷ Δευτερονομίῳ φησίν· "ὥστε εἰδέναι σε, ὅτι κύριος ὁ θεός σου, οὗτος εἷς ἐστι, καὶ οὐκ ἔστιν ἄλλος πλὴν αὐτοῦ." ... ταῦτα μὲν οὖν ὁ Μωυσῆς ἕνα διατεινόμενος μόνον εἶναι θεόν. ἀλλ' οὗτοι τυχὸν ἐροῦσιν· οὐδὲ ἡμεῖς δύο λέγομεν οὐδὲ τρεῖς. ἐγὼ δὲ λέγοντας μὲν αὐτοὺς καὶ τοῦτο δείξω, μαρτυρόμενος Ἰωάννην λέγοντα· "ἐν ἀρχῇ ἦν ὁ λόγος καὶ ὁ λόγος ἦν πρὸς τὸν θεὸν καὶ θεὸς ἦν ὁ λόγος." ὁρᾷς, ὅτι πρὸς τὸν θεὸν εἶναι λέγεται· εἴτε ὁ ἐκ Μαρίας γεννηθεὶς εἴτε ἄλλος τίς ἐστιν – ἵν' ὁμοῦ καὶ πρὸς Φωτεινὸν ἀποκρίνωμαι—, διαφέρει τοῦτο νῦν οὐδέν· ἀφίημι δῆτα τὴν μάχην ὑμῖν. ὅτι μέντοι φησὶ "πρὸς θεὸν" καὶ "ἐν ἀρχῇ", τοῦτο ἀπόχρη μαρτύρασθαι. πῶς οὖν ὁμολογεῖ ταῦτα τοῖς Μωυσέως; cf. also 62, p. 156. See Cook, *Interpretation*, 301f. and Rinaldi, *Bibbia*, vol. 2, 362–65.

96   Cf. Rinaldi, *Bibbia*, vol. 1, 200–3 for Julian's comparative closeness to Arian forms of Christianity, Hunt, "Christian Context," 254–59, and Stöcklin-Kaldewey, *Kaiser Julians Gottesverehrung*, 42–8 for a detailed discussion of Julian's acquaintance with Christianity.

*theotokos* – unless he says somewhere that that which is born from the virgin is the 'only-begotten son of God' and the 'first-born of all creation'."⁹⁷

The same problem is tackled in another fragment, which draws on bits of the Nicene Creed: "But if... the Logos is 'God from God' according to you and 'grew out of the substance of the Father', why on earth do you say that the virgin is *theotokos*? How could she give birth to a god, she, a human being just like us? And, in addition, when God says clearly 'I am [God]' and, 'there is no other saviour beside me', how can you dare to call him who is born of her 'saviour'?"⁹⁸ Here, the difference separating human and divine nature is targeted: a human being cannot give birth to a god – no lower entity can give birth to a higher entity. Julian emphasises the normality of Mary – she is simply an ordinary human being, like anybody else. That which is born of her cannot aspire to the same status as God and accordingly, in the logic of the Christians' own scripture, cannot be understood as a saviour. Underlying both the idea of Mary as God-bearer and of Christ as saviour is the assumption that Jesus Christ is God. According to Julian, this Christian *proprium* hinges on John's prologue and cannot be traced back to earlier Christians: John was the only one who dared to state that Christ was God, even if in a prudently dissimulating, unclear, and vague manner.⁹⁹ Julian's historical exegesis of the development of New Testament Christology reads as follows:

> But you are so miserable that you did not even remain within the confines of the apostolic tradition. And even that was turned to the worse and even more impious by those who came later. For neither Paul nor Matthew nor Luke nor Mark ever dared to say that Jesus was a god. But

---

97    Fragment 64, p. 160 Masaracchia (Cyrill, *Contra Iulianum* 8, 262C–D): ἔστω δὴ καὶ τοῦτο λεγόμενον ὑπὲρ Ἰησοῦ, καίτοι μηδαμῶς εἰρημένον...μή τι θεόν φησιν ἐκ τῆς παρθένου τεχθήσεσθαι; θεοτόκον δὲ ὑμεῖς οὐ παύεσθε Μαρίαν καλοῦντες, εἰ μή πού φησι τὸν ἐκ τῆς παρθένου γεννώμενον "υἱὸν θεοῦ μονογενῆ" καὶ "πρωτότοκον πάσης κτίσεως"; Cf. Rinaldi, *Bibbia*, vol. 2, 203f.

98    Fragment 65, p. 161 Masaracchia (Cyrill, *Contra Iulianum* 8, 276E–277A): ἀλλ' εἰ "θεὸς"... "ἐκ θεοῦ" καθ' ὑμᾶς ὁ λόγος ἐστὶ καὶ "τῆς οὐσίας ἐξέφυ τοῦ πατρός", θεοτόκον ὑμεῖς ἀνθ' ὅτου τὴν παρθένον εἶναί φατε; πῶς γὰρ ἂν τέκοι θεὸν ἄνθρωπος οὖσα καθ' ἡμᾶς; καὶ πρός γε τούτῳ λέγοντος ἐναργῶς θεοῦ "ἐγώ εἰμι" καὶ "οὐκ ἔστι πάρεξ ἐμοῦ σῴζων", ὑμεῖς σωτῆρα τὸν ἐξ αὐτῆς εἰπεῖν τετολμήκατε; See Cook, *Interpretation*, 302f., who points, with Finamore, to Iamblichus' VP 8 as the philosophical background, and Rinaldi, *Bibbia*, vol. 2, 365 and also 172 for Julian's reception of Nicene formulations.

99    Fragment 50, p. 144 Masaracchia (Cyrill, *Contra Iulianum* 6, 213B–C). For an overview of Julian's criticism of Johannine Christology, see Cook, *Interpretation*, 301–06, 334; cf. also Smith, *Julian's Gods*, 202.

the dear fellow John, after he had perceived, on the one hand, that already a great mass of people had been caught in the Greek and Italic cities by this plague, and after he had heard, on the other hand, that the tombs of Peter and Paul were venerated, even thought only secretly, first dared to say that. And after he says a few words about John the Baptist, he leads back to the Logos he proclaims, saying "and the Word became flesh and took abode among us," shamefully shrinking back, however, from actually saying how this happened. However, he never calls him Jesus or Christ when he calls him God and Logos; rather, stealing away our sense of hearing stealthily and slowly, he says that John the Baptist had given that testimony for Jesus Christ, namely that he is the one whom we must believe to be God the Logos.[100]

Julian analyses John's prologue in detail, pointing out the differences between the Logos hymn and the passages relating to John the Baptist; in this composition, he perceives a cunning rhetorical device at work: starting with the divine Logos, which *per se* does not seem to arouse Julian's criticism, John skilfully leads his readers towards the Incarnation and Jesus by using John the Baptist as an intermediary, so as to retain the utmost ambiguity without exposing himself. In another fragment also devoted to further analysis of John's prologue, Julian notes that some Christians distinguish between the Johannine Logos and Jesus Christ, but he underlines that this is a wrong exegesis of John, who intended to make plausible their identity by means of the Baptist as a mouthpiece:

> Look how carefully, quietly and secretly he puts his finishing touch of impiety to the drama; and he is so full of tricks and deceptive that

---

100 Fragment 79, p. 172f. Masaracchia (Cyrill, *Contra Iulianum* 10, 327A–D): Οὕτω δέ ἐστε δυστυχεῖς, ὥστε οὐδὲ τοῖς ὑπὸ τῶν ἀποστόλων ὑμῖν παραδεδομένοις ἐμμεμενήκατε· καὶ ταῦτα δὲ ἐπὶ τὸ χεῖρον καὶ δυσσεβέστερον ὑπὸ τῶν ἐπιγινομένων ἐξειργάσθη. τὸν γοῦν Ἰησοῦν οὔτε Παῦλος ἐτόλμησεν εἰπεῖν θεὸν οὔτε Ματθαῖος οὔτε Λουκᾶς οὔτε Μάρκος. ἀλλ' ὁ χρηστὸς Ἰωάννης, αἰσθόμενος ἤδη πολὺ πλῆθος ἑαλωκὸς ἐν πολλαῖς τῶν Ἑλληνίδων καὶ Ἰταλιωτίδων πόλεων ὑπὸ ταύτης τῆς νόσου, ἀκούων δέ, οἶμαι, καὶ τὰ μνήματα Πέτρου καὶ Παύλου λάθρᾳ μέν, ἀκούων δὲ ὅμως αὐτὰ θεραπευόμενα, πρῶτος ἐτόλμησεν εἰπεῖν. μικρὰ δὲ εἰπὼν περὶ Ἰωάννου τοῦ βαπτιστοῦ, πάλιν ἐπανάγων ἐπὶ τὸν ὑπ' αὐτοῦ κηρυττόμενον λόγον «καὶ ὁ λόγος» φησὶ «σὰρξ ἐγένετο καὶ ἐσκήνωσεν ἐν ἡμῖν», τὸ δὲ ὅπως λέγειν αἰσχυνόμενος. οὐδαμοῦ δὲ αὐτὸν οὔτε Ἰησοῦν οὔτε Χριστὸν, ἄχρις οὗ θεὸν καὶ λόγον ἀποκαλεῖ, κλέπτων δὲ ὥσπερ ἠρέμα καὶ λάθρᾳ τὰς ἀκοὰς ἡμῶν, Ἰωάννην φησὶ τὸν βαπτιστὴν ὑπὲρ Χριστοῦ Ἰησοῦ ταύτην ἐκθέσθαι τὴν μαρτυρίαν, ὅτι ἄρ' οὗτός ἐστιν ὃν χρὴ πεπιστευκέναι θεὸν εἶναι λόγον. A commentary of the whole fragment can be found in Rinaldi, *Bibbia*, vol. 2, 366f.

he draws back again by adding: "No one has ever seen God. The only-begotten son, who is in the bosom of the Father, he made him known." Is now this God the Logos Incarnate, the only-begotten son, who is in the bosom of the Father? And if this is him, whom I mean, then you, too, have certainly seen God for he abode with you and you saw his glory. So why do you say that no one has ever seen God? You have seen, if not God the Father, then at any rate God the Logos; if now the only-begotten God is one and God the Logos another, as I have heard some of your school say, then not even John seems to have attempted this yet [sc. to assert Christ's divinity].[101]

Julian thus deconstructs the Christian Logos incarnate through a comparative historical sketch of New Testament Christology, presenting him as a relatively late newcomer to Christian theology and therefore not a genuine, i.e., original doctrine – a schema that would later be taken up by historical-critical scholars such as Hermann Samuel Reimarus or, later, Adolf von Harnack, and which has exerted an unbroken fascination for Christian theology.[102] His arguments in rejecting the incarnation are mainly scriptural and exegetical and could be adduced also from a Christian emic perspective;[103] he does not enter into a philosophical debate about matter or embodiment and the divine, excepting the rhetorical questions about the absurdity implied in the veneration of Mary as *theotokos*. The pendant to *theotokos* and the god being born from a human being is the dead god: Julian repeatedly labels Christ as a dead body – *nekros* –

---

[101]  Fragment 80, p. 173f. Masaracchia (Cyrill, *Contra Iulianum* 10, 333C–E): σκοπεῖτε οὖν, ὅπως εὐλαβῶς, ἠρέμα καὶ λεληθότως ἐπεισάγει τῷ δράματι τὸν κολοφῶνα τῆς ἀσεβείας οὕτω τέ ἐστι πανοῦργος καὶ ἀπατεών, ὥστε αὖθις ἀναδύεται προστιθείς· "θεὸν οὐδεὶς ἑώρακε πώποτε· ὁ μονογενὴς υἱός, ὁ ὢν ἐν τοῖς κόλποις τοῦ πατρός, ἐκεῖνος ἐξηγήσατο." πότερον οὖν οὗτός ἐστιν ὁ θεὸς λόγος σάρξ γενόμενος, ὁ μονογενὴς υἱός, ὁ ὢν ἐν τοῖς κόλποις τοῦ πατρός; καὶ εἰ μὲν αὐτός, ὅνπερ οἶμαι, ἐθεάσασθε δήπουθεν καὶ ὑμεῖς θεόν. ἐσκήνωσε γὰρ ἐν ὑμῖν καὶ ἐθεάσασθε τὴν δόξαν αὐτοῦ. τί οὖν ἐπιλέγεις, ὅτι θεὸν οὐδεὶς ἑώρακε πώποτε; ἐθεάσασθε γὰρ ὑμεῖς εἰ καὶ μὴ τὸν πατέρα θεόν, ἀλλὰ τὸν θεὸν λόγον. εἰ δὲ ἄλλος ἐστὶν ὁ μονογενὴς θεός, ἕτερος δὲ ὁ θεὸς λόγος, ὡς ἐγώ τινων ἀκήκοα τῆς ὑμετέρας αἱρέσεως, ἔοικεν οὐδὲ ὁ Ἰωάννης αὐτὸ τολμᾶν ἔτι.

[102]  Reimarus, *Apologie oder Schutzschrift für die vernünftigen Verehrer Gottes* (ed. G. Alexander; Frankfurt a. M.: Insel, 1972), part II, book II, 2, "Beschluß," pp. 171–76; Adolf von Harnack, *Das Wesen des Christentums* (ed. C.-D. Osthövener; Tübingen: Mohr Siebeck, 2007²), 75–86; 117f.; 131–34; Hans Küng, *Christ sein* (München: Piper, 1993¹²), e.g. 427–40.

[103]  Here we must keep in mind Julian's own Arian background and connections, cf. Rinaldi, *Bibbia*, vol. 1, 200–4.221–5.

and derides Christian veneration for dead bodies and tombs, which even in the eyes of their founder are unclean.[104]

How does Julian now engage the underlying problem of matter and the divine, of the possibility of divine presence in material bodies? In Iamblichus, we have seen that the *parousia* of the divine in the material realm, which can be confined even to specific bodies, is a necessary corollary of assuming divine providence and demiurgy as well as assuming the possibility of *koinōnia* between humans and the divine. Is there anything comparable in Julian's thought?

In his anti-Christian treatise, Julian presents a relatively simplified sketch of the divine world.[105] In polemical contrast to Moses and his Genesis account of creation, he introduces the demiurge, largely derived from Plato's *Timaeus*.[106] The demiurge produces the invisible, intelligible gods, which in turn produce the visible gods to whom the divided demiurgical operations are assigned.[107] Here, an important distinction emerges: Julian accuses the Christians of bringing together the divine and the material in an unacceptable manner in their account of creation:

> For if there was going to be no difference whatsoever between heaven and man, and, by Zeus, between heaven and beast and, eventually, even the reptiles and the fishes swimming in the sea, it would have been necessary that the demiurge would be one and the same for all things. If,

---

104   Fragment 43, p. 138 Masaracchia (Cyrill, *Contra Iulianum* 6, 194D); 48, p. 142 M. (Cyrill, *Contra Iulianum* 6, 206a); 81, p. 174f. M. (Cyrill, *Contra Iulianum* 10, 335A–C). See Cook, *Interpretation*, 296, 326.

105   For the cosmological simplification in *Contra Galilaeos* see Maria Carmen de Vita, "Un 'agone di discorsi': Genesi e Timeo a confronto nel trattato di Giuliano Contro i Galilei," *Koinonia* 32 (2008): 89–120.

106   For Julian's handling of the speech of the demiurge to the younger gods in the *Timaeus*, see John Finamore, "Θεοὶ θεῶν: An Iamblichean Doctrine in Julian's Against the Galilaeans," in *Transactions and Proceedings of the American Philological Society* 118 (1988): 393–401; Christoph Riedweg, "Julians Exegese der Rede des Demiurgen an die versammelten Götter in Platons Timaios 41 A–D: Anmerkungen zu Contra Galilaeos fr. 10 Mas," in *Culture classique et christianisme: Mélanges offerts à Jean Bouffartigue* (ed. Danièle Auger and Étienne Wolff; Paris: Picard, 2008), 83–95, and Maria Carmen de Vita, "Agone," who engages critically with Finamore, "Θεοὶ θεῶν" and rightly emphasises Julian's connections to Christian apologetics.

107   Fragment 10, p. 97f. M. (Cyrill, *Contra Iulianum* 2, 65A–66A). Cf. De Vita, *Giuliano Imperatore*, 171–80 and also ead., "Agone," 105–16 for the contextualization of Julian's interpretation of the Platonic "gods of gods".

however, there is a great intermediate space between the immortal and the mortal beings, which cannot be increased by addition or decrease by abstraction with regard to the mortal and death-stricken beings, then it is proper that others should be the cause of the former and others that of the latter.[108]

The hierarchy of the cosmos, with the difference between the immortal, mortal, and animalic forms of life in it, requires a hierarchic demiurgy so that the higher beings are kept out of contact with the material and animalic strata of the cosmos. This correlates with Iamblichus' perception of the weakness of human nature or of the material cosmos on the one hand, and, on the other hand, with his emphasis on the fact that the concrete administration of the material cosmos is not undertaken by the immaterial gods, but by those connected with matter.[109]

Besides his notion of hierarchic demiurgy – from which it follows that the higher the divine being, the lesser its involvement with matter – Julian also draws on another idea, which can be traced back to Origen's *Contra Celsum*:[110] the traditional gods are conceived as particular gods of particular peoples.[111] This theory can be correlated with Iamblichus' theory of divine allotments, as described above;[112] comparable ideas are set out by Proclus in his commentary on the *Timaeus*, which also draws on Iamblichus' lost commentary.[113]

---

[108] Fragment 10, p. 98 M. (Cyrill, *Contra Iulianum* 2, 65E–66A): εἰ γὰρ μηδὲν ἔμελλε διαφέρειν οὐρανὸς ἀνθρώπου καὶ ναὶ μὰ Δία θηρίου καὶ τελευταῖον αὐτῶν τῶν ἑρπετῶν καὶ τῶν ἐν τῇ θαλάσσῃ νηχομένων ἰχθύων, ἔδει τὸν δημιουργὸν ἕνα καὶ τὸν αὐτὸν εἶναι πάντων· εἰ δὲ πολὺ τὸ μέσον ἐστὶν ἀθανάτων καὶ θνητῶν, οὐδεμιᾷ προσθήκῃ μεῖζον οὐδὲ ἀφαιρέσει μειούμενον πρὸς τὰ θνητὰ καὶ ἐπίκηρα, αἴτιον εἶναι προσήκει τούτων μὲν ἄλλους, ἑτέρων δὲ ἑτέρους. Cf. also fragment 11, p. 99f. M. (Cyrill, *Contra Iulianum* 2, 69B–D), where Julian states that all humans instinctively associate the divine with heaven, given the celestial realm's eternal beautiful order and, conversely, its distance from matter, decay, and becoming. See also de Vita, "Agone," 111–6, who proposes to read the text as a response to a passage in Origen's *Contra Celsum*.

[109] *De mysteriis* V 17, 222 P., 165f. S./S.

[110] See De Vita, *Giuliano Imperatore*, 181–85.

[111] Fragment 21, p. 113 M. (Cyrill, *Contra Iulianum* 4, 115D–E). Cf. also fragment 28, p. 124 M. (*Contra Iulianum* 4, 148A–D).

[112] Cf. also De Vita, *Giuliano Imperatore*, 182.

[113] The Proclus text is printed in Dillon's collection of Iamblichean Platonic commentary fragments (Dillon, ed., *Iamblichi Chalcidensis in Platonis dialogos commentariorum fragmenta* (Leiden: Brill, 1973) as fragment 14, p. 119.

The traditional gods are presented here as lower gods overseeing specific regions of the divided realm, of the material cosmos. Another fragment emphasises the hierarchy of the divine: on each ethnarchic god depends a chain of lesser beings – an angel, a *daimon*, and "a race of specific souls which ministers to and serves the higher beings."[114] Another fragment presents some traditional gods not as ethnarchs, but as givers of specific goods, presided over by Athena.[115]

Within this cosmic picture of hierarchic and beneficial divine activity, which keeps the demiurge safely separated from contact with matter, Julian presents one particular figure, Asclepius, in terms that suggest a proper pagan counterpart to the Christians' conception of Jesus:

> For Zeus engendered Asclepius among the intelligible [gods] out of himself, and revealed him to the earth through Helios' fertile life. This god [Asclepius] went forth from heaven to the earth and appeared in the shape of a human being in unified manner in Epidauros; thence he multiplied himself by his processions and stretched out his saving right hand everywhere on earth. He went to Pergamum, to Ionia, Tarentum, after that later to Rome, he flew to Kos, hither to Aigai. And now he is everywhere on earth and at sea; he does not visit us individually, but nevertheless he restores our souls when they are in a state of sin and the bodies when they are in a state of infirmity.[116]

The description of Zeus engendering Asclepius cannot fail to recall the Christian birth of the Son from the Father[117] and the Nicene emphasis on *gennasthai*. This birth takes place in the intelligible realm – among the highest

---

114   Fragment 26, p. 121 M. (Cyrill, *Contra Iulianum* 4, 143A–B): ψυχῶν ἰδιάζον γένος ὑπηρετικὸν καὶ ὑπουργικόν τοῖς κρείττοσιν.
115   Fragment 57, p. 151 M. (Cyrill, *Contra Iulianum* 7, 235B).
116   Fragment 46, p. 140 M. (Cyrill, *Contra Iulianum* 6, 200A–C): ὁ γάρ τοι Ζεὺς ἐν μὲν τοῖς νοητοῖς ἐξ ἑαυτοῦ τὸν Ἀσκληπιὸν ἐγέννησεν, εἰς δὲ τὴν γῆν διὰ τῆς Ἡλίου γονίμου ζωῆς ἐξέφηνεν. οὗτος ἐπὶ γῆς ἐξ οὐρανοῦ ποιησάμενος <τὴν> πρόοδον, ἑνοειδῶς μὲν ἐν ἀνθρώπου μορφῇ περὶ τὴν Ἐπίδαυρον ἀνεφάνη, πληθυνόμενος δὲ ἐντεῦθεν ταῖς προόδοις ἐπὶ πᾶσαν ὤρεξε τὴν γῆν τὴν σωτήριον ἑαυτοῦ δεξιάν. ἦλθεν εἰς Πέργαμον, εἰς Ἰωνίαν, εἰς Τάραντα, μετὰ ταῦθ' ὕστερον ἦλθεν εἰς τὴν Ῥώμην. ᾤχετο εἰς Κῶ, ἐνθένδε εἰς Αἰγάς. εἶτα πανταχοῦ γῆς ἐστι καὶ θαλάσσης. οὐ καθ' ἕκαστον ἡμῶν ἐπιφοιτᾷ, καὶ ὅμως ἐπανορθοῦται <τὰς> ψυχὰς πλημμελῶς διακειμένας καὶ τὰ σώματα ἀσθενῶς ἔχοντα.
117   Cf. Jean Bouffartigue, *L'empereur Julien et la culture de son temps* (Paris: Institut d'Études Augustiniennes, 1992), 649.

gods. The description of Asclepius' revelation is couched in ambiguous and paradoxical images: Helios reveals him on earth; Asclepius himself goes from heaven to earth and appears in human shape. The terminology recalls the portrayal of Pythagoras in Iamblichus' *Pythagorean Life* 30 and 92. The counterintuitive multiplication of the unified primordial epiphany, culminating in the assertion of generic ubiquity, contradicts assumptions about how bodies or space behave and underlines both Asclepius' higher nature and the universality of his salvific actions.[118] The emphasis is on the play of appearance and shape; Asclepius does not completely identify with his manifestations. Also, his divine origin is safeguarded: there is no mortal interference, no mother or nativity stories. Finally, he is presented also as a physician of souls and bodies alike, which can be read as an allusion to the similar portrayal of Christ.[119]

Julian's not always perfectly consistent elaborations on the divine hierarchy in his *Contra Galilaeos* as well as his two prose hymns on King Helios, for which he gives Iamblichus as his main source, and the Mother of the Gods have often been discussed in scholarship.[120] In the two hymns, both gods who are celebrated are situated mainly at the level of the intellectual gods, mediating between the highest, intelligible realm and the visible gods, who reign over matter.[121] It is in the intellectual sphere that Julian situates demiurgy proper, identifying Helios with Zeus and presenting the Mother of the Gods as Zeus' consort on the throne.[122] Even if the two mappings of the intellectual gods do

---

[118] See also Stöcklin-Kaldewey, *Kaiser Julians Gottesverehrung*, 252. For another interpretation see Finamore, "Julian," 74 n. 24, who reads the ubiquity of Asclepius' manifestations as intended to outdo the geographical limitations of the Christian incarnation. Petridou, *Divine Epiphany*, 33 points to polymorphy as a distinctive trait of epiphanies of Asclepius.

[119] Cf. de Vita, *Giuliano Imperatore*, 197f., who points to the Christian parallels but does not discuss incarnation.

[120] Cf. Bouffartigue, *L'empereur Julien*, 648 and 652, and, as a recent voice, de Vita (*Giuliano Imperatore*, 198–202), who ponders the idea that incoherencies may be due to Julian's "marcata finalità propagandistica," which may have led him to develop two versions of his system: a simplified one and a more complex one (201). For the theology of the hymns and their cultic background see, e.g., Smith, *Julian's Gods*, 139–78.

[121] The theme of mediation might also be a trace of Christian influence: de Vita (*Giuliano Imperatore*, 152) parallels the centrality of mediation between the mortal and the higher realms, as the key motif in the Hymn to Helios, with the Christian idea of Christ as the mediator, as developed in the Letter to the Hebrews. On the parallel functions and positions of Helios and the Mother of the Gods, cf. de Vita, *Giuliano Imperatore*, 160f. On the importance of the intellectual gods for Julian, see Stöcklin-Kaldewey, *Kaiser Julians Gottesverehrung*, 70–2 and 101.

[122] With an anti-Christian thrust when presenting her as a virgin; de Vita, *Giuliano Imperatore*, 161f., with n. 201.

not overlap perfectly, the idea of a divine hierarchy, in which the higher ranks are far removed from the material world and bestow their beneficence only indirectly, by means of the intellectual and visible gods, emerges clearly. In this picture, the incarnation of higher principles is out of the question, although through lesser deities – such as angels, *daimones*, heroes, or disembodied pure souls – the gods are linked with matter, much like in *Contra Galilaeos* and Iamblichus' *De mysteriis*. Thus Julian can take up the interpretative pattern already used by Iamblichus for Pythagoras as a soul belonging to the retinue of Apollo and present himself as an *opados* of Helios, as his *ekgonos*, in whom a spark of Helios can be found, as he writes in the transparent autobiographical myth in his speech against Heraclius the Cynic.[123]

It is in this work that we encounter an idea that further develops the pattern employed in the presentation of Asclepius as the divine saviour in *Contra Galilaeos* and presents Dionysus and Heracles as counterparts of the Christian incarnation and nativity story.[124] This may be regarded as a continuation of earlier pagan-Christian debates: already Justin Martyr had adduced the three sons of Zeus as pagan parallels for the suffering Son of God.[125] The interpretation occurs in the context of Julian's theory of myth, which he himself traces back to Iamblichus.[126] In the context of establishing that myths encode truth

---

[123] *In Solem* 1, 130B–C; *Contra Heraclium Cynicum* 22, 229C–D. For Julian's self-presentation in *Contra Heraclium* see Heinz-Günther Nesselrath, "Mit 'Waffen' Platons gegen ein christliches Imperium: Der Mythos in Julians Schrift Gegen den Kyniker Herakleios," in *Kaiser Julian 'Apostata' und die philosophische Reaktion gegen das Christentum* (ed. Ch. Schäfer; Berlin/New York: de Gruyter, 2008), 207–19; David Neal Greenwood, "Crafting Divine Personae in Julian's *Oration 7*," *Classical Philology* 109 (2014), 140–49 and de Vita, "Giuliano e l'arte della 'nobile menzogna' (*Or*. 7, *Contro il Cinico Eraclio*)," in *L'imperatore Giuliano: Realtà storica e rappresentazione* (ed. Arnaldo Marcone; Milano: Mondadori, 2015), 119–48, esp. 138f. and 140. For Julian's speeches I have used H.-G. Nesselrath, ed., *Iulianus Augustus: Opera* (Berlin: de Gruyter, 2016).

[124] *Contra Heraclium Cynicum* 14–16, 219A–222C. See Finamore ("Julian," 76–81), who discusses them as part of the dossier for divine descent in Julian. For the passages and their anti-Christian thrust, see also the detailed discussion of de Vita (*Giuliano Imperatore*, 196f.; and ead., "Giuliano e l'arte della 'nobile menzogna'," 130–5), who, however, does not focus on the issue of divine embodiment.

[125] Marcel Simon, "Early Christianity and Pagan Thought: Confluences and Conflicts," in *Religious Studies* 9 (1973): 385–99, 392. See also Stöcklin-Kaldewey, *Kaiser Julians Gottesverehrung*, 250–60 who analyses the three as saviour figures and points to Eusebius' *Praeparatio evangelica* III 13, 15f., were the three are closely associated with the Sun (250).

[126] For Julian's theory of myth and its connections to Iamblichus and Proclus, see the recent discussion of De Vita, *Giuliano Imperatore*, 107–20.

in a symbolic manner, Julian mentions the opinion that Heracles and Dionysus were originally' mortals and were later deified. For Julian, this opinion is false: the birth stories of the two deities are examples of myths encoding higher truths. This can be already seen by the way in which their births – that would make them so very human – indicate "something higher and excelling and transcendent," although to a certain extent comparable to human nature.[127] Heracles may be said to have been a child, to have had a body which grows and increases in divinity, to have had to learn and endure bodily toil and fatigue – but there are signs that he was something greater than a human being.[128] Already at the beginning of his life he could kill snakes; he could expose himself successfully to toils such as fasting and the desert, and he was said to have travelled in a golden cup over the earth, although Julian inclines to the view that he could simply walk on water.[129] For nothing could oppose the "divine and most pure body" of Heracles, as all elements were obedient to the "demiurgic and perfecting power of his immaculate and pure intellect." This is divinely intended: Zeus "sires him as a saviour for the world" and eventually calls his child to himself by means of the fire of his lightning.[130] The parallels with the gospel stories about Christ are clear;[131] the emphasis is, on the one hand, on the fact that the stories are not to be taken literally but as allegories, and, on the other hand, on the pre-eminence and power of the divine: a divine birth and divine child must be larger than life.

While Heracles is said to have actually experienced a birth, Dionysus' birth from the thigh of Zeus is not a birth, but rather the allegory of a "daimonic

---

127  *Contra Heraclium Cynicum* 14, 219B–C: τὸ κρεῖττον καὶ ὑπερέχον καὶ ἐξῃρημένον.

128  On the Greek cultural constructions of divine bodies cf. Petridou, *Divine Epiphany*, 35–9, who points to the "tension between the mortal and the immortal body" (35) involved in corporeal epiphanies, which may manifest itself through signs of the greater nature under the human concealment.

129  *Contra Heraclium Cynicum* 14, 219 C–D.

130  *Contra Heraclium Cynicum* 14, 219D–220A: Τί δ᾿ οὐχ ὑπήκουσεν αὐτοῦ τῷ θείῳ καὶ καθαρωτάτῳ σώματι, τῶν λεγομένων τούτων στοιχείων δουλευόντων αὐτοῦ τῇ δημιουργικῇ καὶ τελεσιουργῷ τοῦ ἀχράντου καὶ καθαροῦ νοῦ δυνάμει; "Ὃν ὁ μέγας Ζεὺς...τῷ κόσμῳ σωτῆρα ἐφύτευσεν, εἶτ᾿ ἐπανήγαγε διὰ τοῦ κεραυνίου πυρὸς πρὸς ἑαυτόν, ὑπὸ τῷ θείῳ συνθήματι τῆς αἰθερίας αὐγῆς ἥκειν παρ᾿ ἑαυτὸν τῷ παιδὶ κελεύσας. See Finamore, "Julian," 76, for a Iamblichean reading: "Heracles is a member of the class of pure souls."

131  See, besides Nesselrath, "Mit Waffen Platons," 213f., Greenwood, "Crafting," 140f., and de Vita, *Giuliano Imperatore*, 196f. and ead., "Giuliano e l'arte," 130–5, Simon, "Early Christianity," 396–8 for a brief overview of the historical background of the rapprochement of Heracles and Christ in Julian, as well as Bouffartigue, *L'empereur Julien*, 166–8 and 341, or Stöcklin-Kaldewey, *Kaiser Julians Gottesverehrung*, 255–9.

apparition" (*ekphansis*), differing in all respects from the birth of human beings.[132] The story itself smacks in Julian's opinion of an overly human description of divine activities, which *per se* points to its own status as encoded truth. In truth, Semele is a wise woman and prophetess, who foresees the epiphany of Dionysus and cannot bear to expect it; she prematurely initiates rites which then provoke a divine fire that consumes her.[133] Her death is thus the result of a ritual mistake. In the pre-ordained course of things, Zeus initiates the return of Dionysus from India and his appearance as a "directly visible *daimon*" who visits the cities together with a host of daimonic beings and bestows on humankind the vine as a symbol of his epiphany.[134] As in the case of Asclepius, Julian emphasises the non-human or superhuman side of the birth and chooses to play with epiphanial terminology to indicate the presence of Dionysus in the world – we have already noted in Iamblichus' *De mysteriis* the ambiguity of epiphanies and the impossibility of making sure whether they are or simply represent the divine being.

The issue of cultic receptacles as temporary *loci* of divine presence, which played an important role in Iamblichus, is also known to Julian, as a brief passage in the *Misopogon* demonstrates: the cult statue of Apollon indicates to Julian that the god had left his temple in Daphne.[135] Another brief mention about divine presence during ritual is linked with secret ritual symbols (*charactēres*) and their efficacy.[136] These symbols are also mentioned in *De mysteriis* as means of divination, and as a means to capture the divine light on walls;[137] this latter passage can be linked with divine presence. Another longer passage on cultic objects shows a slightly but decisively different stance. In the fragment which Bidez counts as Letter 89b, Julian discusses the cultic settings and objects as traditional "symbols... of the presence of the gods."[138] The further discussion indicates a mostly representational meaning of symbols: the

---

132  *Contra Heraclium Cynicum* 15, 220B. See Finamore, "Julian," 77–81, who also notes the contrast with Heracles and the emphasis on epiphany. His interpretation is that Julian wants to place the two in different categories of superior beings. On similar lines also Stöcklin-Kaldewey, *Kaiser Julians Gottesverehrung*, 252–5 for Dionysus and 255–9 for Heracles.

133  Bouffartigue, *L'empereur Julien*, 433, notes a possible parallel between Semele and John the Baptist, and the parallel between Julian's Dionysus and the Christian Logos incarnate.

134  *Contra Heraclium Cynicum* 15, 220D–221B.

135  *Misopogon* 34, 361C.

136  *Contra Heraclium Cynicum* 11, 216C–D.

137  Divination: *De mysteriis* III 13, 129–31 P., 97f. S./S.; divine light: III 14, 134 P., 100 S./S.; cf. Porphyry, *De philosophia ex oraculis haurienda*, fragment 321F Smith, where *characteres* are linked with divine presence on sacralised spatial environment.

138  Ep. 89b Bidez, 293a–b: σύμβολα...τῆς παρουσίας τῶν θεῶν.

cult statues make the immaterial gods accessible in a corporeal way, just like public statues of emperors, to which appropriate reverence is due, represent the emperors. In themselves, however, they remain material objects, whose destruction does not affect the gods themselves.[139] This is also made clear by the introductory statement of the passage: sanctuaries and statues are to be worshipped "as if one saw the gods present."[140] Overall, Iamblichean ideas of material receptacles for the divine are known to Julian but do not determine his interpretation of embodied divine presence.[141]

## 3      Conclusions

These two examples highlight some Neo-Platonic strategies to engage the Christian assertion that the divine became permanently incarnate in a historically graspable human being while fundamentally affirming that the divine is present to the material realm.

When targeting Jesus expressly, Julian dissociates the historical Jesus from the Jesus of the Christians, especially from the Jesus of John, regarding him as a limited, ordinary human being and subject of the Roman emperor. This is a rather negative version of the argumentative move we encounter in Porphyry, who uses the Platonic idea of the immortality of the soul and its kinship to the divine to paint a picture of a Jesus whose soul obtained a high rank after death simply on account of his piety.[142] Julian employs philological arguments to show how the Christians created their abstruse god-man as a product of poor fiction:[143] a close reading of the relevant gospel passages, criticising their

---

139    Ep. 89b Bidez, 293b–295a.
140    Ep. 89b Bidez, 293a: ὥσπερ ἂν εἰ παρόντας ἑώρα τοὺς θεούς.
141    Cf. also *In matrem deorum* 2, 160 and 161a, about the translation of the *xoanon* of the Mother of the Gods to Rome, where Julian insists that the *xoanon* is "not soulless earth, but something ensouled and daimonic;" for the passage, see Charles Guittard, "L'arrivée de Cybèle à Rome: élaboration du thème, de Tite–Live à l'empereur Julien," in *Culture classique et christianisme: Mélanges offerts à Jean Bouffartigue* (ed. Danièle Auger and Étienne Wolff; Paris: Picard, 2008), 191–200, 199f.; and de Vita, *Giuliano Imperatore*, 244–47, who also notes the relationship to Iamblichus.
142    Porphyry, *De philosophia ex oraculis haurienda*, fragment 345F/aF Smith; cf. Smith, *Julian's Gods*, 206. For Porphyry see Ilinca Tanaseanu-Döbler, "Porphyrios und die Christen in De philosophia ex oraculis haurienda," in *Die Christen als Bedrohung? Text, Kontext und Wirkung von Porphyrios' "Contra Christianos"* (ed. I. Männlein-Robert; Stuttgart: Franz Steiner, forthcoming): 137–75.
143    For Julian's notion of fiction and critique of the New Testament, see Cook, *Interpretation*, 286–89.

lack of clarity and their internal contradictions. His quite astute observations regarding the plethora of Christological approaches found in the New Testament lead him to postulate a late high Christology as the product of John's machinations.

If we follow the reading proposed by John Dillon that Iamblichus' *Life of Pythagoras* also engages with John, there we encounter a more ambiguous situation: the lack of an explicit valuation of the various interpretations of Pythagoras and the play with unclear manifestation and revelation produces a heightened aura of divinity and mystery, without resolving it dogmatically. This ambiguity also appears in Julian to describe the possible counterparts to Jesus: the divine sons Asclepius, Dionysus, and Heracles. For all of them, Julian uses epiphanial terminology. The stories involving corporeality – birth, growth, death – are interpreted so as to distract from the human, physiological aspect. They are either symbols of epiphany (Dionysus) or, as in the case of Heracles, a special birth, with mention of Zeus as father but not of the mother,[144] producing a kind of body different from and surpassing that of humans in purity and docility (here echoes from *De anima* and *De mysteriis* may be heard). The same kind of special birth, mentioning only Zeus as father and then going on to employ paradoxical images of ubiquity and epiphanial terminology, is assigned to Asclepius. This contrasts with his emphasis on the Christian conception of *theotokos*, which assumes a real birth and a normal human body.

For both Neo-Platonists, divine presence in the material world is thus not excluded; in Iamblichus it is emphatically asserted and explicitly theorised. In cultic settings, actual divine presence in material receptacles is certainly possible, but only in a specific context and temporarily. In order to maintain the possibility of divine presence, Iamblichus uses various metaphors. Firstly, he employs images of containers and envelopes, thus evoking a paradoxically inverted image: the gods are not in the bodies, but the bodies and the material world are "in" the gods. Secondly, he exploits the potential of light metaphors to assert an incorporeal, although immediate presence. Thirdly, especially in the context of divination, the idea of a *pneuma* as a medium appears. Thus, although present, the gods ontologically remain "outside" the body. The idea of actual divine descent remains an isolated fragment within Iamblichus' theory of sacrifice. The most vivid form of cultic encounter with the divine, the actual epiphanies, are described in their multisensoriality but are never ontologically identified with the gods themselves. The idea of hierarchic divine action and demiurgy further emphasises the strict transcendence of the higher divine

---

144 Bouffartigue, *L'empereur Julien*, 167 points to a possible quasi-motherly role assigned to Athena, but this is disputable.

classes, removing them from matter: the immaterial gods do not act on matter directly (Iamblichus); the demiurge does not directly produce everything, down to humans and animals (Julian).

Against this background, the Johannine incarnation appears problematic in three respects: its purported protagonist, its permanent materiality and its historicity. The idea that an entity from the summit of the divine directly enters the realm of matter contradicts Neo-Platonic hierarchic demiurgy and providence. The permanent divine presence in a human being bursts the safe space of ritual (which can be controlled and kept decent; it would exclude birth or other unwanted and sordid physiological processes) and confuses sacred and profane. Ritual matter is not (necessarily) what it seems; the setting apart and framing which distinguishes ritual contexts from other contexts opens up an undetermined space in which ritually used matter can be endowed with meaning by highlighting or suppressing certain aspects. The idea of a permanent divine presence in a human being brings divine presence into everyday life with all of its materiality. This can be mitigated by downplaying the commonplace materiality of the respective human body, e.g., by the emphasis on super-human traits such as bi-or pluri-location, golden thighs, or the purity and docility of Heracles' body. It can also be mitigated by resorting to narrative and eschewing to explicitly settle the status of the respective being and/or shifting the emphasis from materiality and material presence to the wider and more under-determined conceptual field of epiphany. This corresponds to the way in which the Neo-Platonist Amelius also re-reads John 1 in epiphanial terminology: he plays with terms denoting shape, appearance, and revelation so that the actual incarnation fades into the background.[145] Mythical figures such as Asclepius, Heracles, or Dionysus – or a historical but remote figure, surrounded by legends and quite divine down to its bodily functions, like Pythagoras – lend themselves better to these strategies than does a historical figure of the near past.

---

145   See Vollenweider, "Der Logos als Brücke," 393 and 395f.

# Index of Ancient Sources

1 Corinthians
    2:4   296
    2:6   272
    7:19   314
    13:12–13   182
1 John
    1:9   236
    2:7–8   221, 230
    2:8   236, 241
    2:29   236
    3:2–3   237
    3:3   237
    3:7   236, 237
1 Kings
    5:12   273n115
1 Samuel
    1:15–16   247
1 Thessalonians
    4   182
    4:13–14   164
    4:13–18   181
    5:1–5   182

2 Corinthians
    8:9   192
2 Esdras
    6:16–17   229
2 John
    5   230
2 Kings
    1:8   193
    9:11   247
2 Maccabees   142, 145, 150n44
    4:7–15   229
    6:1–5   229
    6:7   229
    7:9   150n44
    7:11   150n44
    7:14   150n44
    7:22–23   150n44
    8–9   229
    10:1–8   229
    14:33   229
2 Peter   120
    2:1   269n101

3   112n35
    3:13   113n43

4 Maccabees   4, 19, 22, 130, 133, 134, 141, 142, 144
    1:1–3:19   154
    1:1b   149
    1:1–2   143
    1:1–3:18   144
    1:7   143
    1:13–14   143
    1:19   151
    1:30   143
    1:31   151
    2:6   151
    2:6–9   143
    3:1   151
    3:19–18:24   144
    3:20–18:23   154–57
    4:11–12   153
    5:24–25   153
    6:31–55   143
    7:1–5   157
    7:9   157
    7:21–22   314n30
    9:8–9   153
    9:22–25   150
    9:23–24   155
    10:18–21   153
    11:7–8   153
    11:13–16   155
    11:20   155
    11:21–27   155
    12:121   153
    13:1–14:10   152
    13:1–5   143
    13:6–7   157
    13:13–15   150
    13:16–18   152
    13:19–24   152
    14:5–6   150
    15:3   153
    16:1   143
    17:12   150
    18:2   143

# 376  INDEX OF ANCIENT SOURCES

18:23   150

Acts, book of   105n11
   3:11   228n16
   5:12   228n16
   13:6   269n101
   17   243n30, 279
   17:18   279n1
   17:22   279n1
   17:31   243n30
   17:32   243n30
   17:38   243n30
Aelius Aristides, *Orations* 37.2 (ed. Behr; ed. Jebb 9.9)   230
Aeschines, *De falsa legatione*
   98–99   246n10
Aeschines, *In Timarchium*
   126   246n10
   131   246n10
   164   246n10
Aland, *Synopsis of the Four Gospels*   117, 188, 232
*Allogenes* (Nag Hammadi)   329
Ambrose, *Enarrationes in Psalmos*
   36.28   270
Ammonius, *On the Difference of Similar Expressions*
   307   268
Amos, book of
   5:21–24   71
Apocalypse of Peter   112n35, 114, 120
Apollonius   see Pseudo-Apollonius, *Epistles*
Apuleius, *Apology*
   16   285
Apuleius, *Metamorphoses*
   9.14   286, 286n27
   9.15   286n29
Apuleius, *The Golden Ass*   285, 286
Aristophanes, *Clouds*   86n32
Aristophanes, *Wealth*
   582–86   70n7
Aristotle, *Constitution of Athens*
   60.3   70n7
Aristotle, *History of Animals*
   536b   246n9
Aristotle, *Metaphysics*
   357a24ff.   80n16
   1017a27–30   67
   1072a26–27   47–48
   1072a26–29   48
   1072b1–3   48
Aristotle, *Poetics*
   139b34f.   80n16
   1457b6ff.   80n16
Aristotle, *Politics*
   1295a   246n12
Aristotle   see also Pseudo-Aristotle
Athenagoras, *Legatio*   302
   2.3   303n103
   7.3   302
   20.2–5   302
   22.10   302
Athenagoras, *Plea on Behalf of the Christians*   301, 302
Atticus, fragment
   2.4   222
Augustine, *Confessions*
   7.13f.   338n1
Augustine, *De civitate Dei* [*The City of God*]
   10.29   223, 338n2
Augustine, *Letter to Paulinus and Therasia*   223
Augustine, *Letters*
   31   223
Augustine, *On Christian Doctrine*
   2.28   223, 243
Augustine, *Retractations*
   2.4   223
Aulus Gellius, *Attic Nights*
   17.19   106n13

Basil of Caesarea, *Regulae morales*
   56.2   271
Boethus, *Difficult Questions in Plato*   302
Book of Enoch   115n55
Book of the Ten Festivals   190, 216, 217

Cassius Dio, *Roman History*
   52.41.1   246n12
   76.16.2   246n12
*Catena in Matthaeum*   271, 272
Catullus, *Carmina*
   34.1–12   249n25
Celsus, *Alethes Logos* [*True Discourse*]   266, 297, 298, 299
   1.1   297

## INDEX OF ANCIENT SOURCES 377

1.3   297
1.4   297
1.6   297
1.9   299
1.12–13   299
1.26   298
1.28–71   298
2.4–5   297
2.13–20   298
1.30   299
1.44   298
2.47–48   299
2.57–58   298
3.1   298
3.5   297
3.10–12   298
3.41   298
4.6   298
4.8   298
3.11   298
3.14   298, 298n89
3.23   298
4.28   298
4.33–47   298
3.40   298
3.41   299
4.54–61   298
4.74–99   298
5.2   298
5.14   298
5.59   298
5.63   297
6.10   298
6.14   297
6.39–40   297
6.40   297
6.63–64   298
6.72   298
6.74   298n87
6.75–77   298
7.2   298n87
7.13–15   298
7.14   299
7.36   298
7.43   299
7.45   299, 299n90
7.58   297
8.2   297

8.12   298
8.17   297
8.49   297
8.65   297
8.67   297
8.68   297
8.69   297
8.73   297
8.75   297

Censorinus, *On the Natal Day*
  18.11   116

Cicero, *De divinatione*
  2   246n10
  46   246n10
  96   246n10

Cicero, *De officiis*
  11   192n12
  60   192n12
  64   192n12

Cicero, *Letters to Brutus*
  1.14.1   262n73
  2.5.3   262n73

Cicero, *On the Nature of the Gods*
  1.36   107n20, 121

Cicero, *Tusculan Disputations*
  1   170

Cleanthes, *Hymn to Zeus* v.
  39   107

Cleanthes, fragment
  537   249n25

Clement, *Stromata*   301

*Commentary on Plato's Parmenides*   324, 334
  1.4   335
  1.4–5   334
  1.6   334
  1.9   334
  1.17–20   334n24
  1.25   334
  1.25–26   335, 336
  1.29–30   335
  1.30   334
  1.32   335
  1.34   335
  1.34–35   335
  2.10–14   335
  2.13   334
  3.1–9   335
  4.7–9   335

5.10–11   335
6.23   335
9.20–10.35   335
10.16–23   336
11–14   335
11.8   336
11.22   336
11.32   336
11.33   336
12.9   336
*Counsels of Wisdom*
26–30   257n54
*Cynic Epistles, Letters of Diogenes*
34.3   202
38.3   195

Daniel, book of
3:2   229
Democritus, fragment
44   257n53
Demosthenes, *De corona*
180   246n10
Deuteronomy, book of   360
18:15ff.   360
23:24–25   195
*Didache*
8:1–2   245
8:2   244, 247
11:4–12   270
Dio Chrysostom, *Discourses / Orations*
8.20–26   216
10.16   197
11.27   246
36.47–50   112n41
40.37   112n38
Diodorus of Sicily, *Bibliotheca Historica*
1.27.4   249n25
10.9.8   263
34/35.1.4   147
Diogenes Laertius, *Vitae philosophorum* [*Lives of Eminent Philosophers*]   188
1.72   260n63
2.41   242
3.57   327
6.29–30   213
6.37   202, 215
6.39   207, 215
6.41   214

6.42   209
6.63   215
6.85   190n7
6.104   188n4
7.18   260n63
8.10   256n50
Diogenes the Cynic   see *Cynic Epistles, Letters of Diogenes*
Dionysius of Halicarnassus, *Antiquitates Romanae*
1.31.1   232

Ecclesiastes, book of   23, 139, 190, 191
4:17   208
5:2   246
5:2–3   247, 248n19
9:4   190
Epictetus, *Discourses*   310, 320
1.4.26   318n44
1.27.10   318n44
1.27.4–6   313
1.27.7   313
2   282n13
2.9   314
2.9.1–22   282n13
2.9.14   313
2.9.19–21   306, 307, 310, 315, 316, 320, 321
2.9.20   308, 317
2.9.21   317
2.16.44   204
2.18.11   318n44
3.1.8   318n44
3.2.3   318n44
3.21.15   318
3.22   157, 201
3.22.23   203
3.24.15   203
3.24.16   203
4.1.51   309n18
4.1.57   318n44
4.1.123   157
4.7   280, 310
4.7.2   280
4.7.3   280
4.7.4   280
4.7.5   280
4.7.6   280, 306, 307, 310, 320, 321
4.8.28   318n44

# INDEX OF ANCIENT SOURCES

Epicurus, *Epistula ad Menoeceum* 180n44
*Etymologicum genuinum* 271n105
Eunapius, *Vitae sophistarum* 358
   4.2.1–4 (= Origenes fragment 4) 329
Eusebius, *Ecclesiastical History* [*Historia ecclesiastica*]
   3.10.6 143
   4.11.8 300
   4.16.1–9 284n17
   4.16.7 300
   4.18 10n3
   5.10.1 303n103
Eusebius, *Preparation for the Gospel* [*Praeparatio evangelica*]
   3.13 369n125
   3.15–16 369n125
   11.2.4 222
Euripides, *Bacchae*
   641 106n13
Euripides, fragment 852 *TGF* 72
Euripides, *Trojan Women* 123
Exodus, book of
   33:11 205

Galen, *De placito Hippocratis et Platonis*
   7.2.15 246n12
Galen, *De usu partium*
   11.14 296n77, 296n78
   14.7 296n74
Galen, *Epitomes* 294n69
Galen, *On Demonstration* 293, 296
Galen, *On the Differences in Pulses* 293
   2.4 293
   3.3 294
Galen, *On the Unmoved Prime Mover* 293
Galen, *The Best Doctor Is Also a Philosopher* 292
Genesis, book of 108, 117, 122, 231, 298, 365
   2:5 265
   8:22 111
   11:29 266
   11:31 266
   12:17 266
   16:1–4 266
   16:3 266
   18 200
   49:10 360
*Greek Magical Papyri* 248
   I.15–19 248n22
   I.134–43 248n22
   II.1 248n22
   IV.1540–79 248n22
   V.84–90 248n22
   CXXX.6–13 248n22

Hebrews, Epistle to the 368n121
Hecataeus, fragment
   1 89n50
Heraclitus, *Homeric Problems*
   28.2 230
   53 121n78
   55.1 230
   72.4–5 230
Heraclitus, fragment DK 22 B 5 343n19
Herodotus, *Histories*
   4.126 81
   4.155 246, 271n105
   7.48 81
   7.140–44 99
Hesiod, *Theogony* 121
   19 122
   655 81n17
Hesiod, *Work and Days*
   106–201 121
   109ff. 85n28
   207 81n17
   289–92 105
Hesychius, *Lexicon* $\beta$.340 271n106
Hippolytus, *The Refutation of All Heresies*
   6.16 222
   6.24 222
   6.32 222
Homer, *Iliad*
   1.396–406 121
   1.561–62 81n17
   1.579 123
   2.190 81n17
   2.200 81n17
   4.31 81n17
   6.326 81n17
   6.407 81n17
   6.486 81n17
   6.521 81n17
   9.40 81n17
   9.497–501 252
   13.448 81n17

13.810    81n17
16.384–93   124
21    121n78
22.263   123
24.194   81n17
Homer, *Odyssey*   121
  11   77
  1.28   203
  4.274   81n17
  7.118   123
  9.14   122
  9.106   123
  9.123   123
  10.472   81n17
  14.83–84   72
  14.443–45   81n17
  18.15   81n17
  18.406   81n17
  19.71   81n17
Horace, *Carmina*
  1.2   250n28
Hosea, book of   204

Iamblichus, *De anima*   348, 355, 373
  18 F./D.   348n42
  20–21 F./D.   348n42
  21 F./D.   348n43
  28 F./D.   348n43
  44–47 F./D.   348n42
  46f. F./D.   348n43
  56f. F./D.   348n43
Iamblichus, *De communi mathematica scientia*   334n25
Iamblichus, *De mysteriis*   339, 341n15, 344, 344n24, 344n26, 348, 354, 358, 368, 371, 373
  I 8–9   347n36
  I 8, 23f.   344n27
  I 8, 25f. P., 19f. S./S.   345n28
  I 8, 27 P., 20f. S./S.   345n29
  I 8, 28 P., 21 S./S.   345n30
  I 8, 28f. P., 21f. S./S.   346n31
  I 8, 30 P., 22 S./S.   346n32
  I 9, 30f. P., 23f. S./S.   347n33
  I 15, 46 P., 35 S./S.   348n38
  I 15, 47f. P., 36 S./S.   348n39
  I 15, 48f. P., 37 S./S.   348n37
  I 16, 50 P., 38 S./S.   345n28
  I 17, 51 P., 38 S./S.   345n28
  I 17, 51f. P., 39 S./S.   348n40
  I 18, 54 P., 41 S./S.   348n41
  I 18, 55f. P., 42 S./S.   348n41
  II 3–9, 70–90 P., 53–68 S./S.   349n50
  II 3, 70 P., 52f. S./S.   349n47
  II 3, 70 P., 53 S./S.   349n48
  II 4, 76 P., 57 S./S.   349n51
  II 4, 77 P., 58 S./S.   349n52
  II 5, 79 P., 60 S./S.   350n53
  II 6, 81f. P., 61 S./S.   350
  III 1, 100 P., 76 S./S.   350n56
  III 2, 103 P., 78 S./S.   350n57
  III 4–6, 109–112 P., 82–85 S./S.   350n57
  III 7, 114 P., 86 S./S.   350n57
  III 9, 117 P., 88 S./S.   350n57
  III 11, 126f. P., 94f. S./S.   351n58
  III 13   232n21
  III 13, 129–31 P., 97f. S./S.   371n137
  III 14, 134 P., 100 S./S.   371n137
  III 31, 179 P., 134 S./S.   354n70
  V   351
  V 2, 200f. P., 149f. S./S.   348n41
  V 4, 204 P., 152 S./S.   351n60
  V 7, 208 P., 155 S./S.   351n60
  V 9f., 209–211 P., 156f. S./S.   351n61
  V 10, 211 P., 157 S./S.   352n67
  V 14, 218 P., 163 S./S.   349n46
  V 17, 222 P., 165f S./S.   349n45, 352n67, 366n109
  V 21, 228 P., 170 S./S.   351n62
  V 21, 229 P., 171 S./S.   351n63
  V 21, 230 P., 171 S./S.   352n64
  V 23, 232 P., 173 S./S.   353n69, 352n66
  V 23, 233 P., 173f. S./S.   352n65
  V 23, 233f. P., 174 S./S.   352n66
  V 26, 238 P., 177 S./S.   352n67
  V 26, 240 P., 178 S./S.   352n67
Iamblichus, *De vita Pythagorica*   354, 354n71, 355, 356, 358, 358n85, 373
  7f.   355n75
  8f.   354
  29.162   260
  30   357n82, 368
  30f.   357n81
  31   357n83
  65f.   356n78
  72   256n50

## INDEX OF ANCIENT SOURCES

  91 356n79
  92 356n80, 368
  140 357n81
Ibn al-Qifti, *History of Learned Men* 294n69
Ignatius of Antioch, Epistles of 320
Ignatius, *To the Ephesians* 319
  18.2 319
Ignatius, *To the Magnesians*
  5.2 319
Ignatius, *To the Trallians* 319
*Inscriptiones Graecae* II.ii.2311.23–70 70n7
Irenaeus, *Against Heresies*
  1.25.6 221
Isaiah, book of
  1:10–17 71
  5:11 286
  6:1 205
  7:14 361
  7:41ff. 360
  34 112n35
  34:4 111
  65:17 113n43
  66:22 113n43
Isocrates, *Busiris*
  44 259n61
Isocrates, *Panathenaicus*
  88 259n61

Jerome, *De viris illustribus*
  13 143
  23 284n17
Jerome, *Chronicon* 284n17
Job, Book of 23, 139, 204
  11:2–3 246
John, Gospel of 6, 219, 221, 221n5, 222–28,
  231, 231n20, 233, 235–36, 238, 240–42,
  340, 354n72
  1 374
  1:1–2 231
  1:3–4 231
  1:6 204
  1:9 236, 241
  1:12 239
  1:18 228n14
  1:33 232
  1:44 234
  2 224
  2:4 240

  2:19–22 229n18
  2:20–21 229
  3:2 239
  3:14 226
  3:16 228n14
  3:18 228n14
  3:19–21 233
  3:33 234
  4 241n26
  4:1 269n101
  4:5 234
  4:8 234, 241
  4:16–19 234
  4:20 234
  4:20–24 235
  4:21 239
  4:23 236, 239
  4:23–24 234
  4:24 232
  4:28 234
  4:28–30 234
  4:30 234
  4:39 234
  4:39–42 234
  5:8 228n14
  5:18 228, 228n14
  5:31–32 239
  5:37 239
  6 241n26
  6:32 241
  6:55 241
  6:63 232
  7 232n20
  7:6 240
  7:12 231
  7:14 231
  7:20 232
  7:23 240
  7:28 231
  7:32 231, 231n20
  7:36 241n27
  7:39 232
  7:44–46 231
  7:45–46 231n20
  7:47 231
  7:50–51 240
  7:53–8:11 241n27
  8:6 241

8:8   241
8:20   239, 239n24
8:33–58   231
8:41–42   239
8:48   232
8:49   232
8:52   232
8:57   231
9:1   235
9:3–5   235
9:16   233
9:24–25   233
9:31   233
9:38   235
10   229
10:6   232
10:20   232
10:20–21   232
10:22–23   228, 228n15
10:31   240
10:33   228, 228n14
10:34–35   240
10:36   229
10:39   240
11:6   240
11:7–10   240
11:7–8   240
11:47–48   239
11:48   221, 221n7
11:54   234
12   224
12:20–21   235
12:23   240
12:35–36   241
13–17   224
13:1   240
13:10–11   241
13:34   221, 230
14:1–3   241
14:6–17   232
14:18   241–42
14:26   232
15:3   241
15:23   233
15:26   232
16:13–14   232
16:27   233
17:1   240

17:22–23   241
17:25   236
18–19   226
18:3   232n20
18:11   227
18:12   232n20
18:18   232n20
18:19–20   238–39
18:22   231n20
18:36–37   238
19:5   229n17
19:6   232n20
19:7   228, 228n14
19:20   234
19:23   242
19:23–24   242
19:25–27   241
19:28   241
19:30   241
20:17   239
20:22   232
20:24–29   242
21   224
21:25   241n27
John, Gospel of, prologue   338, 361, 362, 363
John Chrysostom, *De Anna*
   2.2   271
John Climacus, *Scala paradise*
   25   271n107
Josephus, Flavius, *Against Apion* [*Contra Apionem*]   242
   2.137   147
Josephus, Flavius, *Life*
   11   194n17
Josephus, Flavius, *Jewish Antiquities*   312n23
   18.116   319
Josephus, Flavius, *Jewish War*
   7.409–421   311
   7.433–450   311
Julian, *Contra Galilaeos* [*Against the Galilaeans*]   340, 359, 368, 369
   164 10   281n8
   fragment 1   359
   fragment 10, 97f. Masaracchia   365n107, 366n108
   fragment 10, 98 Masaracchia   365n108
   fragment 11, 99f. Masaracchia   366n108
   fragment 21, 113 Masaracchia   366n111

fragment 26, 121 Masaracchia 367n114
fragment 31 360n92
fragment 43, 138 Masaracchia 364n104, 365n104
fragment 46, 140 Masaracchia 367n116
fragment 48, 142 Masaracchia 365n104
fragment 50, 144 Masaracchia 362n99
fragment 57, 151 Masaracchia 367n115
fragment 62 Masaracchia 360n93, 360n94
fragment 64 Masaracchia 360n94, 326n97
fragment 64, 159f. Masaracchia 361n95
fragment 64, 160 Masaracchia 361n97
fragment 65, 161 Masaracchia 362n98
fragment 79, 172f. Masaracchia 363n100
fragment 80, 173 Masaracchia 364n101
fragment 81, 174–75 Masaracchia 365n104
Julian, *Contra Heraclium Cynicum* [*Against the Cynic Herakleios*]
    214d 201
    11, 216c–d 371n136
    14–16, 219a–222c 369n124
    14, 219b–c 370n127
    14, 219c–d 370n129
    14, 219d–220a 370n130
    15, 220b 371n132
    15, 220d–221b 371n134
    22, 229c–d 369n123
Julian, *Epistles*
    89b Bidez, 293a 372n140
    89b Bidez, 293a–b 371n138
    89b Bidez, 293b–295a 372n139
Julian, *In matrem deorum*
    2 372n141
    160 372n141
    161a 372n141
Julian, *In Solem*
    I 130b–c 369n123
Julian, *Misopogon* 371
    353a 282n11
    34, 361c 371n135
Julian, *To the Uneducated Cynics*
    199B 206
Justin Martyr, *1 Apology* 269
    6 284
    14.4–5 268–69

    61.10 319
Justin Martyr, *2 Apology* 300
    8 284n17
    8.1 284
    8.1–2 283
    8.2 283, 284
    8.6 284
    12.1 300
Justin Martyr, *Dialogue with Trypho* 299, 301
    1.3 10
    1.5 11
    2.1 11
    2.6 11
    7–8.2 11
    8.1 11, 299
    14.1 317
    18.1 269
    19.2 317
    74.3 319
    97.3 319
Justin Martyr, *Martyrdom of Polycarp*
    3.2 284–85
    9.2 284
    19.1 284
Justus of Tiberius, *The Wreath* 242
Juvenal, *Satires*
    14.98–99 147

Lactantius, *Divine Institutes*
    1.5 107n20
*Letter of Mara bar Serapion* 220
Leviticus, book of
    15 317
*Life of Aesop*
    109 245n7
Lucan, *Bellum Civile*
    1.75–76 113
    1.655–58 113
Lucian, *The Death of Peregrinus*
    13 269n100
Lucian, *The Downward Journey of the Tyrant*
    199
Lucian, *The Life of Demonax* 207
    11 208n37
    52 214n53
    62 214n53
Lucian, *Vitarum auctio*
    8 215

Lucretius, *On the Nature of Things*
    2.1150–52  118
    Book 3  121
    5.380–415  118
    5.925ff.  122
Luke, Gospel of
    239n24 11:9  309n20
    3:8  296n77
    3:10–14  199
    4:18  204
    5:29  195
    6:20  195
    6:27  201n28
    7:36  195
    8:3  195
    10:38  195
    11:1  244b
    11:2b-4  244
    11:5–8  245n6
    11:9  309n18
    16:19–31  199
    21:1–4  239n24
    21:38  241n27
    22:42  227

Marcus Aurelius, *Meditations*  288–89
    1.6  287n35
    1.16  291
    2.13  291
    3.1  291n57
    3.7  291
    3.16  287n35
    5.29  291, 291n57
    7.68  287n35
    8.48  287n35, 291
    8.51  287n35
    11.3  287n35, 288–90, 291
Mark, Gospel of  127, 239n24
    1:6  193
    2:15  195
    2:16  233n22
    2:23  195
    2:27  208
    3:22–26  232
    7:14–15  209
    7:19  209
    7:26  210
    10:38–39  227

    12:41–44  239n24
    14:36  227
    14:54  232n20
    14:65  232n20
    15:41  195
Matthew, Gospel of  245, 255
    3:4  193
    3:9  296n77
    5–8  5
    5:17–19  221n8
    5:21  221n8
    5:33  221n8
    5:44–45  201n28
    5:45  204
    6:2  247
    6:5  244, 247
    6:6  204
    6:7  244, 245, 247, 249, 250, 251n31, 270, 272, 274
    6:7–9a  5, 245
    6:7–8  248, 250–56, 270, 272, 273, 275
    6:8  205
    6:9b-13  244
    6:24  193
    6:25–27  197
    7:7  309n18
    7:12  221n8
    7:15  269n101
    9:17  221n8
    10:9–10  193
    11:8  193
    11:25  204
    12:2  195
    15:3  221n8
    19:17  221n8
    19:21  192
    19:26  296
    19:28  112n42
    21:18–19  195
    21:43  221n7
    22:7  221n7
    22:40  221n8
    24:11  269n101
    24:24  269n101
    26:39  227
    26:42  227
    27:14  321
Menippus, *The Sale of Diogenes*  213

# INDEX OF ANCIENT SOURCES

Micah, book of
   6:6–8   71

Nemesius, *De natura hominis*
   13   326n4
Numbers, book of
   19   317
   21:8–9   226
   24:17   360
Numenius of Apamea, *Concerning the Good*   304–05
   fragment 12.12–14   331
   fragment 13.4–5   331
   fragment 16.2–5   331
   fragment 20.11   331
   fragments 30–38   330

Origen, *Commentary on the Gospel of John*
   5.4   273
Origen, *Contra Celsum* [*Against Celsus*]   222, 297, 366
   Preface 4   297
   1.17   302n99
   1.31   232n21
   2.32   267
   4.38   302n99
   4.48–51   302n99
   4.50–51   302n99
   4.51   304
   4.64   112
   4.87   302n99
   5.5   232n21
   5.15   112
   6.2   199
   6.8   222, 243
   6.29   302n99
   8.65   290n52
Origen, *De oratione*
   21.1.1–2   272
   21.1.8–11   272
   21.2.9–11   273
Origen, *On Daimones*   325n2
Origenes the Platonist
   fragment 7   335
   fragment 9   329n10
   fragment 13   329n10
   fragment 14   329n10

*That Only the King Is Creator*   325, 325n2, 326, 330
*Orphic Hymns*
   32.1   230
Ovid, *Metamorphoses*   108
   Book 1   117
   1.235–61   116n59
   1.285   116n59

Palladius, *Dialogue on the Life of Chrysostom*   224
Parmenides, *Peri physeōs* / Fr. 1,24   97
Paul, Letter to the Galatians
   1:1   204
   2:11–14   282n13
   5:19–21   272
   6:15–16   314
Paul, Letter to the Philippians   339n5
   2:20–24   182
Paul, Letter to the Romans
   9:6–8   317
   12:1–2   229n17
Pausanias, *Description of Greece*
   10.12   116
Phaedrus, *Fables*
   4.21   250n28
Philo of Alexandria, *De aeternitate mundi* [*On the Eternity of the World*]
   47.1   112n42
   76–77   113
   76.5   112n42
   77   214
Philo of Alexandria, *De confusione linguarum*
   106   215
Philo of Alexandria, *De congressu eruditionis gratia*
   71–73   266
   73   266
Philo of Alexandria, *De decalogo*
   175   302
Philo of Alexandria, *De fuga et inventione*
   33–34   217
Philo of Alexandria, *De gigantibus*
   33   214
   61   215
Philo of Alexandria, *De Iosepho*
   28–32   217
   35–36   217

58–60    217
125    216
222    214
Philo of Alexandria, *De migratione Abrahami*
   59    215
   112    296n7
   175    296n79
Philo of Alexandria, *De opificio mundi* [*On Creation*]
   3    215
   46    296n79
   129    265
Philo of Alexandria, *De plantatione*
   151    214
Philo of Alexandria, *De sacrificiis Abelis et Caini*
   12    214
   32    265, 271n106
Philo of Alexandria, *De somniis*
   1.39    215
   1.88    296n79
   1.215    229n17
   1.243    215
   11.60    215
Philo of Alexandria, *De specialibus legibus*
   1.66    190n8
   1.323    215
   2.45    215
   2.46    215
   4.127    296n79
Philo of Alexandria, *De vita Mosis*
   1, 157    215
Philo of Alexandria, *Legum allegoriae*
   Book 2    216
   2.17    214
   Book 3    216
Philo of Alexandria, *On Providence*
   2.61    116
Philo of Alexandria, *On Rewards and Punishments*
   409    105n12
Philo of Alexandria, *Quis rerum divinarum heres*
   5    214
   10    267
Philo of Alexandria, *Quod deterius potiori insidiari soleat*
   19    217

130    265n84
Philo of Alexandria, *Quod omnis probus liber sit* [*That Every Good Person Is Free*]    190, 218
   28    213
   75–87    216
   121–24    213
   157    213
Philo of Alexandria, *On the Virtues*
   27    296n79
Philodemus, *De morte* 38.14–19 (ed. Kuiper)    180–81
Philodemus, *On Piety*    202
   col. vi    121
Philodemus, *On Rhetoric*
   1.357    303n103
Philostratus, *Life of Apollonius*    254
   1.1    256
   1.11    272
   1.11.1–2    254
   1.11.15–16    254n46
   1.14–16    256n50
   1.33    254n46
   4.40.21    254
   4.40.22–23    254
   6.1    256n50
   6.20    256n50
   8.2    259n60
Phlegon, *Book of Wonders*    103
Photius, *Bibliotheca*
   155    302n96
Pindar, *Olympian Odes*
   2.86f.    86n32
Plato, *Alcibiades I*    1
   133c1–6    38n5
Plato, *Alcibiades II*
   149e    72
Plato, *Apology*    5, 37–39, 55n42, 58–59, 78–79, 89, 96, 179, 181, 183, 220, 225, 227, 230–31, 233, 238–40
   17c    238
   20d    82
   20e    50n35, 79, 239
   21b    79
   22e–23a    238
   23b    37
   23c1    37
   24c    79

28b  16
28e–29a  37
29d–30b  37
30c  220
30c–d  156
30c–31b  220
30c7  37
30e–31b  37
31d  79, 239
31d–e  238
33c  50n35
37c–d  238
37e–38a  37
38  220
39c  220
39c–d  220
40a–c  240
40c  237, 241
40c–41d  169
41a–b  220
41d  50n35, 240
42a  240
Plato, *Cratylus*
    400e  249n25
    415a  81
Plato, *Crito*  5, 225, 227, 240
Plato, *Epinomis*
    7.341c–e  78
    980d–983d  84n23
    984e–985a  95n57
    985c  90
    988d  84n23
Plato, *Epistles*  327
Plato, *Epistle II*  323, 327, 330, 331, 336
    312d7  327
    312e  336
    312e1–3  331n18
    312e1–4  331
    312e2–3  336
    312e3  331n18
    312e4–313a6  336
    313a1  336
Plato, *Epistle VI*  323, 327
    323d4  328
Plato, *Epistle VII*  323, 336
    343b8–e1  336
Plato, *Euthydemus*
    282  60n56

290e–291a  81n18
307b6–8  61n59
Plato, *Euthyphro*  3–4, 5, 37–39, 45, 50,
    54–55, 57, 60, 62, 66, 72, 225, 227–30,
    232, 236, 238, 252
    2a  227
    2c  231
    3b  227, 232, 229, 230–31
    3b–c  232
    4e–15e  233
    5a  229, 233
    5b  231
    6a–b  50n35
    7a  233
    8a  233
    9c  233
    9e  42, 47
    9e–11b  56
    9e1–2  67
    10a1–3  56
    10a5–c13  67
    10c1–4  68
    10d–e  233
    10d1–5  66
    10e10–11  67
    11a  233
    11a6–b1  42
    11a8  69
    11e–12a  57
    12d  236
    12e  40
    12e5–8  39
    13b–c  47
    13b–d  40
    14a9–10  40
    14b  233–34
    14b–c  40
    14b3  41
    14c–15c  32
    14e  252n36
    14e10–15a5  66
    15b–c  56n46
    15b1  72
    15c  233
    31d  78
    190b5  56n46
    201d  53
    202c7  56

202e   58
202e3   52
202e4   53
202e5   52
202e6–7   50
202e8   42, 50
203a2   50
204a   53
204b2–5   62
205de   43
206b   53
206c   54
206c–d   47n28
206d1–2   51
207c   53
208b3   47n28, 56n46
208c   53
210a1   41
210b2–3   52
210e6   47
211b   52
211c2   47
211e   51
212a1–6   51, 52, 58
212a4–6   58
212a5–7   56, 58
212b–c   59
215c   53
216a5–b3   53
217a1   53
217b6   53
219b7–c1   59
219c1   53
272e   78
275d   53
Plato, *Gorgias*   119
  449a–c   258n56
  523   120
  525b–c   120
  526e   120
  527e   157
Plato, *Ion*
  553e–534e   86n32
Plato, *Laches*
  199d4   81
Plato, *Last Days of Socrates*   219, 224–26, 234, 236–38, 243
Plato, *Laws*   55n42, 57n50, 60, 61, 78, 90

641e   246, 258n57
643c8–d3   60
643e4–5   60
712b   53n40
713c–d   93
713e–714a   86
716b8–d4   38n5
716c–717a   44
716c   33n46
716d   16
717a–b   90
738b–d   16n13
757b–c   57n50
792c8–d5   38n5
818b–c   92
865b   16n13
885b   16, 252n38
885b–e   32
887e   234
888a–d   32
888c   16
893b   53n40
896b–897d   33
903b–d   55n42
905c–09e   16n13
905d–907b   16, 32
906a7–b3   38n5
948b–c   32
Plato, *Lysis*
  204b1–2   60n56
  204c1   57n48
Plato, *Meno*   42n16
Plato, *Parmenides*   323–24, 326, 332, 332n19, 334–36
  137c–155e   325
  142a   333, 334
  142a3–6   325
  142a3–8   332
Plato, *Phaedo*   5, 13n6, 51, 55n42, 60, 119–20, 225–27, 237, 241, 240, 241n26, 294, 294n69, 332n19
  12d   16
  32c   16
  57a   225
  58c   225
  59c   225, 226
  60b   241
  60d–61b   241

60e2   42n16
61b1   42n16
64b    235
64e    235
65d–e  240
65e    51n37
66e2   60
67a–c  241
67b–c  237
67d    235
67e    33, 235
67e–68b   237
67e5–68a2  60
68a7–b6   60
69c    29n39
69c–d  241
69d    235
70a    237
73b    235
77a    235
80b1   46n27
80e2–1a10  38n5
81a    33
82b10–c1  38n5
83b    235
84a–b  240
84a9   46n27
84d–85b  42n16
87a–c  235
87b    242
87d–e  242
88c–d  235
91c    235
99b–c  51
107a   235
107d   97
108b   97
109e   236
109e–110a  241
112b   120
113a–b  120n74
114a–b  120
114c   237
116a   241
116a–b 241
116b   231n20
117a–c 227
117b   241

117c   53n40, 241
118a   241
Plato, *Phaedrus*   13n6, 25, 30, 31, 60,
        246e–247a, 340n9
   81a    92
   234e   81
   237a   53n40
   242b   78
   242d7  81
   243d1  81
   243e–257b   27, 150
   244b   44n24, 119n71
   246a–249e   150
   246a–256e   27
   246c–d   28n37
   246d   44n24
   246d8–e1   46n27
   246e   28
   246e–247a   340n9
   247a   50n35, 59n53
   247b   28
   247c   16–17, 51n37
   247e   28
   248a1–c5   38n5
   248a–b   28
   248a   33n46 248d 29
   249a   29
   249c   29
   249c4–d3   38n5
   249c6–d3   42n14
   249d   52
   249d3   30
   249d4–257b   30
   249e1–3   42n14
   250ff.   60n55
   250b   340n9
   250b8–c5   42n14
   252c–253c   33n46, 44n24, 340n9
   252d1–3c2   38n5
   253a7–b1   46n26
   265c   27n24
   273e   52
   276a   92
   278b   53n40
   279b–c   53n40
Plato, *Philebus*   51, 326
   16b    53
   16d    52

25b    53n40
27b–30d    326
28d5–29a4    51
30d    326
53cff.    47
61b–c    53n40
64e–65a    51n36
Plato, *Protagoras*    267
   313b–314b    16
   316d    29n39
   329c–d    58n51
   335a–b    258n56
   335c    258n56
   342b–e    259n59
   343a    369
   343a–b    258, 259, 264
Plato, *Republic*    25, 31, 55n42, 60, 78, 90, 294,
     294n69, 332n19
   Book 6    327
   Book 10    96245a 29n40
   248b    29n40
   251a    29n40
   264b–e    252
   327a    53n40
   344d6    81
   362d–364e    97
   362e–365c    29n39
   363e–367a    32
   365d–366a    16n13
   372b–d    224
   372d–373a    224
   377b–383c    16
   379a    16
   414e–415c    91
   427b    42n16
   427b–c    16n13
   432c    53n40
   451a    234
   469a    85
   469a–b    234
   485b    60
   490    60
   490b    51n37
   496c    78
   500c9–d1    38n5, 46n27
   501b1–7    38n5
   501d2    60
   508b–509c    326

   509d2    326
   514a    25
   515b    25
   515d    25
   516a    26
   516c    25
   516e–517a    26
   517b    91
   517bc    26
   517d4–5    46n27
   518c    26, 51n37
   518e    26
   520b–c    26
   521c    26
   522b3    81
   532a    51n37
   540b    85
   613a4–b1    38n5
   613a–b    33
   10.614–21    120
   614c1    97
   617e    97
   620d    97
Plato, *Sophist*
   219b1    47n28
   224c–e    16
   243d–250d    326
   260a    16
Plato, *Statesman (On Kingship)*    108, 327
   269ff.    122
   269d8–9    327
Plato, *Symposium*    39, 41, 43–45, 48, 51, 55,
     57, 59, 60, 88–89, 95, 224–26, 237,
     241n26, 243
   173d6    61
   201d–212c    30n41
   202a–e    95n57
   202b2–3    45n25
   202c7    43
   202c10–d5    44
   202e    77, 79
   202e–203a    41, 52
   203b5–7    45n25
   204c    45
   204c4–5    46
   205a–d    45
   206a4    45
   206cff.    43, 45

INDEX OF ANCIENT SOURCES

206c6  43
207c9–8b4  38n5
207c–209e  33n46
207c5–208b5  43 208b3 43
208b5  46
208c5  44
208e2  43
209b1  44n20
209d–e  46n26
210a1  50
210e–211a  46
211b3–5  46
211e3  46
212a5–6  50
212a6  44
257a  30n41
Plato, *Theages*
  123 8d  78
Plato, *Theaetetus*  38, 237
  66d  60n56
  129b8  78
  142c  237
  150b–d  57n48
  151c–d  57n48
  172b–177c  33n46
  175d  245
  176a–b  12n6, 16, 150
  176a5–6  60
  176a8–b3  38n5
  176b  237
  176c  237
  210d  237
Plato, *Timaeus*  38, 55, 60, 87–88, 91, 96, 119,
    327n5, 329n10, 330, 332, 332n19, 365
  22bff.  103n1
  22c–e  115, 116
  27b–d  53n40
  29d  82, 95
  30b  330
  31b8–32a7  55n45
  34b–41d  327
  34c–36c  32
  39e  329, 330
  39e7–9  329
  40d-2  82
  46d7–e2  60
  47b5–c4  38n5
  48d–e  53n

90a  88n46
90a–d  33n, 58
90b–c  43, 60
90b1–d7  38n5
90c  55n44
269c1–2  327n5
274e1–3  327n5
Pliny the Elder, *Natural History*
  7.73  118
Pliny the Younger, *Letters*
  6.20.17  118
  10.96  306
  10.97  10.96.4 321
Plotinus, *Enneads*
  1.8.2.28–32  331n14
  2.9  329
  2.9.6.10–12  329
  2.9.6.14–24  329
  3.9.1  329n10
  4.3  343n20
  4.11  343n20
  5.1.9  327n8
  5.1.8.10–11  327n7
  5.1.8.14–23  327n8
  5.1.9.30–32  327n8
  6.7.31.10  49
  6.7.42.9–10  331n14
Plutarch, *Aetia Romana et Graeca*
  276–277a  232n21
Plutarch, *Agesilaus*
  7.2  261n69
Plutarch, *Alexander*
  64.1  259
Plutarch, *Amatorius*  226
Plutarch, *Brutus*
  2.2  262n76
  2.4–5  262
  2.5  263
Plutarch, *Caesar*
  50.3–4  261n70
Plutarch, *Conjugalia praecepta*
  142b  261
Plutarch, *Consolatio ad uxorem*  179
  608d  180
Plutarch, *De curiositate*
  519c  246n12
Plutarch, *De garrulitate*  272, 274
  21f  207n36

77e    196n20
169c    147
398c    125
415b    85n27
416c    85n27
417a    97
417b    85n27
502b    264n81
502e7    263
504d    266
511a9–b8    264
511b    269
519d–952d    85n27
566b    97
Plutarch, *De Stoicorum repugnantiis*
    1051c    232n21
Plutarch, *De tranquilitate animi*
    4, 466e    215
    20, 477c    215
Plutarch, *De virtute morali*    247n15
Plutarch, *Demosthenes*
    4.5–7    246n10
Plutarch, *Dion*
    1.1    262n76
    2.6    232n21
Plutarch, *Lycurgus*
    20.6    259, 264
Plutarch, *Obsolescence of Oracles*
    415f.    121
Plutarch, *On the Face of the Moon*    119
Plutarch, *On the Fortune and Virtue of Alexander the Great*
    329a–d    107n20
Plutarch, *On the Oracles at Delphi No Longer Given in Verse*    125
Plutarch, *Phocion*
    5.4–5    261
Plutarch, *Platonic Questions*    222
    1    222
    999d–e    222
Plutarch, *Praecepta gerendae reipublicae*
    803e    261n68
Plutarch, *Quomodo adolescens poetas audire debeat*
    21f    215
Plutarch    see also Pseudo-Plutarch
Porphyry
    fragment 306F Smith    344n22

fragment 321F Smith    343n21
fragment 339F Smith    344n22
fragment 349F Smith    344n22
Porphyry, *De philosophia ex oraculis haurienda* (*Philosophy from Oracles*)
    343, 344
    fragment 321F Smith    371n137
Porphyry, *Letter to Anebo*    344, 344n26
Porphyry, *Life of Pythagoras*    354n71
Porphyry, lost commentaries of    324
Porphyry, *On Images*
    8.103–6    230
Porphyry, *On the Cave of the Nymphs*    330
Porphyry, *Sententiae*    337
    38    333n21
Porphyry, *To Marcella*    255, 267n91
Porphyry, *Vita Plotini* [*Life of Plotinus*]    330
    3 (= Origenes fragment 2)    325, 329, 330
    14    260, 269, 330
    16    329
    17    330
    18    330
    20    330
    21    330
Proclus, *In Alcibiadem*
    61.3–5    49n34
    64    49n34
Proclus, *In Parmenidem* [*Commentary on the Parmenides*]    324, 325n3, 332n19
    VI    325n3
    VI 1065.3    333
    VI 1079.14    333
    VI 1110.9    333
    VII 515.4    325n3, 333
Proclus, *In Timaeum* [*Commentary on the Timaeus*] (= Origenes fragments 9, 13–14)    336, 366, 324, 325n3, 326
    1.31.18–27    324
    1.59.31–60.4    324
    1.63.24–64.7    324
    1.68.3–15    324
Proclus, *Life of Porphyry*    340
Proclus, *Theologia Platonica*    333
    2.4.31.4–22 (= Origenes fragment 7)    325
    2.4.31.12–19 (= Origenes fragment 7)    332
Proverbs, Book of    204
    10:19    246, 248n19, 268, 270, 273
Psalms, book of    205

118:85   247
145:15–16   205
146   205
Pseudo-Apollonius, *Epistles*   256
  16   256n52
  23   256n52
  28   256n52
  48.2   256n52
  50   256n52
  53   256n52
  55.1   256n52
  93   256n51
  94   260n66
Pseudo-Aristotle, *De Melisso Xenophane Gorgia*   302
Pseudo-Clementines, *Epistulae de virginitate*
  1.8.2   245n8
  1.8.2–3   272
  1.12.2   271
  1.12.3   245n8, 271
Pseudo-Plutarch, *Apophthegmata Laconica*
  224c.5–7   258n57
Pseudo-Plutarch, *Consolatio ad Apollonium*   170
Pseudo-Plutarch, *De liberis educandis*   262, 265, 274
  6b–c   263
  6c   246n12
  502e.8   263
  504a9–b6   263n79
Pseudo-Sophocles, fragment 2   109n28
*Pythagorean Sentences*   255, 256, 268, 270, 274
  10   255, 268
  15–16   255, 268

Q (Sayings Source)   202n28

Revelation, Book of
  16:13   269n101
  19:20   269n101

Satyrus, *Life of Euripides*   224
Seneca, *De beneficiis* 4.26, 1   201
Seneca, *De clementia* 3.7, 11   201
Seneca, *De consolatione ad Helviam matrem*
  17.2   168n19
Seneca, *De consolatione ad Marciam*

[*Consolation for Marcia*]   162, 167–68, 170, 175–77, 179, 181
  1.1   166, 168n19
  1.1–4   167
  7.4   176
  16.4   168
  17.1–6   176
  18.1–2   176
  19.3   171n32
  19.4–21.1   170
  19.5   171
  19.6   171
  21.2   172
  23.1   171
  23.2   172n33
  23.3   171, 179
  24.1   171, 179
  25.1   171, 179
  25.2   171
  25.3   164, 168n19, 171
  26.6   113
  26.6–7   172n34
  26.7   172, 173
Seneca, *De constantia*
  16.4   157
Seneca, *Letters / Moral Epistles*   272
  10.4   253
  31.5   250
  31.8   253n42
  32.4   253
  45.6   253n42
  60.1   253
  90   122
  95.45   262n74
Seneca, *Natural Questions*
  3.27–30   115
  3.27.13   116n59
  3.29.1   116
Seneca, *Octavia* vv.
  377–434   114
Seneca, *Thyestes*
  835–84   114
*Sentences of Clitarchus*
  31–32   267
*Sentences of Sextus*   268
  155–57   267
  341   268n95
  430   268

Shepherd of Hermas, *Mandate*
   11.1–2   270n103
   11.4   270n103
   11.7   270n103
   11.11–12   270
*Sibylline Oracles*   4
   Book 1   115, 119, 121
   1.73–76   121
   1.157–58   107
   Book 2   108, 115, 119, 120, 121
   2.5–79   119
   2.34–55   105
   2.145   105
   2.196–213   110
   2.200–2   111
   2.206   112
   2.206–7   111
   2.212–13   111
   2.213   112
   2.231   107
   2.322–29   108
   2.337–38   119
   2.339   123
   Book 3   109n27
   3.1–3   106n14
   3.11   106
   3.55   123
   3.80   111
   3.80–92   109
   3.87   111
   3.90   123
   3.92   113
   3.180   113
   3.187   123
   3.194   113
   3.197   122
   3.247   108n22
   3.278   106n17
   3.294   113
   3.419–25   123
   3.528   120
   3.528–30   123
   3.647   123
   3.704   106
   3.757   107
   3.788   123
   Book 4   108
   4.161   111n33
   4.171–92   111n31
   4.182   113
   5.155–61   111n31
   5.206–13   111n31
   5.265   107
   5.512–31   111n31, 113
   7.139   112
   7.144–45   107
   7.145   113
   8.130   120
   8.319   113
   fragment 1.7   106
   fragment 3.1–3   106n14
Simplicius, *Commentary on Epictetus' Enchiridion*
   37   245n7
Sirach, book of
   7:14   247n16
   29:24–27   191
   32:9   247n16
Sophocles, cf. Pseudo-Sophocles
Statius, *Thebaid*
   2.244   250n28
Stobaeus, *Florilegium*
   2.7.11k   261n66
   3.12.13   257n53
   3.35.11   258n57
   3.36.26   261
   3.36.29   260
Strabo, *Geography*
   14.2.28   246
Suetonius, *Nero*
   16.2   306
Sulpicius Severus, *Dialogues on the Life of St. Martin*   224
Syrianus, *Commentary on Aristotle's Metaphysics*
   109.12–14   332n19

Tacitus, *Annals*
   15.44   286, 306
Tacitus, *Histories*
   5.4.3   147
Tatian, *Diatessaron*   300
Tatian, *Oratio* [*Oration to the Greeks*]   300, 300n92
   19   284n17
   19.1   283n15

# INDEX OF ANCIENT SOURCES

    42.1   300
Tertullian, *Apologeticum*   286
Tertullian, *De praescriptione haereticorum*
[*The Prescription Against Heretics*]
    7   221
    7.9–13   14
    30   221
Tertullian, *On the Flesh of Christ*
    20   222
Theophilus, *Autolycus*
    1.14   301
Theophrastus, *Characters*
    Chapter 3   247n15
Titus, Epistle to   306
    3:12   306

Virgil, *Aeneid*
    6   120
Virgil, *Fourth Eclogue*   104, 108

    4.3   117
Virgil, *Sixth Eclogue*
    31   121

Xenophon, *Cyropaedia*
    1.4.3   246n12, 263n77
    1.4.4   263n77
Xenophon, *Memorabilia*
    254, 272
    1.2.1   206
    1.3.2   253, 274n119
    1.4.2–18   55n42
    4.3.3–8.1.1   55n42
Xenophon, *Symposium*
    4.47   233

Zeno, *Republic*   107
*Zostrianus* (Nag Hammadi)   329

# Index of Modern Authors

Alston, Leonard   160
Annas, Julia   38, 39
Anscombe, Elizabeth   175n39

Balch, David   195–196
Baldwin, B.   286
Beard, W.M.   281
Beardslee, William   263
Bellah, Robert N.   22, 133, 134, 136, 138
Betz, Hans Dieter   251, 264
Birley, Anthony   292n61
Bonhöffer, Adolf   307, 308, 309, 310, 311, 320
Boys-Stones, George   15, 16, 135n14
Breéhier, Émile   216
Brock, Sebastian   219
Brunt, P.A.   288, 289, 289n47, 290, 291, 292
Bultmann, Rudolf   1, 308
Burridge, Richard   223

Collins, J.J.   120
Cook, John Granger   307, 321

Davies, William   247
De Vita, Maria Carmen   359
deSilva, David   145, 146, 157
Detienne, Marcel   87–89, 98
Diamond, Jared   141
Diderot, Denis   160
Dillon, John   2, 333, 354, 355, 372
Donald, Merlin   136, 137n19, 138
Downing, Gerald   117–18
Dressler, Jan   203n32

Edmonds, R.   42, 55
Edwards, Mark   219, 284
Eichstaedt, H.C.A.   288
Elders, L.   48
Engberg-Pedersen, Troels   1n1, 313
Evans, Craig A.   219

Farrar, F.W.   160
Finamore, John   340, 357
Foot, Philippa   175n39
Foucault, Michel   73n2, 77
Frede, Michael   219

Freud, Sigmund   173

Geertz, Clifford   175n39
Goulet-Cazé, Marie-Odile   213
Goulet, Richard   216–217
Grant, R.M.   295, 296
Gruen, Erich   131

Hadot, Pierre   18, 128, 150, 151
Hägg, Tomas   223
Hard, Robin   291
Harrison, S.J.   286
Hays, Richard   226
Hegel, Georg Wilhelm Friedrich   20, 133
Heinemann, Isaak   189, 216, 217
Heininger, Bernhard   145
Heitmüller, Wilhelm   1
Hengel, Martin   2, 130, 208, 211, 311
Hill, David   249
Hunter, Richard   225

Jaspers, Karl   19, 20, 21, 133
Jensen, Jeppe Sinding   17n19

Kant, Immanuel   206
Kennedy, George   143
Kidd, I.G.   88
Kierkegaard, Søren   132

Labriolle, P.   282, 304
Lear, Gabriel   47, 48
Lifton, Robert Jay   173–174
Lightfoot, Jane   106, 111, 117, 119, 120, 122
Lloyd, G.E.R.   96
Long, A.A.   43, 230, 239, 307
Luz, Ulrich   273

Malherbe, Abraham   284
Mansfield, Jaap   302
McPherran, Mark L.   2, 3, 33, 40
Merlan, P.   48
Meyer, Eduard   311, 312
Millar, Fergus   219, 280
Momigliano, A.   116
Morgan, Michael L.   10, 11, 17n16

# INDEX OF MODERN AUTHORS

Mörth, Franz    309, 320
Most, Glenn W.    3, 19, 129, 130

Neujahr, Matthew    115
Neutel, Karin    108
Nikiprowetzky, V.    113
Nolland, John    250
North, J.L.    281
Nussbaum, Martha    128

Oldfather, W.A.    315, 316
Osborne, Catherine    225

Parke, H.W.    125
Pelling, Christopher    262
Perkins, Judith    268
Perron, Anquetil du    133
Porter, Stanley    210
Price, S.R.F.    281

Ramelli, Ilaria    219
Reimarus, Hermann Samuel    364
Renan, Ernest    204, 282
Rilke, Rainer Maria    193
Rist, John    225
Rowe, C.J.    38
Russell, Bertrand    191
Rutherford, R.B.    292
Ryle, Gilbert    175n39

Schenkl, Heinrich    315, 316
Scourfield, David    163n8
Sedley, David    2, 32, 38, 44
Sellar, John    161, 176

Senior, Donald    248
Sharp, Douglas S.    309, 320
Shaw, Gregory    341, 344
Skovgaard Jensen, Søren    73, 83–86, 87, 88, 89n50, 94, 95n57, 99
Sloterdijk, Peter    150, 151
Soskice, Janet    87n33, 89n49

Talbert, C.H.    223
Topper, Kathryn    224

Usher, Mark    115

van der Horst, Pieter    109, 111, 112
van der Sluijs, M.A.    116
van Henten, Jan Willem    145
Vernant, Jean-Pierre    92
Vidal-Naquet, Pierre    92
Vlastos, Gregory    2, 38, 39, 58, 59
Voelke, André-Jean    128
Vollenweider, Samuel    341
von Arnim, Johannes    160
von Harnack, Adolf    1, 364
von Lassaulx, Ernst    20, 133

Walsh, P.G.    285, 286
Walzer, R.    292, 293, 294, 304
Wilken, R.L.    281
Williams, Bernard    175n39
Wilson, Marcus    167, 168, 172, 176
Wittgenstein, Ludwig    99
Wright, Tom    211

Zahn, Theodor    309, 313, 314, 320

# Index of Subjects

Abammon 344
Abaris 356
Abraham 144, 200, 231, 266
Academus 75
Academy (Greek) 14, 77, 82, 83, 99, 128, 167, 262, 301, 302
    academic discourse 90
    academic philosophy 74
    of Plato 189
Acheron 120
'Acherousian lake' 119
action 63, 72
Adam 122
Aemilianus 285n24
afterlife 164, 169, 170, 171, 173, 177, 180, 182, 183, 200, 206, 207, 231
Agapius 294n69
agency 166, 167, 175, 347
Agesilaos / Agesilaus, King of Sparta 207, 261
*agōn* 74
Agora 239
Aidesius 358
Aigai 367
Ajax 220
Akhenaten 20
Alcibiades 53, 59
Alexandria 189, 213, 268, 302n98, 324, 326, 337
Alexandrian Judaism 189
*Allogenes* (Nag Hammadi) 329
ambiguity (of logic) 87, 89, 98
Ambrose 223
Amelius 329, 330, 330n12, 339, 358, 374
Ammonius Saccas 324, 326, 328, 333, 336, 337
anachronism 130
ancient culture 205
ancient Jewish sources 204, 211
ancient Mediterranean (Hellenistic) world 3, 130, 131, 211
ancient moral psychologies 165
ancient philosophical schools (*see* philosophical schools)
ancient philosophical texts 159

ancient philosophy 1, 12, 13, 15n10, 18, 19, 86n32, 99, 103, 118, 126, 159, 168, 180, 258
    discourse 129
    and theology 183
    sources 118
ancient religions 15n10, 19, 129, 141
ancient world 19, 127, 138, 195
*andreia* 91
Anebo 344
angel(s) 205, 349, 360, 366, 368
animals 197, 198
anti-Christian 286, 365
anti-gospel 298
anti-Jewish 317
Antioch 219, 282n13
Antiochus IV Epiphanes 151, 155, 156, 157, 229
Antiochus of Ascalon 262n76
antiquity 19, 35, 74, 104, 125, 129, 133, 159, 183, 211, 279
    Graeco-Roman 141
Antisthenes 187, 202, 212, 213
Antoninus 301
Anytus 156
*apatheia* 167, 168, 171
Aphrodite 329n10
apocalyptic / apocalypticism 115, 122, 125
apocalyptic belief 103
apocalyptic discourse 103
apophthegms 259, 262
Apollo 13, 117, 193, 222, 230, 239, 258, 263, 264, 354, 355, 371
    Festival of 226
    Hyperborean 357
    Pythian 357
    daughters of 76
Apollonius 254, 256, 259n60, 260, 269, 274, 275
apologists, religious 15, 268
Apuleius 285–86, 304
    and Christianity 285n23, 287
Aramaic 211
Aratus 108
archaic philosophers 105n11
Archigenes 293

INDEX OF SUBJECTS 399

Areopagus  239, 243n30
arguments  159, 164–65, 167–68, 173, 177, 257
Arian controversy  339
Aristeas  128–30, 145, 146, 147
Aristippus  214
Aristobulus  145
Aristophanes  56n46, 86n32
Ammonius  6, 267–68
Ambrose  270
Ariston  259
Aristotle  18, 47–49, 56n47, 57n49, 61, 67, 75, 80, 87n33, 89n50, 96, 116, 139, 143, 150n43, 188, 221, 246, 327n8
  school of  348
Aristus  262n76
army  297
Arrian of Nicomedia  280, 306
ascension/ascent of the soul  13, 16, 25–26, 41–42, 44, 51–54, 56–57, 59, 173, 341
asceticism  151
Asclepius  340, 367, 369, 371–74
Asia Minor  142
assimilation  145
'assumptive worlds'  159, 177n41
Assyrians  300
astrologers  116
Aten, god of light and time  20
atheism  284
atheists  279, 283, 284
Athena  230, 366, 372n144
Athenagoras  301, 302
Athene  75, 99
Athenian court  227
Athenian drama  92
Athenian Stranger  (see Stranger from Athens)
Athenians  207, 220, 258n57, 279
Athens  2, 14, 130, 187, 188, 206, 215, 228, 230, 231n20, 242, 243n30, 302n98
  gods of  205
  piety of  42n14
*atheoi*  (see atheists)
Atlantis, story of  324
Atreus  114
Atticus  222
Augustine  14n9, 222–23, 243, 338
Augustus  104, 201
authority  65, 76, 79, 82, 93, 98, 99, 323

Autolycus  301
autonomy  65
Axial Age  19–22, 133
  culture  138
  religion(s)  18, 19–26, 31, 33–35, 139–42, 149, 154 (*see also* religion, Axial Age forms of)
  thinking  139
  transition  150
  types of Judaism  149
axial development  151n48
axiality  20

babble / babbling  245–46, 270
  babbling Gentiles  273
  babbling pagans  251
babblers  244, 264, 271
Bannus  194
baptism  282n13, 314–19
  Christian  317
  counterfeit  317, 319
  of proselytes  317
baptist  314, 317, 319
Bar Hebraeus  294n69
Bar Kochba Revolt  10
barbarians  300
barbarism  297
Basil of Caesarea  271, 272
Battus / Battos  246, 271n105
beauty  29, 30, 41, 42n14, 45–47, 50–52, 54–55, 94, 175, 193, 194
becoming like god  38, 44, 58, 60, 61, 229n17, 236–37; *see also* divinisation, *homoiōsis*
'Begetter of gods'  106n17
beggar / begging  188, 193–96, 200
being  32, 93, 95, 325–26, 328, 330, 333, 335–36 (*see* pure being)
being, divine  371
beings
  higher  344–46, 348, 352–53, 362, 366
  immortal  365
  lesser/lower  345, 348, 353, 362, 366
  mortal  365
belief / beliefs  14, 15n10, 90, 103, 205
beloved disciple  225
bereavement  177n41
Berossus  116
Bias of Priene  258

Bible  199, 204, 216
biblical
    laws  217
    narrative  266
    texts  360
    tradition  204, 267, 268
binding  53, 55, 56, 58, 60 (*see also erōs*)
biocultural evolutionary
    approach/development  136, 138
biographical closure  178, 179, 182, 183
biography / biographies  357
    ancient  223
    Gospels as  223–24
    of Jesus  224
biology  135, 138
blasphemy  228
bodily appetites  91
body (as detached from the soul)  16, 24, 27,
        28, 30–31, 83, 140, 153, 182, 193, 201, 235,
        240, 242, 253, 288, 329, 339, 341, 341n15,
        344–46, 348, 355n77, 365, 367–68, 373
    divine  369n128
    heavenly  348, 348n41
    material  353
Boethius of Sidon  113
Book of Enoch  115n55
Book of the Ten Festivals  190, 216, 217
boundaries  345
brachylogy  258, 260–62, 267
    dialectic  266
    philosophers  265
    sage  269
    wisdom  263
Branchidae  350
bravery  91
brevity  5, 256, 257, 259–66, 268–70, 274
bribing the gods  252
Brutus  261, 265
Buddha  23, 139
Buddhism  23, 139
burial speech  145, 154, 156–57

Caesar  261, 262, 284
Callicles  157
canon  320
canons  313, 314
care and concern for others  38
Carpocrates  221, 223

Cassandra  123
Cato  113
Cebes, disciple of Socrates  235, 242
celestial realm  149
Celsus  222–23, 281, 290, 292, 296–99, 301–4
Cerberos  199
Chaereas  213
chariot  27, 28
children  203, 204, 262, 265, 280, 310, 311, 319
    of god  203, 338
    of Israel  144
Chilon of Sparta  258
China  20, 23, 35, 139
Christ  (*see also* Jesus) 11, 14, 104, 182, 219,
        221–22, 225, 230, 232, 235, 238–43,
        268–69, 293–95, 299, 300, 312n23, 319,
        341, 360–64, 368, 368n121, 370, 370n131
    adherents  128
    charges against  (*see also* Jesus, charges
        against) 228, 228n14
    event  128, 181
    divinity of  360
    followers of  182, 293
    movement  131, 151n48
    religion  14, 127, 131
    suffering of  319
Christian
    apologists  268
    ascetic practices  151
    authors  264, 267, 270
    ethics  178
    believers  253
    community  306, 319
    history of reception  13–14
    literature  268
    ministry  269
    preachers  198
    religion  2, 294
    sources  232
    teachings, philosophical elements in
        306, 310, 320, 322
    texts  118, 245, 271
    thought  304
    tradition  203, 269
    truth  11
Christianity  5, 6, 11–12, 14, 20–21, 120, 131–32,
        134, 139, 160, 206, 210, 221, 223, 268–69,
        279, 281, 282n13, 284–86, 297–99, 302,

INDEX OF SUBJECTS

304, 307, 309, 314, 320–21, 353
Catholic  338
 early  1–5, 13, 125, 127, 270, 337
 relationship with philosophy  12, 14, 304, 321
Christians  3, 5, 6, 14, 118, 130, 161, 181, 223, 245, 250, 279, 281–86, 287–97, 299, 300–4, 306, 307–12, 312n23, 313–16, 319–21, 323, 329, 342, 353–54, 354n72, 360–63, 365, 367
 as heirs of Judaism  320
 criticism of  303
 early  161
 Epictetus' view of  308
 persecution of  306
 Roman sources on  306
 Roman view of  307, 310
 second-century  303
Christology  339n5, 362, 364, 372
Chrysanthius  358
Chrysippus  111–13, 121, 172, 301
chthonian worship  90
chthonic divinities  32, 77, 90
Church  14, 128
church, Christian  338
churches  209, 222
Cicero  165, 170, 183
Cilicia  142
Cinna  201
circumcision  314, 316n37
cities  92, 106, 189, 233, 238, 252, 346, 362, 370
citizens  192, 215, 217, 252
 of Athens  230, 239
 'of the world'  215
citizenship  60
city  234, 282
city gods  79
city-state  90, 98
civic good  291
civilisation  103n1, 109, 134, 196
Classical period (of Greece)  89n50, 92, 96, 97, 103, 128
classical studies / classics  73, 126
classicists  1, 2, 12, 13, 103, 118, 160
Cleanthes  113, 121, 172, 301
Clement of Alexandria  14n9, 301
Cleobulus of Lindus  258
Clitarchus  267

Cocytus  120
Codex Vaticanus  247
cognition  325
'cognitive component' (in consolation)  166
cognitive science  135
cognitive studies  138
Colophon  350
commandment  230
commands  63, 64, 65
'common cultural currency'  3–6, 117–20, 124, 132
common law  107
communism  108
compelling the gods  251
conflagration, Stoic doctrine of  172, 173, 177, 214 (see also cyclic conflagration; universal conflagration)
Confucius  23, 139
consolation  4, 159, 162–65, 168–70, 173, 177, 179, 184
 ancient philosophical and early Christian modes of  164, 170, 181
 'argumentative consolation'  164–68, 170, 177–79, 183
 Epicurean  180
 of Paul  181
 strategy  181n45
 texts, ancient  159, 162, 168, 178, 179
 writing  163n8
consolers  165–67, 178
Constantine  358
containers  353, 358, 373
contemplation  38n7, 51, 54–56, 58–59, 61
contemplative ideal  39
contentment  198
'continuing bonds'  159, 174
 theory of  174n37
contradiction, logic of  87, 89n50, 98
conversion  299, 300, 316n37
 damascene  302
 to Christianity  5, 300
 to Judaism  316
convert, from paganism  301
Corinth  10, 188, 192n12, 215
Cornutus  121
cosmic city  176
cosmic order  114
cosmic regions  346

cosmogony 121 (Stoic)
cosmopolitanism 107, 215
cosmology 325n3, 121 (Epicurean and Stoic)
cosmos 55, 103, 106–7, 111–12, 175, 176, 327, 344–46, 358, 366
   hierarchy of 366
Counter-Reformation 130
court 238, 321
   Athenian 239
craftsmen 90
Crates 190n7, 215
creation 298, 329–30, 361, 365
creator 311, 329–30, 331–32
Cremutius Cordus, Aulus 165, 173, 174
Crescens 283, 284, 284n17, 285, 304
Cretans 258
Criton 81
Cronus 92, 93, 122, 330
cross 321
crucifixion, of Jesus 231n20
cult / cults 15n10, 16n13, 20, 75, 90, 97, 141, 248, 271
   acts / practices 76, 88, 252, 274, 339
   civic 297
   image 343, 352
   observance / obligations 24, 75, 79, 140, 154, 205
   pagan 353
   receptacles 371
   sacred 345
   settings 373
   space 346
   statues 352, 353, 371
   tradition 98
cultural evolutionary perspective / cultural evolution 22, 35, 133–35, 136n16, 137n20, 141–42
cultural history 134, 136
cultural interchanges 127
cultural traditions 127, 135, 146, 164
culture and nature (*see* nature and culture)
culture, homogenised understanding of 127
cultures, relationships between 131–32
cycle of births 92, 97
cyclic conflagration 172 (*see also* universal conflagration)
Cyclopes 123

Cynics 187–89, 195–98, 201–3, 205, 207, 209, 213–15, 217–18
   beggar-like existence 191
   concern 197
   ethics 201, 216, 218
   ideas 191, 212, 216
   life 200, 218
   literature 190, 216 (literary corpus)
   philosophers / movement / philosophy 5, 105, 128n5, 157, 87, 189, 190–97, 200, 202, 203, 208, 210–18
   philosophical tradition 197, 217
   poverty 196, 198, 218
   preaching / preachers 190, 211
   radicalism 190
   school of philosophy 188
   school of thought 214
   spirit 202
   teaching 200
   themes 215
   thought 211
   way of life 191, 195, 196, 206
   worldview 196
Cynicism 189, 204, 210
Cyniscus 199
Cyrenaica 246
Cyrus 263n77

*daemon* / *daimōn* 4, 41, 43, 50, 74–75, 79, 82–84, 87, 88, 90–92, 94–99, 349, 351, 357, 366, 370
   agents 57
   as a mediator 77, 89
   concept 85
   essence 356
   *erōs* 43, 51–52, 58
   intermediaries 54, 57, 59
   passage, the 41, 50, 53
   spirits / men 39, 41, 43, 52, 53
   work 42n16, 52
*daemonic* / *daimonic* 78, 79, 81, 82
   sign 78
   voice 79
*daemonie* 81, 82
*daimones* 324, 340, 340n9, 344, 368
*daimonion* 233
*daimonion*, of Socrates 59, 222, 227, 230–33, 239, 243

INDEX OF SUBJECTS    403

days of judgement   108
dead, cult of   76, 91
death   162, 169, 170–74, 178–83, 198, 220,
    235–37, 241, 242, 282, 283, 290, 291n57,
    295, 297, 300, 313, 319, 321, 372
death-imitation, Pythagorean and Orphic
    rites of   92n55
*deisidaimonia*   279
deists   206
deity   11, 42, 140, 153, 204, 205, 249, 255, 264,
    274, 298, 343, 368, 369
deliberative genre   143
Delphi   42n16, 79n14, 258, 350
Delphic god (authority of)   79
Delphic Oracle   99, 350
demi-gods   196, 203
Demiurge   32, 326, 327n5, 328–30, 330n13,
    332, 341n15, 352–53, 365, 367, 370, 373
    hierarchy of   366, 373
demiurgic causes   351
demiurgy   346, 365, 368, 373
Demonax   207, 214
demonology   4, 73, 83, 84, 86
demons   84, 88 (*see also* daemon; *daimōn*)
demonstration   293, 295, 303, 310, 311, 313
Demosthenes   246n10, 261n68
descendents of the gods   82
desert   370
desire   18n21
destruction   109, 112, 115, 122, 124
Deuteronomian religion   23
Deuteronomian theology   139
devil   299
devotional practices (Graeco-Roman)   244,
    264
dialectic / dialectics   14, 53 74, 75, 82, 89, 98,
    258
    activity   55
    of truth   78
    training   93
    type of discourse   86
    work   55, 56
dialogue   9, 74, 78, 90, 128, 224, 226, 227
    (exchange of) arguments   98, 257
    practice   78, 80
    dialogical principle   96
dialogues of Plato   5, 37, 42n16, 44, 51, 53,
    57n50, 77, 82, 89, 94, 119, 230, 236, 237,

238, 240, 242, 257
    authentic   83
    early   79, 85, 91
    middle   79, 85
    late   90, 93
Diana   249n25
diatribe   105, 198–200, 202, 215
Dion   262
Dio Chrysostom   197, 245, 246, 282
Diogenes Laertius   106n13, 113, 189, 193–97,
    202, 206, 207, 209, 211, 213, 215–17, 242,
    259, 264, 301
Jesus as Diogenes-like figure   212
Dionysus   369, 370, 370n133, 371, 372, 374
Diotima   42n16, 44n20, 52, 53, 54, 57, 58, 59,
    89
disciple
    beloved   241
    of Athenagoras   301
    of Clement   301
    of Jesus   191, 193, 222, 230, 235, 238, 240,
        241, 242, 243, 244, 250, 253, 271, 298
    of Plato   222, 325
    of Socrates   241, 242, 243
discourse   74, 78, 80, 89, 92, 93, 129, 141, 144,
    148, 259, 263, 273, 329
    ancient   327, 327n8
    Christian   359
    fight   146
    formation   86
    interactions   78, 86, 94, 95, 98
    interrelations   74
    Neo-Platonic   339, 359
    on religion   15
    rules   98
divination   42n16, 125, 350, 352, 353, 354, 371,
    373
divine   10n2, 26–28, 30, 41, 42n14, 43, 44, 51,
    53, 58, 61, 72, 106, 239, 336, 339, 343,
    345–48, 351, 354, 364
    communication with   341, 342, 345, 346
    descent   340, 341, 347, 347n36, 351, 352,
        369n124
    father   204
    form   55, 56
    hierarchy   348–49, 353, 366, 368, 373
    knowledge   253
    nature   274

power   78, 85
presence   339, 340–41, 341n13, 343, 346–53, 356, 358, 364, 371, 373
realm   52
relationship with humans   341n15, 365
relationship with matter   344
world   31
union with   344
divinisation   13, 32
emulation of the gods   153
godlikeness   2, 3, 188
of the soul   16
humans becoming like gods   33, 54, 149, 150n43
divinity   43, 88, 327, 334, 356, 372 (*see also* gods)
of Homer   106
divinity, supreme   (*see also* god, supreme)   335
doctrines   173, 189, 314, 326, 329, 336, 364
metaphysical   326
Platonic   329
Stoic   176
Dog, the   188, 193–94, 214
dogma   309
Christian   372
Domitian   306
dreams   246
*doxa*   90
dualism   31, 83–86, 88, 94, 130, 131, 133, 140
duty   262

early Christian texts   1, 320 (*see also* Christianity)
earth   298, 326, 345, 346, 349, 351, 352, 355, 367, 370
earthly world   30, 31
Echecrates   235
ecstasy   10n2
education   60, 91, 260, 262, 266
Egypt   20, 213, 214, 217, 249n22, 268n96
Egyptians   314
religion   20n24
*eidos*   51, 52
Eleazar   153
elenctic practice   59
Eleusinian mysteries   29, 30, 42, 206–7, 318
Eli (priest)   247

Elijah   193, 205
elite (ruling)   24, 141, 154
Elysium   120
embodiment   341, 344, 364
divine   341, 342, 359, 364
emic   12, 16, 18, 35, 146, 359, 364
emotions   165–67
empathy   165, 167
Empedocles   116
emperor   287, 290, 297, 304, 371
empire   304 (*see also* Roman Empire)
*encomium*   145, 154, 157
'end of days' (Judaeo-Christian)   108
Enlightenment   14, 130, 160
envelopes   353, 358, 373
Epameinondas of Thebes   207
Ephesus   10
epic   76, 121, 300
Epictetus   5, 106, 160, 199, 200, 203–4, 280–82, 282n13, 291n56, 299, 300, 304, 306–9, 311–13, 313n27, 314–17, 319, 320–22
as Stoic   307, 308, 320
Christian influence on   309, 309n20, 320
Epicureans   124, 178, 180, 183
ideas   117, 118, 121, 170, 180
Epicurus   183
Epidauros   367
epideictic genre   143–45
*Epinomis*   83
*epiphaneiai*   349, 350
epiphanial terminology   343, 371–74
epiphany   367, 370n132, 371–74
divine   342, 349, 358
Greek   342, 341n18
of Dionysus   370, 371
*epistēmē*   96
epistemology   31, 140, 153
*epithymeia*   91
equality   57n50
Erastus   192n12
*ergon*   39, 40, 43, 50
*erōs*   41–54, 58–62
as a mediator   39, 49, 88
as the binding guide / work   49n34, 51, 52, 54
Eros   29, 30n41, 41, 45, 50, 88, 94

eschatology   4–5, 92, 97, 104, 105, 107–9,
    112–14, 241
  judgement   113
  kingdom   107
  myths   119
  Stoic   177
  visions   109
essence   69
Essenes   216
ethics   2, 18, 104, 108, 120, 121, 126, 127, 135,
    188, 216, 233
  ancient theories of   178
  ethical exhortations   119
  ideal   38n7, 108 (ethical and political)
  instruction   105
  philosophical   297
  reasoning   236
  Stoic   114
  teaching   202
  traditions   126
  virtues   237
Ethiopia / Ethiopians   111n31
*ethos*   126, 128, 158, 199, 201, 282
etic   17, 18, 35, 75, 129, 146
*eudaimonia*   43–46, 56, 59, 61, 97, 178, 179
eulogy   144
Eunapius   358–59
Eurasian cultures   20, 21, 139
Eusebius   10n3, 143, 222, 283, 300, 300n92,
    301, 303, 358
Euthyphro   39, 40, 41, 65–69, 72, 227, 228,
    231, 232, 233, 234
  'Euthyphro Dilemma'   63, 65, 68, 70
  'Euthyphro Problem'   4, 63, 65
Eve   122
evil   29, 30, 31, 168–71, 180, 183, 201, 204, 207,
    208, 222, 253n42, 313, 329
*exōthen*   346, 347, 347n34, 353
experience   84
exteriority   24, 31, 140, 153, 347

faith   2, 14, 293, 295, 301, 307, 316, 314
family   188, 282
farmers   90
fasting   370
fate   81, 93, 97, 171
fatherhood of God   204, 205, 239 (*see also*
    God, as father)

fearlessness   310–14, 319–21
Feast of Renovation   228, 229, 230
feeding of the five thousand   224
Festival of Dionysus   229
festivals   32, 76, 229, 231, 235
fire   350, 353
  divine   351, 370
First Being   299
first cause   325
flood   115, 117, 118
food laws   208, 209n40
foot-washing   224
forms   49, 57n50, 60, 61, 85, 93, 298
  divine   52, 55, 58, 345
  metaphysics of   56
Fortune   166, 176, 177
freedom   196–98, 209, 213, 216, 344
Freudians   174n37
Fronto   290
funeral games   75

Galen   292–96, 294n69, 299, 303, 304
Galileans   280–82, 311–12, 314, 319, 321, 359
Galilee   192, 211, 234, 242, 281
Gentiles   119, 211, 244, 245, 247, 251, 270, 272,
    273, 316
geometry   188
ghettoization   145
Gnosticism   1
Gnostics   329, 332
God   3, 10, 11, 63, 66, 105–6, 110, 115, 124, 149,
    156, 172, 177, 181, 190, 193, 201–6, 214, 217,
    220, 231, 234, 236, 237, 239, 246, 250,
    251, 253, 255, 264, 265, 268, 272, 273,
    280, 289, 292, 296–99, 304, 310, 311, 327,
    334, 334n24, 338, 361–64
  above all   334, 336
  as father   229, 234, 236, 239, 245, 363, 364,
    367
  as Logos   364
  Christian   252, 255
  God from God   361
  nature of   234, 236
  of Israel   71, 153, 360
  of the Old Testament   360
  Stoic   107
god   340n9, 349, 355n77
  demiurgic   331, 331n15

first 331, 332
of Delphi 239
second 331, 332
supreme 335 (*see also divinity, supreme*)
third 330, 332
transcendent 335
godlike (*see* divinisation)
god-loved 67, 68, 69, 72
god-man 372
gods 16, 18, 24, 27, 28–32, 34, 37, 41, 43, 49, 53, 54, 56, 57, 59, 66, 71, 72, 79, 84, 90, 92, 93, 96, 99, 106n17, 121, 149, 169, 178, 196, 201, 202, 206, 207, 227, 228, 236, 237, 238, 245, 249, 251–54, 274, 286, 323, 339, 340, 343n19, 344–48, 348n41, 349–53, 356–58, 360, 368, 371, 373
   for the sake of the 46, 47, 48
   correct thinking about the 206
   immaterial 373
   intellectual 368
   intelligible 365
   invisible 365
   pagan 302
   panhellenic 76
   permissions 64
   role of 50
   traditional 284, 304
   visible 365, 368
Golden Age 93, 108, 122
good 43, 135, 156, 201, 203, 204, 233, 253, 328, 330–33
   of God 272
   idea of the 26, 27
   life 169, 180
   one true 16
gospel(s) 14, 191, 195, 221n5, 222, 223, 305, 357, 372
   Cynic influence in 200
   narrative 357
   stories 370
governor 290, 297, 307
governor, of the universe 329
Graeco-Roman
   antiquity 159
   context 248
   cults 248
   culture 119, 121

literature 103, 108n23, 115, 118, 122, 240, 250, 264
philosophical traditions 149, 252, 262, 264, 268, 273 (*see also* Greek philosophy)
philosophical moral tradition 128, 132, 155–57, 265
philosophy 1–3, 5, 12–13, 126–27, 129, 131, 252
popular philosophy 127, 148, 149, 158
public (non-Jewish) 147
religion 249, 251
texts 251
tradition 132, 274
world 1, 127, 133, 156, 158, 270
Great Year 116, 117
Greece (classical / ancient) 10, 20, 35, 73, 76, 85, 99, 128, 135, 139, 141, 300
Greek (language) 211
Greek
   atomists 180
   authority 123
   biographers 274
   cynics 204, 206
   context 9, 16
   culture 131, 200, 210, 342
   elenchic tradition 148, 154
   hexameter tradition 104
   history 207
   language 210
   miracle 73
   philosophy (ancient) 83, 129, 134, 139, 146, 149, 188, 203, 210, 257, 258, 269
   religion (ancient) 2, 10–12, 23, 76, 99, 205, 250, 343
   thought 256, 343
Greeks (ancient) 5, 99, 103n1, 107, 116, 123, 210, 215, 230, 235, 240, 242, 300, 312n23, 314, 315
grief / grieving 159, 164–68, 171, 176, 177, 235
grief counselling 165
gymnasium 75, 192

habit 313, 313n27, 314
habituation 320, 321
Hades 77, 199, 207
Hadrian 301
Hagar 266

# INDEX OF SUBJECTS

Hanukkah 229
happiness 44n23, 46, 47, 56, 61, 169, 196–98, 207
heaven / heavens 28, 31, 32, 35, 49, 105, 110, 112, 128, 164, 171, 173, 204, 220, 222, 246, 326, 331, 331n15, 345, 346, 365, 367
Hebrew Bible 139, 246 (*see also* Old Testament)
Hebrew festivals 216
Hebrews, the 112
Hector 123
Helios 367, 368, 368n121
    Hymn to 368n121
hell 119, 120, 173
Hellenisation 131, 211, 267n92
Hellenism / Hellenistic world 2, 130, 131, 134, 146, 210, 229
    aphorisms 267
    dichotomy with Judaism 130, 141, 210 (*see also* Judaism and Hellenism)
    Judaism 117, 189, 210
    pagan 218
    period 124, 128, 130
    philosophy 19, 105
    Roman 189, 192, 205, 218
    schools of philosophy 18, 139, 150, 259 (*see also* philosophical schools)
henotheism 24, 32, 140, 153
Hephaestus 122
Hera 123
Heracles 194, 203, 204, 369, 370, 370n131, 370n132, 372, 373, 374
Heraclitus 107n19, 115, 338, 343
Herennius 325n2
heretics 14, 130
hermeneutics 52, 337
Hermes 230
Hermesianax 120
Herod the Great 210, 230
heroes 32, 82, 90, 92, 153, 169, 194, 344, 368
Hesiod 16, 76, 81, 90, 105, 109, 120, 121, 125
    discourse 91
    Iron Age 121
    traditions 124
Hesychius 271n106
hierarchy 84, 85, 90
high priest, Jewish 238
Hinduism 23, 139

Hippolytus 221
historians of ancient philosophy 2
historiographies 159
    of rapprochement 159, 161
    of separation 160, 161, 184
history 73, 298
    of Christianity 14n9, 181
    of philosophy 177
    of reception 14, 129, 130
    of religion 9, 126, 133, 134, 151n48
    writing 145, 148
History of Religions School 1
holiness 233
holy 66n4
    Holy Spirit 301
    spaces 339
Homer 16, 76, 77, 81, 106, 109, 120–25, 203
    discourse 91
    Homeric/Hellenistic Greek hexameters 103
    religion 252n37, 274
    tradition 252
*homoiōsis* 49, 236–37
human being 282, 298, 348, 351, 353
    as differentiated from gods 24, 27, 28, 31, 32, 33, 41, 43, 50, 51, 84, 352, 354
    biology 136
    cognition 137
    "dear to the gods" 42, 51, 54, 56, 61, 62, 233, 255
    flourishing 178
    nature 369
    world 77, 78
humanities 2, 135
*huperesiai* 40
*huperetike* 40
hymns 32, 104
'hypocrites' 244, 245, 247

Iamblichus 260, 264, 339, 341, 341n13, 341n14, 341n15, 342–46, 347n35, 348–51, 353–54, 354n72, 355–59, 364, 366, 368, 369, 369n126, 371, 373
idea(s) 91, 93, 94, 265, 328, 330
ideal city 107
ideal order 93
ideal state 91
identity 145

Ignatius of Antioch  319
ignorance  335
imitation of god  16n13, 150
imitation of the highest good  13
immortal / immortality  43, 50, 51, 54, 56, 57n50, 76, 82, 92, 93, 99, 150, 173, 174, 225 (*see also* mortal / mortality; realm of the mortal and the immortal)
    of the soul  13, 27n35
impiety  56n46, 206, 233, 252, 363
impious behaviour  233
incantations  248, 249n23
incarnation  230, 343, 359, 360, 363, 364, 368, 374
    Christian  339, 340, 354, 355, 369, 372
    divine  341, 355n77
    Johannine  356, 373
    of Apollo  357
India (ancient)  20, 35, 139, 370
initiation  41, 42n14, 53, 76, 89, 94, 95, 241
    esoteric  77, 97
injustice  92
inspiration  85
'integrative concepts'  159, 174–75, 178, 184
intellect  85, 89, 91, 179, 325, 326, 328, 330, 333, 335, 336, 344, 370
    activity  38, 56, 58
    noetic  51
    ritual  208
intellectuals  307
intelligence  84, 196, 197, 299
interiority  24, 31, 140, 153, 347
Internet  136, 138
intuition  81
Ionia  367
Irenaeus  221
irrationality  2, 14, 83
Isaiah  205
Isis, religion of  285
Islam  20
Islamic tradition  216
Isles of the Blest  199, 206–7
Isocrates  106n13, 259n61
Israel (ancient)  20, 23, 35, 139, 141, 149, 217
Israelite religion  135
Israelites  204, 210

Jainism  23, 139
Jeremiah  205
Jerome  243, 284, 284n17
Jerusalem  2, 14, 130, 192n12, 221, 221n6, 228, 229, 234, 239, 240
Jesus  (*see also* Christ) 3–4, 14, 164, 181, 182, 189, 191–93, 195, 197, 199, 201, 202, 204, 205, 208, 210, 211, 216, 217, 219, 221–23, 225–28, 230, 232, 233, 233n22, 234–36, 239, 239n24, 240–43, 243n30, 244, 253, 255, 268, 269, 273, 298, 305, 312n23, 321, 339n5, 357, 358, 360, 361, 363, 367, 372
    as Cynic  5, 211
    as Diogenes-like figure  212
    as pious sage  274
    as sophist  269
    as Stoic sage  275n121
    Cynic influence on  212
    Johannine  5
    Jesus Christ  223, 243, 362
    arrest of  226, 231, 231n20
    body of  229, 298
    charges against  229, 232, 238 (*see also* Christ, charges against)
    death of  243n30
    execution of  225, 226
    response to charges  230, 231
    Socratic  241n27
    tradition  209
    trial of  225, 226, 228, 231, 240
    worship of  235, 236
Jew(s)  3, 104, 118, 131, 145–47, 161, 210, 211, 217, 220, 221, 228–32, 236, 238, 242, 244, 282n13, 286, 292, 294, 297, 298, 302, 312n23, 320, 314–18, 321
    baptised  316
    counterfeit  317
    criticism of  303
    kingdom of  220, 221, 221n6
    real  316, 317, 320
Jewish
    and Graeco-Roman cultural and religious traditions  149
    authors  264
    apocalyptic texts  105
    behaviour  147
    beliefs  131
    convert  282n13
    culture and religion  156

## INDEX OF SUBJECTS

cynic    4, 5, 197, 198, 201, 205
cynicism    190, 204, 208
God    107 (see also God)
eschatology    109
festivals    189, 190, 215
heritage    217
identity    146, 218
intellectual elite    189
law    107, 144, 147, 150, 157, 215, 297
material    103, 107
Orphic material    106n14
people    204
philosophers    205
piety    247
practice    147
preaching / preachers    105, 211
religion    2, 73, 139, 146
resistance    311
roots    360
scriptural traditions    149, 265 (scripture)
sources    232
text    130, 132, 251
thought and practice    190
tradition    104, 131
War    311
way of life    145, 147, 210 (Jewish ways)
wisdom literature    267
world    157
writings    226, 298
Johannine corpus    236, 237
Johannine literature    221
John    5, 221, 221n8, 223–28, 230, 232, 234–35, 237–39, 239n24, 241, 243, 341n12, 358, 361, 362, 364, 372
    knowledge of Plato's dialogues    240
John Chrysostom    271
John Climacus    271n107
John the Baptist    191, 193, 198, 204, 212, 319, 362, 363, 370n133
Joseph    214, 215, 217, 298
Josephus, Flavius    133n12, 146, 194, 202, 210, 242, 311, 319
Judaea    234, 240, 281
Judaism    2, 5, 10, 35, 107, 127, 129, 130–31, 134–35, 146–48, 153, 155, 156, 189, 210, 211, 229, 247, 282n13, 306, 317, 320
Judaism and Hellenism    2, 130, 133, 146, 148, 210

authors    202
binary    132n10
debate    131
discrepancy between    145
interface    118
judgement    109, 110, 113, 120, 124, 220, 225, 227, 234, 238, 243n30, 282, 298
judges    321
Julian    201, 281–82, 358, 362, 365–69, 369n124, 370, 370n131, 370n132, 371, 371n141, 372, 372n143, 373
    as Emperor    339, 340, 341, 343, 359, 361, 363, 364, 371
Juno    220
just, the    201, 254
justice    3, 30, 33, 39, 40, 57, 58, 93, 97, 254, 282, 295
Justin    283, 284, 284n17, 285, 299, 300, 304
Justin Martyr    10, 11, 12, 13, 268, 317, 319, 322, 369
    Christianity of    11
    trial of    290
Justus of Tiberius    242

Kallipolis    32, 42n16
*kalon*    51
King of All    327, 327n5, 331
king, of the Jews    230
king, Plato's    329, 330, 331n17, 331, 332, 336
kingdom of God    113
kings    92, 234
kinship, traditional structures of    24
knowledge    319, 332, 335, 336
Koheleth    190, 191, 192, 208
*koinē*    3
*koinonia*    365
Kos    367
*kosmos*    57n50, 111 (see also cosmos)
knowledge    2, 31, 74, 75, 78, 82, 84, 91, 93, 94, 96, 143, 155, 156, 182, 253, 255, 260
    divine    253
    of God    267
    relitious    155, 274
Kronos-phase    327n5

Lachesis    97
language    137, 210, 211, 212, 335
Lao-tse / Laozi    23, 139

# INDEX OF SUBJECTS

Last Supper  (*see also* Last Symposium)  224–25
Last Symposium  (*see also* Last Supper)  225–26, 230, 240–41
late antiquity  19, 337, 338
law(s)  144, 152, 155, 216, 221, 221n8, 230, 240, 254, 282, 293, 303
  Mosaic  240 (*see also* Jewish law)
  ritual  208
Lazarus  199, 200, 224
letters  163, 164, 166
letters, of John  230
Levi  195
*libri Platonicorum*  338
Licinus  359
life after death  (*see* afterlife)
light  241, 346, 347, 347n35, 349, 350, 353, 358, 371, 373
linguistic turn  86
liturgy  244
Livia, Empress  165, 201
local traditions  76
logic  86, 98, 164, 188
*logoi*  52, 54, 59, 61, 283
*logon didonai*  75, 79
*logos*  4, 73–75, 84, 87, 89n50, 93n56, 94–96, 98, 99n64, 148, 223, 226, 229, 229n17, 231, 263, 272, 279, 282, 354, 361–63
  Christian incarnate  354, 364, 370n133
  divine  363
  hymn  363
  of God  230, 231
Longinus  324, 326
Lord, the  14, 181, 182, 223, 271
'Lord's Prayer'  244, 245, 247, 253, 271
loss  164–67, 169, 176
love  27, 30, 48, 62, 67, 68, 71, 152, 182, 201, 225, 230, 240
love of the enemy  201, 202, 211
Loxias  264
Lucan  114
Lucian  199, 207, 246, 296, 299, 304
Lucilius  253
Lucretius  116–17, 121
Luke  4, 202, 243n30, 244, 245, 279, 358n85, 362
lunatics  310–11, 313
Lysander, Admiral  261, 262

Lysias  80

Maccabean Revolt  229
Maccabeans  129
Maccabees  229
*Maccabees, book(s) of*  107, 118
  as apologetic  145–47, 156
macrology  257–58, 259n61, 266–68
madness  232–33
magic  2, 41, 248, 251, 285
magical formulae  248, 249n23, 264
magicians  249n23
magicoreligious  87
manifestation  342
Mara bar Serapion  219, 220, 221, 223, 230
Marcia  114, 164–67, 169, 171–74, 176–77, 177n41, 179
Marcion  297
Marcionites  297, 298, 298n87
Marcus Aurelius  160, 282, 287–91, 291n57, 292, 297, 299, 300, 303, 304
  and Christianity  287n33, 287n35
  and Commodus, co-regency  297, 301, 302
Mark  4, 128, 132, 362
Martha  195
martyrdom  154, 292, 300
  Christian  303
  of Justin  284
  of Polycarp  284, 284n22
martyrs  144, 146–47, 149, 150–57, 290, 300n91
Mary  361, 362, 364
material
  bodies  364
  bodies, divine presence in  341–42, 347, 374
  objects  341n13, 343, 346, 351, 353, 371
  realm  340
  receptacles  373
  rites  341n15
  rituals  343
  world  341, 349, 368, 373
materiality  339, 345, 373, 374
matter  83, 340, 344, 348–49, 351–53, 356, 358, 364, 368
Matthew  4, 202, 221n7, 221n8, 245, 248–52, 272–74, 362

INDEX OF SUBJECTS 411

Maximus of Ephesus 358
mediation 368n121
mediators (between human and divine knowledge) 84
Mediterranean Diaspora 210
medium 373
Megapenthes 199
Meletus 79, 80, 156, 227, 230, 232, 233
memory 53n40, 84, 136, 137, 138
men (*see* humans)
Mencius 23, 139
mendicancy 196
Menippus 199, 213
messenger of God 204
Messiah(s) 228n14, 312n23
metaphor 80, 87–89, 105, 112, 114 (Stoic)
*metaphora* 80, 98
metaphysics 56, 85
  Neo-Platonic 338, 341
Metilius 164, 165, 170–74, 177 179
*metriopatheia* 167, 168n19, 171
Middle East 212
Mikyllos 199
military life 260
military leaders 261, 262
*mimesis* 96
mimetic culture 137
mind 28, 32, 138, 298, 299, 336
miracle (Greek) 96n59, 295
Mishnah 248
mistaken judgement(s) 166
Moderatus 331n15
modern philosophical tradition / modern philosophy 9, 129
modern religion 129
monologues 74, 78
monotheism 22, 24, 32, 107, 140, 153, 202, 203, 286, 360
moon 357
moral / morality 15n10, 24, 33, 140, 189, 207, 264, 274, 307, 318, 369
  advancement 198
  advice 191
  attitude 141
  corruption 252
  decay 262
  degeneration 251
  depravity 272
  duty 206
  failure 263
  Graeco-Roman 269–70
  Greek popular 264n81
  life 38, 265
  logic 124
  philosophy 128
  values 126, 143
  virtue 38
mortal / mortality 50, 51, 57n50, 58, 76, 77, 82, 83, 90, 92–96, 99, 107, 171 (*see also* realm of the mortal and the immortal)
  beings 179, 207
  realm 54
Moses 204, 205, 226, 265, 266, 274, 293, 294, 296, 298, 360, 361, 365
Mother of the Gods 368, 368n121, 371n141
Muses 29, 53n40, 75, 76, 122
music 188
Myson of Chen 258
mystagogue 77, 94, 97
mysteries 17n16, 41–42, 43, 53, 54, 207, 222, 372
  ascent 59
  cults 206, 207
  initiation 207 (*see also* initiation)
  rites 42
  terminology 44n24, 55
myth / myths 13, 15n10, 17n16, 26n33, 31, 34, 73, 75, 76, 95, 98, 99, 120, 302, 323, 358, 369
  of the soul 27, 30, 31, 33, 34
  Christian 358
  culture 137
  Greek 339n5
  history 104
  Julian's theory of 369, 369n126
  of Er 120
  of the cave (*see* parable of the cave, Plato)
  *Phaedrus* 340, 354
  tradition 90
mythology 103
*mythos* 4, 17, 75, 76, 84, 87, 89n50, 93, 94, 96, 98, 99n64, 148
*mythos-logos*-debate 4, 13, 17, 87, 89n50, 94, 98

Nag Hammadi   329
narrative of the martyrs (in 2 and 4
    Maccabees)   144, 148
nativity stories   368, 369
natural kinds   69, 70
natural law   107, 217
natural philosophy   188
nature / Nature   115, 136, 171–77, 180, 195, 217,
    222, 274, 291
nature and culture, relationship between
    135, 138
nature of reality   325
nature philosophers   139
Near Oriental world   139
Neo-Platonists   6, 49, 61
Neo-Platonic   272n112, 356
    strategies   372
    writings   359
Neo-Platonism   328, 340, 341n12, 358, 359
Neo-Platonists   339, 373
Neo-Pythagoreans   327n6
Neostoics   160
Nero   104, 201, 306
New Testament   1, 2, 126–28, 202, 204, 205,
    221, 232, 244–46, 267, 295, 296, 308,
    309, 317, 320, 339n5, 362, 364, 372,
    372n143
    scholars / scholarship   2, 126
Nicaeno-Constantinopolitanum   339
Nicene Creed   361, 362, 367
Nicias   81
Nicodemus   240
Nicopolis   280, 306
Noachide laws   119
'noetic fire,' Stoic concept of   111n33
non-Christian   342
non-Jew   315, 316
North Africa   285
*nous*   51, 55n44, 60, 61, 87, 89, 91, 93, 95, 97
Numenius of Apamea   304, 329, 330,
    330n12, 331, 332, 332n19
nurture   240, 240n26

obligations   63–65, 90
Oceanos   120
Odysseus   122, 201
Odyssey   264
Oenomaus   206

offerings   71, 205, 254, 255
Old Academy   262
Old Testament   192, 193, 195, 202, 205, 208,
    360 (*see also* Hebrew Bible)
Olympian gods   76, 90
Olympian powers   77
One, the   49, 325–26, 327n8, 332–33, 333n22,
    334, 334n24, 334n25, 335–36
    Plotinian   336
oracle   99, 230, 239, 264
Origen   6, 14n9, 199, 222–23, 225, 243, 266,
    298, 305
Origenes the Platonist   324–25, 325n3, 326,
    328–29, 331, 331n14, 332–37
Orphic
    Cosmogonies   135n14
    discourse   30n43, 91
    fragments   106n14
    initiation   95, 97
    mysteries   29n39
    myth   28
    rites   92n55, 97
Orphics   96
Orphism   88, 120
'Our Father'   244

pagan / pagans / pagan religion   3, 5, 6, 103,
    104, 106, 115, 116, 117, 118, 124, 125, 155,
    156, 219, 223, 232, 245, 251, 262, 264, 265,
    279, 281, 289, 293, 300, 303, 367, 372
    criticism of Christianity   302
    deities   249
    Greeks   235, 236
    Hellenism   218
    Neo-Platonists   343, 359
    piety   248
    philosophical traditions   119
    prayers   253
    relationship with Christians   3, 6, 120,
        369
    sages   271
    sources   120
    worship   249, 250
paganism   282n13
    conversion from   299
    Jewish and early Christian caricature of
        251
Paian   357

INDEX OF SUBJECTS 413

Palamedes  220
Paleolithic culture  137
Palestine  10, 210, 211, 247, 311
Pan  53n40
Panaetius  113
panegyrics  144
*pankalon*  40
Pantaenus  301, 303
pantheon (Greek)  16, 24, 73, 140
parable of the cave (Plato)  27, 30–31, 33–34, 91
parables  295
  New Testament  200
  of Jesus  199
paradise  108, 109, 119, 123
parallelism  132, 142
*pareinai*  (see also *parousia*; presence) 343, 347
Parmenides  93, 97, 327n8
*parousia*  (see also *pareinai*; presence) 347, 349, 350–51, 353, 353n69, 364
participation  347
passions  143, 146, 148–51, 153, 155, 157, 176, 198, 308, 318
Passover  226
*pathos*  94, 154, 314, 316n37, 318, 318n44, 319, 320
Patroclus  124
Paul  4, 126–28, 132, 161, 162n6, 164, 181–84, 204, 210, 273, 279, 282n13, 296, 301, 314, 322, 362
  epistles / letters of  159, 163, 181, 273
  theology of  161n5
  trial of  243n30
peace  170, 198
Penelope  201
Penia  45, 55, 59
Pentateuch  217, 226
Pera  190n7
perception  325, 342
Pergamum  358, 367
Pericles  156
Peripatetics  11, 333
Peripatos  167
Persia  21n26
persuasive speech acts  164
Peshitta  270
Peter  282n13, 362

petitioners (to the gods)  254, 255, 273, 274
petitions (to the gods)  41, 50, 53, 253
Phaedo  225, 235
Phaedrus  80, 81
Pharaoh  298
Pharisaism  247
Pharisee(s)  195, 209n40, 231, 233, 235
Pherecydes  327n8
Philip of Side  301
Philodemus  180, 202
Philo of Alexandria  106nn13–14, 107, 118, 131, 145–46, 148, 189, 190, 202, 210, 212–17, 229n17, 242, 264–67, 274, 296, 302
philosophers (ancient)  4–6, 11, 13, 15, 25–26, 29, 31, 33, 44, 46, 49, 51–52, 55–56, 58n51, 60, 67, 74, 83, 90–92, 117, 123, 161, 168, 177, 179, 188, 192, 193, 196, 200, 203–7, 212, 219, 224, 232, 251, 257–60, 262, 264, 274, 279, 282n13, 283, 284, 292, 294, 295, 299, 300, 301, 304, 310, 321, 331, 338,
  Athenian  301
  Christian  11, 322
  Cynic  283
  Islamic  295
  lay  358
  pagan  221, 223, 279, 322
  second-century  279, 280, 303, 304, 322
  Stoic  314
  true  235
*philosophia*  16
philosophical
  activity / practice  50–52, 57
  argumentation  157, 272
  as a form of theology  11
  biographies  269
  discourse  4, 34, 89, 91, 92, 95, 96, 98, 104, 148, 154, 195
  discussion  311, 337
  doctrines  166, 168
  ideas  161, 204
  insight  92
  life  192, 198, 201, 240
  literature  154
  religion  17, 18, 162
  schools  11, 106, 126, 148, 149, 151n48, 167, 189, 212, 282 (see also Hellenistic schools of philosophy)

speculation  216
theological scholarship / discussion  125, 164
tradition  251, 274
way of life  150, 200
philosophy (term)  9
  ancient  279
  Greek  73, 29
  of Epictetus  280, 313, 318, 320
  Stoic  303, 318
philosophy and religion  4, 9–10, 15–16, 103, 129, 133, 138, 141–42, 158, 184 (see also rapprochement between religion and philosophy in antiquity)
  ancient  12
  categories  13
  Christianity  1, 321
  crossovers / commonalities / interconnections  162, 177–78, 183
  debate  6
  dichotomy  13, 14
  discourse  126, 132, 134, 148
  dualism  19
  relationship/contrast  130, 175
  relationship/continuum  161
  texts  161
Philostratus  254, 256, 274
Philoxena  179, 180
physics  188, 216
  Stoic  112, 121
Phlegon  125
Phocion  260, 261
Phocylides  119
Photeinos  361
piety / pious  3, 13, 15, 16, 33, 39, 40, 56–59, 61–62, 66–70, 72, 144n33, 151, 155, 227, 233, 236–38, 244, 247, 253–55, 270, 274, 303, 372
  Platonic  42
  popular  251–52
  Pythagoraean  256
  Socratic  38
  traditional  297
  work  29
  virtue  38
Pilate  221n5, 228, 312n23
Pittacus of Mytilene  258
physics  108

Plato  3, 4, 9, 10, 12–13, 15–19, 25–38, 39, 42n16, 44, 47–49, 51, 53, 59, 60, 61, 65, 67, 71, 72, 75, 77–79, 81–83, 85–86, 88–95, 98–99, 109, 121, 122, 124, 125, 139, 150, 156, 183, 220–24, 230, 237, 241–43, 252, 259, 262, 300, 301, 309n20, 323–25, 327, 327n8, 328–29
  authority of  326
  beliefs of  323
  dialogues of  219, 224–27, 323–24
  discourse  78–79, 82, 91, 93, 96, 98, 258
  ethics  2
  followers of  327n8
  ideas  265
  interpretation of  324, 327, 329, 330, 332
  interpreters of  326, 328
  myths  119, 120, 122
  philosophy  2, 3, 9, 11, 12, 13n6, 16–18, 19n21, 32, 34, 36, 93, 199, 222, 262, 265
  philosophers  199
  religion / religiosity  2, 9, 12, 18n20, 32–36, 129, 133
  system of  323
  texts  323
  theory  335
  tradition  4, 253, 262, 328
  worldview  158
  writings of  327
Platonism  11, 14, 77, 83, 86, 88, 127, 148, 212, 297, 299, 323, 328, 338
  middle-Platonism  2
Pliny  281, 291, 292n61, 304, 307, 321, 322
Pliny the Younger  306, 310
Plotinus  6, 49, 264, 269, 323–27, 327n8, 328–30, 331n14, 333, 335–37, 339, 343, 345, 358
  as follower of Plato  323
  interpretation of Plato  328
  school of  330
  three hypotheses of  326–28, 333–36
Plutarch  107, 115, 180, 196, 215, 222, 259–65, 269, 272, 330
pneuma  232, 350–53, 358, 373
poem  85, 117, 163, 193, 207
poetry  29n40, 76, 125
poet(s)  16, 17n16, 18, 28, 29n40, 46, 99, 104, 109, 120, 125, 169, 193, 207
polemics  251

Christian-pagan  339
*polis* / polis religion  16, 32–35, 75, 76, 79, 205, 215
political ideals  61
political leaders  274
political life  260
polytheism  22, 24, 73, 75
poor  191, 192, 195, 200 (*see also* poverty)
Porphyry  260, 264, 269, 281, 298, 324, 326, 328–30, 330n12, 333, 335, 337, 339, 343, 344, 349, 358, 372
possessions  191, 192
post-Aristotelian  128, 139, 147, 149
poverty / voluntary poverty  190, 191, 194, 195, 196, 198, 218 (*see also* Cynic poverty; poor)
prayers  16n13, 32, 33, 53, 54, 57, 201, 227, 233, 244, 245, 247, 249, 250–56, 264, 270, 271–74, 348
pregnancy  43, 44n20
Pre-Socratics  15, 18, 135, 139, 300, 327n8
presence  (*see also parousia; pareinai*) 345, 347, 349, 350, 353
priestess  42n16
priesthood  154
priests  41, 42n16, 231, 249, 255
  Egyptian  103n1, 344
  of Hyperborean Apollo  356
Prime Mover  48
prince from Judah  360
principles  315
prison  240, 241
privation  33
processions  75
Proclus  49, 324–26, 328, 330, 330n12, 332–33, 335–36, 340, 347n35, 366, 369n126
  later commentaries of  325n3
prohibitions  63, 64, 65
proof  296, 299
property  197, 282
prophecies  103, 104, 117, 122
prophetess  103, 350, 370
prophets  11, 23, 71, 97, 139, 193, 204, 205, 269, 299, 312n23, 360
  false  270, 274
proselytes  316
Protagoras  258, 301

Protestantism  21
'proto-Trinitarian'  6
'protreptic' discourse  157
proverbs  273
providence  103, 373
prudence  142, 156
Psalmist  247
Pseudo-Clementines  245, 271
pseudo-Platonic  86
Pseudo-Phocylides  105
Pseudo-Plutarch  262, 263
psychology  136
Ptolemy  213
punishment  119, 120, 123, 200, 219, 252
pure being  33, 92, 93, 95, 99 (*see also* being)
purification  112, 241
  ritual  255
purity  208, 237, 373
Pyriphlegethon  120
Pythagoras  220, 221, 253, 256n52, 260, 264, 269, 275, 301, 327n8, 340, 354, 354n72, 355–58, 367–68, 372, 374
Pythagorean / Pythagoreans  11, 83, 88, 89, 92n55, 255, 270, 327n8, 329, 357
  discourse  91
  initiation  256
  philosopher  254, 255
  sage  254, 255, 256
  sources  254
  tradition  253, 254, 256, 267, 268, 270, 273, 274
Pythagoreanism  255n49
Pythia  99n64
Pythian oracle  206

Q. Junius Rusticus  290
Quintillian  87n33

rabbi  298
rabbinic Judaism  248
rabbinic tradition  197
rapprochement between religion and philosophy (in antiquity)  159, 161 (*see also* philosophy and religion)
rational deliberation  87
rationalisation  85, 86, 88, 89
rationality  2, 14, 318
'rational philosophies'  210

'real immortality' 173–74 (*see also* 'symbolic immortality'; immortal/immortality; realm of the mortal and the immortal)
reality  69
realm of the mortal and the immortal  50, 51, 55, 56, 57, 60, 83 (*see also* immortal / immortality; mortal / mortality)
reason  2, 14, 15n10, 83, 84, 107, 143, 144, 148, 149, 150, 155, 157, 165, 179, 263, 280, 310, 313
reasoning  262, 265, 266, 272, 273, 325, 334
rebirth  174, 319
recitations  76
reflection  84
Reformation  14, 130
reincarnation  173
relationship with the gods  39, 40, 42, 52 54 (*see also* humans, as differentiated from gods)
  divine  38, 44, 45, 58, 60
  human  233
  Jesus  239
*religio*  282, 285, 304
religion
  archaic forms of  18, 23, 24, 26, 31, 35, 129, 142, 152–54
  axial form of  21, 22, 27, 149, 150, 152, 153, 158 (*see also* Axial Age religion)
  concept of  15
  critique of  16
  definition of  17
  Israelite  149
  popular  250, 252
  study of  13, 175n39
  term of  9, 16
  traditional  15n10, 17, 24, 33, 140, 154
  tribal forms of  129
  universal  190
religion and philosophy  (*see* philosophy and religion)
religious
  acts  206
  apologists  (*see* apologists, religious)
  authors  161
  discourses  4, 17n19, 78, 96, 129, 255, 256, 264
  ideas  161
  language  13, 56

philosophy  162
practices  15, 84
tradition  76, 251
transformations  133
resilience  166
resurrection  298, 301
  of Jesus  224
  of the body  173
  of the dead  150
revelation  2, 14, 103, 116, 131, 372, 374
revelatory discourse  34
reverence to the god(s)  144n33
rhetoric  87, 99n63, 147, 166, 257, 260, 265, 268, 269
rhetorical education of children  265
rhetorical efforts  257
rhetorical genres  143
righteous / righteousness  93, 107, 119, 120, 155–56, 227, 236–38, 272
rites  41, 50, 53, 55, 59, 207, 316, 352, 370 (*see also* ritual)
ritual  10n2, 16, 24, 26n33, 42, 73, 76, 77, 94, 95, 97–99, 140, 141, 154, 208, 209, 255, 318, 339, 340, 341, 344, 346, 349, 350, 352, 353, 371, 373 (*see also* rites)
  acts  205
  contexts  373
  experiences  83
  Iamblichean  348n44
  Neo-Platonic  344
  practice  256, 307
  practitioners  351
  tradition  90
Rome  103, 114, 182, 221, 297, 306, 311, 367, 371n141
  citizens  321
  culture  342
  emperors  202, 372
  Empire  103, 210, 290, 323
  Imperial Period  201, 203, 327n6
  literature  (*see* Graeco-Roman literature)
  Republic  327n6
  theatre  211
  world  103
Romans  5, 221, 321
rulers (of the state)  90, 92

Sabbath  208, 233, 235

INDEX OF SUBJECTS

sacrifices   27, 32–34, 41, 50, 54, 66, 76, 90,
    153, 154, 205–9, 227, 233, 252, 254, 271,
    349, 351–53
sage(s)   74, 181, 255, 259, 274, 275
    ancient   343
    ideal   269
    pagan   279
    Pythagoraean   254
salvation   19, 97, 234, 285, 355n77, 358n85
Samaria   234
Samaritan woman   224–25, 233–36
Samaritans   236, 242
Samos   220
Samuel ben Meir   248n19
sanctuaries   371
Sarah   266
Sarapion   125
satire   199
saviour   234, 354, 362, 369, 370
scholars of ancient philosophy   13
scholars of religion   13
school
    Christian   293, 294
    Cynic   (see Cynic, school of)
    of Alexandria   301
    of Aristotle   (see Aristotle, school of)
    of Plato   (see Academy)
    of Plotinus   336
    of Pythagoras   301
    philosophical   294, 299
    Stoic   (see Stoic school)
science (Greek)   73
scripture   142, 265, 299, 300, 301, 332, 360
    Christian   359, 362
    Jewish   226
    passages   199
Sea of Tiberias   224, 225
second-order concepts   139
second-order language   152
second-order thinking   149
Second Temple period   129, 130
sect   294
seer   41, 42n16
self-control   295
self-discipline   295
self-improvement   33
self-mastery   151, 156
self-realisation   91–92

self-reflexivity   23, 31, 139, 140, 153
self-restrain   265
self-sufficiency   198, 199
self-training   19
self-transformation   19
Semele   370, 370n133
senator   229
Seneca   112, 114, 160, 161, 165–69, 171–74, 176,
    177, 179, 180, 181, 183, 184, 201, 250
    consolatory letter   181
sense experience   83
Sepphoris   211
Septuagint   124, 232, 246, 247
Sermon on the Mount   5, 205, 221n8, 275n121
service to the gods   37–40, 42, 54, 55
Servius   117
Seven Sages   258, 260n63
Sextus   267–68, 304
Shammai   248
Shepherd of Hermas   270
Shimon ben Gamliel   248
Sibyl   103, 105–9, 111–13, 115, 117, 119, 120–22,
    124
    death of   125
    Jewish background of   108, 120
    Jewish and Christian uses of   116
Sibylline
    authority   104
    'Books'   103
    terminology   111n32
    tradition   119
    writings   118
*Sibylline Oracles*   103–9, 114–16, 119, 124, 125
    Jewish and Christian sources   113
    Jewish sources   117
    Stoic and Platonic sources   4
Sicily   91
Siddhartha Gautama   23, 139
silence   256, 259
Simmias, disciple of Socrates   235, 242
Simon   195
Simon bar Kochba   281n7
Simplicianus   222
sin   115, 122, 227, 233, 246, 267, 268, 273
sinners   119, 120, 121, 124, 233, 233n22, 274
'siren of unity'   163
slave   306
Smyrna   284

social bonding  143
social competition  141, 154
social kinds  69, 70
Socrates  2, 5, 18, 26–30, 34, 37–41, 42n14, 42n16, 43, 45, 50n35, 53, 54n42, 56–59, 65–70, 74, 75, 77–82, 85, 86n32, 89, 91, 92, 94, 95, 97, 139, 156, 169, 170, 180, 187, 188, 203, 205–7, 219–24, 226, 227, 230–33, 236–39, 241–43, 243n30, 253, 254, 257–59, 263, 268, 275, 321, 323
   charges against  227–33, 237
   death of  156, 169, 205, 225
   final words of  227
   indictment of  237
   last days of  242
   response to charges  230
   trial of  227, 238–40, 242, 243n30
Socratic
   alternative  169–73, 178–80, 183
   argument  266
   discourse  96
   monologue  91
   philosophy  2
   tradition  263, 274
Solomon  14, 192, 273
Solon  103n1, 258
son of God  204, 228n14, 230, 355, 356, 360, 361, 363, 367, 369
   Jesus as  298, 299
soothsayer  119n71
Sopatrus  358
*sophia*  74
sophistic rhetoric  269
sophism  32, 74
sophistry  87, 99n63, 258, 260, 263, 274
sophists  16, 74, 257, 258, 268, 269
Sophocles  207
sorcery  297
soul  4, 11, 13, 16, 17n16, 24–32, 34, 35, 44n20, 58, 59, 83, 85, 88, 91, 92, 95–97, 99, 120, 140, 149, 150, 153, 171–73, 179, 206, 215, 229n17, 235, 242, 298, 326, 328–31, 340, 340n9, 341, 344, 349, 350, 355, 355n77, 366–68, 372
   divine  343, 348
   Hellenistic philosophy of  19n21
   hierarchy of  348
   human  348, 348n41
   immortality of  235, 242, 372

   of Pythagoras  354, 355
   pure  355, 355n77, 368, 370n130
   universal  348n41
   wisdom of  16
Sparta  215
Spartan
   brachylogy  262
   brevity  261
   culture  258
   wisdom  258
Spartans  258, 259, 262
spells  41, 42n16
Speusippus  334, 334n25
spirit  253, 291, 298
spiritual activity  76, 235
sporting games  76
stars  84
state  217
statues  339, 343, 343n19, 346
Stobaeus  260
Stoa of Solomon  228, 229n16, 230
Stoa of the King (Athens)  228, 229, 230
Stoic / Stoicism  14, 103, 104, 106–9, 112–15, 116n59, 120, 121, 140, 148, 158, 160–61, 162, 169, 176, 177, 189, 275n121, 303, 308, 309, 314, 316, 321
   'eschatological' thought  109, 177
   discourse  105
   doctrine  172
   ideas  124
   influence on the Sibyl / Sibylline Oracles  111, 125
   moral psychology  167
   philosophy  176
   Stoic school  107, 113
   Stoic-Cynic philosophers  199
   studies  160
   terminology  107
   tradition  117
Stoics  11, 105, 107, 112, 113, 118, 119, 121, 124, 161, 167, 172, 182, 183
Strabo  245
Stranger from Athens  82, 86, 90, 91, 92
Suetonius  281, 306, 310, 314, 307, 321, 322
suicide  289, 290, 291, 291n57
sun  346, 347
sun-King  326
*superstitio*  279, 281
superstition  14, 75, 147, 251, 307

INDEX OF SUBJECTS

symbol 295
symbolic acts 64
symbolic culture 137
'symbolic immortality' 159, 173–74 (*see also* 'real immortality'; immortal/immortality)
symbols 64
*symposioi* 76
symposium 224
sympotic setting 224, 225
synagogue 192, 238, 244, 247
syncretism 249n26
Synesius of Cyrene 358
Synoptic Gospels 4, 227, 229, 231n20, 232, 233, 236, 239, 296, 358
Syria 142
Syriac Curetonian Gospels 247
Syrians 210, 314
Syrianus 328, 332n19

Tacitus 281, 286, 306, 310, 314, 307, 321, 322
Tantalus 200
Tarentum 367
Tartarus 120
Tatian 283, 284, 299, 300, 304
technology 22
Telamon 220
Telesinus 254
temperance 16n15, 30, 33
temple(s) 32, 190, 205, 206, 209, 258, 263, 229n17, 230, 238, 343, 352, 353
   cult 208
   Daphne 371
   Jerusalem 228, 229, 231
   of Herod 235
   treasury of 239, 239n24
Tertullian 2, 14, 130, 221, 222, 285
Thales of Miletus 258, 346
theatrical plays 76
Themistocles 99n64
Theodotus 192n12
*theologia* 16
theology 5, 54n42, 73, 85, 118, 121, 159, 184, 204, 252, 274, 298, 320
   Christian 364
   early Christian 323
   of Iamblichus 340
   of Platonist philosophers 323
   reflection in Judaeo-Christian terms 122

systematic 357
'theo-philosophy' 159, 162, 168, 176, 177, 183–84
   understanding 255
   vs. philosophy 177
   virtues 182
theologians 2
   early Christian 332
   pagan 302
Theophilus 106, 301
Theophrastus 75, 118, 247n15
*theotokos* 361, 362, 364, 373
*therapeia* 40
Therapeutae 217
therapy 166
'therapy of desire' 128
Thetis 121
theurgists 351
theurgy 341n14, 341n15, 344, 344n24, 345
'thick concepts' 175n39
'thinking about thinking' 23, 31, 139, 149, 152
third-order perspective 129
Thomas Aquinas 14n9
Thomas 242
Thucydides 156
Tiberius 165
Timaeus 82, 324
Titans 121
Torah 144, 146, 147, 149, 153, 155, 157
tradition 93, 99, 124, 127, 145
   apostolic 362
   Hellenic 360
   legitimacy of 91
   philosophical 300
   Platonic 94
   respectability of 89
traditional religion / religious practice 208, 210
tragedy (Greek) 156, 300
training (Greek sense of) 24, 33, 140, 150, 151, 153
Trajan 304
transcendence 369, 373
   divine 352
transcendent, the 333, 334
treatises 163
Trinitarian controversies 361
Trinity, the 337
Trojan chariots 124

Trojan War 123
Troy, fall of 121
true being 17n16, 28, 29, 32, 34
　ascent to 26
true philosopher 257
true prophet 270
truth 17n16, 29, 32, 50, 58, 75, 78, 79, 81, 82, 86n32, 89, 90, 91, 94, 95, 99, 135, 140, 149, 153, 169, 180, 234, 236, 238, 260, 272, 298, 332, 369, 370
truths, philosophical 313
Trypho 10
tyrant 280, 310

underworld 119, 120, 121, 168
unity 52, 55, 272
universal conflagration, Stoic doctrine of 108–17 (*see also* cyclic conflagration)
universe 106, 291, 310, 325, 326, 330, 345, 346 (*see also* cosmos)
unjust, the 201
unmoved mover 47, 48, 60n57
urban conventions 193
urbanisation 22, 141

Valentinians 221–22
Valentinus 221–22
Valerius Probus 121
value judgement 166, 167
values 61, 140, 143, 146
vegetarian 188
verbosity 5, 245, 247, 250, 251, 253–60, 263–74
Vesuvius 118
Victorian interpretations 160, 176
Virgil 108
virtue 47, 50, 58, 128, 143, 144, 155, 156, 167, 169–72, 177, 179, 180–83, 188, 237, 248, 291, 295, 321
　life of 189
　path to 105
virtue-ethical argumentative consolatory framework 183
virtue-ethical core 170, 178, 180
Vulgate 270

warriors 90
wealth 188, 190, 192, 193, 198
wedding feast at Cana 224, 225
Western consolation 162n6 (*see also* consolation)
Western consolatory tradition 162n6
Western culture 134, 175
wisdom 37, 39, 46, 54, 55, 58, 60n56, 61, 62, 74, 79, 93, 116, 179, 196, 237, 239, 251, 256, 258, 259, 264, 266, 267, 272, 274, 303, 355
　contemplative 38
　divine 80
　Jewish 197
　literature 85n28
　of the soul 16
　traditions 257
wise / wise man 188, 204, 251, 254, 256, 326
Word of God 231, 272, 273, 338, 363
work 188, 194
world history 104
world religions 35, 36
worship 209, 234, 235, 254, 255, 256, 274, 351, 360
　acts of 206
　in spirit and truth 235, 236, 238
　pagan 249
　public 206, 207
　spiritual 234
　true 234, 235, 236
writers, early Christian 219, 323

Xenocrates 83
Xenophanes 96, 106
Xenophon 54n42, 79n14, 106n13, 206, 253
Xunzi 23, 139

Yahweh 239

Zealots 311
Zeno 121, 259, 260, 301
Zeus 28, 30, 89n48, 99, 106, 107, 121, 123, 124, 202–3, 229, 230, 249n25, 327, 365, 367, 368, 369, 370, 372, 373
Zoroastrianism 21n26, 111n33
*Zostrianus* (Nag Hammadi) 329

Printed in the United States
By Bookmasters